Allies and Adversaries

Allies

and Adversaries

THE JOINT CHIEFS OF STAFF,
THE GRAND ALLIANCE, AND
U.S. STRATEGY IN WORLD WAR II

Mark A. Stoler

The University of North Carolina Press

Chapel Hill and London

Designed by April Leidig-Higgins
Set in Minion by G & S Typesetters, Inc.
Manufactured in the United States of America

The paper in this book meets the guidelines for
permanence and durability of the Committee
on Production Guidelines for Book Longevity of
the Council on Library Resources.

Portions of Chapters 4, 5, 6, 9, 11, 12, and 13
have appeared, in different form, in the following previously published essays; this material is
reused here by permission of the publishers:

"The American Perception of British Mediterra-
nean Strategy, 1941–1945," in *New Aspects of
Naval History: Selected Papers Presented at the
Fourth Naval Symposium, United States Naval
Academy, 25–26 October 1979*, ed. Craig L.
Symonds (Annapolis: Naval Institute Press,
1981), 325–39.

"From Continentalism to Globalism: General
Stanley D. Embick, the Joint Strategic Survey
Committee, and the Military View of American
National Policy during the Second World War,"
Diplomatic History 6 (Summer 1982): 303–21.

"The Joint Chiefs of Staff Assessment of Soviet-
American Relations in the Spring of 1945," in
*Victory in Europe 1945: From World War to Cold
War*, ed. Arnold A. Offner and Theodore A.
Wilson (Lawrence: University Press of Kansas,
2000).

"The Pacific-First Alternative in American
World War II Strategy," *International History
Review* 2 (July 1980): 432–52.

Library of Congress
Cataloging-in-Publication Data

Stoler, Mark A. Allies and adversaries: the Joint
Chiefs of Staff, the Grand Alliance, and U.S.
strategy in World War II / Mark A. Stoler.
p. cm. ISBN 0-8078-2557-3 (cloth: alk. paper)
1. World War, 1939–1945—United States.
2. United States. Joint Chiefs of Staff—History—20th century. 3. Strategy—History—
20th century. 4. Civil-military relations—
United States. 5. United States—Military
relations—Foreign countries. 6. United States—
Foreign relations—1933–1945. I. Title.
D769.1.S76 2000 940.54'012—dc21
00-032589

04 03 02 01 00 5 4 3 2 1

To Diane

For all the reasons. . . .

Contents

Joint Chiefs of Staff luncheon meeting, October 1942. Left to right: Admiral Ernst J. King, General George C. Marshall, Admiral William D. Leahy, and Lieutenant General Henry H. Arnold. (Photograph: U.S. Navy; courtesy George C. Marshall Research Library Collection, no. 4097)

There is only one thing worse than fighting with allies, and that is fighting without them!—**WINSTON S. CHURCHILL,** as quoted in General Alan Brooke's diary, April 1, 1945

When the political perception and guidance by civilian leadership is strong and proves to be sound in historical perspective, the soldier who attempts to interpolate his views will be chided or even clobbered by historians. When civilian and political leadership proves weak in hindsight, the military commander, particularly if he was successful militarily, is likely to be chided for not having shaped his military successes closely to political needs as defined in hindsight.—**BRIGADIER GENERAL GEORGE A. LINCOLN,** October 1970

Allies are the most aggravating of people. They are so difficult to understand, so unreasonable; they approach quite straightforward problems from such extraordinary angles. Even when one agrees with them on common objectives their methods towards obtaining them are so queer, so very queer. They even introduce consideration of their own national politics and hangovers from their past history, none of which have the faintest bearing on the matter of immediate issue. Their most annoying characteristic, however, is that among all the arguing and haggling is the astonishing way they seem incapable of recognizing how sound, how wise, how experienced are our views; how fair, indeed how generous, how big-hearted *we* are. They even at times credit us with the same petty jealousies, narrow nationalistic outlook, selfish maneuvering, that sway them.—**FIELD MARSHAL WILLIAM SLIM,** from his diary

The only bond of the victors is their common hate. . . . We ought to think of something better.—**WINSTON S. CHURCHILL,** February 8, 1945

Preface

During World War II the uniformed heads of the U.S. armed services assumed a pivotal and unprecedented role in the formulation of the nation's foreign policies. Organized soon after Pearl Harbor as the Joint Chiefs of Staff (JCS), these individuals were officially responsible for the organization and strategic direction of the nation's military forces. During the war these functions came to encompass a host of foreign policy issues, however, and so powerful did the military voice become on those issues that only the president exercised a more decisive role in their outcome.

This development constituted a dramatic and permanent change in U.S. civil-military relations. Prior to World War II, military input into the policymaking process had been minimal. Within two years of the war's end, however, the armed forces' new, expanded role in foreign policy had been institutionalized with the passage of the 1947 National Security Act, which made the ad hoc JCS organization of the war years a strong and permanent feature of the foreign policy establishment as well as the new National Military Establishment. Illustrative of this change was the virtual replacement of the term "foreign policy" with the broader, military-oriented "national security policy."[1]

The war years also witnessed a dramatic change in the military's definition of U.S. security requirements. Before 1939 those requirements had been stated in very limited terms centering on defense of the continental United States, its overseas possessions, and the Western Hemisphere. After 1945, however, military planners defined U.S. security requirements in global and indivisible terms whereby events anywhere in the world were considered potentially threatening and therefore of concern to the armed forces. Numerous scholars have analyzed the reasons for this dramatic change and its role in the ensuing Cold War,[2] but little attention has been given to the specific wartime processes by which U.S. security requirements expanded—or to those by which the armed forces gained such an important role in policy formulation. In this book I examine both, as well as the relationship between these processes and the formulation of U.S. military strategy during the war.

The wartime rise of military influence in foreign policy resulted from a host of specific factors and circumstances. Most important was the full-scale U.S. participation after Pearl Harbor in a global and total war. As Army Chief of Staff General George C. Marshall noted during the conflict, "any move in a global war has military implications."[3] Consequently, the Joint Chiefs and their planners found themselves forced to consider numerous foreign policy issues in the process of planning and implementing a strategy for victory.

The fact that World War II was a coalition war as well as a global and total conflict meant that U.S. strategy could not be planned in a diplomatic vacuum. To the contrary, with the United States, Britain, and the Soviet Union aligned and with the nation pledged to deliver supplies to and coordinate global strategy with these two powers, the Joint Chiefs and their planners were forced into intensive and extensive relations with their wartime allies. They were also forced into detailed assessments of the wartime and postwar strategies and policies of their coalition partners as these related to the strategies and policies of the United States.

A precipitous decline in State Department influence during the war years further increased the military's role in diplomatic issues. Although this decline was to some extent the inevitable result of wartime priorities, it was also the self-inflicted consequence of both serious dissension within the department and the artificial dichotomy Secretary of State Cordell Hull maintained between military and political affairs. Unlike the Joint Chiefs, Hull perceived war and diplomacy as separate rather than complementary activities and therefore concluded after Pearl Harbor that the State Department's primary function should be to serve as a diplomatic adjunct to the military effort while planning for the postwar era. Even in this latter realm, however, State Department personnel found the armed forces demanding and receiving a major role on the grounds that postwar policies could not be divorced from postwar military security concerns.

Additional factors in the wartime decline of the State Department and rise of the military in foreign policy include the low esteem in which President Franklin D. Roosevelt (FDR) held the former, his determination to formulate and run his own foreign policy, and his insistence on being a very active commander in chief in direct contact with his armed forces. As early as 1939 he effectively bypassed the civilian secretaries of war, navy, and state by ordering the service chiefs to report directly to him, a practice he continued throughout the war and implemented by providing them with direct access to the White House. Equally important was the very high regard he held for these individuals, one based on their cool professionalism but probably reinforced by their apparent lack of political ambition. Thus no individual save Harry Hopkins was closer to and more influential with FDR than the Joint Chiefs. They accompanied him to all his wartime summit conferences, advised him regularly, composed his conference briefing books, and even drafted many of his telegrams to Allied leaders. By 1944 they had even replaced the ailing Hopkins as the primary presidential advisers.[4]

Traditional interpretations have long held that the Joint Chiefs were neither desirous of nor prepared to accept this new power in the realm of foreign affairs. Strongly imbued with the American belief in civilian supremacy over the armed forces, they supposedly insisted that political leaders should determine the ends of policy while they determined the military means. They consequently limited their thoughts and advice to "purely military" factors and thereby helped to create a vacuum in terms of detailed political advice to the president.[5]

Yet the JCS and their planners were far from being so simplistic. They clearly understood Carl von Clausewitz's famous dictum that war is an instrument of policy and that this necessitated detailed politico-military coordination and political judgments on all facets of the U.S. war effort. Indeed, for many years before Pearl Harbor they had been requesting just such coordination and had been making political assessments on their own as a necessary adjunct to their strategic planning. Throughout the war they continued to do so, and with their greatly expanded wartime influence such requests and assessments carried considerable weight.

The Joint Chiefs and their planners also realized that the war provided them with their long-sought opportunity to achieve coordination with civilian policymakers and to impress on these individuals their view of U.S. security requirements. World War II dramatically altered the geopolitical and military realities of international relations, however, thereby requiring drastic alterations in the prewar military view of those security requirements. Moreover, as civilians were affected by military views on these matters, so military planners were affected during the war by civilian conceptions.

The scope of this book thus encompasses many interrelated politico-military issues, most notably how and why the armed forces expanded their definition of national security and gained such an important role in policy formulation, the evolution of U.S. strategy during the war, the relationship between that strategy and U.S. foreign policy, the interaction between civil and military authority during the war, interservice relations, and the relationship of U.S. strategy and policy to those of its major allies. This latter issue was of particular importance to the armed forces and is my focal point, for in World War II the United States for the first time recognized its own security as intricately and inexorably interwoven with those of allied powers. Yet if total victory over the Axis was to become a reality, those allies would constitute potential postwar adversaries. The Joint Chiefs and their planners were well aware of this fact. Their analyses of appropriate strategies and policies for both the war and the postwar era thus centered on the need to support those allies and promote postwar cooperation while protecting the United States against them should cooperation fail to occur. To a great extent, the history of military concern with U.S. strategy and policy during World

War II is thus a history of military concern with the strategies and policies of Britain and the Soviet Union as both present allies and potential adversaries.

Numerous concepts and words used in this book have multiple definitions, some of which have changed over time. I have taken the liberty of selecting the definitions I found most appropriate but would like to clarify a few of these here to avoid confusing readers who may be aware of and use alternative definitions. "Military" applies to both the navy and the army, though during the time period under study the armed forces used the term to refer only to the latter. Similarly, "foreign policy" is used interchangeably with "national policy," even though the armed forces considered the former to be merely a tool for the accomplishment of the latter, and "Russia" is used interchangeably with "Soviet Union." Finally, "joint" refers to army-navy, whereas "combined" denotes Anglo-American committees and studies.

As originally conceived, this book was limited to the European war and the time period from Pearl Harbor to Roosevelt's death and German surrender. In the process of researching and analyzing these years, however, I discovered that the strategic, diplomatic, security, and civil-military views of the service chiefs and their planners were based to a large extent on events that had taken place before December 7, 1941, and that those views continued to evolve after April/May 1945. Consequently, what had been brief introductory and concluding chapters expanded substantially and led to the present organization and coverage. The thirteen chapters that now constitute this volume break into four overlapping yet fairly distinct time periods, each with its own dominant themes. Chapters 1–3 focus on interservice and civil-military conflicts from World War I through Pearl Harbor, as well as the evolution of U.S. strategy and military thinking about foreign policy and allies during this time period. In Chapters 4–7 I then analyze the massive strategic debates that took place during 1942 and 1943, and the resulting military assessments of British and Soviet strategies and policies vis-à-vis those of the United States. Chapters 8–10 concern the evolution and solidification of these views as the armed forces began to think seriously about postwar as well as wartime issues in 1944 and early 1945, their impact on postwar planning and relations with both the president and the State Department, and the emergence of a global vision of postwar national security. In Chapters 11–13 I consider intra- and interservice as well as interdepartmental debates over postwar policies which had previously arisen but which now escalated, and the ensuing reversal of JCS views and policies as Soviet-American conflict accelerated with first German and then Japanese surrender.

Many documents originally researched in archives and manuscript collections for this volume have been published in edited collections over the last few years. Wherever appropriate and possible I have provided citations to both the original and published versions. Some that remain unpublished have been moved or refiled since my original research. Wherever possible I have changed my citations to reflect these changes.

Acknowledgments

This book has taken much longer to complete than originally anticipated. Indeed, it should have been finished a decade ago, and if human beings were unbreakable physical machines and life predictable, it would have been. Neither "if" is true, however, as I have painfully learned over the years. Delays have resulted from the expanded scope of the study described in the preface, the need and desire to complete other projects, and the uncertainties of life itself. Hopefully the additional years have brought some additional wisdom to this analysis to compensate for the delays. They have definitely extended the list of individuals and institutions deserving acknowledgment.

The University of Vermont granted me the sabbatical leave necessary to complete this volume, while its Committee on Research and Scholarship, Graduate College, and College of Arts and Sciences provided funding for some of the earliest as well as the final U.S. archival research, for research in British archives, and for attendance at many of the national and international conferences during which portions of this book were first presented. Some of these presentations were then published as articles, book chapters, and conference proceedings. I acknowledge permission that has been granted to reuse in revised form these previous publications, as listed on page iv, as well as express gratitude for the university's financial support. I also acknowledge permission to quote from the Edward Mead Earle and James V. Forrestal Papers as granted by the Seeley G. Mudd Manuscript Library, Princeton University, Princeton, New Jersey; the published and unpublished George C. Marshall Papers, Paul M. Robinett Diary, and William Thaddeus Sexton Papers from the George C. Marshall Research Library in Lexington, Virginia; the Henry Lewis Stimson Papers in the Yale University Library, New Haven, Connecticut; and the Albert C. Wedemeyer Papers in the Hoover Institution Archives, copyright Stanford University, Stanford, California.

Although I am not an adherent of the very personal and confessional mode of writing that has become so popular over the last two decades, I do believe that one important aspect of my past has a direct bearing on this volume and those who should be acknowledged: I have never served in the armed forces, and as a member of the 1960s generation, I deeply distrusted those forces for their activities and stated views during the Vietnam War. Indeed, some of my scholarly interest in the wartime Joint Chiefs arose from my desire to trace the origins of what I considered not only incorrect but also extremely dangerous military influence and views. I was at that time totally ignorant of military modes of thinking, however, and victimized by simplistic stereotypes about military officers—and about military history.

Those stereotypes were first challenged by the military historian Edward M. Coffman, who introduced me to many aspects of the "new" military history; by the Marshall biographer Forrest C. Pogue; and by the diplomatic historians John A. DeNovo and William Appleman Williams. While Williams is well known for his seminal "New Left" reinterpretations of U.S. history, few know that he graduated from the U.S. Naval Academy, was a decorated naval officer in World War II, and believed that the real military danger to the nation was militarized thinking by the civilian leadership rather than usurpation of power by the armed forces. He also believed, as he once stated, that the military leader "has a basic and special responsibility to say *no* when he concludes that he cannot defend his country except through means that weaken its structure and violate its principles"—a belief shared by many of the officers analyzed in this study.[1]

My stereotypes were further challenged during the 1981–82 academic year as a visiting professor in the Strategy Department of the U.S. Naval War College in Newport, Rhode Island, and during the 1994–95 academic year as the Visiting Professor of History at the U.S. Military Academy, West Point, New York. These experiences also provided me with invaluable academic insights, most notably in regard to the ends/means relationship of policy to strategy that is fundamental to military thinking—and therefore to this book. Equally important, they provided me with an extraordinary group of scholars and officers with whom I could discuss my work—most notably but far from exclusively George Baer, Marino Bartolomei, Steven Ross, and Robert Wood at Newport, and Michael Bell, Charles Brower, Conrad Crane, Robert Doughty, Cole Kingseed, Judith Luckett, and Scott Wheeler at West Point.

Historians know the importance of archivists in providing not only requested records but also otherwise unknown information about those records; unfortunately, others do not. Such assistance by numerous archivists was critical to the completion of this volume. In the National Archives, William Cunliffe, Timothy Nenninger, and John Taylor in particular provided invaluable aid and advice over the years. I am also indebted to Dean Allard of the Naval Historical Center, Richard Sommers at the U.S. Army's Military History Institute, Alan Aimone and Susan Lintelmann at the U.S. Military Academy Library, John Jacob at the George C. Marshall Research Library, and Dorothy Morales at the public library in Camden, Maine. I am equally indebted to the staffs at the University of Vermont's Bailey-

Howe Library, the Library of Congress, the Franklin D. Roosevelt Library, the Hoover Institution, the Seeley G. Mudd Manuscript Library at Princeton University, the Yale University Library, the Alderman Library at the University of Virginia, the University of Maine Library, and the Public Records Office in Kew, United Kingdom.

I also thank the numerous colleagues whose advice, assistance, willingness to share the fruits of their own research, and general encouragement were equally critical to completion of this study. Charles Brower, J. Garry Clifford, Betty Dessants, Warren F. Kimball, and Theodore A. Wilson graciously shared not only their insights but also their relevant research notes and publications. Along with Norman Saul, Theodore Wilson and Warren Kimball were responsible for organizing and inviting me to participate in a series of Soviet-American colloquia between 1986 and 1992 during which I first organized, presented, and published some of this research. I thank the Russian organizers of these meetings, A. O. Chubarian and G. Sevostianov, and a few of the American and Russian participants whose work and companionship were equally valued: Charles Alexander, Edward M. Bennett, Gregory D. Black, Diane Shaver Clemens, Arthur Funk, Lloyd C. Gardner, David G. Glantz, George C. Herring, Clayton R. Koppes, Elizabeth MacLean, Steven Miner, Vladimir Pozniakov, Oleg Rzheshevsky, Ronald Spector, and V. Zimonin. David Reynolds at Christ's College, Cambridge University, organized the invaluable British additions to these colloquia and was responsible for the exceptional hospitality at the Cambridge meeting of scholars from all three countries; both he and Alex Danchev at the University of Keele also offered incisive criticism and encouragement. Larry Bland, the editor of the George C. Marshall papers, has been a constant source of assistance and information on both this project and my preceding biography of Marshall. He, David Trask, and Theodore Wilson all provided crucial insights that appear in this volume regarding Marshall and the Joint Chiefs, geopolitical thinking, and the linkage between the pre– and post–Pearl Harbor years. Waldo Heinrichs graciously read the manuscript and offered invaluable advice on final revisions, as did David Trask and Randall Woods as University of North Carolina Press readers. Michael Briggs, Keith Eiler, Walter LaFeber, Melvyn Leffler, Thomas Paterson, and numerous History Department colleagues at the University of Vermont furnished not only advice but also constant encouragement to proceed with this project. So did Lewis Bateman, executive editor at the University of North Carolina Press. Assistant managing editor Pamela Upton provided equally valuable guidance in preparing the manuscript for publication. I am grateful beyond words to all these individuals for their assistance and support.

The most important assistance and support came not from any institution, archivist, historian, or editor but from my wife, Diane Gabriel, to whom this volume is dedicated. Her contributions were also the most multifaceted yet for that very reason the most difficult to specify. They were additionally the most personal and the most meaningful. Hopefully the dedication makes all this clear.

Burlington and Starksboro, Vermont

Abbreviations

AAF	Army Air Forces
CAD	Civil Affairs Division, U.S. Army General Staff
CCS	Combined Chiefs of Staff
CIC	Combined Intelligence Committee
CNO	Chief of Naval Operations, U.S. Navy
COMINCH	Commander in Chief, U.S. Fleet
COS	British Chiefs of Staff Committee
COSSAC	Chief of Staff, Supreme Allied Commander (designate)
CPS	Combined Planning Staff
FDR	Franklin D. Roosevelt
F-14	Post War Naval Planning Section
GB	General Board, U.S. Navy
G-2	Intelligence Division, U.S. Army General Staff
G-3	Operations and Training Division, U.S. Army General Staff
JB	Joint Board
JCAC	Joint Civil Affairs Committee
JCS	Joint Chiefs of Staff
JIC	Joint Intelligence Committee
JPC	Joint Planning Committee
JPS	Joint Staff Planners
JPWC	Joint Post War Committee
JSSC	Joint Strategic Survey Committee

JSM	British Joint Staff Mission
JUSSC	Joint U.S. Strategic Committee
JWPC	Joint War Plans Committee
ONI	Office of Naval Intelligence
OPD	Operations Division, U.S. Army General Staff
OSS	Office of Strategic Services
R&A	Research and Analysis Branch, Office of Strategic Services
S&P	Strategy and Policy Group, Operations Division, U.S. Army General Staff
SEAC	Southeast Asia Command
SPD	Special Planning Division, U.S. Army General Staff
SS	Strategy Section, Strategy and Policy Group, Operations Division, U.S. Army General Staff
SWNCC	State-War-Navy Coordinating Committee
WPD	War Plans Division, U.S. Army or Navy General Staff

Code Names

ABC-1	Anglo-American 1941 agreement to Germany-first strategy
ACCOLADE	1943–44 invasion of Rhodes
ANVIL	1944 invasion of southern France
ARCADIA	Anglo-American Conference in Washington, D.C., December 1941–January 1942
BOLERO	Buildup of forces in Britain for a cross-channel attack
BUCCANEER	1944 amphibious assault in Bay of Bengal
CORONET	1946 invasion of Honshu
DRAGOON	1944 invasion of southern France (revised)
GYMNAST	1941–42 invasion of French North Africa
HUSKY	1943 invasion of Sicily
OCTAGON	Anglo-American Conference in Quebec, September 1944
OLYMPIC	1945 invasion of Kyushu
ORANGE	Interwar U.S. plan for war against Japan
OVERLORD	1944 cross-channel attack
PLAN DOG	1940 Navy call for a Germany-first strategy
QUADRANT	Anglo-American Conference in Quebec, August 1943
RAINBOW	1939–41 plans for war against an Axis coalition
RANKIN	Plan for reentry onto European continent in the event of German weakening or collapse before cross-channel attack
RED	Interwar U.S. plan for war against England
RED-ORANGE	Interwar U.S. plan for war against England and Japan

ROUNDUP	1943 cross-channel attack
SLEDGEHAMMER	1942 cross-channel attack
TORCH	1942 invasion of French North Africa (revised)
TRIDENT	Anglo-American Conference in Washington, D.C., May 1943

Allies and Adversaries

The Armed Forces and National Policy before World War II

Military interest in U.S. foreign policy first emerged in the late nineteenth and early twentieth centuries. While clearly linked to America's growing power and international involvements during those years, it also resulted from a simultaneous "managerial revolution" in warfare whereby the principles of large-scale corporate organization and expertise were applied to the rapidly expanding armed forces of the industrialized powers. The United States lagged far behind its European counterparts in this development, but by World War I it did possess, albeit in skeleton form and with very limited powers, the key components associated with the managerial revolution: army and navy general staffs headed by service chiefs, advanced educational systems to train officers for staff work, and a Joint Army-Navy Board (JB) composed of those chiefs and their key strategists.[1]

Foreign policy quickly became a concern of these organizations because of its integral relationship to their planning responsibilities. If war was indeed an instrument of policy as Carl von Clausewitz had emphasized, then strategic planning could proceed only if the armed forces understood clearly the objectives and priorities of the policies they were supposed to defend and promote and if military means were properly matched with political ends. Consequently, military planners began to request guidance from and consultation with the State Department regarding the formulation, prioritization, and implementation of what they referred to as "national policies."[2] Only such guidance and consultation, they maintained, could insure effective politico-military coordination.

Not all officers were comfortable with such requests. "Policy belongs to the Cabinet," Admiral George Dewey asserted in rejecting an early call for coordination. Similarly, the Army General Staff maintained in 1915 that statesmen shaped policy, whereas the armed forces executed it, and where the duty of the "first leaves off the other takes hold"—a judgment the army field manual of the 1930s reiterated in its assertion that politics and strategy "are radically and fundamentally things apart. . . . Strategy begins where politics end."[3]

The State Department forcefully concurred, and throughout the early decades of the twentieth century it ignored or rejected most requests for guidance and coordination on the grounds that they challenged civilian prerogatives in the policymaking process and thus civilian supremacy over the armed forces.[4] That these prerogatives had traditionally belonged to the State Department was probably an additional reason for its refusal to respond positively. But beyond the issues of civilian supremacy and bureaucratic politics, State's position reflected a view of the nature of war and its relationship to diplomacy that differed sharply from the one held by the armed forces.

Although military planners consistently asserted that civil leadership should determine the "what" of national policy, whereas the armed forces should determine the "how,"[5] they simultaneously viewed international relations through a realist framework in which such distinctions could not be so rigidly maintained. To the contrary, they perceived war to be a standard "phase of international politics" resulting from conflicting national policies, with force and diplomacy as interrelated tools to be used as appropriate for the defense and fulfillment of national policies. Along with such beliefs went the need to coordinate civil and military tasks and to view policy, diplomacy, and force in conjunction rather than separately.[6]

Most State Department officials held very different views. With a few exceptions, they maintained the traditional American beliefs that war was an aberration rather than a normal phase of international relations and that force constituted a separate category and last resort to be used only if diplomacy failed. Along with this went the corollary belief that military officers should have no role whatsoever in policy matters until war actually began. As Secretary of State William Jennings Bryan bluntly stated in rejecting a military proposal to conduct fleet movements during the 1913 crisis with Japan, "army and navy officers could not be trusted to say what we should or should not do, till we actually got into a war." President Woodrow Wilson carried this logic a step further. Shocked and intensely angered by the military's efforts to influence his policy and its refusal to accept a contrary cabinet decision in this crisis, he suspended the JB and promised to abolish it and the Navy General Board (GB) entirely if either again attempted to influence policy in any way. Similar anger and threats occurred two years later when the press reported elaborate army plans in progress for war with Germany. By Wilson's standards, the American serviceman should have "nothing to do with the formulation of her policy. He is to support her policy whatever it is."[7]

Presidential hostility to military planning soon dissipated under the impact of World War I, but the general civilian unwillingness to coordinate with the armed forces or even to inform them of national policies and priorities did not. Throughout the 1920s and 1930s, military requests for guidance and coordination thus continued to meet rejection, minimal cooperation, or stony silence. The State Department did occasionally request advice on military issues, such as naval arms limitation, but it usually rejected or modified the advice it received to suit its predetermined conclusions rather than alter policy to meet military objections. The Washington and London arms limitation treaties of 1921–22 and 1930 were thus negotiated and ratified despite strong naval protests as to their contents. Naval warnings were heeded to a greater extent during the Geneva arms limitation discussions in 1927, but the resulting failure to reach an international accord only hardened State Department belief that the military should be bypassed on such issues. The department also consistently refused military requests for high-level consultation and coordination until 1935, when it finally agreed to participate in JB discussions on the Far East. Not until 1938, however, and then only under fear of Axis subversive activities in the Western Hemisphere, did it agree to establish the high-level State-War-Navy Liaison Committee composed of the army and navy chiefs and the undersecretary of state "to perfect the coordination of these three Departments in the execution of national policy."[8]

Even after the committee's establishment and the outbreak of World War II, however, policy guidance and politico-military coordination remained minimal. An army member of the committee later complained that it "became but the mechanism through which the State Department bent the military arms to its short range objectives."[9] The JB's Joint Planning Committee (JPC) complained in 1939 that it still "frequently had to work in the dark with respect to what national policy is with respect to a specific problem, or what it may be expected to be." The Chief of Naval Operations (CNO) noted in early 1940 that despite "frequent consultation" with State, "things are not planned in advance, and often we do not receive advance information of State Department action which might well have affected our activities."[10]

Thus military planners during the interwar years were forced to compose their own definitions of U.S. policies to serve as guidelines in their strategic planning. In these efforts they relied on common knowledge, public statements by high government officials, and their own beliefs regarding the nature of international relations and American society. They rated preservation of the territorial and ideological integrity of the continental United States and its overseas possessions the fundamental national policy requiring military force. Behind this they listed control of the Panama Canal and its approaches, defense of the Monroe Doctrine, and preservation of the Open Door in China. Other policies to be defended and promoted included isolation from European political quarrels and avoidance of any alliances; protection of neutral maritime rights and maintenance of freedom of the seas; continuation of an immigration policy based on quotas for Europeans and exclusion of Asians; maintenance and strengthening of the merchant marine;

expansion of overseas markets, trade, and investments; and the peaceful settlement of international disputes.[11]

Despite strong public support for this last policy of peaceful settlement of disputes, military planners warned that the other policies could easily lead to conflict and war. War was endemic to the existing international system ("another method of effective continuance of state policy," they asserted in one of their paraphrases of Clausewitz),[12] and the economic factors they rated so prominently in U.S. national policies had been and continued to be, in their view, a fundamental cause of international conflict and war. In this conclusion they departed sharply from the traditional U.S. belief that trade provided a peaceful and rational alternative to power politics and war. Furthermore, they noted, the American people had in the past been very willing to go to war for economic reasons—as well as for moral ones, which constituted another fundamental cause of war.

Defense of U.S. national policies thus necessitated preparations for armed conflict, even though Americans believed in the peaceful settlement of international disputes. Indeed, some planners argued, this national policy made military preparedness even more mandatory. In an early version of what would later be called "deterrence theory," they argued that preparation for the "defense of inalienable rights" was "preventative" rather than "provocative of war" and thus the best means to assure success in the policy of peaceful settlement of international disputes.[13]

Military planners saw potential conflicts with numerous foreign powers and developed a series of "color" plans to cover war with each of them. Before 1939 they considered Japan the most likely adversary because of what they labeled the diametrically opposed and mutually exclusive national policies of the two countries, and thus they developed and concentrated on War Plan ORANGE to cover this contingency. Yet the most dangerous potential enemies were Germany (BLACK) and England (RED), who were more powerful, geographically closer, and a threat to the vulnerable Caribbean area and the northeastern U.S. industrial base. In all planning concerning war against a Japan aligned with a major European power, U.S. strategists thus concluded, in a clear precursor to the World War II "Europe-first" approach, that primary emphasis would have to be placed on the Caribbean and Atlantic rather than the Pacific.[14]

War with a European power or a European-Japanese coalition seemed a remote possibility during the 1920s and early 1930s, however, especially after the 1921–22 Washington Naval Conference resulted in the abrogation of the 1902 Anglo-Japanese alliance as well as a general decrease in international tensions. But U.S.-Japanese relations began to deteriorate soon thereafter, and the possibility of conflict with Tokyo appeared more likely with each passing year. Consequently, the planners continued until 1939 to devote most of their attention to War Plan ORANGE.

Conflicts over ORANGE

The planners were far from unified in their assessments of ORANGE, and through-out the first four decades of the twentieth century a sharp intra- and interservice debate took place over its viability and effectiveness. Officially it centered on the mismatch between U.S. ends and means in the Pacific, but beneath the surface debate also swirled around the appropriateness of the policy assumptions on which ORANGE was based. Whereas naval planners argued that the armed forces should demand more funds from Congress or adjust war plans to compensate for military weakness in Asia and the Pacific, some army planners insisted that addi-tional money would not be forthcoming, existing war plans were unworkable and could not be adjusted, and national policy should therefore be altered so as to remove the sources of potential conflict with Japan.

Although the United States had long maintained forces in China and the west-ern Pacific, they had never been sufficient to protect American interests in the area or even to defend the Philippines against a Japanese attack. Nor had the planners been able to reach a consensus on an appropriate strategic response to such an attack. Within the navy, a major disagreement had emerged between "thrusters," who pressed for bases in the western Pacific and a quick confronta-tion there with Japan, and "cautionaries," who argued that the thrusters' re-sponse was a recipe for disaster and that the fleet should only proceed westward against the Japanese slowly and gradually from bases in the eastern Pacific. Most army planners tended to agree with the cautionaries. The result was a highly di-visive debate that severely embarrassed the armed forces while crippling strategic planning.[15]

A host of interwar political decisions exacerbated this ends/means problem and the resulting strategic debate. In the process, they also illustrated the wide gap that separated all military planners from the American government and people on the relationship between force and diplomacy, the danger of conflict inherent in in-ternational politics and defense of U.S. interests, and the subsequent need for military preparedness.

At the end of World War I Japan had been granted a League of Nations mandate over Germany's Pacific island possessions north of the equator. United States mili-tary planners had objected on the grounds that the islands lay athwart their lines of communication and thus posed a threat in Japanese hands, but they were over-ruled by their civilian superiors. Their objections were also overruled at the Washington Conference, when the Harding administration agreed to naval and fortification limits that the navy opposed. From the planners' viewpoint, these decisions gave Japan a tremendous and perhaps insurmountable advantage should any war break out in the Pacific. Throughout the rest of the 1920s and early 1930s, Congress compounded the problems U.S. strategists now faced by refusing to maintain even allowable force levels in the Pacific. Then in 1934 it exacerbated them further by voting to grant the Philippines independence in ten years but to defend it in the interim.[16]

Had these moves been accompanied by a simultaneous change in U.S. Far Eastern policies and improved relations with Japan, the military's strategic problems might not have been so serious. In 1924, however, Congress had infuriated Tokyo by passing an immigration law that totally excluded Asians, and in the ensuing years Washington insisted on maintaining its Open Door policy in China and protested strongly after 1931 against Japan's aggression in Manchuria and China. The planners believed that these administration policies and Japanese aggressiveness were leading the two nations inexorably to war, while the civilian leadership deprived them of what would be needed to win such a war. In this extremely dangerous situation, either military or national policy had to change, and clarification of both was essential. In a joint letter in 1934 the commanders of the Asiatic Fleet and army forces in the Philippines requested clarification of U.S. policies in the Far East, with a clear decision as to whether defense of the Philippines remained a national policy. If it did, then Washington should increase its force levels, renounce the Washington Treaty limitations on fortifications, and build a major base in the Philippines; if defense of the islands was no longer a national policy, then the exposed American forces should be withdrawn.[17]

Along with this letter came demands from some army planners for just such a withdrawal and for even more drastic changes in national policy. U.S. objectives in China and the Philippines, they argued, were militarily indefensible, economically inconsequential, and bound to lead to an unnecessary military conflict with Japan which the American people, insistent on the peaceful settlement of international disputes, would not support. In the light of these facts, Washington both could and should withdraw completely from the Far East and western Pacific and concentrate instead on continental interests and defense.[18]

Navy planners objected vehemently. Withdrawal from the Far East and western Pacific, one contended, would "yield our nation's geographical barrier against the usurpation by the yellow race of the place of the White man in the Far East," constitute "desertion" of the European colonial powers, deny "encouragement and support" to U.S. commerce with Asia, and "encourage Japan to extend and accelerate domination of the Far East and world markets." From a global perspective, such withdrawal would also "weaken our international standing with a resulting weakening of our influence in European and South American affairs." [19]

This disagreement revealed the sharply divergent army and navy policy beliefs that had long existed beneath their surface agreements as to appropriate U.S. strategies and policies. Still relying on conceptions of national greatness posited by Alfred Thayer Mahan during the 1890s, the navy during the interwar years continued to see foreign trade expansion as a vital national policy and the Far East as the great future battleground in an economic and Darwinian struggle for survival and world supremacy. The continued popularity of such beliefs in naval circles was not surprising. They had previously provided the fleet with its chief raison d'être and had always undergirded ORANGE; in the 1930s they continued to do so. Any challenge to those concepts threatened not simply the navy's strategy but also the very worldview, status, and jobs of its officers. Most military statements emphasizing the importance of Far Eastern interests, as well as most of the ensuing ORANGE war plans, thus originated with the planners on the Navy GB.

Army planners at first acquiesced in such statements and plans, but by the mid-1930s they were no longer willing to do so. With their small forces in China and the Philippines hopelessly stranded and surrounded should a war break out, and with the entire army consisting of fewer than 175,000 men and no additional forces or funds available to protect such far-flung interests, these planners labeled the Mahanian worldview dated, incorrect, self-serving, and dangerous. As Secretary of War Henry L. Stimson would later complain, the navy "frequently seemed to retire from the realm of logic into a dim religious world in which Neptune was God, Mahan his prophet, and the United States Navy the only true Church." Deeply affected by the isolationism, pacifism, and antimilitarism then prevalent in society as well as the small size of their forces, some army planners argued in direct opposition to the navy that continental security was the only policy objective the armed forces could or should defend. [20]

The Debate over Great Britain

Beyond this conflict over the importance of Far Eastern interests was an equally important difference over a related and vital policy issue—whether the United States had to plan for unilateral defense of its interests or whether it could rely on potential allies, most notably Great Britain, for help. By the mid-1930s the navy had come to believe that such reliance was practicable and desirous and would enable the nation to concentrate forces in the Far East as well as obtain valuable assistance for a successful defense of its interests in that area. Army planners reached diametrically opposed conclusions and rejected close association with Britain as impractical and as contrary to U.S. traditions and interests in general.

Numerous Anglo-American differences during and after World War I, along with their general emphasis on the economic causes of war, had led military planners during the 1920s to discount the wartime alliance as a temporary aberration, to rate Britain as a "natural" and dangerous potential foe and "our most probable antagonist" in the Atlantic on the basis of commercial rivalry, and to begin developing War Plan RED to cover such a contingency and RED-ORANGE for a renewed Anglo-Japanese coalition. "History indicates that Red has never hesitated to go to war to maintain its dominance in world trade," authors of the 1930 RED-ORANGE war plan asserted. As one scholar has noted, U.S. officers, especially those attending either war college, became "accustomed to regard Great Britain as one of America's most persistent and deadly rivals in a world shaped by commercial economic and racial antagonisms which might very well lead at almost any moment to war between the two powers." [21] Along with such assessments came an intense suspicion of "perfidious Albion" based on its supposedly Machiavellian history. A 1930 Naval War College study labeled Britain "the greatest economic parasite in the world." In 1932 future World War II CNO Ernest J. King argued in his War College thesis that in light of Anglo-American economic competition and the historic British policy of crushing "any serious challenge to their naval and commercial supremacy," London "must be considered a potential enemy and a powerful one, not so much as to questions of security but certainly as to matters involving the growth of our foreign trade, financial supremacy and our dominant position in world affairs." [22]

By the mid-1930s, however, most naval planners had concluded that serious Anglo-American conflict was unlikely and had reverted to their earlier emphasis on bilateral cooperation. Such cooperation, or at least friendly neutrality, had always been an unstated basis of their ORANGE plans, all of which assumed a peaceful and secure Atlantic ocean controlled by the British fleet. Now naval planners made this implicit premise explicit by stating that the two countries might be able to reach an understanding in one or both oceans that would provide the U.S. fleet with direct assistance as well as enable it to concentrate in the Pacific; the result would be a viable ORANGE war plan and no need for any strategic or policy reassessment. [23]

Many army planners objected to this proposed naval "cure" for the dichotomy between U.S. ends and means in the Pacific, with some viewing it as worse than the original problem. Although the subject "participation with allies" had recently been added to strategic planning at the Army War College, [24] these officers viewed naval proposals for actual Anglo-American military collaboration as violating the national policies of isolation from European political quarrels and avoidance of alliances. Furthermore, close association with Britain would tie the United States to an overextended and decaying empire whose fate, they maintained, was in no way linked to the security of a largely self-sufficient United States.[25] They also warned that Britain was a highly manipulative and untrustworthy power that had used and would continue to use bilateral understandings as a means of getting other powers to protect its far-flung interests. In this regard they feared any understanding with Britain would lead to U.S. defense of extensive British interests in Europe and the Far East and thus participation in unnecessary conflicts and wars. Furthermore, despite army agreement in late 1936 that RED was obsolete, some planners still viewed Britain as a potential enemy and insisted on continued development of it and RED-ORANGE.[26]

To an extent this disagreement can be seen as a classic example of bureaucratic politics: whereas in an ORANGE war against Japan the navy would have the primary offensive mission while the army was relegated to secondary defensive tasks, in a RED war against England or a RED-ORANGE scenario the army would play a major role by invading Canada.[27] The issues went far deeper than self-serving bureaucratic interests, however. As the navy's emphasis on cooperation with England was linked to its global view of U.S. national policies, so army distrust of Britain was linked to its more limited, continental vision of national security. Taken as a whole, these divergent perceptions were at least partially the result of the very different histories and tasks of the two services.

From its very inception the navy had been involved in worldwide missions; it was therefore quite logical that the global, economic, and alliance-oriented Mahanian vision of the 1890s would emerge from this service.[28] The army, on the other hand, had for most of its history possessed a continental and unilateral mission—warfare on the North American continent. Indeed, it was still fighting American Indians at the moment Mahan was writing. Moreover, its one large-scale experience with an overseas, coalition war in 1917–18 had been far from pleasant. Constant arguments with the British and French over creation of an independent U.S. force and appropriate strategy against Germany had left bitter tastes in many army mouths.[29]

Equally if not more important, a Congress fearful of militarism had from 1776 onward kept the continental-based army under much closer scrutiny than the overseas and therefore less-threatening navy. As a result, army officers had become ever mindful of congressional and public views and tended to echo them to a much greater extent than did naval officers. During the 1930s these views were overwhelmingly pacifistic, isolationist, and Anglophobic, and army planners accepted them not merely as factors to be considered in war planning but also as valid and key components of national policy. As one officer pointedly noted in pressing for withdrawal from China and the Philippines on the grounds that the public was unwilling to use force to stop Japan, national objectives were not "the whole of national policy any more than the objectives of a war plan are all of that plan. National policy consists of the objectives the nation pursues, plus the means which the nation desires to employ, or is willing to employ in the attainment of those objectives."[30]

Throughout the 1920s and 1930s those means remained extremely limited (as late as 1937 U.S. defense spending was only 1.5 percent of the national income as compared with 28.2 percent for Japan). In light of this fact and the above definition, some army planners felt justified in advocating drastic changes in national policy as well as strategy. A highly limited continental policy and strategy paralleling the isolationist beliefs then prevalent in American society, they believed, was most appropriate.[31]

This isolationist or "continentalist" strand of thought first surfaced within the interwar armed forces during the famous Billy Mitchell controversy in the 1920s. In arguing that air power could replace naval forces, Mitchell had originally limited his concept of military defense to the continental United States and had thereby denied, implicitly if not explicitly, the importance of the navy's overseas missions as well as its forces. Mitchell's arguments thus appealed to many isolationist senators and members of Congress, and although he soon expanded his concept of U.S. interests to win additional support, these individuals continued to speak admiringly of the defensive air alternative to aggressive and provocative naval forces.[32] Meanwhile, an older continentalist strand of thought was being revived and revised by army officers who through bitter experiences had witnessed the dangers and problems inherent in the navy's approach.

Embick and the Continentalist Alternative

Such ideas were most clearly developed and enunciated during the 1930s by an officer who was playing and would continue to play a pivotal role in U.S. strategic and policy planning: Lieutenant General Stanley Dunbar Embick. Born in 1877 and commissioned from West Point in 1899 as a second lieutenant of artillery, Embick had gradually risen to become by the 1930s a coastal fortifications expert and one of the most senior, highly respected strategic thinkers within the army. In the process he had also become one of the foremost exponents of the continental national policy and military strategy. These he vociferously espoused during the 1930s as commander of Philippine coastal defenses, head of the Army General Staff's War Plans Division (WPD), Deputy Chief of Staff, and a corps and army commander.[33]

The key factors in the development of Embick's thought appear to have been his expertise in coastal fortifications and his 1918–19 service in Europe. The expertise resulted in a mentality geared to cautious defense, one that would express itself as opposition to expansive naval plans for western Pacific bases and strategies as early as 1906–7.[34] The wartime service in Europe provided him with a mentor and a series of disillusioning experiences that would heavily influence his later views of U.S. relations with Europe.

As chief of staff of the American section of the Supreme War Council during World War I and a military member of the U.S. delegation to the ensuing Paris Peace Conference, the then Colonel Embick participated in strategic and policy discussions at the highest levels. He also came under the influence of his superior, General Tasker H. Bliss. Former army chief of staff, head of the American delegation to the Supreme War Council, and chief of the U.S. military delegation at Paris, Bliss was one of the highest ranking officers in the army. He was also one of its leading intellectuals.

Like Bliss, Embick appears to have been an internationalist who in 1918 supported both participation in the war and a large postwar role for the United States within the framework of a Wilsonian League of Nations. Technological innovations, both men concluded, had rendered warfare so devastating that it had ceased to be a valid instrument of national policy. After the defeat of German militarism, war would therefore have to be abolished and replaced by a new international order, one in which the United States should play a major peacekeeping role.

Despite these facts and the pressing need to coordinate the Allied effort during the war if the German threat was to be eliminated, Bliss and Embick witnessed what they considered an appalling display of narrow-minded, destructive greed by the Allied powers. Instead of concentrating on the western front for the defeat of Germany, these powers consistently proposed peripheral campaigns to achieve their self-serving political objectives. They also attempted to break up and use the American Expeditionary Force in such efforts. Throughout the war and at the peace conference, Bliss and Embick found themselves opposing such efforts in the Balkans, the Middle East, and Russia. At the peace conference they also witnessed the emasculation of Wilson's proposals for a new international order by Allies still intent on reaping narrow political advantages. By mid-1919 both men had become convinced that this selfishness and greed had planted the seeds for another devastating world war and that under such circumstances the United States might be best off withdrawing from international affairs so as to preserve itself during the coming conflict. As Bliss bluntly concluded in June of that year, "What a wretched mess it all is! If the rest of the world will let us alone, I think we had better stay on our side of the water and keep alive the spark of civilization to relight the torch after it is extinguished over here."[35]

Such thoughts did not stop Bliss and Embick from supporting U.S. entry into the League of Nations, but they did lead Embick on his return into an intensive analysis of international relations in an effort to determine how his country could indeed be left alone if his worst fears for the future materialized. He began this analysis during the early 1920s while an instructor at the Army War College and continued it during ensuing tours of duty in the Philippines and Washington. In addition to extensive reading, his studies included attendance at the Institute of Politics in Williamstown, Massachusetts, and the Institute of Public Affairs at the University of Virginia, as well as publication of some original work on the factors that determined the war-making ability of a state. By the mid-1920s he had become so enmeshed in these studies that he referred to himself in a letter to Bliss as "something of a recluse."[36] In fact, he was becoming for the interwar army what Bliss had been for the prewar army—one of its foremost soldier-scholars.

By the 1930s, Embick's studies had led him to develop an alternative vision of national security which closely paralleled ideas being enunciated by isolationist politicians and such scholars as Charles Beard. His viewpoint was based on the idea that entry into World War I had been a mistake whose repetition could be avoided only if the country recognized its economic and military self-sufficiency, dropped its unnecessary and dangerous overseas commitments, remained wary of British efforts to manipulate it into an unnecessary and catastrophic future war, and concentrated on a continental-based national policy and military strategy.

During the first half of the decade, such beliefs led Embick into an attack on ORANGE and to calls for withdrawal from the western Pacific and rapprochement with Japan. The Philippines, he warned in 1933 as head of its coastal defenses and again in 1935 as chief of the WPD, had become a "military liability of a constantly increasing gravity," and any attempt to carry out ORANGE with the meager resources available "would be literally an act of madness." A buildup of additional resources and retention of a base in the islands, he further argued, would be militarily unsound, "highly provocative," and totally unwarranted, for U.S. Far Eastern interests were relatively insignificant and conflicted with more important national policies.[37]

Those more important policies centered on the fact that the United States was "the most self-sufficient nation in the world." Unlike Britain, it gained little, economically or militarily, from Far Eastern trade, colonies, and bases. To the contrary, these actually weakened the nation by distracting attention from a proper concentration on a continental economy and defense policy. Embick thus dismissed Far Eastern interests for the present. He also dismissed them for the future. Images of vast potential markets in the area which had previously and still motivated U.S. policymakers were mirages. The Pacific was simply incapable of becoming the great trading center Americans since William Henry Seward had incorrectly predicted it would become. The worldwide disposition of arable land and such critical resources as coal and iron, which determined both industrial and military capacity, dictated that the presently dominant areas of the world—the United States, Britain, and the Rhine Valley—would continue their domination.

For both the present and the future, Embick therefore concluded, U.S. interests in the Far East were "relatively inconsequential. Our vital interests lie in the continental United States," a fact that should be "the fundamental premise in the formulation of our military (including naval) policy." Moreover, American national policies included a commitment "to the maintenance of peace and the avoidance of any entanglements which would lead us into war." A continued military commitment to the Philippines would be "the gravest menace to the success of that policy" because it would constitute the most likely source of conflict with Japan. Embick therefore recommended negotiations with Tokyo to "neutralize" the Philippines, as well as withdrawal of all forces from the islands and from China back to Hawaii.[38]

As deputy chief of staff and army commander between 1936 and 1939, Embick applied a similar analysis to warn against any involvement with Britain in either the growing European crisis or the Pacific, and to support appeasement of the Axis powers. His inclinations in this regard were reinforced in 1937 by a visit to Germany and correspondence with his son-in-law, Major Albert C. Wedemeyer, who was a student at the German War College and who shared his belief that the nation could and should stay out of the looming European war. By late 1937 Embick had turned against all naval plans for offensive operations in the Pacific, labeling ORANGE a "potential national disaster" whose aggressiveness violated "the very spirit of America" and threatened its national security. When his defensive alternatives were rejected he fulfilled a previous threat to go public by openly associating with Frederick J. Libby's National Council for the Prevention of War. He also supported the Ludlow Amendment to require a national referendum for war, corresponded with and advised such isolationist leaders as Senator William Borah of Idaho, and attacked both navy and civilian officials who favored a tough Anglo-American stance against Axis aggression in Europe and the Far East. Such individuals, he wrote in April 1939 to Brigadier General George C. Marshall, his successor as deputy chief of staff, "show less historical sense than the average European peasant. They repeat the same fallacies that led to our being duped twenty years ago and that set the stage for the present situation."[39]

A few months earlier Embick had warned Borah that the navy's recently announced desire to fortify Guam as a means of making ORANGE workable was "literally a mad, imperialistic proposal." In the process of explaining why, he made clear the factors that linked his positions on appropriate U.S. policy in the Far East with his previous experiences and anti-European sentiments. British and French "propaganda," he contended, had for years pressed for U.S. retention of a military commitment in the Philippines because it would constitute "a front line trench for the protection of their Asiatic colonies" yet leave them "free to decide in war if, when and to what extent they will supplement our efforts." Fortification of Guam would only put the United States "farther out to the front" and via its "advanced location with reference to their possessions would afford them more plausible pretexts for standing aloof." Strategically, he again argued that "wiser courses" to check Japan would be either unilateral action in the Mandated Islands, the naval "cautionary" position, or participation in an open alliance with Britain and France that would both commit them to "assuming their full share of the burden of the war" and allow U.S. use of the British naval base at Singapore. In terms of overall policy, however, Embick bluntly labeled either approach "a fatal mistake" and "a betrayal of America's vital interests," and he once again noted his preference for withdrawal from the entire area.[40]

Embick's conclusions were by no means unique within the armed forces. Nor were they poorly received. His defensive emphasis had a long history in the army,[41] and many colleagues and superiors supported his assaults on U.S. strategy and policy in the Far East and Pacific. These reached the JB and the White House in 1937–38. The 1937 publication of *We Can Defend America,* a book by the wartime head of Army Services of Supply Major General Johnson Hagood, echoed and brought to public attention Embick's arguments for a continentalist military policy based on U.S. self-sufficiency. Such arguments were also repeated by Colonel Walter Krueger, Embick's successor as WPD chief, in a 1936 rejection of the possible acquisition of European colonial territory as repayment for unpaid war debts.[42]

Many of Embick's colleagues similarly supported his 1939 assault on the Guam base, with Borah inserting into the *Congressional Record* a critique written by Major General William C. Rivers, a former inspector general of the army who was also active in Libby's organization. Embick's comments to Marshall in that same year had resulted from a specific request for his views and were shown to the chief of staff General Malin Craig, who, Marshall noted, had been "equally impressed." Upon succeeding Craig a few months after this exchange, Marshall as army chief continued to request and rely on Embick's advice.[43]

Krueger's 1936 rejection of European colonial possessions added an important corollary to Embick's continentalist thought. Opposition to acquisition of the British and French West Indies had been based on probable Latin American hostility and congressional refusal to fortify the islands rather than their strategic insignificance. To the contrary, the WPD had emphasized their vital importance to defend not only North America and the Panama Canal but also U.S. trade routes—particularly with South America. Although Embick's original directive on this issue had mentioned continued adherence to the policy of restricting acquisitions to areas of value only "in the defense of our continental area," Krueger argued that hemispheric trade was "becoming increasingly important" in light of the fact that the U.S. position in the Far East was "untenable," its interests there "not vital," and its commitments "a danger rather than an advantage, thus pointing to a withdrawal." The "inescapable logic" of these circumstances indicated to Krueger the necessity to focus not merely on continental defense as Embick had directed but on the entire Western Hemisphere as well. By 1938 such arguments would combine with fear of Axis penetration of Latin America to shift army planners from their continental to a much broader hemispheric defense concept.[44]

Civil-Military Coordination and Conflict

Naval planners refused, of course, to accede to either a continental or a hemispheric national policy and strategy, both of which they considered far too limited. Nor could they resolve their own internal disagreements over proper strategy in the Pacific. The ensuing intra- and interservice disputes continued to divide the JB and its planners throughout the 1930s.

In 1935 the State Department entered the conflict when it finally agreed to some limited politico-military coordination: in response to specific requests by the secretaries of war and navy for political advice as well as warnings about U.S. military weakness, Secretary Hull named Far Eastern expert Stanley Hornbeck to participate in JB deliberations regarding ORANGE and the U.S. position in the Far East. Three years later Hull initiated higher-level and more-formal coordination with the establishment of the Standing Liaison Committee composed of Undersecretary of State Sumner Welles and the army and navy chiefs. But Hornbeck openly sided with the navy in the dispute over ORANGE and insisted, as had the State Department previously, that no U.S. forces be withdrawn from the Far East. He also complained that the army was improperly infringing on a foreign policy question that belonged exclusively to State. The army held its ground, however, resulting in split reports by the JPC, while the State Department limited the Liaison Committee's functions to hemispheric concerns instead of the broader, global policy matters desired by the military planners. Deeply disappointed with State's behavior, the army appealed directly to President Roosevelt to overrule Hornbeck on Far Eastern affairs, settle the army-navy dispute over ORANGE himself, and bypass the State Department on other issues by providing the armed forces with direct and detailed policy guidance.[45]

In Franklin Roosevelt the armed forces finally found a commander in chief willing to provide such guidance, though not as much or the kind they desired. Unlike recent predecessors, FDR had a keen interest in and knowledge of military affairs. During World War I he had served as assistant secretary of the navy and

become, in one scholar's words, "the leading civilian exponent of Mahan's doc-
trines in the Navy Department."[46] He also understood the need for politico-
military coordination. Indeed, in 1919 he had made one of the first formal proposals for high-level State-War-Navy cooperation, a proposal never acted upon—
or apparently even opened within the State Department.[47] And while in his first
term Roosevelt had been largely absorbed with domestic matters, in 1937 he
started to provide the direction and guidance his army and navy officers so des-
perately desired. In that year he began to show an interest in their war plans and
requested the creation of new ones, and in the aftermath of the *Panay* sinking he
initiated naval staff conversations with the British as the navy desired. In 1938 he
appealed to Congress for funds to expand the armed forces; by year's end he was
asserting that the revival of German power threatened the hemisphere with invasion "for the first time since the Holy Alliance in 1818" and necessitated the creation of a huge air force as well as an expanded navy.[48] In 1939 he went far down
the seniority lists to handpick his new army and navy chiefs, General Marshall
and Admiral Harold E. Stark, respectively. Equally if not more important, he
provided these men with a direct link to him in July 1939 by transferring the
JB from the existing service departments to the newly created Executive Office of
the President.

This transfer also altered the board's power, influence, and very nature. Formerly a consultative agency to advise the service secretaries and adjust interservice
disagreements, it now became a true national strategy board with greatly increased
powers and independence. From 1936 onward FDR also increased the powers of
the army and navy chiefs within their respective services so that for the first time
they were in full command of their field forces as well as their staffs. With the
shift of the JB to the Executive Office of the President, they also became Roosevelt's foremost strategic advisers, capable of totally bypassing the service secretaries and responsible only to their commander in chief, who, in effect, now became
the "sole coordinating link" between the nation's strategy and foreign policy.[49]

Roosevelt's guidance to the military chiefs at this time was quite nebulous, however, and it often conflicted with what they thought militarily appropriate even
when it did not leave them in a state of utter confusion. Partially this resulted
because, as president, Roosevelt had to consider the numerous political as well
as military consequences of his actions, with the former often outweighing the
latter. It also resulted from his unique personality and bureaucratic operating
procedure. Rather than provide detailed policy guidelines that could tie him to
specific courses of action, he preferred expedient and often illogical compromises
that offered everyone some immediate satisfaction and enabled him to keep numerous options available for as long as possible. Typical of these needs, prefer-
ences, and characteristics was Roosevelt's "solution" to the army-navy dispute

over whether to keep ground forces in China: he removed the army garrison but left its marine counterpart, thereby giving each service what it desired but worsening the mismatch between U.S. ends and means in Asia.[50]

Equally typical were Roosevelt's vetoes of both a major base in the Philippines and withdrawal from the area, as well as his rearmament proposals that called for massive expansion of air and naval equipment but not of personnel or ground forces. Such proposals would hopefully appeal to isolationists as well as internationalists in Congress while providing indirect defense against Germany by enabling France and Britain to buy aircraft. Unfortunately, they would wreak havoc with military plans to develop a balanced armed force, plans based in part on difficulties the armed forces were facing in determining future national policies and military requirements.[51]

With Roosevelt acting in this manner and lacking clear, detailed policy guidance from the White House or the State Department, the military chiefs were once again forced to act on their own. On the insistence of General Craig, who in late 1937 bluntly labeled current war plans "unsound" and "wholly inappropriate to present conditions," the JB ordered a revision of ORANGE and, when their planners deadlocked, directed the then deputy chief of staff Embick and Rear Admiral James O. Richardson to work out a compromise acceptable to both services.[52]

Surprisingly, Embick and Richardson were able to accomplish this seemingly impossible task in early 1938. A key reason was the fact that British priorities in the European theater, as expressed in the Anglo-American naval staff talks taking place simultaneously, were casting cold water on the possibility of assistance to the U.S. fleet in the Far East. This reinforced the logic of the cautionaries within the navy and made CNO Admiral William D. Leahy more amenable to compromise. Equally important, Richardson was in the cautionary camp. Whereas no document could have compromised the diametrically opposed views of army continentalists and western Pacific thrusters, common ground could be found between the former and the cautionaries. Moreover, Craig was amenable to compromise and willing to go further than Embick to obtain it. Consequently, the army dropped its insistence on presidential authority for any western Pacific operations, while the navy dropped its insistence on an early offensive in that theater. Embick and Richardson agreed instead to a progressive westward advance in the Pacific within the context of emphasizing the importance of defending the Alaska-Hawaii-Panama "strategic triangle."[53]

One scholar has concluded that the army triumphed in these negotiations by forcing the navy to recognize both the primacy of continental defense and the need to alter dramatically plans for action in the western Pacific, and that in the process it began the reorienting of U.S. global strategy away from that ocean.[54] In terms of the language and context of 1938, however, the Embick-Richardson revision of ORANGE was acceptable to everyone primarily because it simply ignored continued army-navy disagreements and used vague language so that each service could obtain what it wanted in the new war plan. The result was a series of superficial contingency plans, with the army planning to withdraw ground and air forces to focus on continental defense and the "strategic triangle" while the navy focused on a gradual advance to the western Pacific from a secured defensive line, rather than a joint, binding commitment to a single and clear line of action. Left unresolved were numerous inconsistencies and problems, most notably what would happen to U.S. forces in the Philippines in the event of a Japanese attack.

The plan's political premises were no sounder than its military conclusions. Indeed, they were dated the day the plan was completed, if not earlier. As with its predecessors, this ORANGE plan anticipated a war between the United States and a single hostile power in one theater, but by 1938 Japan was loosely aligned with Germany and Italy in the Rome-Berlin-Tokyo Axis. Furthermore, Japan and China were by this time engaged in a full-scale if undeclared war, while Britain and France appeared to be heading for a war with Germany and Italy. Even though that war was temporarily averted at the Munich Conference in October 1938, U.S. military planners were forced to realize that they might very well face a coalition of hostile nations in multiple theaters rather than merely Japan in the Pacific and that they might have allies in such a conflict.

The RAINBOW Plans

Soon after Munich the JB therefore ordered the JPC to undertake "exploratory studies and estimates as to the various practicable courses of action" open to U.S. forces in the event of violation of the Monroe Doctrine by one or more of the Fascist powers, along with a simultaneous attempt to extend Japanese influence in the Philippines. For planning purposes the JPC was to assume what amounted to a worst-case scenario: a possible German-Italo-Japanese alliance against an isolated United States, with the "democratic nations" of Europe remaining neutral.[55]

Completed in April 1939, the resulting study of more than sixty pages was quite somber. Although the JPC concluded that the Axis powers were not presently a direct military threat to the United States, it insisted that any definition of U.S. security inherently included "not only freedom from invasion, but also freedom from external injury to our world trade, and from interference with our domestic course of life." The Axis did constitute a serious potential threat in this regard, as well as to the Monroe Doctrine and the Panama Canal. Germany might well attempt to establish Atlantic island or West African bases to ferry troops and aircraft to subversive elements in South America, while all three Axis powers were already attempting "economic, political and cultural penetration" of Latin America. And although Japan was preoccupied with China and Russia and thus not likely on the basis of rational calculation to become involved in conflict with the United States over the next few years, it was "not safe to rely on Japanese action being controlled by practicability or logic as these qualities shape up in the American mind." Indeed, given Japan's previous actions and the fact that its "practically foot-loose" navy was capable of acting on its own, Japanese action against U.S. interests was possible "at any time, even in the near future, with little or no warning." [56]

Should Japan act alone, the ORANGE war plan would be put into effect, though the JPC emphasized, as had Embick, Richardson, and others previously, that all plans should be for a gradual advance westward and for a limited war against Tokyo. Should Germany act alone or with Italy, the appropriate U.S. response would be to seek naval predominance in the western Atlantic, "capture or neutralize" Atlantic and West African bases, and send an expeditionary force to neutralize enemy footholds in South America. If all three nations acted simultaneously, the JPC concluded in a reaffirmation of the old RED-ORANGE plan as well as more recent Army War College studies, there could be "no doubt" that U.S. "vital interests . . . would require offensive measures in the Atlantic against Germany and Italy to preserve the vital security of the Caribbean and the Panama Canal," which would necessitate "a defensive attitude in the eastern Pacific." [57]

That was easier said than done, however, and the JPC noted numerous potential problems. Although Germany and Italy could not successfully invade the Western Hemisphere unless the United States had previously committed itself in the western Pacific, for example, the navy could very well be so committed if Japan attacked before any German move. Furthermore, an "aroused" or "emotionalized" public might force unwise military actions, such as an attempted defense of the Philippines. For the time being, the JPC concluded, increased preparedness was needed via larger forces, completion of defenses, additional bases in the Pacific, increased intelligence, and expanded missions to Latin America.

These exploratory studies did not completely satisfy the army or the navy. The Army WPD chief admitted to Marshall on May 2 that they did "represent the best possible compromise between the differing Army and Navy views on the subject," but he pointedly noted that the two services were as far apart as ever on the western Pacific. Indeed, army members of the JPC denied that the public considered Guam and the Philippines to be vital interests worthy or any longer capable of being defended. Worried that naval plans might involve not only a futile defense of these possessions but also U.S. ground forces occupying positions on the Asian mainland and defending European "interests," the WPD chief concluded that before any directive for a new war plan against the Axis, the War and Navy Departments should "obtain from the President a specific indication of our national policy with reference to the Western Pacific in the event of war." Any JB directive to the planners should be "based upon a clear understanding from the President as to our national policies with respect to hemisphere defense, the defense of the Philippines, our position in the Far East, our actual or potential commitments to Great Britain, France, or other democracies, and the specific cooperation that we may rely on from those democracies."[58]

No such indication or understanding from Roosevelt was forthcoming, however, and the JB thus responded in early May by ordering the JPC to prepare a new set of war plans, appropriately named RAINBOW, to cover virtually every possible strategic response to a combined Axis attack. Each plan was to assume the neutrality of Britain, France, and Latin America yet simultaneously clarify the "specific cooperation" desired from each and provide for the "alternative situations" that would develop if the United States received such cooperation.

These rather contradictory directives originally translated into four proposed war plans: (1) unilateral defense of North America above ten degrees north latitude; (2) control of the western Pacific, as rapidly as possible consistent with the defense of North America; (3) defense of the entire Western Hemisphere; and (4) projection of U.S. forces into the eastern Atlantic and Africa or Europe, in a concerted action with Britain and France as rapidly as possible consistent with defense of North America, to defeat Germany and/or Italy. Probably on naval insistence, the JPC quickly complained that alliance with Britain and France might result in projection of U.S. forces to the Pacific rather than the Atlantic, because the Allies could secure the latter while expanded Japanese aggression could be expected in the former against all the coalition's possessions. It therefore proposed creation of a fifth plan to cover such a contingency, with a renumbering so that this addition was listed second and the former plans 2–4 became plans 3–5, respectively.

The JB agreed, and its revised directive thus called for the creation of five plans, to be based on two opposing political premises and five different strategic options. RAINBOWS 1, 3, and 4 would assume the United States had no allies against a combined Axis assault; alliance with Britain and France constituted the basic political assumption behind RAINBOWS 2 and 5. Three strategic options were to be prepared for a war effort without allies: defense of North America above ten degrees north latitude, with a strategic defensive in the Pacific behind the Alaska-Hawaii-Panama line (RAINBOW 1); defense of North America combined with the protection of "vital United States interests in the Western Pacific" (RAINBOW 3); and defense of the entire Western Hemisphere (RAINBOW 4). If Britain and France were U.S. allies and in control of the Atlantic, continental/hemispheric security would not be so pressing an issue. Consequently, the two remaining plans were to explore "forward" strategic options: an offensive to carry out allied as well as U.S. tasks in the western Pacific (the new RAINBOW 2); and a defensive posture in that theater, with forces concentrated for offensive action on the African or European continents (RAINBOW 5).[59]

Although a revised version of RAINBOW 5 would become the primary U.S. war plan by early 1941, it was by no means the favored approach in 1939—or in 1940. The JB and JPC had admittedly reaffirmed their belief that offensive action against the more dangerous European powers had to take precedence over action against Japan, but the possibility of having to fight all three Axis nations simultaneously and without allies led them to give top priority to the development of RAINBOW 1's unilateral, continental, and defensive strategy. The JPC completed this plan on July 27, 1939; the JB and service secretaries approved it in the following month, and Roosevelt (orally) in October.[60]

Beyond that no army-navy agreement existed as to which of the remaining options was most likely and should be developed first. Maintaining that Britain and France would keep the Atlantic secure and thereby free their forces for offensive operations against Japan and encouraged by secret Anglo-American staff talks in Washington that spring regarding possible future collaboration, navy planners called for the development of RAINBOW 2. Army planners acquiesced, but only with grave reservations. Still disagreeing with naval priorities, unwilling to plan on the assumption of defense of the critical Atlantic and Western Hemisphere by dubious European allies, and concerned with the low level of preparedness for any overseas activity, they continued to emphasize the need for a continental strategy as enunciated in RAINBOW 1 and, more and more, the hemispheric strategy associated with RAINBOW 4.[61]

World War II thus began in Europe with the U.S. armed forces disagreeing over appropriate strategy and national policy beyond defense of North America and the eastern Pacific and with minimal civil-military coordination, despite the establishment of recent and important links with the State Department and the president. Such problems were far from new. Ever since the inception of planning staffs at the turn of the century, the armed forces had been requesting policy guidance and coordination but receiving unsatisfactory replies. Thus they had developed their own definitions of national policies to serve as guides for strategic planning but had split over the viability of the ORANGE war plan and the validity of the policy assumptions that underlay it. By the late 1930s the looming world crisis had led the State Department and the president to offer some guidance and coordination, but not enough or the kind to satisfy the planners or to settle their disputes. As a result U.S. war plans remained vague and unworkable. In the absence of detailed policy guidance all possible contingencies were considered, but no consensus existed on what to do beyond unilateral continental defense. The problem went beyond unpreparedness and interservice rivalry to two very different conceptions of proper national security policy, conceptions that reflected the isolationist-internationalist split in American society as a whole as well as the very different missions, histories, and outlooks of the two services.

Although these problems had existed for many years before 1939 without dire consequences, the outbreak and course of the war in Europe made their continuation a very clear and present danger to American security. The next two years would thus witness dramatic efforts by U.S. military planners to achieve greater interservice and civil-military coordination so that appropriate strategies and policies could be agreed on, developed, and implemented. The result would be a major reorientation of American strategy and national policy.

New Strategies and Policies
for a Coalition War, 1939–1941

Interservice disagreements and confusion regarding U.S. strategy and policy continued from the September outbreak of war in Europe into the early months of 1940. During this time the JPC continued to work on the RAINBOW 2 scenario, albeit with growing misgivings and uncertainty in light of wartime events.

These misgivings and uncertainties were visible within the plan itself, which noted the need to revert to RAINBOW 1 should Germany defeat the Allies, the very limited nature of U.S. objectives in any coalition war against Japan, and the fact that allied objectives would be much more expansive than and in conflict with U.S. objectives. They were also visible in the JPC's decision to initiate preliminary studies of RAINBOW 5 before 3 and 4 "in view of the present world situation"— one that had changed "profoundly" from the assumptions of the original RAINBOW directives issued less than a year earlier—and its April request to alter the envisioned scenarios of all five plans. RAINBOWS 1 and 4 would now project Axis violation and unilateral U.S. defense of the Monroe Doctrine after the European war had ended, whereas the remaining three plans would be based on the war still in progress and the United States allied with the European democracies. In RAINBOWS 2 and 3, those nations retained control of the Atlantic and Indian oceans while Japan, supported by Germany and Italy, attacked the Far Eastern interests of the European democracies and the United States. This would lead Washington to join the Allied coalition and, because the Atlantic remained secure, project its power into the western Pacific—either immediately (RAINBOW 2) or from the eastern Pacific "as rapidly as circumstances permit" (RAINBOW 3). RAINBOW 5, on the other hand, envisaged Britain and France on the verge of defeat by Germany, "with a resultant threat to the security of the United States and to the letter or spirit of the Monroe Doctrine." In this situation the United States would project its major forces to the eastern Atlantic and Africa or Europe as soon as possible so as to achieve with Britain and France "the decisive defeat of Germany."[1]

Three of the five revised RAINBOW plans would thus be based on the United States fighting as a member of a coalition and projecting its forces outside the hemisphere. Whether, when, and in which direction it would project those forces remained open questions, however, with the answers partially dependent on the plans and military performance of its potential allies. The planners therefore requested conversations with Britain and France "as soon as the diplomatic situation permits," as well as a new priority order to allow preliminary work first on RAINBOW 3 and then 5, followed by completion of each before beginning work on 4.[2]

Unilateral Hemispheric Defense: The Brief Consensus

The JB approved these changes in the RAINBOW directives on April 10,[3] but within weeks they were totally overtaken by Hitler's stunning military victories in Europe. Hitler's success called into question the basic political assumptions behind RAINBOWS 2, 3, and 5—alliance and concerted action with Britain and France—while posing a potentially mortal threat to U.S. security in the Atlantic and Western Hemisphere. Consequently, in May the JB reversed the priorities it had just approved in April. Work ceased on RAINBOWS 2 and 3, and even though 2 had already been completed it was never forwarded to the board for approval. Instead, RAINBOW 4 for unilateral hemispheric defense, which a month earlier had been downgraded to lowest priority, now was elevated to top priority and completed within the month. "*The date of the loss of the British or French fleets,*" that plan bluntly concluded, "*automatically sets the date of our mobilization.*"[4] The threat of Anglo-French defeat, along with the loss of control in the Atlantic, had temporarily ended U.S. strategic uncertainty and interservice dispute in favor of the army's continental and hemispheric defense plans.

On May 22 the Army WPD clearly explained the logic behind this dramatic shift. Its list of "imminently probable complications of today's situation" included Nazi-inspired revolutions in Latin America, Japanese attacks in the Pacific, the decisive defeat of England and France, and ensuing German aggression in the Western Hemisphere. Although Washington had "vital" interests in the Far East and Europe as well as South America, it could send forces to only one of these areas without risking a dangerous dispersion of forces and would not have the capacity to conduct major operations in Europe or the Far East for at least a year. Consequently, it should concentrate on the Western Hemisphere. An early decision was necessary, the WPD warned, on "what we are *not* going to do" and "what we must prepare to do."[5]

Embick concurred, though he placed greater emphasis on continental than hemispheric security. RAINBOW 4 could be considered sound, he informed the WPD on June 8, only if the proposed extension of U.S. power to South America did not expose the nation's "more vital interests" in North America. The same held true for RAINBOW 3 with its proposal for a delayed extension of U.S. power into the Pacific. He bluntly rejected RAINBOW 2 for leaving exposed "the vital areas" of the continental United States, and he once again called for a reversal of the "past provocative attitude" toward Japan. RAINBOW 5 "appears necessary," he admitted, "since public opinion may force us into the war," but clearly both he and the WPD rejected any such entry or projection of U.S. forces into the Atlantic or Pacific.[6]

Embick and the WPD were far from alone in their continental/hemispheric re-action to Hitler's victories. Indeed, given the paltry size of the U.S. armed forces, any more extensive reaction would have verged on madness. Still ranking nine-teenth in the world in size, the army could field only five divisions totaling eighty thousand men, with air support limited to 160 pursuit planes and 52 heavy bomb-ers. Although in somewhat better shape, the navy was a one-ocean force, and with its April movement to Pearl Harbor, the east coast was virtually defenseless.[7] When Marshall brought the revised May 22 WPD memorandum to the attention of Stark, Welles, and Roosevelt, all concurred that "we must not become involved with Japan, that we must not concern ourselves beyond the 180th meridian, and that we must concentrate on the South American situation."[8] Within days Stark and Marshall were ordering plans for the seizure of European possessions in the hemisphere and, under direct presidential order, military action to check Nazi-inspired revolts in Brazil. These were incorporated into a larger set of military expeditions to secure the hemisphere within RAINBOW 4, and by mid-August that plan had received presidential approval.[9] German victories and U.S. unprepared-ness had apparently ended the Army-Navy split and resulted in a clear and unani-mous civil-military as well as interservice agreement to concentrate on hemi-spheric defense.

This consensus was short-lived, however, if indeed it ever truly existed. By early June Stark was opposing any movement of the fleet from the Pacific on the grounds of the "probable weakening effect on stability in the Pacific against a possible strengthening of the situation in Latin America."[10] In August the GB re-iterated its calls for retention of Philippine bases under U.S. sovereignty unless the government was determined "not to support, under any circumstances, now or in the future, the existing Far Eastern policies or to be a factor in Western Pacific developments."[11] Three weeks later Hornbeck voiced State Department opposition to even a temporary shift of the fleet back to the west coast for maneu-vers and training related to Panama Canal defense on the grounds it would di-minish U.S. influence on Japan and "tend to emphasize the fact that our policy is essentially a policy of defense in our own waters (only)."[12]

More important, Roosevelt refused to remain passive in the Far East and as cautious as his military advisers or to assume as they did that British surrender was imminent and no assistance should be furnished to London. Despite his supposed agreement to the army's sharply limited and hemispherically centered policies and strategies, the president launched a series of major initiatives during the summer, over army and navy objections, in both Europe and the Far East. These included the extension of material aid to Great Britain, the application of early economic sanctions against Japan, and the maintenance of the Pacific Fleet in its new and exposed position at Pearl Harbor in an effort to deter further Japanese aggression. The president also seemed determined not to make the hard choices over strategic and policy priorities that his military advisers now considered mandatory. On June 18 he rejected a proposal to transfer a major part of the fleet from the Pacific to the Atlantic. A week later he theoretically approved the severe limitations on strategy and policy that Marshall and Stark were recommending but characteristically did so with so many generalized qualifiers as to make his agreement meaningless. Throughout the early summer he overruled army and navy objections to sending England military assistance. By September he had further extended that assistance and U.S. commitments via the "swap" of fifty overage destroyers for ninety-nine-year leases on British bases in the Western Hemisphere, and according to navy rumors he had to threaten Stark with relief before winning the CNO's agonized acquiescence in a trade most naval officers opposed. Simultaneously he continued to keep the fleet at Pearl Harbor over army and navy objections, and by October he was proposing, in effect, a long-range blockade against the Japanese should they respond aggressively to Britain's reopening of the Burma Road.[13]

By themselves such presidential moves would have probably forced a reassessment of U.S. war plans and priorities before the end of the year.[14] The main catalysts came from overseas, however: from the Axis Powers in the form of the September Tripartite Pact, which threatened the United States with a multifront war; and from London in the form of a British initiative that included an explanation of their global strategy to U.S. military observers in London, a request for naval assistance at Singapore and revived staff talks, and a proposed accord whereby they would defend the Atlantic while the U.S. fleet assumed responsibility for the Pacific. Then on October 4 British prime minister Winston S. Churchill formally requested from Roosevelt immediate dispatch of a U.S. naval squadron to Singapore for a "friendly visit."[15]

The proposed Anglo-American accord appeared to be exactly what naval planners had previously desired to free their forces for action against Japan. By the fall of 1940, however, they were no longer willing to entrust Atlantic—and with it hemispheric security—to a nation that appeared on the brink of defeat. They were also beginning to face the severe shortcomings within their Pacific war plans, as well as the dangerous imbalance between policy goals and available military means, that Embick and his army associates had been noting for many years. RAINBOW 3 consequently shrank to a token support of the British and Dutch in Southeast Asia, and Stark later admitted to Marshall that he had supported this only because the navy had to be ready to help them in the Far East if so ordered "by higher authority." Such doubts logically extended to RAINBOW 2, leading Stark and Marshall to reject the Singapore proposal and assert the primacy of the Atlantic in early October.[16]

These doubts were heavily reinforced by the January appointment of Richardson as commander in chief of the U.S. Fleet. A noted cautionary within the navy, the admiral had collaborated with Embick on the 1937–38 ORANGE revisions and apparently shared his doubts about the plan, the policy assumptions behind it, and the wisdom of obtaining Britain as an ally.[17] While the GB continued from 1938 to 1940 to support the traditional navy position regarding the western Pacific, Richardson's doubts about any plans for movement into the area and concern for hemispheric security—which he bluntly labeled "the paramount thing for us"— only grew. No naval officer in the long history of ORANGE, Edward Miller has concluded, "so despised the plan as he did."[18] He strongly opposed the decision to move the fleet to Pearl Harbor and made that opposition clear to Roosevelt and the State Department as well as to Marshall and Stark. "His reaction is identical with yours," Marshall told Embick in July, "except that he expresses himself with tremendous vigor on the subject."[19]

In October Richardson returned to Washington to issue more warnings and try, as had Embick in the 1930s, to change U.S. foreign as well as military policies. After a second and apparently disastrous meeting with Roosevelt, he bluntly warned Stark, in what has been aptly labeled "the most scathing condemnation of the Orange plan, and of war planning itself, ever written by a high naval commander,"[20] that ORANGE was unworkable and did not have the wholehearted endorsement of any flag officer, that RAINBOW 2's assumptions were untenable, that U.S. policy in the Pacific was leading toward war with Japan, and that he could not formulate any coherent, alternative war plans "in the absence of a clear picture of national policy, national commitments and national objectives." A "realistic" war plan, he concluded, would be coordinated with national policy and focus on securing the hemisphere before gradually extending U.S. power outward. That would require control of the Western Atlantic; going to war with Japan, naval planners made clear, would necessitate a now unacceptable reliance on a Great Britain teetering on the verge of defeat to exercise such control.[21]

Although naval officers did not share the continental vision of Embick and other army planners, military and political realities were forcing them to similar conclusions, requests for policy guidance, and opposition to what they considered

Roosevelt's provocative policies (Richardson's expression of this opposition to the president in October was so blunt as to result in his removal as commander in chief of the fleet).[22] Moreover, naval planners certainly did share the army's fear of entrusting Atlantic/hemispheric security to Britain, which would be mandatory if war erupted with Japan, as well as a fear of British manipulation of U.S. forces in defense of the British Empire. London's suggestion that U.S. forces defend Singapore reinforced these fears, leading to reassertion of the army belief that U.S. security was in no way dependent on continuation of the empire. Large segments of the public and State Department agreed. As Assistant Secretary of State Adolf Berle had bluntly noted in his diary a year earlier, "we have no necessary interest in defending the British Empire, aside from the fact that we prefer the British as against the German method of running an empire."[23]

Berle carefully added, however, that the requirements of continental and hemispheric security meant the United States did have "a very real and solid interest in having the British, and not the Germans, dominant in the Atlantic."[24] German victories in 1940 brought into question continued British control of that ocean and thereby boldly illustrated that, earlier army comments notwithstanding, American security was related to Britain's fortunes.

This realization did not immediately convert the armed forces into supporters of close Anglo-American cooperation. To the contrary, army and navy strategists opposed aid to Britain during the spring and summer of 1940 on the grounds that London could not survive the German onslaught and that they needed the military supplies to build up their own meager forces for continental and hemispheric defense. As one army planner warned in mid-June, "if we were required to mobilize after having released guns [to Britain] necessary for this mobilization and were found to be short in artillery materiel . . . everyone who was a party to the deal might hope to be found hanging from a lamp post." By the fall, however, two events had forced a change in their views: British survival, and Roosevelt's insistence on aiding London. With German failure in the Battle of Britain and the completion of the destroyer-bases deal in September, the planners were forced to come to grips with an England that remained an active belligerent and a White House–directed policy, supported by the public, of aid to and collaboration with London.[25]

Given these realities, the planners' essential problem was how to reorient U.S. strategy so as to achieve continued British survival and Anglo-American collaboration without falling victim to British manipulation or a dangerous dispersion of forces. Collaboration to ensure London's survival and U.S. security was one thing; defending the entire empire according to British plans was something quite different. In light of the sorry state of U.S. planning and preparation, however, the badly divided Americans had no strategic alternatives to offer. Continental and hemispheric defense via RAINBOWS 1 and 4 were stopgap, internal compromises, too limited in their vision and already made irrelevant by presidential decisions. Indeed, by October new Navy WPD chief Captain Richmond Kelly Turner had concluded that these plans were "defective in the extreme" and canceled supplemental studies. Countering British proposals would require a global rather than a hemispheric alternative, one which would clearly delineate U.S. national interests, which the army and navy could agree on, and which would be accepted by the State Department and a president who so far had refused to outline or prioritize an appropriate course of action—or even define just what U.S. interests and policies were in this crisis. That refusal weighed so heavily on the planners and their chiefs as to lead them now to offer such a definition themselves, along with a new and appropriate strategy.[26]

Plan Dog: Germany-First and Anglo-American Alliance

Galvanized into action by these factors and Richardson's entreaties, Stark went home one day in late October after a three-hour conversation with Turner and sat down "to clear my own mind" on the issues involved. That effort kept him working from early morning until 2:00 A.M. the following morning on the rough draft of a memorandum, which over the next ten days he revised in view of "day and night" discussions with his key planners. In early November he circulated the results as his own analysis of U.S. national policies and appropriate strategy.[27]

Commonly known as the Plan Dog memorandum, this document has received considerable and well-deserved attention because of its conclusion that in any war against the Axis powers the United States should pursue a Germany-first approach in conjunction with England while maintaining a defensive posture against Japan. In asserting what would become the basis of U.S. and Allied strategy in the war, Stark's memorandum was, as Louis Morton notes, "perhaps the most important single document in the development of World War II strategy." But just as important as Stark's strategic conclusions were the policy assumptions and conclusions within the document and the reasons for their enunciation at this time. Composed in the immediate aftermath of Roosevelt's 1940 reelection as well as the British request for naval assistance at Singapore and the Richardson warnings, Plan Dog was clearly directed at the civilian leadership of the nation as well as the armed forces, and at overall U.S. foreign policies as well as military strategies.[28]

Although Stark devoted much attention to attacking ORANGE and emphasizing the importance of Britain's war effort to U.S. security, he made clear that this did not translate into acceptance of British plans. Rather, he emphasized the need to develop a coherent strategy and policy suitable to U.S. rather than British interests by recommending "the prosecution of a national policy, with mutually support-ing diplomatic and military aspects," that would be guided by "a determination that any intervention we may undertake shall be such as will immediately promote our own national interest."[29]

In defining what constituted U.S. national interests, Stark departed sharply from past estimates by openly linking, for the first time, U.S. security to the Eu-ropean balance of power and the continuation of that balance to British fortunes. Preservation of the "territorial, economic and ideological integrity" of the United States and the rest of the hemisphere, the primary national policy, had previously and still depended on a strong British navy and empire to check any military incursion by a hostile Continental power and to keep open the "profitable foreign trade . . . particularly with Europe," without which the U.S. economy could not support the heavy armaments necessary for defense. If Britain fell, Stark warned, the nation would be without these necessary prerequisites for security, and in this weakened condition "we would find ourselves acting alone, and at war with the world." Because "prevention of the disruption of the British Empire" was thus a major national objective related to and subordinate only to continental and hemi-spheric defense, support of Britain against Germany had to be the second funda-mental U.S. national policy in the present crisis.[30]

Stark also listed as a major national objective "diminution of the offensive mili-tary power of Japan, with a view to the retention of our economic and political interests in the Far East," but this was clearly of secondary importance because securing continental and hemispheric defense now required major efforts to aid Britain. Furthermore, the degree to which the CNO wished to diminish Japanese power differed substantially from the degree he wished to diminish German power. Reiterating and expanding on statements in RAINBOW 2 and the JPC as-sessment of 1939 as well as Richardson's entreaties, he considered it "doubtful" that reduction of Japan to "an inferior military and economic power" would be in U.S. interests, noting in this regard that "a balance of power in the Far East is to our interest as much as is a balance of power in Europe."[31] Such a balance, he clearly implied, would have to include a strong Japan.

Restoration of the European balance, on the other hand, would require a clear and decisive victory over Germany, not merely British survival, which in turn would require "the complete, or, at least, the partial collapse of the German Reich." Despite London's "over-optimistic" assertions to the contrary, Stark maintained that Britain could not force such a collapse by itself. Its available military power and peripheral strategy of blockade and bombing were simply insufficient. Even-tual victory would "probably" depend on the ability "ultimately to make a land offensive against the Axis powers"—something Britain could not do alone. Allied ground as well as naval forces and material would be needed, as well as the retention of "geographical positions from which successful land action can later be launched." Stark specifically noted Egypt, Gibraltar, and Northwest Africa in this regard, rating their importance higher than any British possessions in the Far East and mentioning the possibility of launching the "ultimate offensive" from these areas into Portugal, Spain, and France.[32]

In light of these facts, Stark listed four possible long-term strategies, in the form of questions labeled A through D, and rejected three of them as antithetical to the national interests and policies he had just analyzed. Hemispheric defense and continued avoidance of war for as long as possible (A), the Army-Navy-State compromise of the last five months, was ineffective because it would do nothing to aid Britain, whose continued survival was so central to that hemispheric defense. Sending maximum military assistance to potential allies in both the Atlantic and the Pacific (C), the opposite of such a limited effort and the direction in which America seemed to be heading under Roosevelt's policies and London's simultaneous requests for aid in the Atlantic and naval concentration in the Pacific to defend Singapore, would so disperse U.S. forces as to preclude the concentration necessary to conduct successful offensive operations in either theater, and a failure in one or the other would result in a "disastrous" strategic situation. Preparation for offensive operations against Japan (B), the old ORANGE and new RAINBOW 2 and RAINBOW 3 war plans that seemed suitable given British suggestions regarding Singapore, was actually antithetical to both U.S. and British interests. London required massive aid in Europe, not in the Pacific, to defeat Germany. And if Britain lost the war in Europe after this aid had been sent to the Pacific, the United States would have to redeploy its forces, under the worst of circumstances, to the Atlantic. "There is no dissenting view on this point," Stark noted. Furthermore, even a limited war against Japan, consisting primarily of economic blockade, could easily escalate into an unlimited conflict because of "the pressure of public opinion." Stark therefore recommended that diplomatic as well as military policies in the Pacific be extremely limited and defensive.

That left the fourth alternative, Plan D, or "Dog" in naval parlance: concentration for "an eventual strong offensive in the Atlantic as an ally of the British, and a defensive in the Pacific." Such concentration, Stark warned, might eventually expand far beyond naval forces to encompass a full-scale land offensive in the European theater, which public opinion might not support. Despite this potential problem, D was the best strategic alternative for the accomplishment of U.S. policy objectives. Stark therefore recommended its acceptance and the immediate initiation of detailed staff talks with the British, Canadians, and Dutch. U.S. intervention under Plan D would not guarantee victory in Europe, he admitted, and it could result in an inability to check Japanese expansion as well as the possible loss of the Philippines and U.S. "political and military influence" in the Far East.

"Chances for success" in Europe would be "in our favor," however, "particularly if we insist upon full equality in the political and military direction of the war," while disaster in the Far East could be avoided by "a positive effort to avoid war with Japan."[33]

In his extraordinary memorandum Stark had thus done much more than simply state what would become the fundamental U.S. strategic decision of the war. He had outlined a balance-of-power view of American national interests and policies in the present situation, one that for the first time clearly linked U.S. security to Britain. He had also deduced an appropriate strategy in light of these interests and policies, rejecting alternative approaches as counterproductive to them. In the process he had recommended badly needed staff talks with the British, finally buried naval preoccupation with the flawed ORANGE, RAINBOW 2, and RAINBOW 3 war plans, and arrived at a strategy the army and navy could mutually support. Moreover, he had warned the president and the State Department to cease their present military and diplomatic overcommitments, especially in the Pacific, and provided them with a clear strategy-policy match linked to U.S. interests. In doing so he had made presidential action and leadership more likely. As the historian James Leutze has noted, Stark had also arrived at a strategic approach that, when combined with the enormous increase in naval strength recently recommended by the navy and approved by Congress, would make the U.S. fleet the primary naval force in the world by distribution, mission, and size.[34] Far from accidentally he was also proposing a possible U.S. expeditionary force for Europe only a few months after Congress had made such an option possible by passing the first peacetime draft bill in U.S. history and more than quadrupling authorized army strength. Equally important, Stark had accepted the close link between British victory and U.S. security without accepting a strategy that involved manipulation of American forces for British ends. In this conflict, the United States would determine its own strategy in its own interests.

While the navy rethought its strategic assumptions and conclusions regarding the Far East, army planners simultaneously reconsidered their continental/hemispheric views and strategies in light of world realities—economic as well as military. As early as mid-June Marshall had proposed concentration in the Atlantic,[35] and in July a subordinate sent him a summary of what he labeled "an outstandingly significant article" by Walter Lippmann in *Life* magazine that strongly reinforced the logic of such concentration. Titled "The Economic Consequences of a German Victory," Lippmann's article argued that the American free enterprise system could not survive with the other three industrial "workshops of the world"— that is, Western Europe, Russia, and Japan—in totalitarian hands. Attempted competition with "these gigantic government monopolies managed by dictators and backed by enormous armed force" would be equivalent to "naked soldiers trying to stop a charge of tanks." U.S. trade would thus be reduced to North America, and the resulting economic problems would open the nation to foreign agents and influence.[36] Such arguments directly challenged the emphasis of Embick and others on continental self-sufficiency and defense, thereby undermining the logic behind RAINBOWS 1 and 4 while supporting the conclusions that Stark was reaching.

The major points in the CNO's memorandum thus quickly received Marshall's "general agreement" in November, along with army criticism that illustrated continued interservice differences of opinion over national policy and strategy. Despite Stark's clear preference for concentration in the Atlantic, the Army WPD saw a dangerous, continued preoccupation with the Pacific in his inclusion as a national policy the "diminution" of Japanese military power "with a view to retention of our economic and political interests in the Far East." This would result "at the minimum" in an undesirable limited war in the Pacific, along with an unlimited one in the Atlantic. Asserting that it was "extremely dangerous even to intimate that all of the stated national objectives can be sustained simultaneously," the WPD suggested that Stark's strategy and policy conclusions regarding the Far East be deleted and replaced with a policy of no material commitments to that theater and no war with Japan under any circumstances. It also attacked the RAINBOW 3 plan for limited Pacific action and exhibited a much stronger antipathy toward the British and fear of manipulation than had Stark. Faced with Roosevelt's pro-British policy and the existing world crisis, the WPD accepted the CNO's emphasis on the importance of Britain and its fleet to U.S. security, yet it implicitly denied the importance of the British Empire to that security by attacking Stark's notion of an invasion of the Iberian peninsula from imperial bases. It also noted as an additional disadvantage of the hemisphere defense option the fact that any small contingents sent to Europe under such a strategy would probably be merged with British units, thereby making "full control of our forces at a later date more difficult to arrange." Fear of just such a repetition of the World War I experience led the WPD to agree to combined staff talks only if they proceeded "on the basis that the United States shall retain full control of its own forces."[37]

Stark's memorandum and the Army WPD comments were quickly forwarded to Roosevelt, who avoided any direct approval but made clear that he wished his service chiefs to proceed. On November 18 they ordered the JPC to draft a combined statement based on Plan Dog.[38] Simultaneously, Marshall informed Stark of his planners' attacks on RAINBOW 3 as "just what Germany would like to see us undertake" and called for its readjustment on the basis that national interests "require that we resist proposals that do not have for their immediate goal the survival of the British Empire and the defeat of Germany" and that "we avoid dispersions that might lessen our power to operate effectively, decisively if possible, in the principle theatre—the Atlantic." Any aid to Britain in the Far East should focus on "relieving them of naval obligations in the Atlantic." Stark agreed with Marshall's logic but could not concur with this proposal because of Roosevelt's behavior. "Should we become engaged in the war described in Rainbow 3," he replied, "it will not be through my doing but because those in higher authority have decided that it is to our best national interest to accept such a war."[39]

While the service chiefs grappled with this problem, two of their subordinates on the JPC, Turner and Colonel Joseph T. McNarney, worked on the joint statement based on Plan Dog. By December 10 they had successfully compromised army-navy differences, and on December 21 the JB tentatively approved their work. Stark's comments on Far Eastern interests and policies were watered down rather than deleted, as the army had desired, and the statement recommended that "every effort" be made to avoid war with Japan. If such efforts failed, the war should be limited in ends and means, with economic blockade against Tokyo combined with entry into the European war so as to pursue an Atlantic-first strategy. Turner and McNarney also repeated Stark's warning that public opinion might demand escalation to an unlimited war in the Far East, reemphasized that the Philippines could not be held in any conflict, and recommended that Pacific plans be strictly defensive in nature. They also retained the CNO's conclusion regarding the need to prevent disruption of the British Empire but severely modified it via their stand on the Pacific, agreement with Stark that the British position in Egypt and Gibraltar was much more important than Hong Kong or Malaya, and emphasis on the need to check Axis penetration in Latin America. Clearly, Britain's empire in the Far East was of low priority. The army's fear of British manipulation in regard to defending the empire emerged in the reemphasis on Stark's point that U.S. policy "be guided by a determination that any intervention we might undertake should be such as would ultimately promote our own national interests," as well as in the restatement of and addendum to his conclusion that under Plan Dog, chances of success "seem to be in our favor, particularly if we insist upon full equality in the political and military direction of the war." To that they added, "British leadership has not had the competence in any sphere that would justify our entrusting to it the future security of the United States."[40]

Civil-Military Problems

The JB considered taking this document directly to the president but eventually agreed with the JPC first to submit it to Hull, Welles, and the newly appointed secretaries of war and navy, Henry L. Stimson and Frank Knox.[41] Despite their previous support for a strong stand against Japan, the service secretaries quickly endorsed the memorandum, probably because they agreed with the chiefs that, in Stimson's words, the present European "emergency could hardly be passed over without this country being drawn into war eventually." Indeed, they were then pressing Roosevelt for convoys in the Atlantic.[42] Hull, however, proved a good deal more difficult.

Army-navy hopes for State Department concurrence appeared well-founded, for despite their complaints they had found Hull and Welles more willing than their predecessors to coordinate foreign and military policies. The two had, for example, agreed to send Hornbeck to the JB in 1935, and in 1938 they had initiated the Standing Liaison Committee. In 1939 Welles had successfully pressed for expansion of its responsibilities via creation of a special liaison office to deal with European matters, and throughout 1940 he had been extremely cooperative in consultations and had joined the navy in proposing a powerful and permanent interagency committee to coordinate military with foreign policies. While largely the result of the Axis threat, this new willingness to coordinate also reflected a continued determination to dominate future planning. As Welles's representative in the Liaison Office informed his superior, the establishment of a high-powered committee "would tend very strongly to ensure the dominance of the civilian branches of Government over the military in times of emergency."[43]

Hull, however, apparently had a much more limited concept of civil-military coordination. At a January 3 meeting with Marshall and Stark he labeled the JPC memorandum "excellent" and expressed "general agreement" with it, but he "questioned the appropriateness" of "joining in the submission to the President of a technical military statement of the present situation." Astounded that anyone could consider the memorandum a "technical military statement," the service chiefs tried to convince Hull that his signature was both appropriate and badly needed. In the present emergency the nation required a "very definite policy" on which to base military plans, one that "involved broad national questions as well as those pertaining to military and naval operations." The purpose of the memorandum was to "set up" a clear statement of policy "agreeable" to all three departments that "could be submitted to the President for approval" with their full backing.[44] Hull refused to sign, however, and the memorandum thus went to the White House under the signatures of only Stimson and Knox.

Marshall and Stark were a little more successful with the president. After avoiding for two months any direct discussion with them of the key points in the Plan Dog memorandum, during a January 16 White House meeting Roosevelt formally approved combined staff talks, made clear there was to be no curtailment of aid to London even in the event of a concerted Axis attack, and expressed general agreement with many of the key points in the revised memorandum. Most important, he approved the concept of a strategic defensive in the Pacific, recognized the need to avoid committing the army before it was fully prepared and to support Latin American governments against fifth-column activities, and ordered the navy to prepare for Atlantic convoys as well as maintenance of East Coast patrols. He continued to base the fleet at Pearl Harbor, however, and refused to commit himself formally and fully to either U.S. entry or the Europe-first policy and strategy Stark and Marshall had so strongly recommended. He even requested naval exploration of the possibility of bombing Japanese cities in the event of war.[45]

Given the president's method of operation, such behavior was anything but surprising. A master opportunist who disliked rigid planning, FDR had consistently sought throughout his administration to retain his options and flexibility and to make specific decisions only at the last moment and when absolutely necessary. Agreement with the explicit, detailed, and long-range proposals in Stark's memorandum would have been completely antithetical to this method. It would also have committed him to a national policy and strategy far beyond what he thought necessary. Unlike his military advisers, in early 1941 Roosevelt apparently refused to believe that British victory would require either formal U.S. belligerency or an invasion of Europe. Indeed, he had recently proposed Lend-Lease aid as a means of supporting Britain's war effort *without* becoming a belligerent. He had also exhibited little support that summer for the draft and army expansion and since then had shown no interest in creating an expeditionary force for service in Europe ("American mothers don't want their boys to be soldiers," he explained to diplomat Robert Murphy, but they "don't seem to mind their boys becoming sailors"). Thus throughout 1940–41 he saw the U.S. contribution in terms of "arms not armies."[46] He did accept secondary priority and a defensive orientation for the Pacific, but unlike the armed forces he did not view his policies and the continued presence of the fleet in Hawaii as provocative or contradictory to an Atlantic-first approach. To the contrary, he apparently believed that a continued combination of strong words, limited economic sanctions, and a strong naval presence at Pearl Harbor could prevent war in the Pacific by deterring further Japanese aggression. As the British ambassador informed London after a conversation with Turner, although the "military contentions" of Plan Dog had received the "general accord" of Roosevelt and the State Department, "the inference seems that it is not fully subscribed to from the political point of view."[47]

In his effort to clarify national policy and strategy and to force Roosevelt into making some hard decisions, Stark had thus gone far beyond that policy and strategy as perceived by the president, and his logic did not change FDR's mind. Nor did the president totally welcome what was in effect the naval chief's usurpation of his role to define national policy.[48] He therefore responded by approving those sections of the memorandum that echoed his own views, while ignoring or rejecting the sections with which he did not agree. For Roosevelt the "fundamental proposition," as he informed Ambassador Joseph Grew in Tokyo five days later, was recognition "that hostilities in Europe, in Africa, and in Asia are all parts of a single world conflict." U.S. interests were "menaced both in Europe and in the Far East," thus "our strategy of self-defense must be a global strategy."[49] Beyond these points, as well as aid to England and staff talks on the basis of the primacy of the European theater, he was unwilling to commit himself.

Out of this episode and under the prodding of Stimson, additional civil-military coordination would emerge in the form of weekly meetings of the three service secretaries (the "Committee of Three") and more regular meetings between the president, those secretaries, and the service chiefs (the "War Council").[50] But in the minds of many planners these measures could not compensate for the behavior of Hull or the president. From their point of view, they were still operating without specific guidance while the civil leadership irresponsibly refused to heed their warnings regarding the need to limit national policies and make definite military commitments.

ABC-1 and RAINBOW 5: A Coalition Strategy

When the Anglo-American staff conversations began a few days later, the military planners were thus forced again to provide their own policy guidance. The primary task fell once more to the JPC's Turner and McNarney, who relied heavily on their December 21 revision of Stark's memorandum. Now, however, they added a sharp warning to be wary of British manipulation. Citing U.S. ability unilaterally to defend North America and probably the Western Hemisphere, as well as the generally low quality of British political and military leadership in the war, in their memorandum they stated that Washington "cannot afford, nor do we need to entrust, our national future to British direction." British proposals at the forthcoming conference would probably "have been drawn up with chief regard for the support of the British Commonwealth. Never absent from British minds are their post-war interests, commercial and military. We should likewise safeguard our own eventual interests."[51]

To make sure U.S. interests were safeguarded, Embick was appointed to chair the U.S. delegation. He was "worth his weight in gold to the United States," one army officer noted in the midst of the conference, "for he thinks and acts American in his dealings with the British." So did the highly irascible Turner, who quickly emerged as the chief naval spokesman and, according to the historian James Leutze, "seemed to see himself as the sole guardian of American national interest." Supported by the rest of the U.S. delegation, these officers insisted not only on an Atlantic-first policy and no U.S. commitment to defend Singapore but also on receiving copies of any secret treaties Britain had signed and on agreement to separate theaters under U.S. commanders in the event of any alliance.[52] Clearly, bitter memories of World War I experiences remained sharply etched in their minds, along with a determination to avoid any duplication in the present conflict.

Singapore quickly emerged as the major bone of contention during the conference, with the Americans forcefully rejecting British requests for U.S. defense of the base. Agreement to this request, the army delegates informed Marshall on February 12, would not only be "directly and fundamentally at variance" with their instructions but also "a strategic error of the first magnitude" that would commit Washington to a Far East war, lead to cessation of aid to Britain, and leave the Atlantic inadequately defended should Britain fall. "The ultimate fate of Singapore will depend upon the outcome of the struggle in the European Theater," they forcefully asserted, and until Germany was defeated the U.S. contribution to its defense should be limited "to such deterrent and containing influence as may be exercised by our Pacific Fleet operating from Oahu" without any commitment that would preclude sending elements to the Atlantic. Carrying this logic a step further, Embick asserted that it was not yet clear whether the United States would consider even a Japanese attack on the Philippines as a casus belli; Turner emphasized the impossibility of defending the archipelago and explained naval opposition to economic sanctions on the grounds that they would precipitate an unwanted war in the Far East.[53]

In effect, the British were requesting U.S. agreement to the RAINBOW 2 scenario that the armed forces had recently rejected in favor of RAINBOW 5. This request, focusing on U.S. defense of British imperial possessions in the Far East, only reinforced the preexisting suspicion and fear of British manipulation. Indeed, Turner and Stark had warned the British in early December that their views on Singapore "were quite unacceptable as a basis for staff discussions" and would doom any conference to failure. Such warnings had apparently had little effect on British proposals, which only increased U.S. anger. Those proposals, the U.S. delegates insisted, would leave the Atlantic and Pacific coasts exposed and were thus inconsistent with hemispheric security.[54]

New British ambassador Lord Halifax further heightened U.S. anger by informing Hull of the conflict and leaving him a copy of London's position paper, a move the U.S. delegates perceived as a highly improper attempt to exert political influence on them. In response they issued a formal protest and recessed the talks pending an acceptable reply. The British quickly apologized and promised not to approach Hull again. Equally if not more important, a Churchill determined to reach an accord and obtain U.S. entry into the war under any circumstances ordered his representatives to drop the Singapore request and accede to American strategic wishes.[55]

ABC-1, the final conference document, thus echoed the recently enunciated and agreed-on strategic beliefs of the U.S. armed forces by calling for a primary American effort against Germany in the event both powers found themselves at war against the Axis, with a defensive strategy in the Pacific and, aside from some potential combined operations with the small U.S. Asiatic fleet, no direct American commitment to defend Singapore. Indirect assistance would be provided, however, by the Lend-Lease aid Congress was in the process of approving, the continued presence of the Pacific Fleet at Pearl Harbor, and agreement to a naval version of musical chairs: in the event of war, one-fourth of the U.S. Fleet would shift to the Atlantic, thereby releasing a comparable British force for Singapore. Furthermore, the Americans also agreed in ABC-1 to an assertion of Britain's "indirect" approach to German defeat rather than the "direct" approach they would champion a few months later. U.S. planners soon revised RAINBOW 5 to reflect these agreements and made it their primary war plan. On May 14 the JB approved both ABC-1 and the revised RAINBOW 5, as did Stimson and Knox in the next few weeks, whereupon the documents were sent to the White House.[56]

"For the first time in American history," as Steven Ross has stated, "national political and military leaders arrived at basic strategic decisions for the guidance of coalition warfare prior to hostilities."[57] The key catalyst for these unprecedented decisions had clearly been Hitler's 1940 victories, which destroyed almost overnight the foundations of 135 years of American "free security" and forced Americans to rethink their most basic assumptions regarding appropriate foreign and defense policies.[58] Contrary to what is commonly believed, however, the immediate military reaction was to focus exclusively on unilateral, hemispheric defense, not a global approach based on aid to Britain. It was Roosevelt who insisted on such a policy. By that insistence and by his simultaneous refusal to provide detailed policy guidance or face the military consequences of his diplomatic initiatives, he forced the service chiefs and their planners to develop a global strategy. The navy took the lead in this effort, doing so in hopes of simultaneously resolving interservice disputes, educating the president to strategic realities, and pinning him down to a specific and limited line of action.

In developing a new, global strategy, both services harkened back to the fundamental conclusion of all previous U.S. planning for war against a European-Asian coalition: the need to concentrate in the Atlantic and assume a strategic defensive in the Pacific. The definition of "concentration" included policy and diplomacy as well as military forces, however, for in 1940–41 the United States was not a belligerent. The navy's initiative in this realm was stated in balance-of-power terms and focused on entering the war against Germany while avoiding war with Japan. The army agreed in principle but insisted the naval definition of Far Eastern interests remained too expansive, thereby revealing continuation of their interwar disagreement regarding the importance of U.S. interests in the Far East. Those disagreements were resolved by the end of 1940 under the impact of the immediate crisis, but only temporarily.

Resolution of disagreements with the State Department and president was even more limited. Indeed, there was virtually no resolution, for Hull removed himself from considering strategic proposals and Roosevelt merely accepted those sections of the new global strategy with which he agreed while ignoring those with which he disagreed. Most important was whether the United States needed to enter the European war and the appropriate diplomatic stance toward Japan. The points of agreement were sufficiently numerous and important, however, to allow for combined staff conversations with the British. These culminated by the spring of 1941 in agreement on a combined strategy focusing on defeat of Germany, with a defensive effort in the Pacific, should both powers find themselves at war with the Axis. As with the army-navy and presidential agreements, however, the Anglo-American accords of 1941 masked serious, continued disagreements, as well as intense American suspicion.

Thus beneath the surface of the great strategic accomplishments of 1940–41 lay a host of unresolved or only partially resolved interservice, civil-military, and Anglo-American disagreements. These would dominate both strategic and policy planning for the remainder of 1941 as the anti-Axis coalition expanded and the United States approached full-scale belligerency.

Civil-Military and Coalition Conflicts, February–December 1941

Although army and navy planners were able to achieve interservice and Anglo-American strategic accord by early 1941, efforts to reach agreement with their own State Department and president were less successful. Following the narrow logic he had displayed in his prior refusal to endorse formally the Germany-first memorandum, in April Hull did not even look at the ensuing ABC-1 accord. Apparently neither did Roosevelt.[1] Even more worrisome was the president's continued refusal to heed army-navy warnings regarding the Pacific and his continuation of what they considered provocative policies in this theater. They tended to blame the State Department for this situation and in response had previously sought to bypass it and influence Roosevelt directly.[2] A series of disastrous British defeats in Greece, Crete, the Middle East, and the Atlantic in April–May strongly reinforced the urgency of such a move and led the armed forces once again to attempt to force some hard decisions onto FDR directly. Once again, however, they would be foiled by what they considered dangerously flawed State Department advice.

Confusion and Conflict

On April 3, Stark informed his fleet commanders that entry into the Atlantic naval war was now a question of "when, and not whether," and noted the answer could be as quickly as two months hence.[3] For the naval chief speedy entry was most advisable to save both the British and his warships from disaster—the former at the hands of German U-boats, and the latter at the hands of a president who might send them to England under the recently passed Lend-Lease Act were they not committed to battle immediately. Together with Marshall he therefore advised putting ABC-1 into effect by moving naval forces from the Pacific to the Atlantic for convoy duty and shifting the remainder of the fleet from Pearl Harbor to San Diego. Stimson and Knox concurred, but Hull argued that any naval transfer would encourage militarists in Tokyo and weaken his bargaining position. Roosevelt at first agreed to the transfer and extended the hemispheric defense zone to include Greenland and the Azores, but contrary to military advice he rejected both the escorting of convoys to Britain and a concentration of U.S. naval forces in the Atlantic; instead those forces were dispersed for a series of sweeps and patrols to establish "not control but presence." To make matters worse, he backed Hull and chose not to transfer ships from Pearl Harbor to the Atlantic after all (or to San Diego), after which he decided to compromise by transferring some of them.[4]

Thus in spring 1941 the armed forces found themselves even more dispersed and overcommitted than they had been before, and whether correctly or incorrectly, they blamed Hull and his associates for this state of affairs. On April 16 Marshall informed his planners before a White House meeting that he now had to do two things: "begin the education of the President as to the true situation . . . after a period of being influenced by the State Department," and tell Roosevelt whether a decision for war had to be made now and "what he has to work with." According to Marshall, presidential adviser Harry Hopkins agreed that "we are frittering away materiel without tangible results, that the influence and accomplishments of the State Department have been unfortunate . . . , and that the President must be protected against the importunities of those who are not fully aware of the seriousness of the present situation."[5]

Marshall's task was complicated by the disagreement of his advisers over what he should recommend to Roosevelt. While the continued lack of military preparedness led the WPD to view as "highly desirable" the withholding of active participation in the war for "as long as possible," it simultaneously recognized that entry was inevitable and also "highly desirable" before British military defeat or the overthrow of Churchill and his replacement by a pro-appeasement government. In light of recent British losses, many army planners concluded that such a scenario was imminent and agreed with Stark that immediate U.S. entry was now necessary to avoid it. Further delay, McNarney warned Marshall during the April 16 meeting, could lead to the United States "standing alone" against the Axis, and in that situation "internal disturbances may bring on communism. I may be called a fire-eater," he admitted, "but something must be done."[6]

Embick, who Marshall had recently recalled to active duty and asked to participate in the staff and White House discussions, disagreed totally. While now willing to admit that the continued survival of Britain was vital to U.S. security, he refused to equate that survival with continuation of the entire British Empire or the government of Churchill, an individual whose strategic and political judgments he had distrusted since World War I. Indeed, he informed a surprised Marshall on April 16 that neither the loss of the Middle East nor Churchill's fall would weaken England, and he concluded that the United States should not be "duped" again, as it had been in 1917, into entering the conflict voluntarily at this time.[7]

Embick was far from alone in such beliefs. "U.S. policy now follows British policy," Colonel Paul Robinett of the General Staff bitterly complained on March 26 in the privacy of his diary. If a decision was made for war, he informed Marshall on April 16, the United States should follow Embick's advice to assume "effective leadership and control of what is to be left of the English-speaking world," and with it "the naval position England once held," rather than accept "a false leader" such as Churchill and his dated strategy; this would involve, he made clear the following month, securing bases in the Atlantic as well as the Pacific, behind which "a vast fleet could range from continental bases."[8] Colonel Truman Smith, the former military attaché in Berlin, claimed that "no member of the General Staff wants to go to war" and labeled Britain's recent and disastrous decision to send troops to Greece "the worst instance of the political element of the government interfering with the military strategy that has happened since General Halleck" during the Civil War. Attacks within the Intelligence Division (G-2) of the staff on the competency of the Churchill government were so numerous and strong in April as to lead Stimson, who saw continuance of that government as vital to the British war effort, to request from Marshall a muzzling and shakeup of the division's personnel.[9]

Such statements were clearly illustrative of the continued strength of anti-British and continentalist opinion within the army staff, while McNarney's and Stimson's were just as illustrative of the strength of the opposite opinion. In between stood an army chief respectful of both viewpoints and still making up his own mind. Indeed, he appeared to be holding the two contradictory viewpoints simultaneously: although questioning some of Embick's judgments on April 16 via the sharp rejoinder, "For the American people is that all you have to say?," he also recognized the validity of the senior strategist's caution—especially given U.S. unpreparedness. Torn between the need to keep Britain in the war and fear of sending his small and woefully unprepared army into the conflict, Marshall wound up advising the president only to mobilize fully, concentrate in the Atlantic, and continue to meet with Embick, who was assigned on a "confidential capacity at the White House."[10]

A month later Marshall remained both cautious and of two opinions. On May 14 he joined Stark in approving the revised RAINBOW 5 plan, which stated that the army's "primary immediate effort" would be the "building up of large land and air forces for major offensive operations against the Axis."[11] Yet three days later he asserted that "we will not need a 4,000,000 man army unless England collapses," and during a May 21 Standing Liaison Committee meeting he virtually echoed Embick by emphasizing the need to secure Latin America "beyond a shadow of a doubt" and warning that "if we do not have the broader view we are likely to follow Great Britain's example and bleed everywhere." On that same date, however, he twice implied that this "broader view" stretched far beyond the hemisphere: he supported creation of an overall wartime production plan to accomplish the objectives set out in ABC-1 and RAINBOW 5 and rejected Hornbeck's request for Far Eastern reinforcements. Whereas collapse in the Far East would be "serious," he warned, "collapse in the Atlantic would be fatal" and would imperil "vital" U.S. interests. "If the Atlantic is lost," he concluded, "the Pacific is also lost." [12]

For the time being Marshall focused on the lowest common denominators linking the hemispheric and Atlantic/Europe-first viewpoints: no additional forces or provocations in the Pacific, control of the Western Atlantic and approaches to the hemisphere, and the buildup of U.S. ground and air forces as well as movement of the fleet from Pearl Harbor to help exercise such control. He, Embick, and the WPD also discussed the possibility of obtaining in return for Lend-Lease "cessions of British territory in this hemisphere." [13]

That the forces being built up might eventually be used in the eastern Atlantic, North Africa, or Europe remained a possibility if not a probability. Marshall insisted that "eventually" was not the present, however, and throughout the remainder of 1941 he opposed projection of the army beyond the hemisphere on the grounds of unpreparedness and conflict with his primary RAINBOW 5 mission to build up forces. The combination of British successes in the Atlantic during the late spring and the German invasion of Russia in June reinforced his arguments by eliminating the immediate threat to British survival and thus the need for immediate U.S. military action. Such caution "continually irritated" naval planners ready for more aggressive action and reopened the army-navy split. In May Turner persuaded Stark to complain to Marshall that "no plans whatsoever exist for joint overseas expeditions" or even for army-navy cooperation in support of Latin American governments. "If the United States is to succeed in *defeating* the Axis forces," Stark warned, "it must act on the offensive, instead of solely on the defensive." [14] That Marshall remained so hemispherically oriented and that someone with Embick's views could be advising him and the president illustrate the continued power of continental and hemispheric strategic thinking within the army at this time despite Plan Dog, ABC-1, and the revised RAINBOW 5. [15]

Neither Embick nor Marshall, however, was able to limit or direct presidential initiatives. Nor could Stark, who according to Turner's later recollections "spent a lot of time" in mid-1941 "knocking down the hairbrained schemes of the President in regard to the Navy." [16] Throughout the spring and summer Roosevelt continued to pursue what his service chiefs considered provocative and dangerous policies in the Pacific as well as the Atlantic, to disperse U.S. resources via diplomatic and strategic overcommitments, and to refuse to tie himself to a specific and limited course of action. In June he returned ABC-1 and the revised RAINBOW 5 to the JB without specific approval or disapproval. Simultaneously he ordered the preparation of plans and expeditionary forces to seize a host of constantly shifting objectives in the Atlantic theater (including the Azores, the Cape Verde Islands, French North Africa, and the Brazilian "bulge"), extended the navy's duties in the Atlantic, toyed with ordering convoy escorts, and altered specific naval missions and available forces in the Atlantic so frequently as to require creation of four separate "hemispheric defense plans" for the Atlantic between April and July. He also extended Lend-Lease to China in May and material assistance to the Soviet Union when Germany attacked in June. In July he ordered the occupation of Iceland, despite the objections of army planners who had ranked as more urgent the occupation of fifteen other areas out of a total of seventeen. And although he did shift segments of the fleet from the Pacific to the Atlantic to meet these additional commitments, the president also kept the majority of his capital ships in their exposed position at Pearl Harbor to deter further Japanese aggression. By the end of July he had also established a virtual embargo against Tokyo by freezing all of its assets.[17]

As Waldo Heinrichs has effectively argued, these moves were actually quite logical in view of the limited forces available and the numerous, shifting diplomatic, political, and military pressures in the Atlantic, in the Pacific, and at home. They also reveal the existence of two distinct "frameworks of policy" in 1941 and a shift from the "nationalist," hemispheric policy in the spring to the internationalist one in the summer as the German threat to Britain and the hemisphere receded with the invasion of Russia.[18] From the military's perspective, however, Roosevelt's moves were provocative, erratic, and unfocused, with most undertaken despite their opposition. This clearly revealed to the armed forces their lack of influence with the president, who they concluded was still under the baneful influence of the State Department. Equally if not more dangerous, he was also coming under the influence of the British, who were again seeking to manipulate U.S. strategy and policy so as to protect their empire and rescue them from their own military disasters.

The Assault on British Strategy
and the Victory Program

The immediate catalyst for this increased fear of British manipulation was Churchill's open request in May for U.S. entry into the war, followed by detailed strategic explanations and proposals—first to Hopkins during his July visit to London and then to the U.S. military chiefs themselves in August at the Anglo-American summit conference off the Newfoundland coast. On both occasions the British expounded on and strongly defended their peripheral strategy for the defeat of Germany, a strategy based on using naval and air power in conjunction with raids and campaigns in the Middle East and North Africa to weaken German morale and fighting ability to the point of collapse. As part of this effort, which Churchill would refer to as "closing the ring," Britain now requested a U.S. invasion of French North Africa in conjunction with its Middle East campaign and argued that full-scale U.S. belligerency would "revolutionize" the situation and make victory over Germany "certain and swift." Simultaneously, the prime minister pressed for a strong Anglo-American diplomatic stance against the Japanese.[19]

U.S. military planners viewed such expansive proposals as militarily unsound in their refusal to face the need for concentration in one theater and an eventual land offensive against German power on the European continent, as well as diametrically opposed to almost everything they had been recommending during the last few months. The United States, they had consistently argued, remained unprepared for full-scale belligerency and should severely limit its overseas commitments, especially in the Pacific, so as to insure hemispheric security and the buildup of forces for eventual offensive operations in the Atlantic-European theater. London, however, was suggesting an even more provocative policy in the Far East along with an immediate overextension of unprepared American forces into the Atlantic-European theater. To make matters worse, the section of that theater in which it wanted U.S. forces—North Africa and the Mediterranean—also happened to be an area of great imperial interest. As with previous suggestions regarding Singapore, London seemed to be attempting to manipulate U.S. forces and strategy to serve its own imperial goals.

In short, the British were proposing a militarily flawed strategy designed to reap political benefits in peripheral areas rather than defeat Germany, and were attempting to enlist American forces, along with formal U.S. belligerency, as part of that effort. The army's response was explosive. "Under the British strategic concept," the WPD warned, "it appears that if we get into the war, our principal military role would be to protect the British Empire while they take care of the United Kingdom with our material help." That empire, warned Embick's son-in-law, Major Albert C. Wedemeyer of the WPD, was already in a process of disintegration, which was being temporarily checked by the war. Moreover, England's own survival in 1940 had disproven a key component of London's strategic concept—the ability of aerial bombardment to achieve decisive results. Overall, Wedemeyer concluded, Britain's August strategic assessment was disjointed, disconnected, defeatist, and groping for panaceas. "Now they turn to any ally out of necessity," he continued; "they have even risked the consequences of an alliance with Russia, a step which every European knows has dire implications." The WPD chief Brigadier General Leonard Gerow bluntly labeled a complementary strategic explanation provided by British brigadier Vivian Dykes on August 4 a "propaganda effort to bring the United States into the war at the earliest possible date," and London's conclusion that such entry would make victory quick and certain "vastly optimistic." The decision on whether or not to intervene in the war, he concluded, should be determined by American, not British interests, and the United States was not yet ready for full-scale belligerency.[20]

In September the JB approved and forwarded to London a summary of these as well as naval critiques of British strategy that, although using more polite language, clearly rejected Britain's suggestions and strategic approach. The United States, the JB insisted, was not yet prepared to enter the war or invade North Africa and presently had to avoid any "diffusion of effort." London's stated beliefs regarding the impact of U.S. entry were "optimistic," and "at best" such entry at this time would result in "a piecemeal and indecisive commitment of forces against a superior enemy under unfavorable logistic conditions." British strategy also overemphasized bombing and gave insufficient emphasis to the use of land forces necessary to defeat Germany. "Naval and air power may prevent wars from being lost," the board admitted, "and by weakening enemy strength, may greatly contribute to victory," but "dependence cannot be placed on winning important wars by naval and air forces alone. It should be recognized as an almost invariable rule that wars cannot finally be won without the use of land armies."[21]

This conclusion was taken verbatim from a simultaneous, broad review of U.S. strategy and policy that army and navy planners had instituted during the spring on their own initiative and had recently completed under a presidential request for recommendations regarding production requirements needed to defeat America's "potential enemies." Roosevelt had recognized that such recommendations would require "the making of appropriate assumptions as to our probable friends and enemies and the conceivable theatres of operations which will be required," but what he received in September went far beyond such assumptions. Officially titled the "Joint Board Estimate of the United States Over-all Production Requirements" and more commonly known as the Victory Program, this document used his directive as a rationale for providing a comprehensive statement of the military's view of U.S. national policies, as well as the specific military strategies and mobilization that would be required to realize them.[22]

Expanding on the JPC's December 21 revision of Stark's memorandum, the review listed five major national policy objectives related to military policy: preservation of U.S. and hemispheric "territorial, economic and ideological integrity";

prevention of "the disruption of the British Empire"; prevention of the "further extension of Japanese territorial dominion"; the "eventual establishment" of European and Asian balances of power; and, "as far as practicable, the establishment of regimes favorable to economic freedom and individual liberty." These objectives could be fully attained "only through military victories outside this hemisphere" against the Axis powers, victories that would require U.S. entry into the war and offensive operations in the Atlantic and Europe or Africa. Their goal would be "the complete military defeat of Germany," which would probably result in the victorious allies then being able to force Japan "to give up much of her territorial gains." For the immediate future, America's "principal strategic method" should be limited to "material support" of present British and Russian military operations against Germany, reinforced by U.S. air and naval units, and "holding Japan in check pending future developments." In the long run, however, U.S. ground operations would be necessary, for Britain and Russia simply could not defeat Germany by themselves. Furthermore, the Victory Program restated, "naval and air forces seldom if ever win important wars. It should be recognized as an almost invariable rule that only land armies can finally win wars." [23]

Not all military officers were pleased with the Victory Program. "It lays down a five point program which not only entails the defeat of both Germany and Japan but the imposition of our own idalogy [sic] upon the world," Robinett complained, and such objectives were "beyond the means" of the United States. "Our national policy," he argued, "should be cut to conform to our means." [24] Many of his colleagues agreed. The army section of the Victory Program contained a much more limited and specific list of national policies than the final joint statement, which had originated with naval planners. Indeed, three of the five stated policies came directly from Stark's memorandum as revised in the December 1940 JPC report. [25]

While believing that the two additional statements regarding the balance of power and establishing regimes favorable to economic freedom and political liberty "seem purely political and therefore somewhat out of place in this paper," Marshall and his advisers were willing to accede to their inclusion as joint policy assumptions. What they would not agree to was Stark's original emphasis on the immediate use of force, which the Army WPD labeled "premature," or naval production proposals that called for a continued emphasis on the buildup of air and sea rather than ground forces even though the program had openly stated such forces were insufficient to achieve victory. Labeling these proposals "fundamentally unsound," the army in a separate estimate concluded that German defeat would require the creation of a massive ground force. Prepared primarily by Wedemeyer, this estimate called for a 215-division, heavily armored and mechanized army of nearly nine million men to be used in Central Europe, an area labeled "our principal theater of war," by mid-1943. Given the present state of unpreparedness, however (only one infantry division was expected to be ready for combat by October 1 and only six in the following six months), both services agreed that it was "out of the question" to expect "in the near future a sustained and successful land offensive against the center of the German power." They consequently voiced support for the temporary continuation of Britain's indirect strategy.[26]

The Victory Program marked the final, decisive shift of army planners from a continental/hemispheric to a global strategy. Plan Dog, ABC-1, and RAINBOW 5 had mentioned eventual European offensives and the buildup of U.S. forces, but while they were being written and approved, Marshall had continued to focus on an army of sufficient size only for hemispheric defense. Now, the anti-interventionist Embick's equally anti-interventionist son-in-law had completed the logic in Stark's argument: if British survival and German defeat were essential to U.S. security and if this required ground operations beyond British capabilities or competence, then Washington would have to create and deploy the enormous army needed for such operations.[27]

In the process, though, it would have to avoid entry into the war for as long as possible so as to create that force—a position that continued to separate army planners from their naval counterparts and from their own secretary of war.[28] Washington would also have to be extremely careful to avoid British manipulation of its forces, strategy, and policy if it hoped to achieve victory over Germany and preserve its own interests. As Wedemeyer had earlier noted and informed Marshall, alignment of a "virile power" (i.e., the United States) with a "decadent power" (i.e., England) would be a "source of strength" to the former if the latter's geographic position permitted its use as a base of operations but a source of weakness leading to defeat if the virile power "dissipates his strength in the support of the old power or relies upon it for active military assistance." Such old powers "should be used a[s] geographical bases only," while "their interests should be ruthlessly subordinated" to those of the virile power.[29]

Completion of the logic in Stark's argument went even further. Wedemeyer's reasoning had been heavily influenced by his professional readings and scholarly father-in-law. Particularly noteworthy in the former realm had been Sir Halford Mackinder's geopolitical theories, reinforced during his tenure at the German War College with lectures by German geopolitician Karl Haushofer, and numerous works emphasizing the centrality of national policies to strategic decisions. Embick's focus on the economic aspects of war and economic war-making potential of individual nations tended to reinforce this emphasis, as well as Mackinder's focus on the East European "heartland." These came together in Wedemeyer's Victory Program emphasis on the necessity to confront the Wehrmacht before it could fully exploit the resources of its assumed conquests in Eastern Europe.[30] On September 12 in his diary, Robinett wrote a complementary and extraordinarily revealing geopolitical appraisal of the world situation, albeit a gloomy one, which clearly explained why even from an isolationist point of view massive U.S. military intervention in the war was becoming mandatory:

> Germany and Russia are fighting for world domination, which ever wins will be a long way on the road to domination; England cannot win, the best its empire can gain is a respite; Japan fights for domination in order to keep from being destroyed later; the United States does not look out for its own interests, is not united internally, has no objective except the restoration of the status quo, is shot through with elements of weakness and therefore stands to lose regardless of the victor in the present war; finally, *if any one power dominates Asia, Europe and Africa, our country will ultimately become a second class power even if we gain South America and the whole of North America.*[31]

Robinett offered no written conclusion to this analysis save the need to "act in our own self interest in all things." But no written conclusion was necessary on September 12, for the recently completed Victory Program had asserted the now obvious one: the United States in its own interest would have to create an enormous army and send it to Europe to prevent Germany from controlling and exploiting the Eurasian land mass. Even control of the entire Western Hemisphere would be insufficient to keep the United States a first-class power if Washington allowed that to happen.

The New Russian Pivot

How the United States could prevent such an eventuality was another matter, however. With the Victory Program's insistence that U.S. forces were unprepared for large-scale offensive action and British forces insufficient, the obvious question was what would hold the Wehrmacht back, prevent it from controlling all of Eurasia, and keep Britain safe until the United States fully mobilized its forces for a Continental confrontation. The army claimed this process would take close to two more years, and that was an optimistic assessment: Wedemeyer assumed combat in Central Europe by July 1943, whereas Army Air Forces (AAF) planners had concluded that a large-scale invasion of the Continent was "improbable" before 1944.[32]

This conclusion did not worry them because of their faith in strategic bombing. "If the air offensive is successful," they asserted in AWPD/1, their section of the Victory Program, "a land offensive may not be necessary."[33] Army planners had a good deal less faith in airpower, however, and their answer to the present lack of invasion forces was twofold. First, they recommended continuation for the time being of Britain's peripheral approach; "our broad concept of encircling and advancing step-by-step, with a view to closing-in on Germany," Wedemeyer concluded, was "the only practical way in which military and economic pressure may be brought to bear effectively against Germany."[34] Second, they introduced a relatively new factor that would henceforth have a decisive influence on U.S. strategy and policy in the war—the Soviet Union. In both the Victory Program and the September review of British strategy, the JB strongly recommended continuation of the aid Roosevelt had extended to Russia soon after Germany's June attack on that country. Maintenance of an "active" eastern front against Hitler, the board noted in this regard, offered "by far the best opportunity for a successful land offensive against Germany, because only Russia possesses adequate manpower situated in favorable proximity to the center of the German military citadel." Consequently, the arming of Soviet forces would be "one of the most important moves that could be made by the enemies of Germany."[35]

This conclusion, with all the profound repercussions that would flow from it, represented a sharp reversal of military opinion three months earlier when Hitler had first launched Operation BARBAROSSA. At that time the armed forces had opposed aiding Moscow on grounds similar to their 1940 opposition to aiding Britain: U.S. forces needed the supplies, the Soviets could not survive the German onslaught, and the Soviet government could not be trusted.[36] Indeed, such distrust of the Soviets and disbelief in their ability to survive was at least equal to and likely greater than the planners' distrust of British motives and military abilities. Diplomatic relations with the detested and feared Soviet regime had not even existed until 1933, and in late 1939 they had reached a nadir in the aftermath of the Nazi-Soviet Pact. The revised RAINBOW directives of 1940, written while that pact was still in effect, had assumed eventual Soviet entry into the war as a German ally.[37]

Given the very negative Western assessments of the quality of the Red Army, especially in light of Stalin's purge of the officer corps during the 1930s, that possibility was not considered particularly dangerous. "Russia stands unique," G-2 contemptuously informed the WPD on May 26, "a power in its own right but only because of its bulk. In its inherent inefficiency it is a menace to all and of value only to one—Germany—and that because of its raw materials."[38] Two days after the initiation of BARBAROSSA Stimson informed Roosevelt of "substantial unanimity" between himself, Marshall, and the WPD that Germany would be preoccupied with conquering Russia for no less than one but no more than three months and that Washington should take advantage of this opportunity to strengthen defenses in the Atlantic—a reference to full convoy escorts also strongly supported by Stark and Knox. Robinett noted "almost unanimous agreement" in the army that Russia would be "quickly and decisively destroyed," with disagreement over only "how long it would take." [39]

The armed forces' negative view of the Soviet Union was also apparent in Wedemeyer's comment regarding the "dire implications" of Britain's alliance with Russia. It was most clearly and comprehensively expressed, however, in a JPC proposed directive during the summer for conducting staff talks with a Russian military mission. That directive repeated many of the warnings regarding the British which had been given to U.S. representatives in January before the ABC talks, but in a revised form which applied to the USSR and which revealed the deep antipathy of the military planners toward the Russians' ideology, government, and recent policies. Citing the "past history" of Soviet leaders and "the prevalent distrust of the Communistic theory of government in this country," the JPC concluded that "we cannot afford, nor do we need, to disclose to the Russian Military Mission our general plans or specific commitments that have been made with other countries." Conversations therefore should be general in nature and involve no explicit commitments. As with British proposals earlier in the year, Russian proposals "will have been drawn up with chief regard for the interests of the Union of Soviet Socialist Republics. We should likewise safeguard our own eventual interests." Discussions to lay the foundation for future cooperation should proceed on a general basis, but in view of the few existing points of military contact, future cooperation would be "difficult at best." Moreover, the "history of political unreliability of Russia under the present regime," a reference to the Nazi-Soviet Pact, led the JPC to issue an additional warning: "Extreme caution must be observed lest disclosures be made which, following a political turn on the part of that country toward Germany, may be used against the United States or other powers associated with it." [40]

The U.S. armed forces were far from alone in such negative views. They were shared by Churchill's military advisers and by the State Department. Berle issued a similar warning regarding a possible Russo-German separate peace on July 10, and just before the German attack on the USSR, State Department policy in such an event had been to make "no approaches," concessions, or "sacrifices of principle" to the Soviets and to treat any Soviet approaches "with reserve until such time as the Soviet Government may satisfy us that it is not engaging merely in maneuvers." [41] By the late summer and early fall of 1941, however, the military planners' position on the Soviet Union had begun to shift dramatically, and primarily for the same related and mutually reinforcing reasons it had shifted a year earlier on Britain: contrary presidential policy and unexpected military reality. In the White House, Roosevelt refused to sanction the hard line against Russia recommended by the State Department and the armed forces. Despite their objections, he insisted on sending Moscow military aid. Equally if not more important, the Soviets amazed Western military experts by surviving beyond the six weeks many estimates had given them.

United States military planners were quick to realize that Russia's continued survival could drastically alter the strategic outlook and prove to be essential to victory. The exact causal relationship between their dramatically revised assessments, the military situation on the eastern front, and presidential policy cannot be determined with any accuracy, but they were probably mutually reinforcing, with Roosevelt's intuition and pressure providing the original prod.

As early as June 26 the president had predicted that if the eastern front proved to be more than a temporary "diversion," it would "mean the liberation of Europe from Nazi domination"—a clear recognition of Soviet potential to alter dramatically the shape and outcome of the war against Germany.[42] This early recognition led the president to support aid to Russia and to Hopkins's decision, after his July meetings in London, to visit Moscow for a firsthand examination of the situation. Hopkins's positive reports after meetings with Stalin and British ambassador Sir Stafford Cripps reinforced the president's insistence on helping the Soviets "even if the Army and Navy authorities in America did not like it," as Hopkins informed Cripps.[43] So did similar positive assessments by former ambassador Joseph E. Davies and former military attaché Colonel Philip Faymonville. They also apparently convinced the president by midsummer that the odds favored Russian survival, at least into 1942. Consequently, he insisted in strong language on top priority for military assistance to the Soviets, warning that he was "sick and tired" of unfulfilled promises. By the time of his ensuing summit conference with Churchill in August, maintenance of a Russian front against Hitler had become, in the words of Waldo Heinrichs, the "centerpiece of his world strategy." One week after that conference Roosevelt began a White House dinner by pointedly noting that it was the tenth week of Soviet resistance. On August 30 he bluntly informed Stimson that material aid to the USSR was "of paramount importance for the safety and security of America" and that "substantial and comprehensive commitments" of such aid needed to be made at a proposed supply conference in Moscow. By September, according to Heinrichs, "the central dynamic of his policies was the conviction that the survival of the Soviet Union was essential for the defeat of Germany and that the defeat of Germany was essential for American security."[44]

The armed forces' change of heart was more gradual and began later, but not by much. On July 11, G-2 still believed that Germany would be successful by the fall, its invasion had provided merely a "breathing spell" to buttress British defenses, and the "most" that could be expected of Russia "is that she will remain in being in her distant fastnesses after the German onslaught has been spent."[45] On July 18 it predicted German victory and occupation of Russia up to Lake Baikal and perhaps the Pacific. Significantly, however, G-2 now assumed that victory would take place no later than mid-1942, rather than definitely in 1941.[46] Then in late July Hopkins and Faymonville both reported their belief in long-term Soviet resistance, Stimson began to question and criticize the G-2 assessments he was receiving, and Roosevelt began to apply pressure to get more aid to Moscow.[47] Whether the result primarily of that pressure or the extraordinary and unexpected Russian resistance, the armed forces began to shift their position dramatically. By August they had concluded that U.S. aid might be more useful in Russia than in the Middle East. One G-2 officer went much further, arguing that material aid was insufficient and that Russian collapse could and should be averted by the creation of an immediate "diversion front" in Northwest France which could also serve as a base for future Continental operations.[48]

While far ahead of its time, this first U.S. military call for a "second front" clearly revealed the changing attitudes in the War Department toward the Soviets. By early September the planners working on the Victory Program and assessment of British strategy were rating aid to Russia "one of the most important moves that could be made by the Associated Powers." Indeed, in the army's Victory Program the situation on the eastern front virtually defined the deadline by which the United States must invade Europe. At this time the planners still viewed that front as a temporary phenomenon, but they now saw it capable of lasting into mid-1942 and were recommending that it be supported and extended via U.S. aid so as to keep the Germans tied down and preclude their exploitation of Eurasia until the United States could build up its forces sufficiently for large-scale land operations in 1943.[49]

Given the military realities of late 1941, continued Russian resistance was even more important than the armed forces were willing to admit. Army estimates in the Victory Program had concluded that if Russia were defeated, Germany would be able to redeploy 400 divisions. By the historic 2–1 ratio considered necessary for a successful offensive, its opponents would then need 800 divisions, consisting of 25 million men. With only Britain and the Commonwealth nations perceived as allies by 1943, 700 of those divisions rather than the 215 listed in the Victory Program would have to come from the United States. Yet induction of that many men, the Army Victory Program noted, would "definitely" imperil the economic mobilization necessary for victory.[50]

Wedemeyer and his associates had attempted to deal with this problem by dismissing the 2–1 ratio as irrelevant to modern warfare given the power of armored forces supported by air, by arguing that such U.S. forces could be created and deployed before Germany had fully consolidated and exploited its expected victory in Russia, and by emphasizing the ability of strategic bombing, naval blockade, and subversion to weaken German forces substantially before any large-scale invasion of Europe. Paradoxically, however, such a positive evaluation of the effects of indirect warfare ran counter to their simultaneous and extremely negative assessments of the impact of such methods in their attack on British strategy. Furthermore, they seemed to assume that brilliance in armored penetration supported by air would suddenly leave the Wehrmacht and be shifted to the U.S. Army once it landed in Europe.[51]

Such wishful thinking notwithstanding, Germany would become invulnerable were she able to defeat Russia and subsequently exploit the resources of the Eurasian land mass. As noted above, Roosevelt realized this by September, perhaps as a result of reading "between the lines" of the Victory Program in that month, and in October the Army WPD openly admitted it. If Russia were defeated, it warned, Germany's war effort would "not be decisively affected by the tightest sea blockade." Economically and militarily, Germany's position would become "practically invulnerable."[52]

Assessments of whether or when Germany would defeat Russia were inconclusive. Now back in Moscow as a Lend-Lease official, Faymonville concluded that the Germans would fail. Marshall and the staff reported "serious doubts as to his judgment and his impartiality wherever the Soviets are concerned," however,[53] and in October the WPD concluded that the Wehrmacht would be successful. Yet a month earlier G-2 had labeled Russian defeat "possible but not yet probable," and its backup study to the October WPD report noted that in this "titanic" struggle, which was pinning down two hundred of Germany's three hundred divisions including all its armor, the Russians could not be "totally crushed" before the onset of winter. They might be "substantially impotent" by the summer of 1942, however, as posited in the Victory Program. Resistance in Siberia would probably continue, the WPD and G-2 agreed in September, with its intensity dependent on U.S. aid and Japan's position. Another backup study to the October estimate asserted the obvious conclusions from these assessments in blunt, bold language: "The most potent factor in the weakening of Axis war potential is continued active operations on the Russian front. Every effort must be made to prolong this campaign. This should have first priority. Diversions in other theaters such as the Middle East, Africa, or Norway would engage only a very minor portion of Axis forces."[54]

Efforts to aid the Soviets, the estimate made clear, were by no means limited to material assistance—or the European theater. A potentially devastating attack on the Russian rear in Siberia, U.S. intelligence reports throughout the summer and fall incorrectly concluded, was Japan's most likely move.[55] Seeking to assist Russia by preventing such an attack, the WPD temporarily reversed its past insistence on not provoking Japan and in October recommended continuation of existing economic pressures on that nation so as to render it "incapable of offensive operation against Russia" and U.S., British, and Dutch possessions. G-2 concurred and warned against U.S. support for any Sino-Japanese settlement on the grounds that it was now "imperative" to keep the Japanese Army pinned down in China so as to preclude its use against the Soviet Union. Any action which would "liberate" that army for action in Siberia would be "foolhardy." Because the Kwantung Army was expected to pursue such action as soon as it achieved either a 2– or 3–1 numerical superiority over Soviet forces in Siberia, G-2 recommended U.S. aid to Chinese as well as Soviet forces. This policy would admittedly use China as "a cat's paw" and lead to an "initial feeling of revulsion," but it was justified nevertheless "in the light of cold reason"—that is, the need to support Russia in order to destroy Nazism.[56]

Political factors in late 1941 further emphasized the pivotal importance of prolonging Russian participation in the war by calling into question whether 215 divisions would ever be created or allowed to invade Europe. The army's request for such a force and strategy in the Victory Program ignored domestic realities and the contrary views of the president. Congress had recently agreed to an extension of the draft by only one vote and showed no inclination even to enter the war, let alone send an expeditionary force into another European bloodbath. Roosevelt held similar views. Appalled by the World War I slaughter in the trenches, he accepted many of Churchill's views about the power of indirect warfare, and no matter what his true feelings as to the inevitability of some form of U.S. belligerency against Germany at this time, he had no intention of creating or sending to Europe a large army. Indeed, he appears to have viewed continued Russian belligerency supported by U.S. material assistance much as he viewed continued British belligerency with similar support—as a *substitute* for U.S. ground forces and perhaps, even at this late date, for official U.S. entry into the war. The army, on the other hand, insisted that Britain and Russia were incapable of defeating Germany alone and viewed all such assistance as a method of extending their military resistance long enough to allow for full U.S. rearmament, entry into the war, and deployment of major forces into Europe from the English "launching pad."[57] These major policy and strategy disagreements had divided the president from his military advisers for nearly a year, and they continued to do so throughout the fall of 1941. Mark Lowenthal notes that Roosevelt had wanted the Victory Program only to order production rationally so as to continue his aid-to-the-allies policy and thereby avoid more extensive commitments; instead, his military advisers gave him a "comprehensive review of strategy and policy which told him the one thing he did not want to hear, that there really was no alternative to active American participation in the war."[58] The army then made matters worse by insisting that such participation involve a huge U.S. expeditionary force on the European continent.

Roosevelt was far from alone in rejecting the need for such a force. Walter Lippmann in September labeled it "the cancer which obstructs national unity, causes discontent which subversive elements exploit, and weakens the primary measures of our defense, which are the lend-lease program and the naval policy." The army should therefore be reduced in size, and if the United States went to war its contribution should consist "basically of Navy, Air, and manufacturing" while major ground fighting would be left to British and Russian forces. The journalist Ernest K. Lindley voiced similar conclusions, and in November Roosevelt received warning that the American people accepted an air force but were "opposed at present to an A.E.F. [American Expeditionary Force]."[59]

Marshall fought fiercely against such proposals, though he concluded that Roosevelt would not order an actual reduction in army size. "I think he is looking everywhere to find ways and means to secure material for Russia," the army chief stated on September 22. Robinett agreed but concluded there was no place to obtain this material save from the already underequipped army—whether or not its size was reduced. "It was a very trying, maddening situation," Marshall later admitted, "and it was very difficult for one to keep their [sic] temper."[60]

On September 22 Marshall bluntly informed the president that "Germany cannot be defeated by supply of munitions to friendly powers, and air and naval operations alone. Large ground forces will be required"—enough to counter four hundred German divisions dominating Europe from the "Urals to Iberian Peninsula and from Scandinavia to North Africa." Making extensive use of the Victory Program, he insisted that eventually "we must come to grips with and annihilate the German military machine," a task that would require 215 U.S. divisions. The army needed to begin building rapidly and immediately toward this goal, not decrease its size to give more equipment to England and Russia.[61] On the following day Stimson informed Roosevelt that the Victory Program had brought up "fundamental and far reaching questions," all the president's military advisers agreed the country should enter the war, and without such entry Britain could not win or continue resistance indefinitely.[62]

Roosevelt was anything but impressed. Despite Marshall's arguments he deferred army expansion until early 1942 so as to release supplies for Britain and Russia, and in a "very frank" ninety-minute discussion of the Victory Program with Stimson on September 25 he expressed his displeasure over the army's conclusion "that we must invade and crush Germany." Such a conclusion, he noted, would elicit "a very bad reaction" from the public, a judgment with which Stimson concurred.[63] By November Lend-Lease would be extended to Moscow, and despite Marshall's entreaties, tanks and aircraft in large quantities would be sent to Britain and Russia for immediate use rather than being retained for the army as called for in the Victory Program.[64]

Thus, if the naval Victory Program estimate had been "fundamentally un-sound," as army planners claimed, because of its lack of emphasis on the creation of large ground forces, the army estimate was equally unsound because it did not recognize the political impediments to the creation of such a force, Roosevelt's unwillingness to do so, or the impossibility of ever creating one large enough to defeat the Wehrmacht unsupported. On the basis of both political and military realities, Germany simply could not be defeated without continued Russian par-ticipation in the war.

The Search for a Panacea

The Victory Program also did nothing to curb the president's continuing pen-chant for what the armed forces considered premature commitment and over-extension. By the fall of 1941 the result was not only a full-scale shooting war with German submarines in the Atlantic and talk of sending an expeditionary force to North Africa but also a de facto embargo against Japan and a virtual breakdown of diplomatic negotiations. With hostilities in progress and escalating in the Atlan-tic, from a military perspective the president and the State Department seemed to be insanely willing to provoke a second war in the Pacific.

Ironically, however, the president now began to receive some support from the army for his hard line against Tokyo, as well as insistence on a major diversion of U.S. forces to the Far East. Fearful that Japan would attack Siberia and thereby end Russian resistance, in October the WPD, as noted above, reversed past policy and called for continuation of economic pressure to make such a move impos-sible, while G-2 warned against U.S. support for any Sino-Japanese agreement that might free the Japanese army for a movement against Russia. But economic pres-sure risked war, for unless deterred by the threat of major retaliation, Japan would respond with an invasion of Southeast Asia to obtain raw materials and break out of the American vise rather than submit. Given Atlantic events and the depletion of his Pacific fleet, such a war was the last thing Stark needed. Furthermore, naval planners had concluded by September that Japan would not attack Russia in 1941 and no U.S. action was therefore necessary to preclude such an attack. Stark and his subordinates therefore continued to oppose economic sanctions.[65]

During the summer, however, Marshall and his planners had begun to place their trust in a "new" weapon that they viewed as a much more powerful and effective deterrent than the U.S. Pacific Fleet: the B-17 bomber. This turn marked a major reversal of military policy, for the army had previously resisted civilian and air force emphasis on airpower as a cure for U.S. military deficiencies.[66] In the second half of 1941, however, the army decided that the Philippines both could and should be reinforced and defended with airplanes. The reasons for this dramatic shift—in apparent violation of ABC-1, RAINBOW 5, the Victory Program, and twenty years of army doctrine regarding airpower and defense of the archipelago—still defy comprehension. In retrospect they may have been as simple as the arousal of "the fundamental human passion for defending one's own" with the approach of war,[67] and the hope, born of desperation and frustration, that the civilians and air officers were correct and that airpower could provide a panacea to resolve the U.S. strategic dilemmas of 1941.

According to army strategists, such recourse was a hallmark of both British strategy and ignorant civilians. Yet in the Victory Program those very critics had fallen back on airpower when trying to figure out how to combat four hundred German divisions controlling the entire Eurasian land mass. Far from accidentally they began to rely on airpower at approximately the same time to resolve their equally difficult Pacific dilemmas and to prevent Japan from attacking in Siberia. Apparently affected by the power and influence of aircraft in numerous 1940–41 battles as well as the desire to stop presidential dispersion of their planes to Britain and Russia, U.S. military leaders concluded in the summer and early fall that a major reinforcement of the Philippines with new, long-range B-17 bombers might serve as an effective deterrent to any Japanese aggression and, even if it did not, still provide them with a major offensive weapon against the Japanese home islands after the commencement of hostilities.[68]

In late July, at the very moment Roosevelt was freezing Japanese assets, Marshall and Stark thus reversed a decision they had made on July 3 not to defend the Philippines and Malay Barrier with airpower and began to ferry B-17s to the Far East. Simultaneously, the president recalled to active service General Douglas MacArthur, who was then training the Philippine Army, and placed U.S. as well as Filipino forces under his command. By August 7 the president and the War Department had agreed to send him a total of 165 bombers, more than half of those in U.S. possession and three-quarters of the scheduled production for the next six months, including a full air group of 36 new B-17s rather than the squadron of 9 originally planned. Army Air Forces chief General Henry H. Arnold later labeled this a "distinct change in policy," while Marshall informed his British counterpart at the Atlantic Conference that it would act as a "serious deterrent" to Japan.[69] In early September the first B-17s arrived, and the AAF obtained authorization for a broad-based air buildup on the islands. On October 16 Roosevelt and his military advisers decided to accelerate this buildup so that all the heavy bombers would be in the Philippines by March 1942. This potential deterrent was reinforced by the almost simultaneous army decision to commit additional ground forces to the Philippines and the British decision to beef up Far Eastern naval forces.[70]

To Roosevelt's advisers the strategic potential of the bombers was almost limitless. Stimson concluded on September 12 that they "completely changed the strategy of the Pacific" and allowed U.S. power into the Philippines "in a way which it has not been able to do for twenty years." Indeed, those islands could now become "a self-sustaining fortress capable of blockading the China Sea by air power." It was a "reversal of the strategy of the world," he informed Roosevelt and the cabinet. On October 21 he told the president that U.S. strategic possibilities had been "revolutionized." Even the otherwise cautious Marshall saw U.S. bombers operating and moving between Manila, Australia, New Britain, Singapore, the Dutch East Indies and "probably even Vladivostok," thereby covering "the whole area of possible Japanese operations" and forcing them to back down virtually everywhere—including Siberia as well as Malaysia. There was even a "better than 50% chance," he concluded, "of forcing them practically to drop the Axis." With such thoughts in mind WPD and G-2 verbalized their support of continued embargo and toughness toward Japan in October. A month later Marshall shared his beliefs regarding both the deterrent and offensive power of the bombers in an extraordinary secret session with the press bureau chiefs and senior correspondents.[71]

With Stark continuing to oppose the embargo, the army and navy had thus partially reversed the positions they had held in the 1930s. Deeply involved in a shooting war with Germany and with the fleet still being shifted for this conflict, the formerly Pacific-oriented navy now wished to avoid provoking Japan at all costs while pursuing the primary enemy in the Atlantic. Although it agreed that Germany was the primary enemy, the still seriously unprepared army was unwilling to commit forces to the Atlantic theater. Suddenly, however, it appeared willing to reverse decades of opposition to provoking a Far Eastern war and take desperate chances in the Pacific because of the need to keep Russia in the European war and its newfound belief in the deterrent power of bombers.[72]

In November, however, Philippine reinforcement was far from complete, and negotiations with Japan were at the verge of collapse. Furthermore, a shooting war had already begun in the Atlantic, Britain appeared incapable of offensive action or even successful home defense, additional aircraft to England and an expeditionary force to forestall the Germans in North Africa remained distinct possibilities despite continued army opposition, and the likelihood of a Japanese attack on Siberia had diminished considerably.[73] Thus the army reverted to its previous caution regarding the Far East. On the basis of both the Germany-first strategy and the need for more time to reinforce the Philippines (and thus hopefully deter any conflict in the Pacific), Marshall joined Stark in recommending that the United States take no action that might precipitate war unless Japan attacked U.S., British, or Dutch possessions, and he pleaded with the State Department for "some very clever diplomacy" and "minor concessions" to allow Japan to save face and preserve peace for at least ninety days. So did Stimson, who requested from Hull this "very short time" so as to "take advantage of this wonderful opportunity" to strengthen the Philippines and with it his "diplomatic arm." On November 21 the WPD informed Hull that the army considered such a modus vivendi of "grave importance to the success of our war effort in Europe," and Marshall and Stark undoubtedly reinforced that message during a November 25 meeting with him. "The most essential thing now," they informed Roosevelt two days later, "is to gain time."[74]

Hull at first agreed and prepared a three-month modus vivendi that Stark and Marshall rated "satisfactory from a military viewpoint."[75] But he then changed his mind under the impact of negative diplomatic responses and pressure from America's Chinese, British, Dutch, and Australian allies. Without consulting the armed forces he decided on November 26 to reject their request and respond to the final Japanese peace proposal with a rigid, ten-point, moralistic rejoinder that he knew would mean war. Fearing dissension within his emerging Far Eastern coalition of nations as well as domestically over any appeasement of Japan, and furious over Tokyo's apparent duplicity revealed by intelligence of troopship movements and imminent aggression while continuing negotiations, Roosevelt, in a private meeting with Hull, approved this course of action. Neither saw fit to inform the JB, though on November 26 Hull did tell Stimson that he had decided to "kick the whole thing over" and on the next day that he had "washed my hands of it and it is now in the hands of you and Knox, the Army and the Navy." For Hull, foreign and military policy remained separate spheres.[76] Japan attacked Pearl Harbor ten days later. Four days after that Hitler made his conflict with the United States in the Atlantic official by declaring war.

Despite their unprecedented preparations and accomplishments in 1940–41 regarding strategic planning for a coalition war, the U.S. armed forces thus entered World War II under the nightmarish circumstances they had tried to avoid. Their efforts had consistently been foiled, most recently and disastrously by Hull and Roosevelt, and from their point of view this episode was far from unique. To the contrary, Pearl Harbor stood to them as the logical culmination of a long history of civilian refusal to coordinate policy and strategy. Ignoring their warnings and recommendations, the president and the secretary of state had overcommitted the United States, pursued provocative policies unsupported by force, refused to match ends with means, and not even consulted with them on key issues. The result had been the destruction of the Pacific Fleet and the need to fight a global, multifront war which might have been avoided and for which the country was far from prepared.

The validity of such charges remains debatable, as does the appropriateness of the alternative policies and strategies proposed by the armed forces. While Roosevelt and Hull were by no means guiltless in regard to the Far Eastern disaster of late 1941, the basic problem in retrospect was more one of perspective than willful refusal to face facts. As the failure of the armed forces to resolve their strategy/policy differences before late 1940 reflected opposing perspectives based on different historical missions and experiences, so the failure to achieve effective civil-military coordination in 1941 reflected similarly opposing civil-military perspectives. From the armed forces' point of view, recognition of the likelihood of full-scale war against Germany as a result of both the threat posed and presidential policies, as well as the subsequent need for concentration on the Atlantic and Europe while avoiding conflict with Japan, was a commonsense approach to a dangerous situation and an application of the military principle of "concentration of force" to the political realm. But such an application led the armed forces consistently to recommend policies far beyond what the civil leadership considered politically prudent, appropriate, and possible in the European theater given the state of public opinion and policies far too limited in light of such considerations in the Far East. To the military, Roosevelt and Hull were guilty of dangerously mismatching ends and means. Yet the president and Hull felt the armed forces were either ignoring political realities or else incorrectly subordinating them to narrow military considerations. As Roosevelt bluntly responded when Stark in February had opposed a naval "training cruise" through the Philippines because it would disperse the fleet and not affect the Japanese, "this was not a naval or military matter now, but a question of state policy."[77]

The military and civilian viewpoints were each correct from their individual perspectives. In regard to Far Eastern policy, A. E. Campbell notes, Roosevelt "was playing the role appropriate to a domestic political leader and playing it brilliantly, while his military advisers were performing their proper function."[78] And while Pearl Harbor may have illustrated the disastrous consequences of rejecting military advice regarding the relationship between political ends and military means, one cannot conclude that the armed forces' approach could have been put into effect without equally disastrous consequences in the political realm with respect to maintenance of a domestic consensus and the anti-Axis coalition. From Roosevelt's perspective, a "hard" policy toward Japan involved fewer risks than a passive or "soft" one.[79]

Furthermore, there is utterly no evidence that the additional airpower available in the Philippines as a result of a ninety-day modus vivendi would have made any difference. To the contrary, the War Department's sudden belief in the B-17 as a panacea for its Far Eastern strategic dilemmas stands today as one of the most extraordinary delusions of the entire era. Whether such a modus vivendi could have been stretched out sufficiently to avoid any war in the Pacific, however, remains a matter of historical speculation.[80]

Beyond such disputes lay the basic insolubility of U.S. strategic dilemmas in late 1941. As Roosevelt had concluded during the summer, "I simply have not got enough Navy to go around."[81] In truth, he did not have enough planes, troops, or war material either, even if war with Japan could have been avoided. Given the army's beliefs regarding the ineffectiveness of indirect warfare, there was no way Germany could be defeated even with full-scale U.S. participation. During the four months preceding Pearl Harbor, however, military planners had begun to perceive an answer to this dilemma on the Russian front, one they would develop further in the ensuing months. The result would be a fundamental reorientation of U.S. strategy, a massive Allied debate, a new set of civil-military conflicts, and a redefinition of alliance relationships.

Global Strategy Reconsidered, December 1941–July 1942

Pearl Harbor ended the armed forces' uncertainty and confusion regarding American policies. The United States was now a full-scale belligerent and member of a coalition in a global war against the Axis. And even if not officially stated until early 1943, the aim of that coalition was total Axis military defeat and unconditional surrender. Appropriate strategy remained a subject of intense dispute, however, despite the ABC-1 agreement of 1941.

That agreement was reaffirmed at ARCADIA, the Anglo-American summit conference held in Washington immediately after formal U.S. entry into the war, and the ensuing strategic arguments over Mediterranean versus cross-channel operations thus appeared to take place within the context of an agreed-on global strategy. In reality, however, the arguments were far more extensive, for the events of late 1941–early 1942 eliminated many of the essential preconditions on which ABC-1 and related plans had been based. The result was a reopening, albeit on different terms, of all the partially settled disputes of the previous two years. Thus 1942 witnessed a renewed debate over U.S. global interests, priorities, and strategies and a heightening of the army-navy, civil-military, and Anglo-American tensions and disputes of 1939–41. The results by midyear included not only major conflict in all three realms but also a formal proposal by the U.S. service chiefs to abandon ABC-1 in favor of a Pacific-first approach.

New Environments

The institutional framework within which these disputes took place was far different from the one that had existed before Pearl Harbor. At ARCADIA the British and Americans agreed to a merging of their chiefs of staff organizations into the Combined Chiefs of Staff (CCS) to direct their combined forces and plan global strategy. To parallel the British Chiefs of Staff Committee (COS) on the new CCS, the JB was replaced in February 1942 with the U.S. Joint Chiefs of Staff (JCS). In addition to Marshall as army chief and Stark as navy chief, this new interservice body included Air Chief Arnold and the newly appointed commander in chief of the U.S. Fleet (COMINCH), Admiral Ernest J. King. In March, King also replaced Stark as CNO. Because Arnold technically remained subordinate to Marshall, the army in effect now had two votes on the JCS to the navy's one. Furthermore, the JCS still lacked a coordinating link to its civilian superior that the COS possessed. Under Marshall's prodding, Roosevelt in July resolved both problems by agreeing to appoint to the JCS former CNO and ambassador to Vichy France Admiral William D. Leahy in the new position of chief of staff to the commander in chief.

The precursor to the present-day JCS, this wartime body exercised much more power and influence than had its JB predecessor. As a result of King's assumption of the dual titles of COMINCH and CNO as well as separate army and navy staff reorganizations in early 1942, the two service chiefs were able for the first time to exercise complete and effective command over all branches of their forces. Arnold exercised similar control over the AAF as well as a great deal of autonomy within the army. Both as individuals and as a group, the service chiefs now had the power actually to determine strategy and to direct forces and operations, not simply coordinate and advise on planning.[1]

The chiefs' power was further increased by the exceptionally close and direct relationship they developed with Roosevelt. Throughout the war the JCS existed solely at his discretion, with FDR rejecting their request for a formal charter as "superfluous" as well as possibly restrictive and using them as his personal military advisers and planners.[2] They accompanied him to all wartime summit conferences, prepared his briefing books, and were soon drafting many of his messages to other heads of state as well as meeting with him quite frequently—individually and as a group. Leahy's appointment further strengthened and regularized this relationship, though not to the extent the rest of the JCS desired. He maintained a White House office, saw Roosevelt daily, and served as a direct liaison between the other JCS members and the president. But FDR insisted on using him primarily as a "legman" and messenger to the chiefs, not a JCS chairman and personal strategic adviser representing them as Marshall had desired when he first proposed the appointment. Consequently, Marshall himself came to assume these roles in an informal manner.[3]

The service chiefs' increased power and influence occurred largely at the expense of the civilian secretaries of state, war, and navy. Continuing to maintain the artificial dichotomy between diplomatic and military affairs that had marked the prewar years, Hull concentrated on postwar planning while leaving wartime issues to the armed forces. Within the War and Navy Departments, Stimson and Knox, along with their civilian assistants, concentrated on mobilization and domestic issues and worked to a large extent outside the formal chain of command, for by the army and navy reorganizations the chiefs reported directly to and received orders directly from the president rather than through the two secretaries. Thus most policy as well as strategic and operational issues were largely in the hands of those chiefs and their staffs, with only the president above them. Indeed, Hull was no longer invited to military meetings at the White House, and neither he nor the service secretaries were even included on the regular distribution list for JCS papers.[4]

Within the military planning network, a plethora of joint army-navy-air committees and staff divisions began to emerge in 1942 to replace the old JPC, provide qualified members to serve on the new CCS committees, and advise the service chiefs on strategy and policy. They would eventually assume a pivotal role in this latter regard, but not before a 1943 reorganization and expansion.[5] Although a Joint Planning Staff (JPS) and a Joint U.S. Strategic Committee (JUSSC) began to function in early 1942, planning throughout the year lay largely in the hands of the army and navy staff divisions specifically charged with this function.

The most important of these was the Army Operations Division (OPD). The successor to the WPD by the army reorganization of March 1942, the OPD served throughout the war as Marshall's "Washington command post" and the key component of the entire general staff. Its members made up the army sections of the joint strategic planning committees, and its chief served as Marshall's primary strategic planner. So important and powerful was this division that it received a complete and separate volume in the army's official history of the war.[6]

In early 1942, however, the influence of the OPD, the joint committees, and even the chiefs and JCS organization was by no means apparent. Rather, it emerged only gradually and fitfully during the strategic debates that took place throughout 1942 and 1943, debates resulting primarily from the military and political crises that marked the early months of formal U.S. belligerency.

The global politico-military environment within which strategic planning took place in 1942 was as dramatically different from what had existed before Pearl Harbor as was the institutional environment. Beyond the basic structural changes involved in formal U.S. belligerency and the joining of what had been separate conflicts in Europe and the Far East, the early months of 1942 witnessed several devastating military defeats for the Allies. These precipitated a series of political crises and dramatically altered prewar planning assumptions.

In the European theater, Axis forces controlled the entire continent from the French coastline to the gates of Moscow and from Norway to Libya. Moreover, despite the successful Soviet counteroffensive in December, Germany maintained the strategic initiative in the East and was preparing for a massive spring offensive. Simultaneously, Axis surface and underwater naval forces challenged Allied control of the Atlantic, Mediterranean, and Norwegian seas, thereby threatening to isolate Russian and British Middle Eastern forces from outside supplies and cut the critical Atlantic lifeline between Britain and the United States. The situation in the Far East was equally dismal, as the Japanese destroyed the remaining small Allied fleets and successfully invaded the Philippines, Dutch East Indies, and Malaya. By mid-February they had forced the surrender of Singapore and soon thereafter achieved all of their remaining objectives in the Pacific. China, India, Australia, and New Zealand were all threatened. Indeed, Axis forces now controlled more than one-third of the population and mineral resources of the world and appeared capable of taking even more.[7] Most menacing was the possibility of coordinated German-Japanese offensives in the Soviet Union, Middle East, and India which would enable their forces to link up, knock Russia out of the war, obtain the Middle East oil reserves, and probably end the war.

The diplomatic situation was equally threatening. Australia and New Zealand demanded a return of their forces from the Middle East and a reversal of the Europe-first strategy in order to halt Japan. So did the Chinese, who ominously warned of collapse or separate peace without massive U.S. aid. Similar warnings emerged regarding Russia in the absence of Allied military offensives to divert German forces from the eastern front.

Strategic Options and Disagreements

The ARCADIA conferees had responded to this situation by reaffirming ABC-1. The Far East would be stabilized, they vowed, but their forces would remain on the defensive in that theater while attention centered on Europe and the Atlantic. Following the British peripheral approach as outlined by Churchill, they agreed that in 1942 they would reestablish sea supremacy, continue sending supplies to Russia, and launch simultaneous offensives against German forces in Libya from Egypt and French North Africa to clear the Mediterranean and prepare for a 1943 assault on the European continent.[8]

While in accord with ABC-1 and RAINBOW 5, these plans virtually ignored the changed circumstances of early 1942 and were thus, in the words of the official British history, "more formal than real." With respect to material and shipping alone, Britain and the United States could not possibly stabilize the Far Eastern situation and invade North Africa simultaneously, even with French cooperation. Whether they could accomplish either task was an open question. Thus when Britain's offensive in Libya failed, Vichy France remained hostile, and the shipping crisis became acute, Washington and London were forced in March to postpone indefinitely Operation GYMNAST, their proposed invasion of French North Africa.[9]

By this time numerous U.S. planners were no longer willing to abide by ABC-1—

or at least the British interpretation of that document—because of the equally if not more serious situation in the Pacific. Pearl Harbor and the ensuing Japanese onslaught, they argued, had created a new situation in which the Europe-first approach enunciated in early 1941 was no longer applicable. Agreement to that approach had been based on the existence of a strong U.S. fleet at Hawaii, supplemented by a British naval force at Singapore, to hold key defensive positions in what they had hoped could be a limited conflict. By the end of 1941, however, both U.S. and British naval forces had been largely destroyed. Over the next three months the Japanese also destroyed Allied efforts to defend the so-called Malay Barrier and appeared well on their way to conquering all of Asia and the western Pacific. This was far from the limited, defensive scenario the planners had sketched in 1941, and it led to a sharp modification of U.S. priorities in an effort to stop the Japanese onslaught. Lip service was given consistently to the Europe-first approach, but U.S. planners now argued that reinforcements to hold what remained in the Pacific took precedence over any other activities save defense of the Atlantic itself.

Especially vociferous in this regard were navy planners. Desirous of revenge for Pearl Harbor, determined not to take additional losses in an area of naval responsibility, and fearful of the racial and political implications of recent Japanese victories, King and his subordinates returned to the navy's pre-1940 Pacific preoccupation by pleading incessantly in early 1942 for reinforcements sufficient not simply to stem the Japanese advance but also to launch counterattacks. On February 8 King explained his logic to Navy secretary Knox by noting that a static defense in the Pacific was not possible and that any effective defense in the future required a "defensive offensive" now, a strategy to "hold what you've got and hit them where you can, the hitting to be done not only in seizing opportunities but by making them." Throughout February and March the CNO therefore requested army and air forces to garrison islands in the South Pacific and drive northward. Such moves were necessary not only on strategic grounds but also, as he informed Roosevelt on March 5, to avoid Japanese conquest of the "white man's countries" of Australia and New Zealand "because of the repercussions" of such conquests "among the non-white races of the world."[10]

Along with such calls came a major outburst of naval parochialism and a turn away from Anglo-American cooperation. At ARCADIA the Navy WPD chief Turner opposed unity of command and the establishment of the entire CCS organization on the grounds that "British officials would be given half the total authority for matters now solely under US control" and that "US interests would be subordinated to the interests of the British Commonwealth." Although overruled, he appeared so determined in early 1942 to make sure the organization did not succeed that Brigadier Vivian Dykes of the British Joint Staff Mission (JSM) in Washington, labeling him "a stubborn old swine," informally suggested his removal. Turner's subordinate and eventual successor, Admiral Charles M. "Savvy" Cooke, behaved similarly, leading Dykes to refer to him as "that bloody little man" and to question whether combined planning with the Americans could possibly work.[11]

To an extent this shift in naval perspective and behavior was the result of changes in personnel. Unlike his predecessor Stark, King was highly suspicious, aggressive, and often obnoxious in his dealings with others, and his behavior tended to be mirrored by his subordinates, many of whom he had personally selected or, like Turner, possessed their own reputations for obnoxiousness. Marshall uncharacteristically admitted after the war that "I had trouble with King because he was always sore at everybody. He was perpetually mean." One of King's daughters put it more humorously by labeling her father "the most even-tempered man in the Navy. He is always in a rage."[12]

But the naval shift involved more than personalities. Turner, after all, had been one of the authors of Plan Dog and had helped negotiate ABC-1. These experiences had not made him overly trustful of the British, however. Indeed, he had co-authored the warning to U.S. representatives to be wary of British manipulation at the ABC talks.[13] Also important, he realized Britain would oppose the shift to the Pacific now desired by the navy, and he reacted accordingly. Furthermore, King, his new chief, was representative of an anti-British and anticooperation sentiment that had existed within the navy as well as the army before Pearl Harbor but had not been as visible because the two preceding naval chiefs, Leahy and Stark, had strongly supported cooperation. As the British historian D. C. Watt has noted, King's appointment as CNO "marked the return of the Anglophobe nationalism of the 1920's to the high command of the U.S. Navy."[14]

As in the army, this Anglophobia dated back to World War I experiences. Beneath the surface of Anglo-American naval cooperation during that conflict, as personified by Admiral Williams Sims's command, deep differences of opinion had existed. And whereas Stark had served on Sims's staff, King had served during the war as chief of staff to the commander of the Atlantic Fleet Admiral Henry T. Mayo, an officer who strongly objected to Sims's independent command in England and its subordination to overall British direction. Not surprisingly Stark became a strong advocate of Anglo-American naval collaboration, whereas King developed a deep dislike and suspicion of the British. As late as 1932 he had insisted that London remained a potential enemy. Fearing a repetition of the World War I scenario, he had in 1941 suggested a clear geographic division of responsibilities between the eastern and western Atlantic so that no U.S. naval forces could possibly be subordinated to the British Admiralty, a proposal with which Stark had disagreed.[15]

The navy was far from alone in its opposition to ABC-1 and its desire for a Pacific offensive in early 1942. The Chinese, Australian, New Zealand, and Philippine governments all demanded U.S. counterattacks, as did the commander of U.S. forces in the Southwest Pacific, General MacArthur, and large segments of the public. As Stark had warned in 1940, that public was by no means willing to conduct a limited, defensive war against Japan, especially in light of Pearl Harbor. Aroused by this attack and by the humiliating defeats that followed, it demanded immediate revenge. And many of Roosevelt's prewar isolationist opponents now argued that U.S. forces should be concentrated to defeat the "real" enemy that had so viciously attacked the United States rather than "rescue" British chestnuts in the European theater. By March, Roosevelt faced public opinion polls that showed a majority of people rating Japan the primary enemy. Both his Europe-first approach and his military competence were coming under increasing attack.[16]

Army planners had joined in this Pacific emphasis after Pearl Harbor, but by late February they had begun to shift dramatically and to argue for a strictly defensive strategy in the Pacific and the Mediterranean to concentrate forces in England for a 1942 or 1943 cross-channel invasion of Europe. Throughout March they prepared a series of detailed analyses to support this strategic proposal and by month's end had won naval and presidential approval. London concurred in early April. On the surface, the planners thus succeeded not only in stemming the Pacific-first thrust and reaffirming ABC-1, but also in supplementing and revising that rather vague document with specific large-scale ground operations, as implied in the Victory Program, designed to achieve the quick and decisive defeat of Germany before turning against Japan.[17]

Appearances were misleading, however, for within army plans were some very sharp departures from ABC-1—or at least the British understanding of that document. Despite their formal agreement to army plans, Churchill and his advisers had strong reservations regarding their viability and appropriateness, concerns that soon surfaced. Nor were the navy or the president strongly wedded to the army concept, and by May–June they were joining Britain in proposing alternative strategies. But whereas British and presidential alternatives centered on the Mediterranean, those of the navy centered on the Pacific. And, surprisingly, these received army support in July. Indeed, the WPD/OPD chief General Dwight D. Eisenhower had actually suggested such a dramatic shift in two of the earliest army pleas for cross-channel operations. If London rejected the cross-channel approach, he had argued in February and March, "we must turn our *backs* upon the Eastern Atlantic and go, full out, as quickly as possible, against Japan!"[18]

This startling suggestion appeared to violate every strategic principle and priority on which army planning had for years been based. But it was actually a very carefully developed response to what army strategists considered U.S. interests—and the numerous threats to those interests—in 1942.

The Far East, the Soviet Union,
and Army Cross-Channel Plans

Immediately after Pearl Harbor army planners had agreed to send reinforcements to the Pacific as part of a desperate effort to stem the Japanese advance before it reached the resource-rich areas of Southeast Asia.[19] By late February, however, such efforts had obviously and dismally failed. With Singapore in Japanese hands and the Allied fleets virtually eliminated, full Japanese conquest of the East Indies and the Philippines had become simply a matter of time. Consequently, additional reinforcements no longer made sense. Furthermore, such reinforcement would continue the disastrous dispersion of forces that had marked all Allied efforts since Pearl Harbor. It would also commit and subordinate army forces to the whims of a naval campaign that, even if successful, would in no way be decisive from a global viewpoint. As Eisenhower derisively noted in mid-February, King's proposal for army garrisons on Pacific islands would enable the navy to "have a safe place to sail its vessels" but little more. "We've got to go to Europe and fight," he insisted in a private, late-January reaffirmation of Germany-first strategy, "and we've got to quit wasting resources all over the world—and still worse—wasting time." [20]

The problem was that the only existing and approved plan for European action, the invasion of French North Africa in conjunction with a British offensive in Libya, was an anathema to army planners, as was Britain's entire peripheral strategy. As previously noted, those planners had never been enamored with the plan or the overall strategy, and before Pearl Harbor they had labeled both politically inspired attempts to manipulate American strategy and policy in a militarily indecisive area.[21] They maintained this assessment throughout 1942. In January Eisenhower included North Africa as one of the political "side shows" that should not be allowed to interfere with Pacific reinforcement; joined by other planners, he argued that the British should retire in Libya so as to release forces for the Far East. Simultaneously, Embick warned Marshall that London's entire Mediterranean approach was motivated "more largely by political than by sound strategic purposes." Invading North Africa, he insisted, would be "a mistake of the first magnitude," and any belief that the Allies could later invade Europe from this area was so "irrational" as to be "fantastic." [22]

In effect, army planners now rejected not only operations in North Africa and Libya but even the idea that this area was part of the European theater to receive primary attention via ABC-1. As with King's Pacific concerns, British insistence on offensives in this area showed that, in Eisenhower's words, "everybody is too much engaged with small things of his own—or with some vague idea of larger political activity to realize what we are doing—rather *not* doing." [23]

Eisenhower's "everybody" included the president. Despite long-standing army objections, Roosevelt had continued to display an intense interest in North Africa and British ideas of peripheral warfare, an interest army planners saw as illustrative of a dangerous naval and British influence over the president at their expense. As General Joseph Stilwell bitterly noted in his acerbic diary, "the Navy is the apple of his eye" and "the Limeys have his ear," whereas the poor army remained "the stepchild" who had only "the hind tit." [24]

What Eisenhower felt Roosevelt, the navy, and the British were not doing was taking a truly global view of the war and properly prioritizing theaters in order to reach a sound strategy. In a series of brutally frank assessments in early 1942, he and his staff insisted that beyond the assumed safety from major attack of the continental United States, Hawaii, the Caribbean, and South America above the Brazilian "bulge," only three military tasks were truly "necessary": securing the British Isles and Atlantic sea-lanes; holding India and the Middle East to prevent a German-Japanese junction; and retaining the Soviet Union in the war "as an active enemy against Germany." All else, even the defense of Australia, New Zealand, Alaska, and the rest of South America, was "merely desirable" in the present crisis and therefore secondary. Of the three essential tasks, holding the Atlantic sea-lanes and the India–Middle East corridor required only defensive moves at present. The third, keeping Russia in the war, was the most problematic and required "immediate and definite action." The Russian situation thus became the basis of Eisenhower's and the army's strategic planning for 1942. [25]

Eisenhower and his subordinates were far from alone or original in perceiving the overriding importance of continued Soviet participation in the war. As previously noted, in the summer and fall of 1941 Roosevelt and army planners had begun to recognize that victory over Germany might not be possible unless the Red Army continued to tie down the bulk of the Wehrmacht, and they consequently had made assistance to Russia a focal point of their global strategy. The JB had forcefully reiterated this conclusion by informing Roosevelt on December 21 that "Russia alone possesses the manpower potentially able to defeat Germany in Europe." [26] The Soviets' late 1941 success in stopping the German advance on Moscow and launching a counteroffensive, occurring at a time when Axis forces were everywhere else successful, further reinforced this belief. As a result virtually all Allied planning papers in late 1941–early 1942 stressed the critical importance of aiding the Russians so that they could survive a renewed German onslaught. Roosevelt agreed. "Nothing would be worse than to have the Russians collapse," he told Treasury secretary Henry Morgenthau on March 11. "I would rather lose New Zealand, Australia, or anything else than have the Russians collapse." Five days earlier the JUSSC had bluntly stated that "Russia must be supported now by every possible means" because the absence of a Russian front would postpone "indefinitely" the end of the war.[27] And as army planners realized, such postponement would only increase public and naval pressure to turn away completely from the indecisive European theater in favor of the Pacific.

There were two fundamental methods of aiding Russia in 1942: sending Lend-Lease supplies and launching an offensive to divert the Germans from the east and thereby relieve the pressure on Soviet forces. Everyone agreed that both methods had to be pursued as high priorities; the argument was over where to launch the offensive so as to provide the greatest relief.

Indirect relief could be offered by launching either of the already proposed offensives in the North Africa–Middle East area *or* in the Pacific. While the British maintained that the former could decrease the pressure on the Soviets by forcing Hitler to send reinforcements to the area and securing the southern supply line to Russia, the Americans countered that a Pacific offensive could offer more important indirect relief by keeping Japan preoccupied and thus prevent an attack on the Russian rear in Siberia. As far-fetched as this argument might sound, it played a major role in army thinking throughout 1942. Indeed, it bore a striking similarity to fall 1941 army arguments about the importance of both the oil embargo against Japan and air reinforcement of the Philippines to continued Russian resistance. With full-scale hostilities having commenced, Pacific military action replaced embargoes and air deterrence as a means of keeping Japan off Russia's back.

Marshall implicitly supported this position as early as December 20, when he informed Roosevelt that Southwest Pacific action would encourage Russia to stay in the war. On January 15, G-2 warned that, given "a quick and easy victory" by Japan in the Southwest Pacific, "a coordinated joint offensive against the USSR will probably materialize." On March 19 and April 1 it reiterated this warning, adding that such an offensive would be part of an Axis "supreme effort to eliminate one of the United Nations in 1942" before U.S. production was organized and that a separate Soviet peace with the Axis could result from such an offensive, as well as from insufficient aid or high losses.[28] King's Pacific plans could preclude any "quick and easy victory" for Japan by keeping it preoccupied in the south, thus preventing an attack on Russia. Indeed, Embick informed WPD in late January that the "strength shown by Russia," combined with naval losses in the Pacific, had altered the situation assumed in ABC-1 and justified a "greater degree of immediate aid" in the Southwest Pacific so as to retain air and naval bases—not only for the war against Japan but also as "a deterrent to a Japanese attack on Siberia" and encouragement to continued Chinese resistance. A March 8 WPD study concluded that the "most valuable assistance which can be rendered to Russia is to contain Japanese forces . . . in the South Pacific and the sooner our action clearly indicates to Russia that we shall do this the greater the advantage she can gain from that assistance."[29]

As Eisenhower noted, however, action in the Pacific or North Africa could provide only limited, indirect relief via indecisive operations in peripheral theaters. The only way to provide substantial and direct relief, as at least one G-2 officer had noted as early as August 1941, was through a cross-channel invasion of northern France sufficient to force a shift of German forces directly from east to west.[30] Moreover, the OPD argued, only in northern France could the Allies eventually launch a decisive offensive against the citadel of German power, and that offensive could be successfully undertaken only while Russia was in the war tying down the bulk of the German Army. As Eisenhower realized, the reasoning was somewhat circular: only a cross-channel invasion could provide sufficient relief to guarantee continued Russian participation in the war, while only that continued participation could enable Britain and the United States to launch successfully such a decisive operation.[31]

Army cross-channel proposals were also motivated by diplomatic and psychological factors regarding the Soviet Union. The planners were well aware of Soviet dissatisfaction with the low level of Allied aid and veiled threats of a separate peace if more substantial support was not forthcoming. In mid-February G-2 warned of such a possibility if the aid did not improve but concluded that once the Russians were "convinced of our strength and determination, of our desire and ability to fight a war vigorously and victoriously," they would join in active operations against Japan as well as Germany.[32] Ever since the summer of 1941, Soviet leader Josef Stalin had been making clear that only one operation could so convince him and keep Russia in the war—crossing the channel to create a "second front" in northern France. On February 28, in his first formal call for such operations, Eisenhower therefore emphasized that Russia could not be allowed to reach a situation whereby it would be willing to "accept a negotiated peace, no matter how unfavorable," that preventing such a situation required "the early initiation of operations that will draw off from the Russian front sizable portions of the German Army," and that such operations had to illustrate to the suspicious Soviets a willingness as well as ability to provide meaningful assistance. The operations therefore *"must be so conceived, and so presented to the Russians,"* he emphasized, *"that they will recognize the importance of the support rendered."* For Eisenhower, that fact translated into development of "a definite plan" to invade northern France via a cross-channel attack.[33]

Marshall agreed. On March 7 he warned his JCS colleagues that the Soviets would consider a separate peace "justified" if Britain and the United States did "not initiate an offensive on a large scale in the West."[34] By that time Arnold,

Stimson, and Hopkins were also calling for such an offensive. Over the next three weeks, while Eisenhower and his OPD staff clarified their proposals and arguments in several memoranda, these three worked to secure Roosevelt's approval. They were aided by the cancellation of GYMNAST at this time and the president's desire for a substitute 1942 offensive in the European theater to accomplish his own politico-military objectives, most notably the calming of public opinion and diversion of its attention from the Pacific back to Europe, offering encouragement and direct assistance to the Soviets, and preventing an Anglo-Soviet treaty with postwar territorial provisions. By March 8–9 he was informing Churchill of his interest in "definite plans" for "a new front this summer" in Europe, and under Marshall's and Hopkins's prodding he agreed on March 25 to bypass the entire CCS machinery and send the proposal directly to London with the two of them.[35]

As prepared by Eisenhower and the OPD, the proposal called for immediate concentration of forces in Britain for a forty-eight-division, cross-channel attack in the spring of 1943, with provisions for a much smaller, "emergency" operation in the summer or fall of 1942 with whatever forces were then available should Germany be "critically weakened" or the Soviet situation desperate. At an April 1 White House meeting Roosevelt approved the proposal, while Hopkins forced King's acquiescence. The president thereupon cabled Churchill that Hopkins and Marshall were coming to London with "certain conclusions" he had reached which were "vital" and would please both the Soviets and public opinion.[36]

The proposal Hopkins and Marshall carried with them was actually far from being as straightforward as it appeared. Under the surface it contained serious inconsistencies. It also contained a continued hidden focus on the Pacific.

Two essential and related problems faced by U.S. planners were that any cross-channel invasion would be far more difficult to launch successfully in 1942 than either a North African or Pacific offensive and that neither the navy nor the public would tolerate additional losses in the Pacific, despite Eisenhower's downgrading of the importance of the area. In March the JPS had therefore been unable to reach strategic agreement and instead had simply recommended that the JCS choose one of the three courses of action previously analyzed by the JUSSC: total concentration in England for cross-channel operations, even at the risk of further Pacific losses; a Pacific-first approach; or maintenance of presently held positions in the Pacific with concentration of remaining forces in England. On March 16 the JCS chose the third, compromise option, as did Eisenhower, who had been having second thoughts and may have even authored it.[37] Unfortunately, however, maintenance of Pacific positions meant that U.S. forces available for Europe would be far from sufficient to cross the English Channel successfully in 1942. Indeed, given shipping commitments, Washington could send no ground forces to England before July 1 and only sixty-six thousand men by October 1. As the JUSSC concluded, such "delay in the movement of our forces would prevent effective participation in an offensive in Europe at the time deemed essential from strategic considerations." While the planners tried to figure out ways to speed up the transport of U.S. forces, they simultaneously concluded that any 1942 cross-channel assault would have to depend primarily on British troops.[38] To compound this problem, a 1942 cross-channel assault might well end in disaster. But because it would be launched to maintain Soviet resistance in a desperate situation by diverting German forces and because such resistance remained "essential" to the defeat of Germany, the OPD maintained that the operation "should be considered a sacrifice for the common good."[39]

The British might not be willing to play such a sacrificial role, however, and might reject the entire proposal because it ran counter to their peripheral strategy and focus on the Mediterranean. If this occurred the choice for U.S. forces in 1942 would then be North Africa or the Pacific. And although each might offer indirect support to Russia, neither would be decisive, while either by its dispersion of forces would preclude cross-channel operations until 1944 at the earliest.

Choosing either North Africa or the Pacific over cross-channel operations in 1942 would thus mean giving no direct aid to the Soviets not for one but for two years. This would be equivalent to abandoning them and accepting the probability of their defeat or a separate Russo-German peace, either of which would make the European war unwinnable. Even if this did not occur, a two-year delay in crossing the channel would lengthen the European war immeasurably and thus the war in the Pacific. In this choice between the lesser of two evils, army planners adamantly insisted on the Pacific over North Africa. In one sense they had no choice: neither the public nor the navy would tolerate an endless Europe-first approach in the Mediterranean while Japanese forces continued to sweep across the Pacific.[40] Moreover, the JUSSC had stated in March that if Britain refused to cross the channel in 1942, its own "compromise" proposal should be reevaluated with "the possibility of concentrating U.S. offensive effort in the Pacific area considered."[41]

Given the planners' perceptions, choosing the Pacific over North Africa also made diplomatic and military sense. As previously noted, they saw a North African invasion having little if any military value and as being motivated by London's desire to manipulate U.S. strategy and deployments so as to secure British political goals. If only for the negative desire to foil such machinations, U.S. planners would favor virtually any other theater. Furthermore, the Pacific offered possible politico-military gains in regard to Russia. Soviet defeat or a separate peace was the probable but not inevitable outcome of a refusal to cross the channel in 1942, and from the planners' point of view the Pacific alternative would provide Moscow with far more indirect aid, by precluding a Japanese attack on Siberia, than any North African venture. It would also aid and help keep in the war America's allies against Japan while maintaining and extending U.S. influence in Asia and the Pacific. Eisenhower thus included in both his February and March calls for cross-channel operations the threat, if London refused to agree to those operations, to "turn our *backs* upon the Eastern Atlantic and go, full out, as quickly as possible, against Japan!"[42]

The British, of course, had a very different perspective. From their vantage point North Africa and Libya were part of the European theater and still constituted the best areas for offensive action in 1942. To launch a cross-channel assault in light of existing German power in France was suicidal and would not divert any German forces from the east, and for Washington to insist that such an operation be launched with British troops was outrageous. Yet, ever since Pearl Harbor, they had feared a U.S. shift to the Pacific, and Roosevelt and Hopkins played on this fear and that of Soviet collapse to force British agreement.[43] As a result London in mid-April formally accepted the army's cross-channel plans. Forces would immediately be concentrated in England (BOLERO) to cross the channel either in the spring of 1943 with forty-eight divisions (ROUNDUP) or as an emergency in the fall of 1942, with whatever divisions were then available, if Russia appeared to be on the verge of collapse (SLEDGEHAMMER). The British had no intention of launching such a suicide mission, however, and within six weeks Churchill suggested a return to GYMNAST.[44]

By that time King was also having second thoughts. In early May, immediately before the Coral Sea engagement, he had insisted that BOLERO "must not be permitted to interfere with our own vital needs in the Pacific," which he rated just as important and "certainly more urgent." Marshall had disagreed vehemently and in view of apparent presidential support for King had demanded that the White House provide a clarification and straightforward choice between BOLERO and the Pacific. On May 6 Roosevelt reaffirmed the primacy of BOLERO, but as Dykes noted, the army and navy remained "completely divided, the latter going all out for the South-West Pacific and the former for BOLERO." Then, in mid-May, General Walter Bedell Smith of the JCS/CCS secretariat informed Dykes that the Joint Chiefs as a whole were "very worried about the Pacific situation" and fearful of a full-scale attack on their lines of communication to Australia and that the recent Coral Sea battle "was by no means a victory."[45]

The Battle of Midway a few weeks later was a victory, but neither it nor the Coral Sea engagement eliminated the Japanese threat to the lines of communication to Australia. They did open up King's long-desired opportunity for successful counterattacks, however, which the public as well as the navy and MacArthur continued to demand. Consequently, in June, King again proposed a South Pacific offensive.

While Marshall was grappling with these demands, Churchill and the COS arrived in Washington for a strategy conference that the prime minister hoped would replace cross-channel with North African operations for 1942. Marshall and Stimson argued against such a shift and attempted to maintain presidential support for SLEDGEHAMMER by emphasizing its importance in diverting German forces from the eastern front and insisting that GYMNAST, a diversionary operation designed to protect the British Empire rather than win the war, would not do so. The CCS were able to reach a compromise whereby BOLERO would continue but offensive operations would be launched in 1942 only "in case of necessity" or "an exceptionally favorable opportunity," in which case northern France, Norway, or the Channel Islands were all preferable sites to North Africa. This wording suited the COS because it enabled committee members to focus immediately on the defense of Suez against Rommel (Tobruk fell in the midst of the conference), and the JCS because it blocked any North African venture while continuing the buildup in Britain and the possibility of future action. It in no way suited their civilian superiors, however, who rejected their proposal, labeled a 1942 offensive "essential," and emphasized GYMNAST if a successful SLEDGEHAMMER appeared "improbable." [46]

The Churchill-Roosevelt reasoning was political rather than military and not totally unexpected.[47] Because of recent promises to Stalin as well as the state of public opinion, both leaders believed that offensive action in the European theater was mandatory in 1942. Such action had been Roosevelt's primary motivation in agreeing to army plans in the first place, and on May 6, the same day he reaffirmed to Marshall his commitment to BOLERO over the Pacific, he had forcefully reiterated this stand to the JCS and service secretaries. "Active operations" in Europe during 1942 were "essential," he had argued, to divert German forces from the eastern front and thereby fulfill the "principal objective" of helping the Russians. "It must be constantly reiterated," the president wrote in this regard, "that Russian armies are killing more Germans and destroying more Axis materiel than all the twenty-five united nations put together. To help Russia, therefore, is the primary consideration." This necessitated a second front "in 1942—not 1943." [48] Three weeks later he reiterated this conclusion to Churchill, noting that owing to visiting Soviet foreign minister Vyacheslav Molotov's "real anxiety" about the military situation, "I am more than ever anxious that Bolero proceed to definite action beginning in 1942." [49] Now in June the president remained committed to SLEDGEHAMMER. If Britain refused to cross the channel, however, he considered GYMNAST highly preferable to spending the rest of the year merely preparing for a possible 1943 ROUNDUP. Indeed, he would not tolerate such inaction in 1942. For him, the date was much more important than the actual location of the first American offensive action in the European theater.

Churchill clearly realized this and within a few weeks forced the issue. On July 8 he informed Roosevelt that the COS and War Cabinet considered chances of mounting SLEDGEHAMMER to be remote in light of continued defeats in Egypt and the Atlantic, and he proposed an invasion of North Africa in its place as the best way to aid the Russians. "This has all along been in harmony with your ideas," he wrote. "In fact it is your commanding idea. Here is the true second front of 1942."[50]

The Pacific-First Proposal

The Joint Chiefs disagreed strongly. Stimson found Marshall "very stirred up" by what he considered a British breach of faith regarding the April agreements, and on July 10 the army chief called for a "showdown." Stimson heartily concurred.[51] Later that day, Marshall therefore followed the logic of his planners by formally proposing in a JCS meeting that, if London insisted on GYMNAST in place of SLEDGEHAMMER, the United States should "turn to the Pacific for decisive action against Japan." King wholeheartedly endorsed this proposal, after which they forwarded it to Roosevelt in a formal memorandum. They warned that GYMNAST would be indecisive and so disperse U.S. forces as to "curtail, if not make impossible," cross-channel operations for 1943 as well as 1942. It would also heavily drain U.S. resources and jeopardize the entire naval position in the Pacific. If Britain insisted on the operation, they therefore concluded, Washington should "turn to the Pacific and strike decisively against Japan; in other words, assume a defensive attitude against Germany . . . and use all available means in the Pacific."[52]

After the war, Marshall, King, and Stimson insisted that this proposal had been a bluff designed to scare the British into agreeing to SLEDGEHAMMER, and there is no question that the July 10 memorandum did contain an *element* of bluff. Simultaneously, however, Marshall and King were proposing exactly what their advisers had suggested in February and March, and they appear to have been deadly serious. Marshall and King were more than willing to use their proposal as a threat to scare Britain into a reconsideration of SLEDGEHAMMER, but they were equally disposed to make good on the threat if London remained adamant.[53]

This combination of threat and serious proposal emerged clearly in a second memorandum that Marshall sent Roosevelt on July 10. "My object," he bluntly stated, "is again to force the British into acceptance of a concentrated effort against Germany, *and if this proves impossible, to turn immediately to the Pacific with strong forces for a decision against Japan.*"[54] Stimson's diary entry for July 12 exhibited similar logic: "I hope that the threat to the British will work and that Bolero will be revived. If it is not revived, if they persist in their fatuous defeatist position as to it, the Pacific operation while not as good as Bolero will be a great deal better and have a much stronger chance of ultimate effective victory than a tepidly operated Bolero in which the British do not put their whole heart." [55]

Marshall's reasoning was based not only on Eisenhower's February–March presentations but also on military and political events since then which had heavily reinforced the OPD's original conclusions. Once again the focal point was the Soviet Union. "*The retention of Russia in the war as an active participant is vital to Allied victory*," now acting chief of staff McNarney had emphasized on April 12; if German armies were allowed to turn west, "any opportunity for a successful offensive against the European Axis would be virtually eliminated." [56] In mid-June the staff again warned that Russian collapse would necessitate a strategic reassessment, "possibly with the result of directing our main effort to the Pacific rather than the Atlantic." [57]

By month's end the German summer offensive on the eastern front had made such a collapse increasingly probable at the very moment the British were vetoing the one operation Moscow insisted on for its continued participation in the war. "How long Russia can last is the query on everyone's mind," Eisenhower's naval aide wrote in his London diary on July 2. [58] Two months earlier, Colonel Truman Smith of G-2 had informed the diplomat William R. Castle that 50 percent of army opinion held that the Germans would drive successfully "beyond the Volga, bottling the Russians up and opening to German exploitation the entire Ukraine and the oil wells of the Caucasus," while another 25 percent believed Germany would obtain "complete victory and put Russia wholly out of the running." Consequently the Strategy Section of OPD (SS) had begun to explore courses of action open to the United States in the event of Russian capitulation. [59]

The impact of a Pacific offensive in precluding a Japanese attack on the Russian rear also remained a key motivating factor in the Pacific-first proposal. During May and June, G-2, the Combined Intelligence Committee, and the OPD warned that in light of German and Japanese successes, such an attack on Siberia was "possible" anytime, "likely" before October 1, and "probable" before year's end. The JCS had informed Roosevelt of the danger in June and requested the initiation of combined staff conversations with the Soviets. Thus on June 17 the president informed Stalin of "tangible evidence" of a possible Japanese attack and requested such conversations so as to make possible U.S. use of Siberian airfields. [60] At the July 10 JCS meeting Marshall cited the fear of a Japanese attack on Siberia as a reason to shift to the Pacific, noting that second only to BOLERO it would "have the greatest effect towards relieving the pressure on Russia." In their joint memorandum to Roosevelt, Marshall and King noted that Pacific action "would not only be definite and decisive against one of our principal enemies, but would bring concrete aid to the Russians in case Japan attacks them." [61]

The Soviet Union was hardly the only concern in the spring and summer of 1942. Supported by the public, King and MacArthur had continued their requests for reinforcements and offensives to stop the Japanese. In early May MacArthur had fused this request with Soviet and domestic issues by advising Roosevelt that the second front to aid the Soviets "should be in the Pacific theatre. Nowhere else can it be so successfully launched and nowhere else will it so assist the Russians." Establishment of such a front, he further argued, "would have the enthusiastic psychological support of the entire American nation."[62]

It would also have the support of China. Indeed, in the aftermath of a diversion of air forces to aid the British in India and the Middle East and a renewed Japanese offensive in southern China, Chiang Kai-shek had issued a virtual ultimatum in late May, repeated in late June, threatening a collapse or separate peace if massive aid and military operations to reopen the Burma Road were not forthcoming. The U.S. military was "very fearful that behind the scenes China may be dickering with Japan to come to some kind of an agreement," Castle noted after his May 3 conversation with Smith, and by early July the Joint Intelligence Committee (JIC) was bluntly warning that Chinese collapse was quite possible without additional aid. Such a collapse, civilian as well as military officials feared, would enable Japan to unify all Asian peoples against the Allies in a race war that the United States could not win.[63]

Further reinforcing the Pacific-first thrust at this time were military events in and interservice disputes regarding that theater. While the recent U.S. naval victories at Coral Sea and Midway had effectively checked even more dangerous Japanese offensives to the east and south, this result was not clear to planners watching Japan's continued efforts to establish itself in the Solomons astride the line of communications to Australia. The army and navy agreed by June that a counterattack here was both in order and possible, but they disagreed as to exactly where it should take place and who should command it. In a shift in June as political as it was military, King concurred with MacArthur that the attack should be in the South rather than the Central Pacific, the historic focus of naval planning, but insisted that it be in the Solomons, rather than New Guinea and New Britain as MacArthur desired, and under navy rather than army command. Should Marshall not agree, the navy would proceed by itself. Responding to these pressures and fearful that King would cease supporting him in Europe as well as act unilaterally in the Pacific if he did not agree, Marshall in early July agreed to the navy-directed Guadalcanal campaign as the first phase of a three-stage, compromise offensive in the South Pacific. At the July 10 JCS meeting he cited these plans and the fear of Japanese attack on Siberia to support a shift to the Pacific. Such a change, he stated, would be "highly popular" throughout the United States; would find the Pacific War Council, China, and the Pacific Fleet "in hearty accord"; and second only to BOLERO would "have the greatest effect towards relieving the pressure on Russia." In line with such reasoning the JCS on July 10 rejected a suggestion by MacArthur and Admiral Robert Ghormley to postpone the Guadalcanal offensive until additional means became available and instead ordered them to proceed on schedule.[64]

Marshall further explained his reasoning in a July 13 telegram to Eisenhower which was so confidential that he wrote in the margin of one draft, "No distribution, not even in the log." Conditions on the eastern front were now "rapidly developing" toward the "emergency" situation for which SLEDGEHAMMER had been developed, and to launch GYMNAST instead would only add to the possibility of Russian collapse. This would mean the end of cross-channel operations in 1943 as well as 1942. Even if Russia did not collapse, GYMNAST's demands would themselves "curtail, if not make impossible," a 1943 ROUNDUP. GYMNAST would also be indecisive, heavily drain available resources, "definitely jeopardize our naval position in the Pacific," and lead to a situation whereby "we would nowhere be acting decisively against our enemies." If the United States was to "engage in any other operation rather than forceful unswerving adherence to full BOLERO plans," Marshall therefore concluded, he and King believed "that we should turn to the Pacific and strike decisively against Japan with full strength and ample reserves, assuming a defensive attitude against Germany except for air operations."[65]

Such reasoning and conclusions were in complete agreement with those Marshall's staff had been expressing ever since cross-channel operations had first been proposed. Eisenhower thus responded on July 14 that "the views you express are exactly as I understood them when I left Washington," that he had "frequently repeated them" to the British, and that he had also ventured as his "personal opinion" that Russian collapse "would force the United States to go on the defensive throughout the Atlantic and to build up offensive operations against Japan."[66] On the same day the staff presented a draft telegram for Roosevelt to send Churchill emphasizing the same points as Marshall's July 13 message. Continued Russian participation in the war was "essential" to a 1943 ROUNDUP and Hitler's early defeat, and ensuring that continued participation now required the launching of SLEDGEHAMMER. This was admittedly a "desperate measure," but in light of the circumstances, British rejection would lead the United States to "turn to the Pacific and strike decisively against Japan." This would definitely prolong the war and might preclude victory over Germany, but at least "it would be a positive action against one of our enemies," something that could not be said of any other proposed operation save SLEDGEHAMMER.[67]

On July 13 Smith informed Dykes of the JCS Pacific proposal. Both men took the threat quite seriously, as did Field Marshal Sir John Dill, head of the JSM and a close friend of Marshall. Smith, Dykes reported to Dill, was "very concerned about this as he was afraid that it marked the real danger of switching all American effort towards the Pacific." Dykes also noted in his diary that "it looks very much as if BOLERO is going to be thrown out of the window altogether" and that "London can't say we didn't warn them." Two days later Dill informed Churchill that the American service chiefs were serious.[68]

Ironically, the threat had largely passed by the time Dill sent this message, and nothing even approaching the staff's draft telegram was ever sent to Churchill. For by July 15 the Pacific-first proposal had aroused an angry presidential veto. The result would be the worst civil-military and Allied clashes of the war.

**The Great Strategic Debate,
July 1942–January 1943**

The Pacific-first proposal precipitated a crisis in Allied strategy and U.S. civil-military relations. Perceiving it as nothing more than a bluff designed to frighten the British into acceptance of JCS plans, an angry Roosevelt forcefully vetoed it and ordered his military chiefs to agree instead to the North African operation they found so loathsome. Ironically they thus received, finally, the specific presidential guidance they had so long desired—only to find it in direct conflict with their own opinions and advice.

Contrary to FDR's perceptions, the JCS proposal was not merely a bluff. Moreover, despite his explicit orders, the Joint Chiefs did not abandon it. Caught between the duty to obey their commander in chief, on the one hand, and both military realities in the Pacific and the belief that his desires would result in disaster, on the other, they formally submitted to his orders but did so in such a way as to enable them to pursue a modified version of their alternative strategy. The result was a major departure from the Germany-first approach, one that would have a profound impact on Allied relations, U.S. interservice and civil-military relations, and military conceptions of U.S. interests and policies vis-à-vis its allies.

The President versus the Joint Chiefs

After receiving the proposal at Hyde Park, a suspicious Roosevelt telephoned Washington on July 12 to request "a detailed comprehensive outline of the plan for a Pacific-first strategy, as well as advice on the effect of such a shift on the Russian front and the Middle East." In reply the Joint Chiefs were forced to admit that no such outline existed and that the shift would "adversely affect" the Russian front. Nevertheless, they alluded to planned operations in the Solomons and mentioned possible advances along the Truk-Guam-Saipan line as well as through the Malay barrier and Borneo to the Philippines, stated that these operations would have no negative impact on the Middle East, and pointed out that they would aid

Russia if Japan attacked Siberia. They noted in this regard that a "major factor affecting plans for an offensive against Japan is whether or not war breaks out between Russia and Japan." [1]

Receiving this reply around 6:00 P.M., Roosevelt was "quite evidently much annoyed," according to the later recollections of his naval aide, Captain John L. McCrea, and was "soon shaking his head in disapproval as he read." Grabbing a pencil, he dashed off a negative reply to Marshall and signed it "Commander-in-Chief" for emphasis. "My first impression," he wrote, was that the JCS proposal "is exactly what Germany hoped the United States would do following Pearl Harbor." In addition to being strategically unsound, it did not provide for the immediate combat use of U.S. troops "except in a lot of islands whose occupation will not affect the world situation this year or next." Nor would it "help Russia or the Near East." After reading this to McCrea for his reaction and handing it to him for transmittal, Roosevelt dashed off a second reply before the aide could depart telling Marshall to be prepared to go to London with Hopkins. While the two messages were being typed and transmitted, he met with Hopkins and then wrote a third message reiterating his disapproval of the proposal, saying that he had "definitely decided" to send Hopkins as well as Marshall and King to London, and informing the two chiefs of his intention to meet with them the morning of July 15 and with the entire JCS later in the day.[2]

During those July 15 meetings the president once again rejected the Pacific-first approach and insisted that his emissaries fly to London to reach agreement with the British on some 1942 action in the European theater. His first choice remained SLEDGEHAMMER, but if Britain maintained its refusal to cross the channel in 1942, he made clear orally on the fifteenth and in writing on July 16, his envoys would have to agree to operations in North Africa or the Middle East that would bring U.S. troops into action before year's end. Such action was "of the highest importance," and under no circumstances would he agree to turn to the Pacific instead.[3]

Roosevelt's rejection of the Pacific proposal actually reflected his agreement with three previous JCS conclusions: that Japan could not continue to fight if Germany were defeated, that Russia remained the key to German defeat, and that a Europe-first strategy designed to assist the Soviets therefore remained the sound approach to victory. "The whole question of whether we win or lose the war depends on the Russians," he had asserted only a month earlier, and once victory over Germany had been achieved, "we can defeat the Japanese in six weeks."[4] Also in accord with the JCS, he believed that cross-channel operations were superior to GYMNAST and that the Japanese were preparing to attack Siberia. He did not rate this an insurmountable problem for the Soviets, however, or one justifying a shift in U.S. strategy. Perhaps more important, he saw some action along the southern coast of the Mediterranean as the best of the remaining options if

Britain continued to refuse to cross the channel in 1942, one capable of both aiding Russia more than any Pacific offensive and accomplishing a host of additional objectives.[5]

Unlike the JCS, Roosevelt saw the Mediterranean as a vital part of the European theater where military gains against Germany were quite possible. A 1942 offensive here would also serve an important political purpose by relieving public pressure for immediate and successful military activity without overturning Allied strategy and wrecking the coalition. Indeed, such an operation was politically superior to one across the channel for this purpose because of its relative ease and greater chance of success. It was similarly superior in the political realm to Pacific offensives because the latter were being supported by his domestic political opponents, especially those who had never favored aid to England and Russia or involvement in the European war. Nor could the president ignore the potential of Pacific offensives to advance the political career of MacArthur, who his political opponents were mentioning as a possible supreme commander of all U.S. forces and who could well become the 1944 Republican presidential nominee.[6]

In addition, GYMNAST could also serve a diplomatic function. In May, FDR had "promised" the Russians a 1942 second front in northern France.[7] Although British opposition had negated this pledge, the president saw North Africa or the Middle East as a substitute "second front" that would perhaps divert some German forces from the East, despite the warnings of Marshall and Stimson to the contrary. Even if it did not, an offensive here could partially fulfill his promise to Stalin by providing a commitment in blood to the European theater despite the present inability to cross the channel. He also continued to believe, his military advisers' warnings notwithstanding, that 1942 North African or Middle East operations would not preclude a cross-channel assault in 1943. In his mind, therefore, dropping SLEDGEHAMMER did not necessitate a strategic reassessment.[8]

Roosevelt also believed that the JCS were not serious and that even as a bluff their proposal constituted a dishonorable betrayal of America's European allies. He may have been particularly sensitive in this area because of previous military opposition to his coalition policies. Throughout 1940–41, he had had to fight the chiefs on whether to provide Britain and the Soviet Union with aid and, if so, how much. From his perspective their July 10 proposal may have illustrated that the battle was far from over.

Roosevelt stated many of his objections to the Pacific proposal in his first July 14 reply, concerns he reiterated and added to the following day. In a ten-minute session before meeting with Marshall and Hopkins, he informed Stimson that while he remained "absolutely sound" on crossing the channel, he disliked the Pacific alternative and felt it was equivalent to "taking up your dishes and going away." Stimson diplomatically responded that he appreciated this view but that it was essential to use the Pacific threat to force the British into agreeing to cross-channel operations—a comment that only reinforced the president's growing belief, already strong as a result of Marshall's follow-up message on July 10 and lack of detailed plans, that the JCS proposal was pure bluff. In his meeting with the army chief a few minutes later, he thus labeled the proposal "something of a red herring, the purpose for which he thoroughly understood"; angrily rejected it; and even suggested, according to Marshall, that the record "should be altered so that it would not appear in later years that we had proposed what amounted to abandonment of the British."[9] That evening he informed Hopkins that he did not believe GYMNAST would preclude a 1943 cross-channel assault and that he wanted both if SLEDGEHAMMER was out of the question. In his orders to his envoys on the following day, he repeated his commitment to the military reasoning behind the Europe-first approach in one of his most extraordinary wartime overstatements: defeat of Germany, he wrote, "means the defeat of Japan, probably without firing a shot or losing a life."[10]

In retrospect, historians can be thankful Marshall did not follow Roosevelt's suggestion to alter the record, whereas all can be thankful the president did not agree to what could well have been a disastrous strategic shift. But while he may have been correct in his general conclusions and course of action, many of his specific assessments were dead wrong. Japanese defeat did follow German defeat, but hardly "without firing a shot or losing a life." And although GYMNAST would remove public pressure for immediate action, it did not succeed in turning public attention to the European theater. Nor did Stalin accept it as a "second front" of any sort, and his ensuing anger and suspicion resulted in continued separate peace and rumors of Soviet collapse, as well as noncooperation. All of this would reach a fever pitch a year later when Roosevelt's insistence that GYMNAST would not preclude a 1943 ROUNDUP also turned out to be wrong and the more pessimistic JCS calculations proved to be correct, thereby postponing the invasion of France until 1944.[11]

More immediate, Roosevelt's belief that his advisers were bluffing and that he had squelched their scheme was also incorrect. Despite his firm rejection of their proposal and clear directive regarding future operations, neither Marshall nor King had abandoned the proposed Pacific offensives. During the ensuing weeks they would continue to fight for a major revision of Allied strategy and would achieve limited success.

The Joint Chiefs versus the British

As early as their July 14 receipt of Roosevelt's first rejection of their proposal, the JCS had admitted that the president and "our political system would require major operations this year in Africa." [12] Nevertheless, they continued to maintain that Pacific operations were more sound and to press for their acceptance. On July 15, the very day FDR rejected their alternative and ordered them to London, Dill warned Churchill that "King's war is against the Japanese" and that unless London could convince Marshall of its "unswerving loyalty" to cross-channel operations, "everything points to a complete reversal of our present agreed strategy and the withdrawal of America to a war of her own in the Pacific." [13] Marshall's statements pointed to a similar conclusion. On July 16 he requested from Eisenhower, now commanding the U.S. European theater of operations in London, that a "searching analysis" of SLEDGEHAMMER be available for him on arrival. Despite Roosevelt's directives he insisted GYMNAST was "completely out of the question from Pacific naval requirements point of view alone" and that reinforcement both of Britain in the Middle East and of Ireland was possible only "if turn is made to the Pacific." [14]

Eisenhower concurred. Although he stated after the war that SLEDGEHAMMER would have been a mistake, he concluded at this time that it was far preferable to GYMNAST and that it both could and must be launched—even though odds of a successful landing were only one in two and of maintaining a beachhead one in five—because the "prize" of keeping "8,000,000 Russians in the war" justified the risk. As in February, his arguments in this regard were far from "purely military": even if the British were correct that SLEDGEHAMMER would be too small to divert Germany from the East, its psychological effect on the Soviets and on the U.S. and English people and their armies justified launching it. GYMNAST could not help or reassure the Soviets, and it would so disperse Anglo-American forces as to rule out ROUNDUP in 1943 as well as SLEDGEHAMMER in 1942. It thus made sense only as a limited, defensive alternative to these operations, and should be undertaken only if Britain and the United States believed the Red Army was "certain to be defeated." In that case Washington should "go immediately on the strategic defensive in the Atlantic and begin to build up an offensive against Japan." [15]

The British, however, refused to budge. "Just because the Americans can't have a massacre in France this year, they want to sulk and bathe in the Pacific," Churchill grumbled on receipt of Dill's warning. [16] Determined not to allow that massacre to take place and perhaps aware by now via Hopkins or the JSM of Roosevelt's profound disagreement with his military advisers, [17] Churchill and the COS adamantly maintained that SLEDGEHAMMER could not be launched on a sufficient scale to divert any German forces from the East, that it would end in disaster, that they therefore would not agree to undertake it, and that GYMNAST did not rule out a 1943 cross-channel assault. In private sessions lower-level planners were even more blunt, noting that it would be "a disaster" to have a large force on the Continent and still have Russia collapse, and that GYMNAST would be "the best insurance for the Middle East" in the event of such a collapse.[18] The frustrated Americans continued to argue that SLEDGEHAMMER could avoid such a catastrophe, but to no avail. After three days of fruitless debate, they were forced to inform Roosevelt on July 22, a date Eisenhower felt might become known as the "blackest day in history," of complete deadlock. The president responded that he was not surprised and that his representatives had to reach agreement on some 1942 operation against the Germans, preferably in North Africa.[19]

Still, Marshall, King, and their associates refused to give up. In Washington, Stimson warned Roosevelt that GYMNAST would allow Germany and Japan to retain the initiative indefinitely and do nothing to further the destruction of Hitler or keep Russia in the war. While "professing" these two aims, he added, Britain was "equally if not more insistent upon a present attempt to preserve its empire in the Middle East," a motive that explained Churchill's present stance.[20] In London, meanwhile, Marshall and King, supported by Eisenhower and his staff, continued to argue that launching GYMNAST would preclude any effective aid to the Soviets or a 1943 cross-channel assault and therefore made sense only as a defensive move in the event of Russian collapse. Combining these conclusions with Roosevelt's pressure to reach agreement, they came up with two new formulas.

The first, according to General Walter Bedell Smith, was to send two army corps to the Middle East and enough troops to England to insure its security, with the "remainder" of the U.S. effort in 1942 devoted to the Pacific. "Political pressure in the US would force some action by American forces this year," he informed Dykes on July 21, "and if it could not be in Europe it would have to be in the Pacific." Whether this was serious or mentioned informally merely as a negotiating tactic remains unclear. It did represent quite accurately Marshall's thoughts as presented to Eisenhower on July 16, but it was never formally presented to the COS.[21]

What was presented on July 24 was a second formula, authored by Marshall, Smith, and/or King: admit that SLEDGEHAMMER was no longer a "scheduled operation" but continue preparations for it and for ROUNDUP *and* GYMNAST until September 15, at which time a final decision would be made in accordance with the situation on the eastern front. Choosing GYMNAST at that time would in effect equal abandoning hope of Soviet survival, thereby making ROUNDUP "impracticable of successful execution in 1943." Invading North Africa would thus mean "that we have definitely accepted a defensive, encircling line of action for the CONTINENTAL EUROPEAN THEATER" except for air operations. So as not to violate FDR's instructions and rearouse his wrath, security of Britain would remain a "first charge" on military resources, but fifteen air groups and probably sufficient shipping to move a combat division from the West Coast to the Southwest Pacific would be withdrawn from BOLERO "for the purpose of furthering offensive operations in the Pacific."[22]

The British objected vehemently to what one of them called this "most poisonous document," for they did not believe GYMNAST precluded ROUNDUP or that it was defensive in nature. Marshall and King were adamant, however, and the COS feared a complete breakdown in negotiations if they pressed further. They also believed, in the words of one member, that "having got the American Chiefs of Staff to our way of thinking as regards [North Africa], it was a pity to be too critical of the precise wording in which they gave their assent."[23]

The COS therefore agreed to a revised version of the U.S. proposal as an official document (CCS 94) of the Combined Chiefs and convinced a doubting War Cabinet to do likewise.[24] Both the U.S. and the British chiefs agreed that this decision overturned the April decision to pursue a direct, cross-channel approach to victory. But whereas the Americans concluded that it opened the door to a Pacific-first strategy, the COS insisted that it simply gave the JCS some air and shipping reinforcements for the Pacific as a sop while actually maintaining Germany-first. Indeed, they argued that the final wording of CCS 94 was merely a restatement of and return to their original indirect approach to Europe as outlined and accepted by both countries in ABC-1 and again at ARCADIA.[25]

For the moment, Roosevelt and Hopkins made this argument academic. Joined by Churchill, they remained convinced that GYMNAST, now renamed TORCH, did not preclude ROUNDUP or a continuation of Germany-first and that a decision on offensive action in 1942 had to be reached immediately rather than in September. On July 25, Hopkins therefore subverted part of CCS 94 by urging the president, at least partially at Churchill's request and without Marshall's or King's knowledge, to name a definite date for TORCH.[26] Roosevelt responded by informing his envoys that North Africa should be invaded no later than October 30. He then made clear he considered the issue settled for 1942 and that he believed ROUNDUP could and would be launched in 1943. Despite CCS 94, Marshall and King were thus forced to agree that TORCH would occur in the fall. In this civil-military confrontation, the president had apparently triumphed.[27]

The Pacific-First Reality and the Specter of Soviet Defeat

Appearances were again misleading. Although Roosevelt's stance did insure a 1942 invasion of North Africa, it did little to reverse the thinking or the activities of the Joint Chiefs. They continued to believe that ROUNDUP was now out of the question and that what remained of CCS 94 allowed for at least a partial reversal of U.S.

strategy. This became apparent in early August when U.S. forces invaded Guadalcanal and the JCS insisted that in line with CCS 94 TORCH be a small, limited, defensive operation. Dykes complained on August 7 that the Americans "think CCS 94 has changed the basic strategic concept of making Germany the main enemy."[28] Citing their own interpretation of CCS 94 as reaffirmation of the peripheral approach outlined in ABC-1, the COS responded by insisting that TORCH be a large, offensive operation to sweep as far east as possible and conquer Tunisia within a month, thereby helping their Eighth Army efforts to drive the Germans completely out of North Africa and enabling them to use the area, in Churchill's later words, as a "springboard" for further Mediterranean offensives rather than as "a sofa."[29]

Dykes quickly concluded that the problem was King, whom he characterized as both "a man of great strength of character with a very small brain" and "an old shit" who "simply won't play at all."[30] Yet the CNO was only part of the British problem. A "very worried" Dill had contacted Marshall directly on August 8 about the U.S. commitment to TORCH and Europe-first and had received anything but a reassuring response. "At present our Chiefs of Staff quote ABC-4/CS.1 [the ARCADIA strategic accords] as *the* Bible," Dill had quipped, "whereas some of your people, I think, look upon C.C.S. 94 as the revised version!" Marshall did little to disabuse him of this notion, responding that some of CCS 94's provisions were "inconsistent" with ABC-4/CS-1 and would "modify the latter document." Simultaneously he informed Eisenhower of an army "unanimity of opinion" that TORCH "appears hazardous to [the] extent of less than 50% chance of success."[31]

The resulting "transatlantic essay contest" over the size and purposes of TORCH dominated Anglo-American correspondence until September 5, when Churchill and Roosevelt finally settled the issue with a compromise that included landings at Casablanca as the JCS demanded, Algiers and Oran as the COS demanded, but not farther east as London had desired.[32] In the meantime, however, the Guadalcanal campaign began to expand massively as a result of the strong Japanese reaction, and the Chinese situation remained critical, thereby strengthening Pacific-first arguments and calling into question whether TORCH would be launched at all.

Leahy's July addition to the JCS further reinforced those arguments. Officially he served as liaison between the president and the service chiefs, and as Roosevelt defined his tasks he was to represent the president's position to the JCS rather than vice versa. Indeed, FDR had finally agreed to his appointment and defined his position in this way partially to avoid a repetition of what had just occurred.[33] Overall, Leahy fulfilled this role as Roosevelt desired, but he had a mind of his own—one firmly convinced that Japan constituted the primary enemy, that postwar U.S. interests hinged on China, and that a massive effort was now required in the Pacific and Far East. On August 11 he warned his JCS colleagues that any operations that "would not soon provide for aid to China would . . . lead to the collapse of that country's resistance and thence to a very possible U.S. defeat in the Pacific." It was therefore "essential" to make "a specific commitment . . . to open the Burma road and that other means of aiding China should be adopted." Along with King he also insisted that, notwithstanding prior commitments, "our forces now operating in the Southwest Pacific must and will be successfully maintained."[34]

Marshall agreed and further asserted at the August 11 JCS meeting that in the future "the big issues to be decided were whether the major U.S. effort was to be made in the Pacific as against Europe and the Middle East."[35] On August 25 he informed Eisenhower that in light of Japanese attacks then in progress there was "no prospect of withdrawing US naval craft from the Pacific" for North Africa, and on the same date he virtually demanded British agreement to retake Burma in 1943 so as to reopen supply lines to Chiang Kai-shek. "Unless the United Nations increase the visible assistance to China her opposition to Japan may collapse," he warned. Such a collapse would release one-quarter of all Japanese combat divisions for use elsewhere, and a mere ten divisions would be "an important force for employment on the Siberian, Indian or Australian fronts." Reopening the Burma Road, he concluded, was the "only method" of bolstering the Chinese sufficiently to keep them in the war.[36]

Maintenance of China and the U.S. position in the Southwest Pacific involved not only additional troops, shipping, and landing craft but also the fifteen air groups CCS 94 had transferred to the Pacific. JCS discussion of that issue quickly led to a major confrontation between King and Arnold, who had not signed the July 10 Pacific proposal or attended the London Conference during which CCS 94 had been adopted and who remained deeply opposed to both. Although a North African invasion would somewhat disperse the air forces he was attempting to concentrate in England, a Pacific-first reaction would involve even more dispersion and thereby wreck his plans for a major bomber offensive against Germany—an offensive his planners deemed vital both to win the war and to establish an independent postwar air force. Arnold thus rejected the Pacific orientation of his colleagues and by early September had concluded that Britain and North Africa could be considered complementary theaters from an air point of view. King and Leahy disagreed and vehemently argued with him over the disposition of the fifteen air groups. After the August 11 JCS meeting Arnold disgustedly wrote that Smith "came out quite strongly with the idea that perhaps we would never have any operations out of England" and that all the members of the JCS save himself were emphasizing the Pacific as the area "where we would, in all probability, fight the main battle rather than in the European theatre."[37]

Marshall had apparently hoped that such would not be the case. On July 30 he had informed Eisenhower for his "personal and confidential information" that while Arnold and Stimson were "very much disturbed" over possible bomber reductions in England, he regarded "the list of withdrawals for the Pacific as one which gave us liberty of action though not necessarily to be carried out in full." King would "of course" want all fifteen air groups in the Pacific, but Marshall's intention was "to make only the withdrawals that seem urgently required for the Pacific as the situation develops there." By late August that situation was desperate, however, with MacArthur warning of disaster unless reinforcements were immediately sent. "I beg of you most earnestly," he emotionally wrote Marshall on August 30, to order such reinforcements "lest it become too late."[38]

JCS commitment to the Pacific war was heavily influenced not only by the critical battles taking place in that theater and the Chinese situation but also by the somber, simultaneous reports on the Russian front which the chiefs received throughout the summer and fall. All Pacific-first proposals within the army had proceeded on the assumption that a Japanese attack on Siberia was imminent and that such an attack, combined with the German offensive in the east and lack of cross-channel assistance in 1942, could result in a Russian surrender that would effectively preclude any future offensive operations against Germany. By early August G-2's intercepts of Japanese "Magic" traffic had revised these estimates by making clear that Japan would not attack Siberia that summer or fall, but the German summer offensive was simultaneously driving deeply into southern Russia and reinforcing fears of an impending Soviet collapse. On August 5 Marshall forwarded the new G-2 estimates regarding Japan and Siberia to Roosevelt with the recommendation that Stalin be immediately informed so as to provide "at least some encouragement in the present desperate Russian situation."[39]

As early as April–May, OPD, G-2, and the joint committees had begun to explore the appropriate response should this "desperate situation" result in a Soviet collapse, and in early August the JUSSC completed and forwarded to the JPS a massive study of such a contingency. This study indicated that Russian collapse would be a "catastrophe" of such magnitude as to put the United States in a "desperate" situation too, one in which it "would be forced to consider courses of action which would primarily benefit the United States rather than the United Nations." Indeed, it might be the only remaining major member of the United Nations, because the British Commonwealth might collapse and the British public react to Soviet defeat by overthrowing Churchill and agreeing to a negotiated peace that would leave Hitler in control of Eurasia. A revival of isolationism and an "increase in defeatism" within the country were also possible in this scenario. Even without British withdrawal, however, the only sound U.S. response to a Soviet collapse would be to "adopt the strategic defensive in the European Theater of War and to conduct the strategic offensive in the Japanese theater." On August 19 the JPS approved this report, forwarded it to the Joint Chiefs as JCS 85, and ordered the preparation of a strategic plan for the defeat of Japan.[40]

On August 25, the same day Marshall demanded an offensive in Burma to keep China in the war and informed Eisenhower that no naval craft could be released from the Pacific, the Joint Chiefs discussed JCS 85. Leahy labeled it "an excellent statement of policy," but Arnold, who on the previous day had insisted that the danger of Russian collapse required continuation of Germany-first and an air offensive from England to protect the British Isles from the increased danger of German invasion, countered that the Pacific shift recommended in JCS 85 would require England to defend itself without U.S. assistance. This forced Leahy to backtrack and question "whether or not the United States could accept this policy in view of the President's position in favor of conducting the major war effort towards the East." King and Marshall thereupon maintained that even with concentration against Japan, sufficient resources would be left over to maintain the U.S. commitment to the security of the British Isles and thus fulfill the president's policy. At Marshall's suggestion, the chiefs then agreed to return the report to the JPS for inclusion of this point and comment on how TORCH would affect the planners' conclusions and recommendations.[41] On September 1 they responded that even if TORCH succeeded, Russian defeat would keep Britain and the United States on the defensive in Europe and make impossible a successful invasion of the continent. A day later the JIC predicted German success in the Caucasus and subsequent control of its oil.[42]

By this time the British were deeply concerned over not only what Dykes labeled "the continuous drain of US air forces to the Pacific, which Arnold is apparently quite unable to withstand," but also the future of the entire Germany-first approach. The COS even considered placing "on record" its belief that this strategy still held. Marshall apparently convinced the British chiefs that this would be counterproductive, but after listening to King at the August 22 CCS meeting Dykes concluded that "a fundamental difference of opinion on grand strategy" clearly existed and might require direct correspondence between Churchill and Roosevelt. By the end of August he had gloomily decided that combined planning over TORCH had "broken down" and "the whole thing is going to be a flop" and by early September that "the major question of our basic strategic policy will have to be tackled with the Americans as soon as we see the outcome of TORCH. The issue will be whether our main offensive effort next year is to be concentrated against Germany or Japan." The Roosevelt-Churchill resolution of the TORCH controversy left this larger global strategic issue unresolved. "Somehow or other," Dykes noted on September 7, "we must work out between the two nations a common aim." BOLERO had provided one, but now it lay in shambles. Arnold was equally upset, informing Hopkins on September 3 of his "growing apprehension" over the failure to adopt a definite plan for victory and complaining that "little by little our Air Plan has been torn to pieces." [43]

This Anglo-American crisis over global strategy ebbed during the second week of September, but only somewhat. On September 8 the Joint Chiefs accepted the revised recommendations regarding U.S. policy in the event of Russian collapse contained in JCS 85/1 and filed the paper for future reference. They did not forward it to British planners, however, probably because they agreed with Wedemeyer that Russian collapse did not appear "imminent" and that the paper might lead the British to conclude they were abandoning Germany-first.[44] Six days later the U.S. representatives on the Combined Planning Staff (CPS) agreed to reaffirm Germany-first, but the JCS simultaneously agreed to press for the recapture of Burma and reopening of the Burma Road. They also agreed to King's proposal to place additional emphasis on the Pacific in the future by shifting construction priorities from the larger landing craft needed for European operations to combat vessels, a decision they justified on the grounds of CCS 94. By September 21 Dykes had concluded that Anglo-American planning had broken down and was wondering whether it could possibly work in the future.[45] The war against Japan in general and the Guadalcanal/New Guinea campaigns in particular remained the critical issue. King and Arnold continued to argue over the transfer of the fifteen air groups to the Pacific, while Leahy noted in his diary that the U.S. war effort should be concentrated against Japan, for "unless we administer a defeat to Japan in the near future that nation will succeed in combining most of the Asiatic people against the Whites." Such concentration and defeat of Japan "would not be a difficult task," he sardonically added, "if we were not required to distribute both our forces and our war material in support of our allies who, with the exception of Russia, seem incapable of surviving without assistance." [46]

By that time the Japanese had assembled at Rabaul their largest naval concentration since Midway and were in the process of launching massive air and sea attacks on Guadalcanal. In mid-October Admiral Chester W. Nimitz, commander in chief of the U.S. Pacific Fleet, admitted that "we are unable to control the sea in the Guadalcanal area" and that the situation was "critical." On the following day Marshall used the same word in an appeal to MacArthur for air support that would weaken his own operations in New Guinea. MacArthur agreed with the assessment but not the proposed solution, requesting instead a total shift in strategy, if only for the time being, so that the "entire resources of the United States be diverted temporarily to meet the critical situation." Even Roosevelt was forced to conclude on October 24 that diversion of resources to the Southwest Pacific from other commitments, "particularly to England," was now mandatory first to hold Guadalcanal and then to "take advantage of our success." Subsequently he agreed to both a cutback in forces to England and a lower priority for the construction of landing craft. He and Marshall also tried to appease Chiang by promising him on October 12 additional aircraft and their best effort to reopen the Burma Road in 1943.[47] Such strategic gyrations and unilateral decisions deeply upset the British. Dykes concluded that the Americans "are drifting rudderless at present" and that Admiral Cooke was making "a complete mockery" of combined planning; General Sir Alan Brooke, chief of the Imperial General Staff, concluded that the CCS should be abolished.[48]

Continuing uncertainty regarding Russian survival further reinforced the Pacific thrust, while the British victory at El Alamein and the successful TORCH landings did little to halt it. On November 8, with German and Russian forces still locked in hand-to-hand combat amid the rubble of Stalingrad and Anglo-American forces landing in North Africa, the OPD chief General Thomas T. Handy informed Marshall that "our main amphibious operations in 1943 are likely to be in the Pacific" and the larger question of Germany- versus Japan-first was now "largely academic." He justified this conclusion on the grounds of the impossibility of static defense in the Pacific, the fact that offensives in this theater were the best means of preventing a Japanese movement westward to link up with the Germans, and the impossibility of establishing future priorities "until the results of the TORCH operation become apparent and until we have more information concerning Russian present and future combat effectiveness."[49]

During a November 20 meeting of the newly established Joint Strategic Survey Committee (JSSC), Embick provided a forceful rationale for these and future departures from agreed-on strategy. Under ABC-1, he noted, Britain was supposed "to assume responsibility for the Far East" while the U.S. fleet at Pearl Harbor diverted Japanese strength by acting as a threat to their flank. In reality, however, the British had "failed to maintain their positions in the Far East and committed the U.S. to the responsibility for the whole of the Pacific. Having assumed this commitment the U.S. must therefore maintain their position as a first charge," which required no reduction in present forces for operations in the Mediterranean or elsewhere. That did not mean officially overturning Germany-first, but it did allow for such a de facto result—as was occurring. As the committee concluded after additional discussion, "our basic strategy of the strategic offensive in the European Theater and the strategic defensive elsewhere appears sound for the present but must be rigidly interpreted . . . in such a manner as to insure maintenance of our position in the Pacific and to avoid dispersion of our forces elsewhere to unprofitable undertakings."[50]

In line with such thinking, revised War Department plans called for less than half a million instead of 1.2 million U.S. troops to be in England by April 1943. Interpreting this and related comments by Marshall and Eisenhower's deputy as a possible abandonment of BOLERO-ROUNDUP, Churchill in late November fired off an emotional appeal to Roosevelt. Relying on a draft composed by Marshall, the president reassured the prime minister that he had "no intention of abandoning ROUNDUP" but pointed out that ongoing operations in the Southwest Pacific and in North Africa had to take first priority. As a result of such logic and the events and decisions of the summer and early fall, 1942 ended with more U.S. combat forces in the Pacific than in the Atlantic theater.[51]

The Joint Chiefs against Each Other

By year's end, however, the global military situation had changed dramatically from what it had been only a few months earlier. In the Pacific, although fierce fighting continued, Guadalcanal had largely been secured. On the eastern front the successful Soviet counteroffensive at Stalingrad surrounded and sealed the fate of the entire German Sixth Army, ending all talk of Russian collapse. Along the southern shore of the Mediterranean the Alamein offensive and TORCH landings succeeded in trapping all Axis forces in North Africa in a Tunisian cul de sac. Taken together, these victories negated some of the key assumptions behind CCS 94, most notably Russian collapse and the impossibility of crossing the channel in 1943.

Unfortunately, the disposition of U.S. forces made a return to the cross-channel concept highly unlikely, for most of them were now deployed in the Pacific or North Africa. And while defeat no longer appeared likely in either theater, neither did quick victory. Fierce Japanese resistance continued in the Pacific, and in North Africa the Allies lost the "race" for Tunisia and would need six more months to defeat Axis forces there.

For Churchill and the COS, the only logical conclusion was that the armies in North Africa should take advantage of the situation by focusing on the Mediterranean in 1943, while a separate force was built up in England for a cross-channel assault at some unspecified future date. Roosevelt appeared to agree, informing the JCS during a December 10 meeting that U.S. forces should be strengthened in both theaters, with the final decision on 1943 operations postponed until March if necessary.[52]

This proposal received immediate and unanimous condemnation by the Joint Chiefs on the grounds that it would disperse Allied more than German forces and result in a strategically valueless Mediterranean campaign as well as the buildup of a static force in England—all at the expense of the war against Japan. This they considered intolerable. Their unanimity, however, did not extend to any alternative approach. King and Leahy continued to argue for a Pacific-first strategy, whereas Marshall now joined Arnold in pressing for a return to the European theater.

Marshall's reversion to his original concept resulted not only from the dramatically changed military situation but also from production and planning difficulties that had emerged with the lack of a clear strategy and priorities, as well as a subsequent, increasing rivalry between the chiefs over the allocation of scarce troops and supplies. As Wedemeyer noted during an October 21 JPS discussion of war production, because present U.S. strategy was "subject to many interpretations" it did "not provide a sound basis for making estimates" and revision was "essential." His naval counterpart agreed, stating that "CCS 94 had in effect put us on the defensive everywhere and that he would welcome a change to the offensive." The problem was that the navy continued to see that offensive in the Pacific, not Europe. Arnold continued to fight this fiercely, but with his focus on air operations he still viewed the Mediterranean and Britain as complementary theaters, whereas Marshall saw them as competing.[53]

Also threatening to the army chief was that these naval and air proposals, when combined with newly recognized production limits, continued Soviet survival, and British successes in the Middle East, led to a growing belief in Washington that a large army would not be needed after all to defeat the Axis. Marshall had been fighting for over two years and with only limited success against what he labeled in early November "this fallacious and humiliating proposition" (a combination of words that clearly illustrated the inseparability of bureaucratic and psychological from strategic motivations), and from his perspective success in North Africa would only "strengthen this fatal psychology." What was needed was an end to "dabbling" in the Mediterranean and a shift of U.S. forces back to England for cross-channel operations and a decisive confrontation to defeat the Wehrmacht in Europe—not merely to take advantage of a prior crack in German morale. No U.S. forces would be sent to Britain beyond minimal defensive needs, he warned, until London approved an offensive for such a confrontation.[54]

Any return to the cross-channel concept would have to come at the expense of ongoing campaigns in the Mediterranean and Pacific, however. Refocusing for an invasion of Europe would require a virtual halt to operations in these theaters, with no guarantee that the channel could even be crossed before 1944. The result might well be no offensive operation whatsoever in 1943, a situation intolerable politically as well as militarily. Yet continuation of Pacific and Mediterranean offensives would doom any possibility of cross-channel operations for 1943 and probably 1944, thereby calling into question once again whether Russia would continue the struggle without a second front and how Germany could possibly be defeated. Nor could anyone forget Chiang's threats and the need to reopen the Burma Road, an operation that could take place only if *no* European offensives were launched in spring of 1943.[55]

The splits caused by these paradoxes emerged during December within the army staff, the joint committees, and the JCS. In the OPD one group of planners argued for a maximum buildup in England and no further Mediterranean operations; another supported the latter on the grounds that a 1943 ROUNDUP was not possible, surrendering the hard-won initiative in the Mediterranean made no sense, and inaction throughout 1943 might lead Stalin to sign a separate peace. Mediterranean over cross-channel operations in 1943 would also allow for further development of offensive operations in the Southwest Pacific, a fact that led King to support the invasion of Sicily. "In the last analysis," he asserted during one of his off-the-record meetings with the press in late 1942, "Russia will do nine-tenths of the job of defeating Germany." Once again, however, the army and the navy were unable to agree on exactly where Pacific offensives should take place, how extensive they should be, or who should command them.[56]

The full depth of the JCS split emerged during a December 12 discussion of a recent JSSC report that had supported a return to the cross-channel and Germany-first concepts for 1943, albeit within the context of continued, limited offensives in the Pacific and Burma ("full operations in Europe *after* certain things had been accomplished in the Pacific," as one committee member put it). That was insufficient for Leahy, who attacked the paper on the grounds that the entire Germany-first approach was now "considered uncertain." King was more diplomatic, stating his willingness "to accept Germany as the primary enemy in Europe" but objecting to the "offhand" treatment the committee had given the war against Japan—a war that required 25–30 percent of American resources and immediate offensive action in both the Pacific and Burma.[57]

By December 26 the JCS and their planners had succeeded in patching up their differences sufficiently to forward to the British a revised version of the JSSC paper as a summary of their position on operations in 1943. It officially maintained the Germany-first approach by calling for a "strategic offensive in the Atlantic–West European Theater at the earliest practicable date" and a strategic defensive elsewhere. It also maintained the focus on cross-channel operations by calling for the offensive "directly against Germany," only to modify severely if not destroy that focus and the entire Germany-first approach by also calling for continued offensive and defensive operations in the Pacific and Burma "to break the Japanese hold on positions which threaten the security of our communications and positions" and to maintain the initiative in the Solomons and New Guinea.[58]

This "all things for all people" proposal was, in the words of the official army history, "shaky" at best, for it masked rather than resolved strategic differences and could easily come apart if any portion of it were questioned.[59] Such questioning quickly occurred when on January 2–3 the COS responded with a comprehensive attack on the JCS paper and a full description and defense of their Mediterranean alternative for 1943. JCS proposals, they warned, would translate into no

Mediterranean operations in 1943, no Burma campaign, a ROUNDUP too small to overcome German resistance, and one that could be launched no sooner than August. "In other words," they threw back at the Americans, "Russia would get no relief for another 7 or 8 months and the Axis would have a similar period to recuperate." Full exploitation of TORCH in the Mediterranean, combined with a BOLERO buildup and major bombing campaign, on the other hand, could knock Italy out of the war and provide Russia with immediate relief by drawing off German forces to hold a new Italian front, defend against a possible channel crossing, and perhaps deal with the Turks who would join the war in light of Allied Mediterranean action. A late-year offensive in Burma might also be possible, but the Pacific war could not and should not be expanded.[60]

Given the depth of Anglo-American differences as expressed in these papers, it is far from surprising to find the CPS gloomily reporting on December 30 that no accord was possible on future operations because no accepted global strategy for the conduct of the war existed.[61] Nor was there any real agreement within the U.S. armed forces, let alone between them and the president and the British, as to what that strategy should be. On January 5 the JSSC labeled Anglo-American differences over the Pacific as fundamental, and on the following day the JPS concluded that although previous planning directives should be revoked because of "the complete change in the outlook of the Russian situation" as well as JCS approval of the revised JSSC paper, no new directive could be issued owing to continued disputes over basic strategy.[62] Then on January 7, in reply to a direct presidential query as to whether the JCS were "agreed that we should meet the British united in advocating a cross-Channel operation," Marshall responded that "there was not a united front on that subject, particularly among our Planners," and that even within the JCS "the question was still an open one." Given such disarray and disagreement, British victory at the forthcoming strategic summit conference in Casablanca was a foregone conclusion—something FDR realized and warned against when he responded that the British "will have a plan and stick to it."[63]

As 1942 ended the Joint Chiefs could look back on the past year with very mixed feelings. After a series of disasters, they and their allies had succeeded in throwing back Axis offensives in almost all theaters, and they now stood poised to take advantage of these local successes with major offensive actions that would complete the seizure of the strategic initiative begun in the summer and fall. There was no agreement, however, within either the alliance or the U.S. armed forces, as to where such actions should take place or what global strategy should be. Without such agreement material and manpower planning would be crippled, strategic planning would not be possible, the military initiative would be lost, and the alliance might collapse.

Closer to home, 1942 had been almost as disastrous as had 1941 in terms of interservice and civil-military cooperation, as well as extremely disappointing in terms of coalition strategy-making. Formal belligerency had all but eliminated the State Department as a problem and major factor in these issues and had led to much greater power and influence for the service chiefs within their new JCS organization. But the result had not been greater agreement, coordination, or progress. Pearl Harbor had resulted in a virtual reversion to the intense army-navy disputes and suspicions of the interwar years, the only difference being that the army was now focused on European offensives rather than continental defense. The spring army-navy agreement to cross-channel operations provided only a very temporary respite in this dispute and an equally temporary agreement with the president and the British. Indeed, the April accords masked continued serious differences of opinion between the army and the navy, the JCS and the president, and the JCS and the British.

Once those disagreements emerged, the service chiefs formed a new consensus on a Pacific-first approach and pressed in July for a reversal of U.S. strategy, only to be forcefully overruled by their commander in chief. Unable to use this alternative even as a bargaining chip during ensuing negotiations in London, they were soon forced to accept a North African invasion they found loathsome. Both Clausewitz and U.S. law and tradition required military subordination to civil authority, and on the surface the chiefs submitted by agreeing to this operation. Beneath the surface, however, they continued to fight and subvert Roosevelt's strategic priorities. Convinced he was pursuing a militarily and politically disastrous approach as a result of Churchill's baneful influence, they continued to resist the North African invasion and created a de facto Pacific-first strategy in the face of direct presidential orders to the contrary.

To a great extent this decision was admittedly forced on them—first by the enormous and unexpected Allied losses in the Pacific and Southeast Asia, then by the Japanese threat to Australia and New Zealand, and finally by the violent Japanese reaction at Guadalcanal, a response that turned a very limited counterattack into an enormous six-month campaign of attrition. Yet it was they who had agreed to this risky campaign, forced its early launching onto theater commanders who wished to delay, and believed that their own approach dealt better than Roosevelt's with the military and political exigencies of 1942. By late 1942 they had thereby created a Pacific-first strategy, only to discover that their pessimistic global assessments had been incorrect. The result was a reemergence of the interservice split over global strategy, now three-way rather than two-way, and with it a total inability to advise the president let alone receive his support. In such a situation FDR would once again turn to Churchill for advice.

Behind all the arguments of 1942 lay a series of beliefs that dominated U.S. military thinking and would continue to do so throughout the war. The most important of these was that continued Soviet participation remained *the* key to victory, that without it the war in Europe was unwinnable, and that preserving it required specific U.S. military action. These conclusions formed the heart of *both* the cross-channel proposal and, with its rejection by the British, the Pacific-first proposal. If Russia could not be provided with her long-demanded second front in Europe, the planners argued, the best alternative was to establish one in the Pacific which would preclude a Japanese attack on the Soviet rear. Such an alternative would also enable the United States to achieve victory over at least one of the Axis Powers should Russia be defeated. Complementing such conclusions was the belief that while Germany constituted the primary and most dangerous enemy, wartime and postwar political considerations required a much greater emphasis on Japan. Equally important was JCS belief that the Mediterranean was not part of the European theater; that British strategy in this sea was militarily unsound, politically inspired, and contrary to U.S. interests; and that the president was dangerously enthralled by this strategy and would have to be weaned from it.

The failures of 1942 clearly revealed the difficulties the JCS would encounter in any such endeavor. If they hoped to achieve a new united front among themselves and with their president in the future, they would have to be much better organized and show much greater understanding of the specific connections and conflicts between British and U.S. strategy and policy. It was toward such an understanding that the Joint Chiefs turned their attention in early 1943.

6

Britain as Adversary, January–October 1943

The lack of agreement within the armed forces—and between them and the president—was fully revealed during the January Anglo-American strategic summit conference in Casablanca. Taking advantage of these divisions, the better-prepared and coordinated British consistently outargued and overwhelmed the Americans, winning approval for the very strategic approach in 1943 which the JCS so vehemently opposed: continuing offensives in the Mediterranean, focusing on the conquest of Sicily; the buildup of a separate force in the United Kingdom for an "eventual" cross-channel assault of unspecified date; and the continued subordination of the war against Japan to both of these theaters.[1] "If I had written down before I came what I hoped that the conclusions would be," one British planner noted, "I could never have written anything so sweeping, so comprehensive, and so favourable to our ideas." Wedemeyer, the chief army planner at Casablanca, bluntly concluded "that we lost our shirts. . . . One might say we came, we listened and we were conquered."[2]

British success had been the result of their excellent preparations, Wedemeyer and his associates argued, as well as the disunity and lack of politico-military coordination within the American camp. British strategy was clearly linked to British national policies in a way all their military personnel understood and supported. The same could not be said for the United States, and according to Wedemeyer the JCS would never be able to deal competently with London's "super negotiators," who possessed "generations of experience in committee work and rationalizing points of view," unless U.S. military opinion was coordinated and reinforced "by the full weight of national policy as opposed to that of the British."[3] This required greater coordination with both the president and the State Department as well as between the services. It also required a clear assessment of U.S. as opposed to British national policies and the links between these policies and the strategies of the two countries. As two army planners noted in mid-1943, the United States had been "outmaneuvered" at previous conferences "primarily" because British war aims, "based on national aims, have been clear-cut and understood by all concerned. In presenting their strategy and plans they have had the benefit of a nicely integrated politico-economic-military planning organization developed by experience over a long period of time. On the other hand our own war aims have not been so clearly defined and the integration in our strategy of economic, and especially political factors with the purely military factors has not been so thoroughly effected." [4]

Such comments and pleas were not new. British personnel had been appalled by the disorganization they had experienced in Washington, and whether or not they verbalized such feelings, their U.S. counterparts had throughout 1942 experienced on a daily basis the painful contrast between their own and the British system. [5] Even before the debacle at Casablanca, U.S. planners had therefore begun to address the problem.

Coordinating Strategy with Policy:
The New Committee Structure

Within the OPD, in June 1942, Wedemeyer had been placed in charge of the recently formed Strategy and Policy Group (S&P) and had been working to make it the army's "brain trust" on such issues as the coordination of strategy with national policy. [6] On the joint level, in October Marshall proposed the establishment of a new planning organization "with sufficient prestige and disassociated from current operations, which can obtain a good perspective by being allowed time for profound deliberation." On November 3 the Joint Chiefs agreed and established the Joint Strategic Survey Committee as an adjunct to the overworked JUSSC. Composed of military "elder statesman," it was at first charged with advising the JCS on "global and theater strategy" and by the spring of 1943 with matters of "national policy and world strategy." [7]

One day after the JCS established the JSSC, Marshall moved on the presidential level. In a rather extraordinary letter to Hopkins, the army chief complained on November 4 about the continuing lack of coordination between the president, cabinet, and service chiefs. Matters had been improving since Leahy's July appointment, but far from sufficiently, and Marshall now warned that "continuation of this system will sooner or later get us into serious trouble." Unlike the British, the JCS had no clear method of finding out about decisions reached within their own cabinet or between Roosevelt and Churchill, "except as we learn of it through the British here who are immediately informed of every detail." There was not even a clear method of summarizing and circulating decisions reached when the president met with the chiefs, individually or as a group. Marshall therefore proposed that Hopkins get Roosevelt to agree "as a first and very simple adjustment" to have Brigadier General John Deane, the JCS secretary, accompany the chiefs to the White House when they met with the president individually or as a group. Beyond that a secretary should be present at cabinet meetings when war issues were being decided. "I am getting into very delicate ground here," Marshall admitted, "but this is an important business and something should be done to organize it on a sound basis."[8]

Meanwhile, the planners expanded on Marshall's recently approved proposal to establish the JSSC. In an effort to clarify its mission and improve the entire joint committee structure, the JUSSC suggested on December 19 the establishment of a complete war planning system whereby future strategy would flow directly from a clear, "national concept of war," which in turn would "express the national objective, the policies the nation desires to pursue, and the extent and nature of the effort it intends to exert to attain the objective." Of paramount importance in such a system would be a strong and independent JSSC to study and interpret the national concept of war as well as to prepare and keep current a strategic policy for actually conducting the war.[9]

Before his departure for Casablanca, Wedemeyer had supported this proposal and reemphasized the crucial link between national policy and military strategy by reminding Marshall that "national policy determines our military policy" and that strategists therefore required a clear, "intelligent and current understanding of the political and economic aims of the country." The JSSC should therefore be given even broader responsibilities and allowed to submit recommendations directly to the JCS on the "military implications of all executive and legislative action pertaining to the national policy," on basic strategic concepts and objectives, and on all matters "involving global strategy." Additional committees should also be established to deal with other aspects of strategy and policy so that specific operational plans would flow logically from a clear-cut chain that started with national policy and then proceeded to military policy, global strategy, and future plans.[10]

The bitter Casablanca experience strongly reinforced the already recognized need for such a coherent planning network.[11] As a result, in the spring of 1943 the JCS approved a sixty-page report by a special subcommittee on war planning that recommended both an explicit JCS charter and an expansion of the joint planning network so as to guarantee future strategy-policy coordination. Of paramount importance was the total replacement of the overworked JUSSC with two distinct bodies: a Joint War Plans Committee (JWPC) responsible directly to the senior army-navy planners on the JPS, and a totally independent JSSC of military "elder statesmen." Consisting of no more than two navy flag officers and two army general officers, one of whom would come from the AAF, the JSSC was now explicitly charged with advising the JCS on all matters of combined, grand, and global strategy as well as "the relation of military strategy to national policy." Its members were to have no other regularly assigned duties and were given complete freedom to develop their own procedures, call on all military organizations for information, report directly to the Joint Chiefs without going through any part of the committee structure, and initiate their own studies without prior directives. They were also given the freedom to attend meetings of the JCS, CCS, and JPS, "as they may desire."[12]

Implicit within the JSSC charter was the expectation that the committee would inaugurate close ties with the State Department so as to receive appropriate policy guidance and so that political and military factors could be coordinated in planning postwar as well as wartime policies. In March 1943 such contact was indeed established when JSSC members began to meet with Welles and other high-ranking department personnel and to attend meetings of the Security Subcommittee of the department's Postwar Foreign Policy Advisory Committee.[13]

This was by no means the first wartime effort to create civil-military coordination.[14] All previous contacts had been on the individual service level, however, and had been concerned either with informing State of the military situation and resulting diplomatic needs of the armed forces or with postwar planning. The establishment of the JSSC and its liaison with State marked the first formal effort at coordination by the JCS as a body, as well as the first effort to formally link policy objectives with strategic planning for both the war years and the postwar era. Nor was this the only such effort in the spring of 1943. While Wedemeyer suggested to Marshall that a State Department representative sit in on future JCS meetings, the JWPC maintained that even on its own relatively narrow level of strategic planning a State Department representative should be included because it was "impossible entirely to divorce political considerations from strategic planning."[15]

This desire for coordination with State took place despite continuing anger over what had happened in 1940–41. According to Colonel Truman Smith of G-2, the Pacific conflict was "generally known in the War Department as Hornbeck's war," and he derisively asked State Department official William Castle in May 1942 whether the latter "thought Hornbeck was still feeling cheerful about it." Even in mid-1943 OPD chief Handy remained "leery about getting mixed up" with State "based upon [a] feeling of animosity . . . because of past unfortunate incidents."[16] The alternative, however, appeared to be continued defeat and humiliation at the hands of the British. Furthermore, coordination did not have to be on State Department terms. The JSSC and other planners consulted with State on wartime issues to receive information, advice, and issue directives, but they never gave the department representation on any of their committees or a vote on any of their wartime actions.

Desire for coordination with State resulted not only from the superiority of

British arrangements in this regard but also from the need to deal with a host of postwar issues that were arising in early 1943. Enemy territory had by this time been occupied and special divisions established within the service staffs to plan for their governance. As illustrated by the Darlan controversy in North Africa, coordination with State to determine occupation policies had become an urgent necessity. So had preliminary planning for postwar demobilization, with additional staff divisions established by mid-1943 to deal with this issue.[17] Such planning required detailed assumptions about postwar national policies. Furthermore, civilian thinking about a postwar collective security organization had by early 1943 reached a critical phase and resulted in requests for additional military input not only from State but also from the president; as early as December 28, 1942, he had pressed for military consideration of the issue by informing the JCS through his naval aide that "he visualized [that] some sort of international police force will come out of the war" and desired a JCS study "to the end that when the peace negotiations are upon us we will be decided in our own minds where it is desired that 'International Police Force' air facilities be located throughout the world."[18]

In responding to such requests the military began to reassert its prewar insistence on an important role in policy formulation. As it bluntly stated in defense of including the term "grand strategy" within the JSSC charter:

The Military authorities of the nation should share with the diplomatic and economic authorities the responsibility for shaping the national policy in peace as well as war. Since grand strategy looks beyond the war to the subsequent peace, its scope includes all factors which will affect the peace, and extends to the relations of a nation to its allies and to neutrals as well as to its opponents. Among many factors involved, those relating to national security, to communications, and to transportation, both sea and air, are of particular concern to the armed forces. None of these should be resolved without well-considered advice from the Military authorities. Their opinions should be sought, moreover, in regard to all other factors.[19]

The JSSC concurred, noting in mid-March the inseparability of postwar commercial, political, and military issues and insisting that if such issues were to be studied properly and on an integrated basis, the Joint Chiefs would have to be represented on "important groups concerned with post-war planning."[20]

The planners continued to verbalize a theoretical subordination to civil policymakers on the Clausewitzian grounds that "strategy and operations exist only as the implementing measures of national policy" and that the statement of policy was "not a matter which the military should dictate." Implementation of policy, however, required the armed forces to "advise in its preparation, have cognizance of its implications, and be prepared strategically and operationally to carry it out." Moreover, as two army planners emphasized in mid-1943, "the lack of fully defined *post-war* aims" had hurt the Americans in their strategic debates with the British. "Both our national policy and our national war strategy," they maintained, "should certainly envisage steps after unconditional surrender of our enemies," steps that would require "the adoption of strategical measures by the armed forces and the conduct of operations for their implementation."[21] Military and strategic planning, in short, could not be separated from wartime or postwar policy planning.

Although most aspects of the JCS reorganization and emphasis on politico-military coordination were accepted by mid-1943, such expansive proposals met with some opposition—as they had in the past—on the grounds that they interfered with civilian policy prerogatives. Within the State Department's Postwar Foreign Policy Advisory Committee, complaints arose by early April about the "undue domination" of the Security Subcommittee by the military representatives.[22] In the White House, Roosevelt explicitly rejected any JCS charter as "too restrictive," and the Joint Chiefs thus continued to serve totally at his personal discretion. He also rejected Marshall's November plea for secretarial records of his meetings with the members of the JCS and the cabinet. Deane did accompany the JCS to a White House meeting as Marshall had suggested, but the army chief later recollected that the president "blew up" when he saw Deane's "big notebook" and ordered him to "put that thing up."[23] Throughout the war the JCS thus continued to rely on the service secretaries, the British, and one another to remain apprised of presidential decisions.

Opposition also emerged within the Joint Chiefs themselves, as Leahy pointedly warned his colleagues on numerous occasions that they were overstepping their bounds. Whether he was acting under presidential order or his own belief in a clear delineation between strategic and policy responsibility remains unclear. Whatever the cause, he balked at the inclusion of "grand strategy" within the JSSC charter and asked the rest of the JCS exactly what this term meant. He also objected to any JCS concern with postwar commercial issues and throughout the war would consistently take exception to any JSSC reports that seemed to him to be dealing with "purely political" matters.[24]

Leahy's objections notwithstanding, the JSSC would obviously be dealing with a host of political issues and serve a critical advisory role for the Joint Chiefs. That it fulfilled this role is also clear. According to the official JCS history it became "probably the most influential element" of the entire JCS organization, and Brian Villa has aptly described the group as "at times equal in influence" to the Joint Chiefs themselves. Indeed, its numerous reports constitute, in original form, the eventual JCS position on virtually every major wartime and postwar issue with political overtones.[25]

The Joint Chiefs clearly anticipated such an extraordinary role for the JSSC, as is illustrated not only by its powers and responsibilities but also by the exceptionally high quality, rank, and experience of the three officers chosen for membership. Vice Admiral Russell Willson, the navy representative, had previously served as naval attaché in London during the first phases of the Anglo-American staff conversations, superintendent of the U.S. Naval Academy, chief of staff to Admiral King, and deputy commander in chief of the U.S. Fleet. Major General Muir S. Fairchild, the Army Air Forces representative and at forty-eight the youngest member of the committee, had already been assistant chief of staff and director of military requirements for the AAF and was, according to the official administrative history of the JCS, an officer "whose exceptional qualities of mind were widely recognized." The army representative was none other than Embick, probably the army's foremost strategist and soldier-statesman.[26]

Embick's anti-British views were as well known in 1942–43 as his politico-military abilities, and his appointment to this prestigious committee can hardly be considered accidental. Indeed, given the tasks the Joint Chiefs expected the JSSC to undertake, especially those relating to the Anglo-American strategic debate and the links between strategy and policy, Embick by both experience and views was the obvious choice to be army representative. His appointment also reveals that old anti-British feelings within the army had only been strengthened by the strategic dispute of 1942.

The Analysis of Conflicting Strategies and Policies

As expected, the JSSC began to examine the Anglo-American strategic dispute almost immediately upon its establishment, and between January and August 1943 it produced a series of detailed reports in which its members attempted to analyze the key policy differences that they claimed underlay the arguments over strategy.[27] The JWPC and the S&P undertook similar analyses. Taken together, their studies offer detailed insight into the military's view of both British and U.S. strategies and national policies during the war.

According to the JSSC, British emphasis on the Mediterranean was clearly motivated by a need to restore political control in that sea, a control it rated "essential to the maintenance of their present Imperial power" in the postwar world. Coming after Churchill's November "Mansion House" speech with its insistence that he had not become prime minister to preside over the demise of the British Empire, such a conclusion was far from surprising or original. Yet by itself it could not fully explain the logic behind British strategy, for Axis defeat via *any* strategy would restore Britain's prewar Mediterranean position. Given this fact the committee searched for more "fundamental" causes for the divergence between the

British and U.S. strategies. It found these in "the differences in the geographic situation of the two nations vis-a-vis the several enemies, and in the marked contrast between the two nations in respect to their territorial structures and the bases of their power."[28]

A far-flung, island-based empire, Britain's foremost national policies had historically been and remained retention of its overseas possessions and preservation of a balance of power on the European continent. These aims dictated a slow, dispersed strategy of attrition centering on the Mediterranean, not only to restore British control of that sea but also to avoid the heavy casualties that were inherent in cross-channel operations and would result in a "decline in Imperial strength." Furthermore, despite their adherence to the "unconditional surrender" formula enunciated by Roosevelt at Casablanca, the British might have "mental reservations" based on their balance-of-power policy and a subsequent fear of postwar Russian domination of Europe if Germany were to be quickly and totally defeated. A slow, peripheral strategy focusing on the Mediterranean could preserve a balance of power for the postwar era by allowing Germany and Russia to exhaust each other and delaying final German defeat until "military attrition and civilian famine" had significantly weakened the Soviet Union. Such a strategy would also enable Britain to move into the eastern Mediterranean and align with Turkey, thereby successfully continuing its centuries-old policy of blocking Russian control of the Dardanelles while fulfilling Churchill's personal desire to prove correct his "eccentric" World War I ideas regarding peripheral warfare. This desire to invade the eastern Mediterranean, the JSSC held, was a hidden, basic goal of London's Mediterranean approach.[29]

Another basic British goal was the actual expansion, rather than simply retention, of the prewar Mediterranean empire. With India demanding independence and the dominions only sentimentally tied to the mother country, England in the postwar era would face a "crying need for British-controlled raw materials and markets," which the former French and Italian colonies could provide if they were given to London as mandates at the peace conference. Islands in the Mediterranean would be needed as "fortified outposts" for this expanded empire, and these would have to be seized and placed firmly in British hands before the peace conference if London wished to have a solid claim to their permanent possession. These facts explained "the necessity from the British viewpoint" of undertaking militarily ineffective Mediterranean operations "*prior* to undertaking decisive operations against Germany."[30]

The problems with this strategy, according to the JSSC, were both military and political. Eastern Mediterranean operations would require previously committed U.S. naval support, Turkish belligerency the JSSC rated an overall liability rather than an asset, and offensives at the end of long and tenuous supply lines in an area so mountainous and remote from the center of German power as to be indecisive and invite stalemate or defeat. Moreover, such operations were based on the assumption that indirect campaigns in the Mediterranean against Germany's satellites, combined with blockade, bombing, and guerrilla operations, could force a German collapse. Dubious under the best of circumstances, this assumption ignored the fact that an approach relegating to the Soviet Union the brutal task of fighting the bulk of the Wehrmacht while London reaped political benefits in the eastern Mediterranean and Balkans, an area of historic Anglo-Russian rivalry, might so arouse Russia's anger and suspicion as to make it "more susceptible" to German peace feelers—especially ones which would grant Moscow its centuries-old desire to control the Dardanelles. The resulting separate peace would leave Germany undefeated and dominant in Central and Western Europe and would make Allied victory impossible.[31]

Even if such an appalling scenario did not develop, a Mediterranean strategy would involve the use of American forces to achieve British political ends. More threatening than the nationalistic insult involved in this perceived repetition of the attempted World War I manipulation of U.S. forces, Britain's approach would negatively affect America's military position and national policies in the Far East and, with them, Washington's ability to pursue a Europe-first strategy in the future.

The essential problem was that the time-consuming and indecisive Mediterranean approach would delay vital operations against Japan and, in the process, wreak havoc with America's military position, its interests in the Far East, and public support for a global war effort. Even before Casablanca the JSSC had concluded in this regard that the "basic difference" between U.S. and British strategy was not over the appropriate follow-up to TORCH, as London had claimed, but over the "relation of the war in the Pacific to the war as a whole."[32]

Unlike the United States, the JSSC noted, Britain considered China unimportant and assumed Japan's defeat could be postponed indefinitely without serious military or political consequences. Numerous factors led the JSSC to the opposite conclusion. Delay would enable the Japanese to entrench themselves in Asia and the Pacific sufficiently to make U.S. reconquest of the area extremely difficult if not impossible. It would also wreck the long-term and clearly enunciated U.S. policy of preserving and building up China as a great power. Chiang Kai-shek's plight was already desperate, and warnings of a Chinese surrender or separate peace in 1942–43 if massive U.S. aid and an invasion of Burma were not forthcoming had been just as frequent as those concerning Soviet withdrawal from the war without cross-channel operations. In addition to ruining U.S. plans for postwar Asia, Chinese withdrawal would greatly simplify Japan's military task and thereby make U.S. reconquest of the Pacific that much more difficult. And perhaps more menacing, it would enable Tokyo to unify all the peoples of Asia in what would become for the United States a disastrous, unwinnable race war. Indeed, in late 1943 the JSSC noted in this regard that a "successful outcome of the war in the Pacific is of a concern to the United States at least as great as a similar outcome in Europe. An unsuccessful outcome, permitting a coalition under Japan's hegemony of the people of East Asia (about 55% of the world's population), would appear likely to offer, indeed, a greater ultimate threat to the United States than would a similar outcome in Europe."[33]

Equally damaging for the United States would be the domestic repercussions of a time-consuming Mediterranean approach and subsequent delay in the war against Japan. "Only by an intellectual effort," Stimson warned Churchill in August, had Americans "been convinced that Germany was their most dangerous enemy and should be disposed of before Japan." The enemy whom they "really hated, if they hated anyone, was Japan which had dealt them a foul blow." That was an optimistic conclusion: a majority of Americans polled in early 1943 still considered Tokyo their primary enemy. Supported by Roosevelt's political opponents as well as MacArthur, they consistently threatened to force an even greater reversal of the Germany-first approach than had actually occurred in 1942. Behind closed doors, the navy remained equally vociferous in its demands for more resources and offensive action in the Pacific.[34] Indeed, interservice and public unity over the Germany-first approach had originally been forged on the promise of quick victory in Europe via cross-channel operations, and the delays and digressions of 1942 had already destroyed this delicate consensus.

They also threatened serious political and military problems in terms of the limited aid available for the Chinese war effort, whose continuation the president demanded and the JCS considered both precarious and vital. "China is the key to the war with Japan just as Russia is the key to the war with Germany," King asserted in early 1943, "and for exactly the same reasons. China has the manpower and the strategic geographical position to crush the Island Empire." Without China the war would be prolonged ten or fifteen years, he maintained, and indefinitely according to the JPS. A Chinese collapse could result from a lack of Allied military action, especially in Burma; it would be a political and a military disaster because it would lead to a further "loss of face by the United Nations among the peoples of Asia" and disillusionment for the American people who believed, however incorrectly, that China was making a major contribution to the war effort.[35]

Citing these factors, the JSSC concluded the "fundamental difference" between British and U.S. strategies revolved around the importance of swift and decisive action against Japan and that this difference was the result of fundamentally different national policies. The argument over European strategy was merely a reflection, albeit an important one, of this basic disagreement. The "purely military" American approach in Europe via cross-channel operations was designed to defeat Germany as quickly as possible so as to be able to turn against Japan and thereby protect U.S. national interests in Asia and the Pacific. Britain's slow and "political" Mediterranean approach was designed to advance its national interests in that area, but it was militarily flawed and it threatened America's war effort, unity, and wartime and postwar national policies in the Far East by delaying action against Japan.[36]

Within the OPD, Wedemeyer and his Strategy and Policy Group verbalized similar conclusions in memoranda that analyzed in greater depth many of the issues raised by the JSSC. Britain, they maintained, had once again adopted its traditional, naval-oriented, peripheral strategy to preserve its empire rather than win a war as quickly as possible. Indeed, overwhelming seapower, the basis of this strategy, was the key factor that had previously enabled Britain to create, maintain, and defend the empire, and London was therefore depending on it once again. It was also relying on the necessary prerequisite for effective use of that seapower: a continuation of the European balance of power. It therefore favored a slow, Mediterranean strategy which would allow Germany and Russia to exhaust each other and which included Balkan operations to block Russian expansion.[37]

The basic military problem with this approach, according to Wedemeyer and the S&P, was that the ability of seapower to defend the empire—or even the home islands—had been "disputed, if not entirely abrogated by the advent of air power." Furthermore, Japanese military successes had already reduced the empire substantially, while growing U.S. economic influence in Canada, the West Indies, and Australia had left these areas with only a "sentimental" attachment to the mother country.[38] In effect, the British Empire was a decaying and indefensible anachronism already under severe economic and military assault, subsequently reduced to portions of Africa, the Middle East, and India and incapable of surviving even in this smaller form.

Because Britain was a "weak and defenseless island" without the empire, it had geared its wartime strategy and policy to strengthening and expanding the areas it still controlled via its proposed deployment of troops in the Mediterranean. That deployment was also designed to seize or extend influence over new areas, which London could then either "retain or use for bargaining purposes when peace is negotiated." These included Libya, French Morocco, Algeria, Tunisia, Sicily, Sardinia, Palestine, Syria, Iran, Iraq, the Dodecanese Islands, Turkey, and the Balkans.[39]

The heart of this "new" postwar British Empire and point of greatest danger, according to one S&P paper, was Iran and Iraq. Long coveted by Germany and Russia, this was now an area on which British seapower was totally dependent because of its extensive oil fields. Because it could be invaded only by crossing the Dardanelles and advancing through Turkey or via the trans-Caucasian route flanked by Turkey, persuading Ankara to enter the war while simultaneously launching Anglo-American offensives in the eastern Mediterranean and the Balkans was of paramount importance to Britain.[40]

The Strategy and Policy Group thus agreed with the JSSC that the ultimate military objectives of British Mediterranean strategy lay in the east, despite British disclaimers. It also joined the JSSC in pointing out the military deficiencies of such an approach, most notably its overreliance on a dated concept of seapower and dubious assumptions regarding the ability to force a German collapse without a direct military confrontation with the Wehrmacht, and in emphasizing the clashes between British and U.S. national policies which underlay their strategic disputes.

Beyond policy differences over the balance of power in Europe, the priority and timing of operations in the Far East, and the importance of China, the S&P also emphasized the economic threat the United States posed to any continuation of the British Empire. Noting that London might already be attempting to use "the lever of postwar necessity" to undermine American supremacy in commercial air transport, one S&P paper warned that the United States could avoid future conflict with Great Britain "only so long as it does not challenge her supremacy in world trade."[41]

The JWPC repeated this warning in a May 7 report that succinctly linked Anglo-American strategic differences to essential and irreconcilable policy differences. The foremost aims of U.S. national policy, it asserted, were hemispheric security "and the improvement of her world economic position by reciprocal trade pacts," whereas the foremost aims of British national policy were "the maintenance of the integrity of the British Empire and of her supremacy in world trade." In maintaining these goals, the JWPC warned, Britain continued to rely on manipulative and immoral means: "She dominates her empire by controlling the economic destiny of her dominions and crown colonies. She maintains her position in the European area by preserving the balance of power on the Continent. She exploits the resources and people of other nations to insure her position of dominance."[42] Clearly, the JWPC implied, Britain was now trying to exploit America and its other allies to insure that dominance into the postwar era. In addition to using supposed wartime necessities as a means of undermining U.S. supremacy in commercial air transport, London was attempting to manipulate Anglo-American strategy so as to accomplish its policy objectives.

According to the JWPC, British war policy and strategy were heavily influenced by national policies and "post-war economic, territorial and political ambitions." Consequently, Britain desired a war so conducted that "neither Germany nor Russia can emerge in a dominating position in Europe, and that the balance of power in Europe can rest in British hands. She would prefer that operations be so conducted and troops so disposed as to enable her to attain and retain areas which are vital to the maintenance of her empire or which might be used for bargaining purposes at the peace table." London would therefore demand eastern Mediterranean operations "to block Russian designs in the Dardanelles area" and to contribute to a "possible" British ploy of proposing one limited Mediterranean operation after another so that invasion of Europe from the Mediterranean instead of across the channel would "inevitably develop into a commitment."[43]

The JWPC maintained that American national policies dictated a totally different strategy. Unchallenged hemispheric hegemony precluded a need for or concern about the balance of power, it argued, and therefore "current United States policy is not strongly influenced by post-war aims. The aim of United States war policy is to secure the early and decisive defeat of the Axis," and this translated into cross-channel operations in Europe. But the JWPC then contradicted this simplistic strategy-policy dichotomy by noting that the reason U.S. war policy was geared to the early and decisive defeat of the Axis was that "the American people will not countenance a long war of attrition" and that British plans negatively affected U.S. plans for and interest in Asia. Arguing that British objections to the invasion of Burma risked the loss of China in the war, the JWPC emphatically insisted that "everything should be done to maintain the prestige and influence of the United States in China."[44]

The similarities between this analysis and those offered by the JSSC and the S&P were far from accidental. The army section of the JWPC was staffed by members of the S&P and led by the head of the group's Strategy Section (SS), Colonel William W. Bessell.[45] Because that section had been responsible for many of the S&P papers on British strategy and policy, it is not surprising to find numerous S&P concepts and even the same phrases reappearing in the JWPC study. Furthermore, the S&P chief Wedemeyer was Embick's son-in-law and shared many of his views. "If victory is assured," he warned Marshall in language quite similar to that of his father-in-law, "the British may be expected to insist upon operations which will create most favorable circumstances at the peace table while weakening the positions of all other participating nations, particularly Germany and Russia." The sharing worked both ways, however, for according to the later recollections of one planner, Embick often attended S&P meetings, never commenting but always listening carefully to what was being said and, perhaps, repeating those comments in JSSC papers.[46]

Despite the close organizational and family ties, it would be a gross error to conclude that these analyses of conflicting Anglo-American strategies and policies were limited to a small clique and merely an amplification of prewar Anglophobic beliefs by one or two isolationist generals. The JSSC and JWPC papers were composed and signed by navy and air force as well as army officers, and most of them received JCS support and approval with only minor changes. Indeed, Leahy found one of the JSSC analyses (JCS 283) "most forceful and useful" and forwarded a copy to Roosevelt *prior to* JCS approval. He also appears to have requested Embick's Dardanelles memorandum for delivery to the president, and in his diary he echoed many of the planners' conclusions regarding British strategy and policy, as did his JCS colleagues and senior U.S. field officers.[47] In late October one British official described the Joint Chiefs as about as friendly to the British "as they would be to the German General Staff if they sat round the table with them"; King told a press group that Churchill's "main interest was to preserve the British Empire and that cooperating with the United States to win the war took lower priority." In England, Generals Frank Andrews, Jacob Devers, and Ira Eaker all believed the British had no intention of crossing the channel because they did not want to see Germany quickly defeated and Russia dominant on the Continent or in the eastern Mediterranean. Arnold went one step further, concluding that Britain feared Russia more than Germany, wished to maintain the latter as a buffer against the former, and would therefore never agree to operations against Berlin beyond blockade and bombing designed to achieve a negotiated peace.[48]

So widespread and intense was the hostility against Britain within the services that it aroused the concern of both Marshall and Eisenhower, who feared a negative impact on the war effort. "I am not so incredibly naive that I do not realize that Britishers instinctively approach every military problem from the viewpoint of the Empire," Eisenhower wrote Handy in early 1943, "just as we approach them from the viewpoint of American interests. But one of the constant sources of danger to us in this war is the temptation to regard as our first enemy the partner that must work with us in defeating the real enemy." An August OPD paper made a similar point in counseling acceptance of the fact that nonmilitary national policies helped determine "strategic aims" at combined conferences and that "the aims of national policy vital to Great Britain do not always coincide with those of the United States and may in certain cases conflict. This situation should be accepted as a fact and should not excite recrimination." It did, however, with Wedemeyer going so far as to insist on witnesses to and taping of his often bitter conversations with British colleagues.[49]

Anti-British sentiments were by no means limited to the armed forces, however, and the military analysis of conflicting national policies as well as strategies appears to have been based to an extent upon civilian enunciation of similar conclusions. Former ambassador to the Soviet Union Joseph E. Davies echoed Embick's warnings of a resurrected Anglo-Russian clash over the Dardanelles. Stimson discussed the issue with Embick and responded to presidential interest in the eastern Mediterranean by informing FDR in May that as the oldest member of the cabinet, "I could remember the sharp issue between Britain and Russia in the 80's" and that "this antagonism would react sharply against his proposition in Russia." [50] One JSSC paper cited newspaper warnings of British postwar goals in the Mediterranean by *Washington Evening Star* foreign editor Constantine Brown, an individual who often gave such warnings directly and privately to Leahy. State Department official Ray Atherton gave Leahy similar warnings and in May told the admiral England was "principally concerned with post-war control of the Mediterranean"—a conclusion Leahy found to be in agreement "with the evidence that comes to me from many sources." [51] Another JSSC paper on British strategy relied on oral State Department input given in response to a formal request for guidance from Embick, while the JSSC fear of Japan being able to unify the Asian peoples in a race war unwinnable by the United States echoed similar sentiments expressed within the department. [52]

Anti-British sentiments and a belief in conflicting postwar policies were quite widespread and long-standing within the State Department. [53] They were also prevalent among U.S. officers and diplomats in the Far East, most notably General Joseph Stilwell and Foreign Service Officer John Paton Davies in China, though here the emphasis was of course on Britain's determination to focus on its Far East as opposed to its Mediterranean empire. While Stilwell filled his diary with virtually unprintable epithets about the British and their goals, Davies provided an Asian equivalent of the JSSC analysis in questioning British commitment to a strategy designed to defeat Japan on the grounds that "reacquisition and perhaps expansion of the Empire is an essential undertaking if Britain is to be fully restored to the position of a first class power. Therefore reconquest of Empire is the paramount task in British eyes. The raising of the Union Jack over Singapore is more important to the British than any victory parade through Tokyo." [54]

The former Navy League president William Howard Gardiner took this logic a few steps further by warning Joseph Grew of the State Department in a March 1943 letter that Britain might even want to avoid the total defeat of Japan, preferring instead to build up Tokyo "as a counterpose to the United States that would reduce our post-war influence not merely in the Pacific, but in world affairs elsewhere." Grew considered this letter important enough to show to Hornbeck and Welles, to forward copies to both Leahy and Roosevelt, and to discuss it with FDR. [55]

Suspicion of British strategy and policy also extended to the cabinet and the public. Hull and Stimson both objected in April to Britain's plans for administration of territory occupied in the Mediterranean, and in June an interdepartmental effort including State, Interior, Navy, War, and the JCS was launched to beat the British to control of Saudi Arabian oil. [56] Nearly 60 percent of the respondents in a 1942 public opinion poll labeled the British as oppressors who took advantage of their colonies, and Christopher Thorne aptly described the public view of the empire as "a selfish and dangerous anachronism."[57] The armed forces shared this view. "It used to be said," D. C. Watt has wryly noted, "that in Washington war was being waged with five enemies in descending order of priority: with the army or navy, with the Republican Party, with the British, and thereafter with the Germans and the Japanese." For many in the armed forces as well as numerous other departments, "it was the third of these which occupied most of their time and thoughts."[58]

Forging a New Strategic United Front

The near unanimity within the armed forces on conflicting Anglo-American policies unfortunately did not translate directly into unanimity on an appropriate strategic response. Roosevelt had in July 1942 vetoed the JCS Pacific alternative, even as a bargaining tactic, and since that time intra- as well as interservice disputes had continued to cripple U.S. planning. While the offensives instituted by the chiefs in the Southwest Pacific during the summer continued unabated, the service planners argued bitterly over appropriate strategy for the future. Many naval officers favored expansion of the de facto Pacific-first strategy in progress, albeit with a shift in focus to the Central Pacific, while continuing to give lip service to the Europe-first approach. Army and AAF officers disagreed but continued to split over whether to refocus on cross-channel operations or take advantage of the opportunities becoming available in the Mediterranean, especially after the fall of Mussolini in July.[59]

Between late 1942 and the summer of 1943 the JSSC and other strategic planning groups used their analyses of Anglo-American policy differences as well as the ongoing reality of Pacific operations to propose a new global strategy, geared to accomplish American political objectives and capable of receiving interservice support. By its terms the United States would agree to continued offensives in the Mediterranean *provided* they were sharply limited and subordinated *both* to a cross-channel assault with a specified 1944 target date (which the JSSC argued airpower would enable the Allies to successfully launch and exploit) and to continued offensives in the Pacific and Far East. These would include not only the Southwest Pacific and Burma, which the JCS considered as essential to keeping China in the war as cross-channel operations were to keeping Russia in, but also and simultaneously the Central Pacific advance which the navy had long advocated but which Marshall accepted only now and the JSSC recommended be given primacy as necessary to the quick victory the public demanded. If Britain refused to agree, the JCS would take advantage of their unilateral control of both key war production and the war against Japan to transfer unilaterally the needed resources to the Pacific, even if this transfer expanded the de facto Pacific-first strategy that presently existed.[60]

The Mediterranean, in short, was not to be considered part of the European theater. By the new set of priorities being proposed, Anglo-American strategy would focus on defeat of Germany first via cross-channel operations, the Far Eastern/Pacific war and American interests in that area second, and British interests in the Mediterranean third. For the time being operations would continue in this third area because they were already in progress and because the channel could not be crossed until 1944, but only within sharply specified limits designed to promote rather than make impossible a 1944 cross-channel assault, with veteran divisions and landing craft to be transferred to Britain at a specified date.[61] Moreover, if Russia collapsed or signed a separate peace because of the continued delay in crossing the channel, the Joint Chiefs would once again consider a complete and formal reversal of what remained of the Europe-first approach on the grounds that Germany could no longer be defeated.

Although the JCS and their planners agreed on this compromise proposal by the spring of 1943, they were well aware that such agreement in no way translated into its acceptance by the British. Wedemeyer and others had warned that winning approval of a strategy designed to secure U.S. as opposed to British interests would require extraordinary preparations, civil-military unity, and some very hard bargaining.[62] Consequently, the JCS, JSSC, JWPC, and S&P all devoted much time and attention to tactical preparations for the next two Anglo-American strategic conferences, in Washington during May (TRIDENT) and in Quebec in August (QUADRANT). Among the planners' suggestions were the preparation of specific studies designed to counter British and to advance U.S. proposals, additional State Department representation, more joint as opposed to service planning, and closer coordination between the service staffs. Beyond such general points they further suggested the war-gaming of British proposals in advance, the assignment of planners to specific adjoining rooms, detailed JCS rehearsal of all possible arguments, and a series of negotiating tactics to be used in CCS meetings. These tactics included a united front and aggressive argumentation in all negotiations, taking the initiative on specific strategic issues, refusing to be drawn into subjects for which they were unprepared, caution in accepting any British proposal until the staffs had time to examine it in detail, and assignment of specific subjects to individual JCS members.[63] Any British insistence on Mediterranean action should be met by the threat of greater U.S. emphasis on the Pacific and Asia, a threat Leahy and Marshall would verbalize more often than King as a means of strengthening the appearance of JCS unity. Furthermore, if any member of the JCS believed that a subject required further consideration, he was to signal Leahy to press for postponement by saying, "I am having a study made which bears on this subject, which will not be ready until tomorrow." [64]

The planners also emphasized the importance of close coordination with the president to prevent a repetition of what had taken place in 1942. Throughout the spring and summer of 1943, Leahy, Marshall, and Stimson all worked to achieve such coordination and thereby complete their united front. While Leahy forwarded individual JSSC and JWPC papers to the president, Marshall brought forward similar OPD studies as well as papers describing the British secretariat system. He also cautioned FDR concerning both the military problems with British strategy and the negative impact of further Mediterranean operations on public opinion and the war against Japan. [65]

Stimson was equally if not more active. Believing that Anglo-American strategic differences reflected "very deep" differences "in national character and interests" and that the British were "straining every nerve to lay a foundation throughout the Mediterranean for their own empire after the war is over," he consistently warned Roosevelt about the political nature of and dubious military assumptions in British strategy as well as the probable negative consequences of this strategy on U.S. public opinion and postwar interests, continued Russian participation in the war, and postwar Soviet-American relations. Further Mediterranean operations, which he compared in May to holding "the leg for Stalin to skin the deer," would lead to "widespread loss of support for the war among our people" and be "dangerous business for us at the end of the war," because Stalin "won't have much of an opinion of people who have done that and we will not be able to share much of the postwar world with him." In August he amplified these warnings against what he derisively labeled "pinprick warfare" in the Mediterranean. [66]

The degree to which Roosevelt accepted or rejected these conclusions remains a matter of historical controversy. [67] He continued to be attracted to the apparently cheap victories and opportunities in the Mediterranean throughout the first half of 1943. After that time his interest waned, however, and he began to tell the Joint Chiefs of his fears regarding British versus American goals, concerns similar to those they had been expressing to him. He also began to agree with their negative recommendations regarding British requests for action in the eastern Mediterranean and even to use their drafts for his negative replies to Churchill. [68] Clearly, the JCS and their planners had succeeded by the summer of 1943 in forging a formidable united front regarding future strategy.

The result was a new American ability to meet the British on equal if confrontational terms. A series of explosive CCS sessions ensued at both TRIDENT and QUADRANT, with the CCS forced on more than one occasion to clear the room of all assistants for some private and very direct exchanges. Out of these "off-the-record" sessions emerged a compromise strategy that would focus on the Mediterranean in 1943 but then shift to cross-channel operations in 1944, while dual offensives against Japan, designed to bring about Tokyo's surrender within twelve months of Germany's, would be launched in the Pacific. For the most part these compromises reflected the American position and resulted from their superior preparations and negotiating abilities. Indeed, at QUADRANT the U.S. preparations and united front far surpassed Britain's, and the JCS clearly triumphed at this conference in the politics of coalition strategy-making.[69]

The fact that military beliefs regarding the sinister nature of British strategy and policy were so widespread does not, of course, mean that they were valid. In line with JSSC suspicions, COS planners admittedly had begun in late 1942 to consider the Soviet Union a potential postwar enemy and to call for garrisons throughout the Mediterranean, North Africa, and the Middle East.[70] Nevertheless, Britain's true goals and policies in the area were a good deal more limited and its leaders' reasoning considerably more irrational than the Americans thought, and the latter's intense suspicions apparently had little foundation on which to rest. As one British participant in the 1943 debates humorously commented, "Some Americans are curiously liable to suspect that they are going to be 'outsmarted' by the subtle British—perhaps because we sometimes do such stupid things that they cannot take them at face value but suspect them of being part of some dark design."[71] But perceptions were more important than reality in that they created a new reality—one of renewed and intensified U.S. military concern with policy matters within the alliance. That concern, readily apparent in 1940 and 1941, had seemingly disappeared in 1942 under the impact of the Axis assault and multiple military crises. In actuality it had only lain dormant, and the events of 1942 succeeded in reviving and expanding it in 1943.

In explaining the conflict between British and U.S. policies and strategies, however, many of the planners appeared to be explicitly denying fundamental points about U.S. national policies that Stark, the JPC, and the JB had emphasized in 1940–41: the primacy to American security of both a powerful Britain and a European balance of power, and the subsequent secondary nature of U.S. interests in the Far East and Pacific. Enraged by both Pearl Harbor and what had taken place within the alliance in 1942, the planners now appeared to be arguing that the Far East would be more important to the United States than Europe in the postwar world and that neither Britain nor a European balance of power was essential to U.S. postwar security. Nor was the British Empire, for that matter. Implicitly, they seemed to be negating the basic, original rationales for American intervention and strategy, while maintaining that the United States would have no interest in supporting London on any postwar issues, especially in regard to the empire or clashes with the Soviet Union over Eastern Europe. John Paton Davies captured the essence of the ensuing contradictions when he noted that U.S. policy was "based on the conviction that we need Britain as a first-class power," that it could not be such a power without its empire, and that "we are accordingly committed to the support of the British Empire"—after previously noting that "in the minds of most Americans a better world is identified with the abolition of imperialism, and there is a very real danger that the United States may again become isolationist after the war as a result of a feeling by the American people that they have been made dupes of British imperialism."[72]

At least one s&p officer questioned whether the abolition of imperialism was indeed in American interests. The United States should be fighting to preserve the British Empire, he argued in early 1943, but not "merely to perpetuate the British Empire, as such. Far from it. We are fighting for a secure and orderly world wherein we can exploit our American genius. The British Empire is the most satisfactory order-producing agency that is, or will be, available in the Middle East either now or at war's end. So, in simple self-interest, we are—or should be— fighting to preserve at least large slices of the British Empire."[73]

In 1943 most U.S. military planners disagreed, perhaps because they believed that preserving the empire was a hopeless task. Re-creating the balance of power was an equally hopeless task given the extent to which the war had already weakened Britain and revolutionized international relations. Consequently, they contended that both the empire and the balance of power would have to be replaced by a new international security system, one on which they were then working. British efforts to re-create the old system were doomed to failure, in their view, and would only result in Russia's alienation, which in turn would destroy the possibility of creating any postwar security system—as well as the possibility of total victory over Germany.[74]

In these calculations, postwar and wartime, Russia had become the single most important factor. Far from unexpectedly, the planners therefore devoted considerable attention to the Soviet Union in the process of explaining Anglo-American differences and in providing details regarding the new international security system they hoped to put into place at war's end.

Russia as Ally and Enigma,
December 1942–October 1943

Throughout 1942–43, U.S. strategists repeatedly emphasized the critical importance of Russia to the Allied war effort. With the Red Army facing 87–98.5 percent of German divisions on combat fronts and inflicting 93 percent of German battle casualties between June 1941 and June 1944, this emphasis was by no means exaggerated.[1] Soviet withdrawal from the war via military defeat or a separate peace, the planners thus warned repeatedly, would make victory over Germany impossible and thereby necessitate a complete revision of U.S. war aims, policies, and global strategy.

Activities to keep Russia in the war consequently became the focal point of U.S. strategy—even before official entry into the conflict. In the fall of 1941 the armed forces thus reversed themselves and supported diplomatic confrontation with Japan and reinforcement of the Philippines as means of preventing a Japanese attack on Siberia. Throughout 1942–43 they repeatedly justified cross-channel operations in terms of the military and political effects on the Soviets. In 1942 they also justified their Pacific-first alternative in terms of the Soviet war effort: choosing North African over cross-channel operations, they contended, was equivalent to giving up on Russia and accepting stalemate in Europe, thereby negating the Germany-first approach and allowing for the proposed shift to the Pacific. They further justified that shift on the grounds that if the Russians could survive the German onslaught without cross-channel assistance, Pacific action would help them more than any Mediterranean operations by precluding a Japanese attack on Siberia.[2]

Throughout 1943 the JSSC and other planning groups repeated these conclusions and reinforced them with a related warning: acquiescence in Britain's Mediterranean strategy would resurrect and involve the United States in the historic Anglo-Russian clash in southeastern Europe, thereby heightening Russian suspicions and making a separate peace with Germany more likely.[3] It would also increase chances of Soviet refusal to enter the war against Japan, at the very time such entry was becoming an even higher priority for U.S. planners. Heavy casualties in the Pacific and continued problems getting Chiang Kai-shek to commit his forces to major operations against the Japanese had by 1943 led the planners to realize that such entry would be of vital importance in the future and thus to an increasing emphasis on obtaining it.

Given these facts and Moscow's continued insistence on the establishment of a second front in northern France, Soviet and U.S. strategic concepts were remarkably similar in 1943—so much so that the JSSC had no fundamental disagreements to analyze. Postwar policies and objectives were another matter, however, and throughout 1943 numerous military planners joined the JSSC in exploring this controversial issue.

Origins of the Cooperative Policy

Throughout 1942–43 the planners noted a vital political corollary to their strategic assessments regarding the Soviet war effort: if Russia did survive the German onslaught and continue to fight until the Axis powers were totally defeated, it would emerge from the war with enormous power and influence. Moreover, it might still be suspicious of the West and have aggressive designs on its neighbors. In early 1942, G-2 had warned that a victorious Russia would be "certain" to dominate and "very likely" to communize its neighbors in Eastern Europe, the Middle East, and the Far East. "Independent action, imperialistic expansion, and communistic infiltration," it further stated, "must always be expected from the U.S.S.R." Such concerns were repeated in March and April.[4] By mid-1943 military intelligence was further asserting that Russia would delay intervention in the Far East until the last minute and would be guided "only by her own interests. Appeals to gratitude or to the spirit of the Alliance are unlikely to carry weight." Two months later the JIC repeated and amplified these earlier warnings by including as postwar Soviet goals "political hegemony in all European countries east of Germany and the Adriatic Sea"; influence in Germany and Western Europe; interest in the Dardanelles, northern Iran, and perhaps the Persian Gulf; and occupation of northern Manchuria and the southern half of Sakhalin Island should Moscow enter the war against Japan.[5]

Military planners were by no means blind to the dangers this situation could pose to postwar U.S. security, but given Russia's pivotal importance to the war effort and the inevitable expansion of its power should that effort be successful, they concluded that the only viable policy option was to make every effort to erase Soviet suspicion and hostility and to build close relations for the postwar era. As Major General James H. Burns of the President's Soviet Protocol Committee informed Hopkins in December 1942, because Russian defeat "might prevent us from defeating either Germany or Japan" and Allied victory would make Russia "one of the three most powerful countries in the world," good wartime and post-war relations with the Soviets constituted an essential policy objective. "We not only need Russia as a powerful and fighting ally in order to defeat Germany," he maintained, "but eventually we will also need her in a similar role to defeat Japan. And finally, we need her as a real friend and customer in the post-war world." To obtain these objectives Burns suggested a series of moves to improve Soviet-American relations, most notably a Roosevelt-Stalin summit conference, increased Lend-Lease shipments, sending one of the Joint Chiefs as well as a top-ranked ambassador to Moscow, and the offer of postwar aid and friendship to the Soviets.[6]

Eight months later, just before the QUADRANT Conference, Burns sent Hopkins a similar set of recommendations supported by extracts from an unsigned but "very high level United States military strategic estimate of Russia" that carefully noted and commented on Soviet power during and after the war. Partially reprinted in Robert Sherwood's 1950 biography of Hopkins, that estimate remains one of the best known and most widely quoted wartime military assessments of the USSR. "Russia," it bluntly stated "occupies a dominant position and is the decisive factor looking toward the defeat of the Axis in Europe." No future Anglo-American military operations would change this fact. Indeed, they would constitute "decidedly a *secondary*" front compared with the "main effort" in the East. "Without Russia in the war, the Axis cannot be defeated in Europe, and the position of the United Nations becomes precarious." Similarly, "Russia's post-war position in Europe will be a dominant one. With Germany crushed, there is no power in Europe to oppose her tremendous military forces." In this situation proper U.S. policy was "obvious": because Russia "is the decisive factor in the war, she must be given every assistance and every effort must be made to obtain her friendship. Likewise, since without question she will dominate Europe on the defeat of the Axis, it is even more essential to develop and maintain the most friendly relations with Russia." Such relations were also important to insure Soviet participation in the war against Japan. Indeed, the estimate emphasized, "*the most important factor the United States has to consider in relation to Russia is the prosecution of the war in the Pacific.* With Russia as an ally in the war against Japan, the war can be terminated in less time and at less expense in life and resources than if the reverse were the case. Should the war in the Pacific have to be carried on with an unfriendly or negative attitude on the part of Russia, the difficulties will be immeasurably increased and operations might become abortive."[7]

Such statements echoed presidential beliefs and policies regarding the Soviets, and given the positions of both Burns and Hopkins, these documents may very well have been merely military reassertions and amplifications of already established White House policy. It is interesting to note, however, that Roosevelt acted on each of Burns's recommendations *after* the general had submitted them. When efforts to convince Stalin to attend the Casablanca Conference failed, for example, the president suggested to a surprised Marshall during a January 7 meeting with the JCS that the army chief go to Moscow to bolster morale and reassure the Soviet leader, who "probably felt out of the picture" and had "a feeling of loneliness." Marshall could accomplish these goals by informing Stalin of the results of the Casablanca Conference, during which FDR expected to discuss a possible summer summit meeting, postwar disarmament, and "the advisability of informing Mr. Stalin that the United Nations were to continue on until they reach Berlin, and that their only terms would be unconditional surrender."[8]

Although he later dropped the idea of the Marshall journey, Roosevelt did indeed enunciate unconditional surrender at Casablanca. Throughout 1943 he also tried to convince Stalin to attend a summit conference and suggested, as had Burns, that it take place without Churchill. Simultaneously, he tried to replace the overly blunt U.S. ambassador in Moscow, former CNO Admiral William Standley, with the Russophilic former ambassador Joseph E. Davies. When health problems precluded Davies' appointment, the president selected W. Averell Harriman, who had helped negotiate the original Lend-Lease aid package to the USSR. Along with this appointment in the fall went an expanded U.S. Military Mission to Moscow and talk of postwar reconstruction as well as wartime military aid. And soon after QUADRANT, FDR paraphrased portions of Burns's August estimate in telling Francis Cardinal Spellman that Russia would "predominate" in postwar Europe, especially in Eastern Europe, and that while the results might be brutal, "the U.S. and Britain cannot fight the Russians."[9]

As with the 1940 Plan Dog memorandum, the 1942–43 military comments on the Soviet Union appear to have been designed to influence Roosevelt by pointing out to him the implications of his policies and the most appropriate actions to be taken to ensure their success, as well as to provide the armed forces with a clear statement of policy to guide their strategic planning. They also reflect fundamental military agreement with the cooperative policy toward the Soviets. Such conclusions are reinforced by the fact that Burns's memoranda appear to have been heavily influenced and his August strategic estimate perhaps written by an individual who had been directed to examine such broad policy issues and who had previously been quite willing to express policy dissent—Embick.

Although the authorship of Burns's strategic estimate remains undetermined, the document bears a strong resemblance to some previous JSSC assessments and apparent contacts between Embick and Burns. On January 2, for example, Burns noted as "General Embick's own statement of supply policy for Russia" the following sentence, which would reappear *verbatim* in many of Burns's memoranda:

"Russian continuance as a major factor in the war is of cardinal importance, and therefore it must be a basic factor in our strategy to provide her with the maximum amount of supplies that can be delivered to her ports." [10] Furthermore, the August estimate is strikingly similar to an extraordinarily secret set of instructions the JSSC produced the following month in response to a request for advice from General Deane, who was being appointed U.S. Military Observer at the forthcoming Moscow Foreign Ministers Conference and who would remain in Russia after that meeting to head the new U.S. Military Mission.

As forwarded to the JCS on September 18, those instructions directed Deane to inform the Russians of 1944 cross-channel plans and encourage them to enter the Far East war after German defeat. He was also to communicate confidentially to Hull the fact that continued Soviet participation in the war was crucial to the defeat of Germany and that if Moscow withdrew, Allied operations would "have to be restricted substantially" to the air campaign. If Russia did not withdraw, however, and if consequently Germany was defeated, Soviet power in the postwar world would be enormous. The JSSC bluntly concluded in this regard that "when Germany has been defeated, Russia will be in possession of a military machine that cannot be successfully challenged to the eastward of the Rhine and the Adriatic by any Power or combination of Powers." The JSSC also emphasized the importance of Russian participation in the war against Japan, noting that the outcome of this war was "of a concern to the United States at least as great as a similar outcome in Europe." [11] It concluded that a policy "aligned realistically with the military capabilities and interests of the United States" had to include as "cardinal factors" the following:

a. Frank recognition of the fact that the defeat of Germany is so dependent upon the continued full cooperation of Russia.

b. Acceptance of the fact that after that defeat Russia will be in a military position to impose whatever territorial settlements it desires in Central Europe and the Balkans.

c. The great importance to the United States of Russia's full participation in the war against Japan after the defeat of Germany as essential to the prompt and crushing defeat of Japan at far less cost to the United States and Great Britain. [12]

On September 21 the Joint Chiefs in closed session approved these instructions with only minor revisions but extraordinary secrecy provisions: they were to "be carried mentally and . . . the paper itself should not be taken from this country." [13]

The conclusions regarding postwar Soviet power within both these instructions and Burns's August estimate were probably related to recent and ongoing academic analyses for the military of long-term trends in international military power. In June, Edward Mead Earle and Harold Sprout of the Princeton Institute for Advanced Study completed a lengthy study for the Analysis Section of G-2 titled "The Changing Power Position of Great Britain as a Factor in the Defense Problem of the United States," which emphasized the enormous and "continuous decline" in British power that had been taking place "virtually unnoticed" for more than half a century. That decline had resulted not from military factors only, the G-2 section chief William S. Culbertson emphasized a few months later in forwarding this document to the State Department, but "also and quite as much" from "world population trends, new means of communication, advances in metallurgy and manufacturing technology, the uneven growth and spread of industrialization, changes in the structure and social policies of states, and such human factors as health, literacy, discipline, and morale."[14]

Specifically, Britain had suffered a severe relative economic decline as a result of the global spread of industrialization, the subsequent rise of new economic power centers, and an aging population. Simultaneously, its geopolitical position and naval mastery had been subverted by the rapid development of overland communication; the rise of U.S., German, and Japanese power; and such major technological changes as the submarine and the airplane. Nationalist rebellions within the empire and the shifting loyalty to the United States of the dominions had further weakened British power. British influence and its "habit of leadership" were still great, but they no longer bore a close relationship to British power. According to the study, "This is a situation full of potential danger for the United States." Washington could neither afford to follow a weakened British leadership nor "see Great Britain gravitate towards an exclusive association with Soviet Russia, that might eventually align the manpower and resources of Eurasia against us. Our interest demands that the United States, not Great Britain, become the stabilizing balance wheel of the world," with a continued Anglo-Soviet-American alliance or entente as "the strongest deterrent to the resurgency of Germany and Japan."[15]

Whether Embick read this document in 1943 or only later remains unclear.[16] He had previously examined some of these factors himself as they related to military power during the interwar years, however, and he apparently continued to do so.[17] By 1943 his conclusions paralleled those in the G-2 study. In October he discussed them with Marshall, to whom he then forwarded a 1941 memorandum on the influence of industrialization and aviation on military power and, in response to the army chief's specific request, an annex on the specific importance of steel.

The 1941 memorandum emphasized the ability of industrial and airpower to overcome traditional seapower and the consequent dramatic effect on "politico-military organization" and military strategy: projection of ground armies from one continent to another had become "far more difficult"; the world would be "segregated more distinctly than ever" into "distinct politico-military entities"; and empires based on long sea communications would no longer be possible. The 1943 steel annex was even more devastating regarding the future of British power. Labeling steel "the most fundamental basis of modern industry and hence of munitioning capacity," it carefully noted Britain's enormous relative decline in the production of this commodity: as late as 1870 it had produced more steel than the rest of the world combined, but by 1943 global production had increased fifteen-fold, whereas Britain's share had shrunk to 8 to 10 percent, a figure equaled by Japan and far surpassed by the United States, Germany, and Russia. The Russian increase of 300–500 percent and the Japanese of 400 percent in the last twenty years were the most dramatic, but Japan's production was totally dependent on raw material imports, whereas Soviet production was not. Nor was it even close to its full potential: reserves of coal and iron smaller than those in the United States would keep Soviet steel production below U.S. levels, Embick maintained, but not below the production of any other nation.[18]

Interestingly, a similar analysis by world-renowned geopolitican Sir Halford Mackinder had appeared in *Foreign Affairs* only a few months earlier. Russia, he pointed out in reemphasizing the power of controlling the Eurasian "heartland," had in 1938 produced more wheat, barley, oats, rye, sugar beets, and manganese than any other country, ranked second in oil production, was tied with the United States for first in iron production, possessed enough coal to supply the entire world for three hundred years, and was virtually self-sufficient. "All things considered," Mackinder predicted, "the conclusion is unavoidable that if the Soviet Union emerges from this war as conqueror of Germany, she must rank as the greatest land Power on the globe. Moreover, she will be the Power in the strategically strongest defensive position. The Heartland is the greatest natural fortress on earth. For the first time in history it is manned by a garrison sufficient both in number and quality."[19]

The future thus belonged to the emerging Russian and American superpowers, with British decline clear and unavoidable on the basis of economic and military factors. Although the JSSC would fully spell out the implications of these conclusions only in 1944,[20] its 1943 statements regarding the unchallengeable extension of postwar Russian power into Eastern and Central Europe and the need for friendly Soviet-American relations reflected their impact.

In line with those conclusions as enunciated in the instructions to Deane, during the fall of 1943 the JSSC also reiterated its earlier warnings against military operations in the eastern Mediterranean on the grounds they would arouse Russian suspicions and suck the United States into a revived Anglo-Russian conflict, and it pressed for recognition of Soviet wartime and postwar predominance in southeastern Europe. On September 5 the committee expressed to the JCS deep misgivings over any clandestine activities by the Office of Strategic Services (OSS) in this area without prior approval from the Russians. In its original instructions to Deane it stated that U.S. occupation forces after German defeat would be "limited to Western Europe and probably not extend to the Eastward of the Rhine Valley."[21] On October 28 the committee informed the JCS that Rumanian peace feelers should receive consideration only if addressed to Russia as well as to the United States and Britain. "Russia," it maintained, "has the primary interest in Rumania because not only of the Province of Bessarabia, of which she was deprived by the Versailles Treaty, but of the geographical position of Rumania vis-a-vis the Black Sea and the land approach to the Straits." Both the OPD and G-2 approved these conclusions and understood "that there is implicit in recommended action recognition that Russia is to have more or less a free hand in the Balkans." Simultaneously, the JSSC made clear that Russia also had the primary interest in possible Hungarian surrender, Finnish withdrawal from the war, and Turkish entry.[22]

To Leahy such conclusions were much too political for JCS consideration, despite the fact that the State Department had specifically requested JCS opinion on Rumanian surrender talks. Thus the JCS deleted from Deane's top-secret instructions the statement on U.S. occupation policies and revised the JSSC reply to State to read, "Any negotiations between the Rumanians and the Soviet Government are political matters and therefore not within the cognizance of the Joint Chiefs of Staff."[23]

Many planners joined Leahy in objecting to JSSC conclusions, but not on the grounds that they were too political. Rather, these officers felt that JSSC acceptance of enormous Soviet postwar influence in Europe was dangerous to U.S. security and that American strategy and policy should be revised so as to limit or take account of that influence as much as possible.

In this regard, the very arguments that the JSSC and Burns relied on to promote Soviet-American cooperation could be used to promote the opposite conclusion. Although Mackinder himself had emphasized the need for good relations with the Soviets to contain Germany and maintain world peace, for example, his 1943 statements about Russian control of the heartland could easily be interpreted so as to view the USSR as a mortal threat. So could those of the Yale geopolitician Nicholas John Spykman, who in 1942 had warned that "a Russian state from the Urals to the North Sea can be no great improvement over a German state from the North Sea to the Urals." If Eurasia could be organized and controlled by any power or group of powers, he explained, the smaller, far less populous, and strategically indefensible Western Hemisphere would be "politically and strategically encircled" and doomed. "Balanced power, not integrated power," thus constituted the key American interest.[24]

Walter Lippmann's *U.S. Foreign Policy: Shield of the Republic,* published in April 1943, similarly emphasized the historic relationship of American security to the balance of power and the consequent fact that the United States could not allow Hitler—or *any* potential foe—to control Western Europe. Like isolationism and pacifism, collective security was simply another one of the "mirages" Americans had accepted in the process of ignoring this fact. The Atlantic Ocean was not a frontier, Lippmann argued, but "the inland sea of a community of nations allied with one another by geography, history, and vital necessity." Given the much greater military potential of Eurasia over the Western Hemisphere, "the New World cannot afford to be isolated against the combined forces of the Old World."[25]

In this regard, if the Soviets were to emerge so dominant in Eastern and Central Europe at war's end, what would stop them from taking over Western Europe too and thus posing a mortal threat to U.S. security? Although Lippmann echoed Mackinder and Spykman in emphasizing the importance of continuing the Grand Alliance into the postwar era, he also warned that "we are at a decisive turning point in our relations with Russia." The historic friendship between the two nations, despite antagonistic ideologies, had been based on the existence of common enemies, but if Germany and Japan were "never again" to be "great powers of the first magnitude," then "Russian-American relations will no longer be controlled by the historic fact that each is for the other a potential friend in the rear of its enemies. Russia will, on the contrary, be the greatest power in the rear of our indispensable friends." The key question in Europe was thus "whether Russia will seek to extend her power westward into Europe in such a way that it threatens the security of the Atlantic states. The question in the Pacific is whether . . . the United States and Russia move towards rivalry or towards a common ground for understanding. The two questions are inseparable. . . . the crucial question of the epoch we are now entering is the relationship between Russia and the Atlantic Community."[26]

Whether any of the planners or the JCS actually read Mackinder and Spykman remains unclear, though they likely did, given both the subject matter and the growing links between the armed forces and academicians at Princeton and Yale symbolized by the Earle/Sprout study of British decline.[27] They certainly did read Lippmann's book, which became a best-seller and widely popularized an emerging "national security 'orthodoxy.'" It was published by popular magazines in condensed and even cartoon versions, in addition to the complete book form, and distributed to U.S. troops in a twenty-five-cent paperback edition.[28]

Two of the most notable and impressed readers were Stimson and King. The former recommended it to Hull and linked it to his belief that the country had been victimized by a "false history" and needed a "revolutionary effort in a new and correct education to build up a new and correct foreign policy," as well as to his previous conviction that this policy should continue "the same controls as have saved us during the war, namely, close association between the English-speaking countries."[29] King was so impressed that on July 21 he sent Lippmann a personal note of congratulations and thanks in which he asserted that if he could he would "oblige every American citizen to read" the book. Three days later he praised Lippmann in an off-the-record press meeting for having "done the country a great service" and for so well resolving a great "headache" of the navy in general and Naval War College in particular—"to determine what were our foreign policies" so as to be able to support and defend them. "We are grown up now," he continued, "and we have got to evolve a foreign policy and stick to it."[30]

Interestingly, however, King's reading of Lippmann did not lead him to an anti-Soviet position. To the contrary, he asserted at this meeting that Stalin did not want to take over all of Europe, that the Soviet leader would "out of a realistic appraisal of the situation" limit his acquisitions to the Baltic states and eastern Poland, and that he personally favored granting Russia its long-desired, warm-water access to the sea via internationalization of the Bosporus, Skagerrak, and Kattegat. No doubt related, the "essential plan" in Europe, he asserted, remained "to utilize Russia's geographical position and her manpower against Germany"—a restatement of his comments earlier in the year that Russia was "the key to European grand strategy" and would "do nine-tenths of the job of licking Germany." It was also a complement to Marshall's June conclusion that the Red Army was "probably the most important factor" permitting a reduction in planned army combat strength. Secretary of the Navy Frank Knox concurred in King's assessments, informing the press in October that the Russians would be anxious for peace at war's end but would insist on "defensible" boundaries (the Baltic states, eastern Poland, Balkan territory, and a warm-water outlet through the Bosporus) and that the United States could not prevent this "unless we are prepared to maintain a police force in Europe . . . and unless, also, we are prepared to fight Russia right now."[31]

The Confrontation Alternative

Many military planners objected to such conclusions, however, and the newly emerging geopolitics of national security provided them with a good rationale, if not the original motivation, to call instead for a dramatic alteration in U.S. policies toward Moscow. For some this translated into a tougher Lend-Lease policy. In

December 1942, if not earlier, the strongly anti-Soviet Wedemeyer warned of serious conflict with the Russians and recommended a "firm stand" against them. Two months later Arnold informed Marshall that he objected to sending Russia heavy bombers partially because of "growing uncertainty" within the military "as to where Russian successes might lead." Handy concurred and suggested decreasing aid to the Soviets on the grounds that "victory in the war will be meaningless unless we also win the peace. We must be strong enough at the peace table to cause our demands to be respected." The Policy Committee of the Strategy and Policy Group went so far as to recommend continued aid only if "Russia cooperates with us and takes us into her confidence."[32] From Moscow itself came continued complaints from U.S. officers of Soviet noncooperation and requests for retaliation through Lend-Lease, as well as attacks against the pro-Soviet Lend-Lease coordinator Colonel Faymonville. Within the JCS, strong opposition emerged to disclosing any radar or other sensitive information to Russia. Indeed, unlike their British counterparts, the U.S. armed forces until 1944 blocked the sharing of technical intelligence with the Soviets. Their stand was only reinforced by revelations of Soviet espionage in the Berkeley Radiation Laboratory, which Stimson labeled "very alarming" in a September memorandum to Roosevelt.[33]

For others, the probability of extensive postwar Soviet power and hostility necessitated an end to Britain's peripheral strategy. Throughout the spring and summer of 1943 numerous planners and members of the JCS warned that the combination of Soviet victories and relative Western inaction would lead to Russian domination not merely of Eastern but perhaps of all Europe. As early as January 16, King had stated in a JCS meeting that "unless the U.S. and Britain make some definite move toward the defeat of Germany, Russia will dominate the peace table." In August the AAF intelligence chief warned Arnold that unless Anglo-American forces invaded Europe before year's end, "we will merely sit on the sidelines while Russia decides the European politics."[34]

Such fears often merged with the military's anti-British sentiments. In the previously cited March 12, 1943, memorandum in which he warned that Britain might not want a total victory in the Pacific because of a desire to build up Japan as a counterweight to America, the former Navy League president Gardiner also warned that Russia might "dictate the terms of German surrender in Berlin long before Anglo-American forces get within really effective striking distance of that capital—whereupon the major problem of western Europe would be: How to halt the westward and southwestward drive of Russia?" Leahy, who the Soviets considered "bitterly unfriendly," according to Davies, circled that section of the letter, and in April Grew informed Gardiner that the admiral had read his "admirable exposition" with "much interest and with much advantage to his efforts to visualize a correct attitude for America to take at the present time, and in future negotiations with both our present enemies and present friends." Grew also sent the memorandum to Roosevelt and discussed it with him in June.[35]

Gardiner's letter was by no means the only such warning to reach FDR's desk in mid-1943. As previously noted, Stimson consistently reminded the president of possible Soviet anger and refusal to "share" the postwar world if British concepts continued to control Anglo-American strategy. Just as unfailingly, George H. Earle, U.S. naval attaché in Istanbul and former governor of Pennsylvania, cautioned the president about British and Russian expansion goals in the Balkans. In October he bluntly informed Roosevelt that the most important and "most difficult problem you will have to face in post war Europe will be Russia."[36] Former ambassador to Russia William C. Bullitt echoed similar anti-Soviet sentiments in a series of 1943 memoranda to the president and meetings with Leahy in which he called for both a tougher Lend-Lease policy and a dramatic strategic shift to check Soviet advances into the Balkans. Clearly in sympathy with the belief expressed by at least one high-ranking British officer that "to make friends with Stalin would be equivalent to making friends with a python," Bullitt warned the president that the Soviet leader was "a Caucasian bandit whose only thought when he got something for nothing was that the other fellow was an ass."[37]

Fears of postwar Soviet power and behavior also emerged in the Security Subcommittee of the State Department's Advisory Committee on Postwar Foreign Policy, strongly affecting its recommendations. Throughout 1942 and early 1943, army and navy representatives on the committee joined their civilian colleagues in expressing "apprehension" over future relations with Russia and in concluding that such apprehension precluded support for disarmament in Western Europe. As naval intelligence chief Admiral Harold C. Train noted in March 1943, "the shadow of doubt as to what Russia would do had hung over all the armaments discussions he had attended." An early draft summary of subcommittee views warned in this regard that no "realistic discussion" of future arms limitations was possible without "adequate assurance from Russia that she would not exploit the situation to her advantage." Subcommittee chair Norman O. Davis concurred, noting that any plan to disarm postwar France without prior knowledge of Soviet policy was "hazardous in the extreme," that Roosevelt agreed and had therefore changed his mind about French disarmament, that it was "necessary to have France a strong power as part of our own security," and that perhaps Germany should not be totally disarmed after its defeat. "This is the fundamental issue between Russia and the United States," he asserted in May 1943. "We must make it clear that arrangements in Western Europe vitally affect our security," and although future peace would require Allied collaboration, one of the "most important tasks" of the subcommittee must be to consider alternatives in case collaboration was not forthcoming.[38]

Unfortunately, the problems associated with any efforts to force greater Soviet cooperation, limit the extension of postwar Soviet power, or plan for postwar security if the Soviets proved uncooperative were close to insurmountable. Bullitt's proposal for a Balkan invasion to block Soviet expansion, an idea the planners perceived to be a key component of British strategy, promised military disaster or stalemate, the resulting delay of victory against Germany and Japan, and a series of equally disastrous domestic consequences. Such an invasion would also increase Soviet suspicions, perhaps to the point of a separate peace that would make the European war unwinnable and dramatically increase U.S. casualties in the war against Japan. Even the vehemently anti-Soviet Wedemeyer was thus forced to reject this option. As one State Department official concluded about Bullitt's Balkan strategy, "Our friends in the War Department tell us such an attempt would be sheer military fantasy" and that the Soviet Union could not be opposed in Eastern Europe if Germany was to be defeated; the "only way" to implement Bullitt's suggestion would thus be "by means of a coalition between the United States, United Kingdom, and the German military forces."[39] As for using Lend-Lease as a weapon to weaken the Soviets or to force them to be more cooperative, a proposal supported by many military planners as well as Bullitt but rejected by the White House, it also risked increased Russian suspicion and a possible separate peace.[40]

The possibility and disastrous consequences of such a chain of events were boldly highlighted during the spring and summer of 1943 when a series of disagreements with the Soviets, most notably over Poland and the delay of cross-channel operations to 1944, led to a virtual rupture in diplomatic relations and strong separate peace rumors. Those were strongly reinforced by Moscow's enormous military victory at Kursk in July and announcement of the formation of the Free Germany Committee composed of German communists and captured German officers. The details and relative seriousness of this separate peace threat remain unclear, but the panic it induced in Washington was quite evident—and overwhelming.[41] Once again the Joint Chiefs and their planners asserted that such a peace would end any hopes for victory in Europe and necessitate a refocusing on Japan. It would also result in the creation of an unbeatable and highly dangerous Russo-German bloc in control of Mackinder's "heartland" and, in the worst of circumstances, a communized Germany aligned with a hostile, strong and expansionist Soviet Union.[42]

This separate peace crisis also led the planners to recognize fully that a partial answer to what Warren Kimball has aptly labeled their key dilemma—"how to keep the Soviets in the fight without helping to create a monster that threatened American interests"[43]—lay in the cross-channel operations the Soviets were demanding for their continued participation and cooperation. In addition to less-ening its suspicion and hostility by fulfilling one of Russia's major wartime demands, such operations would place a large body of Anglo-American troops in Western and Central Europe, thereby making the Soviets more amenable to postwar compromise and checking their power if cooperation proved impossible. As was noted in one oss-originated jcs Memorandum for Information, while Moscow had made clear that this second front was "indispensable" to postwar cooperation, it was equally indispensable to make a policy of hostility "costly and unattractive" to the Soviets, give the West "an effective" bargaining position in Europe, and check postwar Soviet power if cooperation did not occur.[44]

In line with such reasoning, the jcs and their planners pressed throughout the spring and summer of 1943 not only for cross-channel operations at the earliest practicable date but also for contingency plans to place large numbers of troops in Western and Central Europe if Germany suddenly weakened or collapsed before the channel could be crossed. Marshall, Arnold, King, Hopkins, and Roosevelt expressed interest in such a plan and in being able, in FDR's words, "to get to Berlin as soon as did the Russians." Marshall put an interesting twist on this during the QUADRANT Conference by asking, as had the jic in July, "In the event of an overwhelming Russian success, would the Germans be likely to facilitate our entry into the country to repel the Russians?" The result was the approval at Quebec not only of the OVERLORD plan for a 1944 cross-channel assault but also the RANKIN plans for emergency reentry into Europe in the event of German weakening or collapse, with twenty-four to twenty-six divisions set aside for such a contingency.[45]

The Enigma

OVERLORD and RANKIN were indeed effective wartime plans to cover Soviet cooperation or hostility, but Security Subcommittee members were a good deal less successful in coming up with postwar policies for these contingencies. The problem was that they simply could not determine in 1943 what future Russian policy would be. Some signs pointed to postwar cooperation, especially if cross-channel operations took place as scheduled. Others pointed to hostility and a highly aggressive, expansionist foreign policy, whether in the traditional form of Czarist imperialism, a more contemporary form to spread communism and world revolution, or a combination of both. Hull considered Russia at this time a "complete sphinx" and Churchill "a riddle wrapped in a mystery inside an enigma." Such uncertainty foiled all efforts to formulate plans for postwar U.S. security. Furthermore, Russia's power at war's end would be so enormous that without its cooperation realistic postwar security arrangements would, in the words of Security Subcommittee member Admiral Arthur J. Hepburn, "be almost impossible."[46]

The subcommittee's response to this situation was to insist, in Davis's words, that "every effort be made to ascertain Russia's political and territorial ambitions and to work out a settlement satisfactory to all three powers" as soon as possible. Such a settlement was vital before German surrender not only to see if Russia would cooperate, all subcommittee members agreed, but also to limit the territory Stalin would control after the war. As Davis noted, "Some commitment was needed so that Russia would not be permitted to run loose." But while speed was essential in working out a settlement and trying to bind Russia, the subcommittee agreed that for the present the United States should continue to be friendly and cooperative. As Davis succinctly emphasized, Washington now "had no real alternative" to such a policy "because unless we reach some kind of understanding with Russia, we could not continue to make plans for postwar security arrangements. Once Russia's policy was made known . . . , we could then move ahead quickly in the elaboration of our own plans. Until then we could do very little."[47]

The JSSC's Russian proposals served as the military complement to this policy. The JSSC had concluded, as had Davis, that Washington presently had "no choice" but to continue the cooperative approach and minimize friction. The need for Soviet military power was too great to risk a rupture with a tougher policy; moreover, military realities meant Russia's postwar position in Europe would be unchallengeable no matter what operations were undertaken. To risk provoking or alienating the Russians further when they were so badly needed, when there was no effective way of stopping them, and when their primary postwar concerns in Eastern Europe did not directly affect U.S. security, seemed senseless, to put it mildly.

This approach made eminent military and diplomatic sense for the war itself. The problem was that postwar security planning could not await some future, hypothetical settlement with the Russians. By early 1943 a host of issues had arisen that made specific postwar planning by the military mandatory. Given the uncertain situation, such postwar planning would have to take into account the possibility of both Soviet cooperation and hostility. Cooperation would translate into plans for Allied, international security arrangements. Hostility would mean a unilateral U.S. security policy directed against Russia. Trained to expect the worst from other powers as a result of their *realpolitik* worldview, military planners led by the JSSC responded by giving lip service to international security proposals while emphasizing and developing a very muscular and extensive national security policy for the postwar era.

Early National and International Security Planning

The catalyst for this growing concern over postwar security policy was a December 28, 1942, memorandum from presidential naval aide McCrea informing Leahy that Roosevelt believed "we must keep in mind the peace negotiations and that he visualized some sort of international police force will come out of the war." Consequently, he wanted the JCS to prepare a study "to the end that when the peace negotiations are upon us we will be decided in our own minds where it is desired that 'International Police Force' air facilities be located; this plan to be without regard to current sovereignty."[48]

The Joint Chiefs originally assigned this task to the JPS, but numerous planners soon requested that the JSSC be authorized to undertake a much broader study emphasizing national as opposed to international and naval and commercial as well as military air requirements for the postwar era. Responding to such pleas, the JCS on February 9 canceled their directive to the JPS and referred the matter to the JSSC.[49] On that same date King informed Knox that the subject had "such extensive implications for the Navy" that it should undertake a separate study "with the particular object of recommending policies that the Navy should follow in its negotiations with other government departments and foreign governments." Knox concurred and directed the GB to prepare such a study as well as a separate one on retention of specific bases in the Pacific.[50]

Citing this GB work as well as studies being undertaken by an interdepartmental committee on postwar international aviation, the JSSC on March 6 requested a clarification and expansion of its own directive so that it could produce a study of "a post-war world wide system of air bases" for national as well as international use. Such a study, it recognized, would be "part of the broader subject of world wide military problems which will confront the Joint Chiefs of Staff as soon as the Axis power surrenders—and which, therefore, must be studied now in order that we may be fully prepared." Believing that this broader study would "develop into one of its most important and continuing duties," the JSSC proposed a logical sequence of future papers to define the problem and a method of procedure, to analyze postwar military problems, and to establish additional procedures for production of continued papers as needed.[51]

Once again Leahy objected to military study of what he considered "political" issues beyond JCS concern. The president's directive, he acidly reminded his JCS colleagues and the JSSC, had specifically used the term "international," not national, forces. Restrictive or not, that directive had to be followed. Furthermore, the JSSC members had no business concerning themselves with the commercial aspects of postwar air bases and "would be beyond their field to deal with any matters which had not a military significance."[52]

Leahy quickly found himself to be a minority of one. Willson, King, and the deputy army chief General Joseph McNarney emphasized the impossibility of separating postwar commercial from military use of air bases, with King drawing an analogy to "the many British coaling stations throughout the world for commercial use which eventually became of military importance." Willson also emphasized the JSSC view that any examination of bases for an international police force would "necessarily" require examination "from a point of view of national defense" and pointed out that the creation of an international force might not take place for six to ten years. King further noted that the presidential directive had been transmitted "by word of mouth" and might not consist of Roosevelt's actual words; Embick added that the State Department was also working on these issues and had already requested the military "slant." Under the impact of this verbal barrage, Leahy backed down and on March 9 acceded to a revised and expanded directive for the JSSC.[53]

The resulting JSSC study, completed only a week later, may well have fulfilled Leahy's worst fears. Labeled by William Roger Louis "the genesis of the Joint Chiefs' 'master plan' for a global security network,"[54] it emphasized national over international security preparations for the postwar era; the inseparability of commercial and military problems, especially in regard to aviation; and the fact that the entire question of air bases was but part of a broad series of postwar military problems that should be examined as a whole and from the viewpoints "of national defense, of prospective international military commitments and related national commercial interests." The JCS should therefore be represented on "important groups concerned with post-war planning, as may be necessary to insure that military considerations are integrated with political and economic considerations."[55]

The JSSC based its specific recommendations on the widely held belief, already discussed and analyzed in the Security Subcommittee, that there would be a substantial interim between German surrender and the establishment of any postwar international organization.[56] During that period, the Allies would have to complete the war against Japan while occupying Europe and then maintain world peace as the international organization was being created. They would do so by dividing the world into three areas of responsibility: the Western Hemisphere for the United States; Europe, Africa, and the Middle East for England and Russia; and the Far East for the three of them and China. The United States would obviously have to join its allies in occupying, disarming, and reconstructing Europe as well as be "on guard against post-war tendencies toward the spread of communism," but its concern with the Pacific war and its postwar interests called for limiting military commitments as much as possible to the Western Hemisphere and the Far East.

While emphasizing such limitations, the JSSC insisted that postwar the United States possess wide-ranging air bases in the Atlantic, the Caribbean, Latin America, the Pacific, Asia, and perhaps even Africa and the Middle East, in "the interests of national security and the maintenance of the Monroe Doctrine" as well as for future "international military purposes and U.S. commercial interests." Such factors could not be separated. Furthermore, the JSSC admitted, its assumptions about the future might be incorrect or overly optimistic. Those assumptions had included not only military victory but also the maintenance of Allied solidarity and a desire to cooperate. More pessimistic possibilities included "exhaustion of the will to struggle for a better world, . . . critical economic disturbance, . . . resurgent nationalism, . . . a spread of communism," and "disagreement and strife among the Allies." The JSSC's more optimistic assumptions represented "reasonable expectations," yet the "less favorable" ones could not be overlooked and would need to be studied further.[57]

Such caution translated into insistence that national defense take priority because international organization might not work. Extensive postwar air bases would be "essential" in such a situation, and if international organization did occur the bases could then be transferred to an international authority. Any international police force would be regional in character, however, which meant that U.S. forces would remain primarily responsible for these bases even within an international system. Washington, the JSSC concluded, should therefore begin negotiations immediately to obtain these bases so as to insure its own security and postwar interests as well as to "profit by our present strong position and capitalize on our investments."[58]

Leahy was not pleased. While willing to accept the JSSC's emphasis on national over international security, he objected to mention of the Monroe Doctrine and to the committee's recommendations on "non-military matters with reference to the postwar period." The Joint Chiefs, he warned his colleagues on March 23, "were on dangerous ground when they propose the distribution of post-war aviation facilities from a commercial viewpoint." But Arnold, King, and Willson countered again that the issues could not be separated, with Arnold noting that the British were already "tying post-war commercial matters with military aviation problems." Leahy thereupon agreed to a compromise whereby the Monroe Doctrine would be retained and the JSSC would delete all reference to commercial aviation, provided it "was understood that there is a definite tie between commercial aviation and military aviation, and that the Joint Chiefs of Staff recognize this fact." The JCS then directed the JSSC to revise its study accordingly.[59]

The JCS also directed the JSSC to prepare an additional paper on specific localities where air bases for both an international police force and "national defense" would be necessary. On April 10 it did so by recommending forty-seven specific oceanic base sites in the Atlantic, Caribbean, and Pacific which either were or should be under U.S. control "for national defense and the maintenance of United States interests." Included in the Pacific were sites in the former German islands mandated to Japan after World War I. Establishment of U.S. sovereignty or long-term rights over these islands and all the sites mentioned, the committee recommended, should be an American war aim.[60]

These papers were not prepared in isolation. The JSSC consulted with State as well as War and Navy Department representatives, and its assumptions regarding postwar areas of responsibility and national over international security echoed those being voiced at the same time by the president, members of the Advisory Committee on Postwar Foreign Policy, and numerous military planners.[61] Many of those planners were willing to go much further than the JSSC, however, in explicitly rejecting the possibility of postwar Allied cooperation and an international police force and in specifying national security policies and requirements as well as potential postwar enemies. This occurred despite what Perry McCoy Smith has described as "the unwritten but widely understood rule that no present ally would be specifically identified as a potential enemy."[62]

Throughout 1942 and early 1943 the Security Subcommittee of the Postwar Foreign Policy Advisory Committee had addressed many of the issues raised by the JSSC and reached similar conclusions regarding Allied division of the world before any international organization, the need to plan for the possibility of postwar Allied conflict as well as cooperation, and the importance of national rather than international security measures. The army intelligence chief General George V. Strong and Admiral Harold C. Train, his counterpart in the navy, had emphasized this latter point, speaking out strongly against placing any faith in what they labeled an "unrealistic" international force. For Strong, future peace would depend not on such a force or postwar Allied cooperation but on U.S. willingness to dominate the world both in its own interests and those of world peace. As early as May 1942 he had informed his committee colleagues, in reply to a statement regarding the possible disappearance of the British Empire and the fact that America might "have to take its place," that the United States "must cultivate a mental attitude which will enable us to impose our own terms, amounting to perhaps a pax Americana. If we are to have a stable peace, selfish national interests must be disregarded to a greater extent than at any previous peace conference, and this can be effected only if the United States adopts a tough, hard-boiled attitude in dealing with its allies at the conference."[63]

Within the OPD, the Strategy and Policy Group found all the JSSC assumptions about the postwar world to be sound save one—the "thought that peace will be lasting and that there will never be another war." Clearly linked to an international police force, this thought was "most fraught with danger to our national security—more dangerous by far than any lack of bases or Peace Congress," for it would reinforce the expected public insistence on immediate demobilization after Axis defeat and leave the United States defenseless in the postwar world. As the S&P explained:

We say we are fighting for *peace* but so is the Axis. In reality, we are fighting for *our* peace. Our peace policies are also designed to maintain *our* peace. Our peace and military policy, therefore, have the same purpose. While it is manifestly to our advantage to attempt to maintain this peace for the maximum time, by all possible means (including International Police Force), it is of course utter folly to assume we can do so indefinitely. The thought that there will be a lasting peace leads wishful thinkers naturally to the conclusion that no military force is necessary for national defense.

History has demonstrated that U.S. public opinion will swing sharply after the war, and in a few years the military establishments will have great difficulty in obtaining money from Congress to maintain themselves. Any expressions made now in support of the idea that peace will *last* will boomerang to the detriment of national security in the postwar world. Our present planning and contacts with non-military agencies in postwar matters must take full cognizance of the probable postwar trend of opinion.[64]

In light of these facts and "since national security is the primary postwar responsibility of the JCS," the S&P maintained, "planning and support on postwar measures must emphasize the importance of national defense *over* the importance of an international police force." The JCS must also "exercise due caution that the idea of an international police force does not develop as a substitution for national defense"; plans should be prepared to counter any postwar insistence on drastic reduction in U.S. defense or any thought "that peace may last or that an International Police Force assures it."[65]

The Strategy and Policy Group agreed that an international force would contribute to U.S. security, but it did so only "with reservations." Any international bases not "dominated" by the United States could jeopardize national security because they might "be seized by an aggressive enemy after we have lapsed into our traditional postwar pacifist policies." A revived Germany and Japan were apparently not the major concerns in this regard. "We have no assurance that our present military allies will remain so," it stated. "If they dominate a base it could well be used against us. Italy was our ally 25 years ago as was Japan." The United States should therefore "control all bases essential to our national security."[66]

Although the S&P saw Britain and Russia as potential enemies, Moscow seemed to be of more concern. The group noted that the JSSC's forty-seven base sites did not provide any protection against an attack from the north and therefore recommended inclusion of additional bases in the Greenland–Iceland–North Canada area. It also suggested liaison with the State Department "on a high level" to implement JCS policies, cautioning on April 13 that "*adequate guidance is not given by merely furnishing the State Department with written recommendations* as to the policy it should follow on military matters." Rather, the JSSC should be designated to advise State on "*all* post-war agreements which have a bearing on our future security," and a new committee established to advise State on all postwar matters.[67] By the fall of 1943, some S&P members were questioning a War Department assumption for industrial mobilization purposes that no power or combination of powers would be strong enough to endanger the nation for five years. "There is apparently some question in people's minds, other than G-2," the future S&P chief General George A. Lincoln reported on October 8, "as to whether we can safely count on Russia keeping the peace with the United States for five years."[68]

One focal point of such concern was the AAF. In April its Planning Section chief concluded that U.S. goals after German defeat would require a massive air force of 273 groups with 45,000 tactical aircraft. Although defeating Japan would be one of this force's primary purposes, checking Soviet power was clearly another. "Unless Great Britain and the United States are in a position to join her in doing so," he warned, "Russia may have sufficient provocation to alone occupy and assume control of not only all of Germany, but all of Central and Eastern Europe," after which she might "amend her recently announced intentions as to territorial expansion." Moreover, the strength and mobility of U.S. armed forces relative to those of its allies and in position "to immediately support our views expressed at the peace table will have much to do with the reception which those views receive." Because U.S. ground forces remaining in Europe after German defeat would be smaller than those of Britain or Russia, only airpower could compensate and provide Washington with sufficient bargaining leverage. Two hundred and seventy-three groups would provide such leverage, as well as sufficient forces to defeat Japan, offset Russian ground forces, and provide the U.S. contingent for any international police force that might develop.[69]

Navy planners were equally if not more concerned with these issues. On March 20 the GB responded to Knox's directives with a postwar base study whose wide-ranging conclusions it justified on the basis of the inseparability of national from international, commercial from strategic, and air from naval and ground considerations. Echoing the conclusions of the JSSC and the Security Subcommittee, the board maintained that the creation of a viable international organization would take many years and that in the interim peace would have to be maintained by Allied power. Furthermore, bases required by any international police force would be the same as those required by a "simpler combination" within the present alliance, and the United States should guard against overcommitment to "world-wide agreements, the practicality of which may turn out to be slight or non-existent." The navy needed to "retain a background of realism in all negotiations with other Government Departments, as well as with Foreign Governments."[70]

Echoing the conclusions already reached by the Security Subcommittee, the board emphasized the critical importance of continued Allied cooperation in this interim period, contending that international organization could succeed only if "preceded by, and built upon, a realistic working agreement between these four great powers." It was therefore "highly important" that a four-power accord on postwar policies "be effected without undue delay." As a first step the GB recommended negotiations with the British for division of postwar oceanic responsibility on the basis of U.S. control of the Atlantic west of twenty-five degrees west longitude and the entire Pacific save for specific areas under British or Dutch control, and additional negotiations as needed to obtain rights in key areas for air bases, naval bases, and commercial purposes "as may be desired."[71]

In determining these sites, however, the board ranged far beyond the stated U.S. spheres of responsibility. By its plan, U.S. bases would extend from Hawaii to the shores of China, throughout the Caribbean, along the Canadian and West African coasts, and onto Greenland and Iceland. On March 27 and April 6 it delivered two supplementary reports that detailed and rationalized the numerous changes in sovereignty such a plan would entail in the Pacific. These changes involved not only the Mandated Islands but also British and French possessions. Because all these islands were of value only on strategic grounds, the GB claimed, transfer of sovereignty to the United States "cannot constitute territorial aggrandizement" in violation of the Atlantic Charter.[72] King was even more blunt during a July 24 off-the-record meeting with the press, asserting that "after this war, whether we are criticized for imperialism or not, we have got to take and run the Mandated Islands, and perhaps even the Solomons. We have got to dominate the Pacific. . . . We are in a world in which people play for keeps, and if we intend to survive as a great power we have got to take care of ourselves."[73]

Such logic and rationalizations were hardly the monopoly of the armed forces. Their arguments and conclusions regarding postwar U.S. base requirements and their underlying concern with the Soviet Union bore a striking resemblance to the arguments and concerns of the geopoliticians and realist writers previously noted, particularly Spykman. In his major 1942 work, *America's Strategy in World Politics*, Spykman had labeled collective security a "pious fraud," advising Americans to place their faith instead in the balance of power. An untimely death in June 1943 at age forty-nine prevented completion of his planned second volume, but in late 1942 he had delivered a major lecture on the security position of the United States which constituted the basis of that volume and which his Yale colleagues would edit and publish in 1944. Attacking Mackinder's emphasis on the "heartland," the conflict between British seapower and Russian land power, and the centrality of Eastern Europe, Spykman offered an alternative focus on control of the Eurasian "rimlands" as the key to future U.S. security, with a major emphasis on control of bases along those rimlands for logistics, the projection of airpower, and an appropriate linkage of air-, sea-, and land power. He also emphasized once again, as he had in the 1942 volume, the U.S. need for Continental allies and pointedly noted that "as long as she does not herself seek to establish hegemony over the European rimland, the Soviet Union will be the most effective continental base for the enforcement of the peace." But whether she did seek such hegemony or not, the United States would need to secure the rimland by obtaining extensive bases in the Atlantic and Pacific, with the Mandated Islands and the Philippines as "a minimum arrangement" in the Pacific. Acquisition of such bases, he contended, as had the GB, "would not be a question of imperialistic expansion, but the necessary establishment of a balancing power in certain strategic areas."[74]

As OVERLORD and RANKIN were designed to promote good Soviet-American relations while protecting U.S. interests in case such good relations did not occur, so these plans for an enormous postwar base system irregardless of sovereignty were designed to promote a cooperative international postwar order and simultaneously protect the United States against a hegemonic and hostile USSR—or any other threatening power—should a cooperative order not occur. All such plans now involved an enormous overseas extension of U.S. power in the name of defense against aggression, and interestingly, all could be executed only at the expense of the interests of a rapidly declining and indefensible British Empire.

As early as the spring of 1942, Smith and Dykes had expressed fear of a "very militaristic and imperialistic spirit developing in America as a result of the war" which London would "have to face." In September, a few months before his untimely death, Dykes had admitted that the British would "have a hard job standing up against US imperialism and sentimentalism which in fact will go hand in hand against British interests."[75] One could argue that these naval and academic rationalizations of what was in fact an assault on British imperial possessions, combined with the simultaneous assault on British Mediterranean strategy, constituted the realization of this fear.

In 1942–43 the State Department had steered fairly clear of the strategic disputes with Britain. Postwar bases and sovereignty changes were another matter entirely, however, and here it quickly disagreed with the navy's rationalizations for acquiring territory. It also disagreed with the entire direction of military thinking on the issue. The result would be another major confrontation between the department and the armed forces over politico-military coordination and U.S. national policies.

Civil-Military Coordination and Conflict,
February 1942–November 1943

On one level, Pearl Harbor ended the conflicts between the armed forces and the State Department. With the United States a full-scale belligerent, State ceased to have or desire any role in determining the deployment of U.S. forces for deterrent purposes—deterrence having obviously failed—or in the definition of policy. Wartime policy was clear and understood by all from December 7 onward, even though Roosevelt would not enunciate it until early 1943: total military victory over the Axis in conjunction with the Allies until unconditional surrender had been obtained.

Contact between the armed services and the State Department did not suddenly cease after December 7, however. It actually increased due to the need for co-ordination on numerous politico-military issues that arose throughout the war. Consequently, the army and navy staffs maintained close and direct contact with State, and foreign service personnel worked with U.S. officers in virtually all major theaters of operation. But Roosevelt's refusal to consult with the department on wartime policy issues, combined with the sharp dichotomy Hull continued to maintain between war and peace, kept these contacts low-level and one-way. Thus during the war, the State Department became, in the words of Ernest May, "almost an auxiliary arm of the military services."[1] Most telling was that Hull did not accompany Roosevelt to a single summit conference during the war, whereas the Joint Chiefs accompanied him to all of them. Nor did Leahy put Hull on the distribution list to receive copies of JCS records from those conferences or even agree to give him the Casablanca minutes after he specifically requested them.[2]

While State was clearly subordinate to the armed forces regarding specific diplomatic issues relevant to the military conduct of the war, broader postwar issues were another matter—especially issues of international organization and security. These Hull made the focal point of departmental activity during the war, with the pivotal Advisory Committee on Postwar Foreign Policy beginning to operate as early as February 1942. From their earliest meetings, members of this committee realized the need for some military input into their planning process and invited armed forces participation. They were far from pleased with what they received, however, and by 1943 a new series of civil-military confrontations had begun.

The Armed Forces versus the State Department—Again

On February 21, 1942, Welles suggested the addition of army and navy representatives to the Security Subcommittee of the Advisory Committee. The subcommittee chair Norman O. Davis, president of the Council on Foreign Relations and chairman of the American Red Cross, as well as a former undersecretary of state, "heartily concurred" with this "necessary and desirable" proposal and suggested that an AAF representative also be added. The problem, he realized, would be how to get active officers in wartime. Welles then suggested using retired officers instead, with Embick as a prime example of how valuable such individuals could be, and he promised to discuss the matter with Marshall and Stark.[3]

Embick would indeed join the subcommittee, but not for another year. Davis apparently had his own ideas as to which officers should serve, and they were active as well as high-ranking individuals who had had, in the words of the official department history, "unusual experience with international developments relating to security in the years between the two wars." On April 15 he nominated U.S. Army intelligence chief and former WPD head Major General George V. Strong, who like Davis had attended numerous interwar arms limitation conferences and had been assigned to the State Department from 1932 to 1935, and Admiral Arthur J. Hepburn, another veteran of the arms limitation conferences who was presently a member of the GB and would become its chair in November. The subcommittee and War Department approved, and on April 29 the two attended their first meeting. They were soon joined by numerous technical experts and alternates, most notably naval intelligence chief Rear Admiral Harold C. Train. By December 1942 two additional officers had been assigned to the subordinate Security Technical Committee: Colonel James Olive of G-2 and Captain H. L. Pence of the navy's new Division of Occupied Areas. Then in March 1943 the three JSSC members joined the Security Subcommittee as representatives of the JCS.[4]

During its brief, eighteen-month tenure, the subcommittee produced a large volume of important work. It discussed unconditional surrender months before Roosevelt enunciated the policy, prepared the basic Axis surrender and occupation policies, codrafted key documents dealing with Great Power collaboration after Axis surrender, and formulated basic principles about a proposed international police force and postwar limitation and control of national armaments.[5] Despite these achievements, members of the State Department soon became quite upset with the subcommittee—particularly with its military members.

To an extent these feelings were based on what took place in the subordinate Security Technical Committee, where Pence's often outrageous comments made him a virtual caricature of the uninformed and opinionated military "bull" in State's china shop. Astounding his committee colleagues, the previously retired and now recalled naval captain suggested that Germany was America's "natural" ally, that it was "difficult for him to realize that Russia was today an ally," that Italy should be heavily punished and "taught a lesson," and that Japan should not be allowed to surrender until "nearly one hundred percent" of its population had been destroyed. His rationale for this last suggestion was that the Japanese were "international bandits" who "had accepted Western civilization only recently and should not be dealt with as civilized human beings" and that "it was a question of which race was to survive, and white civilization was at stake." He therefore favored "the almost total elimination of the Japanese as a race. We should kill them before they kill us." When committee chair Grayson Kirk of Columbia University pointed out with tongue at least partially in cheek that such a policy might not be adopted by the United States, Pence replied that this was "because there were not enough naval officers in the world." With classic understatement a 1943 departmental memorandum labeled Pence "a man of strong opinions and prejudices" who was "rather weak in the kind of competence desired" but who had made "a very active contribution" to the committee "within his limitations."[6]

Pence was an exception in an otherwise highly qualified pool of senior officers, however, and by no means the main source of concern. Rather, it was the very high quality of the other officers, as well as their growing numbers and influence, that troubled the department. By 1943 they appeared to be dominating the policymaking process within the Security Subcommittee and, in light of the JSSC and Navy base studies, the government as a whole. This was not what State had had in mind when it first requested military representation, and on April 8, 1943, subcommittee executive secretary Harley Notter complained bitterly to Leo Pasvolsky, special assistant to Hull and the full committee's executive director, about the "undue domination" exercised by the military representatives. Strong in particular, "a forceful and well-informed person," had taken and kept the initiative at most of the meetings, labeling any international police force unrealistic and proposing not only the surrender terms for the Axis but also military control of the ensuing occupation, extensive postwar bases in the Pacific, and the previously mentioned "tough, hard-boiled attitude" in dealing with allies at the peace conference, even if this amounted to a "pax Americana." The United States "could of course pay lip service to the United Nations," he had admitted, but at war's end it "will be in the driver's seat." The general's close friend Admiral Train had supported him as expected, but so had Davis, and when Hepburn attended the meetings, Notter complained, the weight of military opinion "overwhelms" civilian views. To make matters worse, Davis had unilaterally arranged for an air officer to join the subcommittee, invited the entire JSSC rather than one member, and changed the subcommittee's scheduled meeting time and day of the week so as not to conflict with the JSSC schedule! Thus the military representatives now outnumbered as well as outargued and dominated the civilians on the subcommittee.[7]

Notter insisted that the situation had become intolerable, for the State Department was "the civilian branch of Government charged under the President with the formation and conduct of foreign policy," and departmental views based on the "long perspective" were "sounder than those of the armed forces, which are concentrated more on immediate advantages and needs." To make matters worse, this military-dominated group was overstepping its bounds by acting as a "policy-forming committee rather than a body for exploration of security subjects."[8]

Notter would have been even more upset had he been able to read military correspondence on the issue. For whereas he and his colleagues found the military representatives usurping their functions, assuming unacceptable powers, and forcing unsound conclusions on the subcommittee, the armed forces had concluded that State was usurping military prerogatives by even discussing postwar bases, as well as promoting unrealistic, dangerous ideas concerning a postwar international police force.

The military began the war extremely bitter over what it considered to be State Department refusal to heed its views, especially in regard to the Pacific in 1941. While service and congressional boards of inquiry would place the blame for Pearl Harbor primarily on the local commanders, many officers saw Hull and his associates as the real culprits. As noted in Chapter 6, army staff members derisively referred to the war against Japan as "Hornbeck's war." Their anger was not limited to one person, however, or the events of a single year. State's belligerency in 1941 had been preceded by refusal to block Japanese acquisition of German islands in the Pacific in 1919 as the navy had desired or to modify ensuing arms limitation agreements in line with naval recommendations in the 1920s and 1930s. Military warnings, pleas, and recommendations had largely been ignored throughout the interwar years, not simply in 1941. Given this past history, many planners concluded that State had in effect precipitated a war for which it had refused to allow the armed forces to prepare and that it must not be allowed to meddle with security arrangements in the Pacific again.

The Joint Chiefs' suspicions of a repeat performance had probably first been aroused in September 1942, when Davis had requested JCS views on what would become one of the most divisive civil-military issues of the war: disposition of Japanese-controlled islands in the Pacific, especially the former German islands mandated to Tokyo by the League of Nations. In response Leahy had informed him of JCS insistence that Japan be deprived of these and all other islands below thirty degrees north latitude, with the possible exception of the Ryukyus. A September 22 tentative statement of subcommittee conclusions had concurred, with members noting that the United States "should not commit itself as to the ultimate disposition of any territory suitable for air or naval bases until the relevant strategic considerations have been carefully examined." Nevertheless, the armed forces could not have been pleased to see civilians discussing such issues again. Nor were they pleased with the subcommittee's emphasis on an international police force and, with it, collective security. Indeed, the spring 1943 JSSC and navy proposals for an extensive overseas base system in many ways constituted an alternative approach, military statements to the contrary notwithstanding. As an April Military Intelligence report bluntly stated, "Collective security is not a substitute for power."[9]

Former CNO Admiral William V. Pratt clearly verbalized military beliefs on these issues in a handwritten April 10 letter to King after participating in a Council on Foreign Relations study group. The State Department, Pratt feared, was trying to take control of military matters such as the postwar base issue much as it had attempted to "take charge" of military matters belonging to the armed forces after the last war—and with equally disastrous results. It was also pressing for an international police force, which he had told the group was "visionary" and "just a pipe dream." He had further warned that the navy would fight "to the last ditch to prevent the denationalization" of any U.S. forces for this purpose and would demand that the Mandated Islands be "under sole U.S. control." The Pacific, he insisted, was "our baby."[10]

Such beliefs and fears played a major role in the decision to place JSSC members on the Security Subcommittee. In its March 15 postwar base study the JSSC had itself called for such representation, and within the next few days its members moved to initiate it.[11] In an April 14 reply to Pratt, King was quite blunt that this initiative had been approved if not ordered by the Joint Chiefs, and he proceeded to explain why: the State Department as a whole and the subcommittee specifically were concerning themselves with postwar military problems "on an unrealistic basis," and the subcommittee had "consistently shown signs of getting beyond its depth in military matters." Sketching out the recently stated JSSC assumptions about the postwar world, King also noted that the "practicability" of an international police force was "open to serious question" and that the JCS planned to approach the problem of postwar security "from the point of view first of national defense, secondly international military requirements, and thirdly, our national commercial interests, particularly as regards air."[12]

King, Pratt, and the JSSC were far from alone in such views. A consensus existed within the armed forces on the need for an extensive overseas base system that would include control of the Mandated Islands and the entire Pacific, a belief that State had no right to oppose this consensus or even to discuss the issue, and insistence that postwar security needed to be based on national rather than international forces. The armed forces also agreed that memoranda were insufficient to keep State "in line." As the s&p had asserted in calling for the jssc to "advise" State on all postwar issues, "*Adequate guidance is not given by merely furnishing the State Department with written recommendations as to the policy it should follow on military matters.*" [13] The jssc, in short, was to act not merely as adviser to State on military matters and liaison to keep it and the jcs informed of one another's activities but also as "watchdog" to make sure its members did stay "in line" and that the jcs knew if they did not.

In April Welles obtained firsthand knowledge of the armed forces' adamancy on these issues. Perhaps responding to Notter's complaints, he temporarily combined the Security Subcommittee with his own Political Subcommittee, thereby enabling him to bypass Davis by chairing the ensuing sessions and, in the process, to disagree with many of the armed forces' conclusions. This did not silence Strong, however, who often spoke for all the military members and sharply defended their point of view. Particularly noteworthy was the ensuing confrontation over international police *powers* as opposed to the actual force, with Welles asserting that Big Four domination in the subcommittee proposals was "too blatant" and would make "the small states protectorates of the four Great Powers" by requiring them to give up resources and territory for bases—one result of which would be to allow "Russia alone to exercise police power in Eastern Europe." When he proposed an alternative draft, Strong replied for the military that it overthrew all previous thinking and was unacceptable. At one point Welles specifically had to request *non*military views on an issue, only to be met by another verbal salvo from Strong and Hepburn. On another occasion his desire for agreements to bind the Soviets met with military refusal on the premise that such agreements would also bind the jcs. [14]

While such bureaucratic infighting took place within the committee, the armed forces moved to outflank and bypass State by negotiating the issues of postwar bases and national versus international forces directly with the president, who was expressing to the press agreement with the armed forces' overall approach to the postwar world and to the Allies. [15] As early as March 10, Knox had informed Roosevelt of the GB postwar base studies in progress. He suggested a bilateral "understanding" with the British whereby both powers would make their bases available to each other in the postwar world and London would support U.S. possession of both the Mandated Islands in the Pacific and a base in Northwest Africa. Knox made clear that he well understood the objections to such "pre-armistice understandings," but he insisted that they were now warranted by the gravity of the issues involved as well as the fact that "we can get those concessions out of England far more readily and easily now than when the war is over when the British needs and reliance upon us becomes less." [16]

Two days later Roosevelt told Knox to "do nothing further" on the subject of negotiations with the British, but not because he objected to them. Rather, he wished to handle such negotiations personally and on a broader basis than suggested. The British, he noted, "would be delighted" to confine the talks to the Mandated Islands, but he himself was "anxious" to expand them so as to cover all Pacific islands.[17]

Throughout the spring and summer, Roosevelt exhibited intense interest in the subject and in receiving specific military recommendations. In a March 28 discussion of postwar international organization with British ambassador Lord Halifax he specifically mentioned U.S.-controlled bases in Dakar, the Marquesas, and the Tuamotu Islands. At an April 12 luncheon he discussed postwar security with King and made clear his desire for a meeting with a member of the JSSC. The following day, the CNO informed his JCS colleagues that the president "was becoming increasingly interested" in postwar bases and would want to receive army and navy views "in the near future"; under his prodding the Joint Chiefs directed the JSSC to prepare a letter for Roosevelt summarizing their conclusions to date. Then in June the president specifically requested the GB conclusions on air routes and naval bases in the Pacific.[18]

On June 19 Knox sent the president the GB studies on a postwar global base system, which formed, as William Roger Louis has noted, "a blueprint for transforming most of the Pacific into an American lake." [19] Roosevelt read them with "great interest" but replied on June 30 that the "sweeping changes in sovereignty recommended by the Board may not be attainable, and, from an economic point of view, all of the acquisitions recommended may not be desirable." He then clarified, however, that his comments should not be construed as a negative reply to the board's recommendations; rather, they led to the conclusion that the navy should be more specific as to which islands would be particularly valuable, especially for commercial air purposes, and that an investigating team led by Admiral Richard E. Byrd should be sent into the Pacific for this purpose. In August Knox acted on this proposal. Meanwhile, Roosevelt continued to correspond with him and to press the GB to look at additional islands and routes in the Pacific.[20]

The navy was not alone in its 1943 focus on specifying and beginning negotiations to establish an extensive postwar base system. General John Hull of the OPD, Assistant Secretary of War Robert A. Lovett, and AAF chief Arnold and his planners expressed concern during this time over the connection between these issues and the State Department's negotiations with Britain regarding postwar international aviation. They also expressed deep concern over the direction of State's thinking on these issues, and they pressed for priority to military over commercial considerations and for using the negotiations to obtain British agreement to U.S. establishment of specific postwar military bases and air rights around the globe. "Something must be done, and done promptly," Arnold insisted in early August, "to protect our vital interests in this field." The armed forces also urged the State Department once again to recognize that "any American policy of cooperation may fail to bring about cooperation on the part of other nations" and that no agreement should be signed delegating to an international agency authority to determine postwar air routes and facilities needed for U.S. security.[21]

State's negotiations with Britain spurred the armed forces to define their specific requirements as soon as possible so as not to be bypassed and to press them on the department and London. The resulting statements focused once again on the Mandated Islands and may have influenced the jssc's nearly simultaneous endorsement of a major Central Pacific offensive through them. "To insure a continuing peace after the war," the s&p stated, "the U.S. should acquire or control all Japanese owned or mandated islands in the North and Central Pacific."[22]

Nor was that all. In March Lovett specifically warned against "letting the starry-eyed boys who believe that each citizen should be furnished a quart of milk a day free, and that all pay envelopes should contain the same amount of money; and the other group of theorists who wear black Homburg hats, give away the birthright of the United States." By September the planners had informed State that London should be told of the entire global system of bases they were considering and that negotiations should begin at once for their acquisition.[23]

Postwar Policies and Demobilization Planning

By this time the issues of postwar bases and security had become interwoven, as the jssc had predicted, with postwar military requirements and demobilization. Study of these latter issues necessitated making assumptions about national policies and the international situation in the postwar era, and on March 15, the same date the jssc enunciated to the jcs its assumptions about these matters, an army subcommittee on postwar military requirements repeated and amplified them— and the armed forces' rationale for dealing with such issues. "Military commanders and strategists do not determine national policy," it admitted, "but it is their duty to estimate public sentiment and to so guide the military program that forces are at hand to effectuate this policy." Echoing the jssc, the subcommittee divided the future into three periods focusing on Axis defeat, armistice and peace negotiations, and the postwar peace treaty. Military requirements to fulfill national policies throughout these periods included not only the forces necessary to defend the hemisphere but also those needed for the acquisition, maintenance, and defense of "strategically located bases throughout the world, regardless of previous sovereignty, for our military defense and for economic purposes" such as "access to raw materials" and "unhampered use" of commercial air and sea routes. Forces would also be required to garrison "other selected areas" to be used as a "bargaining factor at the peace table." The bulk of U.S. forces therefore should remain mobilized "to give added weight to our policies and plans at the peace conference."[24]

This conclusion translated into resisting expected public pressure for immediate demobilization and retaining an army of five million and a twenty-nine-thousand-plane air force until ratification of the peace treaty. Even then, 1.5 million troops, two-thirds in the air force, would have to be maintained and deployed for hemispheric defense, for control of overseas bases required for that defense and "national economic policy," and to create a strategic reserve. The subcommittee further assumed that no international police force would come into being and that even with peace the "grounds for intense international rivalries still exist." Furthermore, if the Axis were not totally defeated and a negotiated peace resulted, the world would "inevitably" return to a balance-of-power system that would necessitate "maintenance of a tremendous sea and air force with a strong chain of outlying bases and a large, say 60 division strategic reserve."[25]

One month after this report Marshall established a special demobilization study group under Brigadier General William F. Tompkins, and in July he expanded it into the Special Planning Division (SPD). On June 18 the SPD reported that demobilization plans should be "cast against the background" of a slightly revised version of these assumptions. On July 3 the OPD concurred, gave Tompkins its own similar list, and recommended the maintenance of approximately fifty divisions for postwar purposes.[26]

Unlike the base issue, demobilization and postwar military policy planning were the purview solely of the armed forces, even if they did involve policy issues. Thus the State Department was neither invited nor desired as a participant, although Marshall did inform Davis on July 28 of army assumptions and plans.[27] War Department civilians clearly were participants, however, and one quickly objected. On July 12 Assistant Secretary John J. McCloy complained to Marshall that the estimates of needed postwar military strength were too high and not based on an adequate assessment of the postwar situation. He also questioned whether, in light of Anglo-Russian rivalry, any U.S. occupation troops should be placed in the Balkans and criticized the planners for not discussing the postwar positions of Russia, China, the U.S. Navy, and the British Navy. Three days later Handy defended the OPD's work by stating that these variables had been taken into account; above and beyond garrison duties, the most important provision was that of sufficient force to give weight to U.S. positions at the peace conference. The planners had also concluded that a large postwar force would be useful as a "safety valve" to preclude the economic problems that would follow the sudden return of millions of men to the labor force. Furthermore, as noted in a June 30 combined intelligence report, the Soviet position on entry into the war against Japan after Germany's defeat would be, "at best, vague," thus necessitating maintenance of sufficient force to defeat Japan unilaterally.[28]

By this time it had become apparent that future planning would involve some very debatable assumptions. It was equally clear that some sort of interservice coordination was necessary, for navy and AAF planners had also begun to work on the issues. On July 19 the JWPC suggested coordination through the JSSC as the "best qualified" group to prepare an overall postwar strategic plan and keep it current. On July 30 Marshall informed his colleagues of army work already done and seconded the idea of joint planning as soon as possible given that "certain broad assumptions" must and could be made only "in coordination with the Navy Department." He also presented an up-to-date list of army assumptions from the July 22 directive establishing the SPD: the war in Europe would end one year before the war in the Pacific; the United States would furnish four hundred thousand troops in Europe as "a share of the emergency interim forces required to maintain order and to guarantee adequate considerations of American peace aims," as well as a share of any international police force established (probably in the form of air forces); and the nation would probably maintain some form of universal military training.[29]

On August 3 the JCS agreed to forward the entire matter to the JSSC, and by September 21 that committee had revised the army assumptions to be more in line with its own views and what it had learned on the Security Subcommittee. It agreed that four hundred thousand troops would be needed in Europe "to maintain order and to guarantee adequate considerations of American peace aims." But its preliminary discussions with the State Department led to the conclusion that provisional governments would be established in other European countries within a year of German defeat and that U.S. forces would thus be limited to occupation in western Germany as already proposed in the RANKIN plan. In light of the present military and diplomatic situation, the JSSC did not agree that Japan would be defeated within a year of Germany or that an international police force would be created. It therefore changed the date of Japanese defeat to "at least" one year after Germany's, stated that over two million troops would be required, and insisted that the question of U.S. contribution to an international force be deferred until it could see what happened during the occupation period. On September 28 the JCS approved these assumptions with minor changes.[30]

By the time this JSSC report appeared, both the navy and the AAF had also set up postwar planning organizations and produced studies based on their own assumptions regarding U.S. policies in the postwar era. As previously noted, the first air force plan had been completed in April. Its author had noted that because military forces were justified "only as a necessary means of implementing national policies for the accomplishment of national objectives," determination of required postwar strength "hinges upon a discovery and appreciation of our national objectives." After surveying statements made by U.S. officials, he listed five such objectives as of V-E Day to guide air force planning: avoiding chaos in Europe; restoring "sovereign rights and self government to those who have been forcibly deprived of them"; establishing hemispheric "solidarity and security, under United States leadership"; via use of an international military force, ensuring "permanent world peace, and a stabilized world economy"; and effecting an "orderly transition" of the U.S. and the world economy to a peacetime basis. For these purposes, as well as for defeating Japan and checking postwar Soviet power, he recommended 273 air groups with 45,000 tactical craft.[31]

The first draft of the navy plan, created by the newly established Special Planning Section under retired Admiral H. E. Yarnell, was completed in late September and contained yet another list of policy assumptions. Unlike the other lists, however, Yarnell's was very specific and explicit. A strong advocate during the interwar years of better liaison between the armed forces and the State Department, the admiral was also willing to emphasize the need for detailed politico-military coordination.[32] Indeed, he began his draft by bluntly admitting that the armed forces had been unable to fulfill their prewar missions because of four civil-military failures: "Lack of any clear understanding of our foreign policies and commitments. . . . Failure to realize the increasing power of nations that intended to dispute them. . . . Failure on the part of the Government to grasp the elementary fact that policy and the force to support it are interdependent. . . . Failure of the Army and Navy to inform the Government of their inability to support the policies due to the inadequacy of the armed forces."[33] At whose feet to place these failures Yarnell did not say, but he implied that the civilians had failed both to understand the real world and to provide the armed forces with the necessary information and weapons needed. Equally clear was his implication that such errors could not be repeated and the assertion that because the Allies might or might not cooperate after the war, estimates of postwar requirements made at this time would need to be based on no cooperation taking place; should cooperation occur, the estimate could always be reduced.

"It is not the prerogative of the armed forces to enunciate national policies," Yarnell admitted, but certain assumptions about those policies had to be made in order to determine postwar naval requirements. He therefore listed eleven very specific policy assumptions to underlay naval planning:

(a) Protection of the Western Hemisphere (Monroe Doctrine).

(b) Support of an independent Philippine government.

(c) Support of a stable and democratic government in China.

(d) Control of certain island groups in the Pacific such as the Marshalls, Carolines, Bonins.

(e) Interest in Far Eastern Relations.

(f) Interest in Atlantic bases (leased bases, Azores, Cape Verdes, Dakar).

(g) Willingness to cooperate with other nations in maintaining the peace of the world.

(h) Avoidance of any entanglement in European domestic disputes (these to be settled by Great Britain and Russia).

(i) Cooperation with other powers to maintain Germany and Japan in a disarmed status.

(j) Cooperation with other nations to prevent by force, if necessary, similar aggressive powers from acquiring the armed strength to bring about another general war.

(k) Compulsory military training should be a national policy.[34]

Yarnell admitted that U.S. military strength at war's end would be far in excess of the forces needed for these tasks and that partial demobilization was therefore justified. Should Congress insist on reductions beyond what was required to support the policies enumerated, however, the armed forces should request a modification of those policies so that they could be enforced with what was being provided. The admiral also made some additional assumptions worthy of note: Germany would be defeated before the end of 1944, and defeat of Japan would take an additional two years; Great Britain and the United States would be the only great naval powers in the postwar era; Britain could be "disregarded as a future enemy"; future Russian naval power "cannot be foreseen"; and a long period of "unrest or instability" might occur in the postwar world "requiring world-wide policing by military forces."[35]

On October 20 King informed Yarnell of a naval consensus that his plan was "based on acceptable assumptions and that sound conclusions are reached." Yet some of those assumptions met with opposition from Yarnell's colleagues. One argued that Britain would be "a strong commercial rival with very remote possibility of becoming a future enemy" and that Russia was "likely to assume considerable proportions as a naval power." Another called for more emphasis on postwar air commerce and the conflict with Britain over this. Others noted that avoidance of entanglements in European disputes tended to "nullify" cooperation to maintain world peace; pointing out that both world wars had originated in

European disputes, they suggested instead a stated policy of postwar alliance with Britain and Russia to maintain peace.[36]

The navy's first tentative Demobilization Plan, prepared under the direction of Deputy CNO Vice Admiral Frederick J. Horne and distributed on November 17, reflected these comments and Yarnell's draft in its use of most of his assumptions, but with some removed or modified as suggested. Most notable was deletion of the avoidance of entanglements in Europe and the addition of support for "an adequate merchant marine" and "commercial aviation as factors in our future security." The plan stated that to fulfill their mission the armed forces required "a clear understanding of our foreign policies and commitments." And in a vitally important but seldom enunciated point that showed the impact of 1941 events in the Far East and modern war technology in general, it further noted that these forces needed to be "designed and trained to carry on war in enemy waters and territory. Defense of our national interests must envisage the desirability of being able to commence offensive operations without waiting for an initial assault and setback by any future enemy." Furthermore, Yarnell's comments on present allies were altered so as to identify them as potential adversaries: the future of Russia as a naval power "cannot be foreseen," according to the plan, but "it is reasonable to assume that this arm of her military forces will be considerably increased," whereas Britain "will be a strong commercial rival with the attendant possibility of future differences."[37]

Such comments about present allies partly reflected the inability to plan for postwar military forces without a perceived enemy. Indeed, Lincoln in the S&P explicitly stated in October that planning for war in the immediate future was impossible "unless we can name a specific powerful potential enemy with whom we have a specific issue at the present time capable of generating war in the near future."[38] Yet these comments also indicated the deep splits within the alliance in 1942–43 and the planners' fears about the future. Such fears were fueled by their reading of the past. "If history is to be believed," one GB member warned, "we may be certain that at the end of the war each of the Allies will lapse into a resolute pursuit of individual national interests, in spite of any intention at the present or any agreement which can be reached." The United States should therefore "look out for itself" and recognize that present allies could be future enemies.[39]

The Presidential Prod, JCS 570, and the Iowa Talks

While naval planners completed this document, Roosevelt again spurred the JCS to act on the issue of postwar bases. On October 7 he forwarded to them a letter from Vice Admiral William Glassford reporting that the United States was losing out to the British for control of strategic bases in Northwest Africa, along with a presidential request for JCS opinion as to what naval and air bases the United States should seek in the area. The Joint Chiefs' response, written by the JSSC and submitted for JCS approval on November 6, went far beyond the issue of African bases. The committee decided to use Roosevelt's request to present him with a full exposition on its postwar plans, assumptions, and beliefs. As with the Victory Program, a limited presidential directive thus became the excuse for a major policy statement by the armed forces.

In addition to listing desired bases in Africa, the JSSC prepared a massive study on global postwar base requirements and, in an action the official JCS history labeled "unusual," included a list of its politico-military assumptions and recommendations.[40] Taken from its March and April papers, this document stated that the JCS should be represented on "important" postwar planning groups "to insure that military consideration may be integrated with political and economic considerations," and that postwar military problems needed to be studied as a whole. National security "must dominate" in such studies, though "we must be prepared to make concessions to the international organization." In this regard the JSSC assumed that the Allies had maintained their solidarity after winning the war and were "desirous of cooperating." Consequently, the United States should make plans to participate in the postwar occupation of Europe and prepare plans for bases, occupation, and disarmament after Japanese defeat, with military commitments to be based on the dominance of the three major Allied powers and, "in a less degree," China. So far as possible given the above, postwar military commitments should be limited to the Western Hemisphere and the Far East.[41]

As with earlier JSSC papers, the assumption underlying this document was that postwar planning would have to be studied in terms of three distinct time periods: Germany defeated but the war against Japan still in progress; worldwide peace enforced by the Great Powers pending establishment of an international organization; and peace maintained by formal, worldwide machinery emanating from that international organization. The JSSC also reiterated its belief that the overseas bases needed for the third period could not be determined at this time and would have to evolve in light of international developments and experiences in the second period—a nice way of saying that Allied cooperation might break down and an international organization with police powers might never come into existence. Given these facts, the bases proposed for the second phase would have to provide a sound basis to design either a national or an international system for phase 3. In view of the planners' pessimism over international organization, the enormity of the list of bases for phase 2 was not surprising: seventy-two separate sites were listed, thirty-three in the Atlantic, Latin America, Canada, Greenland, and Iceland and the remaining thirty-nine in the Pacific and along the Asian coast, with the focus being a "blue zone" stretching from the Aleutians to the Philippines and back to Hawaii. The key to defense of this zone—and control of the entire Pacific—were bases in the Mandated Islands.[42]

On November 15 the Joint Chiefs approved this study, labeled JCS 570, and later that day gave Roosevelt the document, along with a draft directive for State to begin negotiations for the acquisition of these bases. The president was a step ahead of the chiefs, however, having previously asked the department to explore the possibility of an international trusteeship for the Mandated Islands under U.S. control as a solution to the sovereignty issue first raised by the navy in the spring. During his November 15 meeting with the chiefs he cited a recent memorandum on the subject by Under Secretary of State Edward Stettinius and called trustee-ship "a very satisfactory solution of the government of ex-enemy territory." In another meeting with the JCS four days later, he reiterated his desire that the Man-dated Islands be under "the composite sovereignty of the United Nations," with military bases occupied by U.S. forces. He also expressed his overall agreement with the JSSC study and recommendations, labeling the plan "good," albeit with two caveats: that the time was not "propitious" to begin negotiations for acquisi-tion of bases and he preferred to talk the matter over with Churchill first at the forthcoming Cairo Conference; and that the list of bases was somewhat inade-quate. He therefore expanded the "blue zone" on the JCS map to include the Marquesas, Tuamotu, and Society Island groups in the Pacific. In a November 23 memorandum he formalized his approval of JCS 570, informing the JCS of his "satisfaction" regarding their "very clear and excellent study" and including the expanded map.[43]

Roosevelt's comments on November 15, 19, and 23 did more than establish presidential approval for the Joint Chiefs' proposed global system of military bases. He essentially ratified their new, global concept of national security and, in the process, their rationales for detailed involvement in postwar planning. He also effectively agreed to continuation of the JCS organization after the war, for in approving the base study in JCS 570 he approved the appended JSSC statement of policy assumptions and thus the idea that postwar military problems should be studied as a whole; this meant they would be studied by the Joint Chiefs and their planning committees, not merely the individual services. Moreover, the JSSC list of assumptions indicated that the JCS should be involved in postwar planning, that military considerations in such planning needed to be integrated with eco-nomic and political ones, and that national security concerns would dominate such studies. In a sense, a good portion of the postwar concept of "national se-curity" was thus officially defined by the JCS and accepted by the president at this time. As the planners and their chiefs had envisaged at least since their first responses to Roosevelt's late-1942 directive on bases for an international police force, that definition was global, military, and designed to be appropriate for postwar Allied cooperation or conflict. The armed forces were to be intricately involved in all future activities within this broad definition, with the JCS as their final arbiter internally and their spokesperson externally.[44]

That was only the beginning of the good news for the Joint Chiefs. At least as notable as Roosevelt's approval of JCS 570, with all its implications, was that he gave his approval aboard a U.S. warship, the *Iowa,* en route to planned summit conferences first with Churchill and Chiang Kai-shek in Cairo and then with Stalin as well as Churchill in Tehran. The focus of both conferences would again be on future Allied strategy, for Churchill had by this time reopened the strategic debate by requesting a delay in OVERLORD in order to launch additional operations in the eastern Mediterranean. This issue would be resolved once and for all at Cairo and Tehran.

From late October through mid-November the Joint Chiefs carefully prepared for this next Allied confrontation over strategy. Of particular importance to them, once again, was the formation of a united front both among themselves and with the president before meeting the British. As Deane had suggested, traveling to the conferences with the president provided them with an extraordinary opportunity to achieve that front.[45] Given Roosevelt's expansiveness during the long journey, it also provided them with an extraordinary and unprecedented insight into the president's wartime and postwar thinking.

Roosevelt met with the Joint Chiefs twice on board the USS *Iowa* for a total of more than four and a half hours: on November 15 from approximately 2:00 to 3:30 P.M. and again on November 19 from 2:00 to 5:10 P.M. At these meetings he revealed not only some of his innermost thoughts but also the extent to which he now shared JCS views on both wartime strategy and relations with the Allies. Although only ninety minutes long, the November 15 meeting covered sixteen separate topics. The much longer November 19 meeting covered only five topics but in much greater depth.[46] What linked Roosevelt's comments in the two meetings was the degree to which anti-French and anti-British sentiment, the latter in accord with previously expressed military views, colored presidential directives and opinions on numerous issues.

In regard to future Allied strategy, Roosevelt approved the JCS paper opposing London's call for additional operations in the eastern Mediterranean with the comments "Amen" and that they "should definitely stand on it" at Cairo. He also asserted his decided preference for a unified commander for all U.S., British, French, and Italian forces in the entire European theater, desire that this individual be Marshall, opposition to British proposals for a separate Mediterranean command, and qualms regarding the rearming of French forces. In the political sphere he attacked British wartime and postwar policies regarding France, Italy, and Europe in general. London "wanted to build up France as a first class power, which would be on the British side"—something he implied was not desirable and, he directly added, not possible "for at least 25 years." As for Italy, he warned that "the British are definitely monarchists and want to keep kings on their thrones." The apparent "stalking horse" for these and other postwar machinations, he and Hopkins implied, was the large civil affairs secretariat in London that the British were calling for—something the Soviets would and the United States should oppose.

Roosevelt's suspicions were by no means limited to Europe. They spanned the globe and were integrally linked to his views on JCS 570 and postwar bases. "Undoubtedly," he asserted on November 15, "the British had in the back of their minds the control of Abyssinia." In discussing the rearmament of French forces, he blasted French refusal to circulate the *Reader's Digest* in Arab countries as part of an effort to repress Arab education and bluntly stated, as he had on other occasions in 1942–43, that "we should not commit ourselves . . . to give back to France all her colonies"—specifically not Indochina, New Caledonia, the Marquesas, Tuamotu, or Dakar, which he regarded "as a continental outpost for the Americas which would start on the coast of West Africa." Legal sovereignty here and in the Pacific islands was "immaterial" so long as French fortifications were banned, U.S. bases established, and "commercial traffic open to the world."

It was within this context that Roosevelt redrew the "blue zone" on the JCS map so as to include the Marquesas, Tuamotu, and Society Island groups and proposed international trusteeship for the Mandated Islands. Furthermore, he informed the JCS, "we must soon make up our minds as to what we want to ask the British for regarding Ascension Island." He also supported Stettinius's opposition to the army-navy desire to begin negotiations with Ecuador for postwar bases on the Galapagos Islands because this "might indicate untoward post-war intentions of the United States." International trusteeship, FDR apparently believed, could eliminate such an indication and was thus, as he stated, "a very satisfactory solution." But that solution was not limited to enemy territory. As illustrated by his other remarks while on the *Iowa,* Roosevelt desired to discuss the issue with Churchill before beginning postwar base negotiations because he wanted to place French, Ecuadorian, and perhaps even British possessions under the trusteeship umbrella.

Roosevelt amplified his anti-French and anti-British sentiments during the extensive November 19 discussion of future command in the European theater. He came out strongly in favor of a JCS proposal for unification of all European forces under an American commander rather than the creation of a separate Mediterranean command as the British desired and made clear he would request U.S. commanders for OVERLORD *and* the Mediterranean if Britain insisted on such separation. Its desire for a Mediterranean command, he asserted, "might have resulted from an idea in the back of their heads to create a situation in which they could push our troops into Turkey and the Balkans," a possibility that led him into an attack on recent British military initiatives in the Dodecanese.

Such presidential comments were mild, however, compared with those which followed about the RANKIN plans for occupation of Germany in the event of German collapse, plans the combined cross-channel planning staff under General Sir Frederick Morgan of Britain (COSSAC) had previously prepared and forwarded. United States military planners had quickly recognized the enormous political implications of these plans and that COSSAC had consulted the Foreign Office and War Cabinet in preparing them. Thus they had recommended obtaining guidance from the president and the State Department before proceeding. The Joint Chiefs had concurred and forwarded the appropriate papers to the president, who informed the JCS of his conclusions during the November 19 meeting aboard the *Iowa*.[47]

Morgan's occupation plan for RANKIN Case C had divided Germany into three zones, with the Soviets occupying the eastern zone, the British the northwest, and the Americans the southwest, which the president found highly objectionable.[48] Echoing the planners' conclusions, he asserted on November 19 that "it was quite evident that British political considerations were in the back of the proposals in this paper" and that these were by no means his own considerations. The British would "undercut us in every move we make" in the southwestern zone. So would General Charles de Gaulle, who would move into France behind U.S. forces. France, the president reasserted in an amplification on his November 15 comments, was a British "baby" whose reconstitution was not a U.S. task. Britain should therefore have occupation responsibilities in the southwestern zone as well as in France and the Low Countries, while U.S. forces occupied northwestern Germany, Norway, and Denmark. United States troops should be removed from France and Italy as soon as possible, though some might have to be kept in France to help create a buffer state from Calais, Lille, and the Ardennes through Alsace and Lorraine.[49]

Roosevelt's suspicions of the British regarding RANKIN were linked to those he previously expressed concerning operations and postwar policies in the Aegean and Balkans. Again echoing the conclusions of his military advisers, he insisted that "we should not get roped into accepting any European sphere of influence" and that he did not "want to be compelled, for instance, to maintain United States troops in Yugoslavia." He also made clear, as had his advisers, that in deciding on operations and policies in the Mediterranean and Balkans, "we must be concerned with the Soviet attitude." The president appeared to be no more trusting of his Soviet ally, however. Although willing to give the Russians one-third of the Italian Navy "as a token of good-will," he simultaneously warned that there would definitely be a "race for Berlin" and maintained that the United States should have the German capital within its northwestern zone of occupation. United States forces should therefore be prepared to seize Berlin in the event of German collapse (Hopkins suggested that "we be ready to put an airborne division into Berlin two hours after the collapse of Germany"); 1 million troops should be readied for occupation duty for "at least one year, maybe two." Grabbing a map of Germany he then sketched out an enormous U.S. zone of occupation in the northwest which, he asserted, Stalin "might okay." He also made clear that such a tripartite division should lead to the creation of separate German states, that his proposed boundaries were geographically logical and matched German religious differences ("Prussianism," he claimed, was the major religion in northeastern Germany), and that the RANKIN plans should be rewritten to conform to his proposals.[50]

Roosevelt would alter many of these assessments, some such as unilateral control of Berlin rather quickly and easily, others such as the northwest occupation zone only after many months and arguments.[51] From the Joint Chiefs' perspective, however, the important points were that the president had finally accepted their views, taken them into his confidence, and provided them with very explicit policy guidance based on some of his innermost political thoughts. Leahy's statement that the November 19 meeting "had been of great benefit to the Chiefs of Staff" was, if anything, an understatement. As noted in the official army history, "Never since the United States had entered the war had he given them such a glimpse of his reflections on the political problems that were bound up with the war and its outcome."[52]

In November 1943 the most pressing of these problems concerned Russia. As the JSSC had advised and as he had always desired, Roosevelt was going to Tehran determined to obtain Stalin's agreement to postwar cooperation if at all possible. Whether he could gain such agreement remained the big question in November 1943—for the JCS as well as for the president.

The Big Two,
October 1943 – September 1944

Late 1943 witnessed the long-desired clarification of both Anglo-American strategy and future relations with Russia. Out of a series of Allied conferences emerged firm commitments regarding cross-channel operations, Soviet entry into the war against Japan, postwar collaboration, and international organization. In early 1944, however, additional problems emerged for the armed forces with both the British and the State Department. The JSSC and JCS would respond with a bold reassertion and amplification of their 1943 views on Allied and civil-military relations that would stand as their official position through early 1945.

The Moscow-Cairo-Tehran Watershed

Allied relations improved dramatically during a series of conferences in the fall of 1943: the Moscow Foreign Ministers Conference, the Churchill-Roosevelt-Stalin meeting in Tehran, and the Churchill-Roosevelt meetings in Cairo before and after the Tehran summit. These initiated a "honeymoon" period in Allied relations and fulfilled numerous U.S. military and political desires, largely at the expense of the British. Consequently, the Joint Chiefs, Roosevelt, and Hull emerged from the conferences exceptionally pleased and optimistic regarding future U.S.-Soviet relations.

As had previously been the case, military collaboration remained the prerequisite for postwar political agreement. Before the Moscow Conference the Soviets thus made clear that cross-channel operations would have to be the first item on the agenda. Hull quickly realized the need to "reassure Stalin completely on this point before we could induce him to come in with us on the political decisions" and thus agreed to have Deane brief the Soviets on OVERLORD plans. Joined by General Sir Hastings Ismay of the COS, he did so on October 20 and essentially reaffirmed the operation for 1944.[1] Stating his satisfaction on the following day, Molotov moved on to political issues and, much to Hull's delight, soon agreed to virtually all the secretary's major points on wartime and postwar cooperation. Most notable was Soviet signature to his Declaration on Germany and Four Power Pact, pledging the Allies to unconditional surrender and tripartite occupation of Germany as well as postwar cooperation within the framework of a new League of Nations. Stalin also informally pledged entry into the war against Japan once Germany had been defeated. His military advisers were apparently equally forthcoming and friendly, for Deane, in a dramatic shift from his previous beliefs, left Moscow as pleased and optimistic as Hull. On November 22 he personally informed the JCS that "he had gone to Russia with the idea that the Russians were unwilling to cooperate . . . and were interested only in gaining their own ends," but his experiences had led to a "complete change in his views." The Soviets "entertained no idea of a separate peace," had previously been unresponsive because of their "utter absorption with the war," and were quite willing to cooperate. Furthermore, he now "felt certain" they would go to war with Japan once Germany had been defeated.[2]

The British were less sanguine, for their desire to reach explicit accords on Eastern Europe had met with consistent Soviet rejection and no support from Hull, who refused to allow the major agreements on principles to be torpedoed by boundary issues he considered "piddling little things."[3] That was only the beginning of their disappointment and frustration. The September invasion and surrender of Italy had opened numerous military opportunities in the Mediterranean that Churchill wished to exploit by again postponing cross-channel operations, this time to take the island of Rhodes (ACCOLADE), but unlike 1942 he found the Americans unwilling even to discuss the matter. Now convinced that postwar as well as wartime cooperation with the Soviets was possible if military commitments were fulfilled and Stalin's suspicions could be overcome, the JCS insisted that OVERLORD not be further delayed and even opposed the preliminary meeting that Churchill requested in Cairo. As King informed his colleagues, an Anglo-American conference without the Russians and before the Tehran meeting could be "extremely dangerous to the Allied cause" and would place the United States "in the position somewhat of concerting with the United Kingdom vis-a-vis Russia." Roosevelt and Marshall concurred, but rather than reject the Cairo meeting outright they proposed inviting Soviet officials in order, as Marshall stated, to see that the Anglo-Americans "were not concealing anything from Russia" and "to place the Russians in such a position that they cannot doubt our good faith."[4]

Roosevelt also invited the Chinese, however, which led the Soviets to reject attendance. Nevertheless, the Chinese presence indirectly accomplished his objective by precluding a discussion of European strategy which Roosevelt and the JCS now insisted await the meeting with Stalin. Roosevelt refused even to meet privately with Churchill at Cairo. He did meet privately with Chiang Kai-shek, however, promising him a 1944 amphibious operation against the Andaman Islands in the Bay of Bengal (BUCCANEER). This decision created even more pressure to make clear strategic choices in Europe in light of the landing craft shortage. Indeed, it precluded the possibility, which Churchill desired, of adding landing craft to the European theater at the expense of the war against Japan, and it thereby forced a definite decision between ACCOLADE and OVERLORD on schedule. Under no circumstances would FDR allow U.S. policies in Asia and the Pacific to be threatened by cancellation of Far East operations in order to launch Mediterranean *and* cross-channel operations in 1944. As he bluntly stated at Tehran, "He did not intend to get involved in a discussion as between the relative merits of the Dodecanese and the Andamans."[5]

Roosevelt also discussed his trusteeship idea with Chiang and his desire to apply it at least to portions of the Japanese and French empires in the Far East—and perhaps British colonies too. The ensuing Cairo Declaration stated that Japan would be stripped of the Pacific islands it had acquired since 1914 and territories it had "stolen" from China, that the latter would be returned to the Chinese, and that Korea would become independent. Significantly, Hopkins's first draft of this document did not even imply the return of British possessions after Japanese defeat.[6]

From Churchill's perspective, FDR's behavior in Tehran was even worse than at Cairo. The president consistently supported Stalin against Churchill. Roosevelt also ignored and humiliated him in an effort to "charm" the Soviet leader and illustrate that he did not face any Anglo-American bloc. Much has been made of these supposedly naïve and offensive efforts to impress Stalin, without full recognition that an extraordinary confluence of Soviet-American strategic interests underlay them. Roosevelt was indeed determined to befriend Stalin and establish a basis for postwar cooperation. But that effort was neither naïve nor based merely on a belief in the power of his own personality. To the contrary, it was based on a global strategic quid pro quo that emerged during the first plenary session at Tehran on November 28 and undergirded all discussions that followed.

Roosevelt began the session with a "general survey of the war" from what he aptly labeled "an American point of view" and boldly illustrated the differences between that viewpoint and those of his allies by offering a long disquisition on the war against Japan. Within this he emphasized the importance of planned operations in Southeast Asia to keep China in the war, operations he had already mentioned to Stalin during a private talk beforehand. He thereby made clear his preoccupation with the war against Japan and why the global deployment of U.S. forces remained, even at this date, in violation of Germany-first. Only then did he move on to the admittedly "more important operations . . . of immediate concern to the U.S.S.R. and Great Britain, those against Germany." But his choice of words, lengthy analysis of Far East operations first, and maps of the Pacific kept on the table while talking about Europe—these made American interests and preoccupations abundantly clear.[7]

Roosevelt then emphasized plans to relieve the pressure on Russia via OVERLORD and the choices now available between that operation in the spring of 1944, which he personally favored, and more immediate but "secondary operations" in the Mediterranean that would postpone or cancel the cross-channel assault. Stalin's reply illustrated that he had listened carefully and thoroughly understood the president's remarks, for he began by welcoming U.S. successes against Japan and once again promised, this time formally, to enter the war in the Far East after Germany had been defeated. He then indicated his preference for OVERLORD on schedule over Mediterranean operations he labeled indecisive, and after a lengthy exchange with Churchill he proposed that forces in Italy be used for a previously considered supporting invasion of southern France (ANVIL) after Rome had been captured. Roosevelt immediately concurred. On the following day Stalin reasserted these conclusions and further demanded that they name an OVERLORD commander and set a firm invasion date so that he could launch a supporting operation in the east. Once again FDR agreed, despite Churchill's appeals for delay.[8]

In effect Stalin offered Roosevelt a two-part bargain: on the global level, a Soviet "second front" in the Far East if he dropped his preoccupation with Japan to provide Moscow with the long-desired second front in Europe in 1944; and a supporting operation in Eastern Europe if FDR agreed to cross the channel and provide his own supporting operation in southern France rather than continue Mediterranean dabbling. And if FDR agreed to this strategic bargain, political ones would follow. Roosevelt immediately grasped the significance of the offer and quickly shifted from explaining the options to backing up Stalin's proposals, all at the expense of Churchill's strategy. The prime minister used all his oratorical powers against these proposals for the next three days, but to no avail. Russia and the United States had reached a politico-military accord and now simply outvoted and overwhelmed the British, who for the first time in the war lost a strategy debate and whose weakness was revealed vis-à-vis the two emerging superpowers.

Nor was that all. Seconded by Hopkins and Molotov, Roosevelt and Stalin also agreed that French Indochina, New Caledonia, and Dakar should be placed under international trusteeship as FDR had previously proposed, that strategic points around the globe should be occupied by Allied military forces under international trusteeship, and that the United States would control such points in the Atlantic and the Pacific.[9] Roosevelt also continued Hull's policy of seeking Soviet agreement to broad principles of postwar collective security and cooperation rather than specific accords on Eastern Europe, apparently in the belief that such agreement could help break down Russian suspicion and insecurity and, with them, the desire for extensive territorial gains. So could personal diplomacy, he believed. Thus he attempted to befriend Stalin, refused to meet privately with Churchill, and needled the prime minister mercilessly in the Soviet leader's presence. This was the "icing on the cake," however; the foundation remained the global strategic accord.

The British were deeply depressed. Brooke, chief of the Imperial General Staff, felt like "entering a lunatic asylum or a nursing home." Churchill was appalled at Roosevelt's behavior, and at one point felt it necessary to warn his erstwhile allies that "nothing would be taken away from the British Empire without a war." In truth, however, he was powerless against this emerging Soviet-American entente. As he later admitted, Tehran forced him to realize what a small power Britain had become, with the "great Russian bear . . . paws outstretched" on one side, the "great American buffalo" on the other, and in between "the poor little English donkey." [10]

The JCS, on the other hand, were overjoyed. They were also surprised, for Deane had incorrectly concluded and informed them after Moscow that the Soviets had previously emphasized OVERLORD only "for the purpose of testing Anglo-American sincerity"; now reassured, they viewed British calls for delay with "unconcern" and might even agree in order to obtain immediate Mediterranean benefits. Ambassador to England John G. Winant had seconded this assessment, while Willson had warned the chiefs of JSSC fears that Britain "might effect some understanding or agreement with the Soviets at the expense of the U.S." over Balkan operations. When these fears failed to materialize, Marshall thus reported that the Tehran agreements had been "unexpectedly favorable." [11]

The Americans credited Stalin with responsibility for this outcome. His adamancy on crossing the channel and refusal to be influenced by Churchillian rhetoric had finally succeeded, after two years of acrimony, in forcing British acquiescence. "I thank the Lord Stalin was there," Stimson wrote in his diary after reading the conference minutes. "In my opinion he saved the day." McCloy concurred, informing the secretary after his own perusal of the minutes that "in many cases I got the impression that Marshal Stimson was talking and not Marshal Stalin." [12]

Such happiness was by no means limited to the armed forces. All previous questions about Soviet behavior appeared to have been answered positively, and Hull thus returned from Moscow convinced he had established the basis for a new international order. "There will no longer be need," he informed Congress, "for spheres of influence, for alliances, for balance of power, or any other of the special arrangements through which, in the unhappy past, nations strove to safeguard their security or to promote their interests." [13] With such thoughts in mind, preparations began for a summer conference to create a new League of Nations.

Roosevelt was immensely pleased too, and he returned convinced that strong Soviet-American collaboration was possible and was the key to a peaceful postwar world as well as wartime victory. He also returned apparently agreeing with the belief, previously expressed by numerous military planners, that Britain was a major stumbling block to such collaboration. In mid-December he stated that "he thought he would have more trouble in the Post War World with the English than with the Russians," and in March, that Britain "would take land anywhere in the world even if it were only a rock or sand bar." He also refused to acquiesce in Churchill's proposals to cancel ANVIL and replace it with military operations in the eastern Mediterranean. As he bluntly informed the JCS on February 21, "it took three days at Teheran to get the British to agree to ANVIL," and the Russians had been "tickled to death." Thus "we are committed to a third power" and could not abandon ANVIL without consulting that power—something FDR was not willing to do because "we had made previous promises to the Russians which we had not been able to meet. He felt that we have given up promises in the past and had better not do it again." [14]

In a related political matter FDR also refused to alter his insistence on obtaining the northwestern rather than southwestern occupation zone of Germany and in avoiding any postwar commitment in western or southern Europe. "I do not want the United States to have the postwar burden of reconstituting France, Italy, and the Balkans," he asserted on February 21. "This is not a natural task at a distance of 3,500 miles. It is definitely a British task in which the British are more vitally interested than we are." He forcefully reiterated such sentiments to Leahy, Marshall, and twice to Churchill in that same month. [15]

"The Roosevelt-Stalin Axis is gaining," one U.S. official noted after a cabinet meeting in early 1944, "and the Roosevelt-Churchill Axis is losing strength in approximately the same proportions." [16] As at Tehran the main reasons were power and similar strategic interests, not any naïve presidential belief in his persuasive abilities. "Our strength was declining and the Russians were rising," one British officer commented years later, and FDR "wanted to be in a position where he could deal with Stalin by himself, not tied to anyone else." He therefore kept the British "at arm's length" and with his advisers increasingly "paid no attention to anything we said, unless it happened to coincide with something that they wanted to do." [17]

Those advisers of course included the Joint Chiefs, who with their planners shared this viewpoint and in 1944 produced a series of papers on Allied strategy and postwar relations that spelled out in detail the emerging U.S.-Soviet connection at the expense of the British. Their assessments differed from those of Roosevelt and Hull, however, for they did not share the latter's optimism or rosy view of postwar international organization.

The Joint Chiefs and a Soviet-American World

From the armed forces' perspective, postwar peace as well as wartime victory depended on a Soviet-American collaboration based on very specific strategic and geopolitical understandings rather than Hull's formal international structures. And despite the accords reached at Tehran, those understandings appeared during the spring and summer to be threatened, once again, by British strategy and policy. For although Churchill had been forced at Tehran to accede to OVERLORD and ANVIL, he had by no means given up on his Mediterranean plans.

At the second Cairo Conference Churchill had argued that Stalin's promise to enter the war against Japan lowered the importance of China and that launching ANVIL as well as OVERLORD would require additional landing craft in Europe. He therefore called for cancellation of BUCCANEER and transfer of its landing craft to Europe, where he hoped to use them to break the Italian stalemate and move into the eastern Mediterranean before shifting forces to England for OVERLORD. Roosevelt agreed to the cancellation, thereby ending any possibility of the China theater playing a major role in Japan's defeat and increasing the importance of both U.S. operations in the Pacific and eventual Soviet entry into the war.[18]

More immediately, the result in the Mediterranean was a Churchill-inspired amphibious landing at Anzio in January that failed to break the military deadlock in Italy and required massive reinforcement simply to avert total destruction of the isolated beachhead; by March that reinforcement had made Anzio the fourth largest port in the world.[19] At the same time, newly appointed OVERLORD commander Eisenhower and his staff concluded that the original invasion plan was inadequate and that five rather than three divisions should be landed at Normandy. The ensuing need for additional landing craft and the continued stalemate in Italy led London to call for ANVIL's cancellation and expanded Italian as well as cross-channel operations, followed by a shift of forces from Italy into Yugoslavia instead of southern France. Simultaneously, and not coincidentally, the Red Army advanced beyond Soviet borders and into the Balkans. In May, London and Moscow began to negotiate spheres of military influence in the area, which, their statements to the contrary notwithstanding, possessed enormous postwar implications.[20]

These events deeply upset the JCS and their planners. Detailed Soviet-American military collaboration was about to become a reality, and intelligence sharing was already improving dramatically.[21] The JCS would not tolerate any threat to this via a revival of what they considered British machinations in the eastern Mediterranean. Thus they rejected British requests for cancellation of ANVIL. Instead, they called for launching it after, rather than before or at the same time as, OVERLORD, at one point threatening, should they not get their way, to withhold Pacific landing craft they had previously agreed to divert to the Mediterranean. The JCS also indicated that they would not tolerate a Balkan alternative, which, Marshall warned Roosevelt as well as his JCS colleagues, "would probably be bound to result in a new war." Stimson concurred, labeling such a movement "another diversion in the interest of the British Empire and contrary to our American interests" and noting that Russia "could hardly fail to look with distrust" on any Adriatic substitute for ANVIL. Roosevelt also agreed, with the JCS drafting many of his negative responses to Churchill.[22]

Forced by the preponderance of U.S. power to give in, the British were extremely bitter. "History will never forgive them for bargaining equipment against strategy and for trying to blackmail us into agreeing with them by holding the pistol of withdrawing craft at our hands," Brooke bitterly noted in his diary. Winant thought it necessary to inform the president in mid-July just "how deeply the Prime Minister has felt the differences that have ended in his accepting your decision. I have never seen him as badly shaken."[23]

The JCS ban regarding the Balkans extended to any concern with postwar issues in the area. Reiterating the JSSC warnings and recommendations of late 1943, the planners insisted in March that the Soviets be allowed to dictate unilaterally Rumanian surrender terms much as London and Washington had dictated Italian terms the previous summer, a situation the JSSC termed "analogous." Furthermore, not even minor operations should be undertaken in the Balkans without prior Soviet agreement, Britain should not be supported in any efforts to check Soviet influence there, and no plans should be made for a wartime or postwar U.S. military presence in the area. The OPD and the JCS concurred completely. As Handy stated on March 7, the "basic military policy" of the Joint Chiefs was "not to use U.S. forces in Balkan operations," and "the post-war burden of reconstituting the Balkans is not a natural task of the United States." While the JCS brought these conclusions to the attention of the State Department, Stimson brought them to the White House, where they served only to reinforce the conclusions Roosevelt had himself reached on noninvolvement in this area as well as postwar noninvolvement in Italy, France, and southwestern Germany. Using his statements as their policy directive, the JCS asserted in early June that no U.S. forces were to be employed as occupation troops in southern or southeastern Europe (with only a token occupation division in Austria) and that U.S. participation in civil affairs within this area should be severely limited.[24]

The JPS agreed, citing numerous presidential statements in support of this policy. So did the JSSC, which in May repeated its warnings about the "direct, uncompromising and bitter opposition" between Britain and Russia in the area over the last two centuries, specifically regarding what it called "the most cherished aim of Russian foreign policy"—control of the Dardanelles. Any attempt to move into the Balkans without prior Soviet agreement would arouse Moscow's "resent-ment . . . possibly to such an extent as not only to threaten post-war unity among the three Powers, but to affect adversely their unanimity in further operations against the Axis powers." A "harmonious settlement" of Anglo-Soviet differences in the Balkans was of "fundamental importance to Allied unity" and thus of "di-rect concern" to Washington. Anglo-American occupation policies in the eastern Mediterranean should therefore be settled only after "consultation and agreement with Russia and on the basis of the United States not furnishing occupational forces."[25]

Equally threatening, according to the JSSC, was an issue that had troubled Roo-sevelt since 1941: the negative consequences for Allied unity of preliminary discus-sion of postwar territorial settlements. This concern was linked to those regarding the eastern Mediterranean, for the territories in question included Italy's Aegean colonies. Responding on May 6 to a State Department request for JCS views, the JSSC warned against acceptance of Britain's recently announced desire to discuss the disposition of Italian colonies because of the possible negative impact of such discussion on Allied relations,[26] and it used the occasion to explain in detail the postwar geopolitical and power relationships it had begun to analyze in 1943. "From the narrower view of purely national defense," it admitted, "little" in the British proposals "directly" affected the postwar U.S. military position, but from a "broader aspect of national and world-wide security" there were "implica-tions" the JCS should regard "with considerable concern." These involved possible threats to Big Three solidarity, a national policy of "cardinal importance." Its breakdown would be a "disaster" not only because of its centrality to a successful outcome of the war but also because of revolutionary changes in postwar national strengths that would result from the war.[27]

Summing up and amplifying its 1943 studies, the JSSC asserted that those changes centered on the recent and ongoing "phenomenal development of the heretofore latent Russian military and economic strength," combined with a precipitous de-cline in British power. So great was the former's growth and latter's decline that England could not hope to defeat Russia in a future European war, even with the United States as an ally. "We might be able to successfully defend Britain," the JSSC admitted, "but we could never defeat Russia." Nor could the Soviets defeat the United States. Each nation would emerge from the war effectively invulnerable against the other. Given these facts, U.S. policy must be to prevent such a devas-tating and unwinnable war from taking place. In this regard the JSSC strongly implied that the most likely source of Soviet-American conflict would be Anglo-Soviet conflict, and it stated that no third world war would take place if Britain and Russia collaborated. The greatest threat to collaboration and thus the greatest likelihood of conflict, it admitted, would be if either power attempted to build strength "by seeking to attach to herself parts of Europe." But equally dangerous in light of Russian suspicions would be Anglo-American territorial agreements without prior Soviet consultation—especially in the Aegean given the "ancient" Russian interest in the Dardanelles. Because the Italian territories of Crete and the Dodecanese Islands were in this area and could block Russian exit from the Black Sea, Soviet views should be obtained before agreeing to support British proposals.[28]

On July 28 the JSSC amplified these conclusions and postwar power projections in the process of warning the State Department against discussion of *any* territorial issues at the forthcoming Dumbarton Oaks Conference to plan a postwar collective security organization. Such discussion, it once again argued, would lead to Allied conflict that could weaken the war effort, particularly by delaying or canceling Russian entry into the war against Japan. Should discussion of territorial issues prove unavoidable, however, State should be aware of the military factors involved. These centered on the enormous growth in Soviet power. German defeat would leave Russia "in a position of assured military dominance in eastern Europe and in the Middle East," a dominance only reinforced by the subsequent Anglo-American withdrawal of all but occupation forces from Europe for the war against Japan or demobilization. Furthermore, whether or not Moscow did enter the war in the Far East, Japanese defeat would leave Russia "in a dominant position on continental Northeast Asia, and, in so far as military power is concerned, able to impose her will in all that region." Beyond such specifics, the postwar world would be one so "profoundly changed" with respect to relative national military strengths as to be "more comparable indeed with that occasioned by the fall of Rome than with any other change occurring during the succeeding fifteen hundred years."[29]

Noting the same factors as the 1943 Earle/Sprout and Embick studies, the JSSC asserted that a combination of geography, elimination of Germany and Japan as military powers, the mechanization of warfare and development of aviation, and dramatic changes in the relative economic power and "munitioning potentials" of the Great Powers were creating a situation whereby at war's end the United States and the Soviet Union would be "the only military powers of the first magnitude." Furthermore, the relative strengths and geographic positions of the two would "preclude the military defeat of one of these powers by the other, even if that power were allied with the British Empire." Indeed, that empire would emerge from the war in a much weaker economic and military position, both absolutely and relatively, than it had entered the conflict. As the 1943 studies had pointed out, this was a long-term phenomenon but one that had now reached a critical juncture: whereas British munitioning potential had constituted 50 percent of the world's total seventy years ago, in 1944 it constituted only 8 percent.[30]

The JSSC drew no explicit conclusions from these projections beyond their "fundamental importance" for "future international political settlements." Implicitly, however, the entire paper reinforced its warnings against territorial discussions because of their divisive capabilities and the critical importance of maintaining good Allied relations to ensure Soviet entry into the war against Japan and postwar cooperation. At the same time, the committee reiterated its opposition to any military operations in the Balkans, even if needed to bring Turkey into the conflict as desired by Moscow and London.[31]

The August–September Dumbarton Oaks Conference to create a postwar international organization, a conference in which the members of the JSSC actively participated, reinforced these conclusions. In late August the JSSC thus advised the JCS to "carefully avoid any commitments" to British proposals for future Allied coordinating machinery based on the existing CCS structure, because it would invite Russian suspicion and distrust and thereby destroy future international organization. Success for any such organization would depend on Big Three solidarity, and any continuation of the CCS would be inconsistent with both objectives.[32] In September the new Joint Post War Committee (JPWC) similarly recommended keeping U.S. military participation minimal on the Allied Control Commission for Rumania because of "the risk of becoming involved in possible conflicting interests of the U.K. and the U.S.S.R." as well as the "relatively minor importance" of U.S. interests in the area. The JSSC concurred and reasserted its policy of not challenging Soviet predominance in the Balkans or backing any British attempt to do so. Along with the JPWC and JPS, it also agreed to expand the area covered by this policy to include Czechoslovakia, noting that the forces of West European allies should be equipped only after consultation with the Soviets so as "to avoid any implication to Russia that the United States is supporting the formation of a Western European bloc or is acting bilaterally to assist in rearming such a bloc."[33]

Beyond the issues formally enunciated in their papers, the JSSC, JPWC, and JPS had an additional reason to plead for no Allied discussion of postwar territorial issues. At stake in any such discussion would be their ongoing conflict with the State Department over the future of the Mandated Islands, a conflict that had entered a new and very intense phase.

Civil-Military Conflict over the Mandated Islands

The Joint Chiefs had returned from Cairo and Tehran enormously pleased not only with the conference results but also with the fact that Roosevelt had seemingly accepted their views on Allied strategy and relations as well as the degree to which he made clear to them his own views on various postwar issues. The *Iowa* conversations constituted an unprecedented milestone in this regard and indicated the extent to which he was now willing to take the chiefs into his confidence. Equally illustrative was his extraordinary admission to Marshall that he would not receive the OVERLORD command because "I feel I could not sleep at night with you out of the country."[34] Thus not surprising was the extent to which in 1944 Roosevelt approved drafts of messages to Churchill written by the army chief and other members of the JCS.

In at least one area, however, military recommendations and presidential policy remained partially divergent—the Mandated Islands. Roosevelt and the JCS agreed that they must exercise postwar control over the islands, but the question of where legal sovereignty would be lodged continued to divide them.

As previously noted, Roosevelt saw international trusteeship as a means of obtaining U.S. control of the islands without violating the Atlantic Charter. He and Hopkins also believed that trusteeship would provide international sanction for postwar U.S. and Allied control of additional bases; that control of such "strong points" was, in Hopkins's words, "one of the most important postwar problems"; and that the trusteeship system would additionally provide national self-determination for Japanese and French colonies. Chiang and Stalin had supported these ideas, but Churchill, suspicious of an effort to place portions of the British Empire under such a scheme, objected. He limited his objections so as to protect British possessions rather than attack the entire proposal, however, and Roosevelt thus returned from the conferences convinced he had won tentative approval for the concept and for U.S. postwar control of the Mandated Islands and other bases under it. Thus on January 7 he acted on his November approval of JCS 570, the JSSC base study, by forwarding it to Hull with the request, as recommended by the JSSC, that the State Department "as a matter of high priority" begin negotiations for acquisition of specific postwar bases. Throughout early 1944 he reiterated his desire to place at least portions of the Japanese and French empires, and perhaps British possessions too, under trusteeship.[35]

The JCS remained dissatisfied, however, and in early 1944 turned decisively against trusteeship for the Mandated Islands. On January 4 the JSSC on its own initiative proposed presidential approval of a policy of "no statements, agreements or plans . . . which directly or indirectly might be construed as a basis for any nation other than the United States obtaining sovereignty or any other territorial rights in the Japanese mandated islands," and on January 11 the JCS approved and forwarded the policy proposal to Roosevelt. A few days later FDR sought to reassure them, albeit without specific promises. "There is no danger of our giving away any Japanese Islands in the Pacific," he told his naval aide for transmittal to Leahy, "except that the question of civil administration is still an open one." On February 29 he was a bit more emphatic, setting the JCS memo aside with the remark that "no country but the U.S. will be in these islands."[36]

The JCS found this insufficient, probably because of military and diplomatic events in early 1944. The start of the navy's thrust in late 1943 into the Central Pacific through the Gilbert Islands had already resulted in appalling losses on Saipan, where the marines suffered fourteen thousand casualties in three weeks. According to Lester J. Foltos, the JCS "anticipated that the human cost of liberating the remaining mandates would be terrifying, and the prospect of such losses steeled their determination to insure that American troops would never have to repeat this grisly task." At the same time, Australia and New Zealand, objecting to the Cairo Declaration and their exclusion from postwar planning in the Pacific, finalized a bilateral security agreement that claimed a major role in the future of the Mandated Islands. Hull's February 5 forwarding of this agreement to the Joint Chiefs for comment would serve as the official rationale for their rejection of the trusteeship proposal.[37]

On February 9 Leahy informed his colleagues that the islands should be placed under U.S. sovereignty "without compromise or discussion with any other nation." Then on March 4 the JSSC informed the chiefs that provisions in the Australia–New Zealand accord asserting a right to a "determining voice" in their disposition constituted "implied opposition" to the policy the JSSC had suggested and the JCS had approved on January 11 and were thus unacceptable. The islands had been recognized since 1914 as essential to U.S. security, had become more so since then as a result of aviation developments, and would become even more essential to future security because of an expected increase in the "munitioning capacity of Asia that will result from the progressive industrialization of its vast population." Defense of the islands against a possibly "militant Asia" could be assured only by the United States, and the implication that Australia and New Zealand were capable of doing so had "no foundation in reality." It was therefore "essential" to place them "under the sole sovereignty of the United States," and the State Department should be so informed. "Their conquest is being effected by the forces of the United States," the JSSC draft letter to Hull concluded, "and there appears to be no valid reason why their future status should be the subject of discussion with any other nation." On March 11 the JCS approved and sent this letter. Simultaneously Navy Secretary Knox informed a supportive Congress that in his opinion the islands had "become Japanese territory and as we capture them they are ours."[38]

Roosevelt was not about to let another nation gain control over the islands, but as he informed the chiefs on July 10, he would not openly violate the Atlantic Charter either—especially when he continued to believe that the United States could retain effective military control of the islands within a trusteeship framework that would simultaneously effect global decolonization. Similar thoughts emerged within the State Department, which was then in the process of making the future of the islands part of a compromise with Great Britain over the trusteeship issue at the Dumbarton Oaks Conference.[39]

Territorial trusteeships were high on the State Department's agenda for that conference, though not in regard to the Mandated Islands per se. The general issue had been poisoning Anglo-American relations for months, with London correctly believing that Washington wished to use it as a means of ending European colonial empires in Asia and perhaps Africa. In April 1944, however, an important breakthrough and compromise occurred by which London agreed to place "dependent peoples" on the trusteeship agenda and some form of colonial accountability to the international organization, while Washington agreed that trusteeships need not imply independence, that they be based on collective sovereignty by all members of the international body, and that the Mandated Islands be placed under the system.[40] Failure to do so while demanding imperial concessions from Britain would be so hypocritical as to court a total breakdown in postwar colonial negotiations, the State Department feared, whereas putting the islands under international trusteeship and sovereignty could provide a model for European colonies.

From the armed forces' perspective, however, this was totally unacceptable. The very civilians who had ignored military advice and allowed Japan to retain the Mandated Islands in 1919, who had continued to ignore this advice during the interwar years and then forced the armed forces into an unnecessary war for which they had not allowed adequate preparations, were now planning to give away sovereignty over these vital islands once again in return for strategically meaningless British concessions to the principle of national self-determination. To make matters worse, those civilians apparently had presidential support.

Military opposition to trusteeship for the Mandated Islands may have played a role in the May JSSC paper on Italian colonies, for one way to avoid this was to avoid discussions of *any* postwar territorial issues because of their negative impact on the Grand Alliance. Furthermore, in asserting that the question of national versus international jurisdiction over Italy's colonies should be examined on the individual merits of each case, the JSSC had noted that it was "important to remember that our policy and interests require that we support the concept of national as distinguished from United Nations jurisdiction as regards the Japanese mandates in the Pacific."[41]

The role of this issue in the creation of the July JSSC paper on territorial trusteeships was much more direct. As the date for the Dumbarton Oaks Conference approached, the JSSC made additional efforts to stop the State Department. At Embick's request Strong had visited Grew to show him the JSSC/JCS preceding months' discussions about the Mandated Islands and the Australia–New Zealand accord, a move that resulted in what was probably a desired intercession by Grew with Hull on June 23.[42] A week later the JSSC moved to obtain presidential approval of its policy and explicit orders to Hull. The Joint Chiefs quickly concurred, and on July 4 Leahy forwarded to Roosevelt, as the JSSC had recommended, a JCS-approved restatement by the JSSC of the March 11 assertions. The islands, the chiefs emphasized again, bore "a vital relation" to U.S. defense, and "possession and control" of them was "essential to our security. Together they constitute a single military entity, no element of which can be left to even the partial control of another nation without hazard to our control of that entity." Given these facts and the fact that U.S. forces were conquering them, the islands should be under sole U.S. sovereignty, with no discussion of their future with other nations. On July 10 FDR characteristically responded that, on the one hand, the JCS were correct but, on the other, "they must also realize that we have agreed that we are seeking no additional territory as a result of this war." To resolve this dilemma he was "working on the idea" of the postwar international organization asking the United States to act as sole trustee, which would give Washington civil and military control without the need for sovereignty.[43]

This suggestion remained too vague and insufficient for the JSSC, which was to represent the JCS at Dumbarton Oaks, and it responded by warning State directly, in both meetings and the July 28 memorandum, against any discussion of postwar territorial issues on the grounds of negative inter-Allied consequences as well as the desire to retain the Mandated Islands. On July 18 the JSSC told Hull and the Department Steering Committee that the JCS continued to oppose any such discussions, with Willson focusing on the islands and Embick noting "the importance of any discussion that might in any way reduce the possibilities of Russian assistance being forthcoming in the war against Japan." On July 31 the committee met with Hull and proposed that all reference to territorial trusteeships be eliminated from messages being sent to the Allied governments about Dumbarton Oaks. Hull had previously agreed to this proposal, but reference to the subject had remained in the table of contents for the conference as submitted to the Allies. Realizing that the topic was now bound to come up at Dumbarton Oaks, the JSSC prepared its July statement at this time to serve as a warning and a guideline to State in the ensuing negotiations.[44]

Mention of Soviet-American relations in this context was by no means mere rationalization for postponement of the Mandated Islands issue, however. The JSSC analyses of May and July were far too extensive and detailed for such a limited and narrow purpose, and they clearly flowed from the points first made by its members, Earle and Sprout, and G-2 in 1943. They were also similar to comments on Soviet-American relations that Admiral Yarnell, head of the U.S. Navy Special Planning Section, made within two lengthy June analyses of postwar international relations, most notably his conclusion that there were "no major clashes of policy" between the USSR and the United States and no danger given "realistic statesmanship" of a clash "in the visible future"—despite the fact that "Russia is potentially the most powerful country in the world" and its clear intention to take over at least portions of Eastern Europe—because it was motivated by security concerns, would be preoccupied with postwar recovery, lacked seapower, and would require from twenty to thirty years to obtain it.[45]

The JSSC analyses also reflected a real fear that postwar discussions could seriously weaken relations with the Soviets and thus the war effort. As Willson emphasized to the Steering Committee, the JCS were "primarily motivated by the desire to shorten the duration of the war and thus minimize the expenditure of American lives and treasure." This "major objective," he insisted, "would far outweigh any desire from any political point of view to have the United States in a position to state all of its views on all subjects relating to postwar settlements."[46]

Significantly, however, Willson added that he understood, as other committee members had noted, that the U.S. delegation would have to be "guided by the course of developments" at the conference; if the Russians, for example, insisted on discussion of territorial/trusteeship issues, "then the objective of the Joint Chiefs of Staff would presumably call for a direct reversal of its present recommendations."[47] In other words, relations with the Soviets remained the top priority, not an excuse to obtain sovereignty over the Mandated Islands. The JCS believed that both goals presently necessitated avoidance of territorial issues, but if the Soviets disagreed the armed forces were quite ready to sacrifice this point on the altar of Allied solidarity.

Willson was admittedly a bit disingenuous in his comments, but not with respect to the Mandated Islands. On a broader level, the JCS positions as espoused by the JSSC were far from nonpolitical as he implied. First, the very desire to shorten the war and to minimize U.S. casualties constituted major political objectives,[48] ones that dictated continued wartime cooperation with Russia. Another such objective was the JSSC insistence on trying to maintain close Allied relations into the postwar era. These also happened to be presidential policies. In these papers the JSSC essentially provided military and geopolitical amplification of Roosevelt's cooperative policy vis-à-vis the Soviets—and of FDR's and State's continued opposition to postwar spheres of influence because they perceived such spheres as leading to Allied conflict and future war. Once again the armed forces were spelling out the full rationales and implications of civilian policies, while interpreting them to suit their own purposes.

Once again, however, they were in this process moving beyond civilian policies and proposing some of their own. For despite their opposition to Anglo-Russian spheres of influence in Eastern Europe, committee members were in effect proposing an enormous Soviet-American spheres-of-influence arrangement—or at least an informal understanding—encompassing the entire globe.

Implicit within all the jssc papers on Allied relations, Eastern Europe, and postwar bases was a broad quid pro quo between the two emerging superpowers. The military component consisted of Anglo-American operations in northern and southern France which the Soviets desired rather than the eastern Mediterranean, in return for a major Soviet offensive on the eastern front and eventual entry into the war against Japan which the United States desired. In the related political component as proposed by the jssc, the United States would accede to postwar Soviet hegemony in Eastern Europe by taking no major part in any operations or political negotiations in that part of the world, and Russia in turn would accede to U.S. hegemony in the Pacific, including total control of the Japanese Mandated Islands. The wartime strategies and conquests of each superpower would provide the essential prerequisites for such a settlement, because U.S. forces would at war's end occupy and control the islands much as the Red Army would control Eastern Europe—*provided* no military or political agreements were reached which would limit or disrupt that control. Britain's call for operations and occupation agreements in Eastern Europe constituted just such disruptive accords, but from the armed forces' point of view, State's call for trusteeships in the Pacific and its opposition to territorial acquisitions would be just as disruptive. All these proposals would be equally opposed as dangerous to Allied unity and thus the war effort. As for the linkages between these issues, on the same January day that the Joint Chiefs forwarded to Roosevelt their opposition to trusteeships and insistence on sovereignty over the Mandated Islands, Stimson objected to Hull's insistence on no forceful territorial acquisitions by any of the Allies because Russia had both "saved us from losing the war" and "prior to 1914 had owned the whole of Poland."[49]

The jcs position ran counter to Roosevelt's desires regarding the Atlantic Charter and the Mandated Islands. But it also echoed both his long-held desire to postpone all territorial issues and his assertions that the United States should stay out of the Balkans, his attacks on the French empire, and his insistence on promoting close Soviet-American relations. These facts only added to the proposal's effectiveness and appeal in 1944. It also appeared to reflect what the British historian Keith Sainsbury has labeled Roosevelt's inference at Tehran of a postwar "world of Soviet/American dictatorship,"[50] yet covered the possibility of postwar conflict by providing the United States with absolute control of its desired bases and the world's oceans and, with them, access to the Eurasian rimland.

Anti-Soviet Dissent

The armed forces were far from unified in promoting such a policy, however, and throughout the first half of 1944 opposition surfaced in numerous quarters. Perhaps reflecting Roosevelt's position, Leahy continued to insist that only civilians should be discussing such issues. At the same time, numerous planners argued that Soviet-American postwar collaboration might not be possible and that Britain rather than Russia was America's "natural" ally. The postwar collaboration of all three would, of course, be welcome, but it was highly unlikely. And the very Soviet power that the JSSC had cited to justify a cooperative policy would be an enormous menace to postwar national security, so much so as to justify wartime moves to challenge it in Eastern Europe and elsewhere. Continued Allied disagreement over the future of Poland, combined with the movement of the Red Army into Eastern Europe in early 1944, only reinforced such conclusions.

They were hardly original. As early as 1940–41 U.S. strategists had emphasized the importance of the European balance of power to U.S. security; JSSC proposals negated that emphasis, which by itself would have evoked military opposition.[51] Anti-Soviet sentiments were equally long-standing and had been combined with postwar security concerns in the statements of numerous officers and civilians throughout 1943. The Moscow and Tehran conferences did little to offset their fears. Indeed, Soviet positions at those meetings led Foreign Service Officer Charles Bohlen to offer from Moscow on December 15 a frightening "glimpse of the Soviet idea of post-war continental Europe": with Germany "broken up and kept broken up," no European federations permitted, and France, Italy, and Poland allowed no "appreciable" military force, Russia would be left "the only important military and political force on the continent."[52] Harriman and Deane were more sanguine, but in early 1944 Harriman warned of waning Soviet enthusiasm for cooperation owing to the Polish controversy and began to propose the use of economic aid to Moscow as "one of the most effective weapons at our disposal to influence European political events" and "avoid the development of a sphere of influence of the Soviet Union over Eastern Europe and the Balkans." Deane felt it was "time to revise our soft attitude toward Russia," while Hull became "increasingly concerned" over unilateral Soviet moves in Eastern Europe; by April he had concluded that "the tide of Moscow and Tehran" had ebbed and that it was time for "a very plain-spoken approach" to Stalin.[53]

Marshall and the other JCS members received paraphrases of Harriman's reports.[54] They were also well aware of Bohlen's fears and probably shared them. "Nice friends we have now," Leahy had sardonically told Hopkins at Tehran after listening to Bohlen's assessment of Soviet aims. Privately, the admiral continued to receive warnings and express fear of postwar Soviet and communist expansion. In January the JCS received and forwarded to the White House an OSS warning of a "widespread" impression in occupied Europe that Russia would be the "dominating force" in determining its future. By the spring one member of the British Foreign Office was reporting that some Americans, "particularly in military circles, were saying that their army would be useful in time to fight the Russians."[55]

Such opinions centered during 1944 in the Army General Staff—particularly within the S&P. In 1942–43, perhaps influenced by Wedemeyer, the group had expressed more distrust of the British than of the Soviets. But in September 1943 Wedemeyer departed for Southeast Asia and was replaced by his deputy, Brigadier General Frank N. Roberts. Roberts would in turn be replaced in November 1944 by his deputy, Lincoln, who informed Wedemeyer of a simultaneous and complete turnover in S&P members.[56] Whether the result of these changes in leadership and personnel, other changes in the international situation, or the Bohlen-Harriman warnings, in 1944 the S&P asserted sharp opposition to the JSSC proposals, as well as a pro-British and anti-Soviet orientation with respect to the postwar world.

In April the S&P joined the Civil Affairs Division (CAD) in challenging JSSC policy proposals on Rumanian surrender. The division chief General John J. Hilldring based his opposition on the belief that Washington "should not allow the Balkan door to be completely closed" but instead "protect its right to establish military and political contacts with Rumania should it so desire. . . . [T]o do less than this," he warned, "may jeopardize the position of the United States after the war." The Strategy Section agreed, and in doing so it questioned the JSSC belief that British interests in the eastern Mediterranean were under no circumstances U.S. interests. Any "acknowledgment of the Soviet's hegemony over the Balkans," it contended, "can easily result in a lowering of United States prestige with the U.S.S.R. and an inability to back British interests in the area, even though it might be to our advantage to do so." Thus the SS recommended support for Hilldring's position. Embick continued to disagree. "We are dickering for a small political advantage here," he warned Roberts in an April 10 telephone conversation, which would only open the door to more political questions by the British and more problems that should not impinge on the military importance of quick Rumanian surrender.[57]

Perhaps as a result of this conversation, the OPD supported Embick rather than Hilldring, but dissent within the S&P continued to grow. In commenting on the jssc's May paper on Italian colonies, Lieutenant-Colonel Paul Caraway, ss deputy chief, informed Roberts that the entire section "seriously questions the policy which is advocated," a policy it bluntly labeled "appeasement." Advocates of "feeding the bear to keep him quiet," he warned, "apparently overlook the fact that in every case the bear has turned upon the nations feeding him with the result that either the feeders are themselves eaten or are certainly severely mangled in the ensuing melee." A USSR fighting for its life against a common enemy, he further noted, "can be quite different from a USSR strong enough to feel that she does not require favors from the United States or Britain." [58]

Caraway admitted that the United States had no real conflict of interest with Russia, but "by no stretch of the imagination" could it be considered having been a friend over the last twenty-five years. Britain was far different, and giving up a known friend and ally for an unknown one would be unwise. Furthermore, Russia at that very moment was trying to extend its influence to areas beyond Europe—including Latin America, where it was "attempting to bring nations within her orbit that have always been considered within the hegemony of the United States." Beyond that, "to continue to accede to all Soviet demands and desires merely because we are afraid the Soviets may precipitate another war and be an adversary difficult if not impossible to defeat" would be "the sheerest folly," and "the premise that the USSR must be appeased to keep peace" was "basically unsound"; instead, Washington "must support Britain wherever possible." [59]

Two months later the section further attacked jssc proposals by stating that British control of the Aegean was vital to defend its Mediterranean communications and trade and that this was "of interest to the United States" because "a strong United Kingdom is believed to be of the greatest importance to the defense of the United States." [60] Simultaneously, G-2 objected strongly to Yarnell's June assertion of "no major clashes of policy" with Russia owing primarily to the Soviet lack of seapower and expected preoccupation with postwar recovery. It warned that Russia would maintain large ground and air forces for use in the Far East, Iran, and Europe and would attempt "political penetration" of Latin America, thereby bringing it into serious conflict with the United States. The Intelligence Division agreed with Yarnell that "Russia probably will not engage in armed aggression on a large scale in the immediate postwar period" but disagreed totally with his dismissal of ideology in Soviet national policy by asserting it was "certain" that Russia would "revert to her role of fomenting social unrest and upheavals in all of the capitalistic countries." This would clearly "bring a major clash of policy" with the United States. [61]

The Strategy Section and G-2 were far from alone. During May and June at least two studies of postwar air bases strongly implied that they would be needed against a hostile Soviet Union; one called for additional bases in Alaska and the

Aleutians because "only our erstwhile allies are capable of major military effort and . . . realistic planning must provide for protection against the real threat."[62] Lincoln also challenged the JSSC's call for conceding Russian dominance in Eastern Europe by arguing, in an apparent reference to past workings of the balance-of-power system, that this would eventually result in the rise of Germany once again and another war. He also questioned whether the British decline emphasized by the JSSC was as complete as it had asserted. Britain continued to possess "enormous resources" within its empire, and in a possible reference to the atomic bomb he noted that revolutionary changes in warfare could alter the postwar strategic picture "a great deal."[63]

Beyond these points, Lincoln directly challenged the JSSC assumption of "little or no possibility of a conflict between Russia and the United States." Should Moscow become aggressive in Eastern Europe, the probability of conflict would be great. Furthermore, given its "record of suspicion, unilateral action and non-cooperation," he questioned whether it "should be placed in the same category as Great Britain"—and whether the JCS should even be dealing with such issues. Russia was needed as an ally only while the war was in progress and could not be relied on to remain friendly in the postwar era. Although the JSSC's conclusions might have some validity as long as the war continued, they were based on questionable assumptions, ignored the Asian side of the problem, and would have no meaning once the war ended. Yet they might be broadly applied as JCS postwar policy, he feared, should they be accepted now.[64]

That possibility appeared even more likely with the appearance of the JSSC July paper on territorial trusteeships, a paper specifically designed for that very purpose vis-à-vis the State Department. Handy immediately questioned "whether the JCS should stick their necks out with the State Department on this matter this early in the game" and noted his own doubts about many of the JSSC conclusions. Warnings about a severe weakening of the British Empire had been expressed after World War I, for example, and in his opinion a European confederation could match U.S. or Soviet power. (In this regard he questioned the JSSC assumption "that Germany will be out of the picture for an indefinite period. This may happen, but it certainly did not happen after the last world war.") As for the United States and Russia being incapable of defeating each other, the OPD chief found this true only if defeat equaled physical occupation.[65]

On July 30 Handy informed Marshall that while the OPD agreed with the JSSC's opposition to discussion of trusteeships at Dumbarton Oaks so as not to weaken the alliance or hinder Soviet entry into the war against Japan, the division did not agree with the JSSC proposal that the JCS simultaneously attempt to provide the State Department with a statement of their views on the military situation in the postwar world. Such a statement would not be needed for the conference and would have to be "based on questionable assumptions" concerning the "lineup" of major and minor powers in the postwar world, their economic situation, and the policies each would adopt. Two days later Stimson voiced "general" agreement with the JSSC paper but noted it was "unduly pessimistic about the future of the British Empire" and asserted his belief it was "unwise" for the JCS "to commit themselves in print in so much detail" on the matter.[66]

Despite such negative comments and warnings, Marshall and his JCS colleagues approved all the JSSC papers with only minor revisions. Furthermore, the chiefs forwarded the two memoranda regarding Italian colonies and trusteeship discussions to the State Department, where, exactly as Lincoln had feared, they were interpreted as official JCS policy. Indeed, they eventually became part of the briefing books State prepared before the second Quebec, the Yalta, and the Potsdam summit conferences.[67]

Marshall did take quite seriously OPD objections to the July trusteeship paper, suggesting to his JCS colleagues that most of the postwar paragraphs be eliminated or revised as proposed by Handy. But King and Arnold "agree[d] in general" with the JSSC. At King's suggestion, the JCS informally directed the JPS to meet with the JSSC "and endeavor to reach an agreement on a redraft." Embick was apparently adamant on keeping the postwar sections, arguing that the State Department felt it would have to discuss trusteeships at the conference and "that they therefore need this guidance." Whether because of his arguments or time pressures, the redraft as approved and forwarded by the JCS on August 3 was essentially the same as the original JSSC paper. Indeed, Marshall's cover letter implicitly opposed territorial settlements in general and trusteeships in particular.[68]

Neither Embick's arguments nor the pressure of time accounts for JCS approval of all the additional JSSC papers in 1944, however, and with them the cooperative approach toward the USSR. Other, broader factors, political as well as military, must be taken into account to explain JCS refusal to adopt a tougher stance in regard to the Soviets in 1944—at the very time the British chiefs were reaching diametrically opposed and highly negative conclusions regarding the USSR and were so informing their representatives in Washington.[69] The most important of these were administration policy, the continued importance of the Soviet war effort, and fears that a tougher policy could hurt that effort and perhaps result in a Russo-German separate peace.

This combination of factors was clearly evident in the February–March rejection by the President's Soviet Protocol Committee of a proposal by Harriman that Deane's mission begin to screen and check Soviet Lend-Lease requests, with Marshall providing a key military rationale a few weeks later. Lend-Lease, he informed Roosevelt, was an "important factor enabling the Soviets to seize the offensive and retain it"—an offensive King told his private press group was "regarded by our command as the most magnificent in history." "Should there be a full stoppage" of Lend-Lease, Marshall warned, continued Russian offensives would be "extremely doubtful." So would successful defense. If Russia were deprived of Lend-Lease food and transport, "Germany could probably still defeat the U.S.S.R." [70]

This possibility was particularly noteworthy and frightening given the need for successful and coordinated Russian action if OVERLORD was to succeed and in view of continued separate peace rumors as the Red Army approached its prewar borders. Stimson feared that the Soviets "conceivably might stop" at those borders "with their grand strategic objective of national defense satisfied by the eviction of the invader and the gaining back of all they had lost, plus the Baltic states." Wedemeyer believed Stalin would continue to advance but warned he could order a halt along a line running from Danzig through Warsaw, Bukovina, and Bucharest and duplicitously "give every indication" to his allies that he was "striving to push vigorously forward while they bled and endured heavy losses in the west"; the result would be a weakening of Britain and the United States as well as Germany, "thus creating conditions favorable for the introduction of Karl Marx'[s] ideas." Handy concurred. Marshall disagreed with fears of a Soviet halt short of German surrender but saw Lend-Lease as "our trump card in dealing with U.S.S.R. and its control is possibly the most effective means we have to keep the Soviets on the offensive in connection with the second front." [71]

Marshall was thus far from opposed to using Lend-Lease to achieve U.S. policy objectives vis-à-vis the Soviets. From his perspective, however, the primary objective remained maintenance of full-scale Soviet military action, and threats to cut off aid were militarily counterproductive to such a goal. They could also be politically counterproductive. As Deane informed him in March, negotiating with the Russians was "a good deal like golf—the more you try, the more you press, and the worse you score." [72] Even more revealing was a fascinating letter the army chief received and had G-2 forward to the OPD on March 21, which in one breath warned that the main issue of the war was fast becoming whether "we will let Russia run away with Europe," while in another it maintained that the big danger at the moment was a separate Russo-German peace. Such a peace remained quite "possible" despite Tehran, especially if the cross-channel invasion was further delayed or unsuccessful, and its occurrence would mean "the light would go out over western civilization for a long time to come." [73] For Marshall and the other chiefs, such immediate dangers properly took precedence at this time over the potential danger of postwar Soviet domination of Europe.

In late May Leahy stated the matter quite bluntly to Roosevelt. On May 24 the president had asked him to read some German documents claiming a Soviet desire to communize Europe which Earle had sent from Istanbul and to "let me know what you think I should do about it." In reply Leahy asserted that there was "an element of truth in this German propaganda" but that even if completely true "there appears to be nothing we can do about it until Hitler is defeated."[74]

The successful launching of OVERLORD in June and the ensuing conquest of France did not alter this situation. To the contrary, Anglo-American military successes in Europe remained dependent during this time on German preoccupation in the east, with the Red Army between June and September inflicting nine hundred thousand casualties on the Germans—a figure exceeding by two hundred thousand the total number of German troops engaged against Eisenhower's forces. Furthermore, the War Department decision to create no more than ninety divisions meant that this disparity and reliance on the Red Army would continue for the duration of the war. As Marshall admitted to Stimson, the Americans had "staked our success" in Continental operations on "Soviet numerical preponderance" as well as air superiority and the high quality of U.S. ground units.[75]

The possibility and desirability of Soviet participation in the war against Japan also remained a vital factor in JCS approval of the JSSC proposals. As early as December 2, 1943, the JSSC had proposed that, "in view of the latest information" from Tehran, Pacific war plans be "reviewed and expanded, on the assumption that the USSR will join in the war against Japan promptly after the defeat of Germany."[76] Subsequently, the JCS and their planners began to emphasize the importance of obtaining Soviet entry "at the earliest practicable date," with Deane and Harriman involved in detailed negotiations to establish air bases in Siberia. Soviet entry continued to be considered desirable rather than necessary for victory, with the JSSC and other planning groups placing primary focus on the U.S. Navy's drive across the Central Pacific. Yet they rated such entry as so highly desirable as to be worthy of "every effort" to obtain it—especially in light of the possible need to invade the Japanese home islands and the subsequent desire for a simultaneous Soviet offensive in Manchuria to preclude a redeployment of Japanese troops. Serious Chinese military reverses that spring and summer only reinforced this conclusion, and on September 1 Embick bluntly reaffirmed to Marshall his previous conclusion that Soviet entry "was a matter of the most cardinal importance," particularly to prevent redeployment of the eight-hundred-thousand-man Kwantung Army. Of related interest was the fear, as clearly expressed in a June OSS report, that if at the moment of Soviet entry "the trend in Europe is toward competition among the powers, a corresponding competition can hardly fail to arise in the Far East."[77]

The JSSC refusal to back the British in the Balkans and its emphasis on avoiding Anglo-Soviet territorial clashes also partially echoed State Department views at this time. Excerpting the May JSSC/JCS memorandum, one department briefing paper prepared for the president before the second conference in Quebec (OCTA-

GON) argued that although Britain was trying to play the role of "honest broker" between the United States and Russia as well as maintain a balance between the two, the "absence of any conflict of vital interest" between Washington and Moscow, together with the numerous Anglo-Russian clashes of interest, "make it appear probable that we, whether we choose it or not, may be forced to play such a role" so as to avoid an Anglo-Russian clash. The JSSC proposals also echoed White House policy on the Soviets as expressed by Roosevelt on numerous occasions during the first half of 1944 and presidential fears, as Lloyd Gardner has noted, that Britain wanted "to set up the United States for confrontation with the Soviet Union over spheres of influence when, he fervently hoped, there remained other options."[78]

To what extent military policy followed as opposed to led presidential policy remains an open question. Roosevelt's pro-Soviet policies had been well known to the armed forces since 1941 and may have influenced military assessments—especially those emanating from Burns and the President's Soviet Protocol Committee. But Burns's assessments relied on those of Embick, hardly an FDR follower or an officer afraid to voice dissenting opinions, and the key documents in 1943–44 came from the JSSC, not Burns's committee, and received JCS concurrence. Geoffrey Warner has concluded that these documents and beliefs had an enormous influence on Roosevelt and led him to reject the warnings of Harriman, Hull, and others in early 1944. Indeed, his statements at this time regarding how "friendly" and nonimperialist Stalin was actually constituted a ploy whereby "naivete was deliberately feigned in order to pacify those whom he thought would find it difficult, if not impossible," to accept the real beliefs he held as a result of the JSSC/JCS warnings: that the Soviets would dominate at least Eastern Europe no matter what the United States did. "Do you expect us and Great Britain to declare war on Joe Stalin if they can cross your previous frontier?" he bluntly asked the Polish ambassador. "Even if we wanted to, Russia can still field an army twice our combined strength, and we would just have no say in the matter at all."[79]

Once again the relationship between presidential and JCS policy was in all likelihood symbiotic, with the armed forces translating Roosevelt's general beliefs into explicit policy statements to make him aware of the implications of his actions and help them to fulfill their own agendas. The result was a basic agreement on policy toward Britain and Russia, but one that masked deeply divided opinion within the armed forces—and between them and the president. For Roosevelt once again accepted only those segments of JCS proposals with which he agreed while dismissing the segments with which he disagreed. His continued strong support for placing the Mandated Islands under international trusteeship clearly illustrated this fact, as did his refusal to modify unconditional surrender as requested in 1944 by the JIC, JSSC, and JCS[80] or to accept the northwestern occupation zone of Germany as the armed forces and service secretaries thought appropriate. Unlike them, the president consistently linked his opposition to U.S. occupation forces in southeastern Europe with opposition to their presence in southern Germany or France—often in the same breath or sentence.[81]

At OCTAGON Roosevelt finally agreed to occupy southwestern Germany. He remained adamant on trusteeship for the Mandated Islands, however, an issue that continued to separate him from his military advisers as the Dumbarton Oaks Conference began and postwar planning accelerated.

10

National versus International Postwar Security and Civil-Military Relations, January 1944–January 1945

The 1944 controversy over the Mandated Islands was part of both the debate over Soviet policy and the continued civil-military conflict over postwar security arrangements in general. As in 1943, the armed forces objected vehemently to what they perceived to be State Department efforts to rely on an unproven and as yet nonexistent international organization, as well as an associated and unworkable international police force. Throughout the year they devoted considerable attention to blocking such efforts, preparing alternative security proposals based on large national forces and informal Big Three understanding for postwar security, and ensuring for themselves a major role in future policy formulation.

Politico-Military Coordination and Postwar Planning

The JSSC would continue to play a major role in these efforts. In response to a January 21 State Department request for military input on international security proposals to be put before the Allies, Embick and Willson for the Joint Chiefs and Strong, Hepburn, and Admiral Roscoe E. Schuirman for the War and Navy Departments had been assigned to attend meetings of Hull's Informal Political Agenda Group. That soon proved insufficient for the armed forces, who by March were worried not simply over trusteeship proposals for the Mandated Islands but also the fact that State was becoming, in the words of one document, "very active upon such questions as post-war organization, formation of an international army, and establishment of a world state." Thus on April 4 the JCS approved an army proposal for the JSSC to furnish State with "military guidance" on "all matters of postwar international organization policies except those involving the establishment of broad policies or principles," which the JCS reserved for themselves.[1]

This authorization was part of a 1944 restructuring to enable the armed forces to deal with the host of postwar issues that were rapidly emerging. The JSSC was also charged with representing the JCS at conferences on postwar international organization, and the Deputy Joint Chiefs, with all problems of postwar U.S. military organization. By this time military officers were also serving on the State Department's Working Security Committee to advise the European Advisory Commission on German surrender policies, and on a special JPS subcommittee under JSSC guidance to work with State in negotiating rights for specific postwar military bases. In June this subcommittee was renamed the Joint Post War Committee (JPWC) and expanded via the addition of the high-ranking and powerful Admiral Train and General Strong, who had played such important roles on the Security Subcommittee in 1943. Subordination to JSSC guidance continued, but with a new, broad directive to study, recommend policies for, and work with the State on all specific postwar issues except international organization and civil affairs in occupied territories, which remained the responsibilities of the JSSC and CAD respectively.[2]

The initiative for these moves did not rest solely with the armed forces, for throughout 1944 the State Department consistently requested additional cooperation and coordination. As in the past the armed forces desired this too, though on their terms rather than those proposed by State. In response to Hull's suggestion that army officers be given instruction in political problems before being sent overseas, for example, the JSSC in March proposed instead that his diplomats be given some training in military problems. During the summer Marshall attempted to set up a joint army-navy staff college that diplomatic personnel would attend. McCloy supported this effort to establish and obtain State's participation in what would become the National War College because "our foreign policy in the past has had far too little relation to our military capacities."[3]

As this comment illustrates, beyond the specifics of who should be educating whom lay bitter memories of the interwar years and continuation of the 1943 debate over who should be primarily responsible for postwar security planning and whether that planning should be national or international in character. In the minds of military planners the two issues were closely related: in their opinion, the State Department continued to be ignorant of military realities and possessed unrealistic visions of a postwar international order, as well as international relations in general; the armed services, however, had a more realistic view based on national security and should possess a strong voice in a new, carefully coordinated, policy-planning process.

The navy was at least as vocal as the army in expressing such beliefs. Despite the existence of officers with "a proper conception of the responsibilities that our foreign policies imposed on the Navy," the former ONI director (and Mahan biographer) Captain W. D. Puleston pointedly noted in late 1943, State had in the past "discouraged all efforts" at a "formal discussion which would relate our foreign policies with the strength of our Navy." This could not continue. Preserving postwar peace would require "a cordial understanding" between State and the armed forces, with the navy as the "first line of defense" possessing not merely the right but also actual State Department encouragement "to state the naval necessities required to support a given foreign policy." State also needed to "accept the fact that other first-class nations do regard 'war as an instrument of policy' and the United States cannot, by a unilateral declaration, make armed forces obsolete as an instrument of policy." Educating State to these facts would be the navy's "hardest post-war task," for its officials "consider themselves competent to decide not only the foreign policies but the strength of the Armed Forces necessary to support them." Unless the navy could "overcome this attitude," it would be "kept in ignorance . . . and only called in at the last minute when the diplomats have gotten the nation involved so deeply that war is inevitable." Precluding this scenario required direct access to the president to make clear when "the foreign policies of the country are leading towards war." Such access was a right rather than a privilege, and if it intruded on State's prerogatives, it did not do so as much as the department "habitually" intruded "in presuming to say what the size of the American navy should be." Furthermore, because the secretary of the navy and CNO had in the past "frequently . . . been muzzled by the President and forbidden to state the real needs of the Navy," the GB must be able to report naval needs directly to Congress.[4]

Such beliefs did not translate into a distrust of all civilians. Indeed, the military was well aware of its need for civilian assistance and education in the realm of international politics. As one OPD officer concluded, because war was "an extension of diplomacy by other means," army officers "should be continuously trained along political lines."[5] Given the history of antagonism with the State Department's general ideas about the world as well as its past and present policies, however, the armed forces would not accept such training from Hull or his subordinates. Instead, they turned to a seemingly odd alternative source—the academic world—for instruction in international concepts closer to their own.

The armed forces found such concepts emanating from scholars working in the Research and Analysis (R&A) Branch of the OSS and the previously discussed geopolitical/strategic thinkers at Yale, Columbia, and Princeton. At Princeton in particular, Edward Mead Earle, founder of a special faculty seminar on the relationship between military affairs and foreign policy as well as editor of the 1943 classic *Makers of Modern Strategy*, had previously worked with and produced papers for the armed forces, and he was more than willing to continue to do so. During the summer he met with Embick and Fairchild, while his colleague Harold Sprout and Grayson Kirk of Columbia worked with other officers preparing for the forthcoming Dumbarton Oaks Conference. Either during or soon after these preparations, Sprout met with the deputy ss chief Colonel Paul Caraway to discuss future academic-military collaboration, and on August 11 Earle informed the JSSC that he hoped to draft in the fall a "general statement of certain underlying conditions affecting American security" which they had discussed. He and his colleagues would indeed do so, but meanwhile, with Dumbarton Oaks about to begin, he forwarded a 1941 article he had written on the topic. He also sent material to Caraway, along with a copy of *Makers of Modern Strategy* and strong support for the idea of postwar collaboration between the armed forces and "that lunatic fringe of the academic world which concerns itself with military affairs. This is a subject very close to my heart."[6]

It was also a subject close to the hearts of the military planners. In his August 17 reply, Caraway emphasized the importance of collaboration and the need for the "best minds" in the country to "tackle the problems of our post war national security." Given this fact and Earle's previous work, Caraway questioned his self-description as part of an academic "lunatic fringe," though he did humorously add, "I am certain that after you have dealt with the military for a few years you will either be dead of mental frustration or a lunatic in truth."[7]

Simultaneously, the oss R&A director and noted historian William Langer approached Embick, an officer he considered "a highly educated and keenly intellectual man," to offer the services of his scholars, who had become fed up over their poor relations and disagreements with the State Department and had concluded that working with the armed forces would be more promising. Impressed by the "realpolitik" worldview of these scholars in opposition to Hull's Wilsonianism, Embick "almost immediately recognized" R&A's potential value. He consequently provided Langer a full agenda of work on postwar issues with special focus on Soviet intentions—a subject over which he was "very much concerned." The resulting reports, the JSSC informed Langer in late August, would be of "very great value" to it and to other JCS organizations.[8]

By this time Earle and Sprout had also developed an important correspondence with James Forrestal, the former undersecretary of the navy who had become secretary upon Knox's death in the spring. Perhaps more than any other individual in the War and Navy Departments, Forrestal was deeply concerned with creating appropriate politico-military coordination in postwar planning and proper education in international relations for officers. Consequently, as undersecretary he had commissioned Sprout to develop a course syllabus and textbook for officers in the navy's V-12 educational program. Titled Foundations of National Power, the course was first undertaken experimentally at Princeton, and in September Forrestal and numerous high-ranking naval officers met with Sprout, Earle, Kirk, Arnold Wolfers of Yale, the geographer Isaiah Bowman of Johns Hopkins, and others. Some of these scholars had previously worked with the State

Department and the armed forces as well as on this course, and they were happy to collaborate with the government to expand and institutionalize it. Both the syllabus and the textbook would be published, with the course offered at Princeton, Yale, Northwestern, and the Universities of California at Berkeley, Pennsylvania, and North Carolina.[9]

In a letter to Bowman written during the September meeting, Forrestal referred to the project as "our course on politico-military geographic pragmatism," and on the same date he neatly summarized in his diary the conclusions he had reached regarding "American Problems in Dealing with War, Political Geography, and Military Policy." These were phrased in terms quite similar to those which individuals in the so-called Realist school, from diplomat George F. Kennan to theologian Reinhold Niebuhr, were beginning to use—most notably the "conflict between American idealism and historical reality" and the "American desire to secure finality in dealing with historic and fluid problems." These needed to be overcome, Forrestal concluded, "to achieve accommodation between the power we now possess, our reluctance to use it positively, the realistic necessity for such use, and our national ideals."[10]

Forrestal strongly encouraged younger naval officers to follow his lead in studying U.S. foreign policy (army officers, he maintained in early 1945, "do not view the world from the same global standpoint as the Navy"),[11] thereby offsetting, as Vincent Davis has noted, "any tendencies that might otherwise have existed toward wholly deferring to the renascent State Department in this field. The naval officers for more than thirty years had been more or less forced to do their own thinking about foreign policy, without much astuteness or self-confidence, until Forrestal began tutoring them in this work." In the process he provided them with academic expertise that "did little to instill in them a reliance on the kind of foreign policy that the State Department had often advocated."[12]

Forrestal was also a driving force in the 1944 effort to achieve high-level, politico-military coordination. His aim, he told Hopkins in November, was to create a system similar to the British "for coordinated and focused government action" in the postwar era, one that would continue Hopkins's own White House functions "on a partially formalized basis. . . . [T]here is nothing more important in the coming four years," he maintained, "than the creation of some such machinery." Forrestal remained well aware that the army and navy were "not the makers of policy," but he joined his officers in insisting that "they have a responsibility to define to the makers of policy what they believe are the military necessities of the United States, both for its own defense and for the implementation of its responsibility for the maintenance of world peace." Beyond that, he had come to believe that both service secretaries—and the navy secretary in particular—should play a pivotal role in that definition and in politico-military affairs in general. He consequently moved in 1944 to reinsert those secretaries into the policy-making process from which FDR had excluded them.[13]

Forrestal's concerns and desire to achieve high-level, politico-military coordination were shared by Stimson and Edward R. Stettinius, the undersecretary of state who succeeded Hull as secretary upon the latter's retirement in late 1944. Unlike Hull, Stettinius was a strong proponent of effective coordination, and his experiences with the armed forces in both the planning for and deliberations at Dumbarton Oaks, discussed below, probably played a major role in convincing him of the need to create additional as well as to strengthen existing machinery. Stimson concurred, if for no other reason than to stop Hull's practice, which he found highly objectionable, of corresponding directly with the Joint Chiefs rather than through him and the navy secretary. Only the president, Stimson maintained, should confer directly with the JCS, and this "growing infringement" on his prerogatives, he informed Hull in August, "has troubled me a great deal." Furthermore, all three secretaries desired an end to Roosevelt's policy of keeping them out of the decision-making loop on politico-military matters.[14]

Dissatisfaction with State Department planning for a postwar civil aviation conference in late 1943 provided an additional catalyst for action. The JPWC bitterly noted that although State had "invited coordination" on this issue, it had ignored JCS objections to holding the conference, not apprised them of negotiations in advance, and limited military influence to comments on papers already submitted to the British. In August the JPWC called for the creation of a new civil-military agency to advise the president on the formulation and implementation of a national policy on postwar civil aviation, and in October it joined Stimson and Forrestal in objecting to State's draft agreement and methods. It also expressed "grave concern as to whether the military interests of the United States in this subject are being adequately safeguarded, and whether this country's present aviation supremacy is being needlessly compromised," and it recommended informing State that "highest priority should be given to the determination of a national policy and of a governmentally agreed plan of negotiation."[15]

All these concerns and efforts would culminate in the late 1944 formation of the State-War-Navy Coordinating Committee (SWNCC), formally composed of three civilian assistant secretaries but with uniformed officers serving extensively as advisers, alternates, and subcommittee members. The committee would be responsible for formulating recommendations to the secretary of state on specific politico-military matters and would serve as the conduit for correspondence and requests for guidance between State and the armed forces, which would also now go through the war and navy secretaries. This ended the secretary of state's direct correspondence with the JCS which Stimson had found objectionable, while providing effective interdepartmental coordination. With such coordination, Stimson noted, "we were less likely to get overruled by some fantasy of the President's." At the same time he, Stettinius, and Forrestal began to meet again as a powerful revived "committee of three" while the JPWC charter was revised and the Joint Civil Affairs Committee (JCAC) set up, with both placed under the "general guidance" of the JSSC.[16]

This system, in the words of one official army history, "finally provided a basis for interdepartmental staff work that brought foreign policy formulation into close connection with joint committee work and JCS deliberations."[17] It would not be completed and implemented until early 1945, however. Throughout 1944 the armed forces thus found themselves facing directly a host of postwar politico-military issues, both specific and general, and numerous collisions with the State Department.

Postwar Plans and Conflicts

The most important of these issues concerned State Department planning for a postwar international organization. The Joint Chiefs' objections to such planning extended far beyond the issue of trusteeship for the Mandated Islands. As early as March 1944 they and the JSSC reaffirmed both their postwar base demands and their belief that an international police force was, in Willson's words, "absolutely visionary." This did not mean they opposed postwar international cooperation. To the contrary, they emphasized Great Power cooperation as the sine qua non for postwar order and the accepted basic assumption for postwar planning, and they probably agreed when Pasvolsky told the Informal Agenda Group that "the only two causes of war in the future would be if the big nations fell out or if they fell asleep." They insisted, however, as did their British colleagues, that postwar disarmament and an international police force were not practical and that reliance should be placed on Big Three agreements and national forces for the maintenance of peace. Indeed, they distrusted anything smacking of international military contracts and focused instead on informal understanding between the three great powers—so much so that one British officer concluded after an August discussion with Embick and Fairchild that they "were quite emphatic and were inclined to the policy of the 'big stick.'"[18]

In this regard the armed forces emphasized the importance of planning for and Allied cooperation during the critical time *between* Axis surrender and the establishment and functioning of any international organization. In line with this emphasis, Willson pressed for the establishment of powerful "regional councils" under the interested great powers in each part of the world. His advocacy led to a revealing discussion at the May 25 meeting of the Informal Agenda Group, when Norman Davis objected to the proposal because it would "allow Russia and Great

Britain a free hand in Europe." That concern did not bother Willson. Reflecting both continued congressional/presidential insistence that U.S. military forces not be committed to preserve peace in Europe and naval postwar planning conclusions that would be circulated less than a month later,[19] he replied that "such a solution might be highly acceptable politically." It was not acceptable to Davis or group member Benjamin Cohen, however, who attacked it as an example of the "isolation of the past." Willson disagreed. He also reminded the other group members that international organization remained dependent on a Great Power cooperation that was still hypothetical. Supported by Hepburn, he pointedly noted in this regard that international organization would not be possible unless Russia entered the war in the Far East, for such entry was a critical component of continued Allied cooperation. He also warned that presently "we did not know whether Russia was with us or against us," informed the group that the JCS believed the United States had a strong interest in preventing an Anglo-Russian clash in the Balkans, and suggested expanding the CCS so as to include the Soviet Union.[20]

Willson's comments accurately reflected military thinking about the postwar world—thinking that remained inextricably interwoven with planning the size and shape of the postwar armed forces. Throughout 1944, separate service organizations set up in 1943 to deal with this matter continued to produce plans based on their own views of U.S. postwar national policies and the likely shape of the postwar world. Given the fierce interservice struggles over unification and scarce postwar dollars which were already developing, these plans may very well have been, as some have argued, "window dressing" designed to rationalize ensuing service "wish lists."[21] Yet they offer insight into the political assumptions of the armed forces and their views of the postwar era.

The first army and AAF plans of 1944 provided little if any detail on foreign policy beyond the JSSC assumptions of late 1943.[22] These assumptions included occupation by the Allies of the defeated Axis nations and division of the world into spheres of responsibility. The planners provided U.S. forces for such occupation, as well as for holding extensive overseas bases designed both to protect America and to help secure world peace. Following Roosevelt's repeated insistence from the *Iowa* conversations through the early months of 1944, as well as their own desires, the planners assumed that Britain and Russia would be primarily responsible for the European sphere in terms of ground forces, with U.S. participation limited to the air after a brief occupation of Germany itself. Joint planners reached similar conclusions, noting during the summer that the looming conflict between the need for large-scale occupation forces to prevent chaos in Europe and domestic political pressure for rapid demobilization could be resolved by using airpower as a substitute for ground forces, with the latter limited to occupation duty in Germany and Austria.[23]

As in 1943, navy postwar plans were far more extensive and detailed as to foreign policy problems and objectives. Given the postwar uncertainties with which
they were forced to deal, navy planners had decided to develop three demobilization plans based on different basic assumptions: no agreement between the
Allies regarding postwar cooperation; Allied agreement and a subsequent geographic division of naval responsibilities between the U.S. and British navies; and
establishment of and U.S. membership in an international organization to maintain peace. As previously noted, a plan based on the first assumption had been
circulated in 1943; revisions were completed on May 22, 1944. On June 9 a plan
based on the second set of assumptions was distributed; it included the list of U.S.
postwar policies that Yarnell had originally composed for the first plan as modified by naval suggestions he had received.[24] Five days later the admiral concluded
that a third plan was not necessary because international organization would not
require any appreciable increase in the naval strength projected in the second
plan. The justification for this conclusion consisted of his previously mentioned
assessment of Soviet-American relations, which was in turn part of a seven-page
memorandum on the likely postwar international situation. That memorandum
constituted the navy's first attempt at systematic analysis of the postwar world.[25]

The analysis was not an optimistic one. Axis defeat would be followed "by several years of unrest, minor wars, civil wars, and tensions between major and minor states." These would take place in all parts of the world, with Europe and the
Near East being "more unstable" than anywhere else. Nevertheless, the postwar
U.S. role in this area should be minimal, with all troops withdrawn "as rapidly as
possible." Yarnell justified this conclusion on the explicit grounds that solution of
these problems was "a task for the European nations themselves," particularly
Britain and Russia, and implicitly on the basis of postwar domestic problems that
would include "a strong demand to return our men from foreign stations as soon
as possible, a decrease of interest in foreign commitments, strikes and labor unrest, . . . race riots," and "general disillusionment as a result of selfish interests
abroad, and the squabbles that will take place at the peace conference." Such factors would preclude a policy of global intervention and maintenance of the large
naval force necessary to pursue it, Yarnell implied. Naval forces would obviously
be needed to promote major national policies, but he limited these to membership in an international organization to secure peace, maintenance of the Monroe Doctrine in the hemisphere and the Open Door in the Far East, promotion
of international trade, and the "intention to obtain our share of sea and air
transportation."

Nor did Yarnell believe the United States would face any threat to its national
security in the postwar era. The Axis Powers would be defeated and occupied, and
although there would be "friction" with the Allies, particularly trade rivalry with

Britain, he foresaw "no major differences of policy" with London and "no major clashes of policy" with Russia. None of the Allies would have reason to pursue an aggressive, expansionist policy that would threaten the others, he argued, or the capacity to do so. China simply was not a great power and would not become one in the near future. Britain still was, but its relative decline would accelerate in the postwar era, it would be forced to demobilize as rapidly as the United States, and it would possess neither the motivation nor the ability to go to war with America.

Russia, on the other hand, was "potentially the most powerful country in the world" and would pursue a "realistic and nationalistic" postwar policy that would include takeover of the Baltic States, Bessarabia, portions of Poland and Finland, and perhaps southern Sakhalin and the Kuril Islands as well as neutralization of the Kiel Canal and the Dardanelles. Such a policy would be motivated by a defensive desire for security, however, and in no way threatened the United States. Indeed, Yarnell maintained, as had other naval planners, that Russia could not become a threat to U.S. security without becoming a seapower—a process that would require ice-free ports, internal development, and the building of a powerful navy, which would take twenty to thirty years of peace to accomplish. Consequently, the United States should offer "no objection" to the above-mentioned Russian territorial desires. "With realistic statesmanship on both sides," he maintained, "there is no danger at present or in the visible future of a major clash between the two nations."[26]

On June 16 Yarnell restated and amplified these conclusions, adding detailed arguments opposing any international police force and strongly supporting a regional division of the world into spheres of responsibility that would leave the United States out of Europe but in total control of the Pacific. He also contended that another world war would be unlikely for twenty to thirty years, implied strongly that one could not occur if the Allies remained united, and explained how and why they could and should do so. War with Britain "would be the doom of Anglo-Saxon civilization." British power was rapidly declining, and London clearly feared Russia, "potentially the most powerful nation" in the postwar world. "Extreme communism and world-revolution have been abandoned as national policies" by Moscow, however, and expected Russian demands for territory in Eastern Europe and the North Pacific, free exit from the Baltic and Black Seas, friendly governments in Poland and Germany, and expanded influence in Iran and the Near East did not constitute threats to U.S. security. "There are no major differences of policy between Russia and the United States," he reiterated. "We have no objection to whatever form of government Russia prefers as long as she does not try to force it on us."[27]

The flip side of these conclusions was the expectation that the United States would dominate the Pacific as Russia would Eastern Europe. The degree of "real independence" to be granted the Philippines remained questionable, for example, as did trusteeship for the Mandated Islands. Yarnell's most interesting comments related to the future of European colonies in this U.S. sphere of influence. Picking up on FDR's previous attacks on French colonialism, he proposed that Indochina be made a mandate and either granted independence or returned to France only under condition of better treatment, and that other French possessions in the Pacific be returned only if the United States obtained rights to use the air bases it had built. That was by no means the only precondition. *"It should be asserted as a policy of the United States,"* Yarnell emphasized in proposing extension of the Monroe Doctrine's "no transfer" principle to the Pacific, *"that the United States will not consent to the transfer of sovereignty of any territory in the Pacific unless its approval has been secured."* Nor would it consent to continued control of "vital strategic areas by a nation too weak to defend them." There was also the question of whether the United States should consent to continuation of any colonies in the area, because to do so would collide with the increased nationalism that Japanese conquest had intensified and with the U.S. interest in free trade for these "potential markets of unknown but considerable volume."[28]

Although this June 16 analysis remained within the navy, Yarnell forwarded a copy of his preceding June 14 memorandum to the army, along with a recommendation that interservice agreement be reached before proceeding with postwar planning. New OPD chief General John Hull concurred but took the opportunity to criticize segments of the paper so as to make clear that some army planners were thinking more expansively. Yarnell had ignored U.S. airpower in the postwar world, its existing commitment to maintain occupation forces in Germany "for some time," and the probable occupation of Japan. He had also failed to include the Good Neighbor as a national policy or the conditions under which the United States would use force in the hemisphere, nor had he considered "the need of the U.S. for access to certain strategic raw materials not directly under our control, or to the effect on our national policy of this need." Oil requirements, for example, "may influence our policy with reference to the Persian Gulf area and the NEI [Netherlands East Indies]."[29]

The Intelligence Division was even more critical, arguing that portions of the memorandum constituted unacceptable "opinions as to what should be the future foreign policy of the United States." Most notable was Yarnell's artificial and incorrect isolation of the Americas from Europe, whose nations had previously attempted and would continue to attempt to prevent U.S. hegemony in the hemisphere. Examples given by G-2 included British airline development and "Russian political penetration" of the hemisphere "centered in Mexico." It also insisted that hemispheric defense would require bases in West Africa so as to prevent control of key waters by Britain or France and further warned that "extension of Russian influence into that area through a Communist French Empire is not improbable." Given these facts, as well as likely Soviet maintenance of a large postwar army and air force along with British demobilization and need for U.S. troops to aid in policing Europe, G-2 rejected the limits on European action that Yarnell had posited. It also criticized his failure to consider the Middle East, where Britain's need to maintain both its imperial lifeline and adequate oil supplies would clash with a Russian drive for control of Iran to obtain a warm-water port. United States interests were also emerging in this area, specifically with respect to its oil reserves and "strategic air routes." Thus the United States "can neither ignore the region nor afford not to assist in achieving stability there." [30]

Yarnell was thus incorrect to conclude that there would be no clashes of policy between the United States and the Soviet Union. These would clearly occur in Iran and over the matter of influence in the French and German governments. Furthermore—and again contrary to Yarnell's conclusions—ideology remained an important component of Soviet foreign policy. "While Russia probably will not engage in armed aggression on a large scale in the immediate postwar period," it was "certain that she will revert to her role of fomenting social unrest and upheavals in all of the capitalistic countries. This will bring a major clash of policy between Russia and the United States, and, while not leading to war in the near future, it will certainly entail severely strained relations for a long period of time until a final adjustment is reached either by war or by other means." Yet G-2 was not ready to recommend a confrontation policy. Indeed, it concurred with Yarnell's comments about continued Allied cooperation, albeit with two provisos: that the Big Three proved able to reconcile their differences in the Middle East, and that the United States maintain military forces sufficiently strong to support its policies in any potential conflicts and exhibit a readiness to use them if necessary. [31]

On August 10 SPD chief Tompkins suggested to Yarnell, as Hull had to him, that the entire matter be forwarded to the Joint Chiefs so that the JSSC could study it and prepare a policy paper which the JCS could then take up with the State Department. Yarnell concurred on August 22,[32] but the JSSC could not act, for by this time its members were deeply involved in the Dumbarton Oaks discussions that had begun on postwar security organization.

Dumbarton Oaks

The armed forces would be heavily represented and have a major impact at the Dumbarton Oaks Conference. Six of the eighteen members of the U.S. delegation were in uniform: JSSC members Embick, Willson, and Fairchild for the JCS; Strong and Train for the JPWC and War and Navy Departments; and Hepburn as

GB chairman. Furthermore, as Thomas Campbell has noted, these officers "spoke freely on the basic concepts of the proposed organization" and gave "valuable advice on technical security questions"—as did their subordinates working with State Department personnel on lower levels. Moreover, the military representatives formed a majority in the section of the U.S. delegation constructed to deal with international security arrangements, and Strong and Willson were members of the pivotal U.S. Steering Committee.[33]

By the time the conference opened on August 21, these officers had largely succeeded in turning the official U.S. position against trusteeship discussions and the creation of an international police force. Given their position on the relationship of these issues to Allied relations in general, however, the result was extremely ironic. The JSSC had consistently justified its opposition to discussion of trusteeships, as well as to British moves in the Balkans, on the grounds of maintaining good Soviet-American relations in general and avoiding divisive territorial issues and even the semblance of an Anglo-American bloc in particular. Yet trusteeship discussion would be supported at the conference by the Russians and opposed by the British, who continued to see it as a threat to their empire. A similar division occurred over creating an international air force, with Soviet support facing Anglo-American opposition.[34] The military position on these two issues thereby helped create the very Anglo-American bloc and conflict with the Soviets that the JSSC had sought to avoid at all costs.

That this would occur was by no means clear before or even during the first week of the conference. The opening statements by Hull and Soviet ambassador Andrei Gromyko on August 21 illustrated a similarity between Soviet and JCS views as opposed to those of the State Department as Hull, according to Stettinius, "especially stressed the necessity of justice to all nations, while Mr. Gromyko placed especial emphasis on the responsibility of the Great Powers in maintaining peace and security." Strong further noted in mid-September that the Americans had "in general been in closer agreement with the Soviet delegates than with the British." Moreover, as previously noted, Willson had admitted on July 31 that if the Russians insisted on discussing trusteeship proposals, "then the objective of the Joint Chiefs of Staff would presumably call for a direct reversal of its present recommendations."[35]

That proved unnecessary, for although the Russians at first did question the deletion of the issue and demand that it be discussed, by August 31 they were willing to agree to its removal from the agenda in light of the Anglo-American front that had emerged on this issue. The related issue of an international air force proved more difficult to resolve, however. Strong Soviet support for this concept led to the creation of a special military subcommittee to study the issue and full recognition, as Willson noted on August 25, that the "Russians do really have a different idea than we do about an international air force." Then on August 31 Gromyko argued that given the removal from the agenda of trusteeship, the Allies should agree that small states be obligated to provide bases for such an international force.[36]

The U.S. delegation found this proposal deeply disturbing. By this time most of its members had come to oppose any international military force, even one limited to the air, on both technical grounds and a fear that Congress might view this as a usurpation of its powers and refuse to support or even to join an international organization that included such a force. Of the military representatives only Fairchild remained in favor, and his voice may have been muted by such factors, by his junior status vis-à-vis his uniformed colleagues, and by his late addition to the U.S. delegation and deliberations. Whatever the cause, he soon accepted the negative arguments. As he and Train stated during a later phase of the conference, in addition to the "difficulties of supply, maintenance and training" that would make an international force slower than national units if not totally unworkable, "it would be very difficult to obtain from the United States Congress the authority to establish such an international air force."[37] The U.S. delegation also feared that the smaller states would interpret the obligation to provide bases as a threat and refuse to join the organization, that it was unfair to them, and that the Soviets intended to use any such agreement to acquire control of certain areas under the guise of international authority—specifically Korea, Finland, and Denmark. That this was the same purpose for which the Americans had proposed trusteeship in the Pacific seemed to escape them or to appear, in the words of Robert Hilderbrand, "somehow illegitimate when pursued in this manner by the Soviet Union."[38]

The Soviet stance on these issues remained quite flexible, with their representatives dropping abundant hints that they would readily accede to a proposal to rely on quotas of national forces.[39] Far less resolvable and much more threatening to the outcome of the conference were Soviet demands for sixteen votes in the General Assembly (one for each Soviet republic) and an absolute veto in the Security Council, even on disputes in which it was one of the parties. These demands, the Soviet delegation made clear, were not negotiable.

Nor were they acceptable to the U.S. or British delegations, even though the Americans had originally backed the absolute veto. Stettinius so feared public reaction to the General Assembly proposal, which he labeled "the bombshell," that he instituted special secrecy measures—including no mention in the official minutes and reference to it as the "x matter" in his correspondence. It was the council veto, however, that proved to be the most important and intractable disagreement. Even a meeting between Gromyko and Roosevelt, followed by a special appeal from FDR to Stalin, failed to budge the Soviets on this issue. Instead, on September 12 Gromyko withdrew his international air force and base proposals in a futile effort to obtain Anglo-American agreement to his voting proposals. "We are deadlocked," Stettinius gloomily noted on September 13, and at "the lowpoint of the conversations."[40]

Such conflict was exactly what U.S. military representatives had feared, although they had played an inadvertent role in creating it. Now, however, they moved to prevent any further damage, no matter what the cost in terms of the U.S. position on postwar international organization. On September 14 Hepburn read a memorandum reflecting their opinion that the Americans should concede the absolute veto to the Soviets to maintain the Big Three collaboration necessary for collective security to work. He was strongly supported by Embick, who noted that a rupture over the issue would not only doom collective security but also have dire implications for national security: "He would prefer not to have Russia as strong as she is, but if we fail to establish an organization in which we tie ourselves to Russia, our only alternative is a strong military establishment in the Western Hemisphere."[41]

Later that day Embick suggested and Fairchild supported a compromise.[42] Discussions over the next three days resulted in a formal proposal by all the military representatives and Assistant Secretary of State Breckinridge Long on September 18 whereby the Americans would offer the Soviets two compromises on the veto and, if these failed to resolve the dispute, concede to Moscow's demand. Their reasoning was fully explained in both a memorandum Long drafted and presented on that date, and in their comments during three separate meetings that day to discuss the crisis and military proposals.

During the morning session Embick once again elucidated the dire postwar consequences of a Soviet-American split for both postwar international order and U.S. security. If Russia "does not come along," he warned, "it will be impossible to have any world order" and "we would be powerless to intervene by force in Europe." The memorandum itself, discussed in detail during the late afternoon session, warned of "the most serious, if not fatal, consequences" of failure to achieve accord. Militarily, these would be "very grave" for the United States, "particularly in the Far East," where Russian entry would be delayed and U.S. casualties enormously increased. "The short range military consequences in Europe," the memorandum continued, "will be that Russia will be the dominant power in Europe, at least as far as the Rhine, and possibly over the whole continent." The need to balance such awesome power would necessitate "a greatly increased burden of armament" for England and the United States. A Soviet-American split would also doom the possibility of any but what Hepburn labeled a "useless" postwar international organization that did not include the Soviets, would lead to dissension at home, and would make the unified support necessary for a strong postwar foreign policy extremely difficult. To avoid such catastrophic results, the

United States should attempt compromise on the veto issue and, if that failed, revert to its original position and thereby support the Soviets. The military representatives believed that this position was, in Hepburn's words, "correct" and reflected international "facts of life."[43]

In additional memoranda on September 18 and 19 the military representatives reiterated this point and noted that military sanctions against a great power would never be feasible. They also noted that the Soviet view on the veto would be beneficial to the United States by offering protection against any Security Council action without U.S. approval. Hepburn further informed Forrestal that Long believed "continued lack of agreement" on the veto issue would doom the conference, "which would have serious public repercussions and might result in the decision by the Russians to refuse to attend any further conferences even after the war."[44] It was the military situation, however, that Embick maintained was "of paramount importance." Only Russia could help the United States in the Far East, and delay or cancellation of its entry into the war against Japan because of the Dumbarton Oaks negotiations, he ominously warned, "might double the cost in lives of American men."[45]

The military proposals split the U.S. delegation badly, with Stettinius, Pasvolsky, and Hull in opposition and deeply upset. Stettinius agreed that "relations with the Soviet Union are too important from the standpoint of the prosecution of the war to allow a collapse to occur," but he did not think this could be prevented only by acceding to the Soviet viewpoint on the veto. Indeed, he did not believe that relations with the Soviets were "being impaired to the slightest extent" and concluded that the military representatives had "become panicky, if not hysterical," had "lost their grip," and "are not thinking straight." On September 18, at Hopkins's suggestion, he asked Willson to ascertain whether Marshall and King shared the views of their representatives.[46] Confident that this issue would not threaten relations with Russia but that conference failure would, Stettinius proposed adjourning with the veto left for future resolution.

Roosevelt had previously made extensive use of such postponement tactics and thus agreed on September 21. So did Embick and Willson—provided, of course, that the Soviets agreed. Embick took the opportunity to impress on both Stettinius and the president Marshall's view "that it was very important that whatever course was followed it be handled in a harmonious and workable way so that there would be no prejudice to cooperation with the Soviet Union." Should that cooperation be compromised and Russia not enter the war against Japan, he again warned the U.S. delegation, "it might well double the cost of American lives expended in that conflict." Gromyko accepted the proposal on September 27 but indicated that Soviet participation in any future conference on international organization would be "contingent" on Anglo-American concurrence in Moscow's position on both the veto and the number of Soviet votes in the General Assembly. As he had ominously warned Stettinius a few days earlier, "The moment this principle of unanimity breaks down there is war."[47]

This section of the conference was thereafter able to recess on September 28 with official announcement of success and agreement, in FDR's words to the press, on "90 percent of the issues." A Chinese section ensued, followed by full adjournment and an October 9 public communiqué implying great success.[48]

To an extent, that implication was correct. Agreement had been reached on a large number of issues relating to a postwar international organization, from its official United Nations name through its general structure and powers. Most of the State Department's original proposals for a true international security system had been gutted, however, and largely at the insistence of the armed forces. Indeed, in many ways they emerged from the conference as the great winners. Not only had the serious Soviet-American split they feared been averted, but discussion of trusteeships had been avoided, an international air force squelched, and national sovereignty left unimpaired. In this regard their viewpoint on the Security Council veto was actually closer to that of the Soviets than to the State Department, and it was a view that triumphed at Dumbarton Oaks over State Department internationalism.[49]

Yet the actual success for the armed forces at Dumbarton Oaks was much more limited than it appeared. The trusteeship issue had been postponed rather than resolved, for example, with the president as well as the State Department still supporting the concept for the Mandated Islands and the armed forces still opposed. The conference also left State and the military perhaps more suspicious of and disappointed in each other than they had been beforehand. During the conference, Stettinius in particular had developed and privately begun to express doubts about the competence of Embick, Strong, and Fairchild (ironically at the very moment Stimson was praising Embick), doubts that may have influenced his proposals for higher-level, politico-military coordination after the conference.[50] Much more worrisome, the conference had come dangerously close to total failure and had resulted in exactly what the JSSC and JCS had wished to thwart— Allied conflict pitting the Soviets against an apparent Anglo-American front. A full and formal split had not occurred. Nevertheless, one result of the conference had been the increased suspicion that the JSSC had feared and sought to avoid through their proposals, both before and during the meeting.[51]

Continued Conflict over Trusteeships

These problems were visible in ensuing discussions of the Mandated Islands during the fall and winter of 1944–45. In mid-November Roosevelt reiterated his support for placing them under trusteeship on the grounds that obtaining sovereignty not only violated the Atlantic Charter but also was unnecessary. Its only result, he sardonically maintained, would be "to provide jobs as governors of insignificant islands for inefficient Army and Navy officers or members of the civilian career service." [52] With this backing and a presidential directive to proceed in consultation with the armed forces, Stettinius informed Stimson and Forrestal in late December that although he had agreed not to discuss trusteeships at Dumbarton Oaks in "deference to the wishes of the Joint Chiefs of Staff," he could not continue to keep silent. The Soviets as well as the British, the Chinese, and the American public had raised the issue, and he had received substantial criticism for omitting it. Consequently, the subject would have to be discussed at the next international organization meeting and placed within the UN charter. Hoping to effect a compromise, he then maintained that such discussion could be limited to general principles, with specific territories postponed for later discussions, and he requested War, Navy, and JCS participation in preparation of such a proposal. [53]

Given Roosevelt's stance as well as Stettinius's willingness to postpone discussion of specific territories, the JSSC in early January recommended and the JCS approved a modification of their position, composed by Willson and revised by Leahy, so as to allow for a general Allied discussion of trusteeships—albeit with very strong caveats: military participation in the preparation of any proposals; full consideration of future U.S. defense needs; no discussion of territories under U.S. sovereignty or occupation; and no consideration of any agreement that might give another nation a claim to control over the Mandated Islands. To reinforce this last point, Roosevelt's November 23 statement that these islands were in the "blue zone" required for direct defense of the United States was to be included in the memorandum to the State Department. [54]

Beneath the surface of this unified response lay serious disagreement within the armed forces. Despite his official concurrence with Willson's proposals, Embick indicated that he opposed any modification of the JCS position because it would be impossible "as a practical proposition" to discuss general principles of trusteeship without discussing specific territories and "because the Russians might raise embarrassing questions." Supported by Handy and McCloy, he also warned that any discussion "might bring up matters which would affect Russia wholeheartedly coming into the war against Japan." Willson countered that Moscow had made clear on "several occasions" its desire to discuss trusteeship; if Washington continued to refuse to do so, "we would not only fail to take care of the fears that General Embick has but are likely to make our relationship with the Russians far worse and thereby bring about precisely the undesirable consequences General Embick has in mind." [55]

The JCS had concurred with Willson, but army planners continued to dissent, as did Stimson. Displeased with the JCS compromise and the entire direction of State Department thinking on postwar cooperation and international organization, and perhaps already influenced by progress on the atomic bomb project, he boldly asserted at a January 21 meeting with McCloy, Embick, Handy, Marshall, and Willson (substituting for Forrestal) that not only trusteeship but also the entire question of postwar international organization should be "left open" until the end of the war and "until some of those questions of individual title in reference to these islands had been privately discussed between the parties concerned." Marshall, supported by Willson, responded that the JCS had already approved the policy modification on trusteeships and that final decision was both a political matter and now in the hands of the State Department. He quickly changed his mind, however, when in a rare display of disagreement with his chief of staff Stimson shot back that he had previously been a secretary of state and that in light of his expressed beliefs he intended to discuss the matter directly with Stettinius.[56]

On January 22 in a meeting with Forrestal and Stettinius, Stimson further verbalized why he "dreaded having a general meeting of the United Nations even to discuss the structure of a world organization until certain underlying problems had been ironed out and solved between the four major powers." The following day he sent the secretary of state, upon request, a formal and rather extraordinary memorandum amplifying and explaining the points he had tried to make. Allied discussion of trusteeship and international organization should be postponed, he argued. The 1943 Moscow Declaration had envisaged two different international organizations: one for the future based on open membership and equality, and another, "interim consultative organization of the large four powers" for the period immediately following the war "to establish a guarantee of peace in the atmosphere of which the world organization can be set going." This interim organization would in turn necessitate a settlement of territorial acquisitions for the establishment of defense posts by each of the major powers for their safety in carrying out such a guarantee of world peace. To attempt to create the international organization before all this had been done would be to "put the cart before the horse" and to repeat Woodrow Wilson's blunder of trying to establish an international organization before gaining a solid foundation on which it could rest and before "we have discussed and ironed out the realities which may exist to enable the four powers to carry out their mission."[57]

The Mandated Islands were one such reality, but not one to be discussed under trusteeship. United States acquisition of them would not constitute "colonization or exploitation," he argued, because they were the necessary bases "for the defense of the security of the Pacific for the future world. To serve such purpose they must belong to the United States with absolute power to rule and fortify them." They were "outposts," not "colonies," and as such "their acquisition is appropriate under the general doctrine of self-defense by the power which guarantees the safety of that area of the world."[58]

As the JSSC had done in August, Stimson tied his arguments to relations with Moscow by pointing out that Stettinius would "find the same clash of fundamental ideas and interests with Russia," who would claim that "her own self-defense as a guarantor of the peace of the world will depend on relations with buffer countries like Poland, Bulgaria, and Rumania, which will be quite different from complete independence on the part of those countries." Such "fundamental problems" needed to be "at least discussed and if possible an understanding reached" before trying to establish "principles in a world organization which may clash with realities." To attempt to do so, however, would run the risk of Allied conflict that would be detrimental to the war effort. "Any discussions of territorial matters," Stimson warned in an amplification on the JSSC/JCS warnings of mid-1944, be they "security acquisitions, trusteeships or outright territorial adjustments, are almost certain to induce controversies which put at risk a united and vigorous prosecution of the war itself." Furthermore, to think trusteeships could be discussed without reference to specifics was "fanciful," and to raise the issue while insisting on no discussion of the Mandated Islands was "even more unwise" because it would "immediately provoke a sense of distrust and discrimination . . . which would call marked attention to our aims and poison the general atmosphere of the discussion." The United States should therefore not bring up trusteeship or any other territorial matters "in any form, at least until the war is much further along and Russian participation in the Pacific war is accomplished."[59]

Stimson's memorandum, which Embick and Forrestal both "strongly approved,"[60] in effect reiterated the previous JSSC/JCS arguments against any territorial discussions while the war was in progress owing to their negative impact on Soviet-American relations and the Allied war effort. Beyond that, he now expanded the argument to include no discussion of postwar international organization in general before the Allies first discussed territorial acquisitions for postwar bases, as well as no such territorial discussions until victory in Europe was in sight and the Russians were in the war against Japan.

By this time, however, numerous officers and civilians had begun to question whether postwar cooperation with the Soviets was possible and, if so, whether continuation of present policy was the best way to achieve it. The suspicions engendered at Dumbarton Oaks had by no means been limited to the Soviets. They deeply affected the Americans as well and heavily reinforced calls for a shift in U.S. policy. The result in late 1944 and early 1945 was a renewed, major debate within the armed forces and the government as a whole over that policy and over Soviet-American relations in general.

Second Thoughts on the Allies, September 1944–April 1945

Allied relations had remained relatively harmonious during the great military victories of mid-1944. Those victories raised numerous postwar issues, however, and with them additional fears about Russia. By year's end these were being expressed in numerous quarters, including the armed forces, with increasing frequency and urgency. Equally frequent and urgent were requests for a change in policy. No such change occurred at this time, but the dissent against established policy gained numerous military as well as civilian adherents, thereby setting the stage for the reversal that would take place later in 1945.

The Soviet Menace

Late summer and early fall of 1944 witnessed the initiation of a major effort to reverse U.S. policy regarding the Soviets. Two catalysts for this effort were Soviet behavior as its forces overran Eastern Europe, particularly Poland, and Ambassador Harriman's strong response. The Red Army's sudden halt on the Vistula in August and subsequent refusal to aid the Polish Home Army uprising in Warsaw—or even to allow Anglo-American aid to the beleaguered Poles—created a crisis in the alliance and led Harriman to question whether postwar cooperation was possible. "Gravely concerned" for the first time by Soviet attitude and behavior, he warned that Moscow's refusal to help the Poles was based on "ruthless political considerations" and that relations with Russia had "taken a startling turn" for the worse. "These men are bloated with power," he asserted, and "expect they can force acceptance of their decisions without question upon us and all countries." Washington's "generous attitude" had been "misinterpreted as a sign of weakness and acceptance" and needed to be reversed. The "time has come," he concluded on September 10, "when we must make clear what we expect of them as the price of our good will. Unless we take issue with the present policy there is every indication the Soviet Union will become a world bully wherever their interests are involved." In October he returned to Washington in an effort to convince his superiors to revise U.S. policy accordingly.[1]

Harriman was not alone. He reported that Deane as well as AAF and embassy officers endorsed his views. Indeed, one embassy officer, Counselor George F. Kennan, was simultaneously writing his famous "Russia—Seven Years Later" memorandum, which warned that the Soviets still believed in achieving security via expansion and had agreed to collective security only to guarantee Allied military assistance via a second front. With it established they were now shedding the collective security cloak and would unilaterally move to complete what had been attempted unsuccessfully in 1939: conquest and control of Eastern Europe.[2]

These warnings reached Washington at the same time as conflicts over the UN were erupting at Dumbarton Oaks, which the Americans interpreted as resulting from a change in Soviet mood "from cooperation to intransigence" paralleling their shift in behavior in Poland.[3] A State Department briefing paper for OCTAGON asserted that the Soviets "might mistake friendliness for weakness" and called for "a greater degree of firmness in our attitude and policy." By mid-September the Polish and Dumbarton Oaks conflicts had raised in Hull's mind "the most serious doubts" about Soviet policy, leading him to "wonder whether Stalin and the Kremlin have determined to reverse their policy of cooperation with their Western Allies." At the same time, McCloy opposed plans to make Russia one of the trustees for an internationalized Saar and Ruhr, informing Stimson that he was "alarmed at giving this addition to Russia's power."[4]

The Harriman-Kennan concerns were read in the Pentagon as well as the State Department,[5] and they were far from the only such opinions the armed forces received. Equally if not more antagonistic were the comments of officers who had been dealing with the Soviets directly and who had consistently complained about their noncooperation and hostility. In early September General R. C. Walsh of the shuttle bombing project denounced Soviet failures to collaborate and informed Arnold that the past policy of fulfilling all their aid requests without question, while justifiable to keep Russia in the war, had fostered a Soviet attitude that we "will dance to their tune"; consequently, he recommended a policy revision to force Moscow "to meet us halfway." Arnold concurred, as did Deane and the head of the navy division of the Military Mission in Moscow.[6] A few weeks later Walsh warned that the Soviet ally of today might be the enemy of tomorrow and that they were "drunk with power" yet suffering from "an inferiority complex."[7] Then on December 2 Deane summarized and amplified all previous complaints in an extraordinary letter to Marshall in which he argued, as had Harriman, Kennan, and Walsh, for a major change in policy.

"Everyone will agree on the importance of collaboration with Russia—now and in the future," Deane admitted. "It won't be worth a hoot, however, unless it is based on mutual respect and made to work both ways." What followed made clear his belief that such mutuality had been lacking. "I have sat at innumerable Russian banquets and become gradually nauseated by Russian food, vodka and protestation of friendship," he bluntly stated. "It is amazing how these toasts go down past the tongues in the cheeks. After the banquet we send the Soviets another thousand airplanes, and they approve a visa that has been hanging fire for months. We then scratch our heads to see what other gifts we can send, and they scratch theirs to see what else they can ask for."[8]

Deane admitted the policy of giving "all possible assistance with no questions asked" had been appropriate "when the Red Army was back on its heels" in order to "bolster their morale in every way we could." That was no longer the case, however: "The situation has changed, but our policy has not." It was also important to realize the depth of Russian suspicion and desire to have as little as possible to do with foreigners. "They simply cannot understand giving without taking, and as a result even our giving is viewed with suspicion. Gratitude cannot be banked in the Soviet Union," and any foreigner was viewed as "either a shrewd trader to be admired or a sucker to be despised." United States policy had placed its representatives in the latter category and in a position of being both "the givers and the supplicants. This is neither dignified nor healthy for U.S. prestige."[9]

Despite such statements, Deane insisted, as had Harriman, that he was not proposing a policy of hostility. Individual Russians were "likable" and "would be friendly if they dared to be." Perhaps more important, Russia and the United States had "few conflicting interests, and there is little reason why we should not be friendly now and in the foreseeable future." But Soviet friendship could not be obtained by "pushing ourselves on them"; instead, Washington should "make the Soviet authorities come to us." Labeling this and his other suggestions "simply a question of tactics to be employed," Deane concluded that "we must be tougher if we are to gain their respect and be able to work with them in the future." A month later he reiterated these warnings and recommendations in a fifty-four-page memorandum to the Joint Chiefs containing thirty-four case histories of Soviet noncooperation.[10]

In late December Marshall forwarded Deane's letter to Stimson, along with an expression of his agreement with it "in toto." Stimson in turn sent copies to Stettinius and Roosevelt, noting that Harriman concurred and that he and Marshall "both feel it is an apt presentation with sound recommendations." On January 9 he discussed its contents with Stettinius and Forrestal.[11] He also discussed it directly with the president on December 31, taking the opportunity to link its recommendations to the atomic bomb project by informing FDR "that I knew they were spying on our work but that they had not yet gotten any real knowledge of it and that, while I was troubled about the possible effect of keeping from them even now that work, I believed that it was essential not to take them into our confidence until we were sure to get a real quid pro quo from our frankness. I said I had no illusions as to the possibility of keeping permanently such a secret but that I did not think it was yet time to share it with Russia. He said he thought he agreed with me." [12]

Calls for a policy shift were not limited to U.S. personnel in Moscow, nor was Poland the only area of concern. In reply to a JCS query, for example, Eisenhower in October cited as one reason for recommending recognition of the de Gaulle government the fact that "if France falls into the orbit of any other country the other countries of Europe will do the same," and it would not "be in our interest to have the continent of Europe dominated by any single power." Echoing Embick's concerns a month earlier, he noted that "then we would have a superpowerful Europe, a somewhat shaken British Empire and ourselves," and he asked, "Would we maintain the adequate military, naval and air forces which that would imply?" [13]

Others expressed their fears more directly and did not agree with Harriman and Deane that the question was simply one of the most effective tactics to ensure cooperation of the USSR. By late 1944 many had begun to ask whether cooperation was possible and whether Russia would pose a serious threat to postwar U.S. security and interests. Moscow's sudden declaration of war on Bulgaria on September 5, with only thirty minutes' notice to the British and Americans then in the midst of peace negotiations with the Bulgarians, appalled the OPD Strategy Section chief. Labeling it "highly underhanded," he warned that the Red Army could now occupy Bulgaria and penetrate as far south as Salonika, thereby giving it control of all the Balkans, including Greece, and posing a "threat of further advance of influence in the Middle East." This would be "just as unacceptable to Britain as though she had lost the war to Germany" and might be equally intolerable to the United States. "It may be necessary," he warned, "to decide which of our Allies we shall have to support in the determination of this most crucial political situation." Russia's action had created "a very strong possibility" that Germany had achieved her hope of obtaining easier peace terms by prolonging the war "to effect disagreement amongst her enemies." Not surprisingly, a few months later this officer strongly supported British military intervention in Greece to combat Russian influence. [14]

Reinforcing such comments was a growing interest in Middle East oil and airfields. Following up on a recent State–War Department conference on Saudi Arabia, in October Stimson made clear to State the numerous U.S. military interests in the area and requested advice on the best "means and methods" to safeguard them. State Department representatives simultaneously informed S&P officers that Iran would be critical as a buffer to protect U.S. oil interests in Saudi Arabia, that

Russia was threatening Iran, and that it would be "advisable" to keep a U.S. military mission there "so long as that was necessary and possibly for at least ten years." In late December Stettinius formally requested and Stimson agreed to indefinite continuation of that mission so as to enable the Iranian army to halt "foreign intervention or aggression" as well as prevent the "chaos and disorder" that could lead to postwar inter-Allied "friction." [15]

Growing U.S. military concern over the Soviets encompassed more than the Balkans and Middle East. Contradicting Yarnell's June dismissal of a possible Soviet naval threat, one navy intelligence officer warned in October that Moscow was planning to construct a large postwar fleet and merchant marine and would probably try to obtain naval bases on the Yugoslav and Norwegian coasts as well as in China, Korea, and perhaps even Mexico. In pursuing these objectives it would have the advantage of "the most completely and closely knit government of any great power in history," with every branch "completely synchronized in striving toward any national objective." [16]

Equally strong comments came from Forrestal, who in the summer and fall began to voice a growing suspicion of Moscow, belief that it might constitute a postwar threat, and consequent desire for both a change in wartime policy and a strong postwar national security policy. As early as August 18 he had queried de Gaulle about possible communist influence in France and noted "the widespread fears in America that a Russian menace would be substituted for a German menace." On September 2 he bitterly noted "that whenever an American suggests that we act in accordance with the needs of our own security he is apt to be called a god-damned fascist or imperialist, while if Uncle Joe suggests that he needs the Baltic Provinces, half of Poland, all of Bessarabia and access to the Mediterranean, all hands agree that he is a fine, frank, candid and generally delightful fellow because he is so explicit in what he wants." [17]

By month's end, according to Vincent Davis, Forrestal appears to have concluded that "*Russia was the emerging new enemy* toward which not only naval planning but indeed the whole of postwar U.S. foreign and security policy should be directed." Interestingly, Forrestal began to express his fear of Russia at the same time he was calling for greater politico-military education and coordination, formulation of a strong and comprehensive postwar national security policy, and inclusion of the Middle East within that policy. At the same time, he was precipitating a major shakeup in navy postwar planning, which previously had been inconclusive because of a lack of clarity about the shape of the postwar world and probable U.S. policies as well as the lack of a recognized enemy. Forrestal sought to change this situation by pointing to Russia as the enemy and by making a series of key postwar planning assumptions. [18]

The extent to which this process resulted from a bureaucratic need to compose detailed plans and justify large postwar budgets, as opposed to a real geopolitical and/or ideological fear of the Soviet Union, cannot be determined. In all likelihood a symbiotic relationship developed between the desire to emerge from the war with a strong navy and clear mission, the determination to avoid any repetition of the interwar experiences, the consequent push for geopolitical education and greater politico-military coordination, antipathy toward communism per se, fear of postwar chaos and Soviet power, and anger over Soviet behavior in Eastern Europe. Interestingly, this fusion would resolve the conflict between "idealism and historical reality" that Forrestal had noted in September and achieve the "accommodation between the power we now possess, our reluctance to use it positively, the realistic necessity for such use, and our national ideals" that he so desired.[19] It would also mark the origins of the national security state and the eventual Cold War policy of militant opposition to the Soviet Union on both ideological and power politics grounds. As I have shown, Forrestal did not originate the components of this policy. But he may have been the first to synthesize them into a coherent whole, and he did so at a crucial time.

This anti-Soviet national security policy became more clear on December 26, when the new Post War Naval Planning Section (F-14) produced the first draft of its concept for the postwar navy.[20] The document began by attacking isolationist concepts and any belief that the United States could be immune from events in other areas of the world or avoid participation in another world war, and by asserting that application of overwhelming U.S. force could deter aggressor nations or defeat them quickly. These facts justified a postwar navy with a mission to "contribute to sustaining the peace of the world" as well as "to maintain the security, enhance the welfare and prestige, and ensure respect for the policies of the United States," with minimum naval forces based on what would be necessary for an international force and "effective combat superiority" over the naval forces of any single power or combination of "likely enemies." In an apparent paradox, however, F-14 discounted both bases of determination in noting that the veto arguments at Dumbarton Oaks and "the very nature of political realities" indicated that the UN would act militarily only against "secondary or minor Powers," that only Britain and the United States would be major postwar naval powers, and that Britain could not be considered a potential enemy despite its navy in light of the enormous decrease in British power.[21]

Given such conclusions, what could possibly justify a large postwar navy? The planning section's answer consisted of a detailed projection of the likely postwar world in both ideological and power terms, focusing on the breakdown of world order and initiation of a "revolutionary" era based on a "universal contest between the opposing ideologies of capitalism and socialism, each seeking to attain acceptance as the recognized norm of human organization." Fascism would continue "as an undercurrent among certain peoples," but socialism would be the real threat, emerging triumphant in many areas as the world moved "decidedly to the left." There would also be "emotional and intellectual confusion arising from the conflict between the internationalism inherent in socialist doctrine" and the UN, on the one hand, and the "intensification of nationalism that follows every war," on the other. Equally likely was social unrest, revolution, and civil wars within countries; "tension" between nations over "trade and markets, natural resources, boundaries, and national and ethnic minorities"; and "uncertainty, if not tension, incident to the radical shifts in the balance of world power that will ensure from this war." Economic nationalism would continue; "free trade and untrammeled capitalistic enterprise" would be superseded by an era of "national cartels . . . , monopolies, subsidies and quotas, and state control of international trade and finance," which would turn what had previously been private into government concerns.

The United States would emerge as the only power not devastated by the war and "the most powerful nation in the world," which would "incite envy, animosity and fear" among others. Furthermore, the fact that only Washington would "be making an effort to resist the world current toward socialism and state control of economic life" might "place it in political and economic isolation, and in ultimate conflict with other nations." And it was unlikely to escape the domestic struggle between right and left which would plague the rest of the world and which could nullify much of its power.

That power could also be challenged by the Soviet Union, which would emerge from the war as a dual threat: it would be the second most powerful nation in the world and "potentially" the most powerful, as well as "the dynamic stronghold and exponent of socialism." Thus the USSR would be able to extend influence "far beyond her frontiers" and would "exert a centripetal effect in a Europe and [an] Asia devastated by war, dislocated economically, and unstable socially." This was especially true in Asia, where Western nations were associated with imperialism and colonial exploitation. In Europe loomed the even more frightening possibility of a union of Soviet resources and population with "the technical and organizational skill of a socialist Germany."

Soviet-American interests could clash in Asia, where Moscow would seek to fill the vacuum created by Japan's defeat, but the more serious problem was ideological. "The primary risk of an armed conflict between the United States and Russia," F-14 warned in rather apocalyptic terms, "will lie in the fact that these nations will be the protagonists of the social and economic systems which will be competing in the minds of men for exclusive and universal acceptance and each of which, by the very fact of its existence, represents a continuing threat to the other. The post-war world will pose no greater question than whether or not these two social philosophies and economic systems can concurrently exist without physical conflict or internal stress that would undermine one or the other." Inability to coexist would result in an unwinnable World War III. The "relative strength and geographic positions of these two Powers will be such," F-14 stated in a virtual repetition of JSSC conclusions, "as to preclude the military defeat of one of them by the other, even if that Power were allied with the British Empire."

The Naval Planning Section also updated the specific U.S. policies that Yarnell had previously listed so as to include active participation in a postwar UN, accumulation and maintenance of raw materials stockpiles, "promotion of international trade, with equal access to raw materials and markets," and "competition unrestricted by state or private monopolies or quotas." It also agreed that the United States would be dominant in the Western Hemisphere, whereas Russia would be dominant in Europe, Asia, and the Middle East, and that the USSR "could not . . . become a great sea power within the next decade." Nevertheless, its overall power, along with the projected world situation, made it a serious security threat and called for maintenance of large-scale U.S. naval power.

It was not naval power in the traditional sense, however. Restating and updating Mahan, F-14 asserted that the oceans "must be regarded not as barriers of defense but as open highways for attacking forces" and that the United States should be prepared to deliver offensive naval power before an enemy did to close off these invasion routes. But it included the Arctic Ocean as well as the Atlantic and Pacific as attack routes, warned that old ideas regarding the balance of power should be dropped, and focused on the revolutionary impact of land-based airpower on naval strategy. Land-based airpower would necessitate extensive air bases, including "exclusive" rights in the Japanese-owned and the Mandated Islands, "principal rights" in Japan proper, "reciprocal rights" in the South and Southwest Pacific, long-term leases on British bases in the hemisphere, and reciprocal base rights in the eastern Atlantic and along the west coast of Africa. It would also necessitate major research and intelligence efforts to prevent surprise attack by technologically superior forces. United States naval forces would have to be sufficient to afford combat superiority over any single enemy or combination of enemies, and even though Britain was an unlikely enemy, its seapower should be used as a yardstick to determine U.S. needs.

Airpower and geopolitics as well as ideology thus made Russia a very formidable potential enemy despite its lack of naval power, one requiring large-scale U.S. naval power with a complementary system of air bases for defense and, implicitly, for possible offensive operations against the Soviets. Indeed, within the F-14 analysis was a revolutionary concept, one that Forrestal would verbalize in May, of using naval aircraft against land forces.[22]

Air force planners reinforced naval fears in January by warning that the Soviet

Union would develop strong airpower.[23] Not coincidentally, in a draft of his annual report as AAF commander, Arnold emphasized his belief that "our country's defense line must be established as far from our geographical limits as science and vision will permit and that the system of air bases essential to our security and under our control must extend far beyond our domestic shores." On the advice of his planners, Marshall ordered removal of such statements as "in conflict with the national policy concerning territorial claims by this government." Arnold complied but reaffirmed his belief that defense against future jet and missile attacks required "a system of air bases extending far beyond our domestic shores and not limited to our present insular possessions. Only from such a base system," he insisted, "can we derive adequate assurance of our ability to overpower such attacks at their source and without irretrievable loss of time."[24]

The growing fears of a postwar Soviet threat simultaneously emerged on the JCS level via an extensive JIC assessment titled "Soviet Post-War Capabilities and Intentions," originally prepared by the OSS Research and Analysis Branch on JIC request and circulated on the latter's initiative. As noted in the official JCS history, the assessment "had a fairly ominous ring, somewhat different from earlier appraisals."[25] Overall, the JIC concluded that Moscow would avoid conflict with its allies, at least until 1952, but it balanced this optimism by warning that Soviet ideology preached inevitable conflict, Russia would react violently if it believed its "vital interests" were threatened, and the Soviets would remain "skeptical" of international organization and "fearful" of "capitalist encirclement." They would also insist on postwar control of Eastern Europe; influence equal to the West in Central Europe, China, and perhaps Japan; and "negative power" in Western Europe to preclude formation of an anti-Soviet bloc. Such statements were insufficient for at least one S&P officer, who in a series of handwritten marginal notes sarcastically attacked what he considered still optimistic, "almost naive" conclusions about probable Soviet behavior. He also emphasized Moscow's almost unlimited postwar *capabilities* in the military sphere, as opposed to JIC guesses as to intentions, and warned that those intentions included "a Monroe Doctrine for Eurasia" that would directly contradict what the JIC had listed as a fundamental Anglo-American security objective: "to prevent the domination of the resources and manpower of Europe and Asia by the rising power of the U.S.S.R. if such domination should be attempted."[26]

Maintenance of the Cooperative Approach

Despite these statements and warnings from September onward, no shift in stated JCS policy regarding the Soviet Union occurred in 1944 or during the early months of 1945. Indeed, during this time the Joint Chiefs and their planners frequently reiterated their insistence on avoiding U.S. involvement in Eastern Europe and any Anglo-Soviet conflict there, as well as any confrontation with the Russians or any action that might arouse their suspicions.

Throughout August and September the Joint Chiefs insisted that military support for the Polish uprising in Warsaw was not a matter for their consideration or responsibility.[27] As previously noted, they recommended that their participation on the Allied Control Commission for Rumania be minimal given minor U.S. interests and the desire to avoid involvement in any Anglo-Russian clash, and they reasserted the policy of not challenging Soviet predominance in the Balkans or backing any British attempt to do so. They also explicitly directed all their theater commanders to "adhere to the spirit of tripartite dealing" and avoid bilateral agreements with the British. By month's end they had expanded the area covered by their noninvolvement policy to include Czechoslovakia. They reiterated this policy in November in response to British pleas for a change, and in the following month, their policy of militarily occupying only Germany and Austria.[28]

Also in December came a strong War Department response to reports of anti-Soviet statements and studies in the Command and General Staff School at Fort Leavenworth. On McCloy's request Operations and Training (G-3) chief Major General Ray E. Porter directed the school commandant, by Stimson's order, to investigate, report, and take "immediate steps" to halt these activities and to ensure no repetition. "No form of instruction will be given," Porter forcefully stated, "which could possibly be considered or construed in any way to jeopardize our relations with an allied or neutral country."[29] In January Stimson reiterated JCS and War Department opposition to any discussion of territorial matters with the Soviets, and in February the department considered a "screening process" to exclude from U.S.-Soviet military projects "officers who resent the overall American policy now adopted toward Russia."[30]

Six major factors account for the Joint Chiefs' refusal to propose or sanction any change in their Soviet policy: the need for continued Russian military action and cooperation in the war against Germany; the desire for Soviet participation in the war against Japan; anger at Britain and belief that it was to blame for many of the problems that had arisen; the fact that cooperation remained White House policy; recognition that Axis strategy was to split the Allies; and the belief that everything must be done to avoid an unwinnable World War III with the USSR. None of these was new, but dramatic military and political events from September through February boldly highlighted the continued importance of each. The result was continuation of the existing policy despite the mounting calls for a shift both within and outside the armed forces.

The continued need for military cooperation in the war against Germany was boldly illustrated by Anglo-American military setbacks in the west during the fall and winter of 1944—from the September failure at Arnhem and the revival of German resistance in the west to the fierce German counteroffensive in the Ardennes in December. That offensive came perilously close to breaking American lines, resulted in the commitment of the last U.S. reserves, and led Marshall to warn Stimson that "if Germany beat us in this counterattack and particularly if the Russians failed to come in on their side," the United States would have to adopt a defensive position in Europe and let the American people decide "whether they wanted to go on with the war enough to raise the new armies which would be necessary to do it." Stalin did "come in," however, by ordering the early launching of a major Soviet offensive in response to pleas for assistance from Eisenhower and Churchill—a move Stimson on January 12 called "a very good piece of news for we were all getting a bit anxious about the slowness of Stalin." [31] By late January it had become apparent that the German military bid in the west had been foiled and the 1943 U.S. "gamble" to create only ninety divisions had worked, albeit barely and only because of the Red Army. Clearly, the European war was not over, and continued Allied military collaboration remained a mandatory precondition for victory. As Eisenhower bluntly informed Marshall in mid-January, without a Soviet offensive in the east, "a quick decision cannot be obtained." [32]

The same held true for the war against Japan. In 1944 the United States enjoyed a series of major victories in the Pacific, most notably the conquest of the Marianas, successful landings in the Philippines, and the virtual annihilation of Japanese naval power in the Battles of the Philippine Sea and Leyte Gulf. The cost in U.S. lives was high, however, and the cost rose in the fall as the Japanese introduced new and highly effective suicide tactics. To make matters worse, a successful Japanese offensive in China led to the virtual collapse of that front in the summer and fall amid mutual Sino-American threats and recriminations, culminating in Stilwell's forced recall and replacement by Wedemeyer. By year's end Lincoln was asking whether China would completely collapse and whether the United States should totally withdraw, while rumors spread that the Tokyo government might move to the Asian mainland—a possibility that filled Stimson with "a good deal of foreboding." [33] Although the Japanese government did not move and China remained an official belligerent, it had become obvious that Chiang's forces either could not or would not fulfill the major role U.S. planners had given them—to tie down the bulk of the Japanese army—at the very moment Pacific casualties and European troop shortages were making clear how important that role would be. Soviet entry into the war to fulfill that need thus became more important than ever.

The desire to obtain that entry led to disagreement over the best means of doing so with respect to future strategy in the Pacific. In early September Marshall challenged a JSSC call for blockade and air attack before invasion of the home islands, asking Embick whether this "gradual approach" might result in heavier casualties than a quick invasion, as well as "what consideration" was being given to Russian entry. Embick reiterated that such entry was "a matter of the most cardinal importance" but to invade before it took place would allow Japan to transfer ground forces to the home islands and thus increase U.S. casualties. It would also "surrender our bargaining vis-à-vis Russia, and will involve us . . . in an operation so hazardous and costly that its initiation will prove to be an error in national policy of the greatest gravity." Moscow was "vitally interested in the ejection of Japan from the Asiatic mainland" but would delay entry so as to occupy Manchuria at a "minimum of cost" if led to believe Washington regarded the "time factor" to be of "overriding importance" and invaded before Soviet entry and "regardless of the cost." If, on the other hand, Washington focused first on conquering bases in the Bonins, Ryukyus, and along the China coast, it would be able to "retain a bargaining position with Russia" and exploit its naval and air superiority "at small cost to ourselves." Marshall and the OPD countered that "our bargaining position in this matter would be weakened rather than strengthened by slowing down the tempo of operations against Japan" because the Russians might then "reasonably think that we are maneuvering to get them into the fight in such a manner that they will suffer the major losses." In a pointed reference to the domestic front they also asked whether the JSSC had "considered the political and economic acceptability of deliberately extending the length of the war with Japan," as well as the casualties involved to seize and hold the air bases.[34]

While this debate was going on, Harriman and Deane were discussing with the Soviets the timing and terms of their entry into the Far East war. On November 23, the JPS summarized U.S. military thinking on the issue by reiterating that Soviet entry was not necessary to defeat Japan but that it remained highly desirable, that Russian interests would eventually force them into the war, and that "the factors affecting the timing of Russia's entry will be predominantly those of self-interest." Nevertheless, U.S. logistical and operational support would probably be "significant" in influencing that timing and should therefore be offered—albeit not at the expense of the Pacific offensive. On December 4 the JCS approved these recommendations. In their final late-January survey before the Yalta Conference, the JCS told Roosevelt of their continued desire for Russia's earliest possible entry into the war "consistent with her ability to engage in offensive operations," their willingness to provide the "maximum support possible" to obtain this without interference in the main Pacific drive, and their desire to know both the timing of Russian entry and what could be done to make preparatory military collaboration more efficient and rapid. Clearly, they and their planners continued to view Soviet entry as vitally important and precluding a tougher policy in Europe.[35] Far from accidentally, Stimson, in his January statement on postponing trusteeship/territorial discussions for fear they would weaken relations with Russia, noted that such postponement should continue "at least, until the Russians have clearly committed themselves to their participation in the Pacific war" and until that participation "is accomplished."[36]

Further reinforcing JCS policy toward the Soviets, especially in Eastern Europe, was continued Anglo-American disagreement over appropriate strategy and policy in the Mediterranean, along with continuation of the intense U.S. military suspicion of what Wedemeyer called Churchill's "eternal and infernal Balkan enterprises."[37] From his opposition to ANVIL virtually down to its August 15 launching, through his ongoing advocacy of a movement from Italy northeastward into Vienna and the Balkans, the prime minister appeared to U.S. military planners to remain intent, as he had been throughout the war, on creating a postwar British sphere of influence in Eastern Europe no matter what the cost to the war effort or future Allied relations. This the JCS continued to oppose as counterproductive militarily, highly manipulative, and bound to split the alliance. Stimson and Roosevelt felt similarly and agreed in mid-October to remain "absolutely inflexible" in concentrating all infantry power with Eisenhower and to permit "no more diversions such as Winston Churchill is now asking for again to Italy or to the Balkans." The planners also continued to argue that the United States had no postwar interests in Eastern Europe and should not get sucked into pulling British chestnuts out of the fire. "It is not unnatural that Churchill is a disperser," Stimson told FDR in December, "because he has to disperse his troops to protect the British Empire. On the other hand, we have to win this war. Nobody else can."[38]

Churchill's October trip to Moscow and spheres-of-influence deal with Stalin reinforced such beliefs and conclusions, as did a series of Anglo-American disagreements in the next two months over various politico-military issues. Anglo-American controversy and discord marred the November postwar international civil aviation conference in Chicago.[39] Similar conflict erupted in late fall over Eisenhower's "broad front" strategy and personal command of ground forces in Europe, British policy toward the Italian government, and British military intervention during December in Greece. Indeed, that intervention strengthened the belief of many military planners that Soviet behavior was largely a response to British behavior and that London was at least as much to blame as Moscow for the deterioration in Allied relations.

By late 1944 the public had also become disillusioned with Allied relations owing to British and Soviet behavior. The result was a resurgence of isolationism which so alarmed the military as to lead Strong to recommend that Stettinius "step up whatever missionary work may be in progress or contemplated" to counter such feelings and obtain public support for the Dumbarton Oaks proposals.[40] Although "a plague on both your houses" seemed to summarize public anger against the British and Russians at this time, 54 percent of those polled in one survey blamed London, and only 18 percent, Moscow. According to Robert Hathaway, "public irritation" with Britain reached new heights by December, with the Italian and Greek situations resulting in "scathing denunciations." On December 5 Stettinius issued a press statement widely interpreted as critical of British policy in the Mediterranean. King responded by ordering his naval commander in the area to halt British use of U.S. landing craft to ferry troops and materials from Italy to Greece, while the JSSC and JCS rejected a British request for formal CCS approval of the operation. Stettinius informed the British ambassador on December 18 that the Greek and Polish situations were causing "great resentment in this country" and that "quite a few of our military" were so fed up as to conclude that since Germany was now "boxed in" and "no longer any danger to the United States, . . . we might just as well turn the whole situation over to England and Russia and . . . go to the Pacific now and win the war there." That group may have included Leahy, who on December 15 voiced bitter opposition to any involvement in European politics "except to act against an aggressor with the purpose of preventing an international war."[41]

Such beliefs were reinforced in the armed forces by simultaneous Anglo-American disagreements over threatened military disasters in China and Burma as well as future strategy in the Southeast Asia Command (SEAC), a theater so filled with British postwar political interests as to have its SEAC acronym derisively translated by Americans as "Save England's Asian Colonies." As early as February 1944, the JSSC had recommended rejection of any British proposal for an advance on Japan from this theater rather than the Central Pacific, and during the summer it rejected calls for a single directive for combined staff talks with Portugal because of the strong relationship between Britain's interest in Portuguese Timor and its imperial interests in the area.[42] A British naval presence in the Central Pacific drive was equally objectionable to some planners because, in the words of one OPD document, it would be "the opening wedge toward putting the direction of the Pacific war on a Combined, rather than a Joint level." At OCTAGON King went so far as to attempt to reject the offer of a major British fleet in the Central Pacific, despite presidential agreement to the offer.[43] Wedemeyer informed Marshall in October that Churchill was "torn between two strong desires, namely, operations in the Balkans to counter Russian influence and offensive action with British forces in Southeast Asia to bolster prestige and strengthen British policy."[44] The Joint Chiefs and their planners continued throughout the remainder of 1944 to reject operations in both theaters. "Our national interests," Handy and the JSSC reminded Marshall before a late-September White House meeting, "do not require us to devise operations by United States forces which are not directly contributory to our main effort in order to seize areas of post-war strategic importance." [45]

Continued suspicion of Britain, not the Soviet Union, changed this policy in December as U.S. forces were sent into Clipperton Island, a French possession lying due west of the Panama Canal. The navy officially justified this move as a war measure, but it was actually designed to forestall a feared British occupation and establishment of a military air route across Mexico. White House Map Room officer George Elsey bluntly admitted that it had been "precipitated only by our fear of high-handed British action and our uncertainty of British intentions and activities" and that it was "contrary to our national interests for any European power to develop a new base within striking distance of the Panama Canal." [46]

Many officers joined the public in blaming the British more than the Russians for the deterioration in Allied relations. Indeed, some saw that deterioration as part of a conscious British ploy. One high-ranking general warned Hopkins during the Warsaw uprising that Britain was trying to use the United States as a tool against the Soviets, a judgment with which Hopkins concurred. [47] "Our past efforts to effect closer liaison with the Russians have always been sandbagged by the British," one s&p member concluded in December in supporting jps proposals for greater military collaboration with the Russians in the Far East. "Our future efforts, relating to an area where the common interests of the U.S. and the U.K. are secondary to those of the U.S. and U.S.S.R., must not be similarly obstructed by British national interests." [48]

Roosevelt concurred. Indeed, his cooperative approach with the Soviets and suspicion of the British dominated U.S. policy throughout 1944 and early 1945. In January he expressed bitterness to senators over British moves in Greece and told them he would not oppose Soviet domination of Eastern Europe because the Red Army "had the power in the areas where their arms were present" and "it was obviously impossible to have a break with them." [49] On March 16 he informed his cabinet "that the British were perfectly willing for the United States to have a war with Russia at any time and that . . . to follow the British lead would be to proceed toward that end." [50]

Roosevelt's belief in Soviet-American cooperation and disagreement with the British reached an apogee at the February Yalta Conference. A preliminary Anglo-American conference at Malta had revealed ongoing disagreements over European strategy and how to deal with the Russians, disagreements that were amplified as Roosevelt once again attempted at Yalta to win Stalin's confidence by emphasizing Anglo-American discord over colonialism and other issues. [51] Often ignoring British objections, the president successfully negotiated several critical accords with Stalin which appeared to resolve the major disputes that had erupted in 1944 over the UN, Poland, and German occupation, as well as to guarantee, albeit for a territorial price, Soviet entry into the war against Japan within three months of German surrender and support of Chiang's government in China.

The JCS and their planners were far from prisoners of this presidential policy, however. To the contrary, they had played a major role in creating it, consistently defended it throughout 1944, and strongly supported the ensuing Yalta agreements. Leahy was a notable exception, condemning the Polish accord as "so elastic that the Russians can stretch it all the way from Yalta to Washington without technically breaking it" and concluding that one result of enforcing the Yalta peace terms would be "to make Russia the dominant power in Europe, which in itself carries a certainty of future international disagreements and prospects of another war."[52] The other members of the JCS were quite pleased with the outcome of the conference, however, with Marshall telling State Department official Alger Hiss that "for what we have gained here I would have gladly stayed [in Yalta] a whole month."[53]

Hiss later stated that this comment referred specifically to the military agreement regarding Soviet entry into the war against Japan, but it applied with equal force to the agreements on Poland, Germany, the United Nations, and the entire package of accords. The Allies had gone to Yalta with these issues unresolved and thus capable of splitting the coalition before Germany was defeated—exactly what Hitler was hoping would happen. Success at Yalta precluded that possibility and destroyed this last Nazi hope, something the conference participants clearly realized. "They have always planned on a split of the Allies," Marshall noted for a press talk a few weeks later. "They never for one moment calculated that the Allies could continue to conduct combined operations with complete understanding and good faith."[54]

Marshall had an additional reason to be pleased with the results of Yalta, one that constituted the sixth and final cause for JCS refusal to support a policy shift vis-à-vis the Soviets: the desire to avoid an unwinnable confrontation and possible World War III. Embick and the other members of the JSSC had throughout 1944 made clear their fears in this regard, as well as their belief that the two emerging superpowers possessed no inherently conflicting interests and could cooperate in the postwar world. In their view, failure to do so would probably result in Soviet domination of most if not all Europe and the entire Eurasian land mass. Such dominance would pose a critical geopolitical threat to the United States and necessitate, at the very least, a massive military buildup in the Western Hemisphere. Yet it was unclear whether the public would support such a buildup, let alone the defense of Britain and military involvement in Europe that the possibility of such a situation would require. Given this bleak outlook, every effort had to be made to avoid conflict and to win Soviet trust and agreement to postwar collaboration.

This conclusion was not based on any naïve trust in Russia but rather on recognition of the severe limits to U.S. power vis-à-vis the Soviets—in terms of both physical capacity and public will. As Leahy asserted on a general level during an early 1944 JCS meeting, "enforcement of [U.S.] national policy throughout the world" as recommended by Arnold "would be impossible of accomplishment." In October Handy was more specific, questioning Arnold's call for sufficient postwar forces to "guarantee adequate consideration of American peace aims," which might imply leaving "some forces in Europe to impress the other victorious Allies." They would not be impressed, he predicted, because "if the Russians . . . adopted the same thought they can always outnumber us in divisions."[55]

The ramifications of this situation were fully spelled out for the JCS in an extraordinary memorandum on postwar security signed by seven scholars who had previously worked with the armed forces, the State Department, and/or the Office of Strategic Services: Frederick S. Dunn, William T. R. Fox, David Rowe, and Arnold Wolfers of Yale; Grayson Kirk of Columbia; and Harold Sprout and Edward Mead Earle of Princeton. Drafted by them during a January weekend conference in Rye, New York, and completed in early March, the document constituted the study Earle had previously promised and provided the armed forces with an extensive overview of postwar security issues and their relationship to Soviet-American relations.[56]

"The day when the United States can take 'a free ride' in security is over," the memorandum stated. "From now on it must expect to pay its own way." British power had shielded the United States from Continental aggression in the past but could no longer do so because of its historic and continued deterioration. Henceforth the United States must rely on its own resources while recognizing the need to intervene in European affairs and protect Britain as a vital U.S. interest. The anti-European policies enunciated in Washington's Farewell Address had become dated, and there was "scant evidence" that the nation or even the entire hemisphere could withstand an attack by a power in control of all Europe or Eurasia. Preventing such control must henceforth be a "continuous" U.S. concern.[57]

Potential threats were limited and clear. "In all the world," according to the memorandum, "only Soviet Russia and the ex-enemy powers are capable of forming nuclei around which an anti-American coalition could form to threaten the security of the United States." Given postwar realities only one of these constituted a real threat. "This is the age of the Big Two. Only the Soviet Union will have a power position comparable to that of the United States. If these two stand together, then ex-enemy states can hardly threaten either." If they did not, Germany would be able "to sell herself to the highest bidder," in which case "victory in the present war will have been in vain." Moreover, any ensuing Soviet-German alliance would constitute a mortal threat to American security in its capacity to obtain hegemonic control over all Europe.

The scholars were unwilling to place their trust in Soviet good faith, but they were also unwilling to treat Russia as an adversary without solid evidence that it had truly become one. "Soviet Russia is a power whose good intentions must be assumed until there is incontrovertible evidence to the contrary," they asserted in this regard. "But its intentions are sufficiently unclear so that the United States must in no case place sole reliance for security on Soviet good intentions." Yet "while the United States can afford to make no concessions which leave its security or vital national interests at the mercy of the Soviet Union, there is almost no other concession which it can afford not to make to assure Soviet collaboration in the maintenance of security." This was because the U.S.-Soviet relationship remained "the key to American and to general security." The breakdown of the last Soviet-Western alliance had led to the outbreak of World War II; another breakdown would result in World War III. "Even though history may abound with instances in which 'the allies of today' proved to be 'the enemies of tomorrow,'" they admitted, "it would be criminal folly to jettison our wartime alliance in the moment of victory in the mistaken belief that war with the Soviet Union is 'inevitable.'" It was not. Furthermore, a Soviet-American war "would be protracted and probably indecisive" and would cause irreparable damage to all participants. This fact, together with the joint interest in keeping Germany restrained and neutral, "furnish the bases for intimate and continuous collaboration."

The scholars were also aware of the potential conflict between support for Britain and close Soviet-American relations, and they specifically noted that "support for the British position in Europe need not imply full diplomatic support for all British interests in all parts of the world. In particular, where British diplomatic activity menaces Soviet-American relations," such as the Aegean/Persian Gulf area, "the divergence of British and American policies should be made clear." Conversely, it would "in all probability be necessary to oppose Soviet courses of action in Europe at a number of points," which only highlighted the need *not* to oppose them *every*where their policies conflicted with those of the United States. To "promote in Soviet leaders belief in the good faith of the United States," they argued, "our leaders must be careful not to oppose that country in areas which the Russians consider vital," such as Eastern Europe and Manchuria, "except for patently good cause." The United States admittedly needed to define "the limits of permissible concessions" to the Soviets, prevent the "indefinite westward movement" of their borders, and make clear that it would not permit Germany to fall into the Russian orbit. But they saw the Yalta accords on Poland as fulfilling remaining Russian territorial demands in Eastern Europe while the conference's

Tripartite Declaration on Liberated Europe would be the test of Soviet sincerity with respect to future collaboration, with a lack of good faith serving as a clear warning of what to expect.[58]

The document received widespread circulation. Earle gave copies to Fairchild and Embick, who forwarded it to Willson, Marshall, Arnold, and Leahy. Copies were also sent to the CCS Intelligence Staff, Bessell, Strong, Forrestal, and a host of State Department officials including Stettinius, Archibald MacLeish, Joseph Grew, James Dunn, Benjamin Cohen, Pasvolsky, Hiss, Will Clayton, and Dean Acheson—probably because, as Earle later noted, the scholars had been "very much concerned with the failure of the Department of State to think in terms of overall policy rather than day-to-day procedure." State's response, however, was hardly overwhelming. MacLeish sent a "perfunctory acknowledgment," and a "non-committal letter" arrived from Stettinius's secretary. "None of us expected much from the Department of State in any case," Earle revealingly noted, "so that I am not weeping any tears on that score."[59] Much more important was the circulation within the armed forces.

Unlike State, the JSSC was deeply impressed. On March 29 it formally circulated the document as an official JCS Memorandum for Information, rated it an "excellent study," and expressed agreement, albeit with a few exceptions. Specifically, it felt the importance of Great Britain to U.S. security "as a vital interest to be defended . . . is dangerously overstressed."[60] As Earle explained to Fox, Embick and Fairchild believed Britain was "indefensible as against determined submarine and air attack"—a view he did not share. "On the other hand," he noted, "they are even more convinced than we that the Soviet Union is absolutely unstoppable." They were also "very enthusiastic" about the memorandum and had informed him of their belief "that there is a desperate need for civilian contribution to this type of thinking and strategical planning."[61]

By early April Earle had been informed that the memorandum had been sent to the S&P and that Leahy would bring it to the attention of Hopkins and Roosevelt. Circulation was not limited to government officials, however. Forrestal was so impressed that he apparently recommended publication, a suggestion Embick and Fairchild vetoed as "highly undesirable." So did several of the authors, who felt that some of the material "might very well be offensive to our British and Russian friends." Nevertheless, Earle sent copies in April to numerous journalists and former as well as present government officials, including Hanson Baldwin, Walter Lippmann, Arthur Krock, Walter Millis, George Fielding Eliot, Henry Luce, Sumner Welles, Charles Merz, Raymond Moley, and James Byrnes, while Embick sent copies to McCloy, Nelson Rockefeller, Isaiah Bowman, and numerous other members of the U.S. delegation to the UN Charter Conference then convening in San Francisco.[62]

Ironically, the Yalta accords on Poland and Liberated Europe that Earle and his colleagues had cited as the test of Soviet good faith were breaking down at the moment their memorandum was being circulated in Washington. Prophetically, that breakdown did serve as a clear warning and begin the process by which the Joint Chiefs would reverse their Soviet policy.

12

Victory and Reassessment, April–August 1945

The Yalta Accords began to break down almost immediately after the conference closed, reactivating previously expressed fears of the Soviet Union while adding new voices to the growing chorus opposed to continuation of the cooperative policy. The breakdown also precipitated a fundamental reassessment of that policy within both the armed forces and the government as a whole. Begun in April and continuing through the summer, that reassessment coincided with the end of World War II and in many ways marked the beginning of the ensuing Cold War.

The April Reassessment

The armed forces were well aware of the breakdown in Soviet-American relations after Yalta. Indeed, they participated in it. United States military representatives on the Allied Control Councils for Rumania, Bulgaria, and Hungary all complained bitterly about Soviet behavior in those nations and called for a firm stand in response to what they labeled blatant violations of the Yalta Accords. So did Deane and Harriman in Moscow.[1] On April 3 Marshall informed his JCS colleagues of a series of reports from these two and others "indicating increasing Russian non-cooperation with U.S. military authorities" and violation of the accords. With Harriman's full concurrence, Deane recommended immediate retaliation, as did the U.S. control commissioner in Hungary. Soviet actions might be "indicative of [an] increasing non-cooperative attitude," Marshall warned, though they could be "the result of unrelated causes" or a reflection of diplomatic problems "intended to invite retaliation which could be used as [an] excuse by Soviets to abrogate commitments." Consequently he suggested and the JCS approved sending the matter to the JSSC "for study and recommendation as a matter of priority."[2]

The JSSC was not the only military body advising on this issue. The OPD had previously rejected calls for retaliation by the U.S. representative on the Rumanian

Control Commission,[3] and now the President's Soviet Protocol Committee rejected Deane's call for retaliatory cancellation of a northern convoy because it was impractical and would constitute "a major departure from established policy" reasserted by Roosevelt as late as January 6: that sending supplies to the USSR was "a matter of importance second only to the operational requirements in the Pacific and the Atlantic."[4] The JSSC concurred on April 5, albeit for more extensive reasons. "The maintenance of the unity of the Allies in the prosecution of the war," it insisted in a restatement and amplification of the conclusion it had been emphasizing for over a year, "must remain the cardinal and over-riding objective of our politico-military policy with Russia. The instances of Russian refusal to cooperate . . . , while irritating and difficult to understand if considered as isolated events, are of relatively minor moment. They would assume real importance . . . only if their occurrence should cause our Government to adopt retaliatory measures in kind, and these in turn should be followed by further Russian measures, and thus lead in the end to a break in Allied unity."[5]

Russian actions were the result of their extreme suspicion in areas of primary interest, the JSSC implied, and continued Allied disagreement over the future of those areas. Rather than force a reversal of Soviet policy, retaliation would provoke only further Russian measures and break Allied unity. The episodes cited might also reflect a "very grave misunderstanding" resulting from the secret negotiations in Berne for the surrender of German forces in Italy, negotiations that had led Stalin to accuse his allies of attempting a separate peace. The present crisis, the JSSC further warned, could well be the result of a German ploy to divide the Allies. Consequently, it recommended no retaliation; rather, Roosevelt should personally settle these matters with Stalin at the proper time. The committee even drafted a presidential message inviting Soviet military officials to visit the western front to see that no separate peace was being negotiated. The JSSC did recommend that the JCS restudy all present projects and requests vis-à-vis the Soviets and drop those not essential to the war effort, but the rationale for such a move was the minimization of friction, not any signal of retaliation.[6]

While the JSSC composed this reply, Willson restated in public the broader conclusions it had previously reached. Quoting verbatim from JCS 973 of July 1944, he told the Academy of Political Science on April 4 that postwar changes would be comparable with those occasioned by the fall of Rome, that British power was in decline, that Russia and the United States would emerge as superpowers, and that the key to future peace was not the UN but Big Three unity. Failure to retain that unity would lead to war, either between the Big Three or via a revival of Axis strength and aggression. To guarantee peace and security, the Big Three "must see to it that they maintain control over their former enemies, and find no new enemies among themselves."[7]

The Joint Chiefs considered the JSSC report amid special security precautions and on April 7 once again agreed that no retaliation should be undertaken. Significantly, however, Leahy prodded his colleagues to add "at the present time" to this conclusion and to veto the proposed Roosevelt message to Stalin because the president had already affirmed U.S. good faith.[8]

Roosevelt had affirmed a good deal more, for by this time Soviet-American relations appeared to have reached a breaking point over Stalin's suspicions and accusations regarding a separate peace. An angry Marshall and his staff had drafted a stinging presidential reply to what they labeled these "vile misrepresentations" causing "bitter resentment"—terms Leahy and FDR incorporated into the message sent to Stalin on April 4.[9]

The JSSC had warned that the Berne crisis might very well be the result of a German ploy to split the Allies, and Roosevelt, in what would be his final message to Churchill, tried to minimize what had taken place.[10] Nevertheless, the crisis had aroused further U.S. anger and suspicion—at the very moment German forces in the west were collapsing and the need for continued cooperation thus dissipating. On April 2, one day after Eisenhower's forces had completed the Ruhr envelopment, Marshall had informed Roosevelt and Stettinius that military operations would probably be at a final "mopping-up" stage by month's end.[11]

Ten days later, as U.S. forces reached the Elbe, Roosevelt died. On April 16 the Soviets began their final drive on Berlin, and three days later 325,000 German forces in the Ruhr pocket surrendered. In the space of a few short weeks, two of the major reasons for continuing the cooperative policy with Russia—the war against Germany and Roosevelt's insistence on such a policy—thus disappeared at the same time as Soviet-American conflict appeared to be increasing dramatically.

The increased suspicions of Russia were discussed and heavily reinforced in a twenty-two-page OSS R&A paper, written for Embick by R&A director Langer and Russian section chief Geroid Robinson,[12] that departed from previous R&A assessments in its characterization of the postwar situation as "potentially more dangerous than any preceding one." Russia would be "by far the strongest nation in Europe and Asia," strong enough to quickly become "more powerful than Germany or Japan has ever been" and, if Washington took no counteraction, to dominate all Eurasia and perhaps even "outrank the United States in military potential." With this enormous capability went aims that remained uncertain and a suspicion, based on history and ideology, that could "easily lead Russia to interpret as aggressive the most pacific security measures of the other powers, and then herself to embark upon 'preventive' aggression." If offered "elaborate" security guarantees, Russia might limit itself to spheres of influence in Eastern Europe and northern Asia and equal influence with the West in Germany, China, and Japan.

But it might also "revert to the predatory tradition of Tsarist days or to the dynamism of the Communist International" and pursue an expansionist policy to dominate Eurasia. Success would make it "a menace more formidable to the United States than any yet known."[13]

Such realities called for a policy aimed at convincing Russia of America's pacific intentions "while at the same time demonstrating our determination to safeguard our own interests." This translated into continued efforts both to establish a world security system and international organization and to prepare for possible failure via the creation of a multitiered defense system. In the Atlantic this system would be composed of a West European bloc as the preferred "first line" of defense, bases "from Iceland and Greenland southward through the Caribbean region to the bulge of Brazil, and perhaps even to the straits of Magellan," and a "common defense system for all the Americas," including a long-term security pact as a "fallback" position in case the first two failed. The just-negotiated Act of Chapultepec calling for such a pact was labeled "a stroke of good fortune for us" which "should be exploited to the full" and "under no circumstances . . . set aside in favor of some more inclusive but, for that reason, more diluted formula for world security." Nor should too much faith be placed in it, for if Russia controlled all Eurasia the United States would find itself, even with its island bases and Latin America, in a geopolitical position "somewhat analogous to Japan in the present conflict." Russia might then use Eurasia's enormous resources successfully to attack the United States. "This is the crux of the whole problem," R&A maintained, "and it dictates the urgent necessity of taking all measures to prevent or delay the domination of Europe and/or Asia by a power already so formidable as Russia."[14]

In the European theater, immediate U.S. countermoves were "imperative" to preclude Soviet control of Germany and, with it, the rest of Europe. Most important was the creation of a strong "Western European–Mediterranean–American bloc." In the Far East, Washington should similarly support noncommunist forces to check Russia via a re-created balance of power on the Asian mainland and move to control the Pacific via air and naval bases. Significantly, the paper twice attacked Far East trusteeships as antithetical to U.S. security interests: once, as could be expected, in regard to the Mandated Islands, but also with respect to European colonies. Trusteeship for the Mandated Islands "would be a crippling blow to our security interests," for in an age of long-range bombing they had become "more necessary to our defense than were the Hawaiian Islands in the past." Trusteeships for European colonies were equally dangerous, for the United States had a strong interest in the postwar maintenance of the European empires. Liberalization within them should be encouraged, but primarily "in order the better to maintain them, and to check Soviet influence in the stimulation of colonial revolt." America had "at present no interest in weakening or liquidating these empires or in championing schemes of international trusteeship which may provoke unrest and result in colonial disintegration, and may at the same time alienate from us the European states whose help we need to balance the Soviet power." [15]

Success in these ventures would not eliminate the problem, for if Russian power and influence continued to expand as it had during the last twenty-five years, the United States would face a mortal threat and have to decide whether to meet it in Europe or "abandon Britain and the Continent and fall back on the defense of the Western Hemisphere." That would be a problem for military decision at some future date, however. "About all that can be said now is that, if at all feasible, we should fight abroad rather than at home, and with Allies rather than alone. . . . If we abandoned Europe now, we should be inviting Russia to push her way to the Atlantic, and should thus run the risk of facing her with all Europe organized at her back." [16]

Embick was deeply impressed. He discussed the paper with Langer, Robinson, Bowman, McCloy, and the rest of the JSSC and quickly brought it to the attention of Marshall and Leahy, with special reference to the necessity for hemispheric defense and extensive Atlantic and Pacific bases. Copies also went to the new president Harry S. Truman, the OPD, and the S&P, which had also received a copy of the late-March Earle memorandum. [17]

While the R&A paper circulated, Deane returned to Washington and on April 16 again requested a change in policy. "Not only have we a Russia that is victorious over the Germans," he warned, "but one that is so sure of her strength as to assume an attitude of dominance with respect to her Allies. I have felt this situation developing since my arrival in Russia. It has reached a climax since the Crimea Conference." The basic problem remained that "the Soviet mind can only look for ulterior motive behind our liberality. Failing to find one they conclude that our cooperation springs from fear." [18]

In calling for a change in policy, Deane cited not only this attitude but also Russian violations of the Yalta Accords, the declining need for military collaboration in Europe, his belief that Russian participation in the war against Japan was already "assured in furtherance of their own interests," and the fact that "we have much to offer the Soviet Union both prior to and after the conclusion of hostilities." Rather than suggest retaliation again, he now modified his recommendations and proposed, with Harriman's full concurrence, that the United States "cease forcing ourselves on the Soviet Union, and . . . wait for the Soviet authorities to come to us on matters which require collaboration. Only in this manner can we regain Soviet respect." Specifically, the Joint Chiefs should withdraw from collaborative military projects not essential to the war effort, wait for Soviet initiatives on future collaboration, and approach them only on issues of importance to the United States and "only when we are prepared, in case of an initial refusal, to take positive and effective action to force Soviet cooperation." A separate memorandum listed the specific projects from which the United States should withdraw.[19]

On the following day the Joint Chiefs approved the first four steps Deane had proposed to implement this new policy and referred the rest, as well as the more general recommendations for policy revision, to the JPS "as a matter of priority" and with "special security precautions." Simultaneously, Leahy ordered the White House Map Room Secretariat to prepare major briefing papers for the new president with special emphasis on the Polish and Italian surrender disputes; on April 19 he presented these to Truman with an emphasis on Stalin's "insulting language." Then on April 20, while Harriman personally warned Truman of the need to stand firm against Russia's "barbarian invasion of Europe," Deane explained his problems and recommendations before the CCS, with Marshall implying that the April 17 withdrawal from projects reflected a new firmness in U.S. policy. On April 23 the JPS supported Deane's broad recommendations and in turn proposed JCS approval, which was forthcoming on the following day.[20]

These actions clearly modified JCS policy regarding Russia. They fell far short of a policy reversal, however. First, Deane had not requested retaliation. Indeed, the withdrawal he now proposed was similar to what the JSSC had suggested in its early-April rejection of his previous recommendations: retirement from nonessential projects as a means of minimizing friction. Furthermore, in accepting his new recommendations the JPS toned down his anti-Soviet language and reaffirmed JSSC opposition to retaliation by noting that it was already being practiced by Russia, *might* be practiced by America in the future, but for now it was "important that the U.S. become dependent on the Russians only when necessary" to further its "vital interests." Furthermore, JCS acceptance of the JPS recommendations followed acceptance only three days earlier of a JSSC report that assumed any U.S. action on Italian participation in the war against Japan would be "coordinated" with Russia as well as Britain.[21]

The apparent inconsistencies in JCS policy at this time were likely the result of uncertainty and divided counsel within both the JCS and the administration as a whole; moreover, four of the six major factors previously discussed for supporting the cooperative approach continued in effect. Roosevelt's death and the approaching end to the war in Europe did not negate fear of manipulation by the British, who had continued to call for a strategic shift and race for Berlin, or fear of Axis efforts to split the Allies and of starting an unwinnable and unnecessary World War III. Also remaining was the desire to obtain Soviet entry into the war against Japan, especially on the part of army officials horrified by recent casualties in the Pacific and estimates of the cost of invading the Japanese home islands.[22]

Far from accidentally, these army officials would oppose confrontation with the Soviets as unnecessary and dangerous in the face of navy, State Department, and even presidential comments to the contrary. "We simply cannot allow a rift to come between the two nations without endangering the entire peace of the world," Stimson concluded on April 2. That evening he told Stettinius that "Russia had been very good to us on the large issues. She has kept her word and carried out her engagements. We must remember that she has not learned the amenities of diplomatic discourse and we must expect bad language from her." He also discussed the matter with Marshall, who had anticipated problems with the Soviets "but thought that we must put up with them," and he kept the army chief "close" so as to "have my power in my elbow" for any White House conference on the issue. On April 16 he reiterated in his diary the JCS/JSSC belief that the Russian and U.S. "respective orbits do not clash geographically and I think that on the whole we can probably keep out of clashes in the future." On April 19 McCloy similarly noted in his diary that the true test of U.S. statecraft would be whether "in spite of what all speak of [as] the rudeness and crudities of Molotov and some of the Russians, we go on working out intelligently the issues which arise between us." [23]

The White House conference Stimson had anticipated took place on April 23. At that crucial meeting he directly challenged the beliefs expressed by Truman, Stettinius, Forrestal, and Harriman that the Soviets had broken the Yalta Accords, that this was part of a pattern of domination in Eastern Europe and contempt for U.S. objections, and that Washington must respond firmly even if it meant a showdown and a break. In flat contradiction Stimson repeated his April 2 assertion that "in the big military matters the Soviet Government had kept their word," noting "that the military authorities of the United States had come to count on it." Indeed, the Russians "had often been better than their promise." He also reminded those present that "25 years ago virtually all of Poland had been Russian" and that "without understanding how seriously the Russians took this Polish question we might be heading into very dangerous water." Indeed, "the Russians were perhaps being more realistic than we were in regard to their own security," and while he believed in firmness on "minor matters where we had been yielding in the past . . . , this was too big a question to take chances on." [24]

Stimson received support from Marshall and Leahy. The latter had previously been anything but friendly toward the Soviets or the Yalta protocol on Poland, and he bluntly stated on April 23 "that he had left Yalta with the impression that the Soviet Government had no intention of permitting a free government to operate in Poland." For that very reason, however, he was not surprised at Soviet behavior or prepared to break with them over this. Clearly, "we should tell them that we stood for a free and independent Poland." Yet "the Yalta agreement was susceptible to two interpretations," and breaking with the Soviets "was a very serious matter." Marshall concurred and explained why. Although the military situation in Europe was now "secure," U.S. planners still hoped for Soviet entry into the war against Japan "at a time when it would be useful to us. The Russians had it within their power to delay their entry," he warned, "until we had done all the dirty work." Stimson concurred and added that the Anglo-American definition of "free elections" was neither understood nor practiced elsewhere in the world.[25]

What may have been as extraordinary as this direct rejection of the new president's definition of reality were the counterarguments by those favoring a tough American response. Stettinius challenged Leahy directly by reading part of the Yalta accord on Poland and insisting it was "susceptible of only one interpretation." Harriman questioned Stimson's comment that the Soviets had kept their military agreements. He also stated that a tough U.S. stance would not result in a "real break" with the Russians "if properly handled"—a conclusion based on his previously expressed belief that the Soviets would back down in the face of Anglo-American resolve because they understood the language of force and were far weaker militarily than they appeared. Deane agreed and strongly supported Harriman. In the process he directly disagreed with Marshall, his military superior, by asserting that the Soviets would enter the Far East war in their own interests and as soon as possible "irrespective of what happened in other fields." He also reiterated his belief that "if we were afraid of the Russians we would get nowhere" and that now was the time to be firm.[26]

Truman continued to side with the hard-liners, concluding that "he was now satisfied that from a military point of view there was no reason why we should fail to stand up to our understanding of the Crimean agreements." Such comments may have had an impact on the Joint Chiefs, who approved Deane's recommendations on the following day.[27] They were not ready, however, to move beyond this limited response.

Nor was Stimson, who noted after the meeting his "very grave anxiety . . . as to what will happen"; on April 26 he restated his belief that "our position in the western hemisphere and Russia's in the eastern hemisphere could be adjusted without too much friction." McCloy simultaneously informed Truman that in light of the "collapse going on in Central Europe," unparalleled since the fall of Rome, "we are going to have to work out a practical relationship with the Russians." The army consequently continued to oppose British pleas for a race for territory in Central Europe, and on April 30 Stimson informed Marshall that they should make sure Truman was advised of "past differences between Britain and America" regarding the former's balance-of-power machinations in Central and Eastern Europe and efforts to create an anti-Soviet bloc over such issues. He also warned Undersecretary of State Joseph Grew of these dangers in view of the present crisis with Tito in Yugoslavia, a crisis in which London and the State Department were calling for a tough stand. Marshall was "very much troubled" by such calls. Believing "that every effort at any cost should be made to avoid a military clash," he and the JCS as a whole consistently urged caution on State and the president as the war in Europe ended. Despite their tough rhetoric on April 23, Truman and Stettinius heeded their advice and did not support a race for territory or a military confrontation with Tito. Indeed, Truman would echo Stimson's and Marshall's points by noting in his memoirs that he "did not want to become involved in the Balkans in any way that could lead us into another world conflict" and that he was "anxious to get the Russians into the war against Japan as soon as possible, thus saving the lives of countless Americans." [28] As Germany surrendered on May 7–8, U.S. and JCS policy on Russia was thus modified but still largely uncertain.

Conflicts over Postwar Security

The April reassessment coincided with continued conflicts between the armed forces and the State Department over postwar security planning. These focused once again on trusteeship for the Mandated Islands but also on hemispheric defense measures and the forthcoming conference in San Francisco to prepare a charter for the postwar UN. Both directly and indirectly, these issues intersected with the growing concern over the Soviet Union.

The conflict over hemispheric defense stemmed from the February–March Pan American Conference in Mexico City and ensuing Act of Chapultepec, which had included a hemispheric collective security statement and a call for a full inter-American treaty to this effect. In January the JSSC had strongly endorsed such a regional defense pact as necessary for hemispheric and continental security "in the event that the global structure should disintegrate or prove ineffective." It had further noted that the countries of the hemisphere constituted a military and a geographic entity whose defense was essential to U.S. security and whose high ratio of arable land to sparse population and large mineral resources would "present in the future to the crowded and scantily endowed populations of the old world, particularly those of eastern Asia, the only major world area in which successful aggression would afford them a substantial measure of economic relief." [29]

The State Department feared that a powerful hemispheric pact would violate the Dumbarton Oaks agreement to subordinate regional groupings to the proposed international organization—a subordination opposed by the Latin American nations—and thereby subvert its efforts to establish such an organization at San Francisco. As the JCS representative at the Mexico City conference, Embick sided with the Latin Americans—even though agreement to their demands meant "partial abandonment of the Monroe Doctrine, by the relinquishment of preclusive control over intervention in the Western Hemisphere." He also indicated his willingness to appear before the Senate if necessary to present his case, and on March 29 he informed Leahy that America and Russia would "inevitably be the two post-war great powers and that the Republics of America must remain united against attack from overseas." The resulting Act of Chapultepec quickly became an integral component of the JSSC's postwar security system, with the committee noting in early April that airpower's threat to continental security justified the "change in national policy" involved in giving up the right to intervention.[30]

Simultaneously, the armed forces and the State Department continued to disagree over trusteeships for the Mandated Islands and over international organization in general. Throughout the first three months of 1945, the JSSC fought the State and Interior Departments on this issue, as did Stimson and Forrestal. In March Willson warned King and Forrestal of the need at San Francisco for "considerable vigilance on the part of our military people to counter the utopian ideas of the International Welfare Group," while Embick labeled Pasvolsky "dangerously un-American" for his stand on this and the Act of Chapultepec. Partially as a result of such warnings, the U.S. military delegation to San Francisco was again, as at Dumbarton Oaks, large, powerful, and centered on the JSSC. Stimson continued to express "grave concern" to Forrestal, Stettinius, and Roosevelt over possible "quixotic gestures" to the trusteeship principle. He also continued to maintain that the San Francisco Conference as a whole, along with any trusteeship discussions, should be postponed until Russia entered the Pacific war and the Great Powers privately discussed territorial changes "so that arguments which come up will not interfere with these more important matters"—a position that conference delegate John Foster Dulles supported.[31]

Roosevelt did not, and by March he had become increasingly concerned over the military's demands, intransigence, and apparent lack of confidence in the proposed UN organization and trusteeship system, a system that the Big Three at Yalta had agreed would be established and include League of Nations mandates as well as enemy territory. The army and navy, he noted on March 15, had "no business administering the civilian government of territories" and by implication no business questioning the national policies he was establishing.[32] Their response, already stated repeatedly throughout the war and reiterated during March and April in numerous postwar planning papers, was that national security required them to possess a strong role in the determination of policies with military components. Consequently, throughout the spring they vigorously restated their opinions to the State Department and the White House, as well as a supportive Congress, press, and public. Led by Forrestal, they also continued to emphasize the need for greater civil-military coordination in the postwar era. The United States, Admiral William Halsey informed a congressional committee, needed a special group of civilian *and* military personnel "to minister the *National* Policy" in the postwar era. "If we *don't* find and employ such men . . . , we will lose our shirts as we have in the past."[33]

Throughout March and April the parties involved in the trusteeship dispute attempted to work out a compromise, but to no avail. These efforts coincided with the deterioration in Soviet-American relations. The armed forces' demands clearly did not result from this deterioration, as their positions on trusteeship and related issues had been previously verbalized. Nevertheless, growing conflict with the Soviets reinforced their belief that State Department proposals were premature at best and dangerous to the continued war effort and postwar U.S. security at worst[34]—either because they placed too much faith in continued Soviet-American cooperation or because they prematurely raised issues that could disrupt the alliance. As Stimson noted in the latter regard after the April 23 White House meeting, "I had never felt that it was a wise thing to go ahead with the San Francisco conference without having first adjusted all the problems that might come up between us and Russia and Great Britain first. Now we are reaping the penalty for that piece of heedlessness and we are at loggerheads with Russia on an issue which in my opinion is very dangerous and one on which she is not likely to yield on in substance."[35]

Although postponement of the San Francisco Conference was by this time no longer feasible (it began on April 25), the armed forces continued to oppose discussion of trusteeships, even though it had been mandated in the Yalta Accords, and to insist on a public statement asserting complete, "unrestricted" postwar control over the Mandated Islands. Such control, the jssc maintained and the jcs agreed, was "essential" to future U.S. security. Beyond that, U.S. military advisers to the conference were directed to preserve the inter-American defense system within any global structure and to oppose any further modification of the Monroe Doctrine as well as proposals for an international police force or additional regulation of armaments. Any proposals to modify the Dumbarton Oaks Accords should be analyzed "primarily" for their impact on U.S. security.[36]

By April 9 all parties to the trusteeship dispute had agreed that the secretaries of war, navy, state, and interior and the jcs should meet with the president on April 19 to present their views and reach accord. Roosevelt's death did not substantially alter these plans, but it did convince those involved to try once again to reach agreement before meeting with Truman. On April 14 Stettinius went so far as to press Forrestal, King, and Marshall for such an effort while they awaited the arrival of Roosevelt's funeral train at the railroad station.[37]

Over the next few days several such meetings took place, during which Stimson and Forrestal forcefully reiterated their opposition to trusteeship for the Mandated Islands. Stimson maintained during an April 17 session with the U.S. delegation to San Francisco that the islands were bases, not colonies, with their control vital for U.S. and world security. Responding to the pleas of Embick, who had "begged me to speak out," he informed the delegates that the "error of our ways" in allowing Japan to control these islands after World War I "had been burnt into his soul" by what had occurred in the Pacific during the war and that this situation could not reoccur. Forrestal, who had been similarly and deeply affected by the carnage that he had recently witnessed on Iwo Jima, concurred. He also emphasized the need for an entire system of bases if the United States was to have major responsibility for world peace in the Pacific. "Power," he insisted, "must remain with the people who hate power." [38]

By April 19 a compromise highly favorable to the armed forces had emerged and been approved by Truman. By its terms the delegates could discuss trusteeships at San Francisco, but only in general terms regarding machinery—not specific territories. Furthermore, any trusteeship system would have to provide for U.S. "military and strategic rights" as well as "such control as will be necessary to assure general peace and security in the Pacific Ocean area as well as elsewhere in the world." To assure such rights and control, U.S. proposals for trusteeships would now include a special category of "strategic" trust for the Mandated Islands, with the United States as sole trustee and administration under the Security Council, where America could exercise its veto power if necessary. Many of these terms had originally been proposed months earlier and rejected by FDR. Truman, however, now approved them, thereby ending this long-running dispute with State in the armed forces' favor. [39]

The resulting policy found favor both with those such as Stimson who saw it as a way to avoid conflict with Russia and with those like Forrestal who were coming to see conflict as inevitable and sought to maximize America's strategic position. But it left unanswered a key concern of those who had opposed the armed forces' demands regarding the Mandated Islands: how to prevent the allies from similarly grabbing territory. Following the military's policy, Interior secretary Harold Ickes had warned on April 5, would lead to an "international grab bag" in which the British, for example, might claim absolute title to Middle East territories in which the United States had strategic and economic interests. [40]

A parallel quandary soon emerged with respect to the Act of Chapultepec and regional defense pacts. At Mexico City the Latin American nations had protested the Dumbarton Oaks subordination of such pacts to the UN, a protest renewed at San Francisco and supported by the U.S. military representatives—especially when they learned that via the Yalta Accords regional collective military action could be blocked by a Security Council veto on authorization. But any strengthening of regional defense pacts at the expense of the world organization would open the door to British and Soviet spheres of influence that excluded the United States. Stimson sardonically noted that "some Americans are anxious to hang on to exaggerated views of the Monroe Doctrine and at the same time butt into every question that cómes up in Central Europe"; Willson told the U.S. delegation on April 16 that the basic issue "was whether stress was to be laid on the whole or the parts" and that if the other great powers would possess no veto in Latin America, then the United States would have no veto in their spheres. On May 4 Pasvolsky suggested that such alterations in the UN charter "might result in the creation of three or four spheres of influence, which explains our opposition to such a proposal." [41]

For Embick, such spheres were not a problem. The armed forces, he informed the delegates on April 18, "feel that there are two essential bases for our security— hemispheric solidarity and control of the necessary islands in the Pacific." Notably absent from this short list was an international organization based on collective security, and a shocked Senator Arthur Vandenberg pointedly asked the general "whether he was aware that we are engaged in creating a world organization." Embick bluntly replied that years ago "he had believed in the League of Nations and in world order, but that he believes there was more chance for the League of Nations to endure than for a new world organization to endure" because of "the extent of chaos in the world and the lack of common standards of value. There- fore, the American people must keep a sharp lookout for United States interests." By early May the JCS were insisting that "no other steps be taken to further water down our concept of hemispheric defense," while Stimson pressed for modifica- tion of the Security Council veto over U.S. actions in the hemisphere and Embick asserted the importance of recognizing "that the normal method of action would be by regional organizations as against action normally through the Security Council. It would be essential to maintain our isolation and our preclusive control over this hemisphere," whose solidarity was "indispensable" to U.S. security. [42]

The question was whether such protection of U.S. hemispheric interests could be accomplished, in the words of Thomas Campbell, "without simultaneously acquiescing in Soviet dominance of Europe." [43] The State Department continued to argue that it could not and that a strong UN was the best way to limit Soviet power. United States regional proposals "gave legal sanction to our allies to build up a system that could in time be turned against us," warned Notter, and accord- ing to Harriman the Soviets might "welcome our approach as a reason to get us out of Europe." Having little if any faith in the UN's ability to halt Soviet expansion under any circumstances and still concerned over British efforts to obtain U.S. backing for a confrontation with Russia in the Balkans and Central Europe, the armed forces preferred to rely on conceptions of national security that featured control of the hemisphere and the oceans and to avoid conflict with the Soviets by acceding to their control of Eastern Europe. Such a de facto spheres-of-influence scenario might very well encourage the British and French to create a West European bloc, but as Senator Vandenberg noted, this "might be a healthy thing . . . to prevent control by Russia of the entire European Continent." For Dulles the question had become "whether it was worth it to us to save our position in Western Europe or whether we should trade this off to assure American solidarity." This "would be the highest decision of national policy—whether or not to build hemisphere solidarity alone and throw away all of Europe or whether to save our voice in Western Europe." McCloy favored the latter approach, asserting that it was "essential not to sacrifice our position with the British Empire as well as with Western Europe." Yet he was unwilling to give up hemispheric solidarity. "We ought to have our cake and eat it too," he told Stimson on May 8. Stimson agreed. The U.S. position in Latin America, he rationalized, "doesn't upset any balance on Europe at all," whereas Russia "may upset a balance that affects us."[44]

Embick disagreed totally and in early June offered McCloy and John Hickerson of the State Department his "personal opinion" that in view of the state of relations with the Soviet Union and problems likely to arise during the occupation of Germany, the United States should not press for any unilateral postwar base rights in Iceland. As distinct from rights that might later be obtained as a member of the UN, unilateral rights "will project the United States into the European Theater, cannot be defended as essential to our own national security, and may be expected to arouse Russian suspicions as to Anglo-American intentions." McCloy's response was to label this approach "a rather restricted concept of what is necessary for national defense."[45]

The eventual compromise at San Francisco, again highly favorable to the JCS position, was a new paragraph that became article 51 of the UN Charter. Reversing the Dumbarton Oaks priorities, it raised the status of regional security arrangements by including them within the inherent right to self-defense and requiring only that they be reported to, rather than approved by, the Security Council.[46]

Not surprisingly given these favorable compromises, the JSSC in a formal June 20 paper and Embick in a June 22 telephone conversation asserted that "the military and strategic implications of the draft charter as a whole are in accord with the military interests of the United States" and recommended JCS approval. Lincoln also recommended approval, noting that the military representatives had been "closely integrated" into the conference discussions and that their views on security matters "have been given full weight." On June 23 the Joint Chiefs approved the JSSC conclusions; Stimson and Forrestal followed suit on June 26, albeit with the assumption that in negotiation of any future international agreements involving military matters—"such as the placing of territory under trusteeship," as well as armed forces for the Security Council, regional arrangements, and arms limitation—the War and Navy Departments "will be actively consulted before any definitive action by this Government is determined upon." Clearly, military concepts of national security had triumphed over the State Department's worldview.[47]

Allied Relations and the War against Japan

Meanwhile, the struggle between those favoring and those opposing a harsher Soviet policy continued. Forrestal was particularly active in the former group, hinting at modification of unconditional surrender and modest peace terms for Japan as a means to create counterweights to postwar Soviet influence in Asia. In mid-May he bluntly informed a senator that Marxism was "as incompatible with democracy as was Nazism or Fascism," a conclusion Harriman had expressed to him on April 20, and by month's end he had ordered preparation of a civilian paper exploring the thesis that Stalin was an aggressive dictator like Hitler and Mussolini with similar goals of military expansion.[48]

Forrestal was not alone in his views. On May 12 Acting Secretary of State Grew asked Forrestal and Stimson, at Harriman's prodding, if early Soviet entry into the war against Japan was "of such vital interest" as to preclude reconsideration of the Yalta Accords and obtaining Soviet agreement to "certain desirable political objectives in the Far East prior to such entry." A few days later McCloy and Assistant Navy Secretary Artemus Gates reported a "growing feeling" within the U.S. delegation at San Francisco that, in light of the "freedom of action" afforded the Soviets under existing charter arrangements and the "pattern which Russian policy was disclosing" in Eastern Europe, it might be desirable "to disassociate ourselves from an association that was working out contrary to some of our fundamental beliefs and traditions." They also reported a similar "growing feeling" against disbanding Eisenhower's headquarters and support for Churchill's desire to maintain it "at least until certain concessions were obtained from the Russians."[49]

Others maintained their opposition to confrontation, however, and with it any close association with British policies. In continuing to urge caution on Truman in the Yugolsav crisis, Marshall, Leahy, and Stimson emphasized the lack of U.S. military interest and long-standing antipathy toward involvement in the area, the Anglo-Russian nature of the clash, the dangers of a Soviet-American conflict, and the fact that a settlement agreeable to Britain "can be accomplished only in several years," in Leahy's words, "if ever." In response to reports that the Russians were attempting to communize Rumania and Bulgaria, the JSSC reiterated on May 13 that "it would be impractical to offer successful military opposition to the Russians" in the Balkans, while ominously warning that any Soviet effort to institute similar regimes in Hungary, Austria, and eastern Germany might demand an increase in U.S. forces in Europe which would "adversely affect the war effort against Japan."[50] On May 19 Stimson reasserted that no conflict of vital geographic interests existed between the two nations and that continuation of the Roosevelt policy of mediating between London and Moscow was wiser than "to lock ourselves completely in" with the British against the Russians. As he informed McCloy:

> Our geographical position with respect to Russia, as well as our position in the world, made it perfectly possible for us to get along without fighting; that as long as she did not threaten any of our vital interests . . . we need never fight the Soviets. He [Stimson] felt that the British were more closely involved in Europe; the Russians were more suspicious of them than they were of us and any steps we took now in immediate reversal of our agreement with the Russians would be construed by them as a definite alignment of the Anglo-Americans against the Russians and make it all the more difficult for us to work out an effective relationship with them. Our position and strength justified and made advisable an independent attitude toward Russia in our own right. He said this was the time to put up with a good bit of ill mannered behavior with the Russians in a sincere attempt to work out such a relationship rather than to form what would be construed as a close military alliance against them.[51]

Simultaneously McCloy and Stimson responded to Grew's May 12 queries with a memorandum, produced by the s&p and supported by Marshall, stating once again that Soviet entry into the war against Japan would "have a profound military effect in that almost certainly it will materially shorten the war and thus save American lives." Because that entry would be based on Soviet interests, with U.S. inducements having little effect, military considerations did not preclude an attempt to revise the Yalta Accords. Yet Grew needed to realize that Russia could take most of the territorial concessions granted at Yalta "regardless of U.S. military action short of war," as well as enter the war at the last minute and seize the territories. As in Europe, the United States thus had little leverage, and from a military point of view it remained desirable to have "complete understanding and agreement" with the Russians. Revision of the Yalta Accords would be favored if it could achieve this, but they did not believe "that much good will come of a rediscussion at this time."[52]

Stimson and the jssc were not alone in reiterating the possibility of Soviet-American cooperation, the limits of U.S. power in Eastern Europe, and the need to avoid backing British policy. On May 14 Oscar Cox, Hopkins's aide, echoed similar sentiments in San Francisco. Just before his own departure for Moscow to attempt to resolve the difficulties that had arisen, Hopkins noted the "vital importance that we not be maneuvered into a position where Great Britain has us lined up with them as a bloc against Russia to implement England's European policy." Walter Lippmann publicly asserted a similar position in June, while Joseph Davies informed Truman and Leahy after a trip to London that Churchill was trying to use U.S. muscle in the hope of "sustaining Britain's vanishing position in Europe" and that "Russian knowledge of Churchill's attitude was responsible for much of the aggressiveness and unilateral action on the part of the Soviets since Yalta." Leahy told Truman and Hopkins that relations with Russia were "more important" than those with Britain.[53]

Throughout June the armed forces thus continued to reject British pleas for both a postwar CCS and a tough combined policy against the Soviets because these positions would further and unnecessarily poison Soviet-American relations—with negative consequences for Allied occupation policies, the war against Japan, and the postwar world—as well as fail to produce the desired results and tie Washington to a declining power. Anglo-American military forces in Europe constituted only ninety divisions, approximately one-third of Soviet strength, Leahy noted, and therefore provided very limited bargaining power. General Walter Bedell Smith, now Eisenhower's chief of staff, informed a British associate that Russia "was a nation of the future and Great Britain one of the past. The war had broken British power and the United States would seek a postwar alliance with the Soviet Union." Soviet policies appeared more and more threatening, however. Lincoln consequently concluded in late June that while creation of a central economic authority for the nations of Western Europe would "hold dangers of building toward a very obvious Western European bloc vis-a-vis the Russian eastern bloc," the alternative "may be that the Russian bloc will involve all of Western Europe."[54]

Despite Forrestal's concurrence in the McCloy-Stimson reply to Grew, the division over Soviet policy within the military also reflected disagreement about the need for Soviet entry into the Far East war. The destruction of Japan's remaining naval power and airpower in late 1944, combined with the highly effective submarine campaign against its shipping and the bombing campaign against its cities in 1945, led naval and air force planners to conclude that Tokyo could be forced to surrender without invasion or Soviet assistance. Army planners disagreed, as did MacArthur and Nimitz. Obtaining surrender via blockade and bombing would be a lengthy process that the war-weary public might not tolerate; moreover, any belief that Japan would recognize the hopelessness of the situation and surrender before invasion and conquest had to consider its relentless and suicidal resistance on Iwo Jima and Okinawa.[55]

Because blockade and bombing were essential prerequisites to invasion, navy and AAF planners on the JPS could agree with the army in late April to recommend early invasion of the home islands but still believe it would not prove necessary. Perhaps influenced by the recent modification of JCS policy toward the Soviets and progress on the atomic bomb as well as recent military successes, the JPS noted that U.S. ability to interdict movement between the Asian mainland and Japan meant that early Russian entry into the war "is no longer necessary to make invasion feasible." Yet on May 11 chief naval planner Cooke informed Forrestal and Harriman that although "the necessity for Russia's early participation was very much lessened as a result of recent events . . . , the army didn't share that view." On the following day Marshall informed the head of the JSM that he was determined not to use U.S. forces on the Asian mainland and was still relying on the Russians to deal with the Kwantung Army.[56]

The conflicting service estimates as to the necessity of Soviet entry and how Japan could be defeated intersected with their recommendations on Allied relations. Navy and AAF planners focused on the ability of naval power and airpower to force a Japanese surrender and thus tended to discount the importance of both British and Soviet participation in the war, at the same time as they urged a tougher policy against the no-longer-needed Soviets. Their army counterparts, on the other hand, continued to insist that only land power could win wars and that a U.S. invasion of the home islands and Soviet invasion of Manchuria would be necessary to force Japanese surrender.

Even that might not be enough, however, and the services thus pressed for a modification of unconditional surrender.[57] The JCS also issued a directive for the November 1 invasion of Kyushu, the southernmost Japanese home island (OLYMPIC). As with the JPS report, however, the directive masked ongoing disagreement as to whether this invasion and a later one on the main island of Honshu (CORONET) would really be necessary—and with them Soviet entry—or whether the preceding bombing and blockade, combined with modification of unconditional surrender, could by themselves force Japanese capitulation.

At a June 18 meeting with the JCS and service secretaries, Truman bluntly asked for the military view on OLYMPIC versus other operations or siege warfare and the "necessity for having Russia in the war." All agreed that airpower by itself was insufficient and supported Soviet entry and OLYMPIC as the necessary prerequisites to a siege, bombardment, or CORONET; Marshall noted that the impact of Russian entry "on the already hopeless Japanese may well be the decisive action levering them into capitulation at that time or shortly thereafter if we land in Japan," and Truman stated that one of his objectives at the coming Potsdam summit "would be to get from Russia all the assistance in the war that was possible." Privately, however, King felt OLYMPIC was *not* "essential to a strategy of strangulation," though he voiced no objection when Marshall stated that it was. What the CNO did assert was that "regardless of the desirability of the Russians entering the war, they were not indispensable and he did not think we should go so far as to beg them to come in. While the cost of defeating Japan would be greater, there was no question in his mind but that we could handle it alone." The casualties might be enormous, however, with Truman concluding and the JCS concurring that OLYMPIC "was practically another Okinawa closer to Japan." [58]

Thus at this time and in ensuing weeks, all services called for a modification of unconditional surrender, albeit for different reasons, that would allow the Japanese to retain the emperor. Naval personnel tended to view modification as part of their alternative to Soviet entry and U.S. invasion, whereas army planners saw it as an *addition* to such entry and invasion. "That would certainly coordinate all the threats possible to Japan," Stimson noted on June 19 after Marshall had pressed the Soviet issue. Stimson hoped that these moves would lead Japan to surrender before the invasion began, and a combined intelligence estimate on July 8 concluded that Soviet entry "would finally convince the Japanese of the inevitability of complete defeat." The Strategy and Policy Group was not so sure, however: "Probably it will take Russian entry into the war, coupled with a landing, or imminent threat of a landing . . . , to convince them of the hopelessness of their situation," it concluded on June 4. Implying that the navy's siege strategy was being influenced by desire for postwar control of "particular areas," on July 10 Lincoln wrote Wedemeyer that although Japan might "quit without an invasion" if unconditional surrender was defined, his "personal opinion" was that there would be "two psychological days in the war; that is, the day after we persuade Russia to enter, if we can, and the day after we get what the Japs recognize as a secure beachhead in Japan." Only at these points would the United States be able to obtain a Japanese surrender—and then only provided it had first defined unconditional surrender. These moves were all part of a "cumulative" strategy being proposed by the S&P and supported by Marshall to combine and coordinate all possible measures so as to convince Japan of the hopelessness of its situation. [59]

Both services throughout this time period also continued to express a deep suspicion of British motives in the Pacific. As early as May 19 Lincoln warned of probable British efforts at Potsdam to "out-shuffle us" on Pacific operations, and by late June he was voicing opposition to any expansion of British participation in the campaign if it occurred at the expense of U.S. leadership and control. "Anything smacking of combined command in the Pacific," one of his planners warned, would not only be inefficient but also "might increase the difficulties with Russia and perhaps China." In July the OPD rated a quick Japanese surrender "advantageous" not only because it would shorten the war and save lives but also because "it would give us a better chance to settle the affairs of the Western Pacific before too many of our allies are committed there and have made substantial contributions towards the defeat of Japan." In that same month the Policy Committee voiced opposition to the establishment of Allied occupation zones in the Japanese Empire because the United States would thereby gain "only a partial victory in return for its expenditures in the war, while the U.S.S.R. and possibly the U.K. will have gained greatly. The prizes for which Japan started aggression fifty years ago will simply be passed to other hands." At the same time, the JCS and their planners opposed supporting the British economy with Lend-Lease and rejected British proposals for a combined policy on disclosure of military information to the Soviets in the war against Japan, as well as their participation in strategic decision making for the Pacific. As King told Forrestal, "We will inform and *consult* the British but . . . *we will decide.*" [60]

The July Reassessment

Military planners also attempted to deal with a new set of Soviet territorial demands prior to Potsdam as Moscow renounced its treaty of friendship with Turkey and demanded revision of the Montreaux Convention regarding the Dardanelles, base rights in the straits, and retrocession of territory ceded in 1922. It also called for internationalization of the Kiel Canal, cession of Bear Island from Norway, and joint Soviet-Norwegian control over Spitsbergen Island—partially based on similar steps being taken by the United States and Britain in the Pacific and Mediterranean. The State Department opposed acquiescing in these demands but requested JCS opinion through SWNCC on an "urgent basis" in view of the coming conference. [61]

Any JCS response was, of course, related to their late April revision of Soviet policy, but that revision had been quite limited and had applied *only* to Deane. In early July Lincoln and OPD chief Hull therefore pressed for a reworking of that policy, with Hull informing Marshall that much of it was "inadequate" and "exists only in the minds of the JCS and General Deane." He also noted that London was suggesting a combined policy against the Soviets that the JCS had previously rejected, and he proposed an amplification of the April decisions so as to ensure that America would not be "dependent in any important respect" on the Soviets, to halt unimportant requests where their agreement was unlikely, to place the United States "in the best overall bargaining position" with them, yet to "avoid incidents which might lead to friction." Clearly, military proposals continued to diverge in an effort to cover multiple contingencies. As Marshall informed the British regarding their suggested combined policy toward the Soviets, the JCS "still were very uncertain as to what the right answer is. There have been so many conflicting views expressed here in Washington on the subject that they were reluctant to subscribe too quickly to the idea that had been put forward." [62]

Given these facts the JCS once again turned for guidance to the JSSC, only to find it split. Whereas Embick and Fairchild wished to continue past policy, Willson now recommended direct opposition to Soviet demands.

The Embick/Fairchild majority report on the Dardanelles and Kiel Canal recommended acquiescence in Soviet demands for the same reasons as those cited in the 1944 JSSC papers. Russia was now the predominant power in Europe and would be in northern Asia after Japan's defeat. Unlike its allies, who had fought the war essentially to preserve the status quo, "Russia has aspirations for the rectification of her former status which are quite logical in view of her history." Control of the Dardanelles was the "most historical and cherished" of these, "one that is motivated by national economic need and therefore has moral justification." It was also the one traditionally blocked by Britain. Neither London nor Washington possessed the ability to oppose Moscow here, and "it would appear inconsistent for us to oppose them while ourselves asking for base rights in areas remote from our shores, such as Iceland, the Azores, and the more distant Pacific islands." Washington should therefore approve demilitarization of the straits and Kiel Canal and assume a "detached position" on the question of Russian bases, though keep in mind "the danger inherent in piece-meal satisfaction of Russian aspirations" and the need to satisfy U.S. objectives, most notably in the Pacific. "Our bargaining position vis-a-vis Russia," they concluded, "should therefore be kept in mind and adequately preserved."[63]

Embick further informed the OPD in a separate memorandum that Russian demands regarding the Dardanelles and Kiel were part of a traditional desire for year-round access to the open sea and would probably be accompanied by demands for participation in a condominium over Tangiers, retention of base rights at Bornholm, and cession of Dairen and Port Arthur in the Far East. Since the time of Peter the Great, Russia had focused on obtaining access to the Mediterranean via the Dardanelles. Its efforts had been "consistently thwarted" by other powers "under the leadership of Great Britain," and "no moral justification" existed for continuing this policy. Furthermore, Russia would possess the power at war's end to obtain its aims by force, and any attempt to deny them would both fail and "appear likely to endanger the establishment of the World Order."[64]

Soviet demands regarding Bear Island and Spitsbergen had first been sent to the JPS, who had stated that U.S. strategic interests would not be "seriously affected" provided it had bases on Greenland and Iceland but also cautioned that Russian control of northern Norway could serve as a "springboard for Soviet domination of Scandinavia." Embick and Fairchild concurred with the ensuing JPS conclusions: Washington had "no important military interest" in Spitsbergen, but Norwegian sovereignty was "more desirable than cession to another power for military base purposes"; the issue should be sent to the Council of Foreign Ministers for settlement as part of a package rather than piecemeal to provide more time to define U.S. requirements and preserve its bargaining position; and if this was not possible no objection need be raised to Soviet demands if they agreed to exclusive U.S. base rights in Iceland and Greenland, removal of their troops from and renunciation of any desire to control northern Norway, no demands for Jan Mayen Island, and preservation of Norwegian economic rights on Spitsbergen.[65]

The Strategy and Policy Group attacked these proposals much as it had the 1944 JSSC papers. One planner again labeled them "appeasement" based on the fear "that any other action will endanger future World Peace." Appeasement might be acceptable "if we could be *sure* that, once given her 'vital interest' of year round 'assured' access to the seas, Russia would be content to stop . . . *but* there is no proof that she will and considerable indication that she won't." Indeed, the S&P provided a highly aggressive view of Russian policy and history totally at odds with what Embick and Fairchild had presented, seeing the real aim behind Soviet demands on Turkey as eventual control of the entire Near and Middle East. "There is no historic justification for Soviet claims on eastern Turkey," one draft memorandum insisted, save nineteenth-century Russian aggression. A separate sheet offering historical perspective cited thirteen wars between Russia and Turkey in 250 years, "all motivated by Russian aggression." What, another planner asked, was the Russian definition of "security," and against whom did it need defense? Embick and Fairchild had in effect concluded that Washington could neither stop nor threaten Moscow, but "if we can't, who in the world can?" Furthermore, agreement to internationalize the straits and Kiel Canal would lead to similar demands for Gibraltar, Singapore, Suez, and the Panama Canal.[66]

Many of these comments implied a close relationship between U.S. and British policies and a defense of British interests totally at odds with traditional U.S. military views. An S&P draft letter from Stimson to the new secretary of state James Byrnes noted that airpower had made fortification rights in the Dardanelles useless unless they extended to "covering bases" that would project into vital British areas, and Soviet demands might thus "face us squarely with a problem of choosing between a compromise of British interests or an opposition to Soviet expansion."[67] This and other S&P papers made abundantly clear that the former was incompatible with U.S. security. As noted in one paper, Soviet moves threatened "severance of the British Empire lifeline" and would "affect U.S. oil interests located near the head of the Persian Gulf"; Washington should consider leaving a token military force in Iran both to protect its interests and "furnish backing to Great Britain in her unequal task of protecting her vital strategic interests." Another stated the importance of the Kiel Canal to British control of the North Sea and of that control to U.S. security: "For many years the effective implementation of the Monroe Doctrine has rested on the existence of the British fleet. Any international measure which threatened the effectiveness of British sea power in the Atlantic would unfavorably affect the U.S. position in Latin America." One planner warned that Russia was already "the greatest potential land power in the world," that control of the Dardanelles and Kiel Canal would be part of "the first essential steps on her path to becoming a major naval power" as well as a threat to British power, and that the United States might then be brought into conflict with Russia "at any point in the world." Because that world was presently being divided into spheres of influence and Britain was the buffer between the U.S. and Soviet spheres, it was in America's interest that Soviet demands be resisted and "that Britain remain strong." [68]

The Strategy and Policy Group also rejected Embick's linkage of Soviet demands with U.S. demands for postwar bases because most of the latter consisted of the "ill gotten gains" of the Axis and because "our history clearly indicates that we are not aggressor expansionists. Russia, on the other hand, is presently suspect." Preserving U.S. and British control over Panama and Gibraltar while denying Russia control over the Dardanelles might seem illogical, but it was a "logical illogicality" because "neither the United States nor the British Empire can by the greatest stretch of the imagination be accused of expansionist or aggressive ambitions." That was far from true of the USSR, a "young and vigorous nation of unlimited potential" that was "inextricably, almost mystically related to the ideology of Communism. . . . Russia must be sorely tempted to combine her strength with her ideology to expand her influence over the earth. Her action[s] in the past few years give us no assured basis for supposing that she has not flirted with the thought." [69]

Not surprisingly, the S&P also attacked punitive postwar proposals for Japan because they would force the Japanese to embrace Communism and ignored "the fact that some members of the United Nations . . . translate 'democracy' differently than we do." One officer argued against giving all the Kurils to Russia as agreed at Yalta because they would enable Moscow to control a northern route to Asia half the length of the one through the Mandated Islands. They thus constituted a "springboard of the most possible route of attack on us," and "unless we kid ourselves we know damn well the only Asiatic enemy we are guarding against is Russia." [70]

The Strategy and Policy Group's negative assessments of Soviet aims were reinforced at this time by a G-2 paper that labeled Moscow's intention as "the unlimited expansion of Soviet influence and control whenever and wherever possible" and by whatever means necessary. The issue was raw power rather than Communist ideology by a country "which has never shown itself adept at making any permanent compromises with rival power groups." Russian expansion now focused on Europe and a "solution of their historic problem of lack of warm water ports and free access to open seas." The USSR was already "one of the strongest land powers in the world"; a "fundamental" Soviet national policy was "to ultimately become the greatest air and naval power" too, accomplishment of which the United States could not allow. "The limit has been reached to which the U.S. can subscribe to Soviet expansion." Western Europe was "now the outpost of American ideas" and "must be held. To lose it is to permit Soviet influence to spread over all of Europe, including England, thus concluding one more stage to commence another. The question is no longer one of ideologies; the grasp for world power is the problem." [71]

Some S&P members agreed and warned that although Russian and U.S. strength would in the near future "preclude the overwhelming military defeat of either by the other," Soviet power eventually would surpass America's and pose a mortal threat; Washington must thus oppose "by military force if necessary any further westward expansion by Russia in Europe" and resist demands on Turkey and in Asia. Even those who disagreed with G-2 concurred on the need to pursue "a realistic, common sense, attitude" toward Russia, "demand cooperation, tell her how far we'll go with her and the limits beyond which we will oppose her." [72] On July 6 and 7 Lincoln forwarded some of the S&P studies to Embick and McCloy, along with his "general agreement" to most of the thoughts expressed, his conclusion that while "reasonable" Russian requests should be granted "anything unreasonable or overbearing should be resisted by all means available but short of war," and specific compromise proposals. "Nothing can be done to stop the Russians if they wish to take military action," he admitted, "but we question whether they will choose to do so"—especially if Washington was firm. Otherwise, the Russians would "capitalize on any show of weakness and very soon would be asking for (to us) absolutely impossible things such as a share of the Panama Canal." [73]

These S&P conclusions and disagreements with the JSSC were not new. Now, however, the navy voiced similar dissent. King and his planners had previously expressed a willingness to accede to Russian desire for warm-water ports and access to the open seas on the same grounds Embick and Fairchild had listed, as well as lack of direct U.S. interest in the areas involved. Even in July at least one naval planner still concurred with the two generals that the United States should consent to Soviet demands and avoid getting caught in an Anglo-Russian-Turkish "cross fire" over the Dardanelles. By that time, however, naval opinion as a whole had begun to shift dramatically as a result of Forrestal's efforts and what that naval planner labeled America's "new-found interest in the Mediterranean, not only by reason of our general post-war world position and our strategic relationship to Britain, but because of our extending oil interests in the Middle East." [74] Thus Willson totally disagreed with the Embick-Fairchild position on the Russian demands and filed two minority reports.

Over the past few months the admiral had on occasion implied disagreement with continuation of the old JSSC policy regarding the Soviets and a belief, expressed directly after the war, that insistence on the importance of their entry into the war against Japan had "outlived all its justification." [75] Now he spoke his mind fully. The Allies had previously agreed to leave territorial matters for war's end and to treat them as a whole. "The single but important exception in the application of this principle has been Russia," which had consistently received "preferred treatment" but had reacted by simply demanding further special consideration. The United States did not possess the power to successfully oppose the Russians militarily, Willson agreed, but such compensating factors as war-weariness, overextension, the need for time to recoup losses and rebuild the economy (which would require "substantial" U.S. assistance) might make Moscow unwilling to break with the United States over these issues. Discussion of the Dardanelles and the Kiel Canal should be limited and postponed, he recommended, with final decisions left to the general peace settlement. If this was not possible, Washington should support demilitarization of both waterways but oppose any Russian bases, control, or special position. Soviet proposals regarding Bear Island and Spitsbergen should be flatly opposed as "untimely" and "unnecessary for Soviet security and contrary to the long-range and over-all security considerations from our point of view. This war has been fought to prevent an aggressive nation from dominating Europe," he insisted, "and ultimately threatening the Western Hemisphere. From the long-range security point of view, and until the post-war situation and Soviet policy can be seen more clearly, we should, in so far as practicable, resist demands and policies which tend to improve [the] Soviet position in Western Europe." [76]

The Joint Chiefs and their planners concurred. Indeed, the JPS at Potsdam reversed the recommendations of their deputies in Washington and on July 22 backed Willson. Although Leahy once again questioned the propriety of dealing with such matters, Marshall and King insisted they were well within the JCS sphere. On July 17 and 26 the Joint Chiefs rejected the Embick-Fairchild JSSC reports in favor of Willson's memoranda and forwarded the latter with amendments to SWNCC. [77]

More than the April revision, this July JCS acceptance of Willson's minority report over the Embick-Fairchild majority one marked a fundamental shift in JCS policy toward the Soviet Union. Unlike the situation at the time of the April reassessment, Germany had by now surrendered unconditionally and been occupied, thereby removing any vestigial concern with the European war and Axis efforts to split the Allies. Of perhaps equal importance, Truman had now been in office for a few months rather than a few weeks and had appointed Byrnes secretary of state; both men had made clear their refusal to continue acceding to Soviet demands.

Fear of British manipulation and the desire to avoid being sucked into an Anglo-Russian clash in the Balkans remained, but now countering it was a growing belief that Soviet demands were *not* limited to Eastern Europe or defensive in nature. "They are throwing aside all their previous restraint as to being only a Continental power and not interested in any further acquisitions," Stimson noted in summarizing a July 23 discussion with Harriman, McCloy, and Harvey Bundy, "and are now apparently seeking to branch in all directions." Leahy acidly noted in his diary on July 30 that he had "no doubt" agreement could be reached at Potsdam "if we and the British accede to all the demands made by the Soviet." Along with such comments went a parallel, growing belief that U.S. and British interests coincided in the Middle East and elsewhere.[78] Fear of starting an unwinnable World War III was simultaneously being countered by fear that further Soviet expansion would enable the Russians to win such a conflict and that U.S. acquiescence in that expansion would only encourage Moscow to demand more.

Of the six reasons given for adherence to the cooperative policy, there remained only the need for Soviet entry into war against Japan, a need the navy and AAF had previously called into question. Such questioning was now reinforced by the first successful detonation of an atomic bomb on July 16, before JCS acceptance of Willson's minority reports. That detonation had a decisive impact on some U.S. officials, such as Byrnes, who no longer considered Soviet entry either necessary or desirable and who on July 28 informed Forrestal that he was "most anxious to get the Japanese affair over with before the Russians got in." It also had a powerful effect on Stimson, whose diary reveals intense preoccupation with the weapon as early as February and a belief it would be critical in moderating Soviet behavior. Its impact on the armed forces was far less decisive, however.[79] The atomic bomb appears simply to have reinforced the previous naval and air viewpoint that invasion and Soviet entry would not be necessary, while adding another potential weapon to the army's list of cumulative shocks and pressures.

Stimson did ask Marshall on July 23, at Truman's request, whether he still "felt that we needed the Russians in the war or whether we could get along without them," and he informed the president on the next day that "the implication that could be inferred" from the army chief's reply was that "the Russians were not needed." Yet Marshall's previous arguments had focused not on the necessity of Soviet entry but on its desirability in coordination with other actions, to speed Japanese surrender and minimize U.S. casualties. The final CCS report at Potsdam reaffirmed that desirability, while Marshall's interest in planning for possible tactical use of nuclear weapons on the invasion beaches—even after the August 6–9 bombings of Hiroshima and Nagasaki and Soviet entry into the war—clearly reveals his doubts that this new weapon or any single factor would definitely lead to Japanese surrender.[80]

The bomb's impact on JCS policy regarding the Soviets thus appears to have been minimal before the Japanese agreement to surrender on August 14. It would play a much more decisive role after and along with that surrender, however, in completing the shift in JCS policy on the Soviet Union which was by now well under way.

13 Aftermath and Conclusions

The months following Japan's surrender witnessed a virtual explosion of anti-Soviet statements within the armed forces. That surrender removed the last military rationale for maintaining good relations with Russia, and the ensuing failure of the London Foreign Ministers Conference in September ended any remaining military belief that Soviet desires were limited to defensive needs in contiguous areas. At the same time, military planners began to express fears of U.S. vulnerability owing to atomic weapons and rapid demobilization. The result was the complete abandonment of remaining military hopes for postwar cooperation with Russia and calls for a global anti-Soviet military as well as foreign policy—one that would include defense of British interests and the creation of a new peacetime national security establishment.

Soon after German surrender, on Marshall's suggestion, the JCS had called for review of postwar bases required in the event of another major war as well as for enforcement of the peace. In early July they had been informed that no statement of national military policy existed to determine these requirements and that such a statement, "based upon national interests versus those of other powers," would be "most helpful." Two weeks later the JWPC and the JPWC had informed the JPS that the possibility of a breakdown in Soviet-American relations required the United States to be prepared for a unilateral and active self-defense, one that would require extensive overseas bases.[1]

The JPS had originally deferred action in hopes of obtaining both clarification on postwar national policies and the results of the Potsdam Conference then in session, but on August 3 it met with these committees and the JSSC for what Embick labeled an "exploratory" discussion. Two major problems with any such discussion, Colonel William W. Bessell of the JWPC noted, were a lack of defined policy for some parts of the world and a feeling that specific nations should not be named as objects of any military plan. Yet if the armed forces were to make up a postwar strategic plan, he asked, "can we come out and call a spade a shovel?

We used to do it." Fairchild and Willson concurred, with the latter asserting that he did not "see why we are not old enough to know the facts of life." Those facts, Lincoln explained, would require the power to intervene militarily and unilaterally in Europe or Asia. Extensive military participation within a UN framework, Fairchild insisted, was a popular "misconception" that needed to be corrected; if U.S. military forces were to be employed, "we are going to employ them against a major power" and the UN "will be out the window"—a fact Embick feared the State Department did not yet understand.[2]

The Strategy and Policy Group agreed that a more precise definition of postwar policies was now an "urgent necessity," especially because the existing overseas base study, with its emphasis on the Pacific and Western Hemisphere, did not come to grips with the "primary" U.S. military problem in the postwar era— retention of "the military capacity to intervene in Europe or Asia, or both." Inability to do so would "concede to Russia full freedom of action" on those continents as well as in Africa, which could make hemispheric defense "a meaningless concept."[3] Thus the committees agreed that the JPS, assisted by the others, would prepare a postwar military policy, a global strategic plan, and recommendations for postwar overseas base requirements.

Spurred on by an August 19 suggestion from Marshall and an August 21 directive from Truman as well as Japan's surrender, the planners throughout the month circulated drafts of a military policy statement for review and modification.[4] Strategy and Policy continued to press for greater emphasis on Europe and, joined by the SPD, objected to any repetition of the 1944 JSSC conclusion that neither Russia nor the United States could defeat the other in a war. One S&P member bluntly proposed the addition of "what has been our one and only basic policy in the last 30 years. That is that we prefer to fight our wars in some one else's territory."[5]

The draft sent to the Joint Chiefs on August 30 as JCS 1496 did not include this statement, but neither did it include the old JSSC conclusion regarding a Soviet-American war, and it did list as a major national policy maintenance of "the best possible relative position with respect to potential enemy powers." On Marshall's suggestion the JCS added "ready when necessary to take military action abroad to maintain the security and integrity of the United States." Increased emphasis was placed on such action and an extensive intelligence apparatus to anticipate or prevent an attack, and an entirely new section was added on avoiding via deterrence what everyone agreed would be a devastating third world war. Other national policies included advancing U.S. "political, economic and social well-being"; maintaining its territorial integrity and that of its leased areas, possessions and trust territories, the Philippines, and all nations in the Western Hemisphere; collaboration with these latter nations to maintain hemispheric peace and security; participation in and full support of the UN; and enforcement with the Allies of peace terms upon the Axis. These policies were directed toward maintaining world peace, which in turn depended on Big Three and, especially, Soviet-American cooperation. The "in no way remote possibility" of a breakdown in relations necessitated sufficient military power to maintain U.S. security unilaterally, which in turn required the capacity, given atomic weapons, to "strike the first blow if necessary," as well as "close coordination and mutual understanding" between the State, War, and Navy Departments. With additional revisions that softened some of the anti-Soviet language, the JCS approved this document on September 18 and forwarded it to the service secretaries with the recommendation that it be sent to the State Department and president.[6]

By that time the committees had also prepared and circulated early drafts of the related strategic concept and plan for the employment of U.S. forces. These similarly noted the inability of the UN to handle a Soviet-American confrontation and emphasized that atomic weapons had altered the character of warfare and made mandatory not only overseas bases but also first-strike capacity and a global intelligence system to preclude attack. The earliest of those drafts actually provided a strategic concept and plan for war with Russia, while another bluntly asserted the "most likely" cause of such a war would be "a demonstration of intent on her [Russia's] part to overrun Western Europe." Yet it also harkened back to the 1944 JSSC studies in its conclusion that neither nation could totally defeat the other and that the U.S. aim would therefore be to drive Soviet forces back within their own borders rather than to overrun the USSR. "Such a campaign," according to the draft, "would require an effort on a scale at least as great as World War II," with progress dependent on the "relative state of preparedness of the U.S. and U.S.S.R. to launch the first devastating blow and therefore to sustain an all-out war."[7]

Lincoln and the rest of the OPD strongly concurred on the need to prevent the Russians from overrunning Western Europe, but they did not wish to limit the stated causes of war to one geographic area or U.S. aims in any such conflict. Instead, they called for emphasis "on the instability and unrest which will mark the period of liquidation of the war," along with an expansion of the likely causes of war to include Russian aggression in the Middle East, China, and, "after time for the development of a Russian Navy," the Dutch East Indies. The U.S. aim in such a war "would not be to push Russia back within her frontiers but to destroy her war-making potential. Consequently, the war would have as its objective the final defeat of Russia." Lincoln also argued that although striking the first blow might be "desirable," it was "not politically feasible under our system to do so or to state that we will do so." Such comments were thus removed and replaced with the more defensive sounding necessity to prevent a first strike against the United States. Simultaneously, Lincoln recommended initiation of a paper "in the nature of a backfire to the public sentiment about giving away the atomic bomb. . . . Twenty thousand college professors can be wrong," he sardonically concluded, "but they are hard to convince."[8]

This time, neither Embick nor his JSSC colleagues objected to such strong assertion of anti-Soviet sentiments. Nor did they disapprove the removal of their previous statements about the impossibility of either superpower totally defeating the other in a war. All that remained of the previous position after their own revisions was the emphasis on British weakness and the refusal to agree that the two nations constituted "natural allies," as other planners had claimed. Yet even Embick was now forced to admit that experience suggested the two would probably be allied in any future conflict. On September 19 the JSSC forwarded its revised version of the strategic concept and plan (JCS 1518) to the Joint Chiefs; it was further amended by King and Marshall and then approved on October 13. Joined by the JPWC, the JSSC at this time also concurred in a new JPS report on overseas base requirements that added bases in New Zealand, the Ryukyus, and the Arctic.[9]

In early September Embick also insisted on fully implementing the Act of Chapultepec so as to establish a hemispheric security system rather than place any reliance on the UN. The idea that the world organization would preclude or render unlikely a future major war was "completely erroneous" and if not corrected would pose "grave danger" of congressional refusal to provide adequate postwar military forces. Furthermore, failure to create a full hemispheric security system would open the door to demands from non-American UN nations for bases in the Western Hemisphere, thereby negating the Monroe Doctrine. Embick also noted that "successive recent developments in military weapons, (aviation, rockets, guided missiles, atomic bombs) have tended progressively toward a constantly increasing coalescence of the Western Hemisphere into a distinct military entity," thereby rendering its solidarity in support of the principles of that doctrine "far more essential to our security than heretofore."[10]

The denigration of the UN expressed in these and other planning documents (Lincoln on August 19 had asserted that "there is nothing in the San Francisco Charter which would allow the use of force against anyone except perhaps Liberia") brought forth opposition by McCloy and others and resulted in Marshall rewording that section of JCS 1518 prior to JCS approval.[11] In an October 1 letter to Colonel Herman Beukema at West Point, Lincoln noted that he was "having a little difficulty . . . on the political level" with JCS 1496, which he had enclosed, and that an attempt was being made "to doctor it up politically." He had little sympathy with such an effort, however, and wanted to make sure that none of this became public, for "both Pravda and U.S. college professors might take an interest in a vitriolic and voluminous way." The same held true for the strategic concept and associated intelligence estimate, which he labeled "likely to be the most dangerous document in the English language." Beukema quickly reassured him that JCS 1496 had been placed in a safe with the combination "known only to me" and that "no one save an enemy agent or a full-fledged fellow traveller could cavil at your provisions. Add wishful thinkers." But such people did not dominate academia as much as Lincoln feared, for at a recent conference in Princeton where representatives from fifty-five campuses were being "indoctrinated" prior to introducing the Navy's Foundations of National Power course, Beukema noted, "the hair was down" and "agreement was general that Russia would have to be headed in sharply or else."[12]

Whether Earle expressed such sentiments to Embick during a luncheon and "long talk" in September is not clear.[13] But the general was clearly reversing his position on Russia under the impact of recent events and, perhaps, pressure from his colleagues. In all likelihood he was also affected by the experiences and recommendations of his son-in-law Wedemeyer in China, who wanted to aid Chiang against Mao and on August 14 had warned the JCS of a Soviet and world Communist conspiracy in the area. Furthermore, the JCS now reversed their wartime policy of noninvolvement in the Chinese Civil War and concurred with Wedemeyer's recommendations—ironically at the very moment the State Department turned against such intervention.[14]

Embick's own reversal was completed by early October in the aftermath of Russia's truculent behavior and demands at the failed London Foreign Ministers Conference. Those demands apparently ended any remaining belief that Soviet expansion was defensive in nature and limited to contiguous areas. It also called into question the previously expressed belief that no power or coalition would be strong enough to endanger the United States militarily for five years. Now there appeared "some question in people's minds, other than G-2," Lincoln informed Hull on October 8, "as to whether we can safely count on Russia keeping the peace with the United States for five years."[15]

On the following day the JSSC informed the JCS that it was "seriously concerned" with the U.S. military position "in the light of Russian policy as it has developed in the past year" and as it could be forecast based on its "recent aggressive and uncompromising attitude." Six months ago the United States had been "the greatest military power in the history of the world," whereas Russian power had been limited to contiguous areas. Demobilization had rapidly reduced U.S. military ability to oppose any extension of Russian power, however, with misplaced public faith in the atomic bomb and in the UN reinforcing the demobilization tide. Russia had admittedly cooperated in the conduct of the war and the UN Charter. But by its own statements it planned to keep 5.5 million men under arms, and its territorial "accomplishments" were already "imposing." Also threatening were its demands regarding Turkey, the Dardanelles, the Dodecanese, Bear Island, and Spitsbergen; additional demands at London for a trusteeship over Tripolitania and an equal position in the occupation of Japan; and its "widespread subversive measures" in Latin America.[16]

The time had therefore "now arrived," the JSSC concluded, for the JCS to reexamine "the current and prospective military position of the United States in light of Russian policy." Admittedly, America could not successfully fight the Soviets in the Balkans or Turkey and probably not in South Korea. But "if there is to be any limit to Russian demands," the JSSC insisted, "we must know where we can draw the line and examine our military position and be sure that we are not abandoning our military power so rapidly that we shall be unable to support that line." Soviet policy, it further warned, might well be aiming toward a domination of Europe comparable with German policy, as well as control of the eastern Mediterranean, the Persian Gulf, northern China, and Korea. On October 15, two days after their approval of JCS 1518, the JCS by informal action approved this report.[17]

A week later G-2 weighed in with a preliminary draft in response to a JWPC request for a JIC estimate, "*as a matter of priority*," of the Soviet "political situation with particular emphasis on aims and potentialities for expansion of her sphere of influence by means short of war," as well as the Russian military situation, ability to develop atomic weapons, and economic ability to support a major war in the next five years. The Intelligence Division bluntly concluded that Soviet foreign policy was "one of expansion, nationalistic and imperialistic in character, with no evidence of change in the foreseeable future." Russia was already capable of overrunning Europe and achieving its objectives in Turkey and Iran, and its capabilities would only grow with time. It would avoid the risk of armed conflict for five to ten years, but its caution would decrease as its economic and military weaknesses were eliminated. Revisions in this document over the next few days by members of the Joint Intelligence Staff warned that Soviet development of atomic weapons could occur even more rapidly than expected and that the long-term Soviet goal was control of all Eurasia and its strategic approaches. The JWPC also requested additional information on Soviet capabilities and aims in specific areas, as well as a list of approximately twenty targets for strategic bombing within Russia and Russian-dominated territory. The resulting intelligence document assumed Britain would be a U.S. ally in any such war, while the eventual JWPC war plan of early 1946 labeled Anglo-Russian conflict in Turkey and Iran as the most likely source of war and prevention of British defeat as vital to U.S. security. A December report from Naval Intelligence similarly reversed the wartime insistence on not getting involved in any Anglo-Soviet clash in the eastern Mediterranean by concluding that America had a vital interest in Middle East oil and that "any area in which there is British-Russian conflict is of natural interest to the United States."[18] All of the above led logically to the JPS conclusion of early 1946 that "defeat or disintegration of the British Empire would eliminate from Eurasia the last bulwark of resistance between the United States and Soviet expansion. After this the military potential of the United States together with the military potential of possible allies . . . would probably be insufficient to match those of an expanded Soviet Union. Militarily, our present position as a world power is of necessity closely interwoven with that of Great Britain."[19]

The JSSC in October also produced and forwarded to the Joint Chiefs, in response to a presidential directive, two additional papers opposing any sharing of atomic secrets. Not only would possession of the bomb by another country impair U.S. security, but it would also "not be accompanied by a compensating threat to the security of the only country whose military strength is comparable to ours, and whose policies are most likely to offer serious conflict with the policies of this country." Unlike U.S. industries, which were heavily concentrated and exposed to attack by sea-launched bombs, Russian industry was widely dispersed and inaccessible from the sea. Directly challenging the retiring Stimson's September 11 plea for sharing, the JSSC concluded that disclosure of atomic secrets would not restrict an arms race and considered it "doubtful" that such disclosure would improve relations with Russia or "change her attitude and objectives." Now agreeing with the Harriman-Deane assessments it had previously rejected, the committee concluded that "Russia respects only power and regards generous concessions as a sign of weakness, justifying still greater demands." International control through the UN was unenforceable, leaving secrecy as the only option—even though this could not continue for a long period of time.[20]

Furthermore, the vulnerability of concentrated U.S. industry to sea-launched atomic attack, along with the need to project similar force against Russia, required an ability to intercept enemy aircraft in flight and launch air attacks against Russia. "National security" thus demanded "that our defensive frontiers be well advanced in the Atlantic and Pacific Oceans and to the shores of the Arctic. A system of mutually supporting advanced bases extending far out from the homeland is necessary both for our defense and for the prompt projection of our striking forces against the sources of the military power of the enemy."[21]

Embick's dramatic reversal in effect ended the debate over Soviet-American relations within the armed services and aptly symbolized how far they had come in their views on military and foreign policy. Many of the ideas in the papers cited above could admittedly be interpreted as harkening back to Embick's prewar beliefs in their emphasis on restoring the nation's geographic isolation so as to preserve it from attack.[22] But any such restoration to preclude attack now required its opposite—a global strategy and policy diametrically opposed to the highly limited continental strategy and policy that Embick had espoused during the 1930s.

Embick's reversal also symbolized how far the services had come in their views on specific allies and on alliances in general. Throughout the 1930s he had led the army fight for a unilateral as well as a highly limited strategy and against the navy desire for a close association with Britain so as to be capable of defending a more expansive set of interests. Along with numerous other officers, he had also preferred unilateral rearmament from 1939 to 1941 over material support of Britain and involvement in the European war, as well as a withdrawal from commitments and provocative actions in the Pacific. Opposed by the navy and State Department and overruled by the president on virtually all counts, he had joined and often led other planners in their efforts to devise a strategy that would protect U.S. as opposed to British interests. That strategy became the Germany-first approach and eventually the U.S. insistence on cross-channel rather than Mediterranean operations within the primary European theater.

United States insistence on this strategy dovetailed with recognition by late 1941 that victory over Germany depended on the Soviet Union and that Britain's politically inspired Mediterranean approach would do nothing to preclude Soviet defeat. Thus all JCS strategic proposals in 1942 focused on how best to assist the hard-pressed Soviets. The answer was cross-channel operations, but when the British refused to agree and suggested a 1942 invasion of North Africa instead, the JCS countered with a Pacific-first proposal that they argued would do more to help the Russians than any Mediterranean activity. Roosevelt refused to agree and forced them to accept the North African invasion, thereby creating a major diversionary front in the Mediterranean. But in turn they insisted on launching the Guadalcanal/New Guinea campaign, thereby creating a second diversionary front in the Pacific and, in effect, a de facto Pacific-first strategy for the remainder of 1942. Contrary to expectations, operations in both theaters continued into 1943, thereby precluding any possibility of a channel crossing in that year too and forcing the Joint Chiefs to agree instead to British proposals for additional operations in the Mediterranean.

Humiliated by this failure, during 1943 Embick and other JCS advisers and planners analyzed in depth the conflicts between British and U.S. policies that they believed to be the root cause of Anglo-American strategic disagreement. In the process they defined Britain as an adversary and its politically inspired strategy as a hindrance to victory and the strong relationship with the Soviets necessary for that victory. They also proposed a new set of global strategic priorities that relegated the Mediterranean to a status below Europe and the Pacific, and they successfully created the united front with Roosevelt on those points necessary to win acceptance of their proposals.

The ensuing 1944–45 JSSC position on postwar relations with Britain and the Soviet Union as well as on European strategy flowed logically from these assessments. In what appears to have been a symbiotic relationship with academic geopoliticians, Embick and his associates concluded that Britain would be in serious decline after the war, whereas Soviet and U.S. power would be ascendant. Britain would respond by trying to enlist U.S. assistance in the continuation of its power struggle with Russia in the Balkans and eastern Mediterranean, just as it had been doing via its Mediterranean proposals. The United States, the JSSC insisted, had utterly no interest in this area and conflict save to make sure it did not fracture the alliance or precipitate another war. Indeed, Embick found Russian desires historically justified vis-à-vis Britain. Thus the United States should continue to oppose any British proposals for military operations in the Balkans and eastern Mediterranean and any effort to enlist U.S. assistance against the Russians in this area.

Embick was forced to admit, however, that the United States now had a very real interest in Western Europe and in preventing domination of the Eurasian land mass by any single power, be it Germany or Russia. His fears in this regard, combined with the end of the war against Japan and evidence that Russian desires were not limited to the Balkans and the eastern Mediterranean, led to his reversal of opinion during the late summer and early fall of 1945.

Such timing made Embick one of the last general officers to reach anti-Soviet conclusions, however. Some had been vehemently anti-Soviet or pro-British or both throughout the war, while others became so in late 1944 or early 1945. Yet they remained unable to convince the JCS or any JSSC members to support their approach until July, when Willson shifted and the JCS supported him.

The final papers of Embick and his JSSC colleagues also reveal how far the armed forces had come during the war in obtaining a strong role within the policymaking process. Before the war they had been virtually shut out of that process, and from 1939 to 1941 their advice had often been ignored by a State Department ignorant, in their opinion, of international power realities. Determined to avoid any repetition of this situation, they had dominated policymaking during the war and worked extensively, albeit with mixed success, to win Roosevelt's support. They had also demanded a wide-ranging role in postwar planning and consistently objected to specific State Department proposals that negatively affected them—most notably in regard to the Mandated Islands—and to the entire focus of State's thinking on postwar international organization. Instead, they had proposed a Great Power condominium, whereby the two superpowers would each maintain control over territory it desired and had earned by right of conquest, police its own sphere, and avoid interfering with the other's sphere. The two biggest opponents of such a system in their view were Britain and the State Department, and both were thus defined as adversaries to be watched and checked.

Roosevelt concurred in many of these assessments. Indeed, his own beliefs often formed the basis of JCS papers as the chiefs and their planners consistently attempted to translate his broad policies into specific strategies while simultaneously educating him about the consequences of those policies and leading him to certain conclusions. Their overall record was mixed, for he continued the pattern first established in 1940–41 of accepting the portions of their assessments with which he agreed and ignoring the rest. Yet by late 1943–early 1944 he was in fundamental agreement with them on most major issues—including appropriate global and European strategy, postwar Allied relations, and creation of an extensive overseas base system. He remained insistent on trusteeship for the Mandated Islands despite JCS opposition, however, and that issue remained unresolved when he died in April 1945.

By that time numerous military as well as civilian officials were questioning the cooperative policy with the Soviets and calling for change. The JSSC insisted on cooperation so long as the war was in progress, however, as did Marshall and the rest of the JCS, at least until Germany was on the verge of total defeat in late April 1945. With that defeat now merely a matter of weeks if not days, Roosevelt dead, and the cooperative approach under assault from numerous directions, the Joint Chiefs agreed to a modification of their policy. The war against Japan was still in bloody progress, however, and thus the armed forces, especially army planners unconvinced they could obtain Japanese surrender without an invasion and Soviet entry, remained unwilling to provoke a confrontation. As Marc Gallicchio has aptly noted, the Joint Chiefs and their planners, "particularly the army general staff, had become the custodians of Roosevelt's Soviet policy."[23] Especially interesting is that naval and air force planners who believed Japan would surrender without an invasion or Soviet entry tended to express anti-Soviet sentiments earlier than did army planners who believed such invasion and entry would be necessary.

Conflicting service assessments are not the only or necessarily the best way to analyze the conflict within the armed forces over the World War II allies, for that conflict also tended to pit older against younger officers in all the services. The JSSC and JCS officers who had consistently expressed anti-British and pro-Soviet statements were overwhelmingly in their sixties, whereas others who expressed anti-Soviet and pro-British sentiments tended to be substantially younger. Numerous factors may account for this apparent "generation gap" within the armed forces. Many members of the older generation possessed negative World War I experiences with the British, long-term isolationist or Anglophobic sentiments or both from American society in general, and extensive pre–World War II experience with strategies, policies, and weaponry far more limited than what the younger generation had experienced. One might also argue that these older officers possessed a greater understanding of history, especially that of Anglo-Russian conflicts, and a far less negative view of the policy of appeasement. The failure of that policy during the 1930s made it a dirty word for younger officers and the public in general, but older officers showed an awareness of its long history in international affairs and its numerous, appropriate uses. In this case appeasement of the Soviet Union in Eastern Europe seemed to them a small, acceptable, and unavoidable price to pay for military victory and postwar peace.

Western and Central Europe were different matters entirely. What may have been the most fundamental and important shift in U.S. strategic thinking during World War II was the belief, expressed by academic geopoliticians and by high-ranking officers, that domination of these areas by any single power constituted a mortal security threat. Simply stated, the United States could not defend the Western Hemisphere against a power capable of harnessing the resources of all Eurasia—be it Germany or Russia. Given this fact, many argued, Washington had to adopt London's balance-of-power policy and actually defend Britain as part of that policy. More than any other factor, this belief destroyed the strategic basis of prewar isolationism in its insistence that neither continental nor hemispheric defense could succeed against a hegemonic Eurasian power.

Embick and many other planners fought against these conclusions throughout most of the war. They came to recognize the importance of Western Europe to U.S. security, but their concern over British manipulation, belief in the limited and defensive nature of Soviet postwar goals, and fear of the catastrophic effects of another world war led them to perceive Soviet-American collaboration as an alternative approach, one that mirrored Roosevelt's own views and hopes. Numerous other planners disagreed, but the JCS did not. Indeed, the length of time the chiefs sided with the pro-Soviet and anti-British view is quite surprising in hindsight. Also surprising is the speed with which they then reversed themselves in the summer and fall of 1945. So rapid and total was this reversal that it constitutes a classic example of a "paradigm shift" as first used to explain changes in scientific thought.[24] As with such changes, the Joint Chiefs maintained their "old" paradigm despite growing opposition and evidence to the contrary; they then shifted abruptly to a new one when the evidence and pressure for such a shift reached a critical point in mid-1945. The old paradigm, which included strong anti-British sentiments, had been based on a limited view of U.S. national security concerns that in no way conflicted with what were considered equally limited Soviet security concerns. Conversely, the new paradigm was based on an unlimited, global view of both U.S. national security and Soviet goals, a consequent, fundamental clash of interests between the two superpowers, and a belief that British interests coincided with those of the United States.

Other scholars have emphasized the impact of airpower and the growing lethality of World War II weaponry in the creation and acceptance of this expanded and anti-Soviet definition of U.S. security requirements. They have also noted the bureaucratic desire for a named enemy to serve as a basis for postwar military planning and as a justification for postwar military budgets and a continued major role in policy planning.[25] Rather than merely repeat these conclusions, in the latter chapters of this book I have detailed the process by which each of the major reasons for following the pro-Soviet policy within the old paradigm disappeared for the armed forces in 1945 and thereby set the stage for its reversal. In the process, I have also explored some of the origins of the new and expanded definition of national security that Melvyn Leffler has posited as central to understanding early U.S. Cold War policies—and U.S. foreign relations in general.[26]

As previously noted, the reasons for following a pro-Soviet policy included the need for continued Russian participation in the war against Germany; the desire for their eventual participation in the war against Japan; existing presidential policy; and fears of British manipulation, Axis efforts to split the Allies, and an unwinnable, catastrophic World War III. Interestingly, each of these factors flowed directly from a set of fundamental and related objectives: the achievement of total military victory and establishment of a secure peace, as defined by the civilian head of government, in the quickest period of time and with the lowest possible U.S. casualties. It is no accident that Marshall, Embick, and Stimson were three of the strongest and longest-lasting supporters of the cooperative policy vis-à-vis the Soviets, for it was the army that would have to take the bulk of the additional casualties in any extended war against Germany and Japan without Soviet participation and in any future war against the USSR.

Such goals were anything but "purely military" in nature. In this regard it is time not simply to revise but actually to reverse the old canard about the political naïveté of the wartime service chiefs and their planners. Total victory over the Axis and its accomplishment as quickly as possible and with a minimum of U.S. casualties were *political* goals. They were also the fundamental political goals one would expect of a democratic society at war. Dictatorships may be capable of and willing to conduct long wars with enormous casualties, but they are neither possible nor desirable for a democracy given the nature of its public opinion and the emphasis it places on the importance and sanctity of individual life and freedom.

The Joint Chiefs of Staff and their planners were well aware of these facts and acted accordingly. Marshall regularly placed graphic charts of casualty figures in front of Roosevelt to make sure the president remained equally aware of them.

After the war he stated that the factors constantly on his mind in the European war had been "casualties, duration, expense and the Pacific" and that two of the most important lessons he had learned concerned the need to launch offensives for public opinion and the fact that a democracy "could not indulge in a Seven Years' War."[27] He also informed Dean Acheson that his objections to British strategy had been based not only on his belief that the "soft underbelly" was not very soft but additionally on his fear that this approach would greatly increase U.S. casualties, the time needed to defeat Germany, and thus the time needed to defeat Japan. Acheson correctly concluded from this and other conversations that when Marshall thought about military problems, "nonmilitary factors played a controlling part."[28]

The World War II policies and strategies of the Joint Chiefs were thus not only political but also appropriate for the government and the society those chiefs were sworn to defend. Yet they also helped set the stage for Cold War policies and strategies that often went far beyond what was appropriate. Numerous critics have noted and condemned the chiefs for this. Far fewer have correctly assessed and praised them for their wartime performance.

On November 15, 1945, General Lyman Lemnitzer replaced Embick as army representative on the JSSC. Four days later Eisenhower replaced Marshall as army chief and representative on the JCS, and over the next few months all the other members of the wartime JSSC and JCS save Leahy would similarly retire and be replaced. Simultaneously, the armed forces completed the first contingency plans for atomic war against the Soviet Union. World War II was over and the Cold War had begun. It would be fought by younger officers who possessed a global vision of U.S. security, a belief in alliance with England against Russia, and, thanks to their wartime predecessors, extensive input into the planning process. The era of American globalism and the national security state had begun.

Notes

Abbreviations

AAF	Army Air Forces
ACofS	Assistant Chief of Staff, U.S. Army
AL	Alderman Library, Special Collections, University of Virginia
ASN	Assistant Secretary of the Navy
ASW	Assistant Secretary of War
CAB	Records of the Cabinet Office, Public Records Office
CAD	Civil Affairs Division, U.S. Army General Staff
CCS	Combined Chiefs of Staff
CG	Commanding General
CIC	Combined Intelligence Committee
CM-IN	Incoming message to War Department
CM-OUT	Outgoing message to War Department
CMH	U.S. Army Center for Military History, Washington, D.C.
CNO	Chief of Naval Operations, U.S. Navy
CofS	Chief of Staff, U.S. Army
COMINCH	Commander in Chief, U.S. Fleet
COS	British Chiefs of Staff Committee
CPS	Combined Planning Staff
DCNO	Deputy Chief of Naval Operations
DCofS	Deputy Chief of Staff, U.S. Army
Exec.	Executive File
FDRL	Franklin D. Roosevelt Library, Hyde Park, N.Y.
F-14	Post War Naval Planning Section
FO	British Foreign Office
FRUS	U.S. Department of State, *Foreign Relations of the United States*
GB	General Board, U.S. Navy
GCMRL	George C. Marshall Research Library, Lexington, Va.
G-3	Operations and Training Division, U.S. Army General Staff
G-2	Intelligence Division, U.S. Army General Staff
HI	Hoover Institution on War, Revolution and Peace
JB	Joint Board
JCAC	Joint Civil Affairs Committee
JCS	Joint Chiefs of Staff
JDCS	Joint Deputy Chiefs of Staff
JIC	Joint Intelligence Committee
JPC	Joint Planning Committee

JPS	Joint Staff Planners
JPWC	Joint Post War Committee
JSM	British Joint Staff Mission
JSSC	Joint Strategic Survey Committee
JUSSC	Joint U.S. Strategic Committee
JWPC	Joint War Plans Committee
LOC	Library of Congress, Washington, D.C.
MFNAP	Marshall Foundation National Archives Project
MHI	U.S. Army Military History Institute, Carlisle, Pa.
MID	Military Intelligence Division, U.S. Army General Staff
MRF	Map Room File
NA	National Archives, Washington, D.C.
NH	Operational Archives, Department of the Navy, Navy Historical Division, Washington, D.C.
ONI	Office of Naval Intelligence
OPD	Operations Division, U.S. Army General Staff
OSS	Office of Strategic Services
Phil.	Philippine
PHP	British Post Hostilities Planning Committee
POF	Pentagon Office File
PREM	Papers of the Prime Minister's Private Office, Public Record Office
PRO	Public Record Office
PSF	President's Secretary's File
R&A	Research and Analysis Branch, Office of Strategic Services
RG	Record Group Number, National Archives
S&P	Strategy and Policy Group, Operations Division, U.S. Army General Staff
SEAC	Southeast Asia Command
SGMML	Seeley G. Mudd Manuscript Library, Princeton University
SHAEF	Supreme Headquarters, Allied Expeditionary Forces
SN	Secretary of the Navy
SOF	Special Official File
SPD (NA)	Special Planning Division, U.S. Army General Staff
SPD (NH)	Strategic Plans Division, Office of Chief of Naval Operations
SS	Strategy Section, Strategy and Policy Group, Operations Division, U.S. Army General Staff
SW	Secretary of War
SWNCC	State-War-Navy Coordinating Committee
TS	top secret
UN	United Nations
USMA	U.S. Military Academy Library, West Point, N.Y.
VCNO	Vice Chief of Naval Operations
WDCSA	War Department Chief of Staff Army Files, National Archives
WDGS	War Department General Staff
WPD	War Plans Division, U.S. Army or Navy General Staff
YUL	Yale University Library, Manuscripts and Archives

Preface

1. As Hogan concludes in his outstanding new study, *Cross of Iron*, 68, the result was a system "that institutionalized the National Military Establishment as a major rival to the State Department in the field of foreign policy."

2. See, for ex., Leffler, *Preponderance of Power*, and Yergin, *Shattered Peace*. Sherry, *Preparing for the Next War*; Davis, *Postwar Defense Policy and the U.S. Navy*; and Perry McCoy Smith, *Air Force Plans for Peace*, all examine specific wartime service planning for the postwar era.

3. Cline, *Washington Command Post*, 319.

4. See, for ex., Emerson, "Roosevelt as Commander in Chief"; Kimball, "Franklin Roosevelt"; and Larrabee, *Commander in Chief*.

5. See, for ex., Baldwin, *Great Mistakes of the War*. Huntington, *The Soldier and the State*, 326–33, inverted this argument so as to critique the JCS for accepting naïve civilian views of international relations in place of their own realistic ones.

Acknowledgments

1. Wright and Paszek, *Soldiers and Statesmen*, 165–66. See also Williams, *Some Presidents*, 61–82.

Chapter One

1. The army obtained a general staff and chief of staff in 1903; the navy did so in 1915. Their powers were originally quite limited, and not until the 1930s did the chiefs obtain full operational control over their forces. The original JB, created in 1903, similarly possessed very limited powers as an advisory body composed of U.S. Army General Staff officers and members of the navy's General Board (GB), a body of retired officers established in 1900 to provide advice on broad matters of strategy and policy. In 1919 the JB obtained additional powers, a higher-ranking membership that included the two service chiefs and their key assistants, and the Joint Planning Committee (JPC).

The term "managerial revolution" comes from Millis, *Arms and Men*, 131–210. See also Abrahamson, *America Arms for a New Century*, 105–27; Cline, *Washington Command Post*, 44–45; Watson, *Chief of Staff*, 57–84; Morton, "Interservice Co-operation," 133–38; and Morton, "War Plan ORANGE," 221–25.

2. The terms "foreign policies" and "national policies" are used interchangeably in this study, though the armed forces viewed the former as the diplomatic means used to obtain or defend the latter.

3. Morton, "Interservice Co-operation," 137; Eiler, *Wedemeyer in War and Peace*, xx. See also Miller, *War Plan Orange*, 11–12.

4. Morton, "Interservice Co-operation," 144–48.

5. Cline, *Washington Command Post*, 44. See also works cited above, n. 3.

6. Abrahamson, *America Arms for a New Century*, 152.

7. Morton, "National Policy and Military Strategy," 1–2; Calhoun, *Power and Principle*, 37–38. See also Braisted, *United States Navy in the Pacific*, 125–40; Brune, *Origins of American National Security Policy*, 7–8; Challener, *Admirals, Generals, and American Foreign Policy*, 367–79; Grenville and Young, *Politics, Strategy, and American Diplomacy*, 321–22; Link, *Wilson*, 297–99; and Link, *Papers of Woodrow Wilson*, 27:441–48. According to Link and Chambers, "Woodrow Wil-

son as Commander-in-Chief," 319 and 345–46 nn. 5 and 7, the assertion that Wilson ordered an end to all war planning is "apparently apocryphal." What upset the president, they argue, was the publicity about these war plans.

8. The Liaison Comm. charter is in Notter Papers, box 147, RG 59, NA. See also Morton, "Interservice Co-operation," 142–50; Davis, *Admiral's Lobby*, 146–47; Brune, "Considerations of Force," 389–91, and *Origins of American National Security Policy*, 55–63; Braisted, *United States Navy in the Pacific*, 470–75, 527, 653–54, 670–73; Buckley, *United States and the Washington Conference*, 49–56, 90–92; Wheeler, *Prelude to Pearl Harbor*, 54–69, 131–50, 159–86; O'Connor, *Perilous Equilibrium*, 12–13; Andrade, "Cruiser Controversy," 118; and Weigley, *Towards an American Army*, 232–34. State's continued suspicion of the armed forces was reflected in its original proposal to include only civilian under secretaries rather than the army and navy chiefs. See Watson, *Chief of Staff*, 89–90, and Lowenthal, *Leadership and Indecision*, 1:62–66.

9. "Never once," he further stated, "was there a discussion of objectives, of dangers inherent in our position to the east or to the west, of timing of foreign policy in relation to military strength or of any of the other more important long range affairs that should bind foreign policy and military policy together." Robinett diary, 37–38 (note after 2/12/41 entry), Robinett Collection, GCMRL.

10. Greene, "Military View of American National Policy," 357; Stark to Hart, memo, Feb. 9, 1940, in U.S. Congress, *Hearings before the Joint Committee on the Investigation of the Pearl Harbor Attack* [hereafter *Pearl Harbor Attack Hearings*], pt. 16, 2245.

11. WPD to CofS and SW to Sec. of State, Oct. 31 and Nov. 2, 1921, RG 407, file 381, NA; Greene, "Military View of American National Policy," 360–68; Brune, *Origins of American National Security Policy*, 9–15; Wheeler, *Prelude to Pearl Harbor*, 61 n. 25; Trask, *Captains and Cabinets*, 285–89; and Ross, *American War Plans*, 2:72. See also "Summary of the Report of the Survey of the Military Establishment Prepared by the War Department General Staff," Nov. 1, 1929, WPD 3345, sec. 4, RG 165, NA.

12. "Summary of the Report of the Survey of the Military Establishment Prepared by the War Department General Staff," Nov. 1, 1929, WPD 3345, sec. 4, RG 165, NA.

13. Quotation is from ibid. See also works cited in n. 11, and Grenville and Young, *Politics, Strategy, and American Diplomacy*, 332.

14. The RED, ORANGE, and RED-ORANGE war plans are reproduced in Ross, *American War Plans*, vol. 2. See also Grenville and Young, *Politics, Strategy, and American Diplomacy*, 301; Trask, *Captains and Cabinets*, 288; Braisted, "American Red and Red-Orange Plans," 167–85; Challener, *Admirals, Generals, and American Foreign Policy*, 31–32, 225–64; and Morton, *Strategy and Command*, 21–33.

15. This split between "thrusters" and "cautionaries" is a major theme of Miller, *War Plan Orange*. As early as 1906–7, an interservice split over whether to develop a major base at Subic Bay in the Philippines led President Theodore Roosevelt to lose faith in the JB and warn his officers to consult properly in the future before offering advice on a joint matter. See ibid., 67, and Morton, "Interservice Cooperation," 133–34.

16. Morton, "War Plan Orange," 224; Morton, "Interservice Co-operation," 141–42; Braisted, *U.S. Navy in the Pacific*, 441–62; Buckley, *United States and the Washington Conference*, 49–56, 90–92; Wheeler, *Prelude to Pearl Harbor*, 49–60; and Davis, *Admirals Lobby*, 115–16.

17. Morton, *Strategy and Command*, 36.

18. See army memos in JPC Development File, JB 305, serial 573, RG 225, NA, and directly below in text.

19. "Examination of United States Military (Including Naval) Position in the Far East," unsigned naval memo, Dec. 17, 1935, JPC Development File, JB 305, serial 573, no. 10, RG 225, NA.

20. Stimson and Bundy, *On Active Service*, 506. See also Greene, "Military View of American National Policy," 369–76; Waldo Heinrichs, "The Role of the United States Navy," in Borg and Okamoto, *Pearl Harbor as History*, 201–11; Morton, "War Plan ORANGE," 228–48; Morton, "Army and Marines," 51–66; Wheeler, *Prelude to Pearl Harbor*, 90–95; Watson, *Chief of Staff*, 88–89; and Vlahos, *Blue Sword*, 29–53.

21. Braisted, *United States Navy in the Pacific*, 506; Ross, *American War Plans*, 2:262, 349; Gooch, "'Hidden in the Rock,'" 157–62.

22. Gooch, "'Hidden in the Rock,'" 162–65; Ernest J. King, "The Influence of the National Policy on the Strategy of a War," 1932, King Papers, box 23, Naval War College Thesis Folder, LOC; Buell, *Master of Seapower*, 145. See also Davis, *Admiral's Lobby*, 130; Trask, *Captains and Cabinets*, 352; Allard, "Anglo-American Naval Differences," 76–78; Braisted, "American Red and Red-Orange Plans," 168–77; Doyle, "U.S. Navy and War Plan Orange," 50–58; Braisted, *United States Navy in the Pacific*, 290, 303, 418–40; Reynolds, *Creation of the Anglo-American Alliance*, 10–18; and Watt, *Succeeding John Bull*, 73.

23. Doyle, "U.S. Navy and War Plan Orange," 50–57; Braisted, "American Red and Red-Orange Plans," 180. By 1937 CNO Admiral William D. Leahy was calling for joint action with the British against the Japanese; see John Major, "The Navy Plans for War, 1937–1941," in Hagan, *In Peace and War*, 238–39.

24. Gole, "War Planning," 14–19.

25. See, for ex., unsigned WPD paper, "An American National Policy That Is Unqualifiedly Pro-American," Sept. 14, 1937, WPD Exec. 4, item 5, Defense Policies Folder, RG 165, NA.

26. Gooch, "'Hidden in the Rock,'" 170; Braisted, "American Red and Red-Orange Plans," 180.

27. Ross, *American War Plans*, 2:233, 399; Braisted, "American Red and Red-Orange Plans," 169–70, 177; Miller, *War Plan Orange*, 134.

28. Naval planners had proposed alliances with European powers as part of their ORANGE war plans as early as 1911. See Miller, *War Plan Orange*, 25.

29. See below, this chapter.

30. Memo by Miles, "U.S. Military Position in the Far East," undated, JB 305, serial 573, JPC Development File, no. 9, RG 225, NA. See also Greene, "Military View of American National Policy," 370–74. Ironically, such an argument tended to support the "thrusters" within the navy by emphasizing the public's probable refusal to sanction a long war and the subsequent need for an aggressive strategy that could provide quick and decisive victory; the "cautionaries" countered that it would provide quick and decisive defeat. See Miller, *War Plan Orange*, 29–30.

31. David Reynolds, "Power and Superpower," in Kimball, *America Unbound*, 20; Watson, *Chief of Staff*, 88. See also Chace and Carr, *America Invulnerable*, 12–13.

32. Brune, *Origins of American National Security Policy*, 31–51, 77–82, 90–103, 132–33. Ironically, while Mitchell came to support the acquisition of overseas bases to extend the range of U.S. aircraft, air force planners at Maxwell Air Force Base looked to allies to provide those bases. See Matloff, "American Approach to War," 226–27.

33. A central figure in this volume, Embick has previously been the focus of two scholarly articles: Schaffer's "Embick" and my "From Continentalism to Globalism." Basic biog. data can be found in his West Point obituary in *Assembly* 17 (Fall 1958): 65 and in his biog. file at CMH.

34. Schaffer, "Embick," 90–91; Miller, *War Plan Orange*, 67; Morton, "Defense of the Philippines," 99–104; Linn, *Guardians of Empire*, 65, 186.

35. Trask, "Bliss," 58–60. See also ibid., 7–42, 66–69; Trask, *Supreme War Council*, 131; Schaffer, "Embick," 89–90; Embick, "Notes on Reduction of Armaments," memo, Feb. 3, 1918, Bliss Papers, box 247, LOC; and Embick War College lct., Sept. 6, 1927, WPD 3018, MHI.

36. Embick to Bliss, July 8, 1924, Bliss Papers, box 369, LOC. See also Embick to Bliss, Sept. 29,

1922, ibid., box 368; Embick File, WPD index, RG 165, NA; Embick Biog. File, CMH; Embick address, "Our Present Military Policy," 244–51, WPD 3483, RG 165, NA; and Embick paper, "The World's Major Economic Areas," Sept. 23, 1930, WPD 3483, RG 165, NA, published as "Three Economic Areas Fixed for the Future" in the *New York Times*, Apr. 13, 1930, sec. 11, pp. 4, 9.

37. Embick to CG, Phil. Dept., "Military Policy of the United States in the Philippine Islands," memo, Apr. 19, 1933, WPD 3251-15, RG 165, NA; Embick, "Military Aspects of the Situation That Would Result from the Retention by the United States of a Military (Including Naval) Commitment in the Philippines," memo, Dec. 2, 1935, JB 305, serial 573, JPC Development File, RG 225, NA.

38. Quotes from Embick memos cited in n. 37 and Embick paper, "The World's Economic Areas," Sept. 23, 1930, WPD 3483, RG 165, NA. See also Embick War College lct., "Outline of International Surveys," Sept. 2, 1921, War College Lcts., MHI; Flint, "United States Army on the Pacific Frontier," 154–56.

39. Miller, *War Plan Orange*, 214, 224; Embick to Marshall, Apr. 12, 1939, Marshall Papers, POF, box 67, folder 36, GCMRL. Embick may have introduced Marshall to Libby in 1938; see Marshall to Embick, Sept. 8, 1938, ibid., folder 35. See also Schaffer, "Embick," 91–92; Wedemeyer, *Wedemeyer Reports!*, 25–26, 49–62, 79.

40. Quotations from Embick to Borah, Jan. 13 and Feb. 20, 1939, Borah Papers, box 513, LOC; Embick memo, "Military Aspects," Dec. 2, 1935, JB 305, serial 573, JPC Development File, no. 3, RG 225, NA. For the intranaval debate over fortification of Guam vs. a gradual movement through the Mandated Islands, see Miller, *War Plan Orange*, 73–75, 250–53.

41. See Linn, *Guardians of Empire*, 90; Russell F. Weigley, "American Strategy from Its Beginnings through the First World War," in Paret, *Makers of Modern Strategy*, 408–44.

42. Kilburne, ACofS, WPD, to CofS, "Military Policy of the United States in Philippines Islands," memo, June 12, 1933, WPD 3251-15, RG 165, NA; Miller, *War Plan Orange*, 214–15; Linn, *Guardians of Empire*, 171–72, 179–80, 190, 215–16, 226–31; Hagood, *We Can Defend America*; Gugeler, "George Marshall and Orlando Ward," 35–39; Krueger, ACofS to CofS, "Acquisition of Colonial Territory," memo, Dec. 18, 1936, WPD 3397, MFNAP, reel 298, item 4462, GCMRL. Flint, "United States Army on the Pacific Frontier," 156, concludes that Embick's attack "struck a blow from which War Plan ORANGE never recovered."

43. Rivers to Borah, placed in the *Congressional Record* on Feb. 17, 1939, Borah Papers, box 513, LOC; Marshall to Embick, Apr. 10 and Apr. 14, 1939, Marshall Papers, POF, box 67, folder 36, GCMRL; Schaffer, "Embick," 92. Embick was a strong supporter of Marshall and helped engineer his assignment to the general staff and ascension to deputy chief as a road to the chief of staff position. Marshall also rented Embick's home during his first year in Washington and corresponded with him frequently both before and after the outbreak of hostilities in Europe. See Pogue, *Marshall*, 1:314–15, and Marshall-Embick corres. in GCMRL as cited in this note.

44. Krueger to CofS, "Acquisition of Colonial Territory," memo, Dec. 18, 1936, WPD 3397, MFNAP, reel 298, item 4462, GCMRL. See also Watson, *Chief of Staff*, 88–89. For the later isolationist split over continental vs. hemispheric defense, see Haglund, *Latin America*, 76–77.

45. Strong to CofS, memo, May 2, 1939, JB 325 (634), WPD 4175, RG 165, NA. See also Morton, "Army and Marines," 67–72; Morton, "Interservice Co-operation," 151–55; Morton, "War Plan ORANGE," 238–45; Watson, *Chief of Staff*, 88–91; and Utley, *Going to War with Japan*, 41–42. Ironically, the navy was angry over what it considered Hull's passive policy and opposition to reinforcing the Asiatic fleet. It therefore joined the army in requesting presidential intervention to overrule State, albeit for a more aggressive policy rather than the less aggressive one desired by the army; see ibid., 24–40.

46. Neumann, "Franklin Delano Roosevelt," 718.

47. Freidel, *Roosevelt: The Ordeal,* 19–20; May, "Political-Military Consultation," 167–68.

48. Quotation is in Blum, *From the Morgenthau Diaries,* 3:48. See also Brune, *Origins of American National Security Policy,* 107–8. For the early Anglo-American naval staff talks, see Pratt, "Anglo-American Naval Conversations," 750–52; Lowenthal, *Leadership and Indecision,* 1:19–31; and Watson, *Chief of Staff,* 92–93.

49. Emerson, "Roosevelt as Commander-in-Chief," 183–85. See also Brune, *Origins of American National Security Policy,* 106–10, and Lowenthal, *Leadership and Indecision,* 1:159.

50. Morton, "Army and Marines," 73.

51. As Marshall stated in September 1938, "uncertainties" over future enemies, theaters of war, and national objectives led "inevitably to the conclusion that the only sensible policy . . . is to maintain a conservatively balanced force for the protection of our territory against any probable threat during the period the vast but latent resources of the United States . . . are being mobilized." Roosevelt's approach clearly conflicted with such a "sensible policy," but only Marshall was willing to say so to his face during a 1938 meeting. Marshall later recalled that FDR "gave me a very startled look, and when I went out they all bade me goodbye and said my tour in Washington was over." In reality it was far from over, and less than a year later Roosevelt would appoint Marshall army chief. But neither his dissent nor his appointment led FDR to alter his unbalanced rearmament program or methods of operation. See Bland, *Papers of George Catlett Marshall* [hereafter *Marshall Papers*], 1:633; Lowenthal, *Leadership and Indecision,* 1:91–102; Bland, *George C. Marshall* [hereafter *Marshall Interviews*], 108–9; and Pogue, *Marshall,* 1:322–23.

52. Lowenthal "Roosevelt and the Coming of the War," 416–17; Louis Morton, "Germany First," in Greenfield, *Command Decisions,* 18–20.

53. Lowenthal, "Roosevelt and the Coming of the War," 416–17; Morton, *Strategy and Command,* 39–43, and "War Plan ORANGE," 247–50; Miller, *War Plan Orange,* 224–25; Doyle, "U.S. Navy and War Plan Orange," 58; Matloff, "American Approach to War," 221; Pratt, "Anglo-American Naval Conversations," 757–58; Lowenthal, *Leadership and Indecision,* 1:45–48. The revised plan is in Ross, *American War Plans,* 2:155–227.

54. Flint, "United States Army on the Pacific Frontier," 157–58.

55. JB to JPC, "Study of Joint Action in Event of Violation of Monroe Doctrine by Fascist Powers," memo, Nov. 12, 1938, JB 325, serial 634, RG 225, NA, reproduced in Ross, *American War Plans,* 3:3.

56. "Joint Planning Committee Exploratory Studies in Accordance with J.B. 325 (serial 634)," in Ross, *American War Plans,* 3:4–66.

57. Ibid.; Miller, *War Plan Orange,* 315; Gole, "War Planning," 16–19; Watson, *Chief of Staff,* 97–100; Morton, *Strategy and Command,* 68–70.

58. Strong, ACofS, WPD, to CofS, "J.B. 325 (634)," memo, May 2, 1939, WPD 4175-1, RG 165, NA; Watson, *Chief of Staff,* 98–100.

59. See Ross, *American War Plans,* 3:69–76.

60. Ibid., 87–140. According to a 1940 army memo reproduced in part in Watson, *Chief of Staff,* 90, before becoming army chief Marshall urged CNO Leahy to bring the State Dept. "in on joint plans so that our foreign policy and military plans would be in step." Leahy "seemed to think it unnecessary," but Craig may have given State a copy of the April 1939 JPC study.

61. Far from coincidentally, the War Dept. responded negatively at this time to questions regarding the desirability of acquiring Greenland, whereas the Navy Dept. responded positively. See Fogelson, "Greenland," 60–61; Waldo Heinrichs, "Franklin D. Roosevelt and the Risks of War, 1939–1941," in Iriye and Cohen, *American, Chinese, and Japanese Perspectives on Wartime Asia,* 149; Lowenthal, *Leadership and Indecision,* 1:130–33, 207; and Watson, *Chief of Staff,* 99–100.

Chapter Two

1. JPC to JB, "Joint Army and Navy Basic War Plans—RAINBOW," memo, Apr. 9, 1940, JB 325, serial 642 and 642-1, RG 225, NA, reproduced in Ross, *American War Plans*, 3:77–82. RAINBOW 2 is reproduced on pages 143–83.

2. Ross, *American War Plans*, 3:77–82; Morton, *Strategy and Command*, 73–74.

3. Sec., JB to JPC, memo, Apr. 15, 1940, JB 325, RG 225, NA, reproduced in Ross, *American War Plans*, 3:83.

4. RAINBOW 4, with supporting docs., is in Ross, *American War Plans*, 3:187–222; emphasis in original.

5. WPD, "National Strategic Decisions," memo, May 22, 1940, WPD 4175-7, RG 165, NA, reproduced in Bland, *Marshall Papers*, 2:218–19.

6. Embick to ACofS, WPD (Strong), "Comment on Rainbow Plan," memo, June 8, 1940, WPD 4175-11, RG 165, NA.

7. Dallek, *Roosevelt and American Foreign Policy*, 221–22.

8. CofS to WPD, memo, May 23, 1940, WPD 4175-10, RG 165, NA, reproduced in Bland, *Marshall Papers*, 2:220. See also Watson, *Chief of Staff*, 105–6, and Lowenthal, *Leadership and Indecision*, 1:238–40.

9. Watson, *Chief of Staff*, 106; Simpson, *Stark*, 46–47; Ross, *American War Plans*, 3:187–214; Lowenthal, *Leadership and Indecision*, 1:239–49; Conn and Fairchild, *Framework of Hemisphere Defense*, 33–36.

10. *FRUS*, 1940, 5:1155–56; Haglund, *Latin America*, 158, 178–80.

11. Sexton for GB to SN, "Naval Base in the Philippine Islands," memo, Aug. 28, 1940, GB 405, serial 1953, NH.

12. Hornbeck to Welles, memo, Sept. 21, 1940, in *Pearl Harbor Attack Hearings*, pt. 16, exhibit 97, 2007–9.

13. Matloff and Snell, *Strategic Planning*, 13–21; Morton, *Strategy and Command*, 74–78; Watson, *Chief of Staff*, 110–13; Leighton, "American Arsenal Policy," 226; Heinrichs, *Threshold of War*, 37; Quinlan, "U.S. Fleet," 169–70; J. Garry Clifford, "Bureaucratic Politics," in Hogan and Paterson, *Explaining the History of American Foreign Relations*, 148; Simpson, *Stark*, 48–54, 63–64; Lowenthal "Roosevelt and the Coming of the War," 421–22, and *Leadership and Indecision*, 1:273–76, 295–96, 299–303; Brune, *Origins of American National Security Policy*, 114–15.

14. Indeed, the JB as early as June 7 had directed the JPC to begin developing RAINBOWS 3 and 5, and on June 17 Marshall supported concentration in the Atlantic. Simultaneously, army and navy planners began to echo Roosevelt's assertion that hemispheric defense depended on the continued survival of Great Britain. See Watson, *Chief of Staff*, 108–9, and Haglund, *Latin America*, 214–16.

15. Leutze, *Bargaining for Supremacy*, 162–77; Matloff and Snell, *Strategic Planning*, 21–24; Morton, *Strategy and Command*, 80; and Kimball, *Churchill and Roosevelt*, 1:74.

16. Miller, *War Plan Orange*, 259–63; Simpson, *Stark*, 62; Watson, *Chief of Staff*, 117–18; and Leutze, *Bargaining for Supremacy*, 166. In early October the Army WPD reasserted its belief that U.S. foreign and military policies in the Pacific were "inconsistent" and that "one or the other should be changed." See Utley, *Going to War with Japan*, 112.

17. Embick recalled in 1940 that in 1938 Richardson had "supported me against Leahy and the General Board," while the admiral recalled advising Leahy to "impress on the boss that we do not want to [be] drawn into this unless we have allies so bound to us that they can not leave us in the lurch." Embick to Marshall, July 27, 1940, Marshall Papers, POF, box 67, folder 38, GCMRL; Richardson to Stark, Jan. 26, 1940, in *Pearl Harbor Attack Hearings*, pt. 14, 923–27.

18. *Pearl Harbor Attack Hearings*, pt. 14, 935; Miller, *War Plan Orange*, 219.

19. Marshall to Embick, July 25, 1940, Marshall Papers, POF, box 67, folder 38, GCMRL. See also *Pearl Harbor Attack Hearings*, pt. 14, 946, 954–59, and Dyer, *On the Treadmill to Pearl Harbor*, 278–82.

20. Miller, *War Plan Orange*, 220.

21. COMINCH to CNO, "War Plans," memo, Oct. 22, 1940, in *Pearl Harbor Attack Hearings*, pt. 14, 963–70; Dyer, *On the Treadmill to Pearl Harbor*, 287–92, 399–400; Leutze, *Bargaining for Supremacy*, 181–83. See also Doyle, "U.S. Navy and War Plan Orange," 50–58, and Quinlan, "U.S. Fleet," 157–62.

22. See Dyer, *On the Treadmill to Pearl Harbor*, 435–36; Simpson, *Stark*, 54–61; and Quinlan, "U.S. Fleet," 157–62.

23. Berle and Jacobs, *Navigating the Rapids*, 230. See also Reynolds, *Creation of the Anglo-American Alliance*, 28, 68–70.

24. Berle and Jacobs, *Navigating the Rapids*, 230.

25. Quotation is in Watson, *Chief of Staff*, 312. See also Reynolds, *Creation of the Anglo-American Alliance*, 109–12; Matloff and Snell, *Strategic Planning*, 13–21; Haglund, "Marshall and the Question of Aid to England," 413–40; and Haglund, *Latin America*, 201–6.

26. Turner later stated in this regard that the "greatest single problem" for the JB and its planners at this time was "the lack of any clear lines of national policy to guide the direction of military efforts to prepare for a war situation." With State having "no political War Plan," the army and navy felt forced to undertake "a broad study of the global political situation" that could serve as the basis for civil-military "consultation and agreement." See Dyer, *Amphibians Came to Conquer*, 1:157, 163, and Miller, *War Plan Orange*, 231.

27. Stark to Richardson, Nov. 12, 1940, in *Pearl Harbor Attack Hearings*, pt. 14, 971–72; Dyer, *On the Treadmill to Pearl Harbor*, 292–93; Leutze, *Bargaining for Supremacy*, 183–85; Simpson, *Stark*, 66. Two drafts of the ensuing document with minimal differences were dated Nov. 4 and 12. See below, n. 29.

28. The quotation is in Morton, *Strategy and Command*, 82–83, and Louis Morton, "Germany First," in Greenfield, *Command Decisions*, 35. See also Matloff and Snell, *Strategic Planning*, 24–27. The best analysis of the political aspects of the memo is Lowenthal, "Stark Memorandum," 352–59, and *Leadership and Indecision*, 1:408–14.

Stark asserted his hope that the document would "serve to clarify matters so that, at least, those in authority will be fully aware of the implications of any particular policy that may be adopted with respect to the war." Stark to Hart, Nov. 12, 1940, in *Pearl Harbor Attack Hearings*, pt. 14, 972.

29. CNO to SN, memo, Nov. 12, 1940, OP-12-CTB; copies in WPD 4175-15, RG 165, NA, and Roosevelt Papers, PSF, Safe, Navy Dept., Plan Dog, FDRL. This version is reproduced, along with the Nov. 4 draft, in Ross, *American War Plans*, 3:225–74.

30. Ibid.

31. Ibid. See also Miller, *War Plan Orange*, 315–17.

32. Quotations here and in the next paragraph from CNO to SN, memo, Nov. 12, 1940, OP-12-CTB, reproduced in Ross, *American War Plans*, 3:225–50.

33. All quotes are taken from the Stark memo of Nov. 12, 1940, as reproduced in ibid.

34. Leutze, *Bargaining for Supremacy*, 179, 195, 215. See also Lowenthal, *Leadership and Indecision*, 1:352–59. U.S. naval orders in the second half of 1940 included 9 new battleships, 11 aircraft carriers, 3 battle cruisers, and 8 heavy cruisers, as well as 31 light crusiers and 181 destroyers. See Heinrichs, *Threshold of War*, 10.

35. See above, n. 14. "If we lose in the Atlantic," Marshall asserted in October, "we lose everywhere" (Conn and Fairchild, *Framework of Hemisphere Defense*, 89).

36. Sexton to CofS, memo, July 22, 1940, Sexton Papers, box 2, folder 39, GCMRL.

37. CofS to SW and Anderson to CofS, "National Policy of the United States," memos, Nov. 13, 1940, WPD 4175-11, RG 165, NA. See also Leutze, *Bargaining for Supremacy*, 209; Watson, *Chief of Staff*, 120–21; Pogue, *Marshall*, 2:126–27; and Lowenthal, *Leadership and Indecision*, 1:414–15.

38. Simpson, *Stark*, 71–74; Watson, *Chief of Staff*, 121; Matloff and Snell, *Strategic Planning*, 28.

39. Bland, *Marshall Papers*, 2:360–62; Watson, *Chief of Staff*, 121–22.

40. JPC to JB, "National Defense Policy of the United States," memo, Dec. 21, 1940, JB 325, serial 670, RG 225, NA, reprinted in Ross, *American War Plans*, 3:281–300.

41. Dyer, *Amphibians Came to Conquer*, 1:157; Watson, *Chief of Staff*, 121–23.

42. Stimson diary, Dec. 16 and 19, 1942, YUL, as quoted in Stimson and Bundy, *On Active Service*, 366–67. See also Lowenthal, *Leadership and Indecision*, 1:347, 399–400.

43. Chapin to Welles, memo, Feb. 7, 1940, Notter Papers, box 147, RG 59, NA. See also Chapin memos of Mar. 26 and Apr. 8, 1940, in ibid.; Watson, *Chief of Staff*, 88–91; and May, "Political-Military Consultation," 172.

44. Gerow for CofS, "Conference with Secretary of State," memo, Jan. 3, 1941, WPD 4175-15, RG 165, NA.

45. CofS for WPD, "White House Conference of 16 January," memo, Jan. 17, 1941, WPD 4175-18, RG 165, NA, reproduced in Bland, *Marshall Papers*, 2:391–92. See also Heinrichs, *Threshold of War*, 38; Simpson, *Stark*, 71–74; Leutze, *Bargaining for Supremacy*, 181; Watson, *Chief of Staff*, 123–25; Matloff and Snell, *Strategic Planning*, 28 and n. 43; Morton, "Germany First," 39–41, and *Strategy and Command*, 86.

46. Murphy, *Diplomat among Warriors*, 69; Reynolds, *Creation of the Anglo-American Alliance*, 288.

47. Lothian to London, tel., Dec. 1, 1940, CAB/122/4, PRO.

48. Lowenthal, "Stark Memorandum," 352–59, and *Leadership and Indecision*, 1:412–14, 424–25. Lowenthal defends this usurpation as "necessary" in light of Roosevelt's "virtual abidication of this function" (ibid., 425).

49. Grew, *Turbulent Era*, 2:1259.

50. Watson, *Chief of Staff*, 123; Cline, *Washington Command Post*, 41; Lowenthal, *Leadership and Indecision*, 1:263.

51. JPC to JB, "Joint Instructions for Army and Navy Representatives for Holding Staff Conversations with the British, Including Agenda for the Conversations," memo, Jan. 21, 1941, JB 325, serial 674, RG 225, NA, reproduced with supporting docs. in Ross, *American War Plans*, 3:305–22. See also Dyer, *Amphibians Came to Conquer*, 1:161. These comments were approved not only by Marshall and Stark but also by Stimson, Knox, and Roosevelt.

Army-navy suspicions of the British had by this time been heightened both by renewed requests for a U.S. naval squadron at Singapore and by the recent suggestion of the director of British Naval Intelligence that the two countries reach an informal "understanding" on postwar ship construction to guarantee future Anglo-American control of the world's trade routes. See Leutze, *Bargaining for Supremacy*, 206–8.

52. Quotations are from Robinett diary, Feb. 24, 1941, GCMRL, and Leutze, *Bargaining for Supremacy*, 228. See also ibid., 221–48; Reynolds, *Creation of the Anglo-American Alliance*, 184; and Matloff and Snell, *Strategic Planning*, 32–42. "Every American believes that we are determined to use him as a tool to achieve our own ends," one British representative reported at the beginning of the conference, "and the Navy Department is determined not to be bounced around and made to subordinate their ideas to ours" (Cowman, *Dominion or Decline*, 192).

53. Embick, Miles, Gerow, and McNarney to CofS, "Dispatch of United States Forces to Singapore," memo, Feb. 12, 1941, OPD Exec. 4, item 11, RG 165, NA; Lowenthal, *Leadership and Indecision*, 1:452–53; Leutze, *Bargaining for Supremacy*, 230.

54. Lothian to London, tel., Dec. 6, 1940, CAB/122/4, PRO; "Statement of the U.S. Staff Committee: The U.S. Military Position in the Far East," OPD Exec. 4, item 11, RG 165, NA.

55. Lowenthal, *Leadership and Indecision*, 1:442–45, 454–58; Simpson, *Stark*, 78; Leutze, *Bargaining for Supremacy*, 232, 238–45.

56. ABC-1 and the revised RAINBOW 5 are reproduced in Ross, *American War Plans*, 4:3–66 and 5:3–43, respectively. See also Heinrichs, *Threshold of War*, 39; Reynolds, *Creation of the Anglo-American Alliance*, 184–85; Matloff and Snell, *Strategic Planning*, 32–47; and "History of the JCS: The War against Germany," chap. 1, 32–58, JCS Manuscripts, Transcripts, and Drafts of Historical Studies, box 6, RG 218, NA. I analyze the dispute over the direct versus indirect approach to Germany's defeat in Chaps. 3–6.

57. Ross, *American War Plans*, 3:xiv.

58. See Woodward, "Age of Reinterpretation," 2–8.

Chapter Three

1. Stimson diary, Apr. 24, 1941, YUL. The JPC originally suggested that Welles, who was a member of the Standing Liaison Committee and had consistently shown a broader understanding of the issues involved, be present at and address the first meeting of the ABC talks. At the last minute, however, State Department representation was excluded in order "to preserve the traditional American separation between civilian and military authority and at the same time reduce the level of implied commitment" to the British (Leutze, *Bargaining for Supremacy*, 221). Feis, *Road to Pearl Harbor*, 165 n. 2, notes that FDR himself made this decision.

2. See Chap. 2. In January FDR suggested that the navy consider bombing Japanese cities in case of war, and over the next two months he twice suggested and eventually insisted on a "training cruise" by U.S. warships into the Southwest Pacific, despite Stark's objections to this "childish" and ineffective dispersion; see Bland, *Marshall Papers*, 2:391–92, 416–18, 430–32.

3. Stark to U.S. fleet commanders, "Observations on the Present International Situation," Apr. 3, 1941, in Kittredge, "U.S.-British Naval Cooperation," sec. 4, pt. B, app. A.

4. Heinrichs, *Threshold of War*, 40–47; Quinlan, "U.S. Fleet," 178–80; Brune, *Origins of American National Security Policy*, 118.

5. Watson, *Chief of Staff*, 387–88. In reality Hull was a good deal more moderate on U.S. policy toward Japan than many other members of the cabinet—including Knox and Stimson. But in the armed forces' eyes he and the rest of the State Department were primarily responsible for what they considered Roosevelt's harsh and dangerous policies. See Utley, *Going to War with Japan*, 112–18.

6. Watson, *Chief of Staff*, 388–90; WPD for CofS, "Strategic Considerations, Peace or War Status," memo, Apr. 16, 1941, WPD 4402-9, RG 165, NA.

7. Pogue, *Marshall*, 2:132–33 (quotation); Watson, *Chief of Staff*, 388–90; Matloff and Snell, *Strategic Planning*, 53. Embick's official retirement became effective on January 31, in the midst of the ABC talks; he was recalled to active duty the following day.

8. Robinett diary, Mar. 26, Apr. 16, and May 21, 1941, GCMRL.

9. Smith quoted in Best, *Herbert Hoover*, 1:188; Clifford, "Connecticut Colonel's Candid Conversation," 24–38; Stimson diary, Apr. 15 and 17, 1941, YUL.

10. Pogue, *Marshall*, 2:121, 132–34; Bland, *Marshall Papers*, 2:561–62.

11. Ross, *American War Plans*, 5:7.

12. Robinett diary, May 21, 1941, GCMRL; Watson, *Chief of Staff*, 334–36; Bland, *Marshall Papers*, 2:517–18; CofS to SW, "Paper Presented by Dr. S. K. Hornbeck, Department of State," memo, May 21, 1941, WPD 4402-18, RG 165, NA.

13. Embick to Marshall, "Non-Commercial Repayments by British for Lend-Lease Material," memo, June 5, 1941, WPD 4418-7, RG 165, NA. See also Stimson diary, Apr. 23–24, 1941, YUL.

14. Dyer, *Amphibians Came to Conquer,* 1:172–73; emphasis in original.

15. Robinett noted that Marshall had "complete confidence" in Embick, "could talk with him quite frankly," and "nearly always consulted" him "before making up his mind on an over all strategic problem." Stimson, who had once been a classmate of Embick at the General Staff College, felt similarly—despite his own strong pro-interventionist position and Embick's very negative assessment of that position. In October Stimson would refer to Embick as "one of our best strategists—a retired General whom we all rely on—including the President." Years after the war Marshall labeled him "one of our ablest officers" and noted that Roosevelt "had great confidence in his opinions." Robinett diary, Apr. 16, 1941, GCMRL; Stimson diary, Oct. 1, 1941, YUL; Bland, *Marshall Interviews,* 522, 626.

16. Dyer, *Amphibians Came to Conquer,* 1:173.

17. Matloff and Snell, *Strategic Planning,* 46; Emerson, "Roosevelt as Commander-in-Chief," 189–91; Heinrichs, *Threshold of War,* 47–48, 56–88, 113–15; Reynolds, *Creation of the Anglo-American Alliance,* 198–201, 227–28; Steele, *First Offensive,* 9–18; Kraus, "Iceland," 11–22. The plans for specific operations can be found in Ross, *American War Plans,* vol. 4.

18. Heinrichs, *Threshold of War,* 107–8.

19. Ross, *American War Plans,* 3:325–32, 335–40; Sherwood, *Roosevelt and Hopkins,* 314–18; Wilson, *First Summit,* 120–32; Kittredge, "U.S.-British Naval Cooperation," sec. 5, pt. A, 518–25, and app. A, 349–56.

20. WPD comments on British Staff Paper, Aug.–Sept. 1941; Wedemeyer to Handy, memo, Sept. 1941; and Gerow, memo, Sept. 1941, all in WPD 4402-64, RG 165, NA. Wedemeyer's comments are reprinted in his *Wedemeyer Reports!,* 442–45. See also Lowenthal, *Leadership and Indecision,* 2:657–60.

21. JB to Special Observers in London, "General Strategy Review by the British Chiefs of Staff," Sept. 30, 1941, in Ross, *American War Plans,* 3:341–45.

22. Roosevelt to Stimson and Knox, July 9, 1941, Roosevelt Papers, PSF, boxes 28 and 40, Stimson and Knox Folders, FDRL, reproduced in Ross, *American War Plans,* 5:146–47. Dated Sept. 11, 1941, the Victory Program can be found in JB 355, serial 707, RG 225, NA, and is reproduced in its entirety and with relevant correspondence in Ross, *American War Plans,* 5:143–298.

23. Ross, *American War Plans,* 5:162–69.

24. Robinett diary, Dec. 2, 1941, GCMRL.

25. The army section listed as national policies defense of the Monroe Doctrine, aid to Britain and other anti-Axis nations, freedom of the seas, and disapproval of Japanese aggression with conveyance of determination "to take positive action" but avoidance of any "major military and naval commitments in the Far East at this time." See "Brief of Strategic Concept of Operations Required to Defeat Our Potential Enemies," Sept. 1941, WPD 4494-11, RG 165, NA, reprinted in Ross, *American War Plans,* 5:187. A similar list of national policies can be found in the July and Oct. WPD Strategic Estimates in the Wedemeyer Papers, box 73, folder 5, HI. In preparing the army component of the Victory Program, Wedemeyer had at first requested policy guidance and, after finding policy statements "almost as elusive as the philosopher's stone" and being told to proceed by himself, had come up with his own statement. He later recalled that U.S. objectives as he understood them were "to eliminate totalitarianism from Europe and, in the process, to be an ally of Great Britain; further, to deny the Japanese undisputed control of the western Pacific." See Kirkpatrick, *Unknown Future,* 61–63. For the Stark and JPC lists of national policies, see Chap. 2 of this volume.

26. Marshall to Stark, memo, with enclosed memo from Gerow to Marshall, Sept. 10, 1941, and Marshall to Stark, unused draft memo, Sept. 10, 1941, WPD 4494-10; "Brief of Strategic

Concept of Operations Required to Defeat Our Potential Enemies," WPD 4494-11; and WPD, "Estimate of Army Requirements," Sept. 1941, WPD 4494-21, all in RG 165, NA; Ross, *American War Plans,* 5:169, 187–220; Pogue, *Marshall,* 2:159. Detailed analyses of the Army Victory Program are in Watson, *Chief of Staff,* chap. 11; Kirkpatrick, *Unknown Future;* and Wedemeyer, *Wedemeyer Reports!,* 63–76. Extensive documentation is in the Wedemeyer Papers, boxes 76–77, HI.

27. Wedemeyer's anti-interventionist views were clearly expressed in the early chapters of his memoir, *Wedemeyer Reports!,* most notably on p. 25. He forcefully rejected the isolationist label for such beliefs, however, later asserting that "only fools . . . believe the United States could or should remain isolated in the twentieth century." Eiler, *Wedemeyer on War and Peace,* xvii.

28. Wilson, *First Summit,* 40–41, identifies three policy alternatives (and their adherents) being proposed at this time: all-out aid to Britain first and foremost (Roosevelt and most of his civilian advisers); aid to Britain, combined with the development of U.S. forces and an immediate declaration of either belligerency or a war footing (Stimson, Knox, and Stark); and a holding back on both aid to Britain and U.S. entry so as to build major military forces (Marshall and the Army General Staff). The army section of the Victory Program presented this third alternative and, in effect, challenged existing national priorities.

29. Unsigned typescript, "A Historical Strategic Study," 1940, with handwritten note, "1940—Paper to Marshall," Wedemeyer Papers, box 7, folder 2, HI.

30. See Kirkpatrick, *Unknown Future,* 5–33, esp. 8, 13–14, and 30–31; Wedemeyer, *Wedemeyer Reports!,* 50–53.

31. Quotations here and in the next paragraph from Robinett diary, Sept. 12, 1941, GCMRL; emphasis added.

32. Ross, *American War Plans,* 5:211.

33. Ibid. AWPD/1 is reproduced in ibid., 205–98.

34. Ibid., 197. See also 169.

35. JB, "General Strategy Review by the British Chiefs of Staff," Sept. 30, 1941, in Ross, *American War Plans,* 3:343. See also the similar comments in the Victory Program in ibid., 5:173.

36. Dawson, *Decision to Aid Russia,* 112–15.

37. Ross, *American War Plans,* 3:79–81.

38. Miles to Gerow, memo, May 26, 1941, in *Pearl Harbor Attack Hearings,* pt. 21, exhibit 182, 4757.

39. Stimson diary, June 22–23, 1941, YUL; Stimson to Roosevelt, June 23, 1941, Roosevelt Papers, PSF, box 40, Stimson Folder, FDRL; Bland, *Marshall Papers,* 2:565. See also Quinlan, "U.S. Fleet," 187–88; Dawson, *Decision to Aid Russia,* 113–15; Bradley Smith, *Sharing Secrets,* 3, 73; and Abbazia, *Mr. Roosevelt's Navy,* 213.

40. JPC, "Proposed Directive for Holding Staff Conversations with the Russians," undated, JB 325, serial 728, RG 225, NA.

41. The U.S. ambassador in Moscow concurred, warning on June 17 that it was impossible to create "good will" with the Soviets, who were "not affected by ethical or moral considerations, nor guided by the relationships which are customary between individuals of culture and breeding. Their psychology recognizes only firmness, power and force, and reflects primitive instincts and reactions that are entirely devoid of the restraints of civilization." *FRUS,* 1941, 1:757–58, 765, 790; see also Gorodetsky, *Cripps' Mission to Moscow,* 167–69, 177.

42. FDR to Leahy, June 26, 1941, in Roosevelt, *FDR: His Personal Letters* [hereafter *FDR Personal Letters*], 2:1177.

43. Gorodetsky, *Cripps' Mission to Moscow,* 200. See also 173, 183, 185, 196–99, and 201–4; Sherwood, *Roosevelt and Hopkins,* 323–48; *FRUS,* 1941, 1:826; and Tuttle, *Harry L. Hopkins,* 84–86, 94–97.

44. Quotations are from Heinrichs, *Threshold of War*, 159, 179; Blum, *Morgenthau Diaires*, 2: 264; and Roosevelt to Stimson, Aug. 30, 1941, in Roosevelt, *FDR Personal Letters*, 2:1201–3. See also ibid., 1195–96; Kimball, *Juggler*, 21–41; Offner, "Uncommon Ground," 243; Warren F. Kimball, "Anglo-American War Aims, 1941–43, the First Review: Eden's Mission to Washington," in Lane and Temperly, *Rise and Fall of the Grand Alliance*, 5; Pogue, *Marshall*, 2:72–73; Bland, *Marshall Papers*, 2:581–84, 595–96; Waldo Heinrichs, "Franklin D. Roosevelt and the Risks of War, 1939–1941," in Iriye and Cohen, *American, Chinese, and Japanese Perspectives on Wartime Asia*, 166–67; J. Garry Clifford, "The Isolationist Context of American Foreign Policy toward the Soviet Union in 1940–1941," and Theodore Wilson, "In Aid of America's Interests: The Provision of Lend-Lease to the Soviet Union, 1941–1942," in [Sevost'ianov and Kimball], *Soviet-U.S. Relations*, 46 and 126–31, respectively.

Eliot Cohen, "Churchill and Coalition Strategy in World War II," in Kennedy, *Grand Strategies*, 54, notes that Churchill similarly questioned the pessimistic conclusions of his military advisers regarding Soviet survival and pressed for the delivery of supplies, while ULTRA reports from intercepted German cryptographic messages led the British armed forces by early August to question their original, pessimistic conclusions regarding Soviet resistance (Hinsley, *British Intelligence*, 2:67–68, 78–79). Critics note, however, that such questioning did not lead to any fundamental change in British strategy. See Ben-Moshe, *Churchill*, and Gorodetsky, *Cripps' Mission to Moscow*.

45. Miles, G-2, to ACofS, WPD, "Strategic Estimate of the Situation," memo, July 11, 1941, WPD 4510, RG 165, NA. G-2, Marshall, and Stimson all feared that German success, coupled with Japanese participation, could endanger Alaskan defenses. See Gerow to ACofS, G-2, "G-2 Estimate Regarding the Alaskan Area," memo, July 2, 1941, WPD 4297-4, RG 165, NA; Gerow to CofS, with enclosed G-2 estimate, "Alaskan Security re: the German Russian War," memo, July 1941, and Gerow to Adjutant General, "Priority of Construction at Nome, Alaska," memo, July 15, 1941, both in WPD 4297-3, RG 165, NA; Bland, *Marshall Papers*, 2:564–65.

46. Miles to CofS, "Strategical Estimate of the Situation," memo, July 18, 1941, WPD 4510, RG 165, NA.

47. Sherwood, *Roosevelt and Hopkins*, 327–45; Bland, *Marshall Papers*, 2:579 n. 2.

48. Lt. Col. Edwin E. Schwien, "An Essential Strategic Diversion in Europe," memo, Aug. 1941, WPD 4402-77, RG 165, NA, discussed in Matloff and Snell, *Strategic Planning*, 177.

49. Ross, *American War Plans*, 3:341 and 5:173, 193–95; Kirkpatrick, *Unknown Future*, 72–73; Langer and Gleason, *Undeclared War*, 563; Watson, *Chief of Staff*, 354–55.

50. Ross, *American War Plans*, 5:196. See also Wedemeyer, *Wedemeyer Reports!*, 66. These figures included men needed for maintenance and support of combat divisions.

51. Ross, *American War Plans*, 5:197–99.

52. Marshall to Pres., "Ground Forces," memo, Sept. 27, 1941, in *Pearl Harbor Attack Hearings*, pt. 15, 1636–39; WPD, "War Department Strategic Estimate," Oct. 1941, WPD 4510, RG 165, NA.

53. Bland, *Marshall Papers*, 2:635–36.

54. "War Department Strategic Estimate," G-2 backup, exhibit 1, and SS Theater Studies, no. 13, both in WPD 4510, RG 165, NA; Gailey, WPD, to ACofS, G-2, and G-2 reply, "Strategic Estimate of Situation," memos, Sept. 17–18, 1941, WPD 4494, RG 165, NA; Miles, G-2, to CofS, "Brief Periodic Estimate of the World Situation," memo, Sept. 5, 1941, Wedemeyer Papers, box 73, folder 5, HI.

55. Sherry, *Rise of American Airpower*, 108.

56. "War Department Strategic Estimate," Oct. 1941, WPD 4510, RG 165, NA; G-2 rpts., Kroner to CofS, "Japanese-American Relations," Oct. 2, 1941, and Miles to CofS, "The Kwantung Army versus the Siberian Army," Oct. 21, 1941, in *Pearl Harbor Attack Hearings*, pt. 14, exhibit 33, 1357–61. See also pp. 1347 and 1356–57 for Aug.–Sept. G-2 calls for a tough line against Japan, and

Heinrichs, *Threshold of War,* 193. Interestingly, a Soviet liaison team had on September 15 mentioned to ASW John J. McCloy its desire for preliminary staff discussions regarding military action against Japan. See Bradley Smith, *Sharing Secrets,* 69–70.

57. The term "launching pad" is from Reynolds, *Creation of the Anglo-American Alliance,* 211–12. "There is no evidence," Warren F. Kimball concluded in *America Unbound,* 143, "that FDR became reconciled to the unrestricted use of American military forces in Europe until after the Pearl Harbor attack, although he spoke more and more of naval and air involvement." See also Kimball, *Juggler,* 34; Harriman and Abel, *Special Envoy,* 74; and Wilson, *First Summit,* 116–18.

58. Lowenthal, *Leadership and Indecision,* 2:638.

59. Sherry, *Rise of American Airpower,* 98. See also Heinrichs, *Threshold of War,* 194.

60. Bland, *Marshall Papers,* 2:613–14; Robinett diary, Oct. 6, 1941, GCMRL; Bland, *Marshall Interviews,* 282–83. See also Heinrichs, *Threshold of War,* 174; Steele, "Political Aspects," 69; Pogue, *Marshall,* 2:73–79; and Watson, *Chief of Staff,* 362–65.

61. Marshall to Roosevelt, "Ground Forces," memo, Sept. 22, 1943, in *Pearl Harbor Attack Hearings,* pt. 15, exhibit 60, 1636–39. Marshall used this memo during his September 22 conference with FDR according to supporting documents in the Army Chief of Staff Files, Secretariat, 1938–42, Conferences, 1938–42, box 887, RG 165, NA.

62. Stimson to Roosevelt, Sept. 23, 1941, attached to Roosevelt's July 9, 1941, letter requesting the Victory Program, Roosevelt Papers, PSF, box 40, Stimson Folder, FDRL.

63. Stimson diary, Sept. 25, 1941, YUL. Stimson had noted in his diary on September 13 that he was "rather appalled" by the huge army called for in the Victory Program.

64. Pogue, *Marshall,* 2:72–79. This was one of many reasons why the U.S. wartime army included only 16 rather than the 61 armored and 90 rather than the 215 total divisions called for in the Victory Program. In 1955 the army staff calculated that Lend-Lease had equipped approximately 101 U.S.-type divisions. See Kirkpatrick, *Unknown Future,* 102, 107–8.

65. See Dyer, *Amphibians Came to Conquer,* 1:176, 180–82.

66. Sherry, *Rise of American Airpower,* 101–3.

67. Heinrichs, *Threshold of War,* 131.

68. For studies of this episode see Harrington, "Careless Hope," 217–38; Sherry, *Rise of American Airpower,* 100–115; and Heinrichs, *Threshold of War,* 118–220. See also Heinrichs, "Franklin D. Roosevelt and the Risks of War," 168–73; Matloff and Snell, *Strategic Planning,* 69–79; and Pogue, *Marshall,* 2:186–202.

69. Arnold, *Global Mission,* 249; Heinrichs, *Threshold of War,* 148.

70. Heinrichs, *Threshold of War,* 127–44, 175–76, 194–98. See also Harrington, "Careless Hope," 224–25.

71. Quotations are from Stimson diary, Sept. 12 and Oct. 21, 1941, YUL; Stimson and Bundy, *On Active Service,* 388; Heinrichs, *Threshold of War,* 195–97; and Harrington, ".Careless Hope," 222–26. See also Sherry, *Rise of American Airpower,* 106–10. When asked about the navy at this press conference, Marshall asserted that the new "grand strategy doesn't include the use of much naval force" (Robert Sherrod, "Secret Conference with General Marshall," in Brown and Burner, *I Can Tell It Now,* 43).

72. "It is quite clear that the American Navy and Army authorities have not got together and thought out a joint policy," one British officer noted after hearing conflicting strategic assessments from Marshall and Stark during the Atlantic Conference. See Richardson, *From Churchill's Secret Circle,* 69.

73. On November 2, G-2 rated such an attack "unlikely as long as Russian resistance in Europe continues" and the Red Army in Siberia was not materially reduced (*Pearl Harbor Attack Hearings,* pt. 14, exhibit 33, 1363). In October Embick warned in the aftermath of a visit to England that British forces could do no more than hold in Egypt and that their home defenses were

inadequate. Together with Stimson and Marshall he reemphasized to both FDR and Navy secretary Knox the importance of a cautious, defensive strategy in the Atlantic, retention of U.S. weaponry, and avoidance of any North African diversion. See Stimson diary, Oct. 1–10, 15, and 21, 1941, YUL.

74. Min., Nov. 3, 1941, JB mtg., and Marshall and Stark to Pres., "Estimate concerning Far Eastern Situation" and "Far Eastern Situation," memos, Nov. 5 and 27, 1941, *Pearl Harbor Attack Hearings*, pt. 14, exhibit 16, 1061–65, and exhibit 17, 1083; Stimson Diary, Oct. 28, 1941, YUL; Heinrichs, *Threshold of War*, 200–205, 213.

75. Gerow to CofS, "Far Eastern Situation," memo, Nov. 24, 1941, in *Pearl Harbor Attack Hearings*, pt. 14, exhibit 18, 1103.

76. Stimson diary, Nov. 26–27, 1941, YUL. See also *Pearl Harbor Attack Hearings*, pt. 14, 1084–1201; Heinrichs, *Threshold of War*, 200–214; Langer and Gleason, *Undeclared War*, 898; Sherry, *Rise of American Airpower*, 113–14; Lowenthal, *Leadership and Indecision*, 2:703–4; Brune, *Origins of American National Security Policy*, 394–95, and "Considerations of Force," 394–400. See Hull's *Memoirs*, 2:1080, for his defense of his actions.

77. Marshall to Gerow on White House meeting, memo, Feb. 26, 1941, OPD 165, exec. 4, item 11, RG 165, NA.

78. A. E. Campbell, "Franklin Roosevelt and Unconditional Surrender," in Langhorne, *Diplomacy and Intelligence during the Second World War*, 221.

79. See Heinrichs, *Threshold of War*, 159–60, and "The United States Prepares for War," in Chalou, *Secrets War*, 16–17.

80. "No sadder self-delusion," Edward Miller has aptly concluded in *War Plan Orange*, 62, "is to be found in all the prewar planning experiences." For an analysis of the flaws in both civil and military reasoning on the Far East in late 1941, see sources cited in n. 70 in this chapter. For the argument that the modus vivendi could have been negotiated and extended so as to prevent any Pacific war, see Schroeder, *Axis Alliance and Japanese-American Relations*, and Russett, *No Clear and Present Danger*, 44–62.

81. Ickes, *Secret Diary*, 3:567. In April FDR used King's similar comment that he "did not have enough butter to spread over the bread that he was supposed to cover"; see Stimson diary, Apr. 24, 1941, YUL.

Chapter Four

1. See Cline, *Washington Command Post*, 90–106; Emerson, "Roosevelt as Commander-in-Chief," 191–92; Bland, *Marshall Papers*, 3:127–29; and Albion and Connery, *Forrestal*, 88–90. For additional details on these and other JCS/CCS organizational issues, see Davis, "History of the Joint Chiefs of Staff."

2. See Schnabel, *History of the Joint Chiefs of Staff*, 2 n. 2, and Cline, *Washington Command Post*, 99 and n. 28. By the navy reorganization King as CNO was to be "the principal naval adviser to the President on the conduct of the war," and in the army reorganization Roosevelt specifically directed a rephrasing to make clear his own ability to act "directly through the Chief of Staff." See Albion, *Forrestal*, 89, and Bland, *Marshall Papers*, 3:127–28. The JCS retained its informal status until passage of the National Security Act of 1947.

3. Bland, *Marshall Interviews*, 431–33, 623–24; Bland, *Marshall Papers*, 3:285 n. 6, 338–39; Pogue, "Wartime Chiefs," 71; Marshall interview with Cols. Guyer and Donnelly, Feb. 11, 1949, Oral History Collection, Marshall Folder, GCMRL; Elsey, "Some White House Recollections," 363. According to Marshall's later recollections, King and Roosevelt both originally opposed the Leahy appointment for fear it would usurp their prerogatives. Lowenthal, *Leadership and Inde-*

cision, 2:793, notes that Hopkins more than Leahy informally represented Roosevelt's thinking to the JCS. Croswell, *Chief of Staff,* 89, comments that in light of Leahy's failure to become a true chairman, the JCS were saved from bickering by "the personality of Marshall and the willingness of King to compromise."

4. Schnabel, *History of the Joint Chiefs of Staff,* 1:7; Hull, *Memoirs,* 2:1109–10; Albion, *Forrestal,* 89–90; Bland, *Marshall Papers,* 3:127–28. Roosevelt specifically directed rephrasing of the army reorganization to make clear his ability to act directly through the chief of staff.

5. See Chap. 6.

6. Cline, *Washington Command Post.*

7. Reynolds, "1940," 340.

8. *FRUS: Washington and Casablanca,* 21–37, 210–17. For analyses of ARCADIA see Matloff and Snell, *Strategic Planning,* 97–126, and Butler, *History of the Second World War: Grand Strategy* [hereafter *Grand Strategy*], vol. 3, pt. 1, 325–401.

9. Butler, *Grand Strategy,* vol. 3, pt. 1, 352 (quotation), 565; Matloff and Snell, *Strategic Planning,* 175–77.

10. Quotations are from King to Knox, memo, Feb. 8, 1942, and King to Roosevelt, memo, Mar. 5, 1942, both in King Papers, NH, latter reproduced in Buell, *Master of Seapower,* 531–33. See also King to Marshall, memos, Feb. 18 and Mar. 29, 1942, King Papers, NH; Matloff and Snell, *Strategic Planning,* 154–56, 211; Dyer, *Amphibians Came to Conquer,* 230–45; and A. S. McDill, "Initiation of Operations Leading to Guadalcanal," memo, Sept. 17, 1945, SPD, ser. 3, box 48, Guadalcanal, NH.

11. Danchev, *Very Special Relationship,* 12, 65, and *Establishing the Anglo-American Alliance* [hereafter *Dykes Diaries*], 71–72, 77–78, 85–86, 105. Dykes and U.S. General Walter Bedell Smith served as CCS secretaries in 1942 and established a very close friendship that was as pivotal to Anglo-American military collaboration as the one between Marshall and Field Marshal Sir John Dill, head of the British mission. See Croswell, *Chief of Staff,* 90–93, as well as the Danchev volumes cited above.

12. Bland, *Marshall Interviews,* 593; Larrabee, *Commander in Chief,* 155.

13. See above, Chap. 2.

14. Watt, *Succeeding John Bull,* 74.

15. See above, Chap. 1; Buell, *Master of Seapower,* 50, 145–46; Heinrichs, *Threshold of War,* 112–13; and Allard, "Anglo-American Naval Differences," 75–81. In May 1941 King also blasted the British Navy for "a long series of errors of omission and commission, blunders and mistakes" in the war; see Perry, "*Dear Bart,*" 15.

16. Cantril, *Public Opinion,* 1176; Gallup, *Gallup Poll,* 1:370; Steele, *First Offensive,* 46–53, 81–93; Thorne, *Allies of a Kind,* 156–63, 719; Dallek, *Roosevelt and American Foreign Policy,* 331–33.

17. See directly below in text as well as Matloff and Snell, *Strategic Planning;* Cline, *Washington Command Post;* Steele, *First Offensive;* and Stoler, *Politics of the Second Front.*

18. Chandler, *Papers of Dwight David Eisenhower* [hereafter *Eisenhower Papers*], 1:147, 207; emphasis in original. Eisenhower had become WPD chief on February 16 and the first OPD chief with the March army reorganization.

19. This effort was motivated by political and economic as well as military considerations, which Marshall made clear in a December 20 recommendation to FDR that the Southwest Pacific have priority over West Africa and the Middle East not only to keep East Indies oil out of Japanese hands and stop the Japanese challenge to the entire U.S. position in the area but also because of U.S. obligations to the Philippines, the need to protect Australia and New Zealand as well as to keep China fighting, and, ABC-1 and previous U.S. comments to the contrary notwithstanding, the need now to help Britain defend Singapore. Singapore's fall, he warned, "would be an almost vital blow to the British Empire as well as to our own future commercial interests in the

Pacific." Marshall to Roosevelt, "A Suggested Analysis of the Basic Topics and Their Attendant Problems," memo, Dec. 20, 1941, WDCSA 381, 1, Super Secret, RG 165, NA.

20. Chandler, *Eisenhower Papers*, 1:66, 112.

21. See above, Chap. 3.

22. Embick to Marshall, Jan. 1942, WPD 4511-37, RG 165, NA. See also Eisenhower diary notations for Jan. 1–4 and 17, 1942, OPD Historical Unit File, item 3, CMH, reprinted in Chandler, *Eisenhower Papers*, 1:34, 39, 61–62, and in Ferrell, *Eisenhower Diaries*, 40–44; Embick, "More Important Factors in Current Strategic Situation," memo, Dec. 16, 1941, WPD 4622-37; Embick to Marshall, Dec. 24, 1941, WPD 4628-13; and Embick to Gerow, "Relative Importance of the Far East versus Libya," memo, Jan. 29, 1942, WPD 4596-15, all in RG 165, NA.

23. Chandler, *Eisenhower Papers*, 1:66 (Jan. 22, 1942); emphasis in original.

24. White, *Stilwell Papers*, 15–16; Steele, *First Offensive*, 76–80.

25. Quotes from Chandler, *Eisenhower Papers*, 1:150–51. See also 66, 75, 118–19, 126, 149–55, and 208.

26. JB, "Brief Joint Estimate of the Military Situation of the Associated Powers," memo, Dec. 21, 1941, JB 325, serial 729, RG 225, NA.

27. Blum, *From the Morgenthau Diaries*, 3:81–82; JPS 2/5, "Strategic Deployment of the Land, Sea, and Air Forces of the U.S.," Mar. 6, 1942, CCS 381 (1-30-42) (1), RG 218, NA.

28. Marshall to Roosevelt, "A Suggested Analysis of the Basic Topics and Their Attendant Problems," memo, Dec. 20, 1941, WDCSA 381, 1, Super Secret, RG 165, NA. See also WPD to Pres., "Aid to Russia," unused memo, Dec. 13, 1941, WPD 4557-29, RG 165, NA; G-2 to CofS, "Brief G-2 Estimates of the World Situation," memo, SPD, ser. 3, box 46, Estimates Folder, NH; Military Intelligence Service Rpt., "Situation and Capablities of the Enemy," Mar. 19, 1942, Wedemeyer Papers, box 72, folder 7, HI; War Dept. and CCS Russian Combat Estimate, Apr. 1, 1942, CCS 350.05 USSR (4-1-42), RG 218, NA.

29. Embick to Gerow, "Relative Strategic Importance at Present of the Far East versus Libya," memo, Jan. 29, 1942, WPD 4596-15, and WPD, "An Analysis of the Lines of Action Open to the United States for the Rendition of Assistance to Russia in the Event of Hostilities between Russia and Japan in the Spring of 1942," memo, Mar. 8, 1942, OPD 381 Japan, case 4, RG 165, NA.

30. See above, Chap. 3.

31. Chandler, *Eisenhower Papers*, 1:118.

32. Lee, ACofS, G-2, to CofS, "Possibility of a Negotiated Russo-German Settlement," memo, Feb. 12, 1942, Hopkins Papers, box 105, Russia Folder, FDRL.

33. Chandler, *Eisenhower Papers*, 1:149–55; Eisenhower's emphasis.

34. Min., JCS 4th mtg., Mar. 7, 1942, CCS 381 (3-5-42) (2), RG 218, NA.

35. Kimball, *Churchill and Roosevelt*, 1:398–99; Stimson diary, Feb. 24, Mar. 5–6, 7, 16, 20, 25, 1942, YUL; Arnold to CofS, "Employment of Army Air Forces," memo, Mar. 3, 1942, Arnold Papers, box 39, SOF, 1941–45, LOC; Steele, *First Offensive*, 81–93; Stoler, *Politics of the Second Front*, 32–39.

36. Kimball, *Churchill and Roosevelt*, 1:437, 441. See also Arnold, *Global Mission*, 304–5, and directly below in text.

37. In his February 28 memo Eisenhower admitted that "a desire to concentrate in one direction must not wholly remove protection in another," and on March 25 he informed Marshall that some of his "highly desirable" as opposed to "necessary" tasks were "so important" as to warrant diversion of "at least a small proportion of our strength to their accomplishment. Foremost among these is probably the support of Australia and New Zealand and the lines of communication thereto." See Chandler, *Eisenhower Papers*, 1:151, 205; Matloff and Snell, *Strategic Planning*, 156–62; and Cline, *Washington Command Post*, 147.

38. Quotations are from appendix II to JPS 2/6 in JCS 23, "Strategic Deployment of the Land, Sea, and Air Forces of the U.S.," Mar. 14, 1942, CCS 381 (1-30-42) (1), RG 218, NA.

39. Quotation is from final OPD document as presented to the British, reprinted in Butler, *Grand Strategy*, vol. 3, pt. 2, 675–81. See also Matloff and Snell, *Strategic Planning*, 181–87, 383.

40. King later claimed that he had agreed to cross-channel plans because they could achieve quick victory in Europe and thereby allow him to plan for full concentration against Japan in the foreseeable future; see King and Whitehill, *Fleet Admiral King*, 390–91.

41. "Strategic Deployment of the Land, Sea, and Air Forces of the U.S.," cited above, n. 38.

42. Chandler, *Eisenhower Papers*, 1:147, 207; Eisenhower's emphasis.

43. Roosevelt informed Churchill in early April that U.S. strategic proposals would hopefully be greeted with "enthusiasm" in Moscow and "work out in full accord with [the] trend of public opinion," which demanded a front "to draw off pressure on the Russians" and was "wise enough" to see that the Soviets were "killing more Germans and destroying more equipment than you and I put together. Even if full success if not attained," he insisted, "the *big* objective will be." On arrival in London Hopkins hammered away at the same points, as well as the public's preoccupation with the Pacific, the consensus on the need for action in 1942, and FDR's belief that his proposals "should take the heat off Russia's diplomatic demands," which FDR continued to oppose. See Kimball, *Churchill and Roosevelt*, 1:437, 441; Sherwood, *Roosevelt and Hopkins*, 526, 536–38.

44. Kimball, *Churchill and Roosevelt*, 1:494.

45. Marshall to Roosevelt and Roosevelt to Marshall, memos, May 4–6, 1942, CCS 381 (5-1-42), RG 218, NA; Bland, *Marshall Papers*, 3:183–86; Matloff and Snell, *Strategic Planning*, 210–21; Danchev, *Dykes Diaries*, 139, 145.

46. Butler, *Grand Strategy*, vol. 3, pt. 2, 626–28; *FRUS: Washington and Casablanca*, 433–34, 426–28, 457–60, 465–69, 478–79; Bland, *Marshall Papers*, 3:242–48; Matloff and Snell, *Strategic Planning*, 238–44.

47. Dykes noted in his diary on June 20 that Gen. Sir Hastings Ismay of the COS "anticipates a major explosion from the PM when he is confronted by this document [the original CCS compromise]" (Danchev, *Dykes Diaries*, 159).

48. Roosevelt for Stimson, Marshall, Arnold, Hopkins, Knox, King, and Hopkins, memo, May 6, 1942, CofS 381, 1, Super Secret, RG 165, NA. See also Marshall to Roosevelt and Roosevelt to Marshall, memos, May 4–6, 1942, CCS 381 (5-1-42), RG 218, NA. These memos are reproduced and/or quoted in Bland, *Marshall Papers*, 3:183–86, and Matloff and Snell, *Strategic Planning*, 217–22.

49. Kimball, *Churchill and Roosevelt*, 1:503.

50. Ibid., 520–21; see also Butler, *Grand Strategy*, vol. 3, pt. 2, 629–31, and Matloff and Snell, *Strategic Planning*, 266–67.

51. Stimson diary, July 10, 1942, YUL.

52. Min., JCS 24th mtg., July 10, 1942, CCS 334 JCS (23 June 42), RG 218, NA; CofS and CNO to Pres., "Latest British Proposals Relative to BOLERO and GYMNAST," memo, July 10, 1942, OPD 381 Gen. (sec. 2), 73, RG 165, NA. Arnold did not attend this JCS meeting or sign the document, and Leahy had not yet been appointed to the JCS.

53. King to S. E. Morison, Oct. 27, 1948, King Papers, box 18, LOC; Pogue, *Marshall*, 2:340–41; Bland, *Marshall Interviews*, 593; Stimson and Bundy, *On Active Service*, 425. Most historians also conclude that the proposal was a bluff. Those who question this conclusion include Morton, *Strategy and Command*, 309; Steele, *First Offensive*, 161–63; and Lowenthal, *Leadership and Indecision*, 948–49. Maney, *Roosevelt*, 150–52, views the Pacific-first proposal as a bluff, but one

designed to force Roosevelt's hand as well as that of the British owing to the president's numerous strategic flip-flops since January.

54. Bland, *Marshall Papers*, 3:271–72; emphasis added.

55. Stimson diary, July 12, 1942, YUL.

56. McNarney to Stimson, "Review of Current Situation," memo, Apr. 12, 1942, OPD Exec. 8, book 4, RG 165, NA; emphasis in original.

57. "Memorandum concerning the Occupation of Northwest Africa by U.S. Forces," attached to Marshall to Roosevelt, "Gymnast Operation," memo, June 16, 1942, OPD Registered Doc. 5, RG 407, with draft in OPD Exec. 10, item 53, RG 165, NA.

58. Butcher, *My Three Years with Eisenhower*, 10. Eisenhower had recently been shifted from OPD to command the newly created European Theater of Operations in London.

59. Castle diary, May 5, 1942, Houghton Library, Harvard University, courtesy of Prof. J. Garry Clifford. For the SS studies, see Col. Nevins, "Courses of Action Open to the United States in the Event the Prospective 1942 German Offensive Forces Russia to Capitulate," memo, Apr. 1942, and unsigned memo to Nevins, Apr. 25, 1942, Wedemeyer Papers, box 76, folder 2, HI.

60. Col. Nevins, "Courses of Action Open to the United States in the Event the Prospective 1942 German Offensive Forces Russia to Capitulate," memo, Apr. 1942, and unsigned memo to Nevins, Apr. 25, 1942, Wedemeyer Papers, box 76, folder 2, HI; Givens to ACofS, OPD, "Japanese Plans for Invasion of Siberia," memo, Apr. 15, 1942, OPD 381 Japan, case 4, RG 165, NA; Strong to ACofS, OPD, "Japanese Attack on Russia," memo, May 21, 1942, OPD 381 Japan, case 4, RG 165, NA; JIC, "Japanese Capabilities and Intentions regarding Siberia," memo, June 17, 1942, OPD 381 Japan, case 4, RG 165, NA; Iriye, *Power and Culture*, 90; Bland, *Marshall Papers*, 3:208–9; U.S. Dept. of Defense, *Entry of the Soviet Union into the War against Japan*, 10–11.

61. Min., JCS 24th mtg., and CofS and CNO to Pres., "Latest British Proposals relative to BOLERO and GYMNAST," as cited in n. 52.

62. As quoted in Matloff and Snell, *Strategic Planning*, 215–16. See also 210–14 and 222–26.

63. Castle diary, May 5, 1942, Houghton Library, Harvard University, courtesy of Prof. J. Garry Clifford; JCS Memo for Information no. 14, "Chinese Capabilities," July 4, 1942, CCS 381 China (6-23-42), RG 218, NA. See also Matloff and Snell, *Strategic Planning*, 202–5, 227–29, 247–48; Dallek, *Roosevelt and American Foreign Policy*, 355–56; Thorne, *Allies of a Kind*, 156–58, 175; Schaller, *U.S. Crusade in China*, 107–14; Pogue, *Marshall*, 2:363–66.

64. Min., JCS 24th mtg., July 10, 1942, CCS 334 JCS (23 June 1942), RG 218, NA. See also Matloff and Snell, *Strategic Planning*, 256–65; Pogue, *Marshall*, 2:365–66, 377–81; Bland, *Marshall Papers*, 3:252–56, 261–65; Love, "Fighting a Global War," 275; Buell, *Master of Seapower*, 215–20; "Initiation of Operations Leading to Guadalcanal," memos, Sept. 17 and 24, 1945, SPD, ser. 3, box 48, NH.

65. Bland, *Marshall Papers*, 3:273–74. The draft with Marshall's handwritten note is in OPD Exec. 10, item 36, RG 165, NA.

66. Chandler, *Eisenhower Papers*, 1:380.

67. "Draft of a Proposed Message from the President to the Prime Minister," unsigned memo, OPD Exec. 5, item 9, RG 165, NA.

68. Danchev, *Dykes Diaries*, 167–68, 172, 189. I quote Dill's July 15 message in Chap. 5.

Chapter Five

1. Deane for King and JCS to Pres., "Pacific Operations," memos, July 12, 1942, OPD 381 Gen (sec. 2), 73, RG 165, NA, discussed in Matloff and Snell, *Strategic Planning*, 270–71.

2. McCrea to Director, FDRL, June 14, 1972, McCrea Papers, Accession File, FDRL; FDR handwritten messages in Roosevelt Papers, MRF, box 7-A, folder 2, FDRL; Roosevelt to Marshall, tel., July 14, 1942, WDCSA BOLERO, Super Secret, RG 165, NA.

3. Sherwood, *Roosevelt and Hopkins,* 603–5; Matloff and Snell, *Strategic Planning,* 272–78.

4. Morgenthau Diaries, June 16, 1942, 1131, FDRL, partially quoted in Bennett, *Roosevelt and the Search for Victory,* 57.

5. Roosevelt believed the Soviets could successfully retreat into the interior if the Japanese attacked, and according to Dill he was considering operations in North Africa and the Middle East as well as cross-channel and in the Pacific as ways of assisting the Red Army. See Morgenthau Diaries, June 16, 1942, 1131, FDRL, partially quoted in Bennett, *Roosevelt and the Search for Victory,* 57; Lowenthal, *Leadership and Indecision,* 2:893.

6. Steele, *First Offensive,* 82–84, 90.

7. See Stoler, *Politics of the Second Front,* 42–51.

8. Churchill apparently shared this view, despite disagreement from the COS; see Ben-Moshe, *Churchill,* 190–206.

9. Stimson diary, July 15, 1942, YUL; Marshall to King, memo, July 15, 1942, in Bland, *Marshall Papers,* 3:276. According to his appointments diary, Roosevelt saw Stimson at 10:10 A.M., Hopkins and Marshall from 10:20 to 11:00, King and Hopkins from 11:00 to 11:15, and Hopkins and all three chiefs together from 11:15 to 12:15.

10. Sherwood, *Roosevelt and Hopkins,* 602–5; Matloff and Snell, *Strategic Planning,* 272–78.

11. See Beitzell, *Uneasy Alliance,* 97–99; Stoler, *Politics of the Second Front,* 60–62, 85–86, 91, 96, 102–5.

12. Wedemeyer to Handy, memo, July 14, 1942, OPD Exec. 5, item 1, tab 10, RG 165, NA, quoted in Bland, *Marshall Papers,* 3:275–76.

13. Churchill, *Second World War,* 4:439–40.

14. Marshall to Eisenhower, tel., July 16, 1942, OPD Exec. 5, item 9, RG 165, NA.

15. Chandler, *Eisenhower Papers,* 1:378–81, 388–96, 400–414; Eisenhower, *Crusade in Europe,* 68–71. The pessimistic estimates applied to the LeHavre landing site that Eisenhower's staff originally favored, not the Cherbourg area to which they shifted between July 17 and 20, with members of Lord Louis Mountbatten's Combined Operations Staff providing a detailed and much more optimistic outline plan. See Ambrose, *Supreme Commander,* 71, and Strange, "Cross-Channel Attack," 425–45. Eisenhower may have been more pessimistic than his statements would lead one to believe; see Danchev, *Dykes Diaries,* 178–80.

16. Quoted in Thorne, *Allies of a Kind,* 136.

17. See Danchev, *Dykes Diaries,* 174, 176.

18. Danchev, *Dykes Diaries,* 176.

19. Butcher, *My Three Years with Eisenhower,* 29; Sherwood, *Roosevelt and Hopkins,* 610. The full text of FDR's reply is in the Roosevelt Papers, PSF, box 125, Hopkins Folder, FDRL. The conference minutes are in CCS 334 (26 May 1942), RG 218, and the final Marshall-King rpt. to FDR, July 28, in WDCSA 319.1, Super Secret, RG 165, NA.

20. Stimson to Roosevelt, memo, July 25, 1942, SW Files, Formerly Top-Secret Corres. ("Safe File"), War Plans Folder, RG 107, NA.

21. Danchev, *Dykes Diaries,* 189.

22. Min., CCS 32d mtg., with attached JCS memo, July 24, 1942, CCS 334 (26 May 1942), RG 218, NA. The memo is reproduced in Bland, *Marshall Papers,* 3:278–79. Morison, *History of U.S. Naval Operations,* 11:14, asserted that King wrote the key sections of this memo. Dykes's recollections on August 15, as reproduced in Danchev, *Dykes Diaries,* 189, were that it was written "mainly by Smith, who had a great deal of difficulty putting over the idea of TORCH [the new name for GYMNAST] at all." Marshall's later recollections, in Bland, *Marshall Interviews,* 581,

and *Marshall Papers,* 3:278, were that he wrote the proposal and King accepted it "without a quibble." He also asserted in a different interview that he had feared the Russians might be "licked" and "was ready for any action," including a "sacrifice play" that "would keep the Russians in the war." Marshall interview with Matthews et al., July 25, 1949, MHI.

23. Quoted in Thorne, *Allies of a Kind,* 136.

24. Min., CCS 32d mtg., July 24, 1942, CCS 334 (26 May 1942), RG 218, NA; Butler, *Grand Strategy,* vol. 3, pt. 2, 635–36, 684–85; Pogue, *Marshall,* 2:347.

25. COS to JSM, tel., Aug. 13, 1942, WDCSA BOLERO, RG 165, NA.

26. The message was sent through the British Foreign Office and Washington embassy to circumvent Dill, Marshall, and King, with the secrecy involved linked to the rift between FDR and his military advisers. "I am personally bound to Hopkins for the secrecy and privacy of this telegram," Churchill informed Foreign Minister Anthony Eden, "which has been sent largely at my desire. It is most important that Field-Marshal Dill should not be informed on account of his exceptionally close relations with General Marshall. The President was vexed that Marshall told Dill before this visit the views of the American Chiefs of Staff, with which he, the President, did not agree. We must be very careful not to make bad blood between our American friends." See Danchev, *Very Special Relationship,* 68.

27. Sherwood, *Roosevelt and Hopkins,* 611–12; Howard, *Grand Strategy,* 207; Stimson diary, July 25, 1942, YUL; CM-OUT 7303, McNarney to Marshall, July 25, 1942, and Smith to JCS, "Notes on Conference Held at White House at 8:30 P.M., July 30, 1942," memo, Aug. 1, 1942, both in OPD Exec. 5, item 1, tab 14, RG 165, NA; Matloff and Snell, *Strategic Planning,* 282–84; Danchev, *Dykes Diaries,* 183.

28. Danchev, *Dykes Diaries,* 185–86.

29. Kennedy, *Business of War,* 274.

30. Danchev, *Dykes Diaries,* 196, 199.

31. Ibid., 187–88; Bland, *Marshall Papers,* 3:301–4.

32. Kimball, *Churchill and Roosevelt,* 1:591–92; Chandler, *Eisenhower Papers,* 1:433–99; Howard, *Grand Strategy,* 111–28; Matloff and Snell, *Strategic Planning,* 285–93. See also Sainsbury, *Churchill and Roosevelt,* 180–81.

33. Lowenthal, *Leadership and Indecision,* 2:965.

34. Min., JCS 28th mtg., Aug. 11, 1942, CCS 334 JCS (mtgs. 21–40), RG 218, NA. See also min., JCS 26th and 30th mtgs., July 28 and Aug. 25, 1942, ibid.; Leahy diary, July 20, Sept. 20, and Oct. 2, 1942, Oct. 12, 1943, LOC; and Morison, *History of U.S. Naval Operations,* 9:5. Leahy also believed a separate Russo-German peace remained a constant danger that would make victory in Europe impossible; see his diary, July 23, 1943, and below, Chap. 7.

35. Min., JCS 28th mtg., Aug. 11, 1942, CCS 334 JCS (mtgs. 21–40), RG 218, NA.

36. Bland, *Marshall Papers,* 3:318–19.

37. Memo by Arnold for Record, Aug. 11, 1942, Arnold Papers, box 3, Misc. Corres., Aug.–Dec. 1942 Folder, LOC. See also Arnold to Spaatz, Sept. 3, 1942, box 38, SOF, 1941–45, Corres.-commanders Folder, LOC; JCS 97 series, "Detailed Deployment of U.S. Air Forces in the Pacific Theater," CCS 381 (6-24-42), sec. 1, RG 218, NA; min., JCS 32d, 36th, and 39th mtgs., Sept. 8, Oct. 6, and Oct. 27, 1942, CCS 334 JCS (23 June 1942), RG 218, NA; and Jacobs, "Strategic Bombing," 135.

38. Bland, *Marshall Papers,* 3:284, 330. Leahy later seconded part of Marshall's interpretation by stating that the "main purpose" of the air section in CCS 94 had been "to completely eliminate combined discussions regarding the use of those planes." See min., JCS 36th mtg., Oct. 6, 1942, CCS 334 JCS (mtgs. 21–40) (6-23-42), RG 218, NA. The army chief also reasserted this view of CCS 94 in his Feb. 11, 1949, oral history interview (Oral History Collection, Marshall Folder, GCMRL), but in his July 25, 1949, interview (MHI) he stated that he had hoped to use the Pa-

cific allotments "as a club" against British strategic proposals, only to find that the navy used it against him!

39. Bland, *Marshall Papers,* 3 : 288.

40. JPS 43, "Strategic Policy of the United Nations and the United States on the Collapse of Russia," Aug. 7–8, 1942, and min., JPS 29th mtg., Aug. 19, 1942, CCS 381 (3-5-42) (1), RG 218, NA. See also Nevins, "Course of Action Open to the United States in the Event the Prospective 1942 German Offensive Forces Russia to Capitulate," memo, Apr. 1942, and unsigned memo to Nevins, Apr. 25, 1942, Wedemeyer Papers, box 76, folder 2, HI. The Intelligence Division even considered the possibility of an armistice with Germany should Russia collapse and forwarded its assessment to the State Dept. See S. Doc. 22, "Conditions under Which an Armistice Might Be Negotiated between the United Nations and the European Powers," June 11, 1942, Notter Papers, box 76, RG 59, NA.

41. Min., JCS 30th mtg., Aug. 25, 1942, CCS 334 JCS (mtgs. 21–46), RG 218, NA; Arnold to JCS, "Air War Plan," memo, Aug. 24, 1942, SPD, ser. 5, box 99, folder A16-3 (5) War Plans, NH.

42. JPS 43/2, "Strategic Policy of the United Nations and the United States on the Collapse of Russia," Sept. 1, 1942, modified by JPS and forwarded to JCS on Sept. 4, 1942, as JCS 85/1, same title, CCS 381 (3-5-42), RG 218, NA; JIC 25/3, "German Objectives and Russian Capablities in the Caucasus," Sept. 2, 1942, in United States, Joint Chiefs of Staff, *Records of the Joint Chiefs of Staff* [hereafter *Records of the JCS*], reel 2.

43. Danchev, *Dykes Diaries,* 191–94, 198; Arnold to Hopkins, "Plans for Operations against the Enemy," Sept. 3, 1942, Hopkins Papers, box 128, TORCH Folders, FDRL.

44. Min., JCS 32d mtg., Sept. 8, 1942, CCS 334 JCS (mtgs. 21–40), RG 218, NA.

45. Min., JCS 32d and 33d mtgs., Sept. 8 and 15, 1942, CCS 334 JCS (mtgs. 21–40), RG 218, NA; JCS 97 series, "Detailed Deployment of U.S. Air Forces in the Pacific Theater," Sept. 5, 1942, CCS 381 (6-24-42), sec. 1, RG 218, NA; Danchev, *Dykes Diaries,* 203–6; min., CCS 40th mtg., Sept. 18, 1942, CCS 381 CCS (5-26-42) (mtgs. 21–45), RG 218, NA; Leighton and Coakley, *Global Logistics and Strategy,* 2 : 17–19.

46. Leahy diary, Sept. 20, Oct. 1 and Oct. 2, 1942, LOC. The issue of the fifteen air groups was finally compromised in late October by making them part of a strategic reserve to be used as needs arose. See JCS 97/5 in CCS 381 (6-24-42), sec. 1; min., JCS 39th mtg., Oct. 27, 1942, CCS 334 JCS (mtgs. 21–40) (6-23-42), RG 218, NA; Jacobs, "Strategic Bombing," 135–36; and Craven and Cate, *Army Air Forces in World War II,* 4 : 44–52.

47. Bland, *Marshall Papers,* 3 : 386–87, 401–2, 409–10; Roosevelt to King, Marshall, Arnold, and Leahy, Oct. 24, 1942, Arnold Papers, box 3, Misc. Corres. Aug.–Dec. 1942 Folder, LOC; Romanus and Sunderland, *Stilwell's Mission to China,* 177–81, 222–25; Leighton and Coakley, *Global Logistics and Strategy,* 2 : 17–19.

48. Danchev, *Dykes Diaries,* 212, 217, 221–22.

49. Handy to CofS, "American-British Strategy," memo, Nov. 8, 1942, WDCSA 381, RG 165, NA.

50. Min., JSSC 2d mtg., Nov. 20, 1942, in JCS 1946–47 series, CCS 334 JSSC (11-16-42), RG 218, NA. For further information on this important committee, see Chap. 6.

51. "Notes Taken at Meeting Held in Executive Offices of the President," Nov. 25, 1942, CCS 334 JCS (11-10-42), RG 218, NA; Kimball, *Churchill and Roosevelt,* 2 : 38–42. See also Smith to Marshall, tel., Nov. 26, 1942, WDCSA 381, RG 165, NA. On January 1, 1943, the Pacific theater contained 464,000 troops, 200,000 more than planned, while North Africa and the United Kingdom combined had only 378,000 troops, 57,000 less than planned. See Leighton and Coakley, *Global Logistics and Strategy,* 1 : 662. See also Dallek, *Roosevelt and American Foreign Policy,* 354, 367, and Thorne, *Allies of a Kind,* 163. Calvocoressi, Wint, and Pritchard, *Total War,* 2 : 1079, conclude that the Pacific-first deployment occurred "through the sympathetic connivance of the Chiefs of Staff in Washington."

52. Howard, *Grand Strategy*, 225–36; min., JCS mtg. with Pres., Dec. 10, 1942, CCS 334 JCS (11-10-42) (mtgs. 41–50), RG 218, NA.

53. Min., JPS 42d mtg., Oct. 21, 1942, CCS 334 Jt. Staff Planners (10-14-42), RG 218, NA; JCS 152, Arnold to JCS, "Strategic Policy for 1943," memo, Nov. 16, 1942, CCS 381 (11-16-42), RG 218, NA; and Jacobs, "Strategic Bombing," 135–37.

54. Pogue, *Marshall*, 3:12–15; min., JCS mtg. with Pres., Dec. 10, 1942, CCS 334 JCS (11-10-42) (mtgs. 41–50), RG 218, NA; Ben-Moshe, *Churchill*, 204. See also Maurice Matloff, "The 90 Division Gamble," in Greenfield, *Command Decisions*, 366–68, and Leighton, "American Arsenal Policy," 242–49.

55. Matloff and Snell, *Strategic Planning*, 372–73.

56. Quote from Larrabee, *Commander in Chief*, 187. Matloff and Snell, *Strategic Planning*, 365–70; Stoler, *Politics of the Second Front*, 70.

57. Min., JCS 46th mtg., Dec. 12, 1942, and JCS 167, "Basic Strategic Concept for 1943," Dec. 11, 1942, CCS 381 (27 Aug. 1942), sec. 1, RG 218, NA.

58. JCS 167/1 in CCS 381 (27 Aug. 1942), sec. 1, RG 218, NA, and in *FRUS: Washington and Casablanca*, 735–38.

59. Leighton and Coakley, *Global Logistics and Strategy*, 1:665.

60. *FRUS: Washington and Casablanca*, 738–41. See also 741–52.

61. Lowenthal, *Leadership and Indecision*, 2:1031.

62. JCS 167/3, and min., JCS 49th mtg., Jan. 5, 1943, CCS 334 (11-10-42), RG 218, NA; OPD notes on JPS 53d mtg., Jan. 6, 1943, ABC 381 Japan (8-27-43), sec. 1, RG 165, NA.

63. *FRUS: Washington and Casablanca*, 509–11. For the Casablanca Conf. see Chap. 6.

Chapter Six

1. The British did agree to Pacific and Burma offensives, but only on the condition that they be subject to CCS limitation—and thus British veto—so as not to "prejudice the capacity of the United Nations to take advantage of any favorable opportunity that may present itself for the decisive defeat of Germany in 1943" (*FRUS: Washington and Casablanca*, 761). The CCS also agreed to focus their 1943 efforts on the U-boat war in the Atlantic, continued aid to Russia, and a combined bomber offensive against Germany.

2. Richardson, *From Churchill's Secret Circle*, 165; Wedemeyer to Handy, Jan. 22, 1943, OPD Exec. 3, item 1a, paper 5, RG 165, NA, partially reprinted in Matloff, *Strategic Planning*, 106–7. See also ibid., 18–42, and Pogue, *Marshall*, 3:20–37.

3. Wedemeyer to Handy, Jan. 22, 1943; Wedemeyer to DCofS, "Report of Mission Headed by General Devers," memo, Apr. 28, 1943, OPD 381 Security (sec. 3), 118, RG 165, NA, quoted in Matloff, *Strategic Planning*, 110. See also Wedemeyer to Marshall, memo, June 8, 1943, OPD Exec. 8, book 10, paper 68, RG 165, NA, and Wedemeyer, *Wedemeyer Reports!*, 188–92.

4. Rpt. by Special Subcomm., Cols. W. W. Bessell and R. C. Lindsay, "Conduct of the War," July 25, 1943, OPD 381 Security (sec. 7B), 218, RG 165, NA.

5. See, for ex., Richardson, *From Chuchill's Secret Circle*, 156–57, and Danchev, *Dykes Diaries*.

6. Cline, *Washington Command Post*, 166, 204; author's interview with Wedemeyer, Oct. 1969, Wedmeyer Papers, HI.

7. Min., JCS 38th and 40th mtgs., Oct. 20 and Nov. 3, 1942, CCS 334 JCS; JCS 149/D, Nov. 7, 1942; and JCS 202/12/D, May 10, 1943, CCS 334 JSSC (11-7-42), sec. 1, RG 218, NA.

8. Bland, *Marshall Papers*, 3:423–24. Marshall received copies of Roosevelt-Churchill telegrams not from the White House but from Dill, who received them from London; see Bland, *Marshall Interviews*, 413–14.

9. JPS 97 in JCS 202, "A Proposed National War Planning System," Dec. 19, 1942, CCS 381 (12-19-42), RG 218, NA; Davis, "History of the Joint Chiefs of Staff," 2:379–80.

10. Wedemeyer to CofS, "Reconstitution of Supporting Planning Agencies of the Joint Chiefs of Staff," memo, Jan. 7, 1943, annex C to JCS 202, "War Planning Agencies," CCS 300 (1-8-43), sec. 1, RG 218, NA.

11. Roosevelt's March–April overriding of military objections to helping Britain in its import crisis may have provided the armed forces with additional reinforcement; see Kevin Smith, *Conflict over Convoys*, 174–76.

12. JCS 202, "War Planning Agencies," CCS 300 (1-8-43), sec. 1, RG 218, NA; JCS 202/12/D, May 10, 1943, CCS 334 JSSC (11-7-42), sec. 1, RG 218, NA (quotations); and Davis, "History of the Joint Chiefs of Staff," 2:395, 460. The JCS approved the JSSC charter on June 15, 1943.

13. Notter, *Postwar Foreign Policy Preparation*, 76, 125. See also below, Chap. 8.

14. See Chap. 8.

15. JPS 191, "Joint War Planning Agencies," May 26, 1943, CCS 300 (1-8-43), sec. 3, RG 218, NA. See also Wedemeyer to CofS, June 8, 1943, OPD Exec. 8, book 10, item 68, RG 165, NA, and Cline, *Washington Command Post*, 317–20.

16. Castle diary, May 5, 1942, Houghton Library, Harvard University, courtesy of Prof. J. Garry Clifford; Vittrup to Smith, June 17, 1943, CCS 381 (6-1-42), RG 218, NA.

17. See below, Chaps. 7 and 8, and Pogue, *Marshall*, 3:455–56.

18. McCrea to Leahy, memo, Dec. 28, 1942, Roosevelt Papers, MRF, box 162, A4-2, Air Routes Folder, FDRL. See also Chap. 8.

19. JCS 202/2 and 202/7, "War Planning Agencies," Mar. 25 and Apr. 24, 1943 (quotation), CCS 300 (1-8-43), sec. 3, RG 218, NA.

20. JCS 183/5, "Post-War Military Problems with Particular Reference to Air Bases," CCS 360 (2-9-42), sec. 1, RG 218, NA.

21. JCS 202/2 and 202/7, cited in n. 19 above; Bessell and Lindsay, "Conduct of the War," cited above in n. 4.

22. Notter to Pasvolsky, memo, Apr. 8, 1943, RG 59, Notter Papers, box 76, RG 59, NA.

23. Deane next tried a smaller notebook that he hoped FDR would not notice, but it was also "so small that he couldn't use it" (Bland, *Marshall Interviews*, 623; Pogue, "Wartime Chiefs," 73).

The JCS charter was numbered JCS 202/24/D and dated June 15, 1943. Roosevelt disapproved it in a July 16, 1943, letter in JCS 415, CCS 300 (1-25-42), sec. 2, RG 218, NA.

24. Min., JCS 65th, 69th, 72d, and 79th mtgs., Mar. 9, 23, Apr. 2, May 10, 1943, CCS 334 JCS (3-29-43) (mtgs. 71–86), RG 218, NA.

25. Schnabel, *History of the Joint Chiefs of Staff*, 1:4; Villa, "U.S. Army," 69. Other historians have ignored the committee, perhaps because it did not keep minutes or because of difficulties involved in tracing its papers through the JCS committee structure. May, "Writing Contemporary International History," 111, incorrectly dismisses those papers as "evidence only of the crochets of some elderly officers whom the chiefs of staff had been unable to retire but also unable to use."

26. Quote on Fairchild from Davis, "History of the Joint Chiefs of Staff," 2:375. Biographical data are from Willson Biog. File, NH, and Fairchild and Embick Biog. Files, CMH.

Officers of this caliber should have been given field commands during wartime, but Embick had been retired and recalled and was presently serving on the Inter-American Defense Board. The other two were in poor health: Fairchild had recently been hospitalized, and Willson's physical exam in October had revealed heart problems that dictated removal from strenuous duty. According to Buell, *Master of Seapower*, 176–77, King had wanted to move Willson out of Washington and into the Pacific because their work habits and mental sets were incompatible (Willson "wanted to deliberate on problems for which King wanted quick answers"). The heart problem precluded this movement, but at that moment the JSSC was being formed.

27. One of these resulted from a JCS directive, based on recommendations from the JPS and JWPC, ordering "as a matter of urgency" before the May strategic conference in Washington (TRIDENT) a study on "current British policy and strategy in its relationship to that of the United States." Months before, however, the JSSC had begun to study this issue on its own initiative, and it continued to do so after it had fulfilled the JCS request. JWPC 3 and JPS memo, "Agenda for Next United Nations Conference," Apr. 24–26, 1943, CCS 381 (4-24-43), sec. 1, pt. 1, RG 218, NA; supp. min., JCS 76th mtg., Apr. 27, 1943, CCS 334 (3-29-43), RG 218, NA. See also above, Chap. 5.

28. Quotations are from JCS-ordered study, JCS 283 and 283/1, May 3 and 8, 1943, "Current British Policy and Strategy in Relationship to That of the United States," CCS 381 (4-24-43), sec. 3, RG 218, NA. The other, self-initiated JSSC studies in NA on which the following analysis draws are Embick and Fairchild to Marshall, memo, Jan. 4, 1943, ABC 381 (9-25-41), sec. 7, RG 165; JCS 167/5, "Strategic Concept for 1943," Jan. 10, 1943, CCS 381 (8-27-42), sec. 1, RG 218; JSSC, "Probable Russian Reaction to Anglo-American Operations in the Aegean," memo, May 5, 1943, CCS 381 (5-5-43), RG 218; JCS 286–286/1, "Recommended Line of Action at Coming Conference," May 6–8, 1943, CCS 381 (4-24-43), sec. 3, RG 218; JCS 422/1, "Quadrant," July 25, 1943, ABC 337 (25 May 43), RG 165; and JCS 443 rev., "Quadrant and European Strategy," Aug. 6, 1943, CCS 381 (5-23-43), sec. 1, RG 218, all in NA. See also Embick's comments in min., JCS 80th mtg., May 12, 1943, CCS 334 JCS (3-29-43), RG 218, NA.

29. Embick and Fairchild to Marshall, memo, Jan. 4, 1943, ABC 381 (9-25-41), sec. 7, RG 165, NA; JCS 283/1, "Current British Policy and Strategy in Relationship to That of the United States," May 8, 1943, CCS 381 (4-24-43), sec. 3, RG 218, NA; and JCS 443 rev., "Quadrant and European Strategy," Aug. 6, 1943, CCS 381 (5-23-43), sec. 1, RG 218, NA.

30. Embick and Fairchild to Marshall, memo, Jan. 4, 1943, ABC 381 (9-25-41), sec. 7, RG 165, NA; emphasis in original.

31. JSSC, "Probable Russian Reaction to Anglo-American Operations in the Aegean," memo, May 5, 1943, CCS 381 (5-5-43), RG 218, NA.

32. JCS 167/3, "Basic Strategic Concept for 1943," Jan. 5, 1943, CCS 381 (8-27-42), sec. 1, RG 218, NA.

33. JCS 506, "Instructions concerning Duty as Military Observer at American-British-Soviet Conference," CCS 337 (9-12-43), sec. 1, RG 218, NA. See also below, Chap. 7 on this document.

34. Stimson and Bundy, *On Active Service,* 429–30; Thorne, *Allies of a Kind,* 156–75, 719.

35. Perry, *"Dear Bart,"* 146, 170 (see also *FRUS: Washington and Casablanca,* 590); JCS memo no. 43, in Schaller, *U.S. Crusade in China,* 120; CIC Memo for Information no. 111, "Contribution of China to Allied Strategy," July 5, 1943, ABC 381 Japan (25 June 43), RG 165, NA; Brower, "Sophisticated Strategists," 59–61, 101.

36. This argument appears in virtually all the documents cited above. The "fundamental difference" appears in JCS 283, "Current British Policy and Strategy."

37. Wedemeyer to Marshall, "British Policies as Indicated by Remarks of Prime Minister," undated memo; "Agreements with Respect to Future Operations," unsigned memo, Aug. 8, 1943; and "Strategic Considerations," and "Notes on Strategic Policy—U.S. vs. U.K.," unsigned memos, undated, all in ABC 381 (9-25-41), sec. 7, RG 165, NA. See also SS rpt., "Probable British Proposals for Further Operations in 1943 and 1944 in the European-African Theaters," Apr. 14, 1943, and SS 90, "Conduct of the War in Europe," Aug. 4, 1943, both in ABC 381 SS (7 Jan. 43), tabs 74 and 90, RG 165, NA; unsigned, undated paper, "U.S.-British Strategy," in OPD Exec. 10, item 69, RG 165, NA; and Wedemeyer to CofS, "Observer's Report," memo, app. A, Aug. 24, 1943, Wedemeyer Papers, box 74, folder 3, HI.

38. Quotations are from "Strategic Considerations," ABC 381 (9-25-41), sec. 7, and SS rpt., "Probable British Proposals . . . ," Apr. 14, 1943, ABC 381 SS (7 Jan. 43), tab 74, RG 165, NA.

39. Quotations are from "U.S.-British Strategy," OPD Exec. 10, item 69, RG 165, NA.

40. SS rpt., "Probable British Proposals . . . ," Apr. 14, 1943, ABC 381 SS (7 Jan. 43), tab 74, RG 165, NA.

41. Quotations are from "U.S.-British Strategy," OPD Exec. 10, item 69, RG 165, NA. On China, see also min., JCS 83d mtg. and CPS mtg., May 17, 1943, CCS 381 (3-23-42), pt. 4, RG 218, NA. For the Anglo-American controversies over postwar commercial air transport, see Dobson, *Peaceful Air Warfare*, 125–72.

42. JWPC 14, "Conduct of the War, 1943–1944," May 7, 1943, CCS 381 (4-24-43), sec. 1, pt. 1, RG 218, NA.

43. Ibid.

44. Ibid. See also *FRUS: Washington and Quebec*, 432–34.

45. Cline, *Washington Command Post*, 239–42.

46. Wedemeyer to CofS, "Observer's Report," memo, app. A, Wedemeyer Papers, box 64, folder 3, HI; Caraway Oral History, MHI.

47. Min., JCS 78th mtg., May 8, 1943, CCS 334 (3-29-43), RG 218, NA; Leahy diary, May 2, 7, and 27, Oct. 7, 1943, LOC; Embick to Marshall, memo, May 5, 1943, Marshall Papers, POF, box 56, folder 1, GCMRL. Marshall also sent the one-page Dardanelles memo to Stimson, who relayed its warnings to FDR.

48. Lowenthal, *Leadership and Indecision*, 2:1010–11; Buell, *Master of Seapower*, 272; Ingles to Marshall, May 6, 1943, OPD Exec. 3, item 1c, paper 4, RG 165, NA; and Smart to Arnold, memo, Aug. 16, 1943, Arnold Papers, Diary, Aug. 16–31, 1943 Folder, and Arnold, "Observation Memorandum as of May 1, 1943," Arnold Papers, box 3, Misc. Corres., 1943, LOC.

49. OPD, "Notes on JPS 89th Meeting," Aug. 4, 1943, ABC 337 (25 May 43), RG 165, NA; Chandler, *Eisenhower Papers*, 2:927–29; Bland, *Marshall Papers*, 3:355, 560–61, 581–82; Danchev, *Dykes Diaries*, 206; Wedemeyer, *Wedemeyer Reports!*, 164–65.

50. Stimson diary, May 3 and 11, 1943, YUL; Maclean, *Davies*, 85.

51. Embick and Fairchild to Marshall, memo, Jan. 4, 1943, ABC 381 (9-25-41), Sec. VII, RG 165, NA; Leahy diary, Dec. 9, 1942, and May 7, 1943, LOC.

52. JCS 283, "Current British Policy and Strategy in Relationship to That of the United States," May 3, 1943, CCS 381 (4-24-43), sec. 3, RG 218, NA; Embick to European Div. of State Dept., "Current British Policy and Strategy in Relationship to That of the United States," memo, with handwritten note, "advised orally," Apr. 28, 1943, 711.41/596, RG 59, NA; Sbrega, *Anglo-American Relations and Colonialism*, 16–17.

53. Berle's Anglophobia was far from exceptional. Soon after Pearl Harbor Leo Pasvolsky had warned of possible economic warfare between the two nations. Breckinridge Long believed British policy was "to suck the United States dry"; reach a postwar spheres-of-influence accord with the Soviets that would give London, Iraq, Iran, India, and the Mediterranean in return for Eastern Europe; and then "strangle [the United States] commercially." In early 1943 Welles warned Leahy of the need to maintain control over territory occupied by U.S. troops so as not to be "at a disadvantage in peace negotiations," while another dept. official asserted that Britain wanted U.S. participation in world affairs only "to the extent that we will 'help' either as 'Santa Claus' or in support of British policies and interests. They fear us more than the Soviets because Russia is only a land power and empire and thus has less to fear from her." Pasvolsky to Hull, memo, Dec. 12, 1941, Hull Papers, box 82, Subject File, folder 366, Postwar Planning, LOC; Long diary, Jan. 29, 1942, as quoted in Thorne, *Allies of a Kind*, 99 (see also 146–48); Leahy diary, Feb. 10, 1943, LOC; Achilles to Hull, Welles, and Atherton, memo, Apr. 3, 1943, 740.0011 EW 1939/29067, RG 59, NA. See also Sbrega, *Anglo-American Relations and Colonialism*, 25–26, 82.

54. Davies, memo, Nov. 15, 1943, in OSS E190, box 573, folder 355, RG 226, NA, reproduced in Am. Comm. on History of the Second World War, *Newsletter*, no. 41 (Spring 1989): 30–39. See also Sbrega, *Anglo-American Relations and Colonialism*, 78, 86. For all their saltiness, the excerpts from Stilwell's diaries published in White, *Stilwell Papers*, are mild compared with the original in HI. See, for ex., Danchev, *Very Special Relationship*, 73.

55. Gardiner to Grew, Mar. 12, 1943, Leahy Papers, Add to Diary, vol. 8, LOC. Former FDRL director William Emerson informed me by letter, Apr. 14, 1977, in reply to my queries, that Grew forwarded a copy of the letter to FDR on April 8, along with the comment, "Sumner Welles and I both feel that you will wish to read the enclosed." In an April 26 memo to his aide Gen. Edwin M. Watson, FDR referred to the letter and to setting up a meeting with Grew; that meeting occurred on June 2, 1943. Gardiner's letter was by no means limited to this topic and also included important comments about the Soviet Union that Leahy circled on his copy. See below, Chap. 7; Thorne, *Allies of a Kind*, 293; and Leahy diary, Feb. 10, 1943, LOC.

56. Stimson and Hull to Roosevelt, Apr. 13, 1943, OPD Exec. 3, item 1a, paper 86, RG 165, NA; Stimson Notes after Cabinet Mtg., June 4, 1943, WDCSA 381 War Plans, folder 2, RG 165, NA; Stimson diary, June 4–28, 1943, YUL; Stoff, *Oil, War, and American Security*, 73–80; Rubin, *Great Powers in the Middle East*, 11–14; CCS 463.7 (5-31-43), RG 218, NA; FRUS, 1943, 4:921–30.

57. Thorne, *Allies of a Kind*, 209. See also Anderson, *United States, Great Britain, and the Cold War*, 4–5.

58. D. C. Watt, "U.S. Globalism: The End of the Concert of Europe," in Kimball, *America Unbound*, 48.

59. See Matloff, *Strategic Planning*, 164–67.

60. See supp. min., JCS 79th mtg., May 10, 1943, CCS 334 (3-29-43) JCS, RG 218, NA; JCS 386, "Strategy in the Pacific," June 28, 1943, ABC 384 Pacific (28 June 1943), RG 165, NA; Brower, "Sophisicated Strategists," chap. 3, 82–85, 90–95; and Love, "Fighting a Global War," 278–79. Original plans for the defeat of Japan had extended operations into 1947 and 1948; these revised plans called for ending the war by 1946.

61. See JCS 167, "Basic Strategic Concept for 1943," Dec. 11, 1942, CCS 381 (8-27-42), sec. 1, RG 218, NA; JWPC 14 in JCS 290, "Conduct of the War, 1943–1944," May 7, 1943, CCS 381 (4-24-43), sec. 1, pt. 1, RG 218, NA; JCS 243/3, "Survey of the Present Strategic Situation," Apr. 13, 1943, CCS 381 (8-27-42), RG 218, NA; JCS 286, 286/1, "Recommended Line of Action at Coming Conference," May 6 and 8, 1943, CCS 381 (4-24-43), sec. 3, RG 218, NA; JCS 271, "Operations Subsequent to 'Husky,'" ABC 384 Post-Husky (14 May 43), RG 165, NA; JCS 324, "Agreed Essentials on the Conduct of the War," May 18, 1943, ABC 384 (18 Jan. 43), RG 165, NA; JCS 422/1, "Quadrant," July 25, 1943, ABC 337 (25 May 43), RG 165, NA; JCS 443 rev., "Quadrant and European Strategy," Aug. 6, 1943, CCS 381 (5-23-43), sec. 1, RG 218, NA; "Notes re: Strategic Policy-U.S. vs. U.K.," ABC 381 (9-25-41), sec. 7, RG 165, NA; JCS 386, "Strategy in the Pacific," June 28, 1943, ABC 384 Pacific (28 June 1943), RG 165, NA; "Course of Action for the United States in the Event Russia and Germany Effect a Compromise Peace in July and August, 1943," undated, and "Effect on Overall Strategy of United Nations of Events on Russo-German Front," Nov. 7, 1943, ABC 381 SS (7 Jan. 43), tabs. 111, 131, and 131/1, RG 165, NA; FRUS: Washington and Quebec, 474.

62. Wedemeyer to DCofS, "Report of Mission Headed by General Devers," memo, Apr. 28, 1943, OPD 381 Security (sec. 3), 118, RG 165, NA. Marshall concurred, informing a Senate subcommittee on May 10 "that the thought of political matters was necessarily always on the minds of the Chiefs of Staff," that the COS were "tightly bound" with the War Cabinet and Churchill, that the JCS were "not naive regarding such united front methods," and that they were "now trying to get organized to be in a proper position to meet the British." Min., JCS 79th mtg., May 10, 1943, CCS 334 JCS (3-29-43) (mtgs. 71–86), RG 218, NA; Matloff, *Strategic Planning*, 110–11. See also Bland, *Marshall Papers*, 4:50–52.

63. Leahy was to deal with all organizational, political, and diplomatic matters and to act as JCS leader and representative of the president. Marshall's area was to be European strategy, King's the Pacific and its relation to European strategy, and Arnold's the bomber offensive.

64. Quotation is from JSSC for JCS, "Procedure of Chiefs of Staff at Conference," memo, Aug. 9, 1943, CCS 381 (10-17-43), sec. B, RG 218, NA. See also in RG 218, NA, JCS 283/1, "Current British Policy . . . ," May 8, 1943, CCS 381 (4-24-43), sec. 3; JWPC 30/11, "Thoughts for Quadrant," Aug. 4, 1943, CCS 381 (5-25-43); JPS 189, "Preparations for the Next U.S.-British Staff Conference," May 25, 1943, CCS 381 (5-25-43), sec. 1; and min., JCS 76th, 78–80th, and 101–103rd mtgs., Apr. 27, May 8, 10, and 12, and Aug. 7–10, 1943, CCS 334 JCS (3-24-43) and (8-7-43). See also the following in ABC 337 (25 May 43), RG 165, NA: JCS 422/1, "Quadrant," July 25, 1943; JPS 238, "Exploratory Studies with Respect to Operations in the Mediterranean," Aug. 2, 1943; JWPC 85, "Lessons from Quadrant," Sept. 2, 1943; OPD, "Notes on JPS 89th mtg.," Aug. 4, 1943; and Lincoln to Roberts, "Working Staff to Accompany Planners to the Next Combined Conference," memo, June 15, 1943. For Leahy and Marshall Pacific/Asia-first threats, see *FRUS: Washington and Quebec*, 44, 54, 93, 113, 184–85, and 867–68. Marshall had previously verbalized these threats and portions of the new JCS position to the British at Casablanca; see Pogue, *Marshall*, 3 : 22–29.

65. Min., JCS 78th mtg., May 8, 1943, CCS 334 (3-29-43); Leahy diary, May 2, 7, 24, and Oct. 7, 1943, LOC; Todd to ACofS, OPD, "Special JCS Meeting of July 26, 1943," memo, OPD Exec. 5, item 11, paper 2, RG 165, NA; JWPC 85, "Lessons from Quadrant" Sept. 2, 1943, ABC 337 (25 May 43), RG 165, NA; handwritten notes on Handy memo, "Conduct of the War in Europe," Aug. 8, 1943, OPD 381, sec. 7A, pt. 2, Security Case 217, RG 165, NA; *FRUS: Washington and Quebec*, 432–34, 467–72. For Marshall's interest in the British secretariat system and efforts to get this information to FDR, see Ismay to Marshall, July 3, 1943, with supporting data, Leahy Papers, ser. 1, box 1, British Folder, NH, and Pogue, "Wartime Chiefs," 73.

66. Stimson diary, May 3, 14, 17, and 19, June 1, Aug. 4, 9, and 10, 1943, YUL; Stimson to Roosevelt, memos, Aug. 4 and 10, 1943, Roosevelt Papers, MRF, box 15, FDRL. Excerpts from some of these are in Stimson and Bundy, *On Active Service*, 435–39, 527, and *FRUS: Washington and Quebec*, 444–52. See also below, Chap. 7.

67. Compare, for ex., Matloff, *Strategic Planning*, 124–25, with Leighton and Coakley, *Global Logistics and Strategy*, 2 : 62, and Leighton, "OVERLORD Revisited." Also compare Leighton with Pogue, "Wartime Chiefs," 79–81, 104–5.

68. See, for ex., Stimson diary, Aug. 10, 1943, YUL; Stimson and Bundy, *On Active Service*, 438–39; *FRUS: Washington and Quebec*, 434–35, 482–83, 498–503; and min., JCS 103d mtg., Aug. 10, 1943, CCS 334 JCS (8-7-43), RG 218, NA. See also below, Chap. 9.

69. See *FRUS: Washington and Quebec* for key docs. and min., and Stoler, *Politics of the Second Front*, 94–95, 112–15, for a summary. Ironically, the result of this JCS victory may have been the further postponement of cross-channel operations. Dunn, *Second Front Now*, 269, argues that such operations were possible in 1943 until September, but "over and over, when faced with the need to concentrate forces for the attack, the decision was a trade-off; the Americans would send more to the Pacific, and the British would get deeper into the Mediterranean, while the cross-Channel attack was postponed because of a lack of resources." Indeed, at the end of 1943 more U.S. forces were still deployed against Japan than against Germany; see Matloff, *Strategic Planning*, 397–99.

70. Lewis, *Changing Direction*, 32–34, 40–41.

71. Slessor, *Central Blue*, 358. The most detailed and comprehensive analyses of British strategy and policy are Howard's *Mediterranean Strategy*, esp. 1–18; *Studies in War and Peace*, 122–26; and *Grand Strategy*, 4. See also Ben-Moshe, *Churchill*, 258–99, and Deakin, "Myth of an Allied Landing," 93–116.

72. *FRUS*, 1943, China, 878–80; Thorne, *Allies of a Kind*, 339.

73. Armstrong, SS, OPD, to Chief, S&P, "Report on Visit to Middle East," memo, Jan. 12, 1943, ABC 381 Middle East (3-20-42), sec. 1-A, RG 165, NA.

74. Pogue, "Wartime Chiefs," 84, concludes that the JCS abandoned their earlier balance-of-power comments partially because they never saw the United States as the active balancer and merely hoped to return to the *status quo antebellum*. By 1943, however, it was clear to the Joint Chiefs and their planners that such a return was not possible. See Chaps. 7 and 8.

Chapter Seven

1. Ellis, *Brute Force*, 128–30; Adelman, *Prelude to the Cold War*, 128.

2. See above, Chaps. 3, 4, and 5.

3. See above, Chap. 6, and docs. in Chap. 6, nn. 28–31.

4. Lee, ACofS, G-2, to Marshall, "Possibility of a Negotiated Russo-German Settlement," memo, Feb. 12, 1942, Hopkins Papers, box 105, Russia Folder, FDRL; War Dept. Russian Combat Estimate as of Mar. 1942, in *Records of the JCS*, reel 1; CCS Russian Combat Estimate, Apr. 1, 1942, CCS 350.05 USSR (4-1-42), RG 218, NA.

5. CIC 30, "Russian Intentions," June 30, 1943, ABC 381 Japan (25 June 43), and JIC 129 rev., "U.S.S.R.-Situation, Capabilities, and Intentions," Aug. 20, 1943, ABC 336 Russia (22 Aug. 43), sec. 1A, both in RG 165, NA.

6. Burns to Hopkins, "Importance of Soviet Relationships and Suggestions for Improving Them," memo, Dec. 1, 1942, Hopkins Papers, box 217, Russia Folder, FDRL, reprinted in Sherwood, *Roosevelt and Hopkins*, 641–43.

7. Sherwood, *Roosevelt and Hopkins*, 748–49; emphasis in original. The full memo is in *FRUS: Washington and Quebec*, 624–27.

8. *FRUS: Washington and Casablanca*, 505–6.

9. Gannon, *Cardinal Spellman Story*, 222–24. See also Kimball, *Juggler*, 90; Harriman, *Special Envoy*, 213–30; and MacLean, "Davies," 85–88.

10. Burns's handwritten notes of Jan. 2, 1943, with additional comment, "please file especially carefully," Records of President's Soviet Protocol Committee, 1942–45, box 3, sec. 4, FDRL.

11. The JSSC further explained why this was so, as discussed in Chap. 6.

12. JCS 506, "Instructions concerning Duty as Military Observer at American-British-Soviet Conference," Sept. 18, 1943, CCS 337 (9-12-43), sec. 1, RG 218, NA.

13. Min., JCS 115th mtg., Sept. 21, 1943, and JCS 506/1, "Instructions concerning Duty as a Military Observer at American-British-Soviet Conference," Oct. 5, 1943, both in CCS 337 (9-12-43), sec. 1, RG 218, NA. On revisions, see n. 14 below. The document is summarized in Matloff, *Strategic Planning*, 292–93.

14. "The Changing Power Position of Great Britain as a Factor in the Defense Problem of the United States," Earle Papers, box 32, National Security Folder, SGMML; Culbertson to Hull, Sept. 1, 1943, 860.50/2895, DS, RG 59, NA. Culbertson had appointed Earle an "expert consultant" in late 1942. Earle asserted in a March 1945 letter to Embick that he and Sprout had prepared the memo on the basis of 1940 Princeton seminar discussions. See Culbertson to Earle and Earle to Embick, Dec. 2, 1942, and Mar. 29, 1945, Earle Papers, box 14, Culbertson Folder, and box 5, E-3 Folder, SGMML. An incomplete copy of the study is also in the Notter Papers, S-137, box 78, RG 59, NA.

15. "The Changing Power Position of Great Britain as a Factor in the Defense Problem of the United States," Earle Papers, box 32, National Security Folder, SGMML. The title of Earle's copy was changed from "Defense" to "Security."

16. Earle sent him a copy with the 1945 letter cited above in n. 14.

17. See Chap. 1.

18. Embick to Marshall, memos, Oct. 11 and 29, 1943, Marshall Papers, POF, box 56, folder 1, GCMRL.

19. Sir Halford Mackinder, "The Round World and the Winning of the Peace," *Foreign Affairs* (July 1943): 595–605, as reproduced in the 1962 edition of his 1919 *Democratic Ideals and Reality*, 265–78. The 1942 reissue of this book was an important milestone in the World War II–era reemergence and popularity of geopolitical thought.

20. See Chap. 9.

21. JCS 506, "Instructions concerning Duty as a Military Observer at American-British-Soviet Conference," Sept. 18, 1943, CCS 337 (9-12-43), sec. 1, RG 218, NA, and JCS 484/1, "Subversive Efforts in the Balkans," Sept. 5, 1943, ABC 091.411 Balkans (21 Aug. 43), RG 165, NA. See also JCS 436–436/1, "O.S.S. Plan to Detach Bulgaria from the Axis," Aug. 3–19, 1943, with attached min. of JCS 99th mtg., Aug. 3, 1943, JPS 241 ser., and "Notes on JPS 95th Meeting," Aug. 18, 1943, ABC 384 Bulgaria (3 Aug. 43), RG 165, NA, and CCS 092 Bulgaria, RG 218, NA; Boll, "U.S. Plans for a Postwar Pro-Western Bulgaria," 121–22.

22. JCS 549, "Rumanian Cooperation with Anglo-American Forces," Oct. 28, 1943, with attached OPD, "Notes on JCS 121st mtg.," Nov. 2, 1943, ABC 336 Rumania (26 Sept. 43), sec. 1A, RG 165, NA; JCS 555, "Withdrawal from the War of Hungary and Rumania," Oct. 30, 1943, ABC 384 Hungary Rumania (30 Oct. 43), RG 165, NA; JCS 469/1, "Aid to Finland," Sept. 8, 1943, CCS 092 Finland (9-1-43), RG 218, NA; Willson for JSSC to JCS, "Entry of Turkey into the War," memo, Oct. 26, 1943, OPD Exec. 17, item 22, RG 165, NA.

23. Min., JCS 115th mtg., Sept. 21, 1943, and JCS 506/1, "Instructions concerning Duty as a Military Observer at American-British-Soviet Conference," Oct. 5, 1943, CCS 337 (9-12-43), RG 218, NA; min., JCS 121st mtg., Nov. 2, 1943, and JCS 549/1, "Rumanian Cooperation with Anglo-American Forces," Nov. 6, 1943, ABC 336 Rumania (26 Sept. 43), sec. 1A, RG 165, NA.

24. Quotations are from Spykman, *America's Strategy in World Politics*, 447–48, 460, 466. See also MacKinder, "Round World," 273–74, 278.

25. Lippmann, *U.S. Foreign Policy*, 71–77, 109–11, 135, 164.

26. Ibid., 117–18, 137–54.

27. See Chap. 10.

28. David Reynolds, "Power and Superpower," in Kimball, *America Unbound*, 23–25; Steel, *Walter Lippmann*, 406. *Reader's Digest* published the condensed version, and *Ladies Home Journal*, the cartoon strip. See also Gaddis, *Long Peace*, 22–25.

29. Stimson diary, Dec. 18, 1942, and May 11, 1943, YUL.

30. King to Lippmann, July 21, 1943, King Papers, box 13, Lippmann Folder, LOC; Perry, letter to Keats Spead, July 25, 1943.

31. Perry, letter to Keats Speed, July 25, 1943; Buell, *Master of Seapower*, 486; Bland, *Marshall Papers*, 4:18–19; Perry, *"Dear Bart,"* 146, 168, 203–4.

32. Wedemeyer to Handy, memo, Dec. 19, 1943, OPD 381 Russia; Arnold and Handy to Marshall, "Heavy Bombers for Russia," memos, Feb. 26 and Mar. 5, 1943, OPD 452.1 Russia (sec. 1), case 24; OPD Policy Comm., "The Weekly Strategic Resume," Jan. 23, 1943, OPD Policy Comm. (1 Aug. 42), all in RG 165, NA. Some of these documents are quoted in Matloff, *Strategic Planning*, 282. Wedemeyer later claimed that he unofficially brought his concerns about the Soviets to the attention of his superiors as early as 1941 and that these concerns influenced his strategic recommendations. See his *Wedemeyer Reports!*, 140; interview with Wedemeyer, Oct. 17, 1945, OPD Historical Unit File, item 30a, CMH; author's interview with Wedemeyer, Oct. 1969, Wedemeyer Papers, HI.

33. Stimson to Pres., "FACET Organizational Activities in the Radiation Laboratory," memo, Sept. 9, 1943, Roosevelt Papers, MRF, box 171, FDRL. See also CM-IN 14292 from Michela,

Feb. 27, 1943, OPD Exec. 1, item 20, RG 165, NA; min., JCS 63d mtg., Feb. 23, 1943, CCS 334 JCS (1-14-43) (mtgs. 51–70), RG 218, NA; Bradley Smith, *Sharing Secrets with Stalin*, and "Soviet-American Intelligence and Technical Cooperation in World War Two," 12–15; Pogue, *Marshall*, 3:288–90; Bennett, *Roosevelt and the Search for Victory*, 88–90, and "Challengers to Policy," 19–20, 32–35.

34. Min., JCS 52d mtg., Jan. 16, 1943, CCS 334 JCS (1-14-43), RG 218, NA; Sorenson to Arnold, "Reconsideration of Invasion Timing," memo, Aug. 4, 1943, Arnold Papers, Journals, Aug. 1–5, 1943 Folder, LOC.

35. Gardiner to Grew, Mar. 12, 1943, with cover letter, Grew to Leahy, Apr. 8, 1943, Leahy Papers, box 3, Add to Diary, vol. 8, LOC, as cited above, Chap. 6, n. 55; Davies diary, Oct. 2, 1943, Davies Papers, container 14, Chron. File, 1–29 Oct. 1943 Folder, LOC; Thorne, *Allies of a Kind*, 293; Emerson, FDRL, to author, Apr. 14, 1977. The Soviet assessment of Leahy was correct, as a perusal of his wartime diary clearly reveals.

36. See above, Chap. 6, n. 66; Earle to Roosevelt, Oct. 1, 1943, Roosevelt Papers, PSF, box 146, Earle Folder, FDRL.

37. William Bullitt, "How We Won the War," 91–94. The British quote is from Jacob's diary as quoted in Edmonds, *Big Three*, 302–3. See also Bullitt to Roosevelt, memos, Jan. 27, May 12, and Aug. 10, 1943, Roosevelt Papers, PSF, box 1, Bullitt Folder, FDRL, reprinted in part in Orville Bullitt, *For the President*, 573–80, 591–99; and Leahy diary, Mar 4, 1943, and June 10, 1944, LOC. Bullitt was in all likelihood given a copy of Gardiner's letter, for as Bennett notes in *Roosevelt and the Search for Victory*, 82, its analysis and the one contained in Bullitt's May 12, 1943, letter to Roosevelt were "nearly identical."

38. Quotes from S89 Summary Statement of Security Subcomm. Views, and Security Subcomm. min., Sept. 11, 1942, Jan. 15, Feb. 26, Mar. 19, May 20, and July 23, 1943, Notter Papers, box 76, RG 59, NA. See also ibid., Apr. 29, May 20, Oct. 23, Nov. 13, 20, and Dec. 5, 1942, Mar. 12, 24, May 20, June 10, and June 17, 1943. FDR's shift, Davis reported at the Feb. 26, 1943, meeting, was the result of his having "received a thesis concerning what would happen if Russia was not fully cooperative and France and Germany were both disarmed. In this case Europe would be impotent against aggression. It was necessary to have France a strong power as a part of our own security." The "thesis" undoubtedly was Bullitt's, for a few days later FDR asked visiting British foreign secretary Anthony Eden whether he thought there was any validity to the "Bullitt thesis" that the Soviets were "determined to dominate all of Europe." See *FRUS*, 1943, 3:22. See also Dallek, *Roosevelt and American Foreign Policy*, 410–11. For expressions of similar fears by foreign service officers on the subcommittee and by Welles, see DeSantis, *Diplomacy of Silence*, 94–95, and Kimball, *Forged in War*, 167, respectively. I fully explain military representation on the subcommittee in Chap. 8.

39. European Affairs Div. to Hull, memo, Aug. 10, 1942, as quoted in Lynn Davis, *Cold War Begins*, 79–80. See also Wedemeyer, *Wedemeyer Reports!*, 228–30.

40. In March 1943, G-2 thus rejected requests from its military attaché in Moscow for a retaliatory Lend-Lease policy and Anglo-American discussions before presenting any demands to Moscow on the grounds that "White House policy does not permit using Lend Lease as a basis of bargaining" and such meetings would increase Soviet suspicion; CM-OUT 6583, G-2 to Michela, Mar. 18, 1943, OPD Exec. 1, item 20, RG 165, NA.

41. In *Second World War*, 488, Liddell-Hart claimed German foreign minister Joachim Ribbentropp and Soviet foreign minister Molotov actually met on the eastern front but could not reach agreement. No evidence was cited or has been found to support such a claim, and contacts appear to have been limited to a much lower level in Sweden. Nevertheless, the threat may have been quite real. See Koch, "Spectre of a Separate Peace," 531–49; Mastny, *Russia's Road to the*

Cold War, 73–85; and Mastny, "Stalin and the Prospects of a Separate Peace," 1365–88. See also Samerdyke, "United States and the Free Germany Committee."

42. SS memos, "Comments on Strategic Concept for the Defeat of the Axis in Europe," Aug. 3, 1943; "Course of Action for the United States in the Event Germany and Russia Effect a Compromise Peace in July and August, 1943," undated; and "Effect on Overall Strategy of United Nations of Events on Russo-German Front," Nov. 7, 1943, all in ABC 381 SS (7 Jan. 43) (nos. 131–159), tabs 93, 131, and 131/1, RG 165, NA; Wedemeyer to Marshall, memo, Aug. 5, 1943, ABC 384 Europe (5 Aug. 43), sec. 1A, RG 165, NA; Wedemeyer to CofS, memo, Aug. 10, 1943, with enclosed memo, OSS Planning group to JCS, "Manifesto to German People by Moscow National Committee of Free Germany," Aug. 6, 1943, ABC 381 (9-25-41), sec. 7, PG/1, RG 165, NA; Dunn to Strong, memo, Aug. 11, 1943, OPD Exec. 9, item 11, papers 75 and 103, RG 165, NA; Buell, *Master of Seapower,* 417; Leahy diary, July 23 and Oct. 12, 1943, LOC; and Davies diary, Sept. 24, 1943, LOC. Some of these documents are analyzed in Stoler, *Politics of the Second Front,* 104, 116–18.

43. Kimball, "Stalingrad," 112.

44. JCS Memo for Information no. 121, "Strategy and Policy: Can America and Russia Cooperate?," Aug. 22, 1943, CCS 092 USSR (8-22-43), quoted and analyzed in Stoler, *Politics of the Second Front,* 121–23. The main author of the memo was Prof. Geroid Robinson of Columbia University, head of the Russian section of the OSS R&A.

45. Quotations are from *FRUS: Washington and Quebec,* 910–11, 942. See also ibid., 940, 1010–18; JIC rpt., "Estimate of the Enemy Situation, 1943–1944, European-Mediterranean Area," July 19, 1943, CCS 381 (6-7-43), sec. 1, RG 218, NA; SS, "RANKIN," memo, undated, ABC 381 SS (7 Jan. 43) (nos. 131–159), tab 159, RG 165, NA; Stoler, *Politics of the Second Front,* 89–91, 123; Bland, *Marshall Papers,* 3:620–21; and Buell, *Master of Seapower,* 417.

46. Hull, *Memoirs,* 2:1247–48; Churchill, *Second World War,* 1:449; Security Subcomm. min., Oct. 30, 1943, Notter Papers, box 76, RG 59, NA.

47. Security Subcomm. min., Nov. 20 and Dec. 11, 1942, and Mar. 24, 1943, Notter Papers, box 76, RG 59, NA. See also "Preliminary Report of the Security Subcommittee," Oct. 23 and Nov. 6, 1942, S. Doc. 39a, in ibid. For Welles's expression of similar concerns, see Halifax to FO, Dec. 4, CAB/122/160, quoted in Kimball, *Forged in War,* 167.

48. McCrea to Leahy, memo, Dec. 28, 1942, Roosevelt Papers, MRF, box 162, Naval Aide's Files, A4-2, Air Routes Folder, FDRL. This memo became the first in the JCS 183 series and can also be found in CCS 360 (2-9-42), sec. 1, RG 218, NA.

49. Min., JCS 61st mtg., Feb. 9, 1943, CCS 360 (12-9-42), sec. 1, RG 218, NA.

50. CNO-COMINCH to SN, "Request That the General Board Study the Post War Employment of International Police Force and Post War Use of Air Bases," memo, Feb. 9, 1943; SN to Chmn., GB, "Post War Employment of International Police Force and Post War Use of Air Bases," memo, Feb. 10, 1943; and SN to Chairman, GB, "Pacific Air Bases—Retention of," memo, Feb. 17, 1943, all in SPD, ser. 14, box 199, NB Secs. 1–2 Folder, NH.

51. JCS 183/1, "Air Routes across the Pacific and Air Facilities for International Police Force," Mar. 6, 1943, CCS 360 (2-9-42), sec. 1, RG 218, NA. For the interdepartmental committee on postwar international aviation, see Dobson, *Peaceful Air Warfare.*

52. Min., JCS 65th mtg., Mar. 9, 1943, CCS 360 (2-9-42), sec. 1, RG 218, NA. See also Leahy comments in min., JCS 61st mtg., Feb. 9, 1943, CCS 334 JCS (1-14-43), RG 218, NA.

53. Min., JCS 65th mtg., Mar. 9, 1943, CCS 360 (2-9-42), sec. 1, RG 218, NA.

54. Louis, *Imperialism at Bay,* 261. But see also Converse, "United States Plans for a Postwar Overseas Base System," 10–21.

55. JCS 183/5, "Post-War Military Problems with Particular Reference to Air Bases," Mar. 15, 1943, CCS 360 (2-9-42), sec. 1, RG 218, NA.

56. See Security Subcomm. min., Apr. 29 and Nov. 20, 1942; S. Doc. 13, "Summary of Conclusions," Oct. 23, 1942; and S. Doc. 39a, "Preliminary Report of the Security Subcommittee," Nov. 6, 1942, all in Notter Papers, box 76, RG 59, NA.

57. JSSC 9/1, "Post-War Military Problems with Particular Reference to Air Bases," CCS 360 (2-9-42), sec. 1, RG 218, NA.

58. Ibid.

59. Min., JCS 66th and 69th mtgs., Mar. 16 and 23, 1943, CCS 334 JCS (1-14-43), and JCS 183/5 rev., "Post-War Military Problems with Particular Reference to Air Bases," Mar. 25, 1943, CCS 360 (2-9-42), sec. 1, both in RG 218, NA.

60. JCS 183/6, "Air Routes across the Pacific and Air Facilities for an International Police Force," Apr. 10, 1943, CCS 360 (2-9-42), sec. 2, RG 218, NA. The areas listed in the Atlantic/Caribbean were Newfoundland, Bermuda, the Bahamas, Jamaica, Puerto Rico, the Virgin Islands, Antigua, Santa Lucia, Georgetown, Paramaribo, Cayenne, Cuba, Trinidad, Belem, and Natal; in the Pacific, the Galapagos, Clipperton, Hawaii, Wake, Marcus, Marshalls, Carolines, Palaus, Bonins, Philippines, and Marianas.

61. See, for ex., FDR comments on Nov. 13, 1942, in Roosevelt, *FDR Personal Letters,* 2:1366–67, and below, Chap. 8.

62. Perry McCoy Smith, *Air Force Plans for Peace,* 110. Smith adds that this unwritten rule resulted from "fear of a leak, in conjunction with an acute awareness of the Russian sensitivity toward unfriendly American acts."

63. Security Subcomm. min., May 6, 1942, Notter Papers, box 76, RG 59, NA. See also the minutes from May 20, 1942, Sept. 25, 1942, and Feb. 16 and 26, 1943.

64. S&P, "Notes on JCS 69th Meeting," Mar. 23, 1943, ABC 580.8 (1-1-43), RG 165, NA; emphasis in original.

65. Ibid.; emphasis in original.

66. Ibid.

67. S&P, "Notes on JCS 69th Meeting," and "Notes on JCS 74th Meeting," Mar. 23 and Apr. 13, 1943, ABC 580.8 (1-1-43), RG 165, NA; emphasis in original.

68. GAL to Hull, no title, Oct. 8, 1943, ABC 040 (2 Nov. 43), sec. 5A, RG 165, NA.

69. Smith, *Air Force Plans for Peace,* 40–42, 110–11.

70. Hart, chmn. GB, to SN, "Post-War Employment of International Police Force and Post-War Use of Air Bases," memo, Mar. 20, 1943, SPD, ser. 14, box 199, NB secs. 1–2, NH.

71. Ibid.

72. Ibid., annex A; Hart, chmn. GB, to SN, "Post-War Sovereignty over Certain Islands of the North Pacific," memo, Mar. 27, 1943, and "Islands in the South Pacific: Change in Status Of," memo, Apr. 6, 1943, SPD, ser. 14, box 200, NB Secs. 25–30 Folder, sec. 28-GB 450 (serial 240), NH. Islands to be transferred to U.S. sovereignty included the World War I mandates; the Bonins and Volcanos; Marcus; Ituaba; Samoa; the Lines, Wallis, Phoenix, Union, Ellice, and Gilbert groups; the Marquesas; Society; Tubuai; the Tuamotu archipelago; and the New Caledonia group.

73. Perry, letter to Keats Spead, July 25, 1943.

74. Spykman, *America's Strategy in World Politics,* 462, and *Geography of the Peace,* 46, 57–58. See also the intro. by Frederick S. Dunn, ibid., ix–xii. At a meeting of the Association of American Geographers two weeks after Pearl Harbor, Spykman argued against total destruction of German and Japanese power on the grounds that after the war these "rimland" powers would become U.S. allies against Russian expansionism (Sloan, *Geopolitics,* 19–22).

75. Danchev, *Dykes Diaries,* 138, 146, 208.

Chapter Eight

1. May, "Political-Military Consultation," 174. For contacts, see Gen. John Hull autobiography, Hull Papers, chap. 7, p. 5, and Hull Oral History, 5th sess., 2, MHI; Cline, *Washington Command Post*, 319–21; and Albion, *Forrestal and the Navy*, 191–92.

2. Stimson diary, May 4, 1943, YUL. Welles did accompany FDR to his August 1941 mtg. with Chuchill, and Hull's successor, Edward Stettinius, attended FDR's last summit mtg. at Yalta in February 1945.

3. Joint org. mtg. of Pol., Terr. and Sec. Subcomms., Feb. 21, 1942, Notter Papers, box 76, Security Subcomm. Min. Folder, RG 59, NA.

4. Notter, *Postwar Foreign Policy Preparation,* 76–77, 125, 132; Sec. Subcomm. min., Apr. 15 and 29, 1942, Notter Papers, box 76, RG 59, NA. Davis had headed the U.S. delegation to the 1932 Geneva Disarmament Conference, the second London Naval Conference of 1935–36, and the 1937 Brussels Conference. Strong had served as technical and military adviser at the Geneva Arms Reduction and Disarmament Conferences of 1926, 1927, 1928, and 1932, and Hepburn and Train had both attended the 1930 London Naval Conference.

5. This list is taken from "The Security Subcommittee," annex 3 to an Oct. 4, 1944, memo on State Dept. postwar planning before 1943 in the Pasvolsky Papers, box 5, LOC. See also Notter, *Postwar Foreign Policy Preparation,* 85–86, 125–27.

6. Sec. Tech. Comm. min., Dec. 23 and 30, 1942, Jan. 20, May 7, 12, and 26, 1943, and "Membership of the Security Technical Committee," unsigned memo, Oct. 16, 1943, in Notter Papers, box 79, RG 59, NA. See also Iriye, *Power and Culture,* 123.

7. Notter to Pasvolsky, Apr. 8, 1943; Sandifer to Notter, memo, Apr. 8, 1943; and Sec. Subcomm. min., Mar. 19, 1943, in Notter Papers, box 76, RG 59, NA. For Strong's comments, see page 141. Train stated in his oral history at NH that he was a close friend of Strong and an "old friend" of Embick.

8. Notter to Pasvolsky, Apr. 8, 1943, Notter Papers, box 76, RG 59, NA.

9. Sec. Subcomm. min., Aug. 21 and Sept. 18, 1942, and S. Doc. 38, Sept. 22, 1942, Notter Papers, box 76, RG 59, NA; Leahy to Davis, memo, Sept. 15, 1942, CCS 388 (8-27-42), RG 218, NA; Analysis Sec., Mil. Intell. rpt., "The United States and the Power Cycle," Apr. 1, 1943, SW Files, Formerly Security Classified Rpts., 1940–45 Folder, RG 107, NA; Foltos, "New Pacific Barrier," 318–19.

10. Pratt to King, Apr. 10, 1943, King Papers, box 14, Pratt Folder, LOC.

11. For different versions of the specifics of this initiative, see Sec. Subcomm. min., Mar. 19, 1943, and Sandifer to Notter, "Additions to Membership of the Security Subcommittee," memo, Mar. 25, 1943, Notter Papers, box 76, RG 59, NA.

12. King to Pratt, Apr. 14, 1943, King Papers, box 14, Pratt Folder, LOC.

13. S&P "Notes on JCS 74th mtg.," Apr. 13, 1943, ABC 580.8 (1-1-43), RG 165, NA.

14. Min. of joint mtgs. of Sec. and Pol. Subcomms., Apr. 9, 16, 29, May 5, and 27, 1943, Notter Papers, box 76, RG 59, NA.

15. Forrest Davis, "Roosevelt's World Blueprint," was published in Apr. 1943 and labeled FDR "a geographer and power theorist," deeply concerned with security and future relations with Russia and opposed to an international air force.

16. Knox to Roosevelt, Mar. 10, 1943, Roosevelt Papers, MRF, box 162, Naval Aide's Files, A4-2 Air Routes Folder, FDRL.

17. Roosevelt to Knox, Mar. 12, 1943, ibid.

18. King to Knox, "Postwar Security Force," memo, Apr. 13, 1943, King Papers, NH; min., JCS 74th mtg., Apr. 13, 1943, CCS 334 JCS (3-29-43), RG 218, NA; Roosevelt to Knox, memo, June 12, 1943, Roosevelt Papers, MRF, box 162, Naval Aide's Files, A4-2 Air Routes Folder, FDRL. For the meeting with Halifax, see Gardner, *Approaching Vietnam,* 36–37.

19. Louis, *Imperialism at Bay,* 267; see also 261–66.

20. Knox to Roosevelt with GB enclosures, Roosevelt to Knox, and Knox to King, memos, June 19, June 30, and Aug. 17, 1943, Roosevelt Papers, MRF, box 162, Naval Aide's Files, A4-2 Air Routes Folder, FDRL; Louis, *Imperialism at Bay,* 267–69. These docs., along with related memos between FDR, Knox, King, and the GB, dated July 12–29, 1943, are also in SPD, ser. 14, box 199, H1-23 Air Routes Folder, NH; and GB Records, GB 450, NH.

21. Quotations are from memos between Arnold and ACofS, Air, enclosed within Perrin to ACofS, OPD, "International Aviation," memo, Aug. 18, 1943, ABC 580.82 Efate (2-3-43), sec. 1A, RG 165, NA. See also memos from Deane to OPD, "International Aviation," July 8, 1943; Lovett to Berle, Sept. 1, 1943; and Upston to Chief, S&P, "International Civil Aviation," Sept. 19, 1943, all in ABC 580.82 Efate (2-3-43), sec. 1A, RG 165, NA; and Hull, OPD to Lovett, "U.S. Postwar Requirements for Military Air Bases," memo, Aug. 31, 1943, ABC 389.3 (1-1-43), RG 165, NA.

22. JCS 445, "Buildup of Facilities for Direct Line Air Routes," and S&P, "Notes on JCS 101st Meeting," Aug. 6, 1943, ABC 580.8 (1-1-43), RG 165, NA; Matloff, *Strategic Planning,* 185–93, 205–10; Hayes, *History of the Joint Chiefs of Staff,* 415–31.

23. Anderson to Wedemeyer, "Postwar Aviation Rights," memo, Mar. 11, 1943, ABC 580.82 Efate (2-3-43), sec. 1A, RG 165, NA. See also documents cited above in n. 21 within this file.

24. Rpt. of Special Army Subcomm., "Survey of Current Military Program," app. B, "A Strategic Plan for the United States," Mar. 15, 1943, ABC 381 SS Papers (7 Jan. 43) (nos. 96–126/3), RG 165, NA.

25. Ibid.

26. Marshall to CG, Army Service Forces, "Demobilization Planning," memo, Apr. 14, 1943; Project Planning Div. of Office of DCofS for Service Commands (Tompkins), "Survey of Demobilization Planning," memo, June 18, 1943; and Handy to CG, Army Service Forces (att.: Tompkins), "Demobilization Planning," memo, July 3, 1943, in ABC 381 SS Papers (7 Jan. 43) (nos. 96–126/3), RG 165, NA. See also Sherry, *Preparing for the Next War,* 8–12, and Bland, *Marshall Papers,* 3:633–34, 4:23–24. The SPD assumed that the United States would "emerge as the strongest military power in the world and will remain for at least several post-war years in a state of preparedness for action in widely dispersed areas"; Germany would be defeated before Japan and Washington have an "important share" in occupation forces "for an extended period"; public opinion would demand rapid demobilization but the nation would nevertheless have to maintain sufficient forces to "protect" U.S. interests during the peace negotiation and reconstruction period, "and especially to give sufficient weight to our policies and plans at the peace conference." Furthermore, the permanent postwar military establishment would have to remain sufficiently large to defend the hemisphere and U.S. overseas possessions, carry out any international police force assignments resulting from the peace conference, and occupy strategic bases overseas. These would be required not only for military defense but also for "our economic well-being" because they would ensure access to "essential raw materials," safeguard "unhampered use of sea routes," and provide "military protection of our future global air activities."

27. Marshall to Davis, memo, July 28, 1943, Marshall Papers, POF, box 63, folder 8, GCMRL.

28. McCloy and Handy to Marshall, memos, July 12 and 15, 1943, ABC 381 SS Papers (7 Jan. 43) (nos. 96–126/3), RG 165, NA.

29. Rpt., JWPC to JPS, "Phases of Joint War Planning," report, July 19, 1943, CCS 334 JLPC (7-19-43), sec. 1, RG 218, NA; JCS 431, memo from CofS, "Demobilization Planning," July 30, 1943, CCS 370.01 (7-30-43), sec. 1, RG 218, NA. The SPD was further directed not to consider total strengths needed in the postwar era or the possibility of delaying demobilization "to avoid economic upsets" on the grounds that "these questions are reserved for later determination."

30. Min., JCS 99th and 116 mtgs., Aug. 3 and Sept. 21, 1943, and JCS 431/1, "Demobilization

Planning," Sept. 21, 1943, in CCS 370.01 (7-30-42), sec. 1, RG 218, NA. See also Schnabel, *History of the Joint Chiefs of Staff*, 1:197–99, and Sherry, *Preparing for the Next War*, 22.

31. Perry McCoy Smith, *Air Force Plans for Peace*, 40–42, discussed in Chap. 7.

32. Vincent Davis, *Postwar Defense Policy and the U.S. Navy*, 12–14, 277 n. 34.

33. Special Planning Section, Yarnell draft, memo, Sept. 22, 1943, A16-3/EN, in doc. #95601, CNO-1943, box 666, RG 80, NA. This doc. is also discussed in Vincent Davis, *Postwar Defense Policy and the U.S. Navy*, 15–19.

34. Special Planning Section, Yarnell draft, memo, Sept. 22, 1943, A16-3/EN, in doc. #95601, CNO-1943, box 666, RG 80, NA.

35. Ibid.

36. Memos, CNO to Special Planning, Oct. 20, 1943, A16-3EN, Op-12/eah, serial 0124613; Chief of Ordnance to CNO, Oct. 1, 1943, A16-1(2) PL-001447; DCNO (Air) to VCNO, Oct. 1, 1943, OP-31-2-ESB; Dir., Base Maintenance, to VCNO, Oct. 4, 1943, A16-3/EN, serial 0740430; Dir., Naval Intelligence, to Dir., Central Div., Oct. 14, 1943, A-16-3/EN, serial 02580816, all in CNO-1943 File, box 666, RG 80, NA.

37. "Navy Basic Demobilization Plan no. 1," Nov. 17, 1943, is in both A16-3/EN (Nov.), CNO-1943, box 667, RG 80, NA, and A16-3(5), SPD, ser. 14, NH. It is also discussed in detail in Vincent Davis, *Postwar Defense Policy and the U.S. Navy*, 21–24. Other deletions from the Yarnell draft included specific islands in the Pacific, the word "democratic" in regard to the Chinese government, and universal military training.

38. GAL to Hull, memo, Oct. 8, 1943, ABC 040 (2 Nov. 43), sec. 5A, RG 165, NA. Vincent Davis makes this point in *Postwar Defense Policy and the U.S. Navy*, 16. According to Perry McCoy Smith, *Air Force Plans for Peace*, 35–36, 109, AAF planners resolved the problem by focusing on the U.S. airpower required by the postwar international organization to prevent resurgent German or Japanese airpower, an option the navy did not have because its views on the postwar organization were much more negative. He also notes, however, that air planners did see the Soviet Union as a long-term threat and that some saw it as an immediate threat (40–42, 51–52).

39. Rear Adm. G. J. Rowcliff to chmn., GB, "Navy Basic Demobilization Plan," memo, GB 450, serial 260, RG 80, NA.

40. Schnabel, *History of the Joint Chiefs of Staff*, 1:135.

41. Ibid.; JSSC, "Recommended Policy on Post-War Military Problems," app. B to JCS 570, "U.S. Requirements for Post-War Air Bases," Nov. 6, 1943, CCS 360 (12-9-42), sec. 2, RG 218, NA.

42. JCS 570, "U.S. Requirements for Post-War Air Bases," Nov. 6, 1943, CCS 360 (12-9-42), sec. 2, RG 218, NA. For detailed analyses of the evolution of this doc. over the ensuing months and years, see Foltos, "New Pacific Barrier," 317–42, and Schnabel, *History of the Joint Chiefs of Staff*, 1:299–346.

43. Min., JCS 123d mtg., Nov. 15, 1943, special mtgs. with Pres., Nov. 15 and 19, 1943; JCS 570 and 570/1, "Requirements for Post-War Air Bases," Nov. 6 and 15, 1943; and Roosevelt to JCS, "U.S. Requirements for Post-War Air Bases," memo, Nov. 23, 1943, CCS 360 (12-9-42), sec. 2, RG 218, NA; *FRUS: Cairo and Tehran*, 167 and 197. See also Louis, *Imperialism at Bay*, 271–73; Foltos, "New Pacific Barrier," 319; Sherry, *Preparing for the Next War*, 44–47; and Sbrega, *Anglo-American Relations and Colonialism*, 156. Roosevelt had expressed interest in these islands and Dakar as early as March 28, 1943, and trusteeship for Indochina as early as 1942; see Gardner, *Approaching Vietnam*, 36–37, and Watt, *Succeeding John Bull*, 196–200, 222–23. He had also asked Hull to explore trusteeship with the allies at the conference in Moscow and in early November had requested from Stettinius information on trusteeship. Whether he knew of the JCS study when he made these requests is unclear, though he did know of the navy studies and the looming conflict over sovereignty. Louis claims Roosevelt knew of JCS 570 on November 6, the

date it was forwarded to the JCS, but they did not formally approve and give it to him until November 15. Furthermore, JCS 570 did not demand absolute sovereignty over the bases as the navy studies had done. In all likelihoood FDR was thus motivated to act by navy rather than JCS demands.

44. In *History of the Joint Chiefs of Staff*, 1:135–36, Schnabel notes that FDR's approval became the basis for postwar continuation of the JCS and that the chiefs construed that approval as authorizing them to engage in postwar planning.

45. Min., JCS 120th mtg., Oct. 26, 1943, CCS 334 (9-14-43) JCS, RG 218, NA.

46. The meetings are summarized in Matloff, *Strategic Planning*, 338–46. Excerpts from the official minutes are in *FRUS: Cairo and Tehran*, 86, 194–99, 248–61, and CCS 360 (12-9-42), sec. 2, RG 218, NA. The complete minutes are in army files as described by Matloff, *Strategic Planning*, 339 n. 14; in CCS 334 (JCS), RG 218, NA; and in the Roosevelt Papers, MRF, box 24, Conferences, Minutes of Meetings of FDR with Joint Chiefs of Staff, 1942–1945 Folder. The analysis in the text and quotations therein are taken from the complete minutes.

The sixteen topics covered on November 15 were directives to Ambassador Harriman in Moscow to come to Cairo, floating flight decks, rearmament of French forces, the Galapagos Islands, British opposition to Soviet military representation at Cairo, Allied strategy in the Balkans and eastern Mediterranean, future Allied command arrangements in Europe, declaring Rome an open city, the future of the Italian government, international trusteeship, the preceding Moscow Foreign Ministers Conference, British plans for a civil affairs secretariat, French censorship in Arab countries, U.S. requirements for postwar air bases, the agenda for Cairo, and British interest in Ethiopia. Additional discussion took place on November 19 about a postwar base at Dakar, postwar bases in the Pacific, command arrangements in Europe, proposed agendas for the coming meetings, and postwar spheres of responsibility in occupied Germany.

47. Handy to Marshall, "Brief of Proposed Revision of Outline Plan for RANKIN-Case 'C,'" memo, Oct. 13, 1943, OPD Exec. 9, item 13, paper 82, RG 165, NA; Acting Chief, SS, "Notes on RANKIN," memo, Oct. 26, 1943, ABC 381 SS Papers (7 Jan. 43) (nos. 131–159), tab 159, RG 165, NA; Handy to Marshall, memo, Nov. 2, 1943, OPD 381 Security (sec. 7B), 226, RG 165, NA; JWPC Rpt. 126 to JPS, JCS 577–577/2, excerpts from JCS mtgs. of Nov. 17 and 18, 1943, and Leahy to Roosevelt, "Europe-Wide Rankin," memo, in CCS 381 (8-20-43), sec. 1, RG 218, NA. See also Sharp, *Wartime Alliance and Zonal Division of Germany*, 31–45.

48. Roosevelt first voiced his objections on November 17 and explained why to the JCS two days later; see min., JCS mtg., Nov. 18, 1943, CCS 381 (8-20-43), sec. 1, RG 218, NA, and directly below in text.

49. *FRUS: Cairo and Tehran*, 253–56, and complete min. of Nov. 19 mtg. in Roosevelt Papers, MRF, box 24, FDRL.

50. Min., Nov. 19th mtg, Roosevelt Papers, MRF, box 24, FDRL; *FRUS: Cairo and Tehran*, 255–60. The map is reproduced in Matloff, *Strategic Planning*, between pages 340 and 341. Marshall later reported to Handy that Roosevelt desired joint occupation of Berlin; see ibid., 342.

51. See Chap. 10.

52. *FRUS: Cairo and Tehran*, 261; Matloff, *Strategic Planning*, 345.

Chapter Nine

1. Hull, *Memoirs*, 2:1264; *FRUS*, 1943, 1:583–84, 774–81.

2. Min., JCS 127th mtg., Nov. 22, 1943, CCS 334 (11-15-43) JCS, RG 218, NA. See also Sainsbury, *Turning Point*, 36–123.

3. Harriman, *Special Envoy*, 244.

4. JCS 533/3, "Memorandum from Commander in Chief, United States Fleet and Chief of Naval Operations, Preparations for the Next United States–British Staff Conference," Oct. 24–25, 1943, and JCS 533/5, "Recommended Line of Action at Next U.S.-British Staff Conference," Nov. 8, 1943, both in CCS 381 (10-17-43), sec. 1, RG 218, NA; min., JCS 120th mtg., Oct. 26, 1943, CCS 334 (9-14-43) JCS, RG 218, NA.

5. *FRUS: Cairo and Tehran*, 482.

6. Louis, *Imperialism at Bay*, 274–83; Sainsbury, *Turning Point*, 171–215, 321.

7. *FRUS: Cairo and Tehran*, 484, 488–89, 498–99; Feis, *Churchill, Roosevelt, and Stalin*, 259.

8. *FRUS: Cairo and Tehran*, 489–508, 535–52. ANVIL had been proposed at QUADRANT and mentioned to the Soviets during the Moscow OVERLORD discussion. See ibid., 140–41, and *FRUS: Washington and Quebec*, 1025, 1038.

9. *FRUS: Cairo and Tehran*, 485–86, 509, 532, 554, 568–71, 846; Louis, *Imperialism at Bay*, 283–285; Sainsbury, *Turning Point*, 262–63; Harriman, *Special Envoy*, 275; and Sherwood, *Roosevelt and Hopkins*, 786–87.

10. Bryant, *Triumph in the West*, 64; *FRUS: Cairo and Tehran*, 554; Dilks, *Diaries of Sir Alexander Cadogan*, 582.

11. Min., JCS 127th and 129th mtgs., Nov. 22 and 24, 1943, CCS 334 (11-1543) JCS, RG 218, NA, with abridged versions in *FRUS: Cairo and Tehran*, 301–3, 327–29; Marshall to Stimson, tel., Dec. 2, 1943, OPD Exec. 10, item 63C (2), RG 165, NA.

12. Stimson diary, Dec. 3, 5, and 6, 1943, and McCloy to Stimson, Dec. 2, 1943, YUL. See also Perry, "*Dear Bart*," 247.

13. Hull, *Memoirs*, 2:1314–15.

14. Freidel, *Roosevelt: A Rendezvous*, 493; Campbell and Herring, *Diaries of Edward R. Stettinius, Jr.* [hereafter *Stettinius Diaries*], 40; min. of mtg. between FDR and JCS, Feb. 21, 1944, Roosevelt Papers, MRF, box 24, Conferences, Minutes of Meetings of FDR with Joint Chiefs of Staff, 1942–1945 Folder, FDRL. On ANVIL, see also FDR June 29 message in Kimball, *Churchill and Roosevelt*, 3:221–24.

15. Roosevelt to Stettinius, memo, Feb. 21, 1944, Roosevelt Papers, MRF, box 167, FDRL; Matloff, *Strategic Planning*, 491; *FRUS, 1944*, 1:166, 184, 188–89; Chandler, *Eisenhower Papers*, 3:1727 n. 3.

16. Leo Crowley, in Morgenthau diary, as quoted in Thorne, *Allies of a Kind*, 276.

17. Ian Jacob as quoted in Reynolds and Dimbleby, *An Ocean Apart*, 166. See also Sainsbury, *Churchill and Roosevelt*, 50–52, 74–75.

18. Spector, "Politics of American Strategy," 14; Richard M. Leighton, "Overlord versus the Mediterranean at the Cairo-Tehran Conferences," in Greenfield, *Command Decisions*, 278–82.

19. Higgins, *Soft Underbelly*, 153.

20. For OVERLORD and ANVIL, see Chandler, *Eisenhower Papers*, 3:1659–1908; Maurice Matloff, "The ANVIL Decision," in Greenfield, *Command Decisions*, 383–400. For the Anglo-Soviet negotiations, see *FRUS, 1944*, 5:112–21, and Woodward, *British Foreign Policy in the Second World War*, 3:115–23.

21. See Bradley Smith, *Sharing Secrets*, 170–84.

22. Min. of mtg. between Pres. and JCS, Feb. 21, 1944, Roosevelt Papers, MRF, FDRL, as quoted in Matloff, *Strategic Planning*, 427; Stimson diary, June 21, 1944, YUL. See also Leahy diary, May 12 and June 29, 1944, LOC. For JCS drafts and FDR revisions, see in particular the June 29 msge. to Churchill in Kimball, *Churchill and Roosevelt*, 3:221–24.

23. Bryant, *Triumph in the West*, 134, and Winant to Roosevelt, msge., July 3, 1944, Roosevelt Papers, MRF, box 6. For a useful summary of the debate, see Maurice Matloff, "The ANVIL Decision," in Greenfield, *Command Decisions*, 383–400.

24. Handy to CG, N. Africa, memo, Mar. 7, 1944, OPD 014.1 (sec. 2-A), 73, and Stimson to

Roosevelt, memo, Mar. 8, 1944, OPD 336 Security II, RG 165, NA, both quoted in Lynn Davis, *Cold War Begins*, 78–79. See also in RG 165, NA, Roberts for ACofS, OPD, "Preliminary Data on Possibility of Occupation of Dalmatian Islands," memo, Apr. 14, 1944, ABC 381 SS (7 Jan. 43) (nos. 251–270), tab 270; JCS 778/1, "Withdrawal from the War of Hungary, Rumania, and Bulgaria," Mar. 27, 1944, ABC 384 Hungary Rumania; Cochran to CofS, SHAEF, "Occupation of Certain Areas in the Mediterranean Theatre under Rankin 'C' Conditions," memo, June 7, 1944, SHAEF 381 Rankin; Memo for the Record by L.H.S., "Occupation of Certain Areas in the Mediterranean Theatre under Rankin 'C' Conditions," OPD 381 Security (sec. 7B), 226; and the following docs. in ABC 336 Rumania, sec. 1A (9-26-43): JCS 779/1, "Proposed Procedure for Surrender of Rumanian Forces," Mar. 28, 1944; JCS 812/1, "Rumanian Armistice Terms Proposed by U.S.S.R." and Notes of Embick-Roberts Telephone Conversation, Apr. 10, 1944; JCS 1054, "Allied Control Commission for Rumania, Sept. 26, 1944; and Roberts to Handy and Handy to CAD, "Economic Aspects of Occupation of Rumania," memos, Mar. 11, 1944. JCS 779/1 with the JSSC "analogous comment" is reproduced in *FRUS*, 1944, 4:161–64. See also ibid., 184, 212, 223–32, and 434–35, and Matloff, *Strategic Planning*, 492 and 504–5.

25. JCS 577/12–14, "Occupation of Certain Areas in the Mediterranean Theater under Rankin 'C' Conditions," May 18–26, 1944, ABC 384 NW Europe (20 Aug. 43), sec. 5A, RG 165, NA. See also in this file JCS 820 and 820/2, "Policy for the Surrender of the German Fleet under Rankin Case 'C' Conditions," Apr. 21–May 2, 1944. The JCS and FDR approved the JPS/JSSC recommendations on May 26–27 and forwarded them to London, albeit without the JSSC's detailed fears regarding Allied conflict over the Balkans.

26. Hull to Roosevelt and Leahy, memo with enclosures, Apr. 22, 1944, DS 865.014.210–212A&B, RG 59, NA.

27. JCS 838/1, "Disposition of Italian Overseas Territories," May 6, 1944, ABC 092 Italy (27 Apr. 44), RG 165, NA.

28. Ibid.

29. JCS 973, "Fundamental Military Factors in Relation to Discussions concerning Territorial Trusteeships and Settlements," July 28, 1944, CCS 092 (7-27-44), RG 218, NA.

30. Ibid. For the 1943 studies, see Chap. 7.

31. JCS 973, "Fundamental Military Factors in Relation to Discussions concerning Territorial Trusteeships and Settlements," July 28, 1944, CCS 092 (7-27-44), RG 218, NA. The War Dept. similarly opposed a proposed tripartite railroad agreement in Iran for fear it "would endanger harmonious relations between the U.S. and Russia in the Persian Corridor." See JCS 958 and 958/1, "Severance of Diplomatic Relations with Germany and Turkey," July 15 and Aug. 1, 1944, ABC 384 Sweden-Turkey (25 Oct. 44), sec. 4, RG 165, NA; *FRUS*, 1944, 5:378–80.

32. JCS 1005/1, "Machinery for Coordination of United States–Soviet–British Military Effort," Aug. 31, 1944, in *Records of the JCS*. I will discuss the JSSC role in the Dumbarton Oaks Conference below in Chap. 9 and in Chap. 10.

33. JCS 1954/1, "Allied Control Commission for Rumania," Sept. 26, 1944, and JCS 779/3 and 779/11, "Rumanian Withdrawal from the Axis and Assumption of Co-Belligerent Status with the Allies," Sept. 1944, both in ABC 336 Rumania, sec. 1A (26 Sept. 43), RG 165, NA; JCS 1038, "Proposed Accreditation of Military and Naval Attaches to the Czechoslovakian Government," Sept. 8, 1944, ABC 040 Czechoslovakia (8 Sept. 44), RG 165, NA; JPS 520/1 and JCS 1056, "Assistance to the Slovak Army and Partisans," Sept. 12 and 18, 1944, CCS 381 Czechoslovakia (9-7-44), RG 218, NA; JCS 1039/1, "Policy for the Equipping of the Forces of the West European Allies," Sept. 28, 1944, CCS 400 (7-30-44), RG 218 NA.

34. Sherwood, *Roosevelt and Hopkins*, 803.

35. See Louis, *Imperialism at Bay*, 274–86, 354–57; JCS 570/2, Roosevelt to Hull, Jan. 10, 1944,

CCS 360 (12-19-42), sec. 2, RG 218, NA; Campbell and Herring, *Stettinius Diaries,* 39–40; and Russell, *History of the United Nations Charter,* 174.

36. JCS 656, "Japanese Mandated Islands," Jan. 8, 1944; supp. min., JCS 141st mtg.; and Larsen to JCS Sec., mem, Feb. 29, 1944, in CCS 093 (1-8-44), sec. 1, RG 218, NA; Leahy to Roosevelt and Roosevelt to Brown, memos, Jan. 11 and 14, 1944, Roosevelt Papers, MRF, box 162, Naval Aide's File, A4-2 Air Routes Folder, FDRL.

37. Foltos, "New Pacific Barrier," 320–21. See also Perry, *"Dear Bart,"* 246–51, and Louis, *Imperialism at Bay,* 289–306.

38. JCS 698 and JCS 698/1, "Australia–New Zealand Agreement of 21 January 1944," Feb. 9 and Mar. 4, 1944, ABC 092 Pacific (9 Feb. 44), RG 165, NA; Leahy to Sec. of State, memo, Mar. 11, 1944, in *FRUS,* 1944, 5:1201; Louis, *Imperialism at Bay,* 351.

39. Roosevelt to JCS, memo, July 10, 1944, CCS 093 (1-8-44), sec. 1, RG 218, NA; Foltos, "New Pacific Barrier," 321. After a meeting with Roosevelt at this time, de Gaulle informed the British that FDR was "very insistent" on obtaining French bases and "his preoccupation seemed to be mainly American (as distinct from the general) security, and with American use of bases rather than with United Nations uses in a general security system." See Campbell to Eden, tel., July 10, 1944, CAB/122/1555, PRO.

40. Campbell and Herring, *Stettinius Diaries,* 70–71; *FRUS,* 1944, 3:15–18, 20–22; Louis, *Imperialism at Bay,* 327–36, 358–65; Sbrega, *Anglo-American Relations and Colonialism,* 139–42.

41. JCS 838/1, "Disposition of Italian Overseas Territories," May 6, 1944, ABC 092 Italy (27 Apr. 44), RG 165, NA.

42. *FRUS,* 1944, 5:1266.

43. JCS 656/1, and Leahy for JCS to Roosevelt, "Policy regarding Japanese Mandated Islands," memo, July 1 and 4, 1944, and Roosevelt to JCS, memo, July 10, 1944, all in CCS 093 (1-8-44), sec. 1, RG 218, NA. See also Roosevelt Papers, MRF, box 162, Naval Aide's File, A4-2 Air Routes Folder, FDRL.

44. JCS 973/1, "Fundamental Military Factors in Relation to Discussions concerning Territorial Trusteeships and Settlements," Aug. 4, 1944, CCS 092 (7-27-44), RG 218, NA; informal min. of mtg. in Hull's office, July 18, 1944, and Steering Comm. min., July 31 and Aug. 4, 1944, in Notter Papers, box 173, Minutes—Washington and Steering Comm. Min. Folders, RG 59, NA; Louis, *Imperialism at Bay,* 366, 373–77; Notter, *Postwar Foreign Policy Preparation,* 295–96.

45. Yarnell to VCNO, "Basic Demobilization Plan no. 3," memo, June 14, 1944, SPD, ser. 14, box 198, A16-3 (5) folder, NH. See also Horne to King, enclosing Yarnell letter of June 16, 1944, "Memorandum on Post-War Far Eastern Situation," Nov. 29, 1944, ser. 14, Strat. Plans Div. (WPD), box 195, A-8-Intell. Folder, NH. For analysis of these documents, see Chap. 11.

46. Steering Comm. mtg. min., July 31, 1944, Notter Papers, box 173, RG 59, NA.

47. Ibid.

48. On this point, see Brower, "Sophisticated Strategists."

49. Gardner, *Spheres of Influence,* 176–77.

50. Sainsbury, *Turning Point,* 227.

51. See Chaps. 2 and 3, and Lynn Davis, *Cold War Begins,* 141–42.

52. *FRUS: Cairo and Tehran,* 845–46.

53. *FRUS,* 1944, 4:824–26, 951 (see also 813–43, 862–63, and 1035–37); Deane, *Strange Alliance,* 98; Woodward, *British Foreign Policy in the Second World War,* 3:109–10.

54. See OPD 336 Russia, secs. 45, 46, and 59, RG 165, NA; JCS Geog. series, CCS 350.05 USSR (5-6-44) Folder, RG 218, NA; and Hynes, "Notes on Mr. Harriman's Talk with Members of the MEA Staff," memo, May 5, 1944, CAD 014 Russia (9-1-43) (1), RG 165, NA.

55. Bohlen, *Witness to History,* 158; Leahy diary, May 12, 17, June 10, 1944, LOC; Leahy, *I Was*

There, 238; JCS Memo for Information no. 180, "Report on Political Conditions in Occupied Europe," Jan. 17, 1944, Roosevelt Papers, MRF, box 171, FDRL; Woodward, *British Foreign Policy in the Second World War,* 3:110–11.

56. Lincoln to Wedemeyer, Oct. 30, 1944, Lincoln Papers, box 5, USMA.

57. Informal Notes on JCS 812 and 812/1, "Rumanian Armistice Terms Proposed by U.S.S.R.," Apr. 9, 1944, ABC 336 Rumania, sec. 1A (26 Sept. 43), and Apr. 10, 1944, ABC 381 SS Papers (7 Jan. 43) (nos. 227–240/10), tab 231, RG 165, NA.

58. Caraway to Chief, S&P, "JCS 838/1, Disposition of Italian Overseas Territories," memo, May 13, 1944, ABC 092 Italy (27 Apr. 44), RG 165, NA.

59. Ibid. See also BB, "Notes on JCS 162nd Meeting," undated, ibid.

60. SS 307, "Course of Action in the Balkans and Aegean," July 14, 1944, ABC 384 Sweden-Turkey (25 Oct. 44), sec. 4, RG 165, NA.

61. Bissell and Weckerling, G-2, to Dir., SPD, "Navy's Basic Demobilization Plan no. 3," memo, July 27, 1944, SPD 370.01, RG 165, NA.

62. Perry McCoy Smith, *Air Force Plans for Peace,* 77–81.

63. Lincoln to Handy, "JCS 838/1," memo, May 15, 1944, ABC 092 Italy (27 Apr. 44), RG 165, NA. Lincoln was one of the few OPD officers to be aware of the Manhattan Project.

64. Ibid.

65. Handy, memo, July 28, 1944, OPD Exec. 2, item 11, RG 165, NA.

66. Handy to Marshall, "Fundamental Military Factors in Relation to Discussions concerning Trusteeships and Settlements (JCS 973)," memo, July 30, 1944, and Marshall to Handy, memo, Aug. 1, 1944, both in OPD Exec. 17, item 24, RG 165, NA.

67. On May 16 the JCS approved the Italian colonies paper and forwarded it to Hull. In early September before the second conference in Quebec, he excerpted it in a briefing paper to FDR; see *FRUS: Quebec,* 190–92. On September 27 it was forwarded to U.S. ministers to Commonwealth nations as "personal and secret background information" on postwar Allied relations, and a few months later State reproduced it within the Yalta briefing book as evidence of JCS support for its opposition to spheres of influence. See Hickerson to U.S. Ministers, tel., Sept. 27, 1944, DS, 865.014/5-1644, RG 59, NA, and *FRUS: Malta and Yalta,* 106–7. By informal action on August 3, the JCS approved a slightly revised version of the July JSSC paper on trusteeships, adding "under existing conditions" to the JSSC comment that the United States could not defeat Russia in a war. Marshall then forwarded it to Hull on August 3. It is reproduced in *FRUS,* 1944, 1:699–703, and excerpted in the Potsdam briefing book, *FRUS: Berlin,* 1:264–66.

68. Marshall to Handy, Roberts to Marshall, Cress to JCS Sec., and Handy to Marshall, memos, Aug. 1, 2, and 12, 1944, OPD Exec 17, item 24, RG 165, NA; Memo for the Record by L.H.S., Aug. 7, 1944, OPD 336, sec. 2, RG 165, NA.

69. "Though in the immediate future our security will depend upon preventing the resurgence of Germany," the COS informed the Foreign Office and JSM on July 27, "in the long run the most important factor will be our relationship with Russia." German resurgence remained the major potential threat, yet "the more remote, but more dangerous possibility of a hostile Russia making use of the resources of Germany must not be lost sight of and . . . any measures which we now take should be tested by whether or not they help to prevent that contingency ever arising." Two weeks later the COS instructed the Post Hostilities Planning Committee to face the possibility of conflict with Russia "realistically" and posed a series of questions to their JIC about future Russian intentions and war potential. COS to JSM, tel., July 27, 1944, CAB/22/597, and "USSR-Questionnaire to JIC," Aug. 11, 1944, CAB/81/45, PHP (44) 20 (o) Final, PRO.

Throughout this time period the British Chiefs and the Foreign Office remained at loggerheads over the issue of postwar relations with the Soviets and the need for contingency planning against them. For the COS perspective and activities, see Anthony Gorst, "British Military Planning for Postwar Defense, 1943–1945," in Deighton, *Britain and the First Cold War*, 91–103; Bryant, *Triumph in the West*, 180; Bradley Smith, *Sharing Secrets*, 179, 223–24; Lewis, *Changing Direction;* and Woodward, *British Foreign Policy in the Second World War*, 5:203–10. The Soviet position at this time remains unclear, but Zubok and Pleshakov, *Inside the Kremlin's Cold War*, 29–30, note that former wartime ambassadors to London and Washington Ivan Maisky and Maxim Litvinov argued for postwar cooperation in 1944 and that in July Litvinov saw much hope for such cooperation in the apparent interest of many Westerners in the postwar global "division of security zones" clearly supported by the JSSC and JCS.

That detailed statements on postwar relations were prepared in all three nations during July 1944 was not coincidental and probably resulted from major Allied military victories in Europe as well as the forthcoming Dumbarton Oaks Conference.

70. Matloff, *Strategic Planning*, 497; Perry, *"Dear Bart,"* 270–71.

71. Stimson to Marshall, "Our Military Reserves," memo, May 10, 1944, OPD Exec. 10, item 57, paper 42, RG 165, NA; Matloff, *Strategic Planning*, 411, 497; Wedemeyer to Handy and Handy to Wedemeyer, Apr. 13 and May 4, 1944, Wedemeyer Papers, box 78, folder 9, HI (original in OPD Exec. 7, item 23B, RG 165, NA). Wedemeyer expressed his opinions to Churchill and Eden during a visit to England and reported that Churchill had agreed with his assessment, whereas Eden had disagreed.

72. Deane to Marshall, March 17, 1944, Marshall Papers, POF, box 63, folder 29, GCMRL.

73. Bissell, G-2, to Handy, OPD, memo, Mar, 21, 1944, OPD Exec. 9, book 16, paper 436, RG 165, NA.

74. Roosevelt to Leahy and Leahy to Roosevelt, May 24 and 26, 1944, Roosevelt Papers, PSF, box 146, Earle Folder, FDRL. On May 29 Roosevelt also forwarded a copy of Earle's report to the State Dept., where Bohlen prepared a summary for Hull. See Hull Papers, box 82, Subject File, folder 371, Russia, LOC.

75. Bland, *Marshall Papers*, 4:447–50. See also Buhite, *Decisions at Yalta*, xv–xvi, and Maurice Matloff, "The 90-Division Gamble," in Greenfield, *Command Decisions*, 365–81.

76. JCS 614, "Plan for the Defeat of Japan," Dec. 2, 1943, ABC 381 Japan (8-27-42), sec. 2, RG 165, NA.

77. Embick to Marshall, memo, Sept. 1–2, 1943, Marshall Papers, POF, box 67, folder 40, GCMRL (further discussed in Chap. 11); Matray, "An End to Indifference," 192–93; U.S. Department of Defense, *Entry of the Soviet Union into the War against Japan*, 25–35.

78. *FRUS: Quebec*, 190–92; Gardner, *Spheres of Influence*, 163–65. See also Iriye, *Power and Culture*, 196–97. D. C. Watt concluded that to U.S. policymakers from FDR down, "the biggest danger was an Anglo-Soviet confrontation in which Britain would demand American support" (*Succeeding John Bull*, 103).

79. Warner, "From Tehran to Yalta," 530–36; Gardner, *Spheres of Influence*, 208–9. Huntington, *The Soldier and the State*, 333–35, sharply criticized the JCS for taking on FDR's values in place of their own. In "FDR as Commander-in-Chief," in May, *Ultimate Decision*, William R. Emerson countered that the views of FDR and the JCS on Russia were "identical," though based on different considerations, and that "there was on this question an effective unanimity of opinion" (165). Dallek, *Roosevelt and American Foreign Policy*, 469–70, maintains that at this time Roosevelt remained uncertain and fearful regarding the Soviets.

80. See JCS 718 series, "Effect of 'Unconditional Surrender' Policy on German Morale," CCS 387 Germany (12-17-43), secs. 1–3, RG 218, NA; *FRUS*, 1944, 1:493–94, 501–2; and Matloff, *Strategic Planning*, 428–30.

81. See, for ex., Stimson diary, July 31, 1944, YUL; Roosevelt to Stettinius, msge., Aug. 3, 1944, RG 165, OPD Exec. 10, item 63C (2) RG 165, NA; and handwritten comments by McCloy on occupation zone docs. in OPD Exec. 10, item 71, paper 133, RG 165, NA.

Chapter Ten

1. Notter, *Postwar Foreign Policy Preparation,* 248; min. of Informal Agenda Group, Mar. 23 and Apr. 6, 1944, Notter Papers, box 170, RG 59, NA; JCS 801, "Determination of Joint Agencies to Handle Questions of Post-War Organization," Apr. 1, 1944, CCS 310 (3-31-44), RG 218, NA; and min., JCS 156th mtg., Apr. 4, 1944, ABC 092 (Apr. 44), sec. 1, RG 165, NA. Responding to Leahy's fears that the JSSC and JCS would involve themselves in nonmilitary matters, the JCS added the word "military" after "international" before approving the authorization.

2. JCS 801, "Determination of Joint Agencies to Handle Questions of Post-War Organization," Apr. 1, 1944, CCS 310 (3-31-44), RG 218, NA; JCS 786 and 786/1, "Disarmament, Demobilization, and Demilitarization of Axis Countries," and 786/2/D, "Joint Post-War Committee," Mar. 25– June 7, 1944, in CCS 388.3 Axis (3-24-44), RG 218, NA, and in ABC 334.8 Jt Post-War Cmte (7 June 44) and ABC 381 SS (7 Jan 43) (nos. 271–281), tabs 273 and 278, RG 165, NA; Strong to Dunn, "Joint Post-War Committee of the Joint Chiefs of Staff," memo, DS 840.48/6-744, RG 59, NA; Vernon Davis, "History of the Joint Chiefs of Staff," 2:522–27; Cline, *Washington Command Post,* 323–24. The JWPC had originally proposed that the JSSC be given the JPWC's tasks, but the members of that committee, already overburdened with responsibilities for postwar issues, international conferences, and the State Department, joined the JPS and the OPD in suggesting instead a new body under its guidance. The JSM informed London on June 22 that the JPWC would be "in direct touch" with the State Dept. and that the JCS had given the JSSC "the watching brief." LETOD 143, JSM to War Cabinet, Redman to Jacob, June 22, 1944, CAB/122/417, PRO.

3. JCS 750 and 750/1, "Coordination between the Representatives of the State Department and the Military Commanders," Mar. 7 and 20, 1944, CCS 014.13 (3-7-44), RG 218, NA. See also Pogue, *Marshall,* 3:459–60, and Bland, *Marshall Papers,* 4:519–20.

4. Puleston to Horne, "Comments on 'Navy Basic Demobilization Plan,'" memo, Dec. 24, 1943, CNO Files, 1943, A16-3EN (16–31 Dec.), RG 80, NA.

5. "Probably half the world's important political decisions have been made by military leaders," this officer continued, something the Soviets, Germans, Japanese, and British recognized. So did the navy, which unlike the army was "intelligently setting to dominate" within the postwar U.S. "sphere of influence" in the Pacific. See the unsigned memo to Hull, "Comments on Memorandums to General Hull re Politico-Military Activities," Jan. 25, 1945, ABC 334.8 Post War Planning (19 Mar. 45), RG 165, NA.

6. Earle to Embick, Aug. 11, 1944, Earle Papers, box 15, folder E-3, SGMML; Earle to Caraway, Aug. 11, 1944, Caraway Papers, Personal File, 1941–44, MHI. In early 1945 Earle would also forward to Embick his 1943 paper on the decline in British power discussed in Chap. 7 and an August 17, 1944, paper he coauthored with Kirk and Sprout for the State Dept. titled "The Emerging Power Position of the Soviet Union." This paper echoed many of the JSSC conclusions but warned against overestimation of postwar Soviet power and challenged the belief that neither superpower could defeat the other on the grounds of superior U.S. "alliance-building ability" and difficulties the Soviets would have in controlling Mackinder's "heartland." Earle stated, however, that the paper did "not go as far" as he and the JSSC would "in estimating the full potentialities of the Soviet Union" because "it represents a composite of the views of the three of us." The letter is in the Earle Papers, box 15, folder E-3, and the paper in box 32, National Security Folder, SGMML.

The work of Kirk and Sprout on Dumbarton Oaks is mentioned in the Notter Papers, box 173, RG 59, NA. Information on the academic geopoliticians and their ties to the armed forces can be found above in Chap. 7; Lyons, "Growth of National Security Research," 491–92; and Yergin, *Shattered Peace,* 194, 450 n. 6. Lyons notes that the Government and History Departments at Columbia used the Earle seminar experience to launch their own course titled War and National

Policy in 1941, with the syllabus created by Kirk, Richard Stebbins, John Herz, Lindsay Rogers, Bernard Brodie, Felix Gilbert, and Alfred Vagts. I discuss the security paper Earle promised in Chap. 11.

Earle was also a member of the OSS Board of Analysts in 1941–42 and special consultant to AAF chief Arnold from 1942 to 1945 as well as to G-2 in 1942–43. He cowrote an early 1944 scholarly report, requested by Arnold in November 1943, analyzing whether OVERLORD was necessary or if Germany might collapse as in 1918. Carl Becker, Arthur C. Cole, Henry Steele Commager, Louis M. Gottschalk, Elias A. Lowe, Dumas Malone, Bernadotte Schmidt, and James D. Squires also participated. They concluded that Germany would not collapse this time and that invasion was essential. See Parrish, "Hap Arnold and the Historians," 113–14.

7. Caraway to Earle, Aug. 17, 1944, Caraway Papers, Personal File, 1941–44, MHI.

8. Langer, *Ivory Tower*, 197; Langer to Morse and to Donovan, Aug. 11, 17, 25, and 28, 1944, and Cress to Langer, memo, Aug. 21, 1944, OSS Entry 1, box 84, Langer Personal Files, RG 226, NA; Dessants, "American Academic Community and United States–Soviet Union Relations," 75–76, 84–85, 89–98, 119–23, 133, 225–26, and n. 6; Katz, *Foreign Intelligence*, 150–54. At this time, some R&A analyses concerning the postwar world, U.S. security requirements, and relations with Russia bore a striking similarity to the 1943–44 JSSC analyses discussed in Chaps. 7 and 9. See in particular #2073, "Russian Aims in Germany and the Problem of 3 Power Cooperation," May 11, 1944, and #2284, "American Security Interests in the European Settlement," June 29, 1944, RG 226, NA.

9. Extensive material on the conference and course is in the Forrestal Papers, boxes 10, 11, and 19, SGMML. See also Earle Papers, boxes 25, 30, and 39, SGMML. Princeton University Press published *Foundations of National Power* as edited by Sprout in 1945. It focused heavily on the geopolitical ideas and conclusions that I analyzed in Chap. 7.

10. Forrestal diaries, Sept. 17, 1944, box 1, vol. 1, Forrestal Papers, SGMML.

11. Millis, *Forrestal Diaries*, 26.

12. Vincent Davis, *Admiral's Lobby*, 148.

13. Forrestal diary entries for Nov. 23, 1944, and Apr. 17, 1945, in Millis, *Forrestal Diaries*, 19, 45. Roosevelt had not been the only individual to practice exclusion. According to Hoopes and Brinkley, *Driven Patriot*, 188, King had sought to preserve his direct links to the White House by refusing even to inform Knox of JCS deliberations. Such behavior stood in sharp contrast to that of Marshall, who not only kept Stimson fully informed but even invited McCloy to sit with the JCS as his observer. Forrestal had been able to keep up with JCS discussions since his appointment as secretary only by lunching frequently with McCloy, a situation he wanted to alter. According to Stimson's diary for May 4, 1943, however, Knox claimed that King had kept him informed as Marshall did Stimson (YUL).

14. Stimson to Hull, Stimson diary, Aug. 21–22, 1944, YUL. See also ibid., Sept. 11, Oct. 11, Oct. 26, and Dec. 19, 1944; Dillon to Forrestal, May 6, 1944, Forrestal Papers, box 2, Knox File, RG 80, NA; Dawney, memo, Aug. 9, 1945, ibid., Forrestal File-Carbons; Bird, *Chairman*, 192–93; Campbell, *Masquerade Peace*, 70–71; Campbell, "Nationalism in America's UN Policy," 33–35; Albion and Connery, *Forrestal*, 133–34, 232; and Cline, *Washington Command Post*, 325.

15. JCS 997, "Military Interest in the Planning and Development of Post-War Civil Aviation," Aug. 15, 1944, ABC 580.82 Efate (2-3-43), sec. 1-A, RG 165, NA; JCS 1098/1, "Provisional Arrangements for World Air Transport Routes and Services," Oct. 21, 1944, CCS 360 (12-19-42), sec. 4, RG 218, NA.

16. Quotation is from Campbell, "Nationalism in America's UN Policy," 34–35. The relevant docs. are in *FRUS*, 1944, 1:1466–70; ABC 334.8 Far East (9 Nov. 44), sec. 1-A, and ABC 334.8 Jt. Civ. Affairs Cmte. (18 July 44), RG 165, NA; and SPD, ser. 14, box 197, folder A16-1(1), NH. See also Campbell, *Masquerade Peace*, 70–71; Notter, *Postwar Foreign Policy Preparation*, 347–48; and

Cline, *Washington Command Post,* 325–27. According to White House Map Room officer George Elsey, "Some White House Recollections," 360, in late 1944 Leahy also sought to improve coordination by having Bohlen come to his office each morning to review Map Room traffic and JCS papers for the secretary of state.

Proposals for additional politico-military coordination in the fall had focused on representation for the service secretaries on JCS committees, and on November 7 Forrestal and Stimson informed FDR of these proposals. On November 9 Stettinius suggested a civil-military commission similar to the European Advisory Commission to plan for Japanese surrender and occupation policies in the Far East. King found this "eminently desirable," but Leahy informally objected to direct JCS representation. Whether this reflected his own fears of participation in such "political" issues or those of FDR remains as unclear in this episode as for all the past ones during which he had taken a similar stand, though the navy routing slip for all these proposals contains the penciled notation, "14 Nov/44 President demurs." See Forrestal and Stimson to Roosevelt, Stettinius to Stimson, by King, and MNH for the Record, memos, Nov. 7, 9, 14, and 22, 1944, ABC 334.8 Far East (9 Nov. 44), sec. 1-A, RG 165, NA. The penciled notation is noted on the top sheet covering this correspondence in SPD, ser. 14, box 197, folder A16-1(1), RG 38, NA. Stettinius's November 9 letter to Stimson is also in *FRUS,* 1944, 5:1274–75.

17. Cline, *Washington Command Post,* 326.

18. Pasvolsky quote from min., Informal Agenda Group, Mar. 23, 1944, Notter Papers, box 170, RG 59, NA; see also min. for Mar. 16, Apr 6, and Apr. 27, 1944, mtgs., and JCS 791, "International Regulation of Armaments and Armed Forces . . . ," Mar. 27, 1944, CCS 388.3 (3-20-44), RG 218, NA. British quotation from Welsh, "World Organization Conference," memo, Aug. 19, 1944, CAB/122/598, PRO. Similar COS views on postwar security can be found in COS (44) 282(o), "The Military Aspects of Any Post-War Security Organization," Mar. 29, 1944, CAB/122/15555, PRO.

19. See Hildebrand, *Dumbarton Oaks,* 34–36.

20. Min., Informal Agenda Group, May 25, 1944, Notter Papers, box 170, RG 59, NA. See also min. for Apr. 20 and 27 mtgs.

21. Vincent Davis, *Admirals Lobby,* 148.

22. See Chap. 8.

23. Sherry, *Preparing for the Next War,* 39–41; Perry McCoy Smith, *Air Force Plans for Peace,* 55–64; JCS 942 series, "U.S. Forces Required after Defeat of Germany," esp. JCS 942–942/2 and JPS 549/2 (approved Jan. 1945 as JCS 942/5), July 8, Aug. 23, 31, and Dec. 7, 1944, CCS 370.01 (7-30-43), secs. 1 and 2, RG 218, NA; JCS Memo for Information no. 262, "Planning for Post Hostilities European Theater of Operations," July 11, 1944, CCS 388.3 (7-9-44), RG 218, NA.

24. See above, Chap. 8, and Vincent Davis, *Postwar Defense Policy and the U.S. Navy,* 89–90. The plans are in ser. 14, CNO-1944-1684-A16-3EN May–June 1944, NH.

25. See above, Chap. 9; Yarnell quotations in this and the following two paragraphs are from Yarnell to VCNO, "Basic Demobilization Plan no. 3," memo, June 14, 1944, SPD, ser. 14, box 198, A16-3(5) Folder, NH; see also Vincent Davis, *Postwar Defense Policy and the U.S. Navy,* 91–92. A copy of Yarnell's June 14 memo can also be found in SPD 370.01 April and May 1944, RG 165, NA.

26. Yarnell to VCNO, "Basic Demobilization Plan no. 3," cited in n. 25 above. Puleston had maintained that Russia could "never become a great naval power" because its people were not "skillful on the water" and because its geographic position would require the creation of three separate navies and a large army, a combination the country simply could not afford. See Puleston to Horne, "Comments on 'Navy Basic Demobilization Plan,'" Dec. 24, 1943, in n. 4 above.

27. Horne to King, enclosing Yarnell letter of June 16, 1944, "Memorandum on Post-War Far Eastern Situation," memo, Nov. 29, 1944, SPD, ser. 14, box 195, A-8 Intell. Folder, NH.

28. Ibid.; emphasis in original.

29. Hull to Dir., SPD, "Navy's Basic Demobilization Plan no. 3," memo, July 5, 1944, SPD 370.01 April and May 1944, RG 165, NA.

30. Bissell and Weckerling, G-2, for Dir., SPD, "Navy's Basic Demobilization Plan no. 3," memo, July 27, 1944, SPD 370.01 April and May 1944, RG 165, NA.

31. Ibid.

32. Tompkins to Yarnell, "Navy's Basic Demobilization Plan no. 3," memo, Aug. 10, 1944, and Yarnell to VCNO, memo, Aug. 22, 1944, SPD 370.01 April and May 1944, RG 165, NA.

33. Campbell, *Masquerade Peace*, 31–32. This was insufficient for Forrestal and Stimson, however, who were by this time pressing for their own inclusion in politico-military issues and consequently insisted that they be kept informed during the negotiations, with Forrestal desiring such information in writing; the Steering Committee thus concluded that Hull should meet with both men twice a week during the conference. See Patterson and Forrestal to Hull, July 15, 1944, DS 500.cc/7-1544, RG 59, NA; min. of Aug. 7, 1944, mtgs., Notter Papers, box 173, Steering Comm. Min. Folder, RG 59, NA. See also min. of Aug. 29, 1944, mtg., Notter Papers, box 174, Dumbarton Oaks, U.S. Del. Mtgs. Folder, RG 59, NA, and Notter, *Postwar Foreign Policy Preparation*, 293–94, 302, 308–12.

34. See JSM 220 and 238, JSM to COS, Aug. 25 and Sept. 2, 1944, CAB/122/599, PRO. Despite COS opposition, Churchill supported an international air force and held the mistaken belief, which the British delegation attempted to correct on September 23, that U.S. military opinion favored Russian views on this matter. See CAB/122/599, PRO; FO to DO #7850, Sept. 4, 1944, and PM min. of Aug. 30, 1944, COS (44) 172, PRO; and MM(S) 74, "Report by the Military Members of the UK Delegation," Sept. 23, 1944, CAB/122/600, PRO.

35. Campbell and Herring, *Stettinius Diaries*, 105; Bissell to CofS, "Dumbarton Oaks Conference," Sept. 15, 1944, Army Intell. TS Decimal File, 1942–52, box 1, 350.09-44 Folder, RG 319, NA; Willson quotation in min., Steering Comm. mtg., July 31, 1944, Notter Papers, box 173, RG 59, NA.

36. Min., Aug. 25, 1944, mtg., Notter Papers, box 174, Dumbarton Oaks, U.S. Del. Mtgs. Folder, RG 59, NA; *FRUS*, 1944, 1:710–11, 730 n. 13; Hildebrand, *Dumbarton Oaks*, 143–49, 175–77.

37. Min., Oct. 3, 1944, mtg., Pasvolsky Papers, box 9, Conference File, Dumbarton Oaks minutes, Conv. B minutes—Sp. Mil. Record, OC 1944 Folder, LOC.

38. Hildebrand, *Dumbarton Oaks*, 177–78. See also ibid., 142–45, and Campbell, *Masquerade Peace*, 42–44. The references to Korea, Finland, and Denmark are in the min. of the Sept. 5, 1944, mtg. of the U.S. delegation, Notter Papers, box 174, RG 59, NA.

39. See, for ex., Hildebrand, *Dumbarton Oaks*, 154–55, and "Informal Record of the First Meeting of the Security Subcommittee," Aug. 23, 1944, Pasvolsky Papers, box 9, Conference File, Dumbarton Oaks minutes, A 61944, LOC.

40. Quotations are from Campbell and Herring, *Stettinius Diaries*, 111, 133–35; see also 129–30.

41. Min. of mtg., Sept. 14, 1944, Notter Papers, box 174, U.S. del. mtgs. Folder, RG 59, NA.

42. Min. of mtg. of U.S. Groups 1 and 2, Aug. 14, 1944, Notter Papers, box 173, I.O. Min. Folder, RG 59, NA.

43. Memo and min. of mtgs. on Sept. 18, 1944, in ibid., box 174. See also the Stettinius diary as well as "Calendar Notes," Records of Phone Conversations, and Source Material for Diary, Sept. 14, 18, and 20, 1943, Stettinius Papers, boxes 241, 242, and 270, AL; Campbell and Herring, *Stettinius Diaries*, 139–40; Hildebrand, *Dumbarton Oaks*, 218–19; Campbell, *Masquerade Peace*, 52–53; and Campbell, "Nationalism in America's UN Policy," 30–31.

44. Forrestal diaries, Sept. 19, 1944, box 1, vol. 1, SGMML.

45. Min. of mtg., Sept. 19, 1944, with Sept. 18–19 memos, Notter Papers, box 174, U.S. del. mtgs. RG 59, NA. See also min. of mtg., U.S. groups 1 and 2, Aug. 17, 1944, ibid., box 173, I.O. Minutes Folder; and Stettinius diary, box 241, and "Source Material" for Sept. 20, 1944, box 270, Stettinius Papers, AL.

46. Campbell and Herring, *Stettinius Diaries,* 136–37, 139–40; Stettinius diary, and "Calendar Notes," Sept. 18–19, 1943, Stettinius Papers, boxes 241 and 242, AL.

47. *FRUS,* 1944, 1:831–33; Campbell and Herring, *Stettinius Diaries,* 139, 142–44; Stettinius diary, Sept. 19–21, 1943, box 241, AL; Campbell, "Nationalism in America's UN Policy," 31. According to Hull, *Memoirs,* 2:1705, Embick stated this was the view of the entire JCS. The unpublished Stettinius diary entry for September 19 has Embick reporting that Marshall "shared his view as to the military considerations involved in the case of adjournment" but that he had not discussed the voting issue with the chief of staff, and Willson reporting that King considered this "a political question on which he should not render an opinion" save that "short and long term military considerations should be kept in mind." Campbell, "Nationalism in America's UN Policy," 31, says Marshall was reluctant to agree, whereas according to Hildebrand, *Dumbarton Oaks,* 220, the army chief had replied noncommittally to a query regarding his views on the issue.

48. Campbell and Herring, *Stettinius Diaries,* 145.

49. Campbell, "Nationalism in America's UN Policy," esp. 26–34.

50. Hildebrand, *Dumbarton Oaks,* 145. After a long dinner talk with Embick on August 3, Stimson expressed pleasure that Embick, "one of our best strategists, had also thought over these international problems and in the main agreed with me." After a September 12 conversation on principles of the peace, Stimson concluded that his "breadth of view and temperateness constituted another evidence . . . that it is the soldiers and not the civilians who are most wise and temperate in their proposals as to what we shall do to Germany to secure a lasting peace." Stimson diary, Aug. 3 and Sept. 12, 1944, YUL.

51. Hoopes and Brinkley, *FDR and the Creation of the U.N.,* 146–51.

52. *FRUS: Malta and Yalta,* 57.

53. Ibid.; *FRUS,* 1944, 1:922–23.

54. JCS 973/4, "International Trusteeships," Jan. 9, 1945, ABC 093 (28 July 44), sec. 1-A, RG 165, NA; memo by Pasvolsky of telephone conversation with Willson, Jan. 22, 1945, Pasvolsky Papers, box 3, Int'l. Org.: Int'l. Trusteeship 1 Dec. 1944 Folder, LOC.

55. Memo by Pasvolsky of telephone conversation with Willson, Jan. 22, 1945, Pasvolsky Papers, box 3, Int'l. Org.: Int'l. Trusteeship 1 Dec. 1944 Folder, LOC; Stimson diary, Jan. 21, 1945, YUL.

56. Stimson diary, Jan. 21, 1945, YUL; memo by Pasvolsky of telephone conversation with Willson, Jan. 22, 1945, Pasvolsky Papers, box 3, Int'l. Org.: Int'l. Trusteeship 1 Dec. 1944 Folder, LOC. Stimson's diary reveals extensive discussion of the atomic bomb in the midst of this episode. Indeed, the January 22 meeting that I discuss just below took place immediately after a two-hour discussion of the bomb project. Campbell, "Nationalism in America's UN Policy," 35, concludes that Stimson wanted to delay the proposed UN conference until the United States possessed an A-bomb and that his desire for overseas bases was directly related to this weapon.

57. Stimson diary, Jan. 22–23, 1945, with attached letter, reproduced in *FRUS,* 1945, 1:23–27, and *FRUS: Malta and Yalta,* 78–81.

58. Ibid.

59. Ibid.

60. Stimson diary, Jan. 24 and Feb. 8, 1945, YUL.

Chapter Eleven

1. *FRUS,* 1944, 3:1376, 4:826–28, 988–90, 992–98; *FRUS: Quebec,* 198–200; Harriman and Abel, *Special Envoy,* 340–49, 365–72; Stimson diary, Oct. 23, 1944, YUL. Harriman had wanted to return earlier, in mid-September, but FDR, Hull, and Hopkins demurred. The official ratio-

nale for the return in October was to report on the Churchill-Stalin meeting that had just occurred in Moscow.

2. *FRUS,* 1944, 4:902–14, 989–90; Kennan, *Memoirs,* 503–31.

3. Hildebrand, *Dumbarton Oaks,* 178–79.

4. *FRUS: Quebec,* 192–93; *FRUS,* 1944, 4:991; Stimson diary, Sept. 7, 1944, YUL.

5. As previously noted, paraphrases of Harriman's reports are in OPD 336 Russia, secs. 45, 46, and 49, RG 165, NA, and JCS Geographic series, CCS 350.05 USSR (5-6-44), RG 218, NA. A copy Kennan's memo is in the papers of S&P chief Lincoln, USMA.

6. Bradley Smith, *Sharing Secrets,* 213–14, 222–23, 225; Herring, *Aid to Russia,* 137. Smith concludes that the evidence did not justify such complaints and that the Soviets were more cooperative at this time than they had ever been in the past.

7. Personal Rpt. of Russia Assignment, June–Oct. 15, 1944, Walsh Papers, Russia Shuttle Bombing Folder, MHI, courtesy of Prof. Theodore Wilson.

8. Deane to Marshall, Dec. 2, 1944, ABC 336 Russia (22 Aug. 43), sec. 1A, RG 165, NA, reprinted in *FRUS: Malta and Yalta,* 447–48, and Deane, *Strange Alliance,* 84–86.

9. Ibid.

10. Ibid.; Deane to JCS, "Present Relations between the United States Military Mission, Moscow, and the Soviet Military Authorities," memo, Jan. 22, 1945, in *Records of the JCS,* reel 2. For Harriman's similar position, see *FRUS,* 1944, 4:992–98, and Larson, *Origins of Containment,* 93–106.

11. Marshall to Stimson, memo, Dec. 21, 1944, Marshall Papers, POF, box 63, folder 32, GCMRL, reprinted in Bland, *Marshall Papers,* 4:702–3; Stimson to Roosevelt, Jan. 3, 1945, Roosevelt Papers, PSF, SAFE: Russia, FDRL, reprinted in *FRUS: Malta and Yalta,* 447; Stimson diary, Jan. 9, 1945, YUL; Sherry, *Preparing for the Next War,* 171–72; Pogue, *Marshall,* 3:530–31; Clemens, "Harriman, John Deane, the Joint Chiefs," 289–90.

12. Stimson diary, Dec. 31, 1944, YUL.

13. *FRUS,* 1944, 3:742–43.

14. Billo to Chief, S&P, "Declaration of War by Russia on Bulgaria," memo, Sept. 5, 1944, ABC 380 USSR Bulgaria (5 Sept. 44), RG 165, NA; JJB to Chief, S&P, "Operations in Greece (CCS 750)," Dec. 21, 1944, ABC 384 Greece (20 Dec. 44), RG 165, NA.

15. *FRUS,* 1944, 5:442–44, 748–49; D.Z.Z. to Jones, memo, Oct. 28, 1944, and unsigned memo for Roberts, "U.S. Policy on Iran," Oct. 31, 1944, ABC 334.8 Iran (30 Oct. 43), RG 165, NA.

16. Wylie, "Postwar Aims of the Soviet Navy and Merchant Marine," memo, Oct. 24, 1944, Navy WPD, SPD, CNO, ser. 14, box 195, A8-Intelligence (Oct. 1944–Aug. 1945), NH.

17. Forrestal diaries, Aug. 18 and Sept. 2, 1944, SGMML, the latter entry reprinted in Millis, *Forrestal Diaries,* 14. See also Rogow, *Forrestal,* 126–27, 134, 151–52, 162–63.

18. Vincent Davis, *Postwar Defense Policy and the U.S. Navy,* 101–2, 107–8, and 295–96 nn. 5 and 7; emphasis in original. For Forrestal's interest in the Middle East, see *FRUS,* 1944, 5:755–56.

19. Forrestal diaries, Sept. 17, 1944, box 1, vol. 1, SGMML.

20. Soon after its October creation, F-14 had noted the lack of any basic estimates or integrated framework for postwar planning, despite JCS 570; consequently, it proposed that the JSSC create these while it proceeded with interim naval planning on the "basis of certain arbitrary premises." Douglas to Edwards and Lincoln, memos, and draft memo by Douglas for King to JCS, "Post-War Planning by the Military Services," Oct. 9 and 14, 1944, ser. 14, SPD, box 197, file A16-1(3), folder 1, NH. Interim planning was originally to be based on assumptions in the previous Navy Demobilization Plan no. 2, rev. 1, but by November navy planners had concluded that these were inadequate and that "no authoritative basis" for determining postwar U.S. military needs would be available until agreement had been reached on the nature of the postwar UN. Yet it was

necessary to proceed with tentative plans for the postwar navy. Consequently, F-14 was authorized to prepare an "expression of the facts and assumptions relating to the world situation in the Post-War period, and an evaluation of our national policies and other considerations" that would affect the postwar navy. See directive, Moore for Postwar Plans to Post-War Naval Planning Section Plans Division, "Basis for Establishing the Size, Character, and Disposition of the Post-War Navy," Nov. 22, 1944, ibid., and Vincent Davis, *Postwar Defense Policy and the U.S. Navy*, 105–6. Converse, "United States Plans for a Postwar Overseas Military Base System," 78–81, downplays Forrestal's role in naming the USSR as an enemy.

21. Quotations here and in the following six paragraphs from Naval Planning Section Draft, Dec. 26, 1944, ser. 14, SPD, box 197, A16-1 (1), NH.

22. Vincent Davis, *Postwar Defense Policy and the U.S. Navy*, 148–50.

23. Perry McCoy Smith, *Air Force Plans for Peace*, 68–69.

24. Arnold to SW and CofS, "Report of the Commanding General, Army Air Forces, to the Secretary of War," memo, Feb. 1945, Marshall Papers, box 65, folder 14, GCMRL. See also Pasco to Handy and Marshall to Arnold, memos, Feb. 14–16, 1945, ibid.

25. Schnabel, *History of the Joint Chiefs of Staff*, 1:10. See also Dessants, "American Academic Community and United States–Soviet Union Relations," 132–44.

26. JIC 250 series, "Estimate of Soviet Post-War Capabilities and Intentions," Jan. 18–Feb. 2, 1945, with handwritten marginal notes, ABC 336 Russia (22 Aug 43) sec. 1-A, RG 165, NA; JCS Memo for Information no. 374, "Estimate of Soviet Post-War Capabilities and Intentions," Feb. 5, 1945, ABC 092 USSR (15 Nov. 44), RG 165, NA. See also "Russia's Postwar Foreign Policy," Feb. 7, 1945, Forrestal diaries, box 1, vol. 1, and ONI Memo for Information, "Soviet Capabilities and Possible Intentions," undated, Forrestal Papers, box 24, Russia, SGMML.

27. At first they referred the issue to the British, rejected U.S. daylight air drops, but agreed to night drops. When these resulted in heavy losses, they proposed no further action unless the Soviets allowed them to use shuttle bombing bases, about which they drafted a presidential message that FDR agreed to send to Churchill. One such mission took place, but on September 21 Marshall recommended termination of the project. See Lynn Davis, *Cold War Begins*, 111–12, and memos between Brown and Marshall, Sept. 19 and 21, 1944, Marshall Papers, POF, box 57, folder 4, GCMRL.

28. See above, Chap. 9; JCS 1976, "U.S. Policy for Tripartite Action," Sept.–Oct. 1944, ABC 337 Moscow (13 Nov. 43), RG 165, NA; JCS 1056/1 and CCS 669/2, "Assistance to the Slovak Army and Partisans," Nov. 8 and 11, 1944, CCS 381 Czechoslovakia (9-7-44), RG 218, NA; and JPS 549/2 and JCS 942/5, "U.S. Forces Required after Defeat of Germany," Dec. 7, 1944, and Jan. 4, 1945, CCS 370.01 (7-30-43), sec. 2, RG 218, NA.

29. McCloy to ACofS, G-3, memo, Dec. 2, 1944, and Porter to Commandant, Command and General Staff School, "Alleged Improper Conduct at the Command and General Staff School," memo, Dec. 5, 1944, ASW 336 Russia, RG 107, NA.

30. See above, Chap. 10, and McCloy to DCofS, memo, Feb. 22, 1945, OPD Exec. 17, item 23, RG 165, NA.

31. Stimson diary, Dec. 27, 1944, and Jan. 12, 1945, YUL.

32. Chandler, *Eisenhower Papers*, 4:2430. United States manpower shortages were exacerbated in early 1945 by congressional objections to using eighteen-year-olds in combat and rejection of a national service bill. See Shepardson, "Fall of Berlin," 145, and Pogue, *Marshall*, 3:499–502.

33. Lincoln to Caraway, Dec. 14, 1944, Caraway Papers, Personal File 1941–44, MHI; Caraway to Lincoln, Jan. 4, 1945, Caraway Papers, Official Corres. File, MHI; Iriye, *Power and Culture*, 229; Stimson diary, Dec. 14, 1944, YUL.

34. JCS 924/2, "Operations against Japan Subsequent to Formosa," Aug. 30, 1944, ABC 384 Pacific (1-17-45) sec. 5, RG 165, NA. Marshall-Embick memos, Sept. 1, 2, 30, and Oct. 3, 1944, with

OPD draft, in ibid.; in Marshall Papers, POF, box 67, folder 40, GCMRL; and in Bland, *Marshall Papers,* 4:567–68, 616–17. See also supporting docs. in OPD 381 TS, sec. 19, case 533, RG 165, NA; Pogue, *Marshall,* 3, 527–28; Leahy diary, Sept. 15, 1944, LOC; and Brower, "Sophisticated Strategists," 239–45.

35. JCS 1176 and 1176/6, "Russian Participation in the War against Japan," Nov. 23, 1944, and Jan. 24, 1945, CCS 381 Japan (10-4-43), sec. 3, RG 218, NA; Marshall to Roosevelt, memo, Jan. 23, 1945, Roosevelt Papers, MRF, box 167, Japan Islands Folder 3, FDRL. Some of these docs., as well as docs. on the Harriman-Deane negotiations, are reproduced in *FRUS: Malta and Yalta,* 363–79, 388–400. See also U.S. Department of Defense, *Entry of the Soviet Union into the War against Japan,* 34–46, and Buhite, *Decisions at Yalta,* 88–89.

36. *FRUS,* 1945, 1:23–27. For a full discussion of Stimson's position, see Chap. 10.

37. Wedemeyer to Marshall, Oct. 8, 1944, Wedemeyer Papers, HI.

38. Stimson diary, Oct. 13, Oct. 14, and Dec. 31, 1944, YUL. The JCS did agree to British proposals at OCTAGON in September to consider an amphibious assault against Istria from Italy if practicable, but only because they did not believe it would be—especially in light of their insistence on a prior German withdrawal from Italy, no use of troops or craft required for operations in Europe or the Far East, and a decision by October 15. At that time they flatly vetoed the proposal. See Sainsbury, *Churchill and Roosevelt,* 80; *FRUS: Quebec,* 303, 429; and Bland, *Marshall Papers,* 4:654–56.

39. Dobson, *Peaceful Air Warfare,* 163–72.

40. Strong to Stettinius, memo, Dec. 28, 1944, DS, 500.cc/12-2844, RG 59, NA. See also Campbell, "Resurgence of Isolationism," 46–51.

41. Quotations are from Hathaway, *Ambiguous Partnership,* 97–98; Campbell and Herring, *Stettinius Diaries,* 200–201; and Leahy diary, Dec. 15, 1944, LOC. See also Stimson diary, Dec. 19, 1944, YUL; Anderson, *United States, Great Britain, and the Cold War,* 1–27; Frazier, *Anglo-American Relations with Greece,* 66–70; Sherwood, *Roosevelt and Hopkins,* 840–41; *FRUS,* 1944, 5:147–49; Wittner, *American Intervention in Greece,* 144–46; Buell, *Master of Seapower,* 461–62; and JCS 1210 and CCS 750–750/1, "Operations in Greece," Dec. 23–28, 1944, ABC 384 Greece (20 Dec. 44), RG 165, NA. Hopkins countermanded King's order regarding landing craft; see Harbutt, "Churchill, Hopkins, and the 'Other' Americans," 258–59.

42. JCS 713, "Strategy in the Pacific," Feb. 16, 1944, ABC 384 Pacific (1-17-43), sec. 3-A, RG 165, NA; JCS 953/1, "Staff Conversations with Portugal," Aug. 5, 1944, ABC 384 Portugal (3 Jan. 44), sec. 1-A, RG 165, NA.

43. Hayes, *History of the Joint Chiefs of Staff,* 631, 637–38; Buell, *Master of Seapower,* 445–46; Hathaway, *Ambiguous Partnership,* 61, 330 n. 15; *FRUS: Quebec,* 256–57, 315–18, 330–35. Love, "Fighting a Global War," 281–83, notes that King had been furious at the British ever since they had forced cancellation of BUCCANEER at the second Cairo Conference, thereafter "neither expected nor wanted" their help in the Pacific, and saw their offer as a way to suck the United States into support of SEAC operations. What, he rhetorically asked and answered during an unofficial February meeting with the press, were their 750,000 men in India doing? "They're eating regularly." See Perry, *"Dear Bart,"* 250–51, and Woods, *F.D.R. and the Triumph of American Nationalism,* 567–81.

44. Wedemeyer to Marshall, Oct. 8, 1944, Wedemeyer Papers, box 78, folder 16, HI.

45. Handy for CofS, "Notes for Conference with the President," memo, Sept. 23, 1944, ABC 337 (14 Sept. 44), sec. 1, RG 165, NA. An additional strategic argument, which Leahy labeled a "sharp disagreement," took place in late 1944 when the Joint Chiefs authorized the withdrawal from Burma of Chinese ground and U.S. air forces in an effort to halt the Japanese offensive in China. See Leahy diary, Dec. 6, 1944, LOC.

46. Elsey to Brown, "Clipperton Island," memo, Jan. 17, 1945, Roosevelt Papers, MRF, box 60,

A4-3 Air Bases Clipperton, FDRL. See also Forrestal diaries, box 1, vol. 1, Dec. 31, 1944, SGMML, and Converse, "U.S. Plans for a Postwar Overseas Military Base System," 104–6.

47. Larson, *Origins of Containment*, 100.

48. Unsigned memo for Carter, "Machinery for U.S.-USSR Collaboration in the War against Japan," Dec. 19, 1944, ABC 384 USSR (25 Sept. 44), sec. 1-A, RG 165, NA.

49. Quoted in Campbell, *Masquerade Peace*, 85.

50. Millis, *Forrestal Diaries*, 36–37.

51. See Hathaway, *Ambiguous Partnership*, 118–25.

52. Leahy, *I Was There*, 315–16; Leahy diary, Feb. 11, 1945, LOC; Lynn Davis, *Cold War Begins*, 190–91. On February 11 Leahy also condemned the accords on Germany as "a frightening 'sowing of dragon's teeth' that carries germs of an appalling war of revenge at some time in the distant future," and he concluded that the decision to place France on the Security Council with veto power would lead to disagreements among the Big Three and "destroy the effectiveness" of the UN.

53. Quoted in Reynolds and Dimbleby, *An Ocean Apart*, 174. Even Leahy admitted that he was "deeply impressed" by the agreements on "action that shall be taken to destroy Germany as a military power." Leahy diary, Feb. 11, 1945, LOC.

54. Notes for Off-the-Record Talk to Overseas Press Club in New York City, Mar. 1, 1945, Marshall Papers, POF, box 111, folder 49, GCMRL. See also Bland, *Marshall Papers*, 4:592, 713–14.

55. Supp. min., JCS 144th mtg., Feb. 1, 1944, CCS 334 JCS, RG 218, NA; Handy to CofS, "Composition of USAAF for the Occupation of Germany," memo, Oct. 17, 1944, ABC 381 SS Papers (7 Jan. 43) (nos. 314–326), SS 323, RG 165, NA.

56. JCS Memo for Information no. 382, "A Security Policy for Post-War America," Mar. 29, 1945, CCS 092 (7-27-44), RG 165, NA. The memo itself was dated March 8, 1945. Information on the Rye Conference can be found in the Earle Papers, box 30, 1945 Rye Conf. Folder, SGMML. See also Chap. 10 for Earle's 1944 promise of such a paper.

57. All quotations from the memo are from the March 8 version circulated on March 29 as JCS Memo for Information no. 382, "A Security Policy for Post-War America," CCS 092 (7-27-44), RG 218, NA.

58. Ibid. The memo also emphasized the importance of U.S. economic strength in creating a peaceful postwar world and the need for the UN to appeal to smaller states in order to be effective. Yet its emphasis was clearly on the Great Powers and the importance of future Soviet-American relations to the maintenance of world peace and U.S. security.

59. Quotations are from Earle to Dunn, Apr. 2, 1945, and Earle to Moley, Apr. 28, 1945, Earle Papers, box 30, 1945 Rye Conf. Folder, SGMML. See also Dunn to Earle, Mar. 14, 1945, and Earle to Fox and Earle to Embick, Mar. 26, 1945, ibid.

60. JCS Memo for Information no. 382, "A Security Policy for Post-War America," cited above, n. 57. The JSSC also disagreed with the scholars' conclusion that the UN required the support of smaller states.

61. Earle to Fox, Mar. 26, 1945, and Earle to Baldwin, Apr. 2, 1945, Earle Papers, box 30, 1945 Rye Conf. Folder, SGMML.

62. Quotations are from Earle to Duffield, Apr. 6, 1945, Earle Papers, ibid. See also Earle to Dunn, Embick, Baldwin, Moley, and Embick, Apr. 2, 28, and 30, 1945, and Embick to Earle, May 9, 1945, Earle Papers, ibid.

Chapter Twelve

1. *FRUS*, 1945, 5:816–24, 472–75; Lynn Davis, *Cold War Begins*, 256–59, 267–68.

2. JCS 1301, "Arrangements with the Soviets," Apr. 3, 1945, CCS 092 USSR (3-27-45), sec. 1, RG 218, NA. Harriman's concurrence with Deane's recommendations is in *FRUS*, 1945, 5:824. Specific military complaints included the grounding of all U.S. aircraft behind Russian lines, refusal to repair U.S. aircraft forced to land in the east, a prohibition on further entries by U.S. aircraft into Russian air space, refusal to allow a naval survey party to enter the USSR or Poland, problems with American POWs, and obstruction of the U.S. strategic bombing survey in Russian-occupied areas. Deane's suggested retaliation included a halt in Lend-Lease aircraft shipments, cancellation of the next northern convoy, and equivalent treatment for Russian POWs; the U.S. control commissioner in Hungary recommended suspension of Soviet flights to Italy.

3. Lynn Davis, *Cold War Begins*, 259.

4. JCS 1301/1, "Cancellation of Convoy to North Russia," Apr. 3, 1945, CCS 092 USSR (3-27-45), sec. 1, RG 218, NA.

5. JCS 1301/2, "Arrangements with the Soviets," Apr. 5, 1945, ibid.

6. Ibid. The JSSC asserted that many of the U.S. military requests, while "desirable," were "not of sufficient importance to warrant our insisting upon them in opposition to what is thought to be basic Russian political policy."

7. "Military and Organizational Bases of Security," Apr. 4, 1945, Forrestal Papers, box 25, Adm. Willson Speech Folder, SGMML. See also the undated draft of the Fairchild speech on international organization, Fairchild Papers, box 3, Subject File, Log of JSSC Papers, microfilm, Bolling Air Force Base.

8. Memo for the Record by Col. C. R. Peck, "J.C.S. 1301/2," Apr. 6, 1945, and undated memo on JCS action regarding JCS 1301/2, both attached to JCS 1301–1301/2, CCS 092 USSR (3-27-45), sec. 1, RG 218, NA.

9. Pogue, *Marshall*, 3:565–66; Kimball, *Churchill and Roosevelt*, 3:609–12.

10. Kimball, *Churchill and Roosevelt*, 3:630.

11. Marshall to Pres., "Probable Developments in the German Reich," memo, Apr. 2, 1945, Roosevelt Papers, MRF, box 167, FDRL. Marshall also estimated that a Soviet offensive should begin April 10, U.S. forces would be at the Elbe by April 20, and the two forces would make contact there by May 1. At that point no cohesive German fronts would remain, only isolated albeit large pockets that would offer fanatical resistance as long as Hitler lived. Interestingly, Marshall noted that stories of a Hitlerian Alpine redoubt "are believed to lack substance," though thirty to forty German divisions might be trapped in the area.

12. Dessants, "American Academic Community and United States–Soviet Union Relations," 145–46. Langer noted on his copy of the memo, as graciously provided by Dessants, that he and Robinson had prepared it for Embick and that it was discussed "at length" during the San Francisco UN Conference in a meeting attended by the JSSC, McCloy, Bowman, and others. In his *In and Out of the Ivory Tower*, 190–92, Langer posited that it was "highly regarded" by the JCS and by Embick, that he and Robinson wrote other memos on relations with the Soviets for Embick at this time which the general shared with "a select group of high ranking army officers," and that he and Robinson "had an exciting afternoon of discussion with them."

13. OSS R&A Paper, "Problems and Objectives of United States Policy," Apr. 2, 1945, copies in ASW 336 Russia, RG 107, NA, and in Marshall Papers, POF, box 67, folder 41, GCMRL.

14. Ibid.

15. Ibid.

16. Ibid.

17. Dessants, "American Academic Community and United States–Soviet Union Relations," 145–46; cover note and routing slip, Apr. 2–10, 1945, Marshall Papers, POF, box 67, folder 41, GCMRL; Lincoln to Hull, memo, June 17, 1945, ibid., folder 42.

Embick referred to R&A's emphasis on hemispheric defense and extensive overseas bases because he was then deeply involved in an ongoing struggle with the State Dept. over both issues and their relationship to the postwar UN. The remaining members of the JSSC and the JCS were likewise involved, which may account for the wide distribution of the document.

From the admittedly limited evidence available, the Strategy and Policy Group was not impressed by these memos and found them too optimistic about Soviet intentions. Col. Paul Thompson rated Stalin a new Napoleon, disagreed with Earle and his associates that Soviet good intentions should be assumed, and termed the assertion that the Big Two stand together "wishful thinking." The possibility of Germany selling itself to Russia he considered "damn near a fait accompli," and he concluded that "the greatest danger to U.S. is Soviet Power Politics which includes giving in [sic] its sphere of influence." In May Lincoln asked Colonel Herman Beukema, chair of the Dept. of Economics, History, and Government at West Point, for comments on the Earle paper, but only because of a "general feeling that some additional thought ought to be dredged up" on it before filing. A month later Lincoln dismissed the R&A paper as possessing no "particularly new thought" and proposing "nothing definite," while worrying that "it may have gotten read at the White House with unfortunate results." See Thompson's comments on JCS Memo for Information no. 382 in ABC 334.8 Intl. Sec. Org. (9 Aug. 44), RG 165, NA; Lincoln to Beukema, May 20, 1945, Lincoln Papers, box 3, folder 4, USMA; Lincoln to Hull, memo, June 17, 1945, Marshall Papers, POF, box 67, folder 42, GCMRL.

18. JCS 1313, "Revision of Policy with Relation to Russia," Apr. 16, 1945, CCS 092 USSR (3-27-45), sec. 1, RG 218, NA.

19. Ibid., and JCS 1313/1, "Specific Actions to Be Taken under Revised Policy with Russia," Apr. 16, 1945, CCS 092 USSR (3-27-45), sec. 1, RG 218, NA. Harriman's agreement is in FRUS, 1945, 5:824.

20. Marshall to Deane et al., tel., Apr. 19, 1945; McFarland to JPS, "Revision of Policy with Relation to Russia," memo, Apr. 17, 1945; U.S. Secretariat Notes of Closed CCS Meeting, Apr. 20, 1945; JCS 1313/2 and Decision Amending JCS 1313/2, "Revision of Policy with Relation to Russia," Apr. 23–24, 1945, all in CCS 092 USSR (3-27-45), sec. 1, RG 218, NA; Wilson to COS, tel., Apr. 20, 1945, CAB/122/936, PRO; Yergin, Shattered Peace, 73–74. Harriman's warnings are in FRUS, 1945, 5:231–34.

21. JCS 1313/2, "Revision of Policy with Relation to Russia," Apr. 23, 1945, CCS 092 USSR (3-27-45), sec. 1, RG 218, NA; JCS 1308, "Italian Participation in the War against Japan," Apr. 11, 1945, with supporting docs., ABC 380 Italy (1 April 45), RG 165, NA. For further details with differing conclusions as to the extent of the JCS shift in April, see Clemens, "Harriman, John Deane, the Joint Chiefs," 277–301.

22. See below, n. 56, for details.

23. Stimson diary, Apr. 2, 3, and 16, 1945, YUL; Schwartz, America's Germany, 22–23. Forrestal's diary at this time, on the other hand, was filled with Harriman's warnings regarding the menace posed by Soviet policy and ideology, as well as hints of a united front with Britain. See Millis, Forrestal Diaries, 38–39, 41, 47–48.

24. Quotations are from Bohlen's memo of the mtg. in FRUS, 1945, 5:252–54, and Stimson diary, Apr. 23, 1945, YUL. See also Forrestal's account in Millis, Forrestal Diaries, 49–51.

25. FRUS, 1945, 5:254; Stimson diary, Apr. 23, 1945, YUL.

26. Harriman had previously called the Red Army "an extraordinarily effective but disorganized mass of human beings" from a country "still fantastically backward." He was "therefore not

much worried about the Soviet Union's taking the offensive in the near future" but believed "they will take control of everything they can by bluffing." *FRUS, 1945,* 5:253–55, 840, 844.

27. *FRUS, 1945,* 5:254. Leahy stated that the JCS were going to approve Deane's recommendations "anyway" but incorrectly asserted immediately before this comment and in his diary on April 23 that there was a consensus at the meeting "that the time had arrived to take a strong American attitude toward the Soviet Union and that no particular harm could be done to our war prospects if Russia should slow down or even stop its war effort in Europe and Asia" (*I Was There,* 351). See also Sherry, *Preparing for the Next War,* 175–79.

28. Stimson diary, Apr. 23, 26, 30, May 2, 7, and 10, 1945, YUL; Leahy diary, May 11, 1945, LOC; Truman, *Memoirs,* 1:102, 245; Bird, *Chairman,* 237; *FRUS, 1945,* 4:1127–35; Hathaway, *Ambiguous Partnership,* 137, 140–41; Rabel, *Between East and West,* 47, and "Prologue to Containment," 147; Poole, "From Conciliation to Containment," 12–13. "When men of different races were wandering around with different ideas and one of the races was Yugoslav," Stimson added in a May 3 telephone conversation with Grew, "then the situation was explosive" (*FRUS, 1945,* 4:1134–35).

29. JCS 1233–1233/2, "Military Objectives in Latin America," Jan. 18–31, 1945, ABC 371.3 Latin America (18 Jan. 45), sec. 1, RG 165, NA.

30. Leahy diary, Mar. 29, 1945, LOC; JSSC Rpt., "Preservation of Pan-American Defensive Structure," Apr. 9, 1945, ABC 093 (28 July 1944), sec. 1-A, RG 165, NA; Campbell, *Masquerade Peace,* 116–17; Russell, *History of the United Nations Charter,* 559–66, 688–89. The JSSC said relinquishment was "the maximum concession which should be made" to Latin American nationalism, and Embick later expressed doubts about the implicit loosening of U.S. control over the hemisphere.

31. *FRUS, 1945,* 1:93–94, 122–23, 198–99, 204–6, 209–13; Leahy diary, Mar. 29, 1945, LOC; Stimson diary, Mar. 18–30, Apr. 2–3, and Apr. 6–11, 1945, YUL; Sbrega, *Anglo-American Relations and Colonialism,* 155–56; Louis, *Imperialism at Bay,* 476–78; Notter, *Postwar Foreign Policy Preparation,* 387–88; Russell, *History of the United Nations Charter,* 576–87; Handy to Fairchild, memo, Mar. 30, 1945, Fairchild Papers, microfilm, Bolling Air Force Base. Dulles's support is noted in the Forrestal diaries, Apr. 9, 1945, box 1, vol. 2, SGMML.

Military representation at San Francisco included Embick, Fairchild, Willson, Hepburn, Train, special assistant to Arnold Gen. R. L. Walsh, OPD Pan American Group chief Gen. Kenner Hertford, and numerous army colonels and navy captains and commanders as well as McCloy and ASN Artemus Gates. Officers were heavily represented on the committees dealing with trusteeships and the Security Council. See Notter, *Postwar Foreign Policy Preparation,* 387–88, and Pasvolsky Papers, box 1, Int'l. Orgs (UN) Charter: Drafts, Proposals, etc. Folder, LOC.

32. *FRUS, 1945,* 1:122–23. On the Yalta trusteeship accords, see Louis, *Imperialism at Bay,* 448–60. See also Kimball, *The Juggler,* 148–57.

33. Millis, *Forrestal Diaries,* 45, 62; emphasis in original. For congressional, press, and public support, see Campbell, "Nationalism in America's UN Policy," 32–33, and Thorne, *Allies of a Kind,* 664–65. Throughout early 1945 navy postwar planning papers also continued to insist that the armed forces maintain the ability both to participate in an international organization to maintain world peace and to defend the United States and its interests unilaterally should the Grand Alliance collapse or the international organization prove ineffective or both. See King to Forrestal, "The United States Navy (Postwar)—Basis for Preparation of Plans," memo, Mar. 3, 1945, and "Estimate of Post-War Naval Establishment," memo, Apr. 27, 1945, plus handwritten, undated notes, "Case History: The Vicissitudes of Getting a Basis for Post-War Planning Written and Set Forward," with supporting docs., all in SPD, ser. 14, box 197, A16-1 (3), folder 1, NH; Douglas to Duffield, memo, Apr. 6, 1945, Forrestal Papers, box 1, vol. 2, SGMML; and Vincent Davis, *Postwar Defense Policy and the U.S. Navy,* 108–11.

34. Foltos, "New Pacific Barrier," 323. The Forrestal, Stettinius, and Stimson diaries all reveal

that the three secretaries often discussed the Russian and trusteeship controversies within the same meetings.

35. Stimson diary, Apr. 23, 1945, YUL.

36. JCS 1311, "International Organization for the Enforcement of World Peace and Security," Apr. 14, 1945, CCS 092 (4-14-45), sec. 1, RG 218, NA. See also Millis, *Forrestal Diaries*, 37–38, 41–42.

37. *FRUS*, 1945, 1:204–6, 209–14, 281–83, 290; Marshall to Hull, memo, Apr. 9, 1945, Marshall Papers, POF, box 65, folder 65, GCMRL; draft letter, Forrestal and Stimson to Truman, Apr. 13, 1945, Forrestal diaries, SGMML.

38. *FRUS*, 1945, 1:311–16; Stimson diary, Apr. 17, 1945, YUL; Forrestal diary, Apr. 15–17, 1945, SGMML. For the impact of Iwo Jima on Forrestal, see Hoopes and Brinkley, *Driven Patriot*, 200–201.

39. *FRUS*, 1945, 1:330–32, 350–51, 445–50, 459–60; Stimson diary, Apr. 17, 1945, YUL; Forrestal diaries, Apr. 15–18, 1945, entries and memos, SGMML; Louis, *Imperialism at Bay*, 477–96; Russell, *History of the United Nations Charter*, 576–89; Campbell, "Nationalism in America's UN Policy," 37; "International Trusteeship System," memo, Apr. 14, 1945, Notter Files, box 191, U.S. General Folder, RG 59, NA.

40. *FRUS*, 1945, 1:198–99.

41. Stimson diary, Apr. 26, 1945, YUL; *FRUS*, 1945, 1:305, 596; Stettinius diaries, Apr. 16, 1945, ser. 4, box 224, AL.

42. *FRUS*, 1945, 1:305, 451, 594, 643, 815.

43. Campbell, "Nationalism in America's UN Policy," 40.

44. *FRUS*, 1945, 1:620–24, 633, 643, 807; Sherry, *Preparing for the Next War*, 180.

45. Embick to J. D. Hickerson and McCloy, memos, June 8–9, 1945, and Gerhardt to Hull, "U.S. Base Facilities in Iceland," memo, June 16, 1945, ABC 686 (6 Nov. 43), sec. 18, RG 165, NA. Stimson, who thought very highly of Embick, had previously noted that "he belongs to the classical school and McCloy is suspicious of him for that very reason." Stettinius felt similarly. Stimson diary, Dec. 14, 1942, and Mar. 18, 1945, YUL.

46. *FRUS*, 1945, 1:674–75, 685–86; Campbell, "Nationalism in America's UN Policy," 38–43; Russell, *History of the United Nations Charter*, 688–706.

47. JCS 1390/1–4, "Charter of the United Nations International Organization," June 20–23, 1945, CCS 092 (4-14-45), sec. 1, RG 218, NA; Lincoln to ACofS, "Charter of the United Nations International Organization," June 23, 1945, Lincoln Papers, box 6, folder 2, USMA; *FRUS*, 1945, 1:1430–31.

48. Millis, *Forrestal Diaries*, 47, 52, 57–58; Vincent Davis, *Postwar Defense Policy and the U.S. Navy*, 164.

49. U.S. Department of Defense, *Entry of the Soviet Union into the War against Japan*, 68–70; Harriman, *Special Envoy*, 461; McCloy memo of telephone conversation with Stimson, May 19, 1945, ASW 336 Russia, RG 107, NA. Campbell, *Masquerade Peace*, notes that Grew considered the Yalta issue so sensitive that he personally burned the minutes of a May 11 discussion of it.

50. Quotations are from Schnabel, *History of the Joint Chiefs of Staff*, 1:48, and JCS 1350, "The Current Situation in Rumania and Bulgaria," May 13, 1945, ABC 336 Rumania (26 Sept. 43), sec. 1-B, RG 165, NA. See also *FRUS*, 1945, 4:1155, 1176–77; Schnabel, *History of the Joint Chiefs of Staff*, 1:41–51; Poole, "From Conciliation to Containment," 12–13; and Rabel, *Between East and West*, 56.

51. McCloy memo of telephone conversation with Stimson, May 19, 1945, ASW 336 Russia, RG 107, NA.

52. U.S. Department of Defense, *Entry of the Soviet Union into the War against Japan*, 70–71; Gallicchio, *Cold War Begins in Asia*, 10–11. On May 31 Marshall also stated that most allegations

against the Russians had "proven unfounded," that their "seemingly uncooperative attitude" in military matters stemmed from security concerns, that he personally favored "the building up of a combination of like-minded powers, thereby forcing Russia to fall in line by the very force of this coalition," and that the Russians should be invited to witness the atomic bomb test. See Alperovitz, *Decision to Use the Atomic Bomb,* 170–71.

53. Cox to Hopkins, May 14, 1945, Hopkins Papers, box 337, book 10, Post-Yalta Deterioration Folder, Grp. 24 (folder 2), FDRL; Millis, *Forrestal Diaries,* 58; Steel, *Lippmann,* 422; Leahy, *I Was There,* 378–81; Anderson, *United States, Great Britain, and the Cold War,* 72. Truman asserted in mid-May that he was having as much difficulty with the British as with the Russians; see Leffler, *Preponderance of Power,* 21–22, 31–32.

54. Quotes are from Croswell, *Chief of Staff,* 319, and Lincoln to Hull, memo, June 24, 1945, Lincoln Papers, box 6, folder 2, USMA. See also Lincoln to Hull, "Planners Papers on 'Relations with the Russians' CCS 742," and "Dissolution of SHAEF," memos, June 14 and 26, 1945, ibid.; Dorr and Marshall to McCloy, memos, June 8 and July 3, 1945, ASW 336 Russia, RG 107, NA; and Hathaway, *Ambiguous Partnership,* 137–41, 171–74.

55. U.S. Department of Defense, *Entry of the Soviet Union into the War against Japan,* 54–60; Iriye, *Power and Culture,* 242–43; Brower, "Sophisticated Strategists," 239–54; Cline, *Washington Command Post,* 343. In February, 25,000 entrenched troops on Iwo Jima killed 8,000 Americans, wounded 20,000, and fought virtually to the last man. In the April–June battle for Okinawa, over 100,000 Japanese soldiers and kamikaze pilots would fight similarly and kill 12,500 Americans, wound 36,000, sink 21 ships, and damage 67.

56. JCS 924/15, "Pacific Strategy," Apr. 25, 1945, ABC 384 Pacific (1-17-43), sec. 9, RG 165, NA, also in U.S. Department of Defense, *Entry of the Soviet Union into the War against Japan,* 61–68; Millis, *Forrestal Diaries,* 55; Smith, *Sharing Secrets,* 25.

57. JCS 924/15, "Pacific Strategy," cited in n. 56. See also corres. in Lincoln Papers, box 6, folder 2, and "Military Use of the Atomic Bomb: Summary of Conclusions Based upon OPD Records," undated, box 3, USMA; Villa, "U.S. Army," 66–92; and Brower, "Sophisticated Strategists," 255–75, and "Sophisticated Strategist," 317–37. The JCS temporarily backed away from this position in late May/early June for fear that modification would be interpreted by Japan as a sign of weakness with the Okinawa campaign still in progress and have a negative impact on both public opinion and the Allies, but by mid-June individual members as well as the service secretaries were supporting it once again.

58. *FRUS: Berlin,* 1:903–10. See also Forrestal diaries, box 1, vol. 2, June 18, 1945, SGMML; Roberts to Marshall, "Amplifying Comments on Planners' Paper for Presentation to the President," memo, June 17, 1945, Lincoln Papers, box 6, folder 2, USMA.

59. Forrestal diary, June 18 and 19, 1945, SGMML; Stimson diary, June 19, 1945, YUL; U.S. Department of Defense, *Entry of the Soviet Union into the War against Japan,* 87–89; S&P June 4, 1945, study as quoted in Cline, *Washington Command Post,* 344; Lincoln to Wedemeyer, July 10, 1945, Wedemeyer Papers, box 82, folder 9, HI. See also Stimson diary for June 26–July 2, 1945, YUL; Handy to Hull, Hull to Handy, and Marshall to Stimson with enclosures, memos, June 1–7, 1945, Lincoln Papers, box 6, folder 2, USMA; Villa, "U.S. Army," 66–92; Brower, "Sophisticated Strategists," 260–75, and "Sophisticated Strategist," 317–37; Bird, *Chairman,* 242–48; and Gallicchio, *Cold War Begins in Asia,* 14–17.

60. For the Record by C. D. L., "Forthcoming World Conference," memo, May 19, 1945; Lincoln to JPS, "JWPC 368/2," memo, June 22, 1945; and Roberts to Marshall, "Amplifying Comments on Planners' Paper for Presentation to the President," memo, June 17, 1945, in Lincoln Papers, box 6, folders 1 and 2, USMA; Lincoln to Wedemeyer, July 10, 1945, ibid., box 5, folder 7; "Military Use of the Atomic Bomb," ibid., box 3, folder 1; Roberts to Lincoln, "Occupation and Control of Japan in the Post-Defeat Period," memo with enclosures, July 9, 1945, ibid., box 6,

folder 3, paper 33; Hathaway, *Ambiguous Partnership*, 145–47, 171–74; JCS 1404 and CCS 884/1 "Information for the Russians concerning the Japanese War," June 30 and July 8, 1945, in *Records of the JCS;* "Decision Amending JCS 1404," July 9, 1945, ABC 350.05 (22 June 44), sec. 1-B, RG 165, NA; King to Forrestal, memo, July 22, 1945, King Papers, box 11, Forrestal Folder, LOC (emphasis in original). Forrestal reported in his diary on June 26 that McCloy had justified arms shipments to Latin America partially on the grounds that "the Joint Chiefs of Staff had information that there were British and Russian agents in South America trying to sell armaments of British and Russian manufacture." Forrestal himself feared that some Latin American leaders were "seeking to utilize Russian protection to offset United States influence" in the area.

61. *FRUS*, 1945, 5:91–94; *FRUS: Berlin*, 1:1017–26; JCS 1418, "United States Policy concerning the Dardanelles and Kiel Canal," ABC 093 Kiel Sec. 1-A (6 July 1945), RG 165, NA; Zubok and Pleshakov, *Inside the Kremlin's Cold War*, 92–93. For background on Spitsbergen, see Fogelson, "Tip of the Arctic," esp. 141–42. In August 1944 the CCS had opposed permanent Soviet occupation of Norwegian territory as a "potential threat." They called for avoidance of "any clash with the Russians" in the area while safeguarding "our long term interests." See *FRUS: Quebec*, 399–401.

62. Lincoln to Hull, memo, July 3, 1945, and Hull to Marshall with enclosures, "Policy for Dealing with the Russians," memo, undated, Lincoln Papers, box 6, folder 3, papers 10 and 26, USMA; Wilson to COS, tel., July 2, 1945, CAB/122/943, PRO.

63. JCS 1418/1, Enclosure A, "United States Policy concerning the Dardanelles and Kiel Canal," July 12, 1945, ABC 093 Kiel Sec. 1-A (6 July 45), RG 165, NA. The JSSC similarly continued to oppose dealing with Italian territorial settlements for fear of "bitter disagreement among our Allies" that could negatively affect the war effort against Japan. Simultaneously, the JSSC opposed internationalization of the Ruhr and Saar because it would "inject Russia into the affairs of Western Europe to an undesirable degree" and German dismemberment because it would "tend to enlarge the field for rivalries and schemes of the European powers." See *FRUS: Berlin*, 1:461, 595–96, 685.

64. Embick to Handy, "Position That Should Be Taken by the U.S. Relative to Probable Russian Proposals Relative (1) the Straits, and (2) the Internationalization of the Kiel Canal," memo, with attached memo, "Russian Policy in relation to the Straits," July 4, 1945, ABC 093 Kiel Sec. 1-A (6 July 45), RG 165, NA. Embick also informed the OPD and McCloy that he had written a similar memo for Stimson in 1936 and suggested the secretary "might wish to have his memory refreshed on the historical background." J. E. H. to McCloy, memo, July 8, 1945, ibid.

65. JCS 1443/1, "Soviet Demands with Respect to Bear Island and the Spitsbergen Archipelago," July 17, 1945, Enclsoures A and B, ABC 386 Spitsbergen (14 July 45), RG 165, NA.

66. Handwritten, undated notes on Embick memo by CHB (Bonesteel); "U.S. Position Relative to Soviet Intentions in Turkey and the Near East," draft memo; and Roberts to Lincoln, "Comments on JCS 1418/1," memo, all in ABC 093 Kiel Sec. 1-A (6 July 45), RG 165, NA.

67. Stimson to Byrnes, draft letter, July 8, 1945, ABC 093 Kiel Sec. 1-A (6 July 45), RG 165, NA. The British Foreign Office reached similar conclusions at this time and shifted to a policy of opposing Soviet demands. See John Kent, "The British Empire and the Origins of the Cold War, 1944–49," in Deighton, *Britain and the First Cold War*, 165–68.

68. Quotations are from "U.S. Position," draft memo; Roberts to Lincoln, "Comments on JCS 1418/1"; and S&P Notes on Kiel Canal, all in ABC 093 Kiel Sec. 1-A (6 July 45), RG 165, NA.

69. Roberts to Lincoln, "Comments on JCS 1418/1," and Stimson to Byrnes, July 8, 1945, ABC 093 Kiel Sec. 1-A (6 July 45), RG 165, NA. A similar argument took place in State when one official compared the Dardanelles to the Panama Canal. Loy Henderson "hit the ceiling," reminded the official that he was "no mere academician now but an advocate" of U.S. interests, and argued

that the canal had been built by the United States, whereas the Dardanelles had been built by God. See Paterson, *On Every Front,* 60.

70. TDR (Roberts) to Lincoln, "JCS 1380/1 (SWNCC 150)—'Initial Post Defeat Policy Relating to Japan,'" July 25, 1945, Lincoln Papers, box 6, folder 3, paper 14, USMA; handwritten notes by C. H. B. (Bonesteel) on "U.S. Position Relative to Soviet Intentions in Turkey and the Near East," draft memo, July 6, 1945, ABC 092 USSR (15 Nov. 44), RG 165, NA.

71. G-2 Paper, "Soviet Intentions," July 6, 1945, ABC 092 USSR (15 Nov. 44), RG 165, NA. On July 28 AAF Intelligence would similarly warn that the Soviet Union would develop airpower in the postwar era and that it posed the "greatest threat to [the] security of the United States" (Perry McCoy Smith, *Air Force Plans for Peace,* 113). Arnold, *Global Mission,* 586, said that he and British air chief Sir Charles Portal agreed at Potsdam that "our next enemy would be Russia."

72. Strategy and Policy Group reports on G-2 memo "Soviet Intentions," with handwritten notes by C. H. B. on draft memo, "U.S. Position with Regard to General Soviet Intentions for Expansion," July 6, 1945, ABC 092 USSR (15 Nov. 44), RG 165, NA.

73. Lincoln to McCloy and Lincoln to Embick with enclosures, "Internationalization of the Kiel Canal and Russian Interest in the Dardanelles," memos, July and 7, 1945, ABC 093 Kiel Sec. 1-A (6 July 45), RG 165, NA.

74. Buell, *Master of Seapower,* 415; GB to SN, "Navy Department's Views on Kiel Canal," memo, Feb. 8, 1944, GB 426 (ser. 262), RG 80, NA; Gary to Gardner, memo, July 11, 1945, ser. 14, WPD Records, box 196, A14-1-Foreign Affairs & Policies Jan. 45–July 45, NH. See also Vincent Davis, *Postwar Defense Policy and the U.S. Navy,* 171. King had still believed in May that it was "quite proper" for Russia to have access to the Baltic through the Skagerrak and Kattegat and to the Mediterranean through the Dardanelles, but he now felt that "responsibility for the true freedom of such waters" should be placed in Swedish and Turkish rather than Russian hands, Russia should not be given Port Arthur, and internationalization of the Kiel Canal would raise questions about Gibraltar. By late June Forrestal was thinking that Russia "would like to detach Turkey from the orbit of British influence" and by mid-July had become convinced that "Russia has in mind for Turkey the status of a satellite nation to herself." Forrestal diaries, May 18, June 24, and July 17, 1945, box 1, vol. 2, SGMML; Rubin, *Great Powers in the Middle East,* 64.

75. See Louis, *Imperialism at Bay,* 479, and Brodie, *War and Politics,* 42 n. 19.

76. JCS 1418/1, "United States Policy concerning the Dardanelles and Kiel Canal," Enclosure B, July 12, 1945, ABC 093 Kiel Sec. 1-A (6 July 45), RG 165, NA; JCS 1443/1, "Soviet Demands with Respect to Bear Island and the Spitsbergen Archipelago," Enclosure B, July 17, 1945, ABC 386 Spitsbergen (14 July 45), RG 165, NA.

77. "Decision Amending JCS 1418/1," July 18, 1945, ABC 093 Kiel Sec. 1-A (6 July 45), RG 165, NA; JCS 1443/2, July 22, 1945, and SWNCC 159/3, July 26, 1945, ABC 386 Spitsbergen (14 July 45), RG 165, NA, all three partially reprinted in *FRUS: Berlin,* 2:42, 649–50, 1420–24, and in *FRUS, 1945,* 5:96–97. Leahy's qualms are noted in the July 23 JCS discussion of the Bear Island/Spitsbergen issues in SPD, ser. 3, box 69, Terminal-Rough Notes, NH. The JCS at this time also supported British proposals to shift certain European colonial areas into SEAC and full restoration of British and French rule in Southeast Asia—partially to help their claim to the Mandated Islands but, more important, because of their belief that future U.S. security in Europe now required full British and French cooperation. See Gallicchio, *Cold War Begins in Asia,* 29, and McMahon, "Anglo-American Diplomacy," 1–4. It should be noted, however, that the JCS had never been strong supporters of FDR's anticolonial policy—perhaps because of its link to trusteeship—and that he had modified the policy before his death. See LaFeber, "Roosevelt, Churchill, and Indochina," 1277–95, and Thorne, "Indochina and Anglo-American Relations," 73–96.

78. Stimson diary, July 23, 1945, YUL; Leahy diary, July 30, 1945, LOC. As early as June 8 the

British Embassy in Washington had informed London that the administration and JCS "have persuaded themselves that a strong and prosperous Britain is necessary to the security of the United States" (Balfour for Halifax to Eden, tel., June 8, 1945, CAB/122/1035, PRO). Gallicchio, *Cold War Begins in Asia*, 30–31, concludes that by this time the JCS "favored a full restoration of British and French rule" in Southeast Asia, partially to buttress their own claims to the Mandated Islands but, more significant, because they had decided that "American security in Europe required the full cooperation of England and France."

79. Millis, *Forrestal Diaries*, 78. For Stimson, see diary entries for Feb. 3, 13, 15, Mar. 5, May 14, 15, 16, 28, 31, 1945, YUL. Leahy wrote in his diary on May 20 that Byrnes was "favorably impressed" by the project but that he was not. Alperovitz, *Decision to Use the Atomic Bomb*, 322, notes the lack of formal military involvement in the decision to use the bomb. See Walker, "Decision to Use the Bomb," 97–114, for the historiographical debate on that decision.

80. Marshall's July 23 comments, according to Stimson, were that the Russians were already holding down the Kwantung Army merely by massing their forces on the border, but that "even if we went ahead without the Russians, and compelled the Japanese to surrender to our terms, that would not prevent the Russians from marching into Manchuria anyhow and striking, thus permitting them to get virtually what they wanted in the surrender terms" (Stimson diary, July 23–24, 1945, YUL; *FRUS: Berlin*, 2:1324, 1463). As Sherry noted in *Preparing for the Next War*, 188–89, this hardly constituted the inference Stimson made. "Marshall clearly did not conceive of the use of the atomic bomb on Japan, an American invasion of Kyushu, and Soviet entry into the war as mutually exclusive ways of ending the conflict," Bernstein correctly concluded in "Eclipsed by Hiroshima and Nagasaki," 168. See also ibid., 149–73, and Gallicchio, "After Nagasaki," 396–404. The JCS also continued to press for modification of unconditional surrender; see *FRUS: Berlin*, 2:39–42, 1268–69.

Chapter Thirteen

1. JCS 570/17, "Overall Examination of U.S. Base Requirements for Post-War Military Bases," May 14, 1945, and memo for Leahy (from McFarland), "Post-War Military Bases," July 2, 1945, CCS 360 (12-9-42), secs. 5 and 6, RG 218, NA; JPS 633/4, "United States Post-War Military Policy and Strategic Plan," July 18, 1945, CCS 381 (5-13-45), sec. 1, RG 218, NA.

2. Min. of sp. mtg. of JSSC, JPWC, JWPC, and JPS, Aug. 3, 1945, ABC 381 United Nations (23 Jan. 42), sec. 3D, RG 165, NA. See also Schnabel, *History of the Joint Chiefs of Staff*, 1:137.

3. Unsigned S&P memo for Lincoln, "United States Post-War Military Policy and Strategic Plan (JPS 633/4)," ABC 092 (18 July 45), sec. 1A, RG 165, NA.

4. Sherry, *Preparing for the Next War*, 197–98. The Marshall and Truman documents are in JCS 1478, "Post-War Requirements for Military Forces," Aug. 19, 1945, and JCS 1482, "Proposed Legislation to Fix the Permanent Authorized Strength of the Regular Navy and Marine Corps," Aug. 23, 1945, ABC 040 (2 Nov. 43), sec. 5A, RG 165, NA.

5. C. H. B. (Bonesteel) to Lincoln, "United States Post-War Policy (JPS 633/6)," memo, Aug. 28, 1945, ABC 092 (18 July 45), sec. 1A, RG 165, NA. See also Porter, SPD, to ACofS, OPD, "Comments on U.S. Military Policy," memo, Sept. 10, 1945, and handwritten comments on JPS 633/6, both in ibid.

6. JCS 1496–1496/3, "United States Military Policy," Aug. 30–Sept. 20, 1945, in ABC 092 (18 July 45), sec. 1A, RG 165, and CCS 381 (5-13-45), sec. 1, RG 218, NA. The final draft changed the "in no way remote possibility" to simply "the possibility" of a breakdown in relations. The paper as approved by SWNCC and dated Mar. 27, 1946, is reproduced in *FRUS*, 1946, 1:1160–65. Pasvolsky noted in November that "the general tenor of the paper seemed to reflect the views of

General Embick." For these comments and others by the State Dept., see ibid., 1120, 1123–28. See also Sherry, *Preparing for the Next War*, 198–205; Schnabel, *History of the Joint Chiefs of Staff*, 1: 138–43; and Leffler, *Preponderance of Power*, 41–42. On the intelligence apparatus, see JCS 1181 series in ABC 092 (1 Apr. 44), sec. 2, RG 238, NA. On September 9 Lincoln reported and emphasized that the OPD considered development and coordination of intelligence activities "*to be one of the most vital factors* in the post war era." The JSSC thought similarly, with Embick informing Hull a few weeks earlier that the atomic bomb necessitated "keeping close surveillance on any industrial effort in other countries along that line." See Troy, *Donovan and the CIA*, 293.

7. JPS 744, "Strategic Concept and Plan for the Employment of United States Armed Forces," Aug. 27, 1945, ABC 092 (18 July 45), sec. 1A, RG 165, NA; JPS 744/1, "Strategic Concept and Plan for the Employment of United States Armed Forces," Sept. 4, 1945, CCS 381 (5-13-45), sec. 1, RG 218, NA.

8. Min., JPS 218th and 219th mtgs., Sept. 5 and 12, 1945, CCS 381 (5-13-45), sec. 1, RG 218, NA; Lincoln to Hull, memo, Sept. 9, 1945, Lincoln Papers, box 6, folder 3, paper 15, USMA; JPS 744/ 2, "Strategic Concept and Plan for the Employment of United States Armed Forces," Sept. 14, 1945, ABC 092 (18 July 45), sec. 1A, RG 165, NA; Lincoln to Chief, Strategic Policy Section, memo, Sept. 10, 1945, Lincoln Papers, box 6, folder 3, paper 17, USMA.

9. JPS 744/3 and JCS 1518–1518/3, "Strategic Concept and Plan for the Employment of United States Armed Forces," Sept. 14, 19, Oct. 1, 9, and 13, 1945, in CCS 381 (5-13-45), secs. 1 and 2, RG 218, NA, and ABC 092 (18 July 45), sec. 1A, RG 165, NA; JCS 570/34, "Over-All Examination of U.S. requirements for Military Bases and Rights," Sept. 27, 1945, RG 218, NA. See also Schnabel, *History of the Joint Chiefs of Staff*, 1:145–49, 305–9, and Sherry, *Preparing for the Next War*, 204.

10. Embick to CofS, "Fundamental Importance to the Security of the United States of the Full Implementation of the Act of Chapultepec," memo, with attached draft memo, Sept. 6, 1945, Marshall Papers, box 61, folder 46, GCMRL; memo left by Embick for Marshall, "United Nations Organization: Its Limitations for the Enforcement of Peace; Its Relation to the Monroe Doctrine," ibid., box 67, folder 42, GCMRL. Marshall concurred in these views, as did his JCS colleagues. See JCS 1507–1507/2, Sept. 6–19, 1945, CCS 092 (9-10-45), sec. 1, RG 218, NA, and Schnabel, *History of the Joint Chiefs of Staff*, 1:353.

11. Lincoln to Chief of Policy Section, memo, Aug. 19, 1945, Lincoln Papers, box 6, folder 4, paper 61, USMA. See also McCloy to CofS, "U.S. Military Policy in Relation to the United Nations Organization (see JCS 1496/2 and 1511)," memo, Sept. 23, 1945, OPD 336 TS (2 Oct. 45), case 192/4, RG 165, NA; McCloy to CofS, "JCS 1518," memo, Sept. 26, 1945, ABC 092 (18 July 45), sec. 1A, RG 165, NA; and JCS 1518/2, Oct. 9, 1945, CCS 381 (5-13-45), sec. 1, RG 218, NA. McCloy told Stettinius on Sept. 29 that "Embick was still having a bad influence in the Army of thinking in narrow terms of the defense of the Western Hemisphere rather than of the world." See Campbell and Herring, *Stettinius Diaries*, 429.

12. Lincoln to Beukema and Beukema to Lincoln, Oct. 1 and 4, 1945, Lincoln Papers, box 3, folder 4, USMA.

13. Earle to Embick, Sept. 11, 1945, box 15, folder E3, and Earle to Fairchild, Oct. 3, 1945, box 16, folder F3, Earle Papers, SGMML; Fairchild to Earle, Oct. 4, 1945, Fairchild Papers, microfilm, Bolling Air Force Base.

14. See Schaller, *U.S. Crusade in China*, 262–75, and Gallicchio, *Cold War Begins in Asia*, 119–20. On November 10 Embick informed Hull via telephone that it was "urgent" to have the State Department defend Wedemeyer against Communist attacks and that it was not doing so because of a "Leftist" within the department—that is, John Carter Vincent. See telephone conversation 1350 between Embick and Hull, Nov. 10, 1945, ABC 336 China (26 Jan. 42), sec. 1-C, MFNAP, GCMRL; Pogue, *Marshall*, 4:59–60.

15. Lincoln to Hull, Oct. 8, 1945, Lincoln Papers, box 6, folder 3, paper 12, USMA. Schnabel, *History of the Joint Chiefs of Staff*, 1:73–74, and Poole, "From Conciliation to Containment," 13, both emphasize the impact of the failed London Conference on the armed forces.

16. JCS 1545, "Military Position of the United States in the Light of Russian Policy," Oct. 9, 1945, CCS 092 USSR (3-27-45), sec. 1, RG 218, NA.

17. Ibid. See also Sherry, *Preparing for the Next War*, 213–16.

18. JIC 250/3/M and JIS 80/6/M, "Memorandum of Request—Russian Capabilities," Oct. 18 and 22, 1945; JIS 80/5/M, "Memorandum of Request—Bombing Targets in Russia," Oct. 22, 1945; JIC 329 and 329/1, "Strategic Vulnerability of the USSR to a Limited Air Attack," Nov. 3 and Dec. 3, 1945, all in ABC 336 Russia (22 Aug. 43), sec. 1-A, and (16 Aug. 43), RG 165, NA; JIS 80/7, 9, and 10, "Russian Capabilities," Oct. 23, 25, and 26, 1945, *Records of the JCS*; Schnabel, *History of the Joint Chiefs of Staff*, 1:149–54; ONI Report, "Basic Factors in World Relations," Dec. 1945, Navy SPD, ser. 3, box 106, A-8 Intell., RG 38, NA.

19. JCS 1641/1, "U.S. Security Interests in the Eastern Mediterranean," Mar. 10, 1946, ABC 382 (1 Sept. 45), sec. 1-A, RG 165, NA. See also Schnabel, *History of the Joint Chiefs of Staff*, 1:108–11.

20. JCS 1471/2, "Military Policy as to Secrecy Regarding the Atomic Bomb," Oct. 19, 1945, ABC 471.6 Atom (17 Aug. 45), sec. 1, RG 165, NA. Stimson's September 11 plea is reproduced in Stimson and Bundy, *On Active Service*, 642–46. Forrestal disagreed strongly with the Stimson point of view, writing in his diary that the Russians, "like the Japanese, are essentially oriental in their thinking, and until we have a longer record of experience with them on the validity of engagements . . . , it seems doubtful that we should endeavor to buy their understanding and sympathy. We tried that once with Hitler. There are no returns on appeasement" (Forrestal diaries, Sept. 21, 1945, box 1, vol. 3, SGMML).

21. JCS 1477/1, "Overall Effect of Atomic Bomb on Warfare and Military Organization," Oct. 30, 1945, ABC 471.6 Atom (17 Aug. 45), sec. 2, RG 165, NA. Both papers received extensive critiques and the JCS wound up deleting much of this language, including the specific references to Russia, as "politically undesirable," in Marshall's words. Memo for Asst. Sec., WDGS, "JCS 1471/2," Oct. 22, 1945, ABC 471.6 Atom (17 Aug. 45), sec. 1, RG 165, NA. See also remainder of JCS 1471 and 1477 series with attached memos in ibid., secs. 1 and 2; Sherry, *Preparing for the Next War*, 209–13; and Schnabel, *History of the Joint Chiefs of Staff*, 1:257–61, 277–83. On October 23 the Joint Chiefs approved the revised base study, JCS 570/40, with its greater focus on the Atlantic and Arctic; see Converse, "U.S. Plans for a Postwar Overseas Military Base System," 170–72, and Leffler, *Preponderance of Power*, 56–59.

22. This point is made by Foltos, "New Pacific Barrier," 325.

23. Gallicchio, *Cold War Begins in Asia*, 20.

24. Kuhn, *Structure of Scientific Revolution*. For an application of this approach to late-nineteenth-century U.S. foreign policy, see Beisner, *From Old Diplomacy to New*.

25. See, for ex., Sherry, *Preparing for the Next War*; Perry McCoy Smith, *Air Force Plans for Peace*; Vincent Davis, *Postwar Defense Policy and the U.S. Navy*; and Yergin, *Shattered Peace*.

In his introductory essay in *Containment*, Etzold commented that "the interest in reorganizing the government for foreign and military affairs took on such momentum that one may suspect certain officials of longing for war's end less in anticipation of the blessings of peace than in hope of a timely opportunity to institutionalize the improvised arrangements of the war years regarding defense and diplomacy." Of interest in this regard is Lincoln's September 22 conclusion that the armed forces had "carried" the State Department during the war by producing and implementing policy statements and that the military had been able to "get away" with this "because it has fairly consistently stuck to problems that had to be solved in the near future in order to get on with the war, even though they were political." United States aims could "no longer be cloaked under the guise of military necessity," however, and State would therefore have to "carry the ball in public" in the face of possible foreign and public criticism of the military arguments for specific actions. Lincoln to Hull, memo, Sept. 22, 1945, responding to memo, McCloy to Handy, Sept. 18, 1945, Lincoln Papers, box 6, folder 5, paper 47, USMA.

26. Leffler, *Preponderance of Power,* and Leffler, "National Security," in Hogan and Paterson, *Explaining the History of American Foreign Relations,* 202–13.

27. Marshall interview, July 25, 1949, MHI; Bland, *Marshall Interviews,* 529–30, 622; Matloff, *Strategic Planning,* 5. "The political and military considerations were thoroughly merged with each other so that one could not separate them even in our own thinking," Lincoln later stated. "Our strategic planners did not separate the two concepts." See Brower, "Sophisticated Strategists," 131.

28. Acheson, *Sketches from Life,* 163–64. Marshall specifically noted that the Mediterranean strategy might "stretch out the time for decision in Asia into the congressional elections of 1946," and he drew historical parallels regarding the "hazards which inhered in the election of 1864, of that of 1918, and of the great strain of five years of war." Acheson concluded that his primary concern in the strategic debate was thus as political as was Churchill's, albeit different: "to reach a decision in Asia before war-weariness might weaken American will." Brower correctly emphasizes this fear throughout "Sophisticated Strategists."

Bibliography

Primary Sources

Unpublished Manuscript, Archival, and Oral History Collections

Alderman Library, Special Collections, University of Virginia, Charlottesville, Va.
    Edward R. Stettinius Jr. Papers
        Edward R. Stettinius Jr. Diary
Bolling Air Force Base, Washington, D.C.
    Muir S. Fairchild Papers. Microfilm
Franklin D. Roosevelt Library, Hyde Park, N.Y.
    Harry L. Hopkins Papers
    John L. McCrea Papers
    Henry L. Morgenthau Presidential Diary
    Franklin D. Roosevelt Papers
        Map Room File
        Official File
        President's Personal File
        President's Secretary's File
    Records of the President's Soviet Protocol Committee, 1942–45
George C. Marshall Research Library, Lexington, Va.
    Harvey A. DeWeerd Papers
    James B. Faichney Collection
    Frank B. Hayne Papers
    Frank McCarthy Papers
    Reginald N. MacDonald-Buchanan Papers
    George C. Marshall Foundation National Archives Project
    George C. Marshall Papers
    Oral History Collection and Reminiscences about George C. Marshall
    John McAuley Palmer Papers
    William D. Pawley Papers
    Paul M. Robinett Collection
        Paul M. Robinett Diary
    William Thaddeus Sexton Papers
Hoover Institution on War, Revolution and Peace, Stanford, Calif.
    Joseph Stilwell Papers
    Albert C. Wedemeyer Papers
Library of Congress, Washington, D.C.
    Henry H. Arnold Papers
    Tasker H. Bliss Papers
    William L. Borah Papers

Joseph E. Davies Papers
    Joseph E. Davies Diary
Cordell Hull Papers
Ernest J. King Papers
Frank Knox Papers
William D. Leahy Papers
    William D. Leahy Diary
Leo Pasvolsky Papers
Robert P. Patterson Papers
National Archives and Records Service, Washington, D.C., and College Park, Md.
  Record Group 38, Records of the Office of the Chief of Naval Operations
  Record Group 59, Records of the Department of State
  Record Group 80, Records of the Department of the Navy
  Record Group 107, Records of the Office of the Secretary of War
  Record Group 165, Records of the War Department General and Special Staffs
  Record Group 218, Records of the Joint and Combined Chiefs of Staff
  Record Group 225, Records of the Joint Army-Navy Boards
  Record Group 226, Records of the Office of Strategic Services
  Record Group 319, Records of the Assistant Chief of Staff, G-2
  Record Group 331, Records of Allied Operational and Occupational Headquarters,
      World War II
  Record Group 332, Records of United States Theaters of War, World War II
  Record Group 334, Records of Interservice Agencies
  Record Group 407, Records of the Adjutant General's Office
Operational Archives, Department of the Navy, Navy Historical Center, Washington, D.C.
  Biographical Files
  James V. Forrestal Papers
  Ernest J. King Papers
  Frank Knox Papers
  William D. Leahy Papers
  Samuel E. Morison Collection
  Navy General Board Studies
  Harry L. Pence Papers
  Harold C. Train Oral History
  Records of the Operational Division (FX-03), COMINCH
  Records of the War Plans (Strategic Plans) Division, Office of the Chief of Naval Operations,
      Series 3, 5, 7, 9, 12, 14, and 15
Public Record Office, Kew, United Kingdom
  Records of the Cabinet Office (CAB)
      CAB 79, Chiefs of Staff Committee Minutes
      CAB 80, Chiefs of Staff Memoranda
      CAB 81, Chiefs of Staff Committees and Subcommittees
      CAB 84, Joint Planning Committee Minutes and Memoranda
      CAB 88, Combined Chiefs of Staff Papers
      CAB 98, Miscellaneous
      CAB 99, Commonwealth and International Conferences
      CAB 119, Joint Planning Committee Staff Files
      CAB 122, British Joint Staff Services Mission, Washington Office Files

Papers of the Prime Minister's Private Office
  PREM 1, Miscellaneous Correspondence and Papers
  PREM 3, Operational Papers
  PREM 4, Confidential Papers
Records of the Foreign Office (FO)
  FO 371, Political
  FO 409, Indexes to General Correspondence
  FO 800, Others
  FO 881, Confidential Print
  FO 954, Photocopies of Papers of Anthony Eden
  FO 934, Potsdam
Seeley G. Mudd Manuscript Library, Princeton University, Princeton, N.J.
  Edward Mead Earle Papers
  James V. Forrestal Papers
    James V. Forrestal Diary
U.S. Army Center for Military History, Washington, D.C.
  Biographical Files
  Operations Division Diary
  Operations Division Historical Unit File
U.S. Army Military History Institute, Carlisle Barracks, Pa.
  Paul W. Caraway Papers
  Guy Vernon Henry Papers
  John E. Hull Papers
  Lawrence J. Lincoln Papers
  Oral Histories—Senior Officer Debriefing Program
    Paul W. Caraway
    Paul L. Freeman
    Andrew Goodpaster
    Thomas T. Handy
    John E. Hull
    Albert C. Wedemeyer
    Robert J. Wood
  Forrest C. Pogue Interviews for *The Supreme Command*
U.S. Military Academy Library, Special Collections and Archives Division, West Point, N.Y.
  George A. Lincoln Papers
Yale University Library, Manuscripts and Archives, New Haven, Conn.
  Henry Lewis Stimson Papers
    Henry L. Stimson Diary

Published Documents, Papers, Memoirs, and Other Primary Sources

Acheson, Dean. *Sketches from Life of Men I Have Known.* New York: Harper and Brothers, 1959.
———. *Present at the Creation: My Years in the State Department.* New York: W. W. Norton, 1969.
Arnold, H. H. *Global Mission.* New York: Harper and Brothers, 1949.
Berle, Beatrice Bishop, and Travis Beal Jacobs, eds. *Navigating the Rapids, 1918–1971: From the Papers of Adolph A. Berle.* New York: Harcourt Brace Jovanovich, 1973.
Bland, Larry I., ed. *George C. Marshall: Interviews and Reminiscences for Forrest C. Pogue.* Lexington, Va.: George C. Marshall Research Foundation, 1991.

———. *The Papers of George Catlett Marshall.* 4 vols. Baltimore: Johns Hopkins University Press, 1981–96.

Blum, John Morton, ed. *From the Morgenthau Diaries: Years of War, 1941–1945.* Vol. 3. Boston: Houghton Mifflin, 1967.

Bohlen, Charles E. *Witness to History, 1929–1969.* New York: W. W. Norton, 1973.

Brown, Richard, and W. Richard Burner, eds. *I Can Tell It Now.* New York: E. P. Dutton, 1964.

Bryant, Arthur. *The Turn of the Tide: A History of the War Years Based on the Diaries of Field-Marshal Lord Alanbrooke, Chief of the Imperial General Staff.* Garden City, N.Y.: Doubleday, 1957.

———. *Triumph in the West: A History of the War Years Based on the Diaries of Field-Marshal Lord Alanbrooke, Chief of the Imperial General Staff.* Garden City, N.Y.: Doubleday, 1959.

Bullitt, Orville H., ed. *For the President: Personal and Secret: Correspondence between Franklin D. Roosevelt and William C. Bullitt.* Boston: Houghton Mifflin, 1972.

Bullitt, William C. "How We Won the War and Lost the Peace." *Life,* Aug. 30, 1948, 82–97.

Butcher, Harry C. *My Three Years with Eisenhower.* New York: Simon and Schuster, 1946.

Campbell, Thomas M., and George C. Herring. *The Diaries of Edward R. Stettinius, Jr., 1943–1946.* New York: Franklin Watts, 1975.

Cantril, Hadley, ed. *Public Opinion, 1935–1946.* Princeton: Princeton University Press, 1951.

Chandler, Alfred D., Jr. *The Papers of Dwight David Eisenhower: The War Years.* 5 vols. Baltimore: Johns Hopkins University Press, 1970.

Churchill, Winston S. *The Second World War.* 6 vols. Boston: Houghton Mifflin, 1948–53.

Danchev, Alex. *Establishing the Anglo-American Alliance: The Second World War Diaries of Brigadier Vivian Dykes.* London: Brassey's, 1990.

Davis, Forrest. "Roosevelt's World Blueprint." *Saturday Evening Post,* Apr. 10, 1943, 20–21, 109–10.

Deane, John R. *The Strange Alliance.* New York: Viking, 1947.

Dilks, David, ed. *The Diaries of Sir Alexander Cadogan, 1938–1945.* New York: G. P. Putnam's Sons, 1972.

Dyer, George C. *The Amphibians Came to Conquer: The Story of Admiral Richmond Kelly Turner.* 2 vols. Washington, D.C.: U.S. Government Printing Office, 1969.

———. *On the Treadmill to Pearl Harbor: The Memoirs of Admiral James O. Richardson.* Washington, D.C.: U.S. Government Printing Office, 1973.

Eiler, Keith, ed. *Wedemeyer on War and Peace.* Stanford: Hoover Institution Press, 1987.

Eisenhower, Dwight D. *Crusade in Europe.* New York: Doubleday, 1948.

Elsey, George M. "Some White House Recollections, 1942–1953." *Diplomatic History* 12 (Summer 1988): 357–64.

Embick, Stanley D. "Our Present Military Policy." Address delivered to the Institute of Public Affairs at the University of Virginia. In *Summer Quarterly Bulletin of the University of Virginia* 1 (Oct. 1, 1927): 244–51.

———. "Three Economic Areas Fixed for the Future." *New York Times,* Apr. 13, 1930, sec. 11, 4.

Etzold, Thomas H., and John Lewis Gaddis. *Containment: Documents on American Policy and Strategy, 1945–1950.* New York: Columbia University Press, 1978.

Ferrell, Robert, ed. *The Eisenhower Diaries.* New York: Norton, 1981.

Gallup, George H. *The Gallup Poll: Public Opinion, 1935–1971.* 3 vols. New York: Random House, 1972.

Grew, Joseph C. *Turbulent Era: A Diplomatic Record of Forty Years, 1904–1945.* 2 vols. Edited by Walter Johnson. Boston: Houghton Mifflin, 1952.

Hagood, Johnson. *We Can Defend America.* Garden City, N.Y.: Doubleday, Doran and Co., 1937.

Harriman, W. Averell, and Elie Abel. *Special Envoy to Churchill and Stalin, 1941–1946*. New York: Random House, 1975.

Hull, Cordell. *The Memoirs of Cordell Hull*. 2 vols. New York: Macmillan, 1948.

Ickes, Harold. *The Secret Diary of Harold Ickes*. 3 vols. New York: Simon and Schuster, 1954.

Kennan, George F. *Memoirs, 1925–1950*. Boston: Little, Brown, 1967.

Kennedy, Sir John. *The Business of War*. London: Hutchinson, 1957.

Kimball, Warren F., ed. *Churchill and Roosevelt: The Complete Correspondence*. 3 vols. Princeton: Princeton University Press, 1984.

King, Ernest J., and Walter M. Whitehill. *Fleet Admiral King: A Naval Record*. New York: W. W. Norton, 1952.

Langer, William L. *In and Out of the Ivory Tower*. New York: Neale Watson Academy Publications, 1977.

Leahy, William D. *I Was There*. New York: Whittlesey House, 1950.

Link, Arthur S., ed. *The Papers of Woodrow Wilson*. 69 vols. Princeton: Princeton University Press, 1966–94.

Lippmann, Walter. *U.S. Foreign Policy: Shield of the Republic*. Boston: Little, Brown, 1943.

Mackinder, Sir Halford. *Democratic Ideals and Reality*. Edited by Anthony J. Pearce. 1919. New York: W. W. Norton, 1962.

McCloy, John J. "Turning Points of the War: The Great Military Decisions." *Foreign Affairs* 26 (Oct. 1947): 52–72.

Millis, Walter, ed. *The Forrestal Diaries*. New York: Viking, 1951.

Ministry of Foreign Affairs of the USSR. *Russia: Correspondence between the Chairman of the Council of Ministers of the U.S.S.R. and the Presidents of the U.S.A. and the Prime Ministers of Great Britain during the Great Patriotic War of 1941–1945*. 2 vols. Moscow: Foreign Languages Publishing House, 1957.

Murphy, Robert. *Diplomat among Warriors*. Garden City, N.Y.: Doubleday, 1964.

Perry, Glen C. H. *"Dear Bart": Washington Views of World War II*. Westport, Conn.: Greenwood, 1982.

———. Letter to Keats Speed, July 25, 1943, in *Pull Together: The Newsletter of the Naval Historical Foundation* 30 (Fall/Winter 1991): 6.

Robinett, Paul M. "Grand Strategy and the American People." *Military Affairs* 16 (Spring 1952): 30–34.

Roosevelt, Elliot. *As He Saw It*. New York: Duell, Sloan, and Pearce, 1946.

———, ed. *FDR: His Personal Letters*. 4 vols. New York: Duell, Sloan, and Pearce, 1947–50.

Ross, Steven T., ed. *American War Plans, 1919–1945*. 5 vols. New York: Garland, 1992.

Slessor, Sir John. *The Central Blue: Recollections and Reflections*. London: Cassell, 1956.

Sprout, Harold H., ed. *Foundations of National Power*. Princeton: Princeton University Press, 1945.

Spykman, Nicholas John. *America's Strategy in World Politics: The United States and the Balance of Power*. New York: Harcourt, Brace, 1942.

———. *The Geography of the Peace*. Edited by Helen R. Nichol. New York: Harcourt, Brace, 1944.

Stimson, Henry L., and McGeorge Bundy. *On Active Service in Peace and War*. New York: Harper and Brothers, 1947.

Truman, Harry S. *Memoirs*. 2 vols. Garden City, N.Y.: Doubleday, 1955.

United States, Joint Chiefs of Staff. *Records of the Joint Chiefs of Staff, Part 1, 1942–1945: The Soviet Union*. 2 reels. Frederick, Md.: University Publications of America. Microfilm.

U.S. Congress. *Hearings before the Joint Committee on the Investigation of the Pearl Harbor At-*

tack, pursuant to Senate Cong. Res. 27, 79th Cong., 1st sess., 39 parts. Washington, D.C.: U.S. Government Printing Office, 1946.

U.S. Department of Defense. *Entry of the Soviet Union into the War against Japan: Military Plans, 1941–1945.* Washington, D.C.: Department of Defense, 1955.

U.S. Department of State. *Foreign Relations of the United States.* Annual volumes, 1940–1945. Washington: U.S. Government Printing Office, 1955–1969.

———. *Foreign Relations of the United States. The Conference of Berlin.* 2 vols. Washington: U.S. Government Printing Office, 1960.

———. *Foreign Relations of the United States. The Conferences at Cairo and Tehran, 1943.* Washington: U.S. Government Printing Office, 1961.

———. *Foreign Relations of the United States. The Conferences at Malta and Yalta, 1945.* Washington: U.S. Government Printing Office, 1955.

———. *Foreign Relations of the United States. The Conference at Quebec, 1944.* Washington: U.S. Government Printing Office, 1972.

———. *Foreign Relations of the United States. The Conferences at Washington, 1941–1942, and Casablanca, 1943.* Washington: U.S. Government Printing Office, 1968.

———. *Foreign Relations of the United States. The Conferences at Washington and Quebec, 1943.* Washington: U.S. Government Printing Office, 1970.

War Reports of General of the Army George C. Marshall, Chief of Staff, General of the Army H. H. Arnold, Commanding General, Army Air Forces, and Fleet Admiral Ernest J. King, Commander-in-Chief of the United States Fleet and Chief of Naval Operations. Philadelphia: J. P. Lippincott, 1947.

Wedemeyer, Albert C. *Wedemeyer Reports!* New York: Henry Holt, 1958.

Welles, Sumner. *Seven Decisions That Shaped History.* New York: Harper and Brothers, 1950.

White, Theodore, ed. *The Stilwell Papers.* New York: William Sloan Associates, 1948.

Secondary Works

Books

Abbazia, Patrick. *Mr. Roosevelt's Navy: The Private War of the U.S. Atlantic Fleet, 1939–1942.* Annapolis: Naval Institute Press, 1975.

Abrahamson, James L. *America Arms for a New Century: The Making of a Great Military Power.* New York: Free Press, 1981.

Adams, Henry H. *Witness to Power: The Life of Fleet Admiral William D. Leahy.* Annapolis: Naval Institute Press, 1985.

Adelman, Jonathan R. *Prelude to the Cold War: The Tsarist, Soviet, and U.S. Armies in the Two World Wars.* Boulder: Lynne Rienner, 1988.

Albion, Robert G., and Robert H. Connery. *Forrestal and the Navy.* New York: Columbia University Press, 1962.

Aldrich, Richard J., ed. *British Intelligence, Strategy, and the Cold War, 1945–1951.* London: Routledge, 1992.

Alperovitz, Gar. *The Decision to Use the Atomic Bomb and the Architecture of an American Myth.* New York: Alfred J. Knopf, 1995.

Ambrose, Stephen E. *Eisenhower and Berlin, 1945: The Decision to Halt at the Elbe.* New York: W. W. Norton, 1967.

———. *The Supreme Commander: The War Years of General Dwight D. Eisenhower.* Garden City, N.Y.: Doubleday, 1969.

Anderson, Terry H. *The United States, Great Britain and the Cold War, 1944–1947*. Columbia: University of Missouri Press, 1981.

Baldwin, Hanson. *Great Mistakes of the War*. New York: Harper and Brothers, 1949.

Beisner, Robert. *From Old Diplomacy to New, 1865–1900*. 2d ed. Arlington Heights, Ill.: Harlan Davidson, 1986.

Beitzell, Robert. *The Uneasy Alliance: America, Britain, and Russia, 1941–1943*. New York: Alfred A. Knopf, 1972.

Ben-Moshe, Tuvia. *Churchill: Strategy and History*. Boulder, Colo.: Lynne Rienner Publishers, 1992.

Bennett, Edward M. *Franklin D. Roosevelt and the Search for Victory: American-Soviet Relations, 1939–1945*. Wilmington, Del.: Scholarly Resources, 1990.

Best, Gary Dean. *Herbert Hoover: The Postpresidential Years, 1933–1964*. 2 vols. Stanford, Calif.: Hoover Institution Press, 1983.

Bird, Kai. *The Chairman: John J. McCloy, the Making of the American Establishment*. New York: Simon and Schuster, 1992.

Blake, Robert, and William Roger Louis, eds. *Churchill*. New York: W. W. Norton, 1993.

Borg, Dorothy, and Shumpei Okamoto, eds. *Pearl Harbor as History: Japanese-American Relations, 1931–1941*. New York: Columbia University Press, 1973.

Braisted, William R. *The United States Navy in the Pacific, 1909–1922*. Austin: University of Texas Press, 1971.

Brands, H. W. *Inside the Cold War: Loy Henderson and the Rise of the American Empire, 1918–1961*. New York: Oxford University Press, 1991.

Brodie, Bernard. *War and Politics*. New York: Macmillan, 1973.

Brune, Lester H. *The Origins of American National Security Policy: Sea Power, Air Power, and Foreign Policy, 1900–1941*. Manhattan, Kans.: MA/AH Publishing, 1981.

Buckley, Thomas H. *The United States and the Washington Conference, 1921–1922*. Knoxville: University of Tennessee Press, 1970.

Buell, Thomas. *Master of Seapower: A Biography of Fleet Admiral Ernest J. King*. Boston: Little, Brown, 1980.

Buhite, Russell D. *Decisions at Yalta: An Appraisal of Summit Diplomacy*. Wilmington, Del.: Scholarly Resources, 1986.

Butler, J. R. M., ed. *History of the Second World War: Grand Strategy*. 6 vols. London: Her Majesty's Stationery Office, 1957–72.

Calhoun, Frederick. *Power and Principle: Armed Intervention in Wilsonian Foreign Policy*. Kent, Ohio: Kent State University Press, 1986.

Calvocoressi, Peter, Guy Wint, and John Pritchard. *Total War: The Causes and Courses of the Second World War*. 2 vols. Rev. 2d ed. New York: Pantheon, 1989.

Campbell, Thomas. *Masquerade Peace: America's UN Policy, 1944–1945*. Tallahassee: Florida State University Press, 1973.

Chace, James, and Caleb Carr. *America Invulnerable: The Quest for Absolute Security from 1812 to Star Wars*. New York: Summit Books, 1988.

Challener, Richard D. *Admirals, Generals, and American Foreign Policy, 1898–1914*. Princeton: Princeton University Press, 1973.

Chalou, George C., ed. *The Secrets War: The Office of Strategic Services in World War II*. Washington, D.C.: National Archives and Records Adminsitration, 1992.

Clemens, Diane Shaver. *Yalta*. New York: Oxford University Press, 1970.

Clifford, J. Garry, and Samuel R. Spencer Jr. *The First Peacetime Draft*. Lawrence: University Press of Kansas, 1986.

Cline, Ray S. *Washington Command Post: The Operations Division.* In *United States Army in World War II.* Washington, D.C.: Government Printing Office, 1951.

Coles, Harry L., ed. *Total War and Cold War: Problems in Civilian Control of the Military.* Columbus: Ohio State University Press, 1962.

Conn, Stetson, and Byron Fairchild. *The Framework of Hemisphere Defense.* In *United States Army in World War II.* Washington, D.C.: U.S. Government Printing Office, 1960.

Cowman, Ian. *Dominion or Decline: Anglo-American Naval Relations in the Pacific, 1937–1941.* Oxford: Berg, 1996.

Craven, Wesley F., and James L. Cate, eds. *The Army Air Forces in World War II.* 7 vols. Chicago: University of Chicago Press, 1948–49.

Croswell, D. K. R. *The Chief of Staff: The Military Career of General Walter Bedell Smith.* Westport, Conn.: Greenwood, 1991.

Dallek, Robert. *Franklin D. Roosevelt and American Foreign Policy, 1932–1945.* New York: Oxford University Press, 1979.

Danchev, Alex. *Very Special Relationship: Field-Marshal Sir John Dill and the Anglo-American Alliance, 1941–1944.* London: Brassey's, 1986.

Davis, Lynn E. *The Cold War Begins: Soviet-American Conflict over Eastern Europe.* Princeton: Princeton University Press, 1974.

Davis, Vincent. *The Admirals Lobby.* Chapel Hill: University of North Carolina Press, 1967.

———. *Postwar Defense Policy and the U.S. Navy, 1943–1946.* Chapel Hill: University of North Carolina Press, 1962.

Dawson, Raymond. *The Decision to Aid Russia, 1941: Foreign Policy and Domestic Politics.* Chapel Hill: University of North Carolina Press, 1959.

DeSantis, Hugh. *The Diplomacy of Silence: The American Foreign Service, the Soviet Union, and the Cold War, 1933–1947.* Chicago: University of Chicago Press, 1979.

Deighton, Ann, ed. *Britain and the First Cold War.* New York: St. Martin's, 1990.

Divine, Robert A. *Roosevelt and World War II.* Baltimore: Johns Hopkins University Press, 1970.

Dobson, Alan P. *Peaceful Air Warfare: The United States, Britain, and the Politics of International Aviation.* Oxford: Clarendon, 1991.

Dunn, Walter Scott, Jr. *Second Front Now, 1943.* University: University of Alabama Press, 1980.

Edmonds, Robin. *The Big Three: Churchill, Roosevelt, and Stalin in Peace and War.* New York: W. W. Norton, 1991.

Ellis, John. *Brute Force: Allied Strategy and Tactics in the Second World War.* New York: Viking, 1990.

Eubank, Keith. *Summit at Teheran.* New York: William Morrow, 1985.

Farnsworth, Beatrice. *William C. Bullitt and the Soviet Union.* Bloomington: Indiana University Press, 1967.

Feis, Herbert. *Churchill, Roosevelt, and Stalin: The War They Waged and the Peace They Sought.* Princeton: Princeton University Press, 1957.

———. *The Road to Pearl Harbor.* New York: Atheneum, 1964.

Frazier, Robert. *Anglo-American Relations with Greece: The Coming of the Cold War, 1942–1947.* New York: St. Martin's, 1991.

Freedman, Lawrence, Paul Hayes, and Robert O'Neill, eds. *War, Strategy, and International Politics: Essays in Honour of Sir Michael Howard.* Oxford: Clarendon, 1992.

Freidel, Frank. *Franklin D. Roosevelt: A Rendezvous with Destiny.* Boston: Little, Brown, 1990.

———. *Franklin D. Roosevelt: The Ordeal.* Boston: Little, Brown, 1954.

Gaddis, John Lewis. *The Long Peace: Inquiries into the History of the Cold War.* New York: Oxford University Press, 1987.

———. *Strategies of Containment: A Critical Appraisal of Postwar American National Security Policy.* New York: Oxford University Press, 1982.

———. *The United States and the Origins of the Cold War, 1941–1947.* New York: Columbia University Press, 1972.

Gallicchio, Marc S. *The Cold War Begins in Asia: American East Asian Policy and the Fall of the Japanese Empire.* New York: Columbia University Press, 1988.

Gannon, Robert I. *The Cardinal Spellman Story.* Garden City, N.Y.: Doubleday & Co., 1962.

Gardner, Lloyd. *Approaching Vietnam: From World War II through Dienbienphu, 1941–1954.* New York: W. W. Norton, 1988.

———. *Architects of Illusion: Men and Ideas in American Foreign Policy, 1941–1949.* Chicago: Quadrangle, 1970.

———. *Spheres of Influence: The Great Powers Partition Europe, from Munich to Yalta.* Chicago: Ivan R. Dee, 1993.

Gellman, Irwin F. *Secret Affairs: Franklin Roosevelt, Cordell Hull, and Sumner Welles.* Baltimore: Johns Hopkins University Press, 1995.

Gorodetsky, Gabriel. *Stafford Cripps' Mission to Moscow, 1940–1942.* Cambridge: Cambridge University Press, 1984.

———, ed. *Soviet Foreign Policy, 1917–1991: A Retrospective.* London: Frank Cass, 1994.

Graff, Frank Warren. *Strategy of Involvement: A Diplomatic Biography of Sumner Welles.* New York: Garland Publishing, 1988.

Graham, Dominick, and Shelford Bidwell. *Coalitions, Politicians and Generals: Some Aspects of Command in Two World Wars.* London: Brassey's, 1993.

Greenfield, Kent Roberts. *American Strategy in World War II: A Reconsideration.* Baltimore: Johns Hopkins University Press, 1963.

———, ed. *Command Decisions.* Washington, D.C.: U.S. Government Printing Office, 1960.

Grenville, John A. S., and George Berkeley Young. *Politics, Strategy, and American Diplomacy: Studies in Foreign Policy, 1873–1917.* New Haven: Yale University Press, 1966.

Hagan, Kenneth J., ed. *In Peace and War: Interpretations of American Naval History, 1775–1984.* 2d ed. Westport, Conn.: Greenwood, 1984.

Haglund, David. *Latin America and the Transformation of U.S. Strategic Thought, 1936–1940.* Albuquerque: University of New Mexico Press, 1984.

Hammond, Paul Y. *Organizing for Defense: The American Military Establishment in the Twentieth Century.* Princeton: Princeton University Press, 1961.

Harbutt, Fraser J. *The Iron Curtain: Churchill, America, and the Origins of the Cold War.* New York: Oxford University Press, 1986.

Hathaway, Robert. *Ambiguous Partnership: Britain and America, 1944–1947.* New York: Columbia University Press, 1981.

Hayes, Grace Person. *The History of the Joint Chiefs of Staff in World War II: The War against Japan.* Annapolis: Naval Institute Press, 1982.

Heinrichs, Waldo. *Threshold of War: Franklin D. Roosevelt and American Entry into World War II.* New York: Oxford University Press, 1988.

Herring, George C. *Aid to Russia, 1941–1946: Strategy, Diplomacy, and the Origins of the Cold War.* New York: Columbia University Press, 1973.

Higgins, Trumbull. *Soft Underbelly: The Anglo-American Controversy over the Italian Campaign, 1939–1945.* New York: Macmillan, 1968.

Hilderbrand, Robert C. *Dumbarton Oaks: The Origins of the United Nations and the Search for Postwar Security.* Chapel Hill: University of North Carolina Press, 1990.

Hinsley, F. H. *British Intelligence in the Second World War.* 5 vols. New York: Cambridge University Press, 1979–90.

Hodgson, Godfrey. *The Colonel: The Life and Times of Henry Stimson, 1867–1950*. New York: Alfred A. Knopf, 1990.

Hogan, Michael J. *Cross of Iron: Harry S. Truman and the Origins of the National Security State, 1945–1954*. Cambridge: Cambridge University Press, 1998.

Hogan, Michael J., and Thomas G. Paterson, eds. *Explaining the History of American Foreign Relations*. Cambridge: Cambridge University Press, 1991.

Hoopes, Townsend, and Douglas Brinkley. *Driven Patriot: The Life and Times of James Forrestal*. New York: Alfred A. Knopf, 1992.

———. *FDR and the Creation of the U.N.* New Haven: Yale University Press, 1997.

Howard, Michael. *Grand Strategy.* Vol. 4 of Butler, ed., *History of the Second World War: Grand Strategy.*

———. *The Mediterranean Strategy in the Second World War*. London: Weidenfeld and Nicolson, 1968.

———. *Studies in War and Peace*. New York: Viking Press, 1972.

———, ed. *The Theory and Practice of War: Essays Presented to Captain B. H. Liddell Hart on His Seventieth Birthday*. New York: Frederick A. Praeger, 1965.

Huntington, Samuel P. *The Soldier and the State: The Theory and Politics of Civil-Military Relationships*. New York: Vintage, 1957.

Iriye, Akira. *Power and Culture: The Japanese-American War, 1941–1945*. Cambridge: Harvard University Press, 1981.

Iriye, Akira, and Warren Cohen, eds. *American, Chinese, and Japanese Perspectives on Wartime Asia, 1931–1949*. Wilmington, Del.: Scholarly Resources, 1990.

Jones, Matthew. *Britain, the United States, and the Mediterranean War, 1942–1944*. New York: St. Martin's, 1996.

Katz, Barry M. *Foreign Intelligence: Research and Analysis in the Office of Strategic Services, 1942–1945*. Cambridge: Harvard University Press, 1989.

Kennedy, Paul, ed. *Grand Strategies in War and Peace*. New Haven, Conn.: Yale University Press, 1991.

Kimball, Warren F. *Forged in War: Roosevelt, Churchill, and the Second World War*. New York: William Morrow, 1997.

———. *The Juggler: Franklin Roosevelt as Wartime Statesman*. Princeton: Princeton University Press, 1991.

———, ed. *America Unbound: World War II and the Making of a Superpower*. New York: St. Martin's, 1992.

Kirkpatrick, Charles E. *An Unknown Future and a Doubtful Present: Writing the Victory Program of 1941*. Washington, D.C.: Center for Military History, 1990.

Kitchen, Martin. *British Policy towards the Soviet Union during the Second World War*. New York: St. Martin's, 1986.

Kolko, Gabriel. *The Politics of War: The World and United States Foreign Policy, 1943–1945*. New York: Random House, 1968.

Kuhn, Thomas. *The Structure of Scientific Revolution*. Chicago: University of Chicago Press, 1962.

Lane, Anne, and Howard Temperly, eds. *The Rise and Fall of the Grand Alliance, 1941–1945*. New York: St. Martin's, 1995.

Langer, William L., and S. Everett Gleason. *The Undeclared War, 1940–1941*. New York: Harper and Brothers, 1953.

Langhorne, Richard, ed. *Diplomacy and Intelligence during the Second World War: Essays in Honor of F. H. Hinsley*. Cambridge: Cambridge University Press, 1985.

Laqueur, Walter, ed. *The Second World War: Essays in Military and Political History.* London: Sage, 1982.

Larrabee, Eric. *Commander in Chief: Franklin Delano Roosevelt, His Lieutenants, and Their War.* New York: Harper and Row, 1987.

Larson, Deborah Welch. *Origins of Containment: A Psychological Explanation.* Princeton: Princeton University Press, 1985.

Leffler, Melvyn P. *A Preponderance of Power: National Security, the Truman Administration, and the Cold War.* Stanford, Calif.: Stanford University Press, 1992.

Leighton, Richard M., and Robert W. Coakley. *Global Logistics and Strategy.* 2 vols. In *United States Army in World War II.* Washington, D.C.: U.S. Government Printing Office, 1955, 1968.

Leutze, James R. *Bargaining for Supremacy: Anglo-American Naval Collaboration, 1937–1941.* Chapel Hill: University of North Carolina Press, 1977.

Levering, Ralph B. *American Opinion and the Russian Alliance, 1939–1945.* Chapel Hill: University of North Carolina Press, 1976.

Lewis, Julian. *Changing Direction: British Military Planning for Post-War Strategic Defence, 1942–1947.* London: Sherwood Press, 1988.

Liddell Hart, B. H. *History of the Second World War.* New York: G. P. Putnam's Sons, 1970.

Link, Arthur S. *Wilson: The New Freedom.* Princeton: Princeton University Press, 1956.

Linn, Brian M. *Guardians of Empire: The U.S. Army and the Pacific, 1902–1940.* Chapel Hill: University of North Carolina Press, 1997.

Louis, William Roger. *Imperialism at Bay: The United States and the Decolonization of the British Empire.* New York: Oxford University Press, 1978.

Love, Robert W., ed. *The Chiefs of Naval Operations.* Annapolis: Naval Institute Press, 1980.

Lowenthal, Mark M. *Leadership and Indecision: American War Planning and Policy Process, 1937–1942.* 2 vols. New York: Garland, 1988.

Lukas, Richard C. *Eagles East: The Army Air Forces and the Soviet Union, 1941–1945.* Tallahassee: Florida State University Press, 1970.

Lundestad, Geir. *The American Non-Policy towards Eastern Europe, 1943–1947: Universalism in an Area Not of Essential Interest to the United States.* New York: Columbia University Press, 1978.

Lytle, Mark H. *The Origins of the Iranian-American Alliance, 1941–1953.* New York: Holmes and Meier, 1987.

McJimsey, George. *Harry Hopkins: Ally of the Poor and Defender of Democracy.* Cambridge: Harvard University Press, 1987.

Maclean, Elizabeth. *Joseph E. Davies: Envoy to the Soviets.* New York: Praeger, 1992.

McNeill, William Hardy. *America, Britain, and Russia: Their Cooperation and Conflict, 1941–1946.* In *Survey of International Affairs, 1939–1946,* edited by Arnold Toynbee. London: Oxford University Press, 1953.

Maney, Patrick J. *The Roosevelt Presence: A Biography of Franklin Delano Roosevelt.* New York: Twayne, 1992.

Marks, Frederick W., III. *Wind over Sand: The Diplomacy of Franklin Roosevelt.* Athens: University of Georgia Press, 1988.

Mastny, Vojtech. *Russia's Road to the Cold War: Diplomacy, Warfare, and the Politics of Communism, 1941–1945.* New York: Columbia University Press, 1979.

Matloff, Maurice. *Strategic Planning for Coalition Warfare, 1943–1944.* In *United States Army in World War II.* Washington, D.C.: U.S. Government Printing Office, 1959.

Matloff, Maurice, and Edwin Snell. *Strategic Planning for Coalition Warfare, 1941–1942.* In

United States Army in World War II. Washington, D.C.: U.S. Government Printing Office, 1953.

May, Ernest R., ed. *Knowing One's Enemies: Intelligence Assessment before the Two World Wars.* Princeton: Princeton University Press, 1984.

———, ed. *The Ultimate Decision: The President as Commander in Chief.* New York: George Braziller, 1960.

Messer, Robert L. *The End of an Alliance: James F. Byrnes, Roosevelt, Truman, and the Origins of the Cold War.* Chapel Hill: University of North Carolina Press, 1982.

Miller, David Aaron. *Search for Security: Saudi Arabian Oil and American Foreign Policy, 1939–1949.* Chapel Hill: University of North Carolina Press, 1980.

Miller, Edward. *War Plan Orange: The U.S. Strategy to Defeat Japan, 1897–1945.* Annapolis: Naval Institute Press, 1991.

Millis, Walter. *Arms and Men: A Study of American Military History.* New York: G. P. Putnam's Sons, 1956.

Morison, Elting E. *Turmoil and Tradition: A Study of the Life and Times of Henry L. Stimson.* Boston: Houghton Mifflin, 1960.

Morison, Samuel E. *History of U.S. Naval Operations in World War II.* 15 vols. Boston: Little, Brown, 1947–62.

Morton, Louis. *Strategy and Command: The First Two Years.* In *United States Army in World War II.* Washington, D.C.: U.S. Government Printing Office, 1962.

Notter, Harley. *Postwar Foreign Policy Preparation.* Washington, D.C.: U.S. Government Printing Office, 1949.

O'Connor, Raymond. *Diplomacy for Victory: FDR and Unconditional Surrender.* New York: W. W. Norton, 1971.

———. *Force and Diplomacy: Essays Military and Diplomatic.* Coral Gables: University of Miami Press, 1972.

———. *Perilous Equilibrium: The United States and the London Naval Conference of 1930.* Lawrence: University Press of Kansas, 1962.

Paret, Peter, ed. *Makers of Modern Strategy: From Machiavelli to the Nuclear Age.* Princeton: Princeton University Press, 1986.

Paterson, Thomas G. *On Every Front: The Making and Unmaking of the Cold War.* Rev. ed. New York: W. W. Norton, 1992.

———. *Soviet-American Confrontation: Postwar Reconstruction and the Origins of the Cold War.* Baltimore: Johns Hopkins University Press, 1973.

Pogue, Forrest C. *George C. Marshall.* 4 vols. New York: Viking, 1963–87.

Pratt, Julius W. *Cordell Hull.* Vol. 13 in *The American Secretaries of State and Their Diplomacy,* edited by Robert H. Ferrell and Samuel Flagg Bemis. New York: Cooper Square, 1964.

Rabel, Roberto G. *Between East and West: Trieste, the United States, and the Cold War, 1941–1954.* Durham: Duke University Press, 1988.

Reynolds, David. *The Creation of the Anglo-American Alliance, 1937–1941: A Study in Competitive Cooperation.* Chapel Hill: University of North Carolina Press, 1981.

Reynolds, David, and David Dimbleby. *An Ocean Apart: The Relationship between Britain and America in the Twentieth Century.* New York: Random House, 1988.

Reynolds, David, Warren F. Kimball, and A. O. Chubarian, eds. *Allies at War: The Soviet, American, and British Experience, 1939–1945.* New York: St. Martin's, 1994.

Richardson, General Sir Charles. *From Churchill's Secret Circle to the BBC: The Biography of Lieutenant General Sir Ian Jacob.* London: Brassey's, 1991.

Rogow, Arnold A. *James Forrestal: A Study of Personality, Politics, and Policy.* New York: Macmillan, 1963.

Romanus, Charles F., and Riley Sunderland. *Stilwell's Mission to China*. In *United States Army in World War II*. Washington, D.C.: U.S. Government Printing Office, 1987.

Roskill, Steven. *Naval Policy between the Wars*. London: Collins, 1968, 1976.

Rubin, Barry. *The Great Powers in the Middle East, 1941–1947: The Road to the Cold War*. London: Frank Cass, 1980.

Russell, Ruth B. *A History of the United Nations Charter: The Role of the United States, 1940–1945*. Washington, D.C.: Brookings Institution, 1958.

Russett, Bruce M. *No Clear and Present Danger: A Skeptical View of United States Entry into World War II*. New York: Harper and Row, 1977.

Sainsbury, Keith. *Churchill and Roosevelt at War: The War They Fought and the Peace They Hoped to Make*. New York: New York University Press, 1994.

———. *The Turning Point: Roosevelt, Stalin, Churchill, and Chiang Kai-shek, 1943: The Moscow, Cairo and Teheran Conferences*. Oxford: Oxford University Press, 1985.

Sbrega, John J. *Anglo-American Relations and Colonialism in East Asia, 1941–1945*. New York: Garland Publishing, 1983.

Schaller, Michael. *The U.S. Crusade in China, 1938–1945*. New York: Columbia University Press, 1979.

Schild, Georg. *Bretton Woods and Dumbarton Oaks: American Economic and Political Postwar Planning in the Summer of 1944*. New York: St. Martin's, 1995.

Schnabel, James F. *The History of the Joint Chiefs of Staff: The Joint Chiefs of Staff and National Policy*. Vol. 1, *1945–1947*. Wilmington, Del.: Michael Glazier, 1979.

Schroeder, Paul. *The Axis Alliance and Japanese-American Relations, 1941*. Ithaca: Cornell University Press, 1958.

Schwartz, Thomas Alan. *America's Germany: John J. McCloy and the Federal Republic of Germany*. Cambridge: Harvard University Press, 1991.

[Sevost'ianov, G. N., and W. F. Kimball, eds.] *Soviet-U.S. Relations, 1933–1942*. Translated by Kim Pilarski. Moscow: Progress Publishers, 1989.

Sharp, Tony. *The Wartime Alliance and the Zonal Division of Germany*. Oxford: Clarendon, 1975.

Sherwood, Robert. *Roosevelt and Hopkins: An Intimate History*. Rev. ed. New York: Grosset and Dunlap, 1950.

Sherry, Michael S. *Preparing for the Next War: American Plans for Postwar Defense, 1941–1945*. New Haven: Yale University Press, 1977.

———. *The Rise of American Airpower: The Creation of Armageddon*. New Haven: Yale University Press, 1987.

Simpson, Mitchell B., III. *Admiral Harold R. Stark: Architect of Victory, 1939–1945*. Columbia: University of South Carolina Press, 1989.

———. *War, Strategy, and Maritime Power*. New Brunswick: Rutgers University Press, 1977.

Sloan, G. R. *Geopolitics in United States Strategic Policy, 1890–1987*. New York: St. Martin's, 1988.

Smith, Bradley F. *Sharing Secrets with Stalin: How the Allies Traded Intelligence, 1941–1945*. Lawrence: University Press of Kansas, 1996.

———. *The Ultra-Magic Deals and the Most Secret Special Relationship, 1940–1946*. Novato, Calif.: Presidio, 1993.

Smith, Gaddis. *American Diplomacy during the Second World War, 1941–1945*. 2d ed. New York: Alfred A. Knopf, 1985.

Smith, Kevin. *Conflict over Convoys: Anglo-American Logistics Diplomacy in the Second World War*. Cambridge: Cambridge University Press, 1996.

Smith, Perry McCoy. *The Air Force Plans for Peace, 1943–1945*. Baltimore: Johns Hopkins University Press, 1970.

Smith, R. Harris. *OSS: The Secret History of America's First Intelligence Agency.* Berkeley: University of California Press, 1972.

Steel, Ronald. *Walter Lippmann and the American Century.* Boston: Little, Brown, 1980.

Steele, Richard. *The First Offensive, 1942: Roosevelt, Marshall, and the Making of American Strategy.* Bloomington: Indiana University Press, 1973.

Stein, Harold, ed. *American Civil-Military Decisions: A Book of Case Studies.* Birmingham: University of Alabama Press, 1963.

Stoff, Michael B. *Oil, War, and American Security: The Search for a National Policy on Foreign Oil.* New Haven: Yale University Press, 1980.

Stoler, Mark A. *George C. Marshall: Soldier-Statesman of the American Century.* New York: Twayne, 1987.

———. *The Politics of the Second Front: American Military Planning and Diplomacy in Coalition Warfare, 1941–1943.* Westport, Conn.: Greenwood, 1977.

Thorne, Christopher. *Allies of a Kind: The United States, Britain, and the War against Japan, 1941–1945.* New York: Oxford University Press, 1978.

Trask, David F. *Captains and Cabinets: Anglo-American Naval Relations, 1917–1918.* Columbia: University of Missouri Press, 1972.

———. *General Tasker Howard Bliss and the "Sessions of the World," 1919.* Transactions of the American Philosophical Society, new series vol. 56, pt. 8. Philadelphia: American Philosophical Society, 1966.

———. *The United States in the Supreme War Council: American War Aims and Inter-Allied Strategy, 1917–1918.* Middletown, Conn.: Wesleyan University Press, 1961.

Troy, Thomas F. *Donovan and the CIA: A History of the Establishment of the Central Intelligence Agency.* Frederick, Md.: University Publications of America, 1981.

Tuttle, Dwight William. *Harry L. Hopkins and Anglo-Soviet-American Relations, 1941–1945.* New York: Garland, 1983.

Utley, Jonathan G. *Going to War with Japan, 1937–1941.* Knoxville: University of Tennessee Press, 1985.

Vlahos, Michael. *The Blue Sword: The Naval War College and the American Mission, 1919–1941.* Newport, R.I.: Naval War College Press, 1980.

Watson, Mark S. *Chief of Staff: Prewar Plans and Preparations.* In *United States Army in World War II.* Washington, D.C.: U.S. Government Printing Office, 1950.

Watt, D. Cameron. *Succeeding John Bull: America in Britain's Place, 1900–1975.* Cambridge: Cambridge University Press, 1984.

Weigley, Russell F. *The American Way of War: A History of United States Military Strategy and Policy.* New York: Macmillan, 1973.

———. *Towards an American Army: Military Thought from Washington to Marshall.* New York: Columbia University Press, 1962.

Wheeler, Gerald E. *Prelude to Pearl Harbor: The United States Navy and the Far East, 1921–1931.* Columbia: University of Missouri Press, 1963.

Williams, William Appleman. *Some Presidents: Wilson to Nixon.* New York: New York Review Book/Vintage, 1972.

Wilson Theodore. *The First Summit: Roosevelt and Churchill at Placentia Bay, 1941.* Rev. ed. Lawrence: University Press of Kansas, 1991.

Wittner, Lawrence. *American Intervention in Greece, 1943–1949.* New York: Columbia University Press, 1982.

Woods, Randall Bennett. *A Changing of the Guard: Anglo-American Relations, 1941–1946.* Chapel Hill: University of North Carolina Press, 1990.

Woodward, Sir Llewellyn. *British Foreign Policy in the Second World War.* 5 vols. London: Her Majesty's Stationery Office, 1971.

Wright, Monte D., and Lawrence J. Paszek, eds. *Soldiers and Statesmen: The Proceedings of the 4th Military History Symposium, United States Air Force Academy, 22–23 October 1970.* Washington, D.C.: Office of Air Force History, 1973.

Yergin, Daniel. *Shattered Peace: The Origins of the Cold War and the National Security State.* Rev. ed. New York: Penguin, 1990.

Zubok, Vladislav, and Constantine Pleshakov. *Inside the Kremlin's Cold War: From Stalin to Khrushchev.* Cambridge: Harvard University Press, 1996.

Journal Articles and Book Chapters

Allard, Dean C. "Anglo-American Naval Differences during World War I." *Military Affairs* 44 (Apr. 1980): 75–81.

Ambrose, Stephen E. "Applied Strategy in World War II." *Naval War College Review* 22 (May 1970): 62–70.

Anderson, Irvine H. "Lend-Lease for Saudi Arabia: A Comment on Alternative Conceptualizations." *Diplomatic History* 3 (Fall 1979): 413–23.

Andrade, Ernest, Jr. "The Crusier Controversy in Naval Limitations Negotiations, 1922–1936." *Military Affairs* 48 (July 1984): 113–20.

Barker, Thomas M. "The Ljubljana Gap Strategy: Alternative to Anvil/Dragoon or Fantasy?" *Journal of Military History* 56 (Jan. 1992): 57–85.

Beloff, Max. "The Special Relationship: An Anglo-American Myth." In *A Century of Conflict, 1850–1950: Essays for A. J. P. Taylor,* edited by Martin Gilbert, 148–71. London: Hamish Hamilton, 1966.

Bernstein, Barton. "Eclipsed by Hiroshima and Nagasaki: Early Thinking about Tactical Nuclear Weapons." *International History Review* 15 (Spring 1991): 149–73, and ensuing correspondence in 16 (Winter 1991–92): 204–21.

Boll, Michael M. "U.S. Plans for a Postwar Pro-Western Bulgaria: A Little-Known Wartime Initiative in Eastern Europe." *Diplomatic History* 7 (Spring 1983): 117–38.

Braeman, John. "Power and Diplomacy: The 1920's Reappraised." *Review of Politics* 44 (July 1982): 342–69.

Braisted, William R. "On the American Red and Red-Orange Plans, 1919–1939." In *Naval Warfare in the Twentieth Century, 1900–1945: Essays in Honour of Arthur Marder,* edited by Gerald Jordan, 167–85. London: Croon Helm, 1977.

Brower, Charles F., IV. "Sophisticated Strategist: General George A. Lincoln and the Defeat of Japan, 1944–1945." *Diplomatic History* 15 (Summer 1991): 317–37.

Brune, Lester H. "Considerations of Force in Cordell Hull's Diplomacy, July 26 to November 26, 1941." *Diplomatic History* 2 (Fall 1978): 389–405.

Buhite, Russell D., and Christopher Hamel. "War for Peace: The Question of an American Preventive War against the Soviet Union." *Diplomatic History* 14 (Summer 1990): 367–84.

Campbell, Thomas M. "Nationalism in America's UN Policy, 1944–1945." *International Organization* 27 (Winter 1973): 25–44.

———. "The Resurgence of Isolationism at the End of World War II." *American Diplomatic History: Issues and Methods, West Georgia College Studies in the Social Sciences* 13 (June 1974): 41–56.

Chase, John I. "Unconditional Surrender Reconsidered." *Political Science Quarterly* (June 1955): 258–79.

Clemens, Diane S. "Averell Harriman, John Deane, the Joint Chiefs of Staff, and the 'Reversal of Co-Operation' with the Soviet Union in April 1945." *International History Review* 14 (May 1992): 277–306.

Clifford, J. Garry. "Both Ends of the Telescope: New Perspectives on FDR and American Entry into World War II." *Diplomatic History* 13 (Spring 1989): 213–30.

———. "A Connecticut Colonel's Candid Conversation with the Wrong Commander-in-Chief." *Connecticut History* 28 (Nov. 1987): 24–38.

Cohen, Eliot. "The Strategy of Innocence? The United States, 1920–1945." In *The Making of Strategy: Rulers, States, and War,* edited by Williamson Murray, MacGregor Knox, and Alvin Bernstein, 428–65. Cambridge: Cambridge University Press, 1994.

Conn, Stetson. "Changing Concepts of National Defense in the United States, 1937–1947." *Military Affairs* 27 (Spring 1964): 1–7.

Deakin, F. W. D. "The Myth of an Allied Landing in the Balkans during the Second World War." In *British Policy towards Wartime Resistance in Yugoslavia and Greece,* edited by Phyllis Auty and Richard Clogg, 93–116. New York: Barnes and Noble, 1975.

Doyle, Michael K. "The U.S. Navy and War Plan Orange, 1933–1940: Making Necessity a Virtue." *Naval War College Review* 32 (May–June 1980): 49–63.

Eiler, Keith E. "The Man Who Planned the Victory." *American Heritage* 34 (Oct./Nov. 1983): 36–47.

Emerson, William. "Franklin D. Roosevelt as Commander in Chief in World War II." *Military Affairs* 22 (Winter 1958–59): 181–207.

Flint, Roy K. "The United States Army on the Pacific Frontier, 1899–1939." In *The American Military and the Far East: Proceedings of the Ninth Military History Symposium, United States Air Force Academy, 1–3 October 1980,* edited by Joe C. Dixon, 139–59. Washington, D.C.: U.S. Air Force Academy and Office of Air Force History, 1980.

Fogelson, Nancy. "Greenland: Strategic Base on a Northern Defense Line." *Journal of Military History* 53 (Jan. 1989): 51–63.

———. "The Tip of the Iceberg: The United States and International Rivalry for the Arctic, 1900–1925." *Diplomatic History* 9 (Spring 1985): 131–48.

Foltos, Lester J. "The New Pacific Barrier: America's Search for Security in the Pacific, 1945–1947." *Diplomatic History* 13 (Summer 1989): 317–42.

Franklin, William M. "Yalta Viewed from Tehran." In *Some Pathways in Twentieth-Century History: Essays in Honor of Reginal Charles McGrane,* edited by Daniel Beaver, 253–301. Detroit: Wayne State University Press, 1969.

———. "Zonal Boundaries and Access to Berlin." *World Politics* 16 (Oct. 1963): 1–31.

Gaddis, John Lewis. "Intelligence, Espionage, and Cold War Origins." *Diplomatic History* 13 (Spring 1989): 191–212.

Gallicchio, Marc. "After Nagasaki: General Marshall's Plan for Tactical Nuclear Weapons in Japan." *Prologue* 23 (Winter 1991): 396–404.

———. "The Other China Hands: U.S. Army Officers and America's Failure in China, 1941–1950." *Journal of American East-Asian Relations* 4 (Spring 1995): 49–72.

Gole, Henry G. "War Planning at the U.S. Army War College, 1934–1940: The Road to Rainbow." *Army History* 25 (Winter 1993): 13–28.

Gooch, John. "'Hidden in the Rock': American Military Perceptions of Great Britain, 1919–1940." In Freedman, Hayes, and O'Neill, eds., *War, Strategy, and International Politics,* 155–73.

Gormly, James L. "Keeping the Door Open in Saudi Arabia: The United States and the Dhahran Oilfield, 1945–46." *Diplomatic History* 4 (Spring 1980): 189–205.

Greene, Fred. "The Military View of American National Policy, 1904–1940." *American Historical Review* 66 (Jan. 1961): 354–77.

Gugeler, Russell A. "George Marshall and Orlando Ward, 1939–1941." *Parameters* 13 (Mar. 1983): 28–42.

Haglund, David. "George C. Marshall and the Question of Aid to England, May–June, 1940." *Journal of Contemporary History* 15 (Oct. 1980): 413–40.

Haines, Gerald K. "Under the Eagle's Wing: The Franklin Roosevelt Administration Forges an American Hemisphere." *Diplomatic History* 1 (Fall 1977): 373–88.

Harbutt, Fraser. "Churchill, Hopkins, and the 'Other' Americans: An Alternative Perspective on Anglo-American Relations, 1941–1945." *International History Review* 8 (May 1986): 236–62.

Harrington, Daniel F. "A Careless Hope: American Air Power and Japan, 1941." *Pacific Historical Review* 48 (May 1979): 217–38.

———. "Kennan, Bohlen, and the Riga Axioms." *Diplomatic History* 2 (Fall 1978): 423–37.

Heinrichs, Waldo. "President Franklin D. Roosevelt's Intervention in the Battle of the Atlantic, 1941." *Diplomatic History* 10 (Fall 1986): 311–32.

———. "The Russian Factor in Japanese-American Relations, 1941." In *Pearl Harbor Reexamined: Prologue to War,* edited by Hilary Conroy and Harry Wray, 163–77. Honolulu: University of Hawaii Press, 1990.

Herring, George C., Jr. "Lend Lease to Russia and the Origins of the Cold War, 1944–1945." *Journal of American History* 56 (June 1968): 93–114.

Hess, Gary R. "Franklin Roosevelt and Indochina." *Journal of American History* 59 (Sept. 1972): 353–68.

Higgins, Trumbull. "The Anglo-American Historians' War in the Mediterranean, 1942–1945." *Military Affairs* 34 (Oct. 1970): 84–88.

Jacobs, W. A. "Strategic Bombing and American National Strategy, 1941–1943." *Military Affairs* 50 (July 1986): 133–39.

Kimball, Warren F. "Churchill and Roosevelt: The Personal Equation." *Prologue* 6 (Fall 1974): 169–82.

———. "Franklin Roosevelt: 'Dr. Win-the-War.'" In *Commanders in Chief: Presidential Leadership in Modern Wars,* edited by Joseph G. Dawson III, 87–105. Lawrence: University Press of Kansas, 1993.

———. "Lend-Lease and the Open Door: The Temptation of British Opulence, 1937–1942." *Political Science Quarterly* 86 (June 1971): 232–59.

———. "Naked Reverse Right: Roosevelt, Churchill and Eastern Europe from TOLSTOY to Yalta—and a Little Beyond." *Diplomatic History* 9 (Winter 1985): 1–24.

———. "Roosevelt and the Southwest Pacific: Merely a Facade?" In *The Making of Australian Foreign Policy: The Contribution of Dr. H. V. Evatt,* edited by David Day, 10–29. St. Lucia, Australia: Queensland University Press, 1993.

———. "Stalingrad: A Chance for Choices." *Journal of Military History* 60 (Jan. 1996): 89–114.

Koch, H. W. "The Spectre of a Separate Peace in the East: Russo-German Peace Feelers, 1942–1944." *Journal of Contemporary History* 10 (July 1975): 531–49.

LaFeber, Walter. "Roosevelt, Churchill, and Indochina, 1942–1945." *American Historical Review* 80 (Dec. 1975): 1277–95.

Langer, John D. "The Harriman-Beaverbrook Mission and the Debate over Unconditional Aid for the Soviet Union, 1941." *Journal of Contemporary History* 14 (July 1979): 463–82.

Langer, William L. "Turning Points of the War: Political Problems of a Coalition." *Foreign Affairs* 26 (Oct. 1947): 73–89.

Leffler, Melvyn P. "Adherence to Agreements: Yalta and the Experiences of the Early Cold War." *International Security* 11 (1986): 88–123.

———. "The American Conception of National Security and the Beginnings of the Cold War, 1945–1948." *American Historical Review* 89 (1984): 346–400.

Leighton, Richard M. "The American Arsenal Policy in World War II: A Retrospective View." In *Some Pathways in Twentieth-Century History: Essays in Honor of Reginal Charles McGrane*, edited by Daniel Beaver, 221–52. Detroit: Wayne State University Press, 1969.

———. "OVERLORD Revisited: An Interpretation of American Strategy in the European War, 1942–1944." *American Historical Review* 68 (July 1963): 919–37.

Leutze, James R. "Technology and Bargaining in Anglo-American Naval Relations, 1938–1946." *United States Naval Institute Proceedings* 103 (June 1977): 50–61.

Link, Arthur S., and John Whiteclay Chambers. "Woodrow Wilson as Commander-in-Chief." In *The United States Military under the Constitution of the United States, 1789–1989*, edited by Richard H. Kohn, 317–75. New York: New York University Press, 1991.

Love, Robert William, Jr., "Fighting a Global War, 1941–1945." In Hagan, ed., *In Peace and War*, 263–89.

Lowenthal, Mark M. "Roosevelt and the Coming of the War: The Search for United States Policy, 1937–1942." *Journal of Contemporary History* 16 (July 1981): 413–40.

———. "The Stark Memorandum and American National Security Process." In *Changing Interpretations and New Sources in Naval History: Papers from the Third United States Naval Academy History Symposium*, edited by Robert William Love Jr., 352–59. New York: Garland, 1980.

Lukas, Richard C. "The Velvet Project: Hope and Frustration." *Military Affairs* 28 (Winter 1964): 145–62.

Lyons, Gene M. "The Growth of National Security Research." *Journal of Politics* 25 (Aug. 1963): 488–508.

McFarland, Stephen L. "A Peripheral View of the Origins of the Cold War: The Crisis in Iran, 1941–1947." *Diplomatic History* 4 (Fall 1980): 330–52.

MacLean, Elizabeth. "Joseph E. Davies and Soviet-American Relations, 1941–1943." *Diplomatic History* 4 (Winter 1980): 73–93.

McMahon, Robert J. "Anglo-American Diplomacy and the Reoccupation of the Netherlands East Indies." *Diplomatic History* 2 (Winter 1978): 1–23.

Mark, Edward. "American Policy toward Eastern Europe and the Origins of the Cold War, 1941–1946: An Alternative Interpretation." *Journal of American History* 68 (Sept. 1981): 313–36.

———. "October or Thermidor? Interpretations of Stalinism and the Perception of Soviet Foreign Policy in the United States." *American Historical Review* 94 (Oct. 1989): 937–62.

Mastny, Vojtech. "Soviet War Aims at the Moscow and Teheran Conferences of 1943." *Journal of Modern History* 47 (Sept. 1975): 481–504.

———. "Stalin and the Prospects of a Separate Peace in World War II." *American Historical Review* 77 (Dec. 1972): 1365–88.

Matloff, Maurice. "The American Approach to War, 1919–1945." In Howard, ed., *Theory and Practice of War*, 213–43.

———. "Franklin D. Roosevelt as War Leader." In Coles, ed., *Total War and Cold War*, 42–65.

Matray, James. "An End to Indifference: America's Korean Policy during World War II." *Diplomatic History* 2 (Spring 1978): 181–96.

May, Ernest. "Political-Military Consultation in the United States." *Political Science Quarterly* 70 (June 1955): 161–80.

———. "Writing Contemporary International History." *Diplomatic History* 8 (Spring 1984): 103–13.

Miscamble, Wilson D. "Anthony Eden and the Truman-Molotov Conversations, April 1945." *Diplomatic History* 2 (Spring 1978): 167–80.

Morton, Louis. "Army and Marines on the China Station: A Study in Military and Political Rivalry." *Pacific Historical Review* 29 (Feb. 1960): 51–73.

———. "Interservice Co-operation and Political-Military Collaboration, 1900–1938." In Coles, ed., *Total War and Cold War,* 131–60.

———. "Military and Naval Preparations for the Defense of the Philippines during the War Scare of 1907." *Military Affairs* 13 (Summer 1949): 95–104.

———. "National Policy and Military Strategy." *Virginia Quarterly Review* 36 (Winter 1960): 1–17.

———. "Soviet Intervention in the War against Japan." *Foreign Affairs* 40 (July 1962): 653–62.

———. "War Plan ORANGE: Evolution of a Strategy." *World Politics* 11 (Jan. 1959): 221–50.

Neumann, William L. "Franklin Delano Roosevelt: A Disciple of Admiral Mahan." *United States Naval Institute Proceedings* 78 (July 1952): 713–19.

Offner, Arnold A. "Uncommon Ground: Anglo-American-Soviet Diplomacy, 1941–42." *Soviet Union/Union Sovietique* 18 (1991): 237–57.

Parrish, N. F. "Hap Arnold and the Historians." *Aerospace Historian* 20 (Sept. 1973): 113–15.

Paterson, Thomas G. "The Abortive Loan to Russia and the Origins of the Cold War, 1943–1946." *Journal of American History* 56 (June 1968): 70–92.

Pogue, Forrest C., et al. "The Wartime Chiefs of Staff and the President." In *Soldiers and Statesmen: Proceedings of the 4th Military History Symposium,* edited by Monte D. Wright and Lawrence J. Paszek, 69–105. Washington, D.C.: Office of the Air Force History, Headquarters USAF and U.S. Air Force Academy, 1989.

Poole, Walter S. "From Conciliation to Containment: The Joint Chiefs of Staff and the Coming of the Cold War, 1945–1946." *Military Affairs* 62 (Feb. 1978): 12–16.

Pratt, Lawrence "The Anglo-American Naval Conversations on the Far East of January 1938." *International Affairs* 47 (Oct. 1971): 745–63.

Quinlan, Robert J. "The United States Fleet: Diplomacy, Strategy, and the Allocation of Ships (1940–1941)." In *American Civil-Military Decisions: A Handbook of Case Studies,* edited by Harold Stein, 153–202. Birmingham: University of Alabama Press, 1963.

Rabel, Roberto G. "Prologue to Containment: The Truman Administration's Response to the Trieste Crisis of May 1945." *Diplomatic History* 10 (Spring 1986): 141–60.

Resis, Albert. "The Churchill-Stalin Secret 'Percentages' Agreement on the Balkans, Moscow, October, 1944." *American Historical Review* 83 (1978): 368–87.

———. "Spheres of Influence in Soviet Wartime Diplomacy." *Journal of Modern History* 53 (1981): 417–39.

Reynolds, David. "The 'Big Three' and the Division of Europe, 1945–48: An Overview." *Diplomacy and Statecraft* 1 (July 1990): 111–36.

———. "1940: Fulcrum of the Twentieth Century?" *International Affairs* 66 (1990): 325–50.

———. "Roosevelt, Churchill, and the Wartime Anglo-American Alliance, 1939–1945: Towards a New Synthesis." In *The Special Relationship: Anglo-American Relations since 1945,* edited by William Roger Louis and Hedley Bull, 17–41. Oxford: Clarendon, 1986.

Schaffer, Ronald. "General Stanley D. Embick: Military Dissenter." *Military Affairs* 37 (Oct. 1973): 89–95.

Shepardson, Donald E. "The Fall of Berlin and the Rise of a Myth." *Journal of Military History* 62 (Jan. 1998): 135–53.

Small, Melvin. "How We Learned to Love the Russians: American Media and the Soviet Union during World War II." *Historian* 36 (May 1974): 455–78.

Smith, Bradley F. "Sharing Utra in World War II." *International Journal of Intelligence and Counterintelligence* 2 (Spring 1988): 59–72.

Steele, Richard W. "American Popular Opinion and the War against Germany: The Issue of a Negotiated Peace, 1942." *Journal of American History* 65 (Dec. 1978): 704–23.

———. "Political Aspects of American Military Planning, 1941–1942." *Military Affairs* 35 (Apr. 1971): 68–74.

Stoler, Mark A. "From Continentalism to Globalism: General Stanley D. Embick, the Joint Strategic Survey Committee, and the Military View of American National Policy during the Second World War." *Diplomatic History* 6 (Summer 1982): 303–21.

Strange, Joseph L. "The British Rejection of Operation SLEDGEHAMMER: An Alternative Motive." *Military Affairs* 46 (Feb. 1982): 6–13.

Tarr, Curtis. "The General Board Joint Staff Proposal of 1941." *Military Affairs* 12 (Summer 1967): 85–90.

Thorne, Christopher. "Indochina and Anglo-American Relations, 1942–1945." *Pacific Historical Review* 45 (Feb. 1976): 73–96.

Tillapaugh, J. "Closed Hemisphere and Open World? The Dispute over Regional Security at the U.N. Conference, 1945." *Diplomatic History* 2 (Winter 1978): 25–42.

Villa, Brian L. "The U.S. Army, Unconditional Surrender, and the Potsdam Proclamation." *Journal of American History* 63 (June 1976): 66–92.

Walker, J. Samuel. "The Decision to Use the Bomb: A Historiographical Update." *Diplomatic History* 14 (Winter 1990): 97–114.

Warner, Geoffrey. "The Anglo-American Special Relationship." *Diplomatic History* 13 (Fall 1989): 479–99.

———. "From Tehran to Yalta: Reflections on F.D.R.'s Foreign Policy." *International Affairs* 43 (July 1967): 530–36.

Watt, D. C. "Every War Must End: War-Time Planning for Post-War Security in Britain and America in the Wars of 1914–18 and 1939–45. The Roles of Historical Example and of Professional Historians." In *Transactions of the Royal Historical Society*, 5th ser., vol. 28, 159–73. London: Butler and Tanner, 1978.

Weigley, Russell F. "Military Strategy and Civilian Leadership." In *Historical Dimensions of National Security Problems,* edited by Klaus Knorr, 38–77. Lawrence: University Press of Kansas, 1976.

Wilt, Alan F. "The Significance of the Casablanca Decisions, January 1943." *Journal of Military History* 55 (Oct. 1991): 517–29.

Woods, Randall Bennett. "F.D.R. and the Triumph of American Nationalism." *Presidential Studies Quarterly* 19 (Summer 1989): 567–81.

Woodward, C. Vann. "The Age of Reinterpretation." *American Historical Review* 66 (Oct. 1960): 1–19.

Unpublished Manuscripts, Papers, and Dissertations

Bennett, Edward M. "Challengers to Policy: Proponents of an Inevitable Soviet-American Confrontation." Paper presented at the Second Soviet-American Colloquium on World War II History, October 1987, Roosevelt Library, Hyde Park, N.Y.

Brower, Charles F. "Sophisticated Strategists: The Joint Chiefs of Staff, Political Considerations, and the Defeat of Japan." Unpublished manuscript.

Converse, Elliot V., III. "United States Plans for a Postwar Overseas Military Base System, 1942–1948." Ph.D. diss., Princeton University, 1984.

Davis, Vernon E. "The History of the Joint Chiefs of Staff in World War II: Organizational Development." 2 vols. Historical Division, Joint Secretariat, Joint Chiefs of Staff, 1972. In Record Group 225, National Archives, Washington, D.C.

Dessants, Betty Abrahamsen. "The American Academic Community and United States–Soviet Union Relations: The Research and Analysis Branch and Its Legacy, 1941–1947." Ph.D. diss., University of California–Berkeley, 1995.

Kittredge, Tracy. "U.S.-British Naval Cooperation, 1940–1945." Navy Historical Center, Washington, D.C.

Kraus, Theresa L. "Planning for the U.S. Occupation of Iceland, 1940–1941." Paper delivered at the annual conference of the Society for Historians of American Foreign Relations, Aug. 2, 1990, Washington, D.C.

Mead, Dana George. "United States Peacetime Strategic Planning, 1920–1941: The Color Plans to the Victory Program." Ph.D. diss., Massachusetts Institute of Technology, 1967.

Samerdyke, Michael F. "The United States and the Free Germany Committee, 1943–1945." Paper presented at the annual conference of the Society of Historians of American Foreign Relations, Boulder, Colo., June 23, 1996.

Smith, Bradley F. "Soviet-American Intelligence and Technical Cooperation in World War Two." Paper presented at the Fourth Soviet-American Colloquium on World War II History, Oct. 1990, Rutgers University, New Brunswick, N.J.

Spector, Ronald. "The Politics of American Strategy in the War against Japan." Paper presented at the Fourth Soviet-American Colloquium on World War II History, Oct. 1990, Rutgers University, New Brunswick, N.J.

Strange, Joseph J. "Cross-Channel Attack, 1942: The British Rejection of Operation Sledgehammer and the Cherbourg Alternative." Ph.D. diss., University of Maryland, 1984.

Index

AOUT 2013